Europe Since 1870

By the same author

THE SECOND INTERNATIONAL
INTELLECTUALS IN POLITICS
THE ANARCHISTS

EUROPE SINCE 1870
An International History

JAMES JOLL

Harper & Row, Publishers
New York, Evanston, San Francisco, London

Europe Since 1870: An International History

Copyright © 1973 by James Joll

All rights reserved. Printed in the United States of America. No part of this book may be used or reproduced in any manner whatsoever without written permission except in the case of brief quotations embodied in critical articles and reviews. For information address Harper & Row, Publishers, Inc., 10 East 53rd Street, New York, N.Y. 10022.

First U.S. Edition

Library of Congress Cataloging in Publication Data

Joll James
    Europe since 1870.

    Bibliography: p.
    1. Europe—History—1871-1918. 2. Europe—
History—20th century. I. Title.
D395.J64 940 73-13828
ISBN 0-06-043415-5

CONTENTS

CONTENTS

MAPS

MAPS

ACKNOWLEDGEMENTS

Any adequate expression of the debts I have incurred in the preparation of this book would have to include the titles of most of the books I have read and the names of all the students, colleagues and friends with whom I have discussed these problems over the past twenty-five years.

I should however particularly like to mention some of the people who have given me ideas, facts and corrections, or have answered queries, during the last stages of writing the book: M.J.Dorling, Theodore Draper, Felix Gilbert, Austin Gough, Ragnhild Hatton, Max Hayward, George F.Kennan, Walter Laqueur, David Luke, Norbert Lynton, Eino Lyytinen, T.W. Mason, Arno J.Mayer, Otto Pflanze, Stuart Samuels, Carl Schorske, Fritz Stern, Anthony Vidler, D.C.Watt, Richard Wollheim and Theodore Zeldin.

I am very grateful indeed to those who have read, checked, and commented on the whole or large parts of the final draft – R.F.Bridge, Mary Dysch, John Golding, Margaret Lim, Anthony Polonsky and J.M.Roberts. The many mistakes which remain are however mine, not theirs. Margaret Lim has also very kindly prepared the index.

I have received invaluable secretarial help from Mrs P.Joseph, Mrs M. Van Sant, Miss Monica Anvoner and Miss Carol Hargraves.

The Institute for Advanced Study, Princeton, New Jersey provided the opportunity for me to complete this work, already long delayed, and I am glad to take this occasion to thank the Director and the School of Historical Studies for their generous hospitality and financial assistance, as well as thanking my colleagues in the Department of International History at the London School of Economics and Political Science who undertook additional teaching loads in order to permit me to take leave to go to Princeton and to finish the book.

INTRODUCTION

The hundred years of European history since 1870 have been filled with such dramatic and rapid changes, social, economic, cultural and political as to make it almost impossible to write about them in a single volume. Yet these have been years in which certain historical experiences were common to Europe as a whole, and in which European developments were sharply differentiated from those in most other parts of the world; and they were also years in which the course of European history profoundly affected society in countries outside Europe. It is with these common experiences that this book attempts to deal.

While it tries to describe and analyse the great mass movements which have provided the main themes of the history of the past century – liberalism, imperialism, fascism, socialism, communism – these movements have been described in their historical and chronological context. History is concerned with actual men in actual situations; and for this reason it is important to remind the reader of the sequence of events in which these general movements have been embodied, to provide him, so to speak, with a chart with which he can begin to navigate in these stormy seas.

This is a period in which the impact of political events on the lives of individuals has been particularly strong, and while it is valuable, as many social and economic historians now try to do, to write history with the politics left out, in terms of wage rates, the cost of living or the incidence of unemployment, as being the historical factors which condition the experience of the ordinary man, such studies make sense only within a political and ideological framework, and it is this which in outline I have tried to provide.

While history can be written in terms of vast global movements or of economic cycles in which events such as the Second World War only cause a momentary tremor on the instrument readings, the precise form in which changes occur is determined by the actions of individuals. It would be unrealistic, in writing about a period which starts with Bismarck and in which Lenin and Hitler, to say nothing of Churchill or de Gaulle or Freud or Einstein, are leading figures, to deny the impact of personality on history or to maintain that the course of the twentieth century would have been the same without these particular personalities. If this seems old-fashioned, then this is old-fashioned history.

The author of a general book of this kind is bound to take arbitrary decisions about what to put in and what to leave out, where to begin and where to end. Some of the gaps are the result of my own ignorance, of physics for example, or of technical economic history. Other gaps are the result of lack of space: in discussing intellectual and artistic developments I have limited myself to those which seem to me to have affected or reflected the quality of European society and the presuppositions of its members; and the result has been that some of the greatest imaginative writers, painters and musicians, as well as the most original natural scientists, have not been mentioned. On the other hand I have tried to relate these developments to the political and social history of the period, rather than treating them separately.

All books reflect the interests and tastes of the writer, especially when, like this one, they have to be highly selective, but they are also, especially if dealing with contemporary history, influenced by the author's own social, economic and national status. No doubt this book bears the mark of having been written by someone who has lived through over half of the period covered, and who for some forty years of it was old enough to observe what was happening from the comparative safety and detachment of an English middle-class life. Yet one of the justifications for any kind of historical writing is that it enables the writer and the reader to make the effort to transcend his own limitations. History, like art, offers us an opportunity to enlarge our own experience. Writing this book has made me look again at the period through which I have lived and to question much which I have taken for granted. Its only justification will be if it arouses the reader's interest sufficiently to fill the gaps and to challenge the conclusions for himself.

But if history is like art, it is also like psycho-analysis. Just as the psycho-analyst helps us to face the world by showing us how to face the truth about our own motives and our own personal past, so the contemporary historian helps us to face the present and the future by enabling us to understand the forces, however shocking, which have made our world and our society what it is.

Finally any general work which attempts a broad synthesis of a long and crowded period of history inevitably imposes a pattern on what it describes. Each sentence must compress, and so distort, the events and ideas which it summarises. Moreover it is impossible to avoid what W.L.Langer has called 'the greatest mistake a historian could make . . . to construct a neat, logical pattern when in actual fact everything was confusion and contradiction.' And here, too, the only justification for trying to fit the last hundred years into a manageable frame will be if the reader reacts against the pattern which I have suggested and plunges back into the confusion and contradiction which is the substance of historical research. This confusion and contradiction are even more noticeable a feature of contemporary history than of earlier history. Every day new evidence becomes available, and new research is being published disproving our assumptions and forcing us to revise our ideas. Moreover our perspective on the recent past is always changing. We can now see for instance that the First World War was not such a total break as it appeared to be, and that the movements and ideas which have conditioned the experiences of the later twentieth century had nearly all made their appearance before 1914.

Episodes which seemed immensely important at the time sink into insignificance in a wider view. This is especially true of the history of Europe in the last twenty-five years. Since the end of the Second World War it is hard to decide what is important and what is ephemeral in our history. Down to the end of the Second World War we at least now know, when writing history, what was going to happen. For the more recent past we do not know the outcome of historical events in which we are still personally involved. At least we can be aware of the endlessly unpredictable and surprising turns which history can take and share the excitement of feeling that we too are part of history, and that whether we like it or not we are caught up in events as important as any in the European past.

London   James Joll
January 1972

THE NEW BALANCE
OF POWER

In November 1870, after hearing the news of the fall to the Prussian army of the French fortress town of Metz, the venerable British philosopher and historian Thomas Carlyle, a lifelong admirer of German culture, wrote to *The Times*: 'That noble, patient, deep, pious and solid Germany should be at length welded into a nation and become Queen of the Continent instead of vapouring, vainglorious, gesticulating, quarrelsome and over-sensitive France, seems to me the hopefullest public fact that has occurred in my time.' His optimism was not shared by everyone. Although many voices were raised in Europe to welcome the final unification of Germany under Prussian leadership and the proclamation, in the Hall of Mirrors at Versailles on 18 January 1871, of the King of Prussia as German Emperor, there were others who expressed misgivings at the emergence of a new great power in Europe as the result of a short, successful, but bloody war. Of the importance of the new 'public fact' however, there could be no doubt.

The military success of Prussia and the other German states – for the war had been a truly national one in which all the German states had been involved, even those which Prussia had defeated in the war of 1866 – was due to the careful military planning which had preceded the war, but it also reflected important economic and political developments. The years between 1860 and 1871 had been a period of extraordinary industrial growth in Germany, and Germany's production of coal was already greater than that of France and Belgium combined; it was to increase steadily, and by 1913 Germany's 219,000,000 tons a year rivalled the 292,000,000 tons of Britain, the world's greatest coal-producing country. The pattern was similar for the other basic materials necessary for the expansion of heavy industry. German iron and steel production increased about five times between 1850 and 1874, and the annexation of the French province of Lorraine after the war brought further important deposits of iron ore under direct German control, so that Germany was soon to be the second iron-producing country in the world. The rapid growth of basic heavy industries was accompanied by the development of new techniques and of new products: in 1867 Werner von Siemens invented the dynamo, and the electrical industry rapidly became a very important branch of the German economy and a source of economic and industrial influence abroad, as did the manufacture of chemicals after the discovery of important potash deposits at Stassfurt in central Germany in 1860 and the development by German chemists of the synthetic dye industry (one of the earliest colours being appropriately named Bismarck Brown), so that by 1870 Germany produced about half the world's requirements of dyestuffs and by the end of the century ninety per cent.

The unification of Germany, bringing as it did the removal of the last barriers to internal trade as well as a common banking and currency system, helped to speed the industrial development which was already under way before 1870. The war was followed by a great boom in investment, in part due to the increased capital made available by the payment by France of a heavy war-indemnity; indeed there was temporarily a serious financial crisis caused by over-speculation. In general however, Germany's emergence as the strongest military power in Europe was paralleled and sustained by her emergence, in a short period of time, as a leading industrial power; and in turn this rapid industrialisation led to radical changes in the structure of German society and imposed many strains which were never wholly removed.

The manpower essential for the industrial revolution in Germany was provided partly by a shift in the distribution of population and partly by a rapid population increase. Germany's replacement of France as the leading power on the Continent is nowhere more strikingly demonstrated than in a comparison between their population figures. In the 1840s they had been more or less equal at approximately 35,000,000; by the 1870s Germany had risen to 41,000,000 compared to France's 37,000,000, while in 1910 the German figures had shot up to 65,000,000, whereas in 1911 the French had only reached 39,500,000. These additional resources of manpower in Germany were fully utilised by the expanding industrial economy. By 1890 emigration from Germany dwindled almost to nothing; the movement which had provided the United States with millions of citizens of German stock had come to an end. The growing cities, too, attracted workers from the land to swell the urban industrial proletariat, and this in turn created further problems. Many of the large estates in East Germany came to depend on seasonal labour, much of it from over the border of Russian Poland, and this produced new racial and social tensions.

Germany's preponderance in the new balance of power in Europe was therefore firmly based on industrial and demographic factors. But her military victory in 1870, as well as her subsequent economic growth, was due to a number of other causes – educational and technological progress, administrative efficiency and careful planning. In military terms the great armaments factory of Krupp at Essen, in the heart of the Ruhr basin, Germany's key industrial area, was turning out breech-loading steel cannon which had shown their effectiveness in the war, even though the latest French weapons, the *chassepot* rifle and the *mitrailleuse*, an early type of machine gun, had held their own in their own sphere. (It was ironical that Krupp had also offered his new cannon to the French government, but the War Minister had rejected it.) Yet the German victory had been as much the result of long-term strategic planning as of the technical superiority of German weapons. The railway system had been planned and developed so as to enable the armies to be concentrated rapidly and to be supplied efficiently once in action, whereas it was the French failure to make the best use of their railways which was one of the major elements in their defeat. Certainly the German success in producing a superior concentration of man-power in the decisive early stages of the campaign had been extremely important.

Universal liability for military service had been a principle of Prussian military organisation since the reforms of 1814–15. The army was regarded as 'the training school of the entire nation for war'. Prussian military organisation had been reformed again in 1862 – a measure which had provoked a constitutional crisis and led to the summoning to power of Otto von Bismarck – to tie the reserve army more closely into the regular forces. Every male Prussian spent three years of his youth with the colours and then passed into the reserve. Napoleon III had tried unsuccessfully to introduce a comparable system of universal military service in France in 1866, both to replace the drafting by ballot (which enabled a rich man who had drawn a *mauvais numéro* to buy a poor man to substitute for him), and to increase the numbers of properly trained men available on mobilisation, but political opposition was too great, and the French army reform of 1868 was, from the standpoint of military efficiency, a somewhat unsatisfactory compromise.

Nevertheless, after the fall of the empire, conscription was introduced in France, and indeed universal military service was to remain a feature of life in most European countries until our own time. Only in Britain was it regarded as an emergency measure, barely tolerable in time of war or extreme danger, but not otherwise. (It was introduced in 1916 after bitter political debates; in May 1939 its adoption was seen as a symbol of Britain's determination to resist Germany.) Conscription was bound to have consequencer that were as important socially and politically as militarily. In the words of a leading military historian, 'the difficulty which was to face the Governments of Europe during the nineteenth century was how ... to fashion armies which would be not only politically reliable but also militarily effective.'[1] On the one hand, conscription gave every citizen a taste of military discipline, and some governments hoped that the experience would continue to condition conscripts for later life. On the other hand, the fear was sometimes expressed that universal military service would open the army to subversive civilian influences. In fact, conscription came to be accepted as a part of life, and there was remarkably little discontent, as the patient endurance by the soldiers of all the belligerent countries for at least three years of the First World War was to show. While the idea of a conscript army commanded by a professional officer corps was repugnant to many liberals who dreamed of a national part-time militia, and of the 'nation-in-arms' ready to defend its liberties, such a citizen army could only function efficiently in the case of a small state such as Switzerland, which never envisaged fighting anything other than a strictly local defensive war. For the modern warfare which the Prussian campaigns of 1866 and 1870 had inaugurated, conscription alone seemed to provide the trained manpower required. Yet, even if it did not serve either the conservative or the subversive ends which were feared early in the century, it did give every young man a period away from his home and some experience of other ways of life; and while he might in some cases respond to a training in obedience and discipline, he might, in those countries which did not yet have universal suffrage, also be struck by the argument that, if a man could be compelled to fight for his country, he should be allowed to have a say in the election of its government.

The new Germany was a state which had both conscription and universal suffrage, but in this respect as in many others it was marked by curious contrasts. The political force behind Bismarck in his creation, first of the North German Confederation after the war of 1866, and then of the German Empire after the victory over France, was the National Liberal Party. One of the measures which overcame liberal suspicions of Bismarck's aristocratic origins and unconstitutional behaviour during the struggle for the Prussian army reforms in the early sixties, had been his introduction, in 1866, of universal suffrage in the elections to the Diet of the North German Confederation, and this had also applied to the elections to the Imperial Parliament (*Reichstag*) after 1871. This concession to liberal ideas was perhaps not as important as it seemed: the government, embodied in the office of the imperial chancellor and in the person of Bismarck, remained responsible to the emperor alone and not to the Reichstag; and, while the Reichstag on paper had considerable powers of budgetary control over the executive, Bismarck found ways of limiting these, such as keeping the army out of the range of parliamentary discussion for long periods at a stretch by means of voting the military credits for seven years at a time. Moreover, many of the individual states which composed the German Empire, and notably Prussia, did not have universal suffrage for the elections to their own parliaments, while their governments retained control over important areas of administration directly affecting the ordinary lives of their citizens – including education, direct taxation, the police and the laws regarding the press and public meetings.

However, although constitutionally the German Empire was far from being a liberal state, it had been the National Liberal Party which had mobilised the political support that Bismarck needed to create the new united Germany. It was the massive middle-class enthusiasm for the idea of national unification which had overcome the resistance of the rulers of the smaller states, reluctant to give up their power to the new *Reich* – and it was the National Liberals on whom Bismarck relied for support in standing out against the opposition of many of his fellow Prussian *Junkers* to the idea of submerging their 'specific Prussian qualities' (*spezifisches Preussentum*) in a new, liberal, united Germany. For the moment in the early 1870s the National Liberals were content with what they had: a strong, united Germany, a policy of free trade, universal suffrage and a parliamentary system for the empire as a whole which they still hoped to transform into a genuinely responsible parliamentary government.

It was the liberal enthusiasm for national unification that had given Bismarck the popular backing he needed, but he himself was far from willing to grant the liberals' demands for responsible government. It was characteristic that when, in 1878, Bismarck decided that he could now do without liberal support, and set out to break the National Liberal Party, he dismissed their opposition with the words, 'They can force me to retire, but they will not make me construct a party ministry of National Liberals and entrust them with the conduct of affairs while they place me like a worm-eaten apple as an ornament on the table.'[2] Bismarck had been indispensable to the liberals, German unification, as the experiences of 1848–9 had shown, was impossible to attain except with the backing of Prussian power; but they were not indispensable to him. The imperial constitution was custom-made to fit his relationship with Emperor Wilhelm I, to whom alone he was responsible; and, although he needed a majority in the Reichstag for certain budgetary and legislative proposals and to guard against the possibility that Crown Prince Friedrich Wilhelm, who was believed to have liberal sympathies, might on his succession introduce true parliamentary government, he did not need any permanent political following. He was nearly always able to produce a majority when required – sometimes by making the parties strike a bargain over tariffs and appealing to their sectional economic interests as in 1879, sometimes by calling for national solidarity in the face of an external threat largely of his own invention, as when in 1887 he seized on the popularity in France of General Boulanger and his policy of revenge for the defeat of 1870 to proclaim that there was an imminent danger of war, thus winning an electoral success and incidentally confirming Boulanger's popularity in France.

Germany's emergence as a great power was largely Bismarck's work, a fact that was recognised both in Germany and abroad. And Germany's place in the new European balance of power created by her victory in 1870 was also determined by Bismarck. He had decided in the 1860s that Germany was to be united without Austria, but by signing an alliance with Austria–Hungary in 1879, he ensured that Germany could restrain the Habsburg Empire if its rivalry with Russia in the Balkans threatened the equilibrium of Europe. He realised that France's resentment at the loss to Germany of Alsace and Lorraine as a result of the war of 1870 would make it likely that, in the event of another war in Europe, France would be bound to take sides against Germany. For this reason alone he saw that the preservation of peace was in Germany's interest. Germany was, he declared, 'a satiated power', and the virtuosity and the unscrupulousness of his diplomatic methods aimed at preserving the balance of power in Europe and maintaining the situation he had established. 'Always try to be one of three in a world of five great powers', was the maxim on which his foreign policy was based. Until his dismissal in 1890 – when he was unable either to retain the confidence of the young Emperor Wilhelm II or to produce a majority to support him in the Reichstag – Germany's military and economic preponderance in Europe served to preserve the peace. After Bismarck had gone, his successors were not so conservative; and the history of international relations between 1890 and 1914 was dominated by the spectacle of the ever growing resources, military, technological and industrial, of Germany being used for new ends which were bound to affect the balance of power in Europe.

While the emergence of a powerful united Germany was to have a profound effect on the international scene and on the whole subsequent development of Europe, another state with pretensions to be a European great power was also able to complete its unification as a result of the events of 1870. This was Italy. The *Risorgimento*, the movement for a united Italy, was one of the great liberal causes of the century, and its leaders, Cavour, Garibaldi and Mazzini, whatever their political differences, had each contributed to its various stages. In 1859 the French had supported the King of Sardinia and Piedmont, King Victor Emanuel, and his minister Cavour, and had expelled the Austrians from Lombardy; in 1860 Garibaldi had led the expedition of his famous Thousand to Sicily and had overthrown the rule of the Bourbons in Naples and brought the states of central Italy into the new kingdom. In 1866, in alliance with Prussia and in spite of being themselves defeated, the Italians had profited by Prussia's victory over Austria to acquire Venetia. Yet until 1870 the city of Rome itself still remained outside the Italian kingdom, and the Pope's sovereignty was protected by a detachment of French troops sent by Napoleon III. For Italian liberals, the unity of Italy would never be truly attained until Rome was the capital of the new kingdom, and on two occasions Garibaldi made unsuccessful attempts to seize the city. With the French defeat by the Prussians however, the French garrison was withdrawn and on 20 September 1870 Italian troops entered the city.

The possession of Rome seemed to be the crowning achievement of the movement for Italian unity, yet it was to produce problems and aspirations which were to complicate Italian political development over the next fifty years. In the first place, the end of the Pope's temporal sovereignty alienated the Church from the new State, and the Roman question was yet another of the many points of conflict between liberals and Roman Catholics. The Pope had never formally renounced his temporal power and so did not recognise the Italian kingdom, and many Catholics refused to take any part in its politics. The old Pope Pius IX, as his temporal power waned, increased his spiritual claims, and the Vatican Council which assembled at the end of 1869, proclaimed in July 1870 the doctrine of Papal Infallibility and claimed divine and incontrovertible authority for the formal pronouncements of the Pope on questions of faith and morals. Although Catholics said that this was merely the formalisation of something they had believed for generations, the doctrine of Papal Infallibility not only confirmed the liberals' belief in the doctrinaire arrogance of the Church, but also led to deep divisions in the Church itself, so that in Germany a few prominent Catholics even left the Church and formed a schismatic group of 'Old Catholics'.

In Italy, to the embarrassment of King Victor Emanuel, himself a devout Catholic, the breach between Church and State was marked by the Pope's forbidding Catholics to take any part in politics: they were to be 'neither electors nor elected'. Although not all members of the Church obeyed the ban, it was not lifted till 1904, and it was not until 1919 that a Catholic political party was formed, so that in the intervening years, it has been suggested, the working of democracy in Italy suffered from the absence of a responsible conservative party. It was only in 1929 that the Pope's own position was clarified, with the establishment of the Vatican City as an independent sovereign state.

The repercussions of the Roman question, moreover, affected the political attitude of Roman Catholics in a number of other states. In France, they remained hostile to the Third Republic, and it was not until 1893 that Pope Leo XIII allowed them to support the republican regime; but this brief *ralliement* ended in the bitter partisanship of the Dreyfus affair (see pp. 64–5, 107–8 below), and in 1905 the Church was legally separated from the French State and deprived of many of its privileges. Bismarck too made use of the liberals' anti-clerical feelings for his own ends. By embarking on what one of the German liberals called the *Kulturkampf*, the struggle for culture, and asserting the State's control over the Catholic Church in Prussia, Bismarck hoped both to bind the liberals more firmly to him and to check any possibility that the Catholics might encourage separatist tendencies in South Germany. (In fact this turned out to be one of Bismarck's greatest mistakes, for the *Kulturkampf* only served to harden Catholic opposition to him and to turn the Catholic political party, the Centre Party, from a small sectarian group into a powerful national party which played a key part in German politics right down to 1933.)

For the Italians the winning of Rome not only symbolised and exacerbated the conflict between Church and State, it also seemed to confer great-power status on the new kingdom. 'What do you intend to do in Rome ?' the great German historian of ancient Rome, Theodor Mommsen, asked an Italian acquaintance, 'You cannot be in Rome without having cosmopolitan projects.'[3] How, the argument ran, could the possession of the city of Rome not involve a revival of the glories of the Roman Empire ? Even the republican followers of Mazzini shared in these dreams, for Mazzini had spoken of the *Terza Roma*, the Third Rome, that of the peoples, which would succeed the Rome of the Caesars and the Rome of the Popes. For some seventy years Italy was haunted and bedevilled by dreams of empire, for which she lacked the economic and military resources, while her strategic position in the Mediterranean gave her an international importance she was not always able to sustain.

Italian unification was political rather than social and economic. The North possessed an expanding industry in Milan and Turin and in the textile mills of the Alpine valleys; the agricultural area of the Po valley was rich and productive and Cavour himself had set an example on his own estates of what modern agricultural methods could do. The South, on the other hand, together with the islands of Sardinia and Sicily, was desperately poor. Its industrial resources, except for the sulphur mines of Sicily, were very small, and suffered from exposure to northern competition after unification; its agricultural potentialities were ruined by deforestation and erosion and by the neglect of generations of absentee landlords. Brigands infested the mountains; from time to time desperate peasants revolted in a vain attempt to achieve a better life. In Sicily these threats to the safety of property led to another abuse – the Mafia, a secret society formed to give landowners the security the State could not guarantee, and which soon became the true governing party in the island.

The economic and social problems of the South of Italy – still not wholly solved today – made it hard for a coherent national political system to emerge, while at the same time the lack of the raw materials for industry restricted industrial development. Although Italian liberals had realised one of their great ideas with the achievement of unity, the Republicans were disappointed with the maintenance of the monarchy, and parliamentary life, based as it was on a franchise which, even after the reform of 1882, included only 2,000,000 out of some 30,000,000 citizens, soon became a struggle for power and personal advantage in which it was hard for even the most high-minded to maintain their principles. In 1876 the prime minister Agostino Depretis coined the term *trasformismo* to describe what he hoped would be a 'fertile transformation of parties and the unification of all shades of liberal in parliament in exchange for those old party labels so often abused'; but in practice the transformation was not for the better, and political groups lost

8

any principles they may have once had in an attempt to win and retain power at all costs. The result in the generation which grew up after the achievements of the Risorgimento was a growing disillusionment about Italian life and politics and a growing desire for a radical change, whether by revolution or by a war for national expansion.

The rise of national states in Germany and Italy had a profound effect on the balance of power in all Europe, but no country was more affected than Austria. The Habsburg Emperor Franz Joseph had lost Lombardy in 1859 and Venetia in 1866. At the same time the war with Prussia in 1866 had finally destroyed the possibility of the Habsburgs playing a leading role in Germany. Austria now had to come to terms with the heterogeneous races which made up the empire, races bound together simply by an allegiance to the House of Habsburg. In an age when national states were taking the place of dynastic ones, such allegiance could no longer be taken for granted. In 1867 the Emperor made a compromise (*Ausgleich*) with the Hungarian nationalist leaders by which the empire was transformed into a Dual Monarchy, with Hungary linked to Austria simply by the fact that they had the same sovereign and that the conduct of foreign and military affairs was in the hands of joint ministries. In 1868 the Hungarian leaders Deák and Eötvös promised a measure of autonomy to the Croats, and undertook to respect the rights of the other national groups in the kingdom, but these promises were never fulfilled; and the Hungarians firmly suppressed any movement for national independence by the six million Croats, Serbs, Roumanians, Slovaks and others within their borders, while keeping alive a reputation for liberalism by maintaining a parliamentary system in which two parties, representing only a small proportion even of the Magyar inhabitants, alternated in power under a system reminiscent of the eighteenth-century parliament in England.

Hungary could at least claim to be a national state with traditional boundaries, even if it was at the expense of denying the national rights of the subject peoples. The Austrian half of the monarchy, on the other hand, was a collection of provinces without even a common name. (Its official title was 'The provinces and countries represented in the *Reichsrath* [the Parliament in Vienna]'.) Inhabited by different races – Germans, Czechs, Poles, Ukrainians, Slovenes, Croats, Italians and others – and with widely differing levels of economic development, it was the emperor and the imperial army and administration which alone gave it any sort of unity. However, in Vienna, the period between 1880 and 1914 was one of exceptional cultural brilliance, in which many of the seminal ideas and movements of the twentieth century were being developed. But it was also a period of anxious discussion of the 'problem of nationalities' and of the role of the Habsburg monarchy in the modern world. By 1870 indeed the idea of 'national self-determination' was already widespread and had already had profound political consequences. One by one those nations of Europe which had not already achieved a national state were becoming aware of their cultural, linguistic and historical traditions, and their intellectual leaders were demanding the embodiment of these in some sort of autonomous state. While Germany and Italy were being united and becoming European great powers, smaller states were finding a place on the map. The growing awareness of nationality had produced the Greek revolt against the Turks in the 1820s; it kept alive in the hearts of liberals all over Europe the idea of the restoration of Poland, partitioned between Russia, Prussia and Austria since 1795. In the Ottoman Empire other peoples such as the Bulgarians were eager to follow the example of the Greeks whose independence had been recognised by the European great powers in 1830, and of the Roumanians, freed from formal Turkish sovereignty in 1856, while in Western Europe the Irish question was entering a new phase with the growth of an active movement demanding home rule.

Mazzini, perhaps the most influential theorist of the new nationalism, had believed that, in a newly regenerated Europe based on national states, the interests of each nationality would ultimately coincide and each contribute its own specific qualities to a harmonious whole. In fact however the growth of one nationality tended to be, or at least appeared to be, at the expense of another. And in Austria–Hungary especially, the Germans, excluded from the new German Empire by the war of 1866 and deprived of their influence in Hungary by the Compromise of 1867, tended to regard the strivings of the subject nations as a direct threat to their traditional position, while the claims of nations with a proud historical past – the Czechs or the Poles, for example – often extended to territory now occupied by people of different nationality. The growth of national states inevitably raised the problem of national minorities.

Once the right of nations to independence had been recognised, then it was hard to know where to draw the line, and the success of the Serbs, Greeks, Roumanians or Bulgarians in obtaining in various degrees their independence from Turkey had its repercussions elsewhere. As the great French historian Albert Sorel wrote of the Eastern question, the problem of the Ottoman Empire, at the end of the nineteenth century, 'On the day we think we have solved it, we shall be faced with the Austrian question.'[4] To a greater or lesser extent, from 1867 on, each of the nationalities in Austria–Hungary challenged the German or Hungarian right to rule, and began to demand some sort of autonomy, even though until 1914 this generally stopped short of proposing the complete dissolution of the monarchy. These national movements ranged from those based on well-organised, urban middle-class support – as in the case of the Czechs in Bohemia, who had a traditional capital in Prague and a growing awareness of their culture, expressed for example in the foundation of the Czech National University in 1882 or in the music of Dvořák or Smetana – to the struggling efforts of village priests or schoolmasters to fan a spark of national feeling in the remote villages of Slovakia. It is possible that, had these questions remained the internal concern of the monarchy, change might have been postponed almost indefinitely: once they acquired international ramifications – as, with the existence of an independent Italy, Roumania or Serbia to which the nationalists inside the monarchy could look across the frontier, they were bound to do – then they were no longer problems for Austria–Hungary alone but came to affect the whole of Europe. In the early part of the century Metternich had managed to convince the European powers that the maintenance of Austria was essential for the European balance of power; by the beginning of the twentieth century the failure of the Habsburgs to find a solution to the national problem in their empire was one of the principal factors upsetting that equilibrium.

At the end of the war of 1866 Bismarck had prevailed on the King of Prussia and the generals not to impose a harsh peace on Austria. Within a few years Austria–Hungary, although her financial position had been greatly weakened by the cost of the unsuccessful campaigns of 1859 and 1866, leaving her with a prolonged budget deficit, and although, as we have seen, her internal problems were made worse rather than better by the Compromise of 1867, nevertheless maintained her rank as a great power, and gave up all ideas of revenge against Germany, so that in 1879 the two empires signed an alliance. Relations between Germany and France after the war of 1870 were very different, however. Under the Treaty of Frankfurt, which formally ended the Franco-Prussian War, France was not only obliged to pay a large cash indemnity, but her two eastern provinces of Alsace and Lorraine were annexed to Germany. The loss of Alsace–Lorraine had both military and economic consequences. By extending her territory west of the Rhine, Germany would now have an initial advantage in any new war with France, while the iron ore of Lorraine was particularly valuable for the manufacture of steel. Production had quadrupled over the previous decade, and there was to be a further increase when two English inventors, Gilchrist and Thomas, introduced a new method of smelting steel which overcame the chemical problems caused by the high phosphorus content of the Lorraine ore.

But perhaps as important as the military and economic loss of the provinces to France was the emotional and political effect. Even if Alsatians spoke a dialect of German, they remained firm in their allegiance to France, and the Germans never succeeded in assimilating them, while Lorraine was solidly and unchangeably French. The memory of the lost provinces, kept alive by patriotic propagandists and by those inhabitants of Alsace and Lorraine who left their homes rather than come under German rule, was a constant factor in French foreign policy up to 1914 and ensured that France would always side against Germany in any international alignment. President Wilson was later to assert that the annexation of the provinces poisoned the public life of Europe for forty years; and, even if after 1890 the demands in France for revenge were less insistent, the hope of recovering the lost territory never disappeared.

In addition to military defeat and territorial losses, France was faced with a political crisis as the result of the war. The empire collapsed in the defeat and Napoleon III, already a sick man, did not long survive his surrender and captivity. A new provisional government headed by the moderate liberal Adolphe Thiers, a politician who had been active since the reign of Louis Philippe, had to cope with an insurrection in Algeria and in March 1871 with the fierce revolt of the people of Paris, exasperated by defeat and by the hardships of a long siege. The Paris Commune was to take its place as a legendary revolutionary act in the annals of the European Left (see chapter 3 below), but, in spite of the bitterness which its repression caused, it had failed to do more than arouse the fears of moderate people all over France, and it confirmed the conservatism of the National Assembly, elected in February 1871, which expressed the country's need for peace and quiet. For a few years indeed it looked as though the power of conservatism might be strong enough to produce a restoration of the Bourbon monarch; but the difficulties which the rival claimants – descendants of Charles X and Louis Philippe respectively – had in coming to an understanding weakened their appeal, and the revival of republican feeling, under the leadership of Léon Gambetta, led in 1875 to the adoption of constitutional laws which, without formally declaring France to be a republic, inaugurated a republican regime – 'the regime which divides Frenchmen least' – which lasted until 1940.

In May 1877, indeed, the President of the Republic, Marshal Macmahon, who regarded himself somewhat as a regent for a non-existent monarchy, tried to impose his own candidate as Prime Minister and to appoint his own nominees to a large number of posts in the provincial administration, and dissolved the Chamber of Deputies. However the newly-elected Chamber was firmly opposed to the President's policies and to the Prime Minister designated by him, and asserted once and for all the supremacy of parliament over the presidency, so that, after Macmahon's resignation and his succession by Jules Grévy, who had led the parliamentary revolt against him, the importance of the President of the Republic began to decline, and his power to dissolve parliament was never again exercised during the history of the Third Republic. The effects of this crisis on the political and constitutional development of France were profound. Each parliament now by convention served its full term, so that the government was not able to use the threat of dissolution and a general election as a means of asserting its authority and keeping its majority. As a result government crises were frequent and French ministries notoriously unstable, as each parliamentary group tried to improve its own position and win its share of government posts. The parties of the centre, sometimes looking to the right for support, sometimes to the left, formed a succession of government coalitions in which the same names recurred in different positions and combinations. On the other hand, at elections, under a system of universal suffrage in which for most of the period there was a second ballot if no candidate obtained an overall majority at the first round, it paid the parties to form loose groupings or mutual agreements for the second ballot; consequently at such moments it was often possible to distinguish a broad division between Right and Left, between what one writer has called the party of order and the party of movement, and to see where Frenchmen's political allegiance lay, before the parliamentary game was resumed again.

It was a system which was best suited to a period when the government was not expected to intervene in economic life or to engage in long term planning; but in the decades after 1870 it produced a number of prominent personalities – Jules Ferry for example, a Protestant who gave to the French educational system a lay, republican foundation; Théophile Delcassé, foreign minister for seven years from 1898 to 1905 and the architect of the Anglo-French *Entente Cordiale*; or Georges Clemenceau who, after a long and chequered parliamentary life in which he did not conceal his contempt for his fellow parliamentarians (*'C'est une chambre de sous-vétérinaires'*, he is once reported to have remarked), gave France the leadership needed to survive the last gruelling year of the First World War. But although capable of moments of vigour and resilience – after the Dreyfus affair or during the First World War for example – the political system of the Third Republic reflected the underlying conservatism of much of French society and the desire of provincial France to get on with its own affairs; and the most successful politicians of the Third Republic were those who knew how to manipulate the parliamentary and governmental machine in such a way as to further the interests of the rural areas and quiet country towns where their political support lay, at a time when 60 per cent of the population still lived in towns of less than two thousand inhabitants.

The surprising fact about France in the 1870s was the speed with which she recovered from the material losses and the emotional humiliation of the defeat, and the comparative ease with which political stability was achieved in spite of frequent changes of government. Although during the next thirty years there were to be a number of political crises and scandals – about the sale of honours by members of the president's household in 1887, about the bribing of deputies in the interests of the Panama Canal Company in 1892 for example – and although the Dreyfus affair in the late 1890s aroused passionate feelings and divided families and lifelong friends, the new republican regime was never seriously in danger. As a contemporary Frenchman re-

hmarked: 'We present te spectacle of a tranquil people with agitated legis-
lators.'[5] This tranquillity was in part due to the slow rate of change of French
society. France remained at the end of the nineteenth century a predominantly rural country: 68 per cent of the population was classified as rural in
1876 and 56 per cent in 1911, whereas in Germany at the beginning of the
twentieth century only 28 per cent remained on the land. And, while
Germany was feeling the disturbing effects of rapid industrialisation and a
very fast growth of population, the population of France was only increasing
very slowly. France's natural resources and the capital invested abroad,
especially in the earlier part of the century, still gave France economic
strength and stability, and it was a measure of her social and economic
resources that she was able to survive victoriously the war with Germany in
1914–18, as well as to maintain, in the years before the war, a level of artistic,
scientific and literary activity which could stand comparison with any period
in European cultural history.

Within a few years of the defeat of 1870 France had regained her position
among the great powers of Europe. She paid off the indemnity to Germany
by the end of 1874, six months before it was due; and in 1875 Bismarck was
apparently sufficiently worried by France's military recovery to create an
artificial war scare in the hope of alarming the French government with suggestions that a preventive war by Germany against France might be a possibility – an episode, however, which did Germany no good and gave the other
powers of Europe an opportunity of expressing their sympathy and support
for France. Three years later, in 1878, a great International Exhibition in
Paris seemed to assert France's undimmed prestige and cultural supremacy.
France's recovery was due in part to the success of the loans which the
government raised to meet the indemnity – a sign both of the stability of the
new regime and of the capital resources which France could still mobilise.
And, although it was not until the 1890s that the industrial population began
to increase in numbers, much was done to make good the loss of resources
in Lorraine by the transference of factories and the development of mines in
the part of Lorraine still left to France, particularly in the area of Briey and
Longwy, which consequently was to become an object of German covetous-
ness during the 1914–18 war.

The Franco-Prussian War and the emergence of the German Empire as the
strongest military and potentially the strongest industrial power on the
Continent were bound in the long run to affect the position of Great Britain.
For the moment, however, the British were able to regard the events in
Europe with a certain detachment. During and immediately before the
Franco-Prussian War the main preoccupation of the Liberal government
under the leadership of William Ewart Gladstone had been to reaffirm
Britain's concern with the maintenance of Belgian neutrality guaranteed by

the great powers in 1839; in words which Sir Edward Grey was to recall in the crisis of 1914, Gladstone stated, 'We have an interest in the independence of Belgium which is wider than that which we may have in the literal operation of the guarantee.'[6] In 1870 however neither the Prussians nor the French needed to invade Belgium in the execution of their military plans, and the question of British intervention on the Continent did not arise; and indeed England would have had difficulty in finding the necessary forces if it had done.

Britain could still afford to be isolationist in the 1870s. She had been the first country to experience the economic benefits – and the social evils – of the industrial revolution and was still the leading trading nation in the world. The introduction of a policy of free trade and low tariffs from the 1840s on contributed to London's position as a world centre for banking and shipping. The British merchant fleet was larger than that of any other nation. British capital had contributed much to the industrial development of the countries of continental Europe and was now actively engaged overseas, in Egypt or South America, for example. The British navy remained much stronger than that of any other power – though from time to time it became apparent that its strength lay perhaps more in its reputation than in the actual state of its equipment, and radical reforms were required in 1888–9 and 1893–4 to bring it up to date. The Royal Navy had been used for a variety of purposes all over the world; it had fought the slave trade; it had twice forced the Chinese to open their ports and markets to British trade; it had intimidated small powers if the interests of British citizens were at stake. It could also be used for a political role, as when its command of the Mediterranean had tacitly ensured that no other power could intervene to stop Garibaldi's expedition to Sicily in 1860.

Britain's interests, however, were mainly outside Europe. Her army was designed for service in India or for colonial expeditions and not for service on the Continent. In the only war against a great power which Britain had fought since 1815 – the Crimean War against Russia in 1854–5 – its deficiencies had been as striking as its gallantry. Indeed, British strategy was dominated by the fact that she ruled India and needed to protect the routes to India and the security of India's frontiers. For this reason she was suspicious of Russia's expansion eastward into central Asia; and for this reason too she was concerned with the fate of the 'Sick Man of Europe', the declining Ottoman Empire. Preoccupation with India underlay Britain's interest in Egypt, and Britain became increasingly involved in Egypt after the opening of the Suez Canal in 1869. In turn this involvement created its own strategic needs, and led in the 1880s and 1890s to a further involvement in central and southern Africa.

It was, indeed, Russia rather than Germany or France which remained Britain's main rival until the end of the century, for it was Russia which seemed to have both the motive and the geographical position to enable her to threaten India and the routes to it, and it was this rivalry which provoked the most serious international crisis in the twenty-five years after the Franco-Prussian War. In 1875 the Christian populations in the Balkans – Serbs and Bulgarians – rose against the Turks; the Russians went to war with Turkey to support their fellow-Slavs and fellow Orthodox Christians, and the Turks' hold not only on their remaining possessions in Europe but also on Constantinople itself seemed threatened. In Britain the Conservative government, which under Benjamin Disraeli, Lord Beaconsfield, had come to office in 1874, threatened to intervene in support of the Turks; but divisions within the Cabinet and the vigorous and eloquent opposition of Gladstone and the Liberals, appealing for the right of Christian peoples to freedom and castigating the Turkish atrocities in Bulgaria, led to a more moderate policy. In spite of Disraeli's desire for unilateral action against the Turks and Queen Victoria's hysterical bellicosity ('Oh if the Queen were a man, she would give those Russians such a beating', she wrote), the British eventually agreed with Bismarck that the Eastern question should be the subject of a congress at Berlin, which assembled in June 1878. The congress met Britain's demands by limiting Russian gains; the Turks retained Constantinople; a small independent Bulgaria was created; Austria–Hungary occupied and took over the administration of Bosnia and Herzegovina though these provinces, like Bulgaria, remained nominally under Turkish suzerainty. Britain was also conceded the island of Cyprus by Turkey and the government ignored Gladstone's suggestion that this should be handed over to Greece (nor did Gladstone attempt to do so when the Liberals returned to power in 1880).

By the Congress of Berlin Bismarck had succeeded in averting a clash in the Balkans which would have forced him to choose between Austria and Russia. France obtained the sanction of the powers for the extension of her North African empire by the declaration of a protectorate over Tunisia. The countries which left the congress dissatisfied were Russia, whose hopes of Constantinople had been thwarted and who had failed to establish a large Bulgarian state under Russian protection, and Italy who had hoped to obtain Tunisia as a first step towards a new Roman Empire in Africa. In general, however, the Congress of Berlin settled the map of Eastern Europe for some thirty years, although its provisions regarding Bulgaria were soon abandoned since the Bulgarians were not satisfied with the small state allotted to them and in 1885 amalgamated with the Turkish province of Eastern Rumelia to form a 'big Bulgaria', whose rulers soon disappointed their Russian sponsors by showing a determination to pursue a policy independent of them.

Disraeli returned to London from the Congress of Berlin claiming that he had brought 'Peace with Honour', but in fact the success of the Congress was due as much to Bismarck as it was to Disraeli and his Foreign Secretary, the Marquess of Salisbury. In retrospect we can perhaps see the Congress of

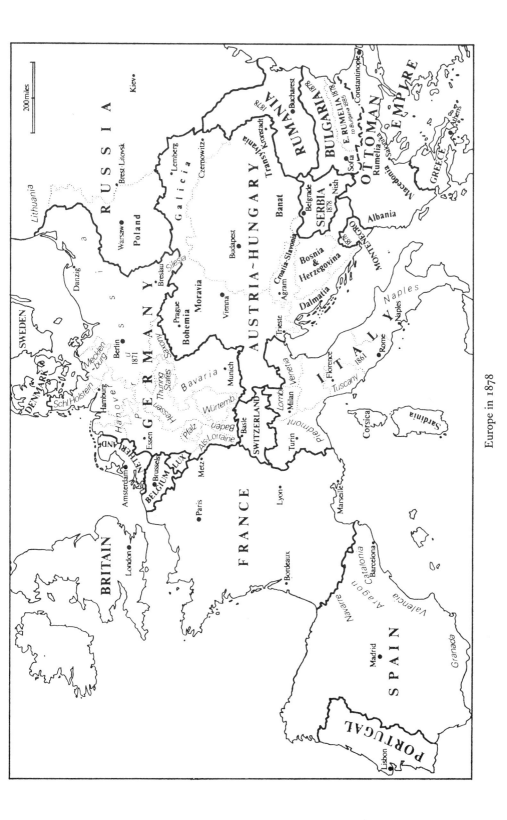

Europe in 1878

Berlin as marking Germany's emergence as the predominant power in Europe, but although in the 1880s and 1890s some people in Britain began to feel anxiety about her international position, in the 1870s she seemed to be at the height of her power and political influence. Constitutionally the two-party system was working efficiently, and Liberals and Conservatives, under their great leaders Gladstone and Disraeli, succeeded each other in office and vied in reforms intended to remove some of the abuses of *laissez-faire* industrial society. The franchise had been extended in 1867 and in 1884 a further measure of liberal reform gave the vote to nearly all the adult male population. The development from aristocracy to democracy seemed to be following a pattern of smoothness and good sense and England was widely regarded as a society in which political differences could be solved by compromise and in which, to quote the Queen herself, 'the lowest were able to rise by their own merits to the highest grade of society'.[7] Even if this claim was exaggerated, the English ruling class had shown its capacity to absorb new elements from the industrial middle class, while as far as the government was concerned, the administration was increasingly open to the talented – or at least to such of them as had been trained in the older universities, Oxford and Cambridge – after the introduction in 1872 of a competitive examination for entry to the civil service. The other side to Victorian England – poverty, hypocrisy, exploitation – to which reformers and critics were increasingly drawing attention, does not invalidate the success of Victorian political developments and constitutional achievements. There was, however, one question which began in the 1870s to increase in political importance and soon came to dominate the political scene, providing a challenge to the functioning of parliament and to the claim of the British that they were able to resolve their difficulties by sensible compromise. This was the Irish question.

Ireland had been formally united with England and Scotland by the Act of Union of 1800, and members representing the Irish constituencies sat in the parliament at Westminster. The political emancipation of the Roman Catholics (who formed the overwhelming majority of the population of Ireland), the extension of the franchise by the Reform Bills of 1832 and 1867 and above all the introduction in 1872 of the secret ballot, so that the landlords could no longer know which way their tenants voted, made it possible for an Irish nationalist party to become a parliamentary force; and in the early 1880s, under the leadership of Charles Stewart Parnell, the Irish party pursued tactics of obstruction in the House of Commons which brought business to a standstill, while their increased numbers enabled them to hold the balance between the Liberal and Conservative Parties. In 1886 Gladstone introduced a bill to give Ireland Home Rule, but he split his party by doing so and failed to carry the measure, as he was opposed not only by the Conservative Party but by the Whig elements in the Liberal Party (many of whom owned vast estates in Ireland which they seldom visited) and by some of the radical wing of the Liberal Party led by Joseph Chamberlain, who wanted the reorganisation of the Irish Government to be carried out within a general framework of reform and decentralisation for the other parts of the United Kingdom, and who in any case was now ready to challenge Gladstone's leadership of his party. Although Gladstone remained in active politics until the age of eighty-five, mainly in order to try and solve the Irish question, he again failed to carry Home Rule in 1894, and Ireland was still unreconciled in 1914, when the situation had deteriorated to such an extent as to face England with the threat of civil war and the breakdown of parliamentary government at a moment of growing international tension (see chapter 7).

Gladstone's great merit in dealing with Ireland was that, in spite of personal and tactical mistakes in handling the problem, he was almost alone among Englishmen in seeing that in Ireland Britain was confronted with a phenomenon similar to that which the Habsburg Emperor and the Ottoman Sultan were facing. The Irish were a nation, like the Italians, whose unification Gladstone had applauded in 1860, or the Bulgarians, to whose cause he had devoted his immense oratorical powers in 1876-7. They were not in the long run to be satisfied just by the recognition of their religious liberty – the Protestant State Church was disestablished in 1867 – or even by the agrarian reforms which Gladstone introduced and which the Conservatives, in an attempt to 'kill Home Rule by kindness', extended in 1891 and 1903. Once the idea of national self-determination had been launched in Europe, it was bound to affect Ireland, as it was later to affect the countries in Asia and Africa under alien rule. For Britain Ireland provided a continuous test of the sincerity of British belief in liberalism and democracy, and the failure of British governments always to pass this test was interpreted by foreign critics as yet another example of British hypocrisy. However, in the last quarter of the nineteenth century, for all the profound effects of the Irish question on English internal politics and party alignments, and although to many Liberals the cause of Home Rule provided a real crisis of conscience, it did not directly affect Britain's international position or her role as a great power. It was imperial questions, and especially those arising out of the possession of India and of the need to control the route to the East which conditioned British foreign policy. Throughout the nineteenth century Russia had been expanding her power eastward, first into central Asia and then into Siberia, and at each stage Britain had been alarmed by what seemed to be a Russian threat to the northern borders of India or to the communications between Britain and her eastern empire. In the 1830s Britain had been worried at Russian expansion to the north of Persia and towards the Caspian; by the 1880s the Russians were on the frontiers of Afghanistan and seemed to be already within reach of India itself. By the end of the century Russian ambitions in northern China provoked a diplomatic crisis which was to lead to a realignment of British policy.

This vast movement of internal colonisation was one of the great achievements of Russia in the nineteenth century and made Russia a power that was at the same time both European and Asian. Russia was undoubtedly a European great power. The immense size of her territory, a population that was shooting up – seventy-four million in 1861, a hundred and thirteen million in 1887 – and the influence which she had exercised in international affairs since the end of the eighteenth century, and more especially since her contribution to the defeat of Napoleon in 1812 and 1815, all ensured her position in the world. The Russian government, moreover, had used the opportunity presented by the Franco-Prussian War to free itself from the restrictions which had been imposed as a result of Russia's defeat in the Crimean War of 1854–5; she once more asserted her right to send ships freely through the Bosphorus and Dardanelles from the Black Sea to the Mediterranean and to maintain a fleet and fortifications in and around the Black Sea.

Yet Russia's internal development had certain marked differences from that of the rest of Europe. The traveller from the centre of the Continent, going eastwards into Russia or westwards into Spain had, and indeed still has, to change trains at the frontier, or at least to feel his carriage being lifted onto other wheels, since these two countries alone in Europe used a different gauge for their railway tracks from that of other railway systems. Although doubtless this was due to good engineering reasons, the change seems perhaps to symbolise the extent to which Spain and Russia both remained outside the mainstream of European development. For Russia in the second half of the nineteenth century the problem of how far and by what means to adapt herself to European methods of industry, government or finance was all-important. The Crimean War had shown that Russia was not militarily the equal of Britain and France. During the war Tsar Nicholas I, who had seemed to liberals in Russia and indeed all over Europe, the very pattern of unbending reactionary autocracy, died, and his successor Alexander II, faced with the results of military defeat and with growing unrest among peasants, felt obliged to do something new.

Alexander II was forced to face the fact, as he himself admitted in March 1856, of the 'hostile feelings between the peasants and their owners', and decided that if a change was to be made, 'it is much better for it to happen from above rather than from below'.[8] Of the series of reforms which he introduced in the 1860s much the most important was the emancipation of the serfs, the very large number of peasants who were literally the property of the landowners. The emancipation edict of 1864 – almost contemporaneous with the abolition of slavery in the southern states of the United States – was complicated in form and execution, and its effect varied widely from one part of the country to another. Although in the long run it was to act as a stimulus to further modernisation and to industrialisation, its immediate results solved few of Russia's problems. Although some landowners turned to more modern agricultural methods, many of them (some of whom are unforgettably portrayed in the novels of Turgeniev and a generation later in the plays of Chekhov) found the difficulties of running their estates with free rather than serf labour more than they could manage. For the peasants, too, the liberation created many new problems. Although they were now entitled to the permanent use of their land, in some cases the actual holdings were smaller than those they had farmed as serfs, and in all cases they were obliged to pay redemption dues out of which the landlords received compensation. Permission to leave the village community was only granted when the peasants had met these fiscal obligations, so that they were tied to the soil almost as firmly as before, while often their allotments of land were too small to give them much hope of ever paying their dues.

Five-sixths of the population of Russia consisted of illiterate and land-hungry peasants with little prospect of improvement in their condition. The abolition of serfdom did not put an end to recurrent peasant unrest, which came to a climax in the years after 1900 and in the Revolution of 1905 (see p. 73-4, 122-3), after which the redemption dues were finally abolished and a further programme of land reform undertaken; but by then it was too late. By 1914 Nicholas II had been no more successful than his grandfather in winning and retaining the loyalty of the peasants who still formed some 70 per cent of his subjects.

Alexander II was also only partially successful in the other reforms by which he attempted to move Russia in the direction of becoming a modern Western state. A reform of the curriculum and administration of the universities which might have produced a bureaucratic class competent to modernise the country was largely revoked when the students used their new freedom to criticise the authorities. A reform of the army in 1874 introduced conscription and reorganised the system of command and supply, but the army's equipment remained old-fashioned, and this limited the use which could be made of Russia's enormous resources of manpower. Nevertheless the economic system was beginning to change and consequently to speed up the Westernisation of Russia. Between 1866 and 1876 there was an intensive building of railways. A modern banking system was introduced, and a start made with industrial development, although it was not until after 1890 that industrialisation in Russia took a great leap forward.

Russia's international position had led to her involvement with the rest of Europe and necessarily forced comparison with the standards and achievements of the great powers of the West. Even the abolition of serfdom, the institution which, in the words of a recent economic historian of Russia, 'more than anything else had tended to make Russia different from the

West',[9] did not make Russian society and political institutions comparable with those of other countries in Europe, even the most conservative such as Austria–Hungary. Consequently, both among supporters of the Tsarist autocracy and among its revolutionary critics, there was a constant debate as to whether Russia's future should lie in the wholehearted adoption of Western methods or whether on the contrary it was traditional Russian institutions and modes of behaviour that would enable Russia to meet the challenge of Western political and technological progress. Until the Revolution Slavophils and Westernisers, Populists and Marxists each offered their rival solutions, and Nicholas II alternated between taking the advice of men such as Count Witte, Finance Minister from 1892 to 1903, who was working to make Russia a modern industrial and capitalist state, and K.P.Pobiedonostsev, Procurator of the Holy Synod of the Russian Orthodox Church and tutor to both the emperors Alexander III and Nicholas II, who saw in the hierarchical structure of traditional Russia and in the rigorous exclusion of Western ideas the only hope of salvation for the country. The contradictions to which these rival policies led were not resolved until the Revolution of 1917 – and even then perhaps not completely.

After 1870 Germany, France, Britain, Austria–Hungary and Russia were undoubtedly the great powers of Europe, with Italy staking a claim to be regarded as one of them. The balance of power in Europe consisted in the shifting balance between them and in the various alignments they adopted – the Dual Alliance between Austria–Hungary and Germany in 1879, the Franco-Russian alliance of 1893 and the *Entente Cordiale* between France and Britain in 1904 for example. But during the period up to 1914 the situation was changing, not only in the changing relations of the great powers to each other in their attempts to tip the balance of power in their own favour and in their reactions to the rise of Germany, but also in the emergence of new forces in international politics. Some of these changes were caused by the expansion of Europe overseas and by the rise of two new non-European great powers, the United States and Japan, but in Europe itself the smaller states were beginning to affect the international balance and play a part in international relations. We have seen how Italian national sentiment demanded that Italy should assume the posture of a great power. Even though she lacked the economic and military resources to do so, her history and cultural achievements seemed to justify her in this role. Moreover, the desire to assert their national identity through an active foreign policy was something that was experienced by nearly all the new states which had emerged as Ottoman power receded and the peoples of European Turkey became independent. It was their aspirations which caused many of the international crises of the period between the Franco-Prussian and the First World Wars and contributed to the outbreak of war in 1914.

Small states of this kind depended on the backing of great powers for the attainment of their goals, and Austria–Hungary and Russia tended to try to use them for their own aims and as a means of establishing control in the Balkans. In the 1880s and 1890s Serbia was relying on Austrian support, while Russia stood behind Bulgaria, but when, after a military coup had led to a change of dynasty in Serbia in 1903, the Serbs embarked on a policy of direct hostility to Austria–Hungary in the hope of freeing the southern Slavs under Habsburg rule, the ruling group in Serbia looked to Russia for support. For a brief period in 1911 and 1912 Serbia and Bulgaria, under Russian influence, were persuaded to combine and to join with Greece in driving the Turks out of the last areas of Europe still under their rule, but such an alliance was short-lived and the victors soon began to fight each other for the newly-won territory (see pp. 174–5 below). Bulgaria drew nearer to Austria–Hungary and Germany and eventually entered the First World War on their side. The rise of small states in the Balkans, first at the expense of Turkey and then with hopes of succeeding to the heritage of the Habsburgs, was the consequence of the growing belief in the principle of 'national self-determination'. Once it was accepted as a basis of international organisation it enabled small states to emerge, with their own national and historic claims, and to affect the balance of power and give them an importance which their own resources would not justify.

However, there were other states which by their strategic position were bound to enter into the calculations of the diplomats in the chancelleries of the great powers. The international position of Belgium or Spain, commanding the approaches to the English Channel and the Western Mediterranean respectively, was a matter of major concern to Britain, for example, while Spain, Portugal and Holland all still had great overseas empires which gave them importance, especially in the imperial rivalries of the last twenty years of the nineteenth century. Belgium and Spain are in some ways typical of two different kinds of development. Belgium, which had been joined to Holland by the Treaties of 1815, had broken away in 1830 to form an independent kingdom. In spite of including two distinct linguistic groups – French and Flemish – Belgium had in the nineteenth century achieved a considerable measure of political stability as a constitutional monarchy with parliamentary government. The great internal political struggle for universal suffrage continued till 1919, with each stage gained after an impressive and disciplined demonstration of peaceful strength by the organised working-class movement. This degree of political organisation was only possible because Belgium was one of the most highly industrialised areas in Europe as well as one of the most densely populated. The Belgians, with French capital, had early developed their coal mines, and textile and other industries rapidly followed, so that, of the small countries of Europe, Belgium could claim to be in the forefront of industrial and political progress. The international guarantees of Belgian neutrality helped to keep Belgium out of the rival power groupings of Europe and enabled her to concentrate on her industrial and commercial growth, but once that neutrality was threatened, it was impossible for Belgium to remain outside the struggles of the great powers.

Spain, on the other hand, had remained largely isolated from many of the main developments of the rest of Europe. The government was weak and unpopular; and the attempt in 1868 to establish a federal republic, after discontent with the rule of Queen Isabella had become so widespread that she was forced to abdicate, had ended in disorder and failure. After vainly searching for a new monarch – and the possibility of a Hohenzollern candidate on the Spanish throne had of course served as the pretext for the outbreak of the Franco-Prussian War, a sign of how sensitive the French were as to what happened on the other side of the Pyrenees – the Bourbon dynasty had been restored and things went on much as before. Industrial development was very limited; and in and around Barcelona, where there was an active textile industry, the anarchist influence on the workers was added to the Catalonian separatism which was one of the factors which made Spain hard to govern. The central power was continuously if unsuccessfully opposed both by the industrial workers and by the desperately poor peasants in the southern provinces who had nothing to gain by preserving the present regime and everything to gain by revolutionary change. The monarchy itself was challenged not only by Republicans but by a rival faction, the Carlists, who had denied Queen Isabella the right of succession to the throne, claiming that this was a right only to be inherited through the male line, and who represented some of the extreme conservative elements in a deeply conservative country. In vast areas of the south absentee landlords owned huge estates on which the peasants could barely earn a livelihood and were faced with famine in a bad year. Few of those conditions existed in Spain which produced the political and economic changes experienced by most of the countries of Europe in the later nineteenth century; and Spain remained isolated, often deliberately, from the rest of the world, at least until 1898 when defeat by the United States and the loss of her remaining colonies in America and the Pacific forced some Spaniards to ask questions about the destiny of Spain and Spain's place in the modern world and showed that, unaided, a weak power, however grand its historical past, could not hold its own without allies in the power struggle of the contemporary world.

Between 1870 and 1914 Europe reached a degree of technical progress and economic development higher than ever before. Yet there were many factors which prevented the establishment of the era of permanent peace and progress to which many liberal thinkers earlier in the century had looked forward. The change in the international balance of power caused, among other things, by the rise of Germany, produced further changes, and the technical and economic progress itself posed international problems and led to new international developments. In the period up to 1890, while Bismarck was still in power in Germany, it is true that he tried to maintain international stability and believed that by doing so he was serving the interests of Germany, yet it is also true that by the very subtlety and skill with which he attained his aim, he introduced a new degree of complication, cynicism and duplicity in international relations – 'It is the lees left by Bismarck that still foul the cup,'[10] Sir Edward Grey, the British foreign secretary, remarked in 1907. At the same time the governments of all the great powers were arousing, often for reasons of purely domestic politics, forces and movements for national expansion or for colonial development which tended to upset the existing international situation. The opening up of new areas of the world for development by Europeans led to an increase of international rivalry, while the insistent claims for national rights put forward by small or oppressed nations complicated the international scene still further.

Moreover, to an increasing extent international affairs became the concern of ordinary people: even the most autocratic government could not wholly neglect public opinion or the increasingly powerful press. Foreign policy could not be conducted independently of domestic policy and, as we shall see, some governments were fatally attracted by the idea of seeking in foreign adventures a release from the tensions within their own society. The desire for national greatness or for national self-determination as well as that for overseas expansion was experienced by the mass of the people as well as their rulers, even if they were not always aware of the implications of the policies presented to them, and these desires in turn contributed to the outbreak of war in 1914, a war which was to have profound effects on the structure of European culture and society. Yet there were in these years other forces – social, economic, political, intellectual – which were affecting the ordinary lives of Europeans and transforming even those countries which were able by their geographical position or lack of political importance to remain outside the rivalries between the great powers. If the First World War speeded up the transformation of European society, the forces making for change were already there before 1914, and the stability which observers a century later are sometimes inclined to attribute to European society at the end of the nineteenth century was already being undermined. How were the beliefs, circumstances and modes of expression of Europeans changing in the half-century after 1870? It is to some of these questions that we must now turn.

2

SOCIAL CHANGE AND
SOCIAL REFORM

The balance of international power in Europe had been profoundly changed by the emergence of a strong, united Germany; and the demand by the lesser states for national independence and a national foreign policy contributed to the instability of international politics. But in the internal development of each society in Europe there was, in the years between 1870 and 1914, an ever more marked shift in the balance of power between classes, and a growing demand for the recognition of the rights of the under-privileged, together with a continuous debate about the means by which this recognition could be achieved. The 'social question' had, of course, been raised in the early stages of the industrial revolution, and political philosophers and economists had been discussing it since the 1830s or before, but the rapid urbanisation of much of Western Europe, the growth of industry in countries where there had been little before (parts of the Austro-Hungarian Empire and Russia for example) as well as the increasing size and complexity of the whole industrial process and the spread of ideas about universal suffrage and representative government, all combined to make the problems of industrial society more acute than ever before. At the same time scientific and technological discoveries suggested that many of the evils of human existence which had been regarded as inevitable could in fact be removed or brought under men's control by rational means.

Britain had been the first country to experience the economic benefits and the social evils of the industrial revolution and, since the beginning of the nineteenth century, successive British governments had been taking steps to moderate and diminish at least some of the most glaring social abuses. During the 1840s the principle was finally established that the State could and should have the power to impose certain limitations on the freedom of employers to exploit their workers, so that, for example, in 1847, a law limited the length of the working day to ten hours in certain industries. In 1874 these gains were consolidated in an act prescribing a 56-hour week.

The legal limitation of the hours of labour became one of the most important demands in any movement for the betterment of the conditions of the working class: it had been a major item, for example, in the radical programme of the French workers in the revolution of 1848 and, in the growing international working-class movement of the 1880s, the demand for a working day of eight or at least ten hours remained a crucial point in all programmes of reform, and one on which all members could agree. In Prussia, laws aiming at securing adequate working conditions had been introduced in the 1830s and 1840s; it was a country where the idea of state control was part of the national tradition, but it was also a country where the right of the landowner – a right extended in the minds of many factory-owners to their own enterprises – to rule with patriarchal justice over his own people was widely recognised. In 1878 Bismarck introduced legislation which consolidated and extended the previous Prussian measures and forbade the employment of children under twelve years old and limited the hours of work for older children, while laying down certain safeguards for women workers. In Italy – where both industrialisation and social legislation were less developed than in Germany – child labour was prohibited in 1886, but until 1902 children under twelve were still working eleven or twelve hours a day in the mines.

State interference with the right of employers to exploit their workers was only slowly accepted in France – and the novels of Emile Zola, such as *Germinal* (written in 1884 but based on research into conditions some twenty years earlier), show just how appalling were the conditions in the mines and factories of France. It was not until after 1900 that there was any great improvement and then only as the result of widespread political and trade union agitation. In fact, although France like many other countries had introduced factory legislation as early as the 1840s, there was very little effective means of enforcing it, particularly in times of economic difficulty and unemployment, and the government inspectors were mostly unable to intervene successfully until an act of 1900 increased their powers. The same is true of Austria for example where, although on paper the factory legisla-tion was as advanced as anywhere in Europe, it was rarely strictly enforced.

While governments, under pressure from organised humanitarian bodies and indeed in some cases from the consciences of their own members, had made some attempt to alleviate the worst of the evils of the factory system, it was only with the emergence of large and powerful working-class pressure groups that the rulers of Europe were obliged to take social reform seriously if the loyalty of the masses to the State was to be maintained. As Bismarck himself put it when embarking on an extensive programme of social insurance in 1884,[1]

That the state should concern itself with those of its citizens who need help to a greater degree than hitherto, is not just a duty of humanity and Christianity, which should inspire all the institutions of the state, but also a conservative policy which has as its goal to encourage the view among the unpropertied classes of the popula-tion . . . that the state is not only a necessary institution but also a beneficent one.

If the improvement of working conditions in the industries of Europe was only achieved gradually, and never completely, in other respects growing control over the physical environment made possible profound changes for the better in the lives of ordinary people. While life in the industrial cities was bleak and harsh, and while the growth of towns had increased the danger of infectious disease, the problems of public health were nevertheless gradually being solved. The epidemics which had decimated the cities of Europe since the Middle Ages were being controlled or even eliminated. In the 1880s cholera, for example, was still a major threat – 55,000 people died of it in Italy between 1884 and 1887, while in the city of Hamburg 5,000 died as late as 1892 – but within a few years it was no longer a danger. These improvements were due in part to the new knowledge of the causes and nature of infectious disease and in part to government and municipal action to put this knowledge to practical effect.

In the 1850s the French chemist Louis Pasteur was investigating the process of fermentation and this led him to the discovery that it was caused by living organisms. His first practical successes were in dealing with the silkworm disease which ruined the French silk industry in the 1850s and 1860s, and in suggesting ways of dealing with the phylloxera which attacked the vines of France, threatening in the 1870s and 1880s to put an end to the production of French wine. Pasteur applied his discoveries to the cattle disease of anthrax in 1877; and a year earlier the German doctor Robert Koch had independently reached similar conclusions. The modern science of bacteriology had been invented; and during the rest of the nineteenth century the germs which caused some of the most serious and widespread diseases were isolated and identified. With the discovery of the organisms which caused disease, it was gradually possible to suggest methods of immunisation and cure. (Pasteur himself had one of his most sensational successes when in 1885 he successfully treated a boy who had been bitten by a mad dog and prevented him from developing rabies.) By the end of the century the bacilli which caused diphtheria, plague, tetanus and typhoid had all been discovered, and the means of curing or preventing at least some of these diseases made available: a serum against diphtheria was on the market by 1892 (and immunisation against the disease was possible by 1913). A method of immunisation against typhoid fever was first prepared in 1896 and was proved to be successful in the British army during the South African War. While it sometimes took many years for the discovery of a means of cure to follow the discovery of the cause of a disease – Koch discovered the tuberculosis bacillus in 1882, but it was only with the development of anti-biotics after the Second World War that a cure was found, and the question of immunisation against tuberculosis is still a matter for medical controversy

– the cure or elimination of many diseases now seemed to be in man's power and increased the belief in the possibility of more and more complete control by man over his natural environment.

Earlier in the century the possibilities of surgery had been enormously increased, first by the introduction of anaesthetics to kill the pain of operations and then by the use of antiseptics to control the gangrene which was so frequent and dangerous an after-effect of surgery. The use of gas for dentistry had been developed in America in the 1840s and in 1847 a British surgeon had used chloroform as a general anaesthetic. These and other methods, largely developed in the United States, spread rapidly in Europe and were considerably improved. More important still, in 1865 Joseph Lister first introduced the use of antiseptics into surgery, while the experiences of the Franco-Prussian War showed how essential something of this kind was if surgeons were to have much chance of dealing effectively with wounds: out of 13,000 amputations carried out on war casualties, 10,000 proved fatal. Indeed both the Franco-Austrian War of 1859 and the war of 1870 showed that war, with the introduction of new, more powerful weapons, was becoming increasingly bloody; and these and each subsequent war led both to advances in medicine and surgery and to demands that war should somehow be made more human. It is reported that Napoleon III wept at the sight of the slaughter on the battlefield of Solferino in 1859. More practically, again as a result of his experiences at the same battle, a Swiss observer, Jean-Henri Dunant, set about founding the International Red Cross in an attempt to mitigate the sufferings of war and to establish some conventions for limiting its effects.

New methods of treatment and new ideas about running hospitals gradually increased the chances of recovering from serious illness or injury and, although the reform of hospitals was slow – and in many parts of Europe is still by no means completed – the work of single-minded pioneers like the Englishwoman Florence Nightingale at the time of the Crimean War, and of enlightened patronesses like Queen Victoria's eldest daughter, the wife of the German Emperor Frederick, gave an example of what might be achieved. Medical discoveries and improved methods of treatment could only bring widespread benefits, however, within a general improvement of public health administration, with better water supply and sewage disposal (the means by which the eradication of cholera was achieved), better housing and better food. Here too the determined administrator could achieve profound changes in the lives of ordinary people. Perhaps the most famous of these was Baron Haussmann, Napoleon III's prefect of the metropolitan district, who had completed his replanning of Paris before 1870. Much of the old city had been demolished and replaced by the wide boulevards and broad prospects characteristic of Paris today. A new sewage system contributed to public health; a new water supply reduced the risk of cholera. Haussmann's town-planning had also had the effect, very much in his mind and in that of Napoleon III, of making the old traditional revolutionary tactics of fighting behind barricades in narrow streets harder to use. Yet at the same time the development of new quarters of the city inhabited solely by the rich tended to mark the contrast between classes all the more strongly, while the gradual removal of much of the working-class population to the inner suburbs surrounded the centre of Paris with a 'Red belt' which was to affect the nature of Parisian politics for several generations.

Haussmann had benefited from the strongly centralised administrative system which Napoleon I had given France. In England, and especially in London, the multiplicity of different local authorities hindered municipal reform and, although the London parks had so aroused the admiration of Napoleon III during his exile in England that he constructed the Bois de Boulogne and other Paris parks in imitation of them, in many respects London was behind Paris in municipal government, at least until 1888 when a central London County Council was set up. London was certainly behind Birmingham, where Joseph Chamberlain's career as a statesman was preceded by one as the reforming mayor. He claimed that during his term of office as mayor between 1873 and 1876 the death rate in the city fell by seven per thousand. Birmingham, with its municipally owned gas and water supply and scientifically planned drainage system was indeed in advance of most European cities and served as a model of what might be achieved by energetic municipal government.

Similar examples could, however, be found in other great cities of Europe, where active leaders were trying to deal with the problems caused by rapid growth: Vienna, for instance, was given a first large-scale water supply in 1873, and at the end of the century her mayor, the radical Catholic social reformer Karl Lueger, not only added a second reservoir, municipally owned gas and tramway systems and a municipal funeral organisation, but made the city one of the most imposing in Europe by increasing its parks and by putting a green belt round the city. As the population in the cities grew – and, to quote one authority, 'the larger the city, the faster the growth'[2] – the housing problem increased and in many of the great cities of Europe the inhabitants moved outwards, leaving large sections of the centre empty at night, since these districts were used solely for offices and government buildings. The development of the suburbs was hastened by improvements in local transportation systems: the electric tramway was introduced in 1881 for instance, while in 1883 a British act of parliament subsidised suburban railways to enable workers to be brought cheaply from the outskirts to the centre. The age of the commuter had begun.

Although the state was assuming the power to impose at least certain minimum standards of public hygiene and labour conditions, in many other respects – particularly in urban housing – the rights of property were still secure. For all the improvements brought about by individual philanthropists and by government action, large sections of the industrial population were still at the end of the nineteenth century living under appalling conditions. It was estimated that in Britain in the 1880s for example, 'a person born in one of the "selected healthy districts" of England may expect to live . . . nearly twice as many years as a person born in urban Manchester.'[3] In less developed countries the situation was even worse and the slums of Naples, for instance, remain a scandal in the mid-twentieth century. Nevertheless the accumulated effect of the changes briefly mentioned, as well as, for some of the population at least, an improved and more varied diet, meant that Western Europeans were living longer than ever before. In Britain, for example, the expectation of life at birth was 40 years in 1871, 51 in 1901 and 68 in 1959; in Italy 35 in 1874 and 44 in 1905, while fifty years later the Italians had caught up with the more advanced countries of Europe with an expectation of life of 66. To show how fortunate even the most backward of European countries was compared with other parts of the world in this period, it is worth noting that in India in 1881 the expectation of life was 25 years and that this had only risen to 35 in 1955.

If in the last quarter of the nineteenth century life for the working classes was only gradually improving, there is no doubt that for the wealthier classes of Europe it was physically more comfortable than ever before and offered a greater possibility of choice in all sorts of fields. The main streets of the cities had been lit by gas for several decades, and private houses also had gas lighting and electricity before the end of the century – Wagner's Festival Theatre at Bayreuth was lit by electric light in 1881 and the British Prime Minister Lord Salisbury was one of the first people in Britain to use incandescent lamps, which he had installed in his great house of Hatfield in 1880. In that same year the invention of the electric lift made possible the construction of taller buildings than had ever been seen before. The ideal of 'modern comfort' – running hot water and efficient plumbing – was slow to be put into practice, however, at a period when domestic servants were still available in plenty to stoke fires, carry hot water to the bedroom or empty chamber pots, and many of those who could have afforded to install the luxuries of piped hot water or steam heating did not do so. For those with money to spend there were new types of shops which offered a much wider range of commodities than previously. By 1870 the era of the department store was already under way. In Haussmann's Paris the new stores – the Bon Marché from 1852, the Magasins du Louvre from 1855 – set an example of a new kind of retail shop which was soon copied in the other great capitals of Europe. Félix Potin developed the first chain of grocery stores, also incidentally winning a reputation as a model of civic morality by his refusal to make an excessive profit from selling his wares during the siege of Paris in the winter of 1870; and after his death in 1871 the firm began to set up factories to manufacture the products sold in its stores, pointing ahead to some of the great twentieth-century commercial empires in the distributive trades.

Paris, in spite of the defeat of 1870 and the Commune of 1871, soon recovered its reputation as the '*ville lumière*', the city of fashion, glamour and luxury which other capitals could emulate but never equal. London, though it too had its department stores and its grandiose architectural projects such as the Royal Albert Hall (1867–71), as well as its popular parks, remained a less flamboyant city than Paris, a less ostentatious city than Berlin, its quiet residential squares still preserving something of the eighteenth century and the office buildings of its bankers and merchants often belying the wealth of the occupants. Berlin was not really a national capital at all; as a centre of German culture it was outshone by Munich or Dresden, to say nothing of Vienna, and as a financial or commercial centre Frankfurt and Hamburg were equally important. However, in the boom of the 1870s the city was transformed from being the somewhat provincial capital of a comparatively small state; between 1860 and 1914 its population increased six times and the new stores, apartment buildings and town houses of the new rich had a heavy vulgarity, unequalled in Europe, to set against the charm of the lakes, forests and waterways which surround the city. Vienna, whatever the problems of the empire of which it was the capital and which had contributed so many streams – Magyar, Slav, German, Italian – to its cultural life, kept the air of a great imperial capital. The Ringstrasse, on the site of the old ramparts demolished in 1857, and its new buildings such as the Opera House, were as grand, if not as beautiful, as the mediaeval or baroque palaces in which the aristocracy of the empire still lived in state, while, as we have seen, at the end of the century Karl Lueger gave the city municipal government and public services modern enough to stand in sharp contrast to much of the administration in other parts of the empire.

These urban improvements and the growth in consumption of most classes of European society hardly affected the mass of the peasantry who remained, even after the coming of the railway, in a condition which had changed little since the end of the eighteenth century. Although improved methods of farming and the development of a new mass market in the cities contributed to the general rise in living standards by making possible a better and more varied diet, it was only in a few countries that the peasants benefited from the changing conditions of life. The industrial revolution touched them very little and in some areas, such as the south of Italy, methods and equipment had not changed since antiquity; nevertheless most European peasants were now using iron ploughs instead of wooden ones, while their homes were lit with oil lamps instead of with tallow candles, even if it was only the richer landowners or more prosperous farmers who could afford to use the new agricultural machinery which had come onto the market in the middle of the century. Over much of Europe – in Spain, in Hungary or in the eastern provinces of Prussia – the power of the old landowning class was unchallenged in the countryside; and even those landlords who introduced scientific farming methods and equipment did little to alter the social organisation on their estates.

Yet almost imperceptibly the years before 1914 were a period of slow change on the land: production increased and a new specialisation grew up in certain areas to meet the demand of the cities for particular products, a demand which improved transport and storage methods had made it possible to satisfy. In some countries too, France for example, this is the period of the first attempts at the organisation of rural workers to protect their interests and of agricultural producers to develop their technical facilities, to improve their marketing methods or to exert pressure on politicians for their own economic ends; agricultural cooperatives became a feature of some parts of Germany, while in other countries such as the Netherlands and Denmark the development of a specialised and technically advanced agriculture (in this case dairy farming) forced farmers to cooperate and to assimilate their methods of production and distribution to those of industrialists. In general, though, the biggest factor making for change in the countryside was the appeal of the growing cities. Although the increased population of the cities was largely the result of the increasing survival rate of their existing inhabitants, the attraction of the town for the young peasant was very great, and led in many areas to complaints about the destitution of the villages and the shortage of rural labour. The barriers between town and country were gradually being broken down, even if the greatest changes were only to come in the twentieth century, when the motor-bus and radio and television were to transform what Marx had called 'the idiocy of rural life' and to suggest other standards and codes from those of traditional peasant society.

With the development of new industries and the beginning of a mass market for consumer goods as well as of a search for new fields of investment abroad, new forms of financial and commercial organisation had grown up. New investment banks provided capital for fresh enterprises, while various types of banking houses mobilised the savings of large numbers of small investors and enabled them to contribute to new undertakings and to subscribe to the loans raised by foreign governments. In commerce and industry, the individual merchant or factory-owner, taking the risks and responsibilities of his own business on his own shoulders alone, was giving place to the joint-stock company with limited liability – a form of organisation recognised by law in Britain in 1862, in France in 1863 and in Prussia in 1870.

In Germany especially, where the rate of industrial growth after 1870 was astonishingly rapid, these forms of organisation tended to coalesce; companies would make price-fixing agreements to avoid mutual destruction, even if such agreements were at the expense of the consumers; banks provided the capital for industrial development and their directors became directors of the new companies which they sponsored and financed; manufacturers tried to win control of all stages in the production of their own commodity – from the mines which produced the raw material to the machine tools which made the final product. A firm like the great German electrical combine, the AEG (*Allgemeine Elektrizität Gesellschaft*) thus became closely linked with mines and banks, as well as forming companies abroad. (It owned the municipal electricity supply in Genoa and Barcelona for example.) The concentration of capital and economic power went further in Germany than in the other industrial states of Europe, but the tendency was felt everywhere; and if it was an exaggeration to say, as the German industrialist and director of the AEG, Walter Rathenau, wrote in 1909, 'Three hundred men all acquainted with each other control the economic destiny of the continent',[4] this nevertheless certainly expressed the direction in which financial and economic organisation was developing in the years before 1914, and perhaps more important still it confirmed what was instinctively believed by the Left throughout Europe.

The establishment of London as the most important centre in the world for shipping, banking, insurance-broking and buying and selling generally, as well as the growth of British industry, had been based on a policy of free trade. In the 1840s Richard Cobden, the British publicist and politician, had succeeded in persuading members of both political parties that tariffs must be reduced or abolished, and at least until the end of the nineteenth century it was assumed, rightly or wrongly, that Britain owed her prosperity and pre-eminence to the adoption of this policy. But Cobden also became an international figure: he lectured before the sovereigns of Europe; he was a respected visitor to the meetings of liberal businessmen in Belgium or the Rhineland; shortly before his death he had successfully negotiated, in 1860, a commercial treaty between Britain and France, under which French tariffs were considerably reduced and France seemed to be on the way to becoming a free-trade country.

The attraction of Cobden's doctrine for the liberals of Europe was not based on an appeal to their economic interests alone. For Cobden, free trade was a means of improving international relations and the whole morality of international society. If trade flowed freely and if the middle classes of Europe could substitute their own enlightened self-interest for the traditional diplomacy of aristocratic foreign ministers and bellicose generals, then, he believed, the interests of each country would harmonise with each other and ensure peace and prosperity for all nations. Just as for Mazzini the development of each of the peoples of Europe into a nation would contribute to the advancement of the whole continent, so for Cobden the pursuit of the individual interests of each group of traders and the cooperation and competition of enlightened businessmen would produce the greatest happiness of the greatest number, since in the long run their interests would lead in the same direction. In the decade after Cobden's death in 1865 the liberals of Europe regarded his doctrines as axiomatic; and belief in free trade was as essential a part of liberal ideology as belief in national self-determination.

The lowering of the French tariffs against British trade by the treaty of 1860 was followed by similar moves in other countries. When the German Empire was founded in 1871, one of the first acts of the National Liberal Party in the Reichstag was to vote a gradual reduction of tariffs, with the intention that by 1877 a large number of foreign manufactured goods would enter Germany freely. Cavour, an avowed and enthusiastic disciple of Cobden, had introduced free trade in grain in Piedmont and at the time of his death in 1861 was working for further reductions; the tariff of the Piedmontese kingdom was applied to the whole of Italy after unification, so that until 1878 Italy too seemed to belong to the ranks of the liberal, free-trade nations. Even Russia, always the most protectionist of the European great powers, industrially backward and needing to safeguard her inefficient agriculture, lowered her tariffs during the twenty years following the great reforms of the 1860s.

However, during the last quarter of the nineteenth century the free-trade era was coming to an end. The economic climate was changing and low tariffs had not brought the benefits which had been expected of them. Indeed, during the years from 1873 to 1896 all Europe experienced the effects of a long recession after the boom of the preceding decades. The main symptom was a widespread if uneven fall in world prices, facing manufacturers with the need to find new outlets and to increase production, and tempting them to cut wages, thus adding to working-class dissatisfaction with the existing order. The long-term reasons for this downward trend are numerous, complicated and still disputed among economic historians; the industrial and railway-building boom was over, and it was only in the last decade of the century, with the development of new industries and techniques – electrical engineering, the internal combustion engine, synthetic textiles – that what has been called the 'second industrial revolution' gave opportunities for fresh industrial expansion. The world supply of gold was diminishing, as the effects of the gold rushes in California and Australia in the 1850s and 1860s passed. This coincided with the decision in the 1870s of many of the leading countries to follow Britain's example and use gold rather than silver as the basis of their currency – Germany in 1871, France in 1876 for example – so that the demand for gold rose just as the supply was temporarily declining. This in turn led to some doubt about the use of a gold standard and to much discussion about 'bi-metallism' and about the possibility of restoring silver to its place as the metal on which the world's currency should be based, though this movement had more success in the United States than in Europe, where gold had now established itself firmly. By the 1890s however the discovery of new gold deposits in South Africa, Western Australia and Canada put an end to these discussions and uncertainties, as far as currency was concerned, for some fifty years.

Alongside these industrial and financial difficulties – often exacerbated in particular cases by additional complications such as the crisis caused in Germany in 1873 by the over-speculation after the influx of capital as a result of the French indemnity, or made more acute by serious bank failures, such as that in Vienna in May 1873, that of the French Union Générale in 1882 or that of the London firm of Baring Brothers in 1890 – there was also a long term change in the position of European agriculture. The existence of this agricultural crisis was underlined by bad harvests throughout Europe in 1878–9, but the downward trend was not just the result of temporary difficulties. New sources of supply of the basic foodstuffs had been opened up in America and in Australia; wheat from the Mid-Western plains of the United States and Canada, now that railways and steamships had made transportation cheaper and quicker, could be sold more cheaply in Europe than most European-grown grain. The development of artificial refrigeration, exploited commercially from the early 1880s, enabled meat and dairy products from Argentina, Australia and New Zealand to compete in the European market. To meet these challenges and to enable the European farmer to hold his own, two courses were possible. One was to increase and modernise agricultural production, as was done effectively, for example, by the dairy farmers of Denmark and the Netherlands; the other was to introduce a protective tariff; and it was the latter that the majority of European landowners and peasants demanded. In some countries, notably Britain, agriculture never wholly recovered from the experiences of the late 1870s and 1880s, which led to a reduction by half of the area growing wheat, and a drop of over 40 per cent in the number of workers on the land. It was only during the two world wars and because of the difficulties of feeding the population in the face of hostile blockade that efforts were made to increase the supply of home-grown food.

It was the practical experience of these varied economic difficulties which led to the questioning of the principles of liberal economic doctrine and to the abandonment by many liberals, when their own economic interests were threatened, of free trade as an item in their programme. In Britain alone the majority remained convinced of the practical benefits of free trade, while, within the Conservative Party, many of whose members were by the end of the century pressing for tariff reform, those whose fortunes depended on shipping or insurance or banking or the other activities of which London was the centre, succeeded in maintaining the low tariff until a later great world economic crisis, that of 1931.

In Germany the end of the brief period of free trade marked also the end of Bismarck's alliance with the liberals and the beginning of a new era in German politics. By the mid-1870s Bismarck was looking for a new basis of parliamentary support and he found it in two policies which he used to split the National Liberal Party and to do permanent harm to the liberal movement in Germany – protection and anti-socialism. The introduction of a protective tariff as the basis for a new policy was, however, not easy, because the interests of those who were demanding protection were by no means identical. The industrialists wanted protection for their growing concerns, especially against British competition; but they would have preferred the new tariff to have been limited to industrial goods, enabling foreign food to continue to enter Germany at a cheap rate and thus to keep wage-demands down. The landowners and peasants, on the other hand, and especially the best established political pressure group in Germany, the Prussian *Junkers* with estates east of the Elbe, were anxious to be able to buy clothes or agricultural implements as cheaply as possible. To construct a conservative bloc therefore, Bismark was obliged to negotiate with both groups and to produce a tariff acceptable to each. This he succeeded in doing in 1878–9, but the agreement was precarious and in 1902 under the chancellorship of Bülow the bargain had to be struck afresh in order to maintain the solidarity of the two conservative interest groups; it was, as one writer has pointed out, an alliance between iron and rye which delayed the coming of democracy in Germany.

The German tariff of 1879 had important consequences for internal politics. Many of the National Liberals were themselves industrialists and for them the immediate attractions of protection outweighed their theoretical loyalty to the principle of free trade and split them from other members of their party on this issue. The Catholic Centre Party, united as it was by a solid confessional tie rather than by a bond of economic interest, included a cross-section of those who wanted protection – manufacturers from the Rhineland as well as peasants from Bavaria – but used the opportunity to bargain with Bismarck and in return for their support obtained part of the revenue from the new tariff for the purpose of social welfare schemes to be administered by the individual states and not by the central government, thus demonstrating, as they thought, both their interest in social reform and their support for the rights of the states against the central authority.

In no other country did the raising of the tariff issue as a result of the economic difficulties of the 1870s have as far-reaching political effects as in Germany, but everywhere the attitude of each section of society showed the interest groups into which each country was divided, and the move towards protectionism was a general one. By 1900 Austria–Hungary and Russia as well as Roumania, Greece, Portugal, Switzerland and Sweden had all followed the German example.

In France during the 1880s tariffs were raised piecemeal by a complicated system of bilateral commercial treaties, in response to pressures from the various groups of agricultural producers, until in 1892 a new consolidated tariff was introduced which contributed to making France self-supporting in food but also to discouraging French efforts in the field of international trade. It was perhaps a sign of the extent to which France was dominated by the pressure groups from the rural areas and by the interests of the provinces in spite of the centralised administrative system and the power of Paris itself.

The new tariffs had international consequences and contributed to mutual accusations and suspicions among the European states. Some governments kept the prices of their own products down with the help of subsidies; others used tariffs as a means of political pressure against a neighbour, as when from 1889 to 1892 the Austro-Hungarian government conducted a 'pig war' against Serbia, and prevented the import into the monarchy of pork, one of Serbia's most important products, in the hope of keeping the Serbian government as a satellite.

In the 1880s relations between France and Italy, already bad on account of France's success in declaring a protectorate over Tunisia, and Italy's subsequent adherence to the Triple Alliance with Germany and Austria-Hungary, were made worse by a 'tariff war' in which each country discriminated against the other's products, with the result, among others, that French wine merchants, who needed to import wine because of the fall in home production owing to the phylloxera epidemic which destroyed most of the vineyards of France in the decade after 1873, turned to Spain rather than Italy for the wine which they blended with their own. It was only in 1898, as part of an attempt to loosen Italy's ties with Germany and Austria-Hungary, that normal trading relations between the two countries were restored. Again, in the last years of Bismarck's rule relations between Germany and Russia deteriorated as a result of increased tariffs on both sides, in spite of Bismarck's apparent success in maintaining collaboration between the two countries on the diplomatic level.

The demand for protection, whether from agricultural producers or from industrialists, found a theoretical basis in the belief that a country which had achieved national independence politically must also aspire to economic independence and self-sufficiency. This view contributed much to the protectionist movement in Italy, and in Germany it seemed to mark a return to traditional German doctrines, which had prevailed before Cobden's influence had linked liberalism and free trade. Both Fichte during the Napoleonic Wars and Friedrich List a generation later had preached the necessity for national autonomy in social and economic affairs as well as in culture and politics; and List indeed had contemporaneously with Cobden produced a rival school of economic thought based on the advocacy of protection, and had pointed out that England's industrialisation had been carried out under a protectionist system and that it was only after her industrial supremacy had been established that her rulers began to extol the virtues of free trade. The fact that Britain's spokesmen and especially Cobden himself should be preaching to others the abandonment of protection just at the moment when it might help other countries to increase their production and thus become a rival to Britain could easily be represented as an example of British hypocrisy, and the doctrine of free trade described as the doctrine of the 'free fox in the free chicken-run'.

The rise of protectionism in the 1870s and 1880s was accompanied by a growing challenge to the other great principle of liberal political doctrine – the principle that the government had no right to interfere in the lives of its citizens except in so far as was necessary to maintain law and order and to hold the ring for the working out of economic forces. At the moment when, with the achievement of national unity in Germany and Italy, with the overthrow of the empire and the establishment of a republic in France, with the spread of the doctrine of national self-determination, with a growing belief in many countries in the virtues of parliamentary government and the merits of a broad franchise, liberal ideals seemed to be triumphant, many of the most fundamental of those ideas were already being questioned.

In the last quarter of the nineteenth century the way in which industrial society was developing, its economic difficulties and its social inequalities and abuses, forced people to accept a new concept of government and new political theories to justify it. In the early days of the industrial revolution most liberals had believed that the duty of the state was to leave its citizens alone; if the weaker members of society suffered at the hands of the stronger, if the rich grew richer and the poor poorer, this was simply the result of the laws of economics, and no government was expected or indeed considered able to do much about it; it was even thought that interference would only make things worse. We have seen however how men's consciences had been pricked by some of the more obvious abuses of the industrial system and how the governments of Europe had nearly all been obliged to pass legislation to limit, for example, the exploitation of small children or to regulate hours of labour in certain industries. By the 1880s a more positive view of the role of the State began to be put forward, according to which the duty of government was to offer its citizens not only negative protection but also positive advantages. It was a doctrine based on conservative prudence as well as on liberal and humanitarian idealism. Now that in almost all the states of Europe a growing industrial proletariat was beginning to organise itself and to express demands of a more or less revolutionary kind, governments felt that it was in their own interest to try to keep the working class contented.

One of the most important and in some ways most advanced of the exponents of this view was Bismarck himself. During the 1870s, as will be seen in the next chapter, the German Social Democratic Party was growing in numbers and effectiveness of organisation and in Bismarck's view represented a real threat to the stability of German society and of the newly established empire. In 1878 two attempts on the life of Wilhelm I gave him the opportunity he wanted and, although the would-be assassins had no real links with the Social Democratic Party, Bismarck used the opportunity for an all-out attack on the socialists. It was characteristic of Bismarck's political actions that each should serve more than one purpose: by introducing legislation – modelled, so it is said, on the laws which the British parliament had felt obliged to pass from time to time to curb revolutionary nationalist disorder in Ireland – to restrict socialist activity by banning party organisations, publications and meetings and by expelling socialist militants from their homes, Bismarck intended not only to stop socialist activity but also to divide the liberals, caught between their dislike and fear of socialism and their belief in civil liberties. The anti-socialist law was an integral part of Bismarck's breach with the National Liberals, for it was passed at the same time as the new tariffs were introduced, so that the liberals were split on two issues essential to their liberalism – individual liberty and free trade. Moreover the new tariff, providing as it did a new source of income for the central imperial government, was an essential part of the other half of Bismarck's programme to curb socialism by sponsoring schemes for social welfare.

Bismarck realised that to prevent the emergence of an organised working-class political movement, the anti-socialist law alone was not likely to be enough, and he accompanied his oppressive measures with a programme of social benefits which went further than anything of the kind previously seen in Europe, and which was to serve as a model for similar schemes in other countries, for instance in England under the Liberal government in the years immediately before the First World War. From 1883 on Bismarck introduced a scheme of social insurance to protect the workers against the hazards and misfortunes of life and against the loss of their power to earn for themselves, through sickness, accident or old age. The new legislation brought the various voluntary insurance schemes previously introduced by paternalist employers or by the old artisans' guilds or workers' cooperative societies into one national compulsory scheme. Although the financial burden of the new insurance system fell on the employers, who paid about two-thirds of the contributions, and on the workers themselves, the State also made a supplementary contribution to the old-age insurance fund.

Bismarck's social legislation failed in its immediate purpose. The Social Democratic Party steadily increased in strength and the workers remained unimpressed by Bismarck's policies. But the plan nevertheless represented something new in European society, a first step on the road to the welfare state of the mid-twentieth century. Two features of Bismarck's programme marked a breach with the beliefs of liberalism. First the State took over the responsibility of running a compulsory system which both employers and workers were legally obliged to join. The State, that is to say, was deciding what was good for its citizens and forcing them to accept it, whatever their own inclinations. Secondly by itself making a contribution, however modest, the government was using money obtained by taxation as a means of financing social benefits. So far this was at the cost of the consumer, for the revenue so used came to a large extent from customs and excise duties; but there were already people in Germany putting forward the idea of a progressive income tax, so that what was taken from the rich in the form of taxation might be given to the poor in the form of practical social benefits, and it was this system which was to be widely used by the advanced states in the twentieth century.

The idea of the State having the right to decide what was in the citizen's best interest was perhaps more traditionally familiar in Germany than in most other countries. The Prussian government had a paternalist tradition; both Fichte and Hegel had taught that the State was more than the sum of its citizens and that in obedience to a rational state and in serving its purpose a man would be fulfilling his own true role as an individual; Friedrich List had already in the 1830s and 1840s linked the idea of protection with the ideal of social reform and progress. Moreover Bismarck's legislation was supported and discussed by the academic economists and social thinkers of his own day. In 1872 a group of professors founded the *Verein für Sozialpolitik* (Association for Social Policy) and contributed much to creating a new climate of opinion about social reform. These 'professorial socialists' (*Kathedersozialisten*) were genuinely concerned with raising the level of life of the workers and with analysing the economic and historical nature of industrial society. Their 'socialism' did not go very far; but they did believe that the State must intervene to adjust the glaring inequalities of contemporary society; and they did believe that a scientific study of the laws of economics could serve as a basis for rational legislation and reform.

Even in England, where the *laissez-faire* liberal doctrines of the 'Manchester School' had been widely regarded as axiomatic and accepted as the basis of British prosperity, classical liberal beliefs were already being questioned in the 1880s. Although the demand for protection, first launched as a demand for 'fair trade' in the early 1880s, did not get very far in the face of the vested interests which decades of free trade had produced, the need for an active policy of positive social reform, based on a taxation system which would provide the government with the necessary financial basis, was becoming accepted as part of radical political thinking. Inside the Liberal Party the doctrine of *laissez-faire* and Gladstone's stern insistence on the reduction of government spending were being challenged and Joseph Chamberlain, who had started his political career as a leader of practical municipal reform in Birmingham, in 1885 put forward an 'unauthorised' election programme which contains many points on which the social policies of the twentieth century are based. 'What is to be the nature of the domestic legislation of the future?' Chamberlain asked. 'I cannot help thinking that it will be more directed to what are called social subjects than has hitherto been the case. How to promote the greater happiness of the masses of the people, how to increase their enjoyment of life, that is the problem of the future.'[5] To promote these ends Chamberlain was willing to tax the rich, to make them, as he said, pay a 'ransom' for the security of property which they enjoyed. Although Chamberlain did not carry the Liberal Party with him in 1885, and early in 1886 broke with Gladstone over the Irish question, with the result that within a few years he was working with the Conservatives on a policy of imperial expansion and reform, the ideas he propounded were gradually accepted by the Liberals. Even Gladstone in his last government could not withstand the demand for a radical programme and shortly after his retirement in 1894 the government took a decisive step in the direction of the redistributive taxation demanded by the social reformers by introducing, in spite of expressions of alarm from the landed aristocracy and the Queen herself, a tax on inherited property, the 'death duties', which have continued to provide British governments with a substantial source of revenue ever since.

Just as in Germany the academic reformers of the *Verein für Sozialpolitik* were concerned to find a new intellectual and theoretical basis for a new social policy, so too in England a new approach to social reform was being developed by a number of people. Among these the Fabian Society founded in 1884 was perhaps to have the most lasting influence, in spite of modest beginnings. This group of middle-class intellectuals, although including a man as talented and brilliant as George Bernard Shaw, really exercised its influence through the patient methods of social research especially associated with the names of Sidney and Beatrice Webb. They believed that society could be reformed by piecemeal practical means, by 'permeation' of any political organisation that could serve these ends – a Fabian tactic of slow progress as opposed to the immediately revolutionary hopes of some of the other socialist groups. Above all, and in this they were heirs of the philosophical radicalism of Bentham and his followers at the start of the nineteenth century, they believed that social legislation must be scientifically based, that the ills of society could be studied and diagnosed and an appropriate remedy prescribed as a result. It was in the hope of developing studies of this kind that the Fabians sponsored the foundation in 1895 of the London School of Economics. Thus the work of the Fabians led to the collection of a great deal of statistical and documentary material which went far to justify their claim to be scientific social reformers of a disinterested kind; and in their work in municipal government, especially in London, as well as in the tireless dissemination of facts and figures, they contributed much to the climate of opinion which made possible the rise of the Labour Party and the creation of the welfare state. In advanced industrial countries such as England and Germany the nature of progressive thought about the State was changing; the old tenets of liberalism were no longer unchallenged and new doctrines of State action and social justice were gradually accepted both by intellectual and academic thinkers and by practical politicians. As Gladstone's friend and biographer John Morley put it in 1889,[6]

If Socialism means a wide use of the forces of all for the good of each; if it means the legal protection of the weak against the strong; if it means the performance by public bodies of duties which individuals could not perform either so well, or not at all, for themselves, why, then, the principles of socialism are admitted all over the field of our social activity.

The awareness that times were changing and that, if existing institutions were to survive, they would have to be adapted to new needs and new ideas was shared by conservatives like Bismarck and by democratic radicals like Joseph Chamberlain. There was one other important body of opinion in Europe, traditionally linked with the deepest conservatism, which also had to come to terms with modern industrial society and at least to consider how far it should adapt itself to new social and intellectual movements if it was to retain its hold over men's minds: this was the Roman Catholic Church. Throughout the last years of the pontificate of Pius IX, who died in 1878, the Church seemed to be the embodiment of the conservative desire to resist change and to oppose the main intellectual, political and social trends of the day. Pius IX had in the Syllabus of Errors of 1864 condemned most contemporary literature and philosophy; he had reasserted his dogmatic authority at the Vatican Council of 1870 with the proclamation of the doctrine of Papal Infallibility; he had refused to accept the loss of his temporal dominions in Italy and had as a result remained bitterly hostile to the new Italian state. In Germany, though the fault was Bismarck's rather than the Pope's, Catholics had suffered for their beliefs at the hands of the Prussian government; between 1872 and 1878 the Prussian authorities asserted their right to approve the nomination of Catholic bishops and refused their assent in several cases; they controlled Catholic schools; they expelled the Jesuits. As a result the Church found itself in unremitting opposition to Bismarck and his policies. In France too, although vast sums were subscribed to build the church of the Sacré Cœur on the heights of Montmartre in Paris as a token of the nation's penitence in defeat, the new republic soon developed into a secular state whose government often seemed to act on Gambetta's slogan 'Le cléricalisme, voilà l'ennemi!' In 1882, for example, the government established a nation-wide system of lay education, destined to weaken the power of the Church in the schools.

Throughout Europe, therefore, the Catholic Church seemed to be hostile not only to the newly emerging socialist movement but also to the liberal state. Leo XIII, who succeeded Pius IX and reigned till 1904, at least listened to advisers who were pressing a change of attitude on him. Bismarck indeed had by 1878 come to realise that the *Kulturkampf* had been a mistake. It had been popular with the liberals even though it had forced them to compromise their principles, since their willingness to accept measures allowing individual Jesuits to be expelled from their place of residence made it harder for them to oppose comparable measures against socialist agitators when Bismarck asked for it. Nevertheless the campaign against the Catholic Church had not only led to a large growth of support for the Catholic Centre Party but had also alarmed many Protestant Prussian conservatives, who saw in Bismarck's liberal and anti-clerical policies a threat not just to the Roman Catholics but to the Christian religion in general. By 1878 Bismarck was ready to break with the liberals; and he needed the support of the conservatives and also of the Centre Party for his new protectionist policies. Accordingly, with the cooperation of the new Pope, relations between the Church and the German State gradually improved and over the next ten years most of the anti-Catholic laws were revoked or allowed to lapse.

Inside Germany too some Catholics, many of whom had been deeply worried by the Vatican decrees of 1870, were anxious not only to come to terms with the imperial state but also to show that the Church was ready to play an active part in movements for social reform and in mitigating the evils of the new industrial society. In particular, already before 1870 Wilhelm Emmanuel Ketteler, the Bishop of Mainz, was preaching the necessity of Catholic participation in the working-class movement; and it was under his influence that the first Catholic trade unions were founded.

Bishop Ketteler's influence extended beyond the Catholics of the German Empire, and his ideas had a considerable following in Austria. There the Catholic Christian Social doctrine was given a wider theoretical base by one of Ketteler's converts from Protestantism, a nobleman from North Germany, Karl von Vogelsang. Vogelsang's ideas about social reform were accompanied by a belief that a truly Christian state should be organised not on the modern democratic principle of one man, one vote, in a parliamentary system based on universal suffrage, but rather on what some nineteenth-century conservative thinkers believed to have been the basis of mediaeval political organisation, the organisation by 'estates', in which a man only had any political personality as part of a professional group, as a member of a trade or guild or of a recognised class in society. The attempts of the Catholic Church to find an alternative basis for political organisation to that of parliamentary democracy continued into the twentieth century, and indeed in the later years of the inter-war Austrian Republic an attempt was made to put some of Vogelsang's ideas into practice.

44

More immediately effective however than Vogelsang's theories was the movement launched under his influence by the reforming mayor of Vienna, Karl Lueger. Lueger used some of the ideas of Christian Socialism to create a successful demagogic movement, primarily aimed at improving conditions in Vienna, and there is no doubt that, as we have seen, he did achieve a considerable degree of modernisation in the administration and public services of the city. In this case genuine aims of social reform and sincere indignation at the conditions of urban life were accompanied by a virulent anti-Semitism in which the Jews were held responsible for the social evils which the movement was attacking. (For a further discussion of anti-Semitic movements, see chapter 4 below.) In the German speaking countries, although these attempts to bring the Church into contact with the needs of modern society had some support, they were bitterly opposed by some members of the hierarchy. In France these divisions were deeper still.

Ever since the French Revolution the power of the Church in France had been under attack, even though Napoleon III had restored some at least of its privilege and influence in the field of education. But French Catholics were themselves often divided about the best way to meet the challenge to their Church provided by the ideas of the Revolution. Under the Second Empire most of the church authorities had been careful not to espouse too strongly the claims of the legitimist claimant to the throne, the Count of Chambord, and had been willing to give conditional support to Napoleon III, whose troops were maintaining the territorial sovereignty of the Pope in Rome. At the same time for many French Catholics the House of Orleans was tainted with associations of free thought and liberal ideas. Some had retained the old ideal of a Gallican church, independent of Rome in its internal affairs, while others subscribed to the claims made by the Pope at the Vatican Council of 1870. After the defeat of 1870 and the fall of the empire, the royalist cause in France had renewed hopes of success, and the National Assembly elected in 1871 contained a majority of royalist deputies, spokesmen, so it seemed, for the French provinces who expressed the desire for peace and order after the shock of the defeat and the adventures of the empire. These hopes were disappointed; the Count of Chambord, after years of exile, refused to accept the tricolour flag which had been France's national emblem since the revolution. His insistence on the white flag of the Bourbons symbolised his total rejection of the values of the nineteenth century and he forfeited therewith his chances of restoration. The Orleanist candidate, the Count of Paris, finally made his peace with the older branch of the Bourbons and was recognised by the childless Chambord as his heir, but this prevented him from coming forward as the champion of a different kind of monarchy, constitutional and parliamentary rather than absolute. By the 1880s the opportunity for a royalist restoration had passed, never to return.

The hopes of the Catholic Church in France had been closely bound up with the possibility of a royalist restoration, and the avowedly anti-clerical policies of many republicans, and especially the introduction of a general system of lay education by Jules Ferry in 1882, alienated the Church from the new regime. It was only gradually during the 1880s that some French Catholics tried to overcome this hostility to the republic, and to sponsor movements of social reform. The move towards a new social Catholicism was largely the work of two monarchist aristocrats, the Marquis de la Tour du Pin and Count Albert de Mun. La Tour du Pin had been directly influenced by Vogelsang's theories which in their anti-democratic aspect appealed to some of the more intelligent of those royalists who visited the Comte de Chambord during his long exile in Austria. Under the leadership of La Tour du Pin and de Mun a real effort was made to bring the Church into contact with the workers and to promote social reform. In 1889 a pilgrimage of ten thousand artisans made its way to Rome to receive the papal blessing. This movement did not however have much lasting success: the deep anti-clericalism of most French workers, the rival appeal of various socialist and revolutionary doctrines, the divisions in the Church itself between conservatives and moderate reformers all made a Catholic social movement hard to sustain, and it was characteristic that the younger, more radical and democratic Catholic social reformer Marc Sangnier, whose movement *Le Sillon* (the Furrow) founded in 1894 was the forerunner of some twentieth-century developments in the Roman Catholic Church, should have been denounced by the Vatican in 1910.

Many Catholics were still in the 1890s irrevocably opposed to the idea of the republic as such; and what was important about de Mun's political career was the fact that he had accepted the republican regime and was trying to work within it. In November 1890 one of the senior Catholic prelates, Cardinal Lavigerie, gave his official approval to this conservative 'rallying' (*ralliement*) to the republic:[7]

When the will of a people has been clearly declared, when the form of government has nothing in itself ... contrary to the sole principles by which Christian and civilised nations can live, since only a sincere adherence to the form of government can save the country from the horrors that threaten it, the time has come to ... put an end to our divisions, to sacrifice all that conscience and honour allow.

Even this degree of reluctant adhesion to the republic was too much for many French Catholics who even, or so it is said, offered up prayers for the conversion of the Pope, so that when in the late 1890s the Dreyfus affair reopened and extended the breach between Catholics and Republicans, the *ralliement* was soon forgotten. It was another thirty years or more before an effective Christian social movement was to develop, even though the formal

46

relations between Church and State were settled in 1905 by a law completely separating the two.

The movement within the Catholic Church to meet the challenge of modern industrial conditions and of the nineteenth-century liberal state was only slowly supported by the Vatican itself, entrenched in its hostility to the Italian kingdom (which was in 1895 still celebrating its triumph over the Church by declaring that 20 September, the anniversary of the entry into Rome of Victor Emmanuel's troops, should be a public holiday). However in 1891 Pope Leo XIII issued a comprehensive statement of Catholic social policy in the encyclical *Rerum Novarum*, and in the following year gave his approval to the efforts of those Catholics in France who were working for a reconciliation between Church and State. As in the case of Bismarck's social legislation the Church's social doctrine was an attempt to check the danger of social revolution: it was only if the governments of Europe realised their moral responsibility to protect the working class from exploitation that the workers could be prevented from listening to dangerous revolutionary leaders and from putting the whole social structure in jeopardy. As the encyclical *Rerum Novarum* put it:[8]

> The elements of a conflict are unmistakable; in the growth of industry and the surprising discoveries of science; in the changed relations between masters and workmen; in the enormous fortunes of individuals and the poverty of the masses; in the increased self-reliance and closer mutual combination of the working population; and finally in a general moral deterioration.

In these circumstances the State must intervene to avoid the class conflict which these conditions would produce. 'The richer class have many ways of shielding themselves and stand less in need of help from the State; whereas the mass of the poor have no resources of their own to fall back upon and must chiefly depend upon the assistance of the state.'

'The increased self-reliance and closer mutual combination of the working population': it was this as much as the humanitarian conscience of the governing class that prompted the various movements of social reform discussed in this chapter, and it seemed that neither the efforts of governments nor those of the Church were going to satisfy the demands of the newly awakened urban masses. The liberal movement had challenged accepted beliefs and thrown doubt on ancient institutions; and the liberal leaders of Europe as well as conservative rulers were faced with new forces which, once unleashed, they could not control. As Jean Jaurès, the great French socialist, pointed out to the radicals who had led the attack on the Catholic Church in France, 'You have finally torn the people away from the protection of the church and its dogma . . . You have interrupted the old song which lulled human misery, and human misery has risen up and is crying out.'[9]

From 1870 onwards the demands were growing more insistent and the

Church vs. 47 socialists

organisations which put them forward were becoming better organised. An international socialist movement was in being which seemed to offer the possibility of a totally new society.

3

THE SOCIALIST CHALLENGE

In March 1871 an insurrection broke out in Paris. For months the population had suffered the hardships of a siege by the Prussian army. The economic life of the capital had broken down; food was desperately scarce. When in January the provisional government finally made an armistice with the Prussians, the temper of the Parisians was bitter and resentful both because of their economic situation and because their patriotic resistance had been in vain. The government, in an attempt to restore normal economic conditions, declared that the promissory notes which had served as currency during the siege must now be honoured in full and that rents in arrears because of the siege should now be paid, so that many of the middle class in Paris faced financial disaster. Shortly afterwards, on 18 March, Thiers, the head of the provisional government now established outside Paris at Versailles, ordered the National Guard in Paris to hand over the artillery in their possession, and sent troops to enforce the order. The reaction of outraged patriotism and general exasperation took the form of an immediate revolt against the government's authority. (Some people have suggested that Thiers had foreseen this and had deliberately provoked it in order to make an opportunity to suppress the revolutionary movements which had been developing in Paris during the previous few months, but it is more probable that the government's tactless handling of the affair of the cannons was unintentional.)

Under the leadership of a miscellaneous group of revolutionaries – followers of Proudhon, veterans of 1848 or disciples of Auguste Blanqui, the old insurrectionary hero who had spent most of his life in prison as a result of his dedication to the cause of violent revolution – elections were held in Paris, and on 28 March a new government for the city took office. For two months the revolutionaries ruled Paris, giving their regime the name of the Commune, after the revolutionary government of Paris set up by the extreme Jacobins of 1793. Eventually, however, after some weeks of siege the government's regular troops were able to occupy the city and suppress the Commune. The fighting was bitter, with acts of terrorism on both sides, including the murder of the Archbishop and other hostages and the burning of the Tuileries

Palace by desperate supporters of the Commune. Very many participants and even innocent bystanders were shot out of hand, while many others were punished with sentences of death, transportation and imprisonment.

In spite of its short life and lack of success the Paris Commune at once became a legendary episode. For the Left all over Europe it seemed to show that the age of revolution was not yet over and that a successful insurrection might after all still lead to a new social order. Each group among the revolutionaries claimed to have inspired the Commune; for the anarchist disciples of Proudhon and Bakunin it was 'simply the City of Paris administering itself',[1] the first of thousands of independent communes which would set up a new federalist, anarchist society. For the Marxists – after an initial hesitation on the part of Marx himself – it soon became an example of the dictatorship of the proletariat in action, 'the glorious harbinger of a new society',[2] which Marx and Engels celebrated in one of their most famous pamphlets, *The Civil War in France*, and although in the years before his death in 1883 Marx seems to have regarded the episode as less important than it had appeared at the time, the legend was launched and played its part in later socialist history, especially in the thought and practice of Lenin.

For the rulers of Europe, however, the Commune confirmed all their worst fears of an international revolutionary movement and of the dangers of an imminent social revolution. The dramatic events in Paris from March to May 1871 firmly convinced many people all over Europe that the International Working Men's Association (the First International, as it has become known subsequently), which had been founded in London in 1864 and which Karl Marx had almost immediately made into the vehicle for his ideas and policies, really was a kind of general staff for a universal revolution. In fact few of the leaders of the Commune were more than very loosely connected with the International and it was only after the event that Marx was to proclaim its virtues. The International itself was, in 1871, on the verge of dissolution because of internal quarrels and because Marx believed that it had served its purpose, and in 1872 it split irrevocably. Nevertheless, the ideal of a Socialist International had been born and one of the results of the Commune was to give the International a popular significance greater than it had had in its own lifetime. Above all, the First International had provided a means for the dissemination of Marx's ideas and this was to have an incalculable influence on the new working-class movements in Europe and beyond.

Karl Marx was a philosopher and an economist. That is to say that from his early writings in the 1840s down to his death in 1883 his theoretical work was always in the long run more important to him than the organisation of the International Working Men's Association – although this did not prevent him from dominating the International and interfering in the German Social Democratic Party or from involving himself for a brief period in English working-class politics. He wrote one major theoretical work, *Capital*, and a large number of shorter books, pamphlets, essays and articles; he conducted a large correspondence with a number of his associates, and this correspondence was continued after his death by his lifelong friend and colleague Friedrich Engels, who in the years between Marx's death in 1883 and his own in 1895 continued to spread Marx's ideas in the increasingly important socialist parties of Europe. All this writing has, since the deaths of Marx and Engels, been subjected to intensive and voluminous analysis, interpretation and reinterpretation, so that it is difficult to disentangle what were the elements in Marx's thought which made an immediate impact on his own generation and that immediately following.

Marx's influence on European thought has been at many levels. While much of his theoretical economic analysis of the nature and development of capitalist society is no longer accepted outside those countries where Marxism is an unassailable official dogma, and while many of his predictions were already falsified by events in his own lifetime, his doctrine that all historical change, the development of legal and social systems, the emergence of philosophies and ideologies, are to be explained in terms of economic causes and of changes in the nature of economic production and organisation, has had a profound influence on the methods of historical research and on the procedures of the social sciences, and has affected many people who by no means accept the rest of Marx's doctrines. While Marx's economic interpretation of history and his emphasis on the economic motives behind human conduct have had a far-reaching effect on our way of looking at the world, it was his doctrine of the class struggle and of the inevitable triumph of the proletarian revolution which gave his teaching an immediate political appeal to the industrial workers, at a moment when they were just beginning to organise themselves and to formulate their demands. As Engels said at Marx's graveside, deliberately if misleadingly linking the names of the two most influential thinkers of their generation, 'Just as Darwin discovered the law of evolution of organic nature, so Marx discovered the law of evolution of human history.'[3]

Marx inherited from Hegel the belief that history moved on a pre-ordained pattern. But whereas for Hegel the universal dialectical pattern, in which the contradictions of each stage were transcended into a higher synthesis, applied on the spiritual and metaphysical level, Marx's dialectic was based on what was subsequently known as dialectical materialism and was a law of change firmly rooted in the realities of the material world and of economic life. For Marx, as he and Engels had written in the *Communist Manifesto* of 1848, 'All history is the history of class struggles.' At each stage of historical development, as the means of production change and the economic structure of society alters, a new class takes over. The feudal aristocracy made way for the bourgeoisie; and this in turn is bound by the inexorable laws of history to make way for the proletariat. There, however, according to Marx and Engels the process will stop. After the proletarian revolution and a period of enforced radical change under the 'rule of the proletariat', a new order will emerge, in which the problems of the old class-dominated society will vanish and a new era of social justice will begin in which eventually, in Engels' words, 'The political authority of the state dies out. Man, at last the master of his own form of social organisation, becomes at the same time the lord over Nature, his own master – free.'[4]

It is this aspect of Marx's ideas, especially as made popular by the later writings of Engels, rather than his more sophisticated and subtle economic and sociological doctrines, which made Marxism so attractive a creed to the industrial working classes. History was on their side and they were bound to triumph against their oppressors and in so doing to fulfil a mission of universal emancipation. All that was needed was a greater degree of organisation and an awareness of where their true class interest lay, and they would sooner or later be able to take over the state. In this they might be helped and guided by the few members of the bourgeoisie enlightened enough to see which way history was moving, and so detach themselves from their own class and move forward with the proletariat, but ultimately 'the emancipation of the working classes must be the work of the working-classes themselves'. The means of that emancipation must be political; it was by organising so as to be able eventually to take over the machinery of government that the proletariat would be able to win power. (This was indeed one of the fundamental differences between the followers of Marx and the anarchists inspired by Proudhon and Bakunin, for whom the revolution consisted not in taking over, but rather in abolishing the machinery of the state, and in winning immediate possession of the economic sources of power and direct control of the means of production.)

For Marx's followers the class war transcended national boundaries. 'Workers of the world unite, you have nothing to lose but your chains,' the 1848 *Communist Manifesto* concluded, and the First International had firmly established the idea that the working-class movement must be organised on an international basis if it was to triumph. It was of course this proclamation of its essentially international role that aroused the suspicions of the governments of Europe and inspired the belief that the International Working Men's Association was behind the Paris Commune. Throughout the next twenty years there was in the minds of many European leaders, and notably of Bismarck, a real fear of the danger of an imminent outbreak of revolution on an international scale.

In fact the history of the First International showed that Marx, for all the power of his intellect and the strength of his personality, was by no means the only prophet of a revolutionary solution of the evils of nineteenth-century society. Pierre-Joseph Proudhon, who died in 1865, Michael Bakunin, who died in 1876, and Ferdinand Lassalle, who died in 1864, had each started movements before their deaths which were based on different assumptions and different methods from those of Marx. Proudhon had preached a doctrine of federalism, in which society would consist of small communities cooperating to run their own economic activities with little or no central administration. With the abolition of property and the abolition of government, men would be free to develop the best part of their nature, and the reign of justice would set in. Proudhon's analysis was based on a deep and realistic view of human nature, for he believed that the attainment of justice was the result of a constant struggle against the violent and irrational elements in man, instincts which the desire for property and the desire for political power encouraged. For his disciples, however, what was important was less his view of the world and of man's nature, but rather his insistence on decentralisation, on mutual cooperation and on the reduction of governmental power. The world which they envisaged was one of self-reliant peasant farmers or of skilled artisans running their own factories and workshops, and it was an ideal which seemed to fit the structure of economic life in France reasonably well. France had been a peasant society since the revolution had broken up the noble estates and given land to peasant owners, while heavy industry was much less developed than in Britain or Germany, so that the industrial pattern of France was that of a number of small industrial areas widely distributed over the country, with most factories employing comparatively few workmen. Proudhon himself, disillusioned with the experiences of 1848, had repudiated political action, but his disciples had already in the 1860s taken part in elections and it was they who had formed the French section of the International. There was thus in France already a strong tradition in the working-class movement which favoured decentralisation and mutual economic cooperation rather than the organisation of large political parties aiming at the control of a strong centralised State machinery. The ideas of Marx therefore, with their emphasis on political action and central government control of the economy, only made slow headway in France, and the federalist tradition of Proudhon and his suspicion of political as opposed to economic action by the workers lasted on into the twentieth century.

In the International the Russian anarchist Michael Bakunin had reinforced the libertarian ideas of Proudhon's followers, and had brought to them a belief in insurrection and conspiracy which was in direct contradiction to Marx's insistence on the necessity of patiently building up a strong, class-conscious political party in order to seize power. Bakunin believed that the true revolutionaries were those with nothing to lose – the landless agricultural workers of Italy or Spain or Russia, for example. And whereas the Marxists thought that it was the industrial proletariat in advanced societies who would be the spearhead of the next revolution, Bakunin maintained – rightly perhaps as things have turned out – that the industrial working class was already enjoying the benefits of economic progress and that it already had a stake in existing society which it would be reluctant to throw away. Bakunin's ideas were therefore applicable to societies where Marx, with his insistence on the necessity of industrialisation as a prerequisite for the proletarian revolution and his belief that the middle-class revolution must precede that of the workers, had less appeal. In Italy, Spain and Russia Bakunin found much support and his doctrines, especially in Spain, left a deep mark on the development of the working-class movement.

It was Bakunin's quarrel with Marx which had split the First International and had led in 1872 to the decision virtually to wind up its activities. Although the breach was largely over organisational questions and was provoked by Bakunin's belief that he could organise a clandestine and conspiratorial network within the International to support and supplement its overt political activities, and by Marx's refusal to tolerate any rival to himself in the international movement, the two men seemed to embody two rival conceptions of the revolution and of the society which should follow it: the one based on a disciplined political party working towards the conquest of the political institutions of the state and the centralised direction of the entire life of society; the other based on a libertarian belief in the loose association of independent groups in a federal system, where central government should be abolished completely or at least be reduced to a minimum and where the means of production should be directly controlled by the workers who were using them. What was common to the followers of both Marx and Bakunin was a belief that the new working-class movement must be international and that the community of interests between the proletarians of all lands transcended their national differences. This did not prevent Marx himself from being anti-Slav, because he felt the Slav peoples were less developed than those of Western Europe and therefore likely to delay the revolution by falling under the control of reactionary Russian rule; equally Bakunin was both anti-German and anti-Jewish (both of which prejudices were strongly reinforced by his dealings with Marx). Nevertheless the idea of an international socialist movement was one which has never been wholly abandoned, even though its supporters have often been disappointed, for it was often hard for the socialist leaders to persuade their followers to look beyond their immediate environment and their immediate interests. However, the two leading followers of Marx in Germany, Wilhelm Liebknecht and August Bebel demonstrated the genuineness of their international sentiments in 1870 by refusing in the North German parliament to vote in favour of the credits required for the war against France and by voting against the annexation of Alsace–Lorraine.

This opposition to the Franco-Prussian War resulted partly from a reluctance to see a Germany united under Prussia and was not shared by all the members of the German working-class movement. Not only was Marx himself at first prepared to welcome German unification as a step towards the creation of a strong centralised state which the socialists would eventually take over – though he disapproved of the methods used by Bismarck to obtain unification – but the followers of the other founder of the German labour movement, Ferdinand Lassalle, believed passionately in the necessity of creating a strong German state under Prussian leadership. Lassalle was a far less original thinker than Marx and, although his writings covered a wide range of subjects and included classical philosophy as well as modern legal theory, it was as a political agitator that he made his reputation. By reiterating a few simple points he had a profound influence on the German working-class movement and, even if his ideas were later overlaid and officially replaced by those of Marx, the practice of the German Social Democratic Party as opposed to its theory remained very much in the tradition of Lassalle. Lassalle was the first person to see the potential strength of an independent working-class movement, relying on the workers themselves and not on any of the middle-class liberal parties. The essential condition for mobilising the numerical strength of the workers – 'the poorest and most numerous class' as Saint-Simon and Proudhon had called them – was universal suffrage. At the same time the only way to deal with economic problems and to provide for economic development in the interest of the nation as a whole instead of a particular class was by state ownership and state planning. Thus Lassalle envisaged that under a system of universal suffrage the organised working class would ultimately be able to win political control of a strong state machine and to use it for the benefit of the masses. Although he explicitly rejected the idea of a bid for world power by any single country, for Lassalle the self-contained national state – which Germany of course in the early 1860s, when Lassalle's agitation was at its height, had not yet become – was the essential unit within which socialism could be realised.

It is characteristic that Lassalle should have been a passionate supporter of Prussian leadership in the movement for German unification, and equally characteristic that he should have reminded Marx that he was a German socialist and should work for Germany. Indeed, Lassalle's ideas about universal suffrage and about Prussia's role in uniting Germany even aroused Bismarck's interest and the two men met and expressed a guarded admiration for each other. Lassalle's early death prevented the association from continuing, but one of his close associates, Lothar Bucher, ended up as one of Bismarck's confidential secretaries. By the time of Lassalle's death the idea of a mass working-class party in Germany was launched, and when in 1875 his supporters united with those of Marx to form the German Social Democratic Party, the Germans were pointing the way to the other socialist parties of Europe and showing what could be done by determined organisation of the growing industrial masses.

By the 1870s, therefore, there were in Europe a number of traditions and theories of socialism to which the leaders of the new working-class movements could look for guidance; but what made the new socialist movement formidable and enabled it to arouse the anxiety and dismay of European governments was less the myth of the International and the bloody interlude of the Paris Commune than the fact that, with the spread of universal suffrage and the growth of the industrial proletariat, socialism was becoming a mass movement.

There were two ways in which the growing urban proletariat of the industrial countries of Europe could hope to better their condition. On the one hand they could organise themselves into political parties and, in those countries with universal suffrage or at least a wide franchise, use the force of their numbers to win parliamentary seats and thus gain reforms by political means. On the other hand there was a strong tradition in the working-class movement, reinforced by the disappointments of 1848 and expressed in the teachings of Proudhon and Bakunin, which rejected parliaments and elections as a fraud by the employers on the working classes, and which maintained that the only way to obtain improvements in working conditions, higher wages, shorter hours and even, eventually, control over the running of the economy, was by direct action, either by means of strikes or else by violent insurrection.

In practice the labour movements of Europe mostly combined both these methods or else oscillated between them. In the two countries where industrial development was farthest advanced, Great Britain and Germany, it was possible both to organise mass political parties and to found effective trade unions, so that the development of the working-class movement in both these countries depended on a close association between their political and industrial wings. In other ways however the development in these two countries was strikingly different.

In England by 1884 virtually all adult males had the vote; but in a country where the Liberal Party was dedicated to the cause of reform and had an influential radical wing calling for social change, and where even the Conservative Party had shown itself when in office from 1874–80 to be capable of tackling some of the evils of industrial society, it seemed to most of the newly enfranchised working men that their best hope of change lay in exerting pressure within the existing political parties rather than by founding a new one. Thus, although Marx had originally hoped to see a strong socialist party in Britain, he had soon been disillusioned, and although attempts were made in the 1870s and 1880s to found a specifically socialist party, the Social Democratic Federation, it attracted little support and was further weakened by quarrels among its mainly middle-class leaders. An Independent Labour Party was founded in 1893 and its leader James Keir Hardie was one of the first members of the working class to sit in the British parliament. However, it lacked mass support until 1901 when, as a result of a decision by the courts that members of a trade union were liable to pay damages to the employers for losses caused by strike action, the trade union leaders realised that they needed their own political party to press for the legal reforms necessary to make union action possible. In 1900 a Labour Representation Committee had been founded with the aim of returning workers to parliament. This became the means of political expression for the trade union movement and more than doubled the number of its supporters in the year 1902-3, when it became clear that the Conservative government was not prepared to amend the legislation controlling trade union activity. From then on the Labour Party (which took its name in 1906) could rely on the mass support of the organised trade unions and thus became of increasing political importance and influence.

During the earlier part of the nineteenth century the workers' unions in Britain had been mainly concerned with maintaining professional standards and carrying on in a sense the traditions of the mediaeval guilds. Gradually, however, as many of the old trades disappeared and as the demand for unskilled industrial labour grew, the old type of union though surviving in some crafts no longer seemed appropriate to the mass of the industrial workers. By the 1880s a 'new unionism' was developing, more militant and with a broader basis than the old unions had possessed. To many Englishmen the great strike in the London docks in 1889 was a revelation of an impressive new political and social force, and at least it showed that effective organisation could win a measure of recognition for the workers' aims and lead to practical reforms – in this case an increase in the wages for the dockers. During the next twenty years the organisation in trade unions of unskilled as well as skilled labour gave the workers in many industries a real bargaining power. However, although the Labour Party increased its parliamentary strength in the elections of 1910, there were still many trade unionists who believed that strike action was more effective than political action, while on the other hand there were also people who still believed that the Liberal Party – which since taking office at the end of 1905 had introduced an extensive programme of social insurance and other reforms and which had leaders such as David Lloyd George who seemed committed to even more radical measures – offered more hope of social change than did the Labour Party.

Thus, up to the First World War, while the strength of the organised labour movement in Britain was increasing and while an independent Labour Party had had some electoral success, the British working class was primarily concerned with practical gains and immediate reforms. The increasingly strong British labour movement remained pragmatic, with little ideological interest, seeking the improvements which were practically possible in a social and political system that allowed for gradual and peaceful change. Although some of the strikes, especially in the years 1910-14, threatened to turn into a more violent class war, the possibility of successful action, whether industrial or political, kept the British working-class organisations for the most part peaceful and reformist in tone. Because of its pragmatic purposes and practical achievements the British labour movement was very little influenced by the socialist ideologies of continental Europe, and its atmosphere and beliefs seemed nearer to non-conformist Protestantism than to the Marxist or anarchist parties in other European countries. Many of the early trade union organisers and labour political leaders in Britain had had their first experience of public speaking or of committee work in the activities of their local chapel, and phrases from the Bible always came much more readily to them than sentences from Marx's *Capital*.

The lack of a theoretical doctrine was one of the main things which distinguished the British labour movement from that which was growing in power and importance in Germany. The two branches of the German socialist movement – that inspired by Marx and that inspired by Lassalle – had united in 1875 to form the Social Democratic Party and its leaders August Bebel and Wilhelm Liebknecht were in close touch with Marx up to his death in 1883; and after Marx's death Friedrich Engels survived till 1895 to codify, disseminate and popularise Marx's teachings and to offer advice to the socialist parties of Europe and especially to the German Social Democratic Party. The growth in numbers of the German Social Democrats paralleled the growth of German industry. In 1877 they won 500,000 votes and 12 seats in the elections to the Reichstag; in 1890 they had 35 seats and 1,500,000 votes, while by 1912 they were the largest single party in Germany with 110 seats and 4,500,000 votes. On the eve of the First World War one German voter in three was voting socialist.

This impressive success was achieved in the face of considerable difficulties and indeed the achievements of German social democracy were less than its numerical strength might lead one to expect. Bismarck, especially after the frightening example of the Paris Commune, was genuinely afraid of revolution and had an exaggerated fear of the socialist movement. He tried to stop its growth both by a programme of social insurance (see pp. 40-1 above) and by, using the excitement aroused by the two unsuccessful attempts on the life of the Kaiser in 1878, by legislation imposing severe restrictions on the political activity of the socialists. Although they still took part in elections and sent an increasing number of members to the Reichstag, they were forbidden to publish newspapers or to hold meetings, and known socialist agitators were liable to expulsion from their homes. The effect of the anti-socialist law was the opposite of what Bismarck intended: it increased the solidarity of the Social Democratic Party by giving it martyrs so that a tradition of persecution survived, and it made the workers unwilling to place any confidence in Bismarck's social security schemes. When in 1890 the law was allowed to lapse after Bismarck's fall, the Social Democratic Party had an efficient organisation, a loyal membership and a clear doctrine and political programme.

However, even after the lapsing of the anti-socialist laws, there were considerable limitations on the freedom of action of the German socialists. Each individual state in the German Empire – Prussia, Bavaria, Saxony and the rest – controlled its own police force and made its own laws about such matters as the right of assembly, so that in some parts of Germany it was harder for the socialists to operate than in others. But the most important check on the efficacity of the Social Democratic Party was the actual constitution of the German Empire. Even though the Social Democrats might become the biggest single party in the imperial parliament, they were largely powerless to influence policy because the Reichstag itself had only very limited powers. It is true that it controlled taxation and had the right to amend or reject legislative proposals, but though it sometimes exercised these rights, it had no power to overthrow the executive, since the Imperial Chancellor was responsible to the Emperor alone. Thus large areas were left free for executive action independent of all parliamentary control, and the socialists could have little hope of affecting the conduct and policies of, for example, the army and navy.

Moreover, in some of the individual states the state parliaments, unlike the Reichstag which was elected by universal male suffrage, were chosen on a very restricted franchise. In Prussia, the largest state in the empire, it was scarcely worth the socialists putting up candidates in elections to the state diet, the *Landtag*; and in Saxony the government abolished universal suffrage in 1896 when the socialists showed signs of becoming too strong. It was this contrast between the numerical and organisational strength of the German socialists and their comparative political impotence which struck many foreign observers. In 1904, for instance, Jean Jaurès, the great French socialist leader and orator, attacked both the doctrinaire nature of German socialism and its political weakness: 'Behind the inflexibility of theoretical formulas . . . you concealed from your own proletariat, from the international proletariat your inability to act.'[5]

One of the peculiarities of the German Social Democratic Party was the extent to which its members were isolated from the rest of German society. It was extremely rare for a worker to rise into the bourgeoisie, and the tone of the middle class itself was largely set by the old aristocratic military caste. Germany still showed traces of feudalism alongside its highly developed capitalism. The Prussian landowner still had extensive control over local government, and the new industrialists were anxious to run their factories on similar lines to the hereditary estates of the aristocracy: in the Saar basin, for example, the great mine- and factory-owner Stumm dominated every aspect of life. In these circumstances, the workers seemed cut off from the classes above them, and many people were worried by the extent to which the working class in general and the socialists in particular appeared to be alienated from German life. Moreover, the avowed internationalism of the socialists made them suspect – the Kaiser himself once referred to them as 'fellows without a country' (*Vaterlandslose Gesellen*) – while the gap between the workers and their employers made the Marxist doctrine of the proletariat as the revolutionary class in an inevitable class-struggle a plausible one.

The role of the German Social Democratic Party therefore was a far broader and more general one than that of the British Labour Party. It was more than just a political organisation with electoral ambitions; it provided a whole range of activities for its members – cultural, educational and recreational; it developed vigorous women's and youth groups and a wide selection of newspapers and periodicals, ranging from high theoretical reviews to children's magazines. It was a way of life officially based on Marxist doctrine and on the expectation that the forces of history would lead inevitably to the triumph of the proletariat. The official party programme – the Erfurt programme of 1891 – gave an analysis of the future development of society:[6]

> The economic development of bourgeois society . . . divides the worker from his means of production and turns him into a proletarian without property, as the means of production become the monopoly of a comparatively small number of capitalists and large landlords . . . Hand in hand with this monopolisation of the means of production . . . goes the transformation of the tool into the machine and a gigantic increase in human productivity . . . For the proletariat and the working middle class – petit bourgeois and peasants – it means the increasing uncertainty of their existence, misery, oppression, servitude, humiliation and exploitation.

In this belief the socialist workers were to work for the inevitable day when the revolution would come and a whole social system in which they had no part would be ineluctably swept away.

In practice, however, these predictions seemed only partly true in the Germany of the 1890s. Even if wealth was inequitably distributed, the workers nevertheless had their share in Germany's growing industrial prosperity. Rather than sinking into increasing misery, their standard of living was rising. Moreover, even in the political field there seemed to be possibilities of action. Although the powers of the imperial parliament were limited, in some of the individual states, especially Baden and Württemberg in the south-west, where there was a live liberal tradition, there were possibilities of cooperation with other parties. Above all the Social Democratic Party needed to win elections and therefore was obliged to have an immediate programme to appeal to the voters as well as a long-term vision of a remote revolutionary future. One of the great problems for all socialist parties was how to win the support of the peasants. The doctrine of Marx, which assumed that the peasant would be squeezed out by the large landowner and be turned into a landless rural proletarian, was hardly one which would attract the votes of the prosperous independent peasants of Bavaria, for example, and the problem of finding a suitable agrarian programme which would not alienate the peasantry forced socialist parties into a compromise with the existing order of society at the expense of some orthodox Marxist ideas.

Thus the need for winning elections and broadening the basis of support for the Social Democratic Party inevitably obliged its leaders to come to terms with the political institutions of Germany. In the south there was some cooperation with bourgeois parties in local politics; programmes were modified to win the support of classes other than the industrial proletariat. Above all, the growth of a powerful trade union movement more concerned to secure higher wages, shorter hours and better working conditions than to carry out any fundamental revolutionary reorganisation of society, affected the party deeply. Although in Germany – in contrast to England – a strong socialist party had come into being before a strong trade union movement, during the 1890s the unions grew in strength. In 1889 – the same year as the great London dock strike – there had been a major strike in the Ruhr coalfield which demonstrated the potential strength of the organised working class and led to an increase in union membership. By 1900 the Free Trade Unions, as the socialist unions were called, were by far the strongest of the workers' organisations and their membership of 680,000 in 1900 increased to 2,574,000 by 1913. Inevitably they came to have an increasing importance in the shaping of Social Democratic policy and in directing the party towards the immediate practical reforms with which their members were most concerned.

However, while both socialist parliamentarians and union leaders were working for reforms within the framework of existing German society, the official doctrine of the Social Democratic Party remained committed to a Marxist belief in the class struggle and the inevitable revolutionary triumph of the proletariat. Because of the strong theoretical interests of the party leaders, the contrast between the party's revolutionary theory and its reformist practice was discussed in largely theoretical terms. In 1899 one of the leading intellectuals and journalists of the party, Eduard Bernstein, published a famous book, *Die Voraussetzungen des Sozialismus* (The Presuppositions of Socialism, though it was published in English under the title *Evolutionary Socialism*), which questioned the official Marxist doctrine at many points. Bernstein had lived in London and had been much impressed by the work and ideas of the Fabian Society, and he maintained that the working-class movement, instead of fixing its eyes on a distant revolutionary goal, should concentrate on immediate reforms. Thus he pointed out that Marx's prediction of the progressive impoverishment of the working class had not come true and that the workers would do best to concentrate on obtaining a fair share of the country's increasing wealth, while at the same time he questioned the rigid materialism of contemporary Marxists and tried to leave room in socialist belief for independent, individual, ethical choice.

Bernstein's criticisms of orthodox Marxism gave rise to an extensive theoretical discussion, both in Germany and elsewhere, and his 'revisionist' ideas were officially condemned by the German Social Democratic Party, although he himself remained a member. Thus in the years before the First World War the German Social Democrats were in the position of pursuing revisionist tactics while condemning revisionist theory. They were, that is to say, in spite of criticism from left-wing militants such as Rosa Luxemburg, the young Polish intellectual who made her reputation in Germany as a formidable controversialist during the revisionist debates, in practice committed to the acceptance of the existing order of things and to working for reform within it, while at the same time reiterating their theoretical belief in the class struggle and the inevitability of revolution. As a result the Social Democratic Party occupied a peculiar position in imperial Germany. It was by 1912 the largest single party in the country and the largest and most important socialist party in Europe, to which other socialists looked for leadership and guidance. On the other hand, its parliamentary effectiveness was limited by the comparative weakness of parliament itself and the practical reforms which the Social Democrats were able to obtain in Germany came either through working with other parties at the local level or through the collective bargaining power of the unions. At the same time, the party was committed to a Marxist materialist view of history, to the idea of the class struggle and of the revolution, and this inevitably increased the hostility and suspicion of the ruling classes towards the socialists, so that the workers were often regarded as somehow unintegrated into the German community and the Social Democratic Party as forming a state within the state.

It was its numerical strength and organisational efficiency, even though this could lead to criticisms of bureaucratization, that made the German Social Democratic Party so impressive to the other socialist parties of Europe, and many of them – the Belgian party founded in 1885 and the Austrian and Swiss parties founded in 1888 for example – looked to the Germans as a model, while the German party was able from its considerable financial resources to give help to those groups such as the Dutch socialists which were trying to establish themselves in the face of competition from rival anarchist groups. However German methods and the full rigour of Marxist doctrine were not everywhere applicable. Whereas in Germany the rapid growth of heavy industry had produced a concentrated urban proletariat which could readily be organised in a centralised mass party, in many other countries, even where industry was already an important part of the economy, its geographical distribution was less concentrated and the factories were smaller and employed fewer workers, so that the workers' organisations differed accordingly.

Thus of the major countries of Europe France showed marked differences from either Britain or Germany, both in the structure of its industry and the nature of its labour movement. Although there were, in the coalfields and textile centres of the north-east for example, parts of France with large-scale heavy industry and a concentrated mass proletariat, French industrial resources were spread over many parts of the country, and before the First World War the most characteristic industrial undertakings in France were those in medium-size provincial towns employing a comparatively small number of workers. Accordingly the doctrines of Proudhon, with his insistence on decentralisation and small units and his respect for the dignity of the individual artisan, genuinely corresponded to the structure of the French economy in a way that Marx's teachings did not. The French labour movement, therefore, was much less homogeneous and much less centralised than that of Germany, and its nature and forms were dictated both by the traditions of French social and political thought and by France's geographical and economic structure.

The practical organisation of the labour movement in France had been delayed by the repression following the Commune. However, an amnesty in 1879 allowed many of the socialist leaders who had been exiled to return, and in 1884 the formation of trade unions was made legal. At the same time the establishment under the Third Republic of a genuine parliamentary democracy based on universal male suffrage made possible the formation of an active socialist parliamentary group pressing for practical social reform.

Between 1880 and 1900 various trends in the French socialist movement developed independently, and it was not finally till 1905 that a united party was formed; and even then there remained an important body of working-class opinion opposed to any sort of political or parliamentary action and trusting instead to direct strike action to achieve its ends. In the shifting and complicated groupings of the 1890s three main tendencies can be traced. First there was the growing influence of Marxism in France. This was largely due to the efforts of Jules Guesde, a dedicated professional politician who, although lacking in personal charm, nevertheless had the powers of exposition to spread Marx's ideas and the organising ability to found a major socialist party. Marx's major works were not published in France until the 1890s (translated by Marx's son-in-law, Paul Lafargue), and indeed his ideas were never universally accepted in the French labour movement where rival ideological traditions were still strong. Guesde himself was not a very profound Marxist theoretician compared to his German or Italian socialist colleagues, and French socialism remained an eclectic doctrine embracing ideas derived from Blanqui and Proudhon as well as elements of liberal humanism not to be found in stricter Marxist sects. However in certain areas, and especially among the miners in the north of France, Guesde's ideas of a disciplined, centralised Marxist party found considerable support and started a line of development which, after the Russian revolution, was to contribute to the foundation of the French Communist Party.

However, Marxism, with its emphasis on the class struggle and the impending catastrophic crisis of capitalism, had only a limited appeal in a country whose population was still largely rural and which had a real parliamentary life and a genuine possibility of achieving social reforms by constitutional means. Thus, the second main tendency in the French socialist movement was that developed within the Chamber of Deputies. During the 1890s a parliamentary group of independent socialists was formed, men for whom the ideal of social and economic reform had taken the place of the constitutional liberalism of the older generation of republicans. Although several of them – Alexandre Millerand, René Viviani and Aristide Briand for instance – later left the socialist ranks and went on to hold high ministerial office, the most important of them was Jean Jaurès, the principal architect of a united socialist party in France, and the man who more than anyone gave French socialism its particular flavour, combining a liberal ethical humanism and a deep sense of social justice with elements drawn from Marx's analysis of historical development. Jaurès himself was an orator of genius, whose inexhaustible optimism gave confidence both to himself and his followers. He was attracted to socialist ideas (after first entering politics as a Radical) because they seemed to provide hope of a society based on justice, in which the sufferings of the poor would be eliminated. And once he had become a socialist, he saw in socialism a movement which could create a new international order in which the workers of the world would combine to prevent war, and in which nations, after agreeing to disarm, would solve their differences by arbitration and by peaceful negotiation. For him social justice and international harmony were part of the same vision. It was characteristic of him that he should have become a passionate Dreyfusard in 1897, and it was partly through his actions that the case of Dreyfus – a Jewish officer on the general staff, unjustly accused and convicted of espionage for the Germans and sentenced to imprisonment in appalling conditions on Devil's Island off the coast of French Guiana – became a major political *affaire*, which divided French society into two bands of passionate partisans. While Guesde and his followers saw the issue as a quarrel between two groups of the ruling class which was of no concern to the masses (a judgement which was largely supported by the elections of 1898, in which the Dreyfus case was only a secondary issue), for Jaurès Dreyfus' condemnation was an act of injustice, irrespective of the class or status of the victim, and as such must be reversed if the French Republic were ever to progress towards being a society based on justice.

Those who believed Dreyfus innocent declared that the military authorities who had accused and judged him had stopped at nothing to conceal their duplicity and incompetence; they had, the Dreyfusards pointed out, forged and suppressed evidence and conspired to prevent justice, in the interest of what appeared to the Left to be an anti-Semitic, anti-Republican officer caste. To the opponents of Dreyfus, on the other hand, the army seemed the defender of the security and greatness of France and its officers the representatives of an institution that should be immune from criticism, especially when that criticism came from what they considered a conspiracy of Jews and freemasons. In some ways it was an artificial crisis in that, although the supporters of Dreyfus declared that his antagonists were endangering the republican regime, there was in fact no organised group on the right capable of overthrowing the republic, so that the violent anti-republicanism of Dreyfus' opponents remained rhetorical rather than practical. Nevertheless, the virulence of the propaganda on both sides was enough to convince many republicans that the constitution was seriously in danger. The situation therefore produced declarations of support for the liberal republic against its royalist, Catholic and authoritarian opponents, from all those whose interests were by now vested in the republican regime, ranging from politicians making a career in the Chamber of Deputies to village schoolmasters who owed their jobs to the system of universal lay education which the republican government had introduced in the 1880s.

The result of the Dreyfus crisis and of the rallying of support for republican institutions was the formation in 1899 of a government of republican solidarity, and it was this event which produced a controversy within the French socialist movement comparable to that aroused by Bernstein's theoretical revisionism in Germany. To Jaurès and many others it seemed the duty of the parliamentary socialists to support the new government, committed as it was to the safeguarding of republican institutions and to a revision of the verdict and sentence on Dreyfus. In fact one of the leading independent socialists in the Chamber, Alexandre Millerand, without consulting his colleagues, accepted a ministerial appointment in the government. This provoked a bitter discussion about the circumstances, if any, which justified collaboration between socialists and bourgeois political parties.

It was a debate which echoed through the history of French socialism in the twentieth century, but its immediate effect was to widen the breach between the followers of Jaurès and those of Guesde, since Jaurès believed that when the republic was in danger it was worth saving and that to do this it was legitimate for socialists to collaborate with other republican parties, while Guesde followed the German Social Democrats in rejecting any such collaboration in any circumstances. When the French socialist parties finally united in 1905, it was Guesde's views which became the official party line, and indeed the unification took place under the direct influence of the German socialists, for it was carried out as the result of a decision taken after a long and heated discussion at the International Socialist Congress at Amsterdam in 1904, in which the Germans supported the view that there should be no cooperation with other parties, and persuaded the congress to recommend that this should be the basis on which the unification of the French socialists should be effected.

Thus until 1914 the French Socialist Party was committed to permanent opposition – a prospect which led some of its politically ambitious members such as Briand and Viviani to leave a party which could offer them no hope of ministerial office. This refusal to participate in government did not however prevent the French Socialist Party (which, on unification, had taken the name of *Section Française de l'Internationale Ouvrière* – French Section of the Workers International) from being an important and effective parliamentary force: by 1914 they had 103 seats in the Chamber and around 1,400,000 votes. Jaurès was an outstanding speaker and parliamentary figure, but nevertheless his influence and that of the party was necessarily circumscribed by their refusal to enter a government, even though their votes could help to pass measures of social reform or to hinder proposals for increased armaments or colonial expansion.

However in spite of Jaurès' leadership and in spite of a considerable measure of parliamentary and electoral success, the united socialist party which combined some of the Marxist elements in French socialism with the practical experience of the independent parliamentary socialists was not the only focus of loyalty for the French working class. The Socialist Party had to face the competition of a third trend in the French working-class tradition. Among many French workers there was a deep-rooted feeling of suspicion of parliamentary methods and indeed of parliament as such, which found intellectual justification in the doctrines of Proudhon or in Blanqui's advocacy of direct revolutionary action. While in the 1880s and 1890s much of the feeling had expressed itself in anarchist acts of terrorism – the murder of the President of the Republic in 1894, the throwing of a bomb into the Chamber of Deputies – and in more generalised acts of protest against the whole of bourgeois society such as the dynamiting of cafés or apartment blocks, by the turn of the century a new movement was becoming important which combined an anarchist belief in the virtues of direct action with the development of a vigorous militant trade union movement.

The fusion in France of the trade union organisation with some of the ideas and methods of the anarchists led to the development of anarcho-syndicalism, a movement which not only affected the later history of the labour movement in France but provided an example which was followed elsewhere, notably in Spain but also in South America, while similar techniques were employed contemporaneously but independently by the Industrial Workers of the World (IWW) in the United States. The anarcho-syndicalists combined a distrust of politics and parliaments with a belief in the efficacy of direct action as a means of securing control of the economy. The workers were to be guided, trained and educated by a group of dedicated militant leaders who would prepare them for the general strike which, it was hoped, would give them control of the means of production and thus eventually of the whole of society. The movement found a theorist in Georges Sorel, a retired engineer who, in a series of original and exciting even if somewhat disjointed books, of which the most famous is *Reflections on Violence* published in 1908, expounded his view that the leaders of the proletariat would provide a new force for the regeneration of society and that direct violent action by the workers could at once both purge and transform the corrupt old order. The form of action most suited to this end was the general strike, the most powerful weapon at the disposal of the proletariat. Sorel developed from his belief in the efficacity of the general strike a wider doctrine of the significance of the myth in politics. Men, he believed, are moved to action by irrational beliefs as much as by rational methods; and the belief in the general strike would be effective even if the strike itself remained in the future. Myths, he taught, are in politics as effective as reality, and if the proletariat believed firmly enough in its own strength, then the opposition of the ruling classes would be undermined and finally overcome.

Sorel's work is of interest because it reflects many of the ideas current at the turn of the century and links the ideas of Marx, Nietzsche and Bergson (see chapter 5 below) with the practice of the French labour leaders, who themselves would never have worked out so elaborate a theoretical basis for their tactics. During the years before 1914 the militant trade unions in France succeeded in calling a number of effective and impressive strikes, but for all the success of syndicalist ideas of direct action, the effects of these fell short of the revolutionary intentions of some of their leaders and resulted in minor immediate gains for the workers rather than in the transformation of French society. The vigour of the syndicalist movement masked its comparative lack of numerical strength – far behind that of the German trade unions – while at the same time posing problems for the parliamentary socialist party by obliging it in some cases to adopt a more militant left-wing attitude than it might otherwise have done. Above all, however, it was the comparative numerical weakness of the French syndicalist movement that limited its effectiveness and ensured that the myth of the general strike and the direct seizure of power remained a myth instead of becoming reality. It was not until the First World War that the syndicalist organisation, the *Confédération Générale du Travail* (CGT), became a major force in French society, accepted by and accepting the government of the republic which necessarily needed its cooperation in wartime.

With the labour movement in Britain standing apart from the main stream of continental socialism, the German and French socialist parties were typical of the different roads to socialism followed elsewhere in Europe. In Austria, Switzerland and Belgium, for example, the German pattern was followed, while in Italy there were similarities both with Germany and with France. The Italian socialist movement included some important Marxist theorists and in the industrial centres of the north, such as Turin and Milan, an effective trade union organisation, but there was also a strong anarchist tradition which found expression both in outbreaks of rural violence and in militant syndicalist action, as in the famous 'Red Week' of June 1914 when it looked for a few days as if the myth of the insurrectionary general strike was about to be realised, until the nerves of the syndicalist leaders failed and the strikes were called off. However, for all the unevenness of Italian economic development and the backwardness of most of the south, Italy was nevertheless a parliamentary country and as in France there were socialist leaders anxious to play a part in the normal political game, who in 1911 broke away from the orthodox socialists. However, even within the official Italian socialist party there were deep divisions between Right and Left, reformists and revolutionaries, which were never wholly healed and led to further splits during and immediately after the First World War and to the creation in 1921 of a strong Italian communist party. (See chapter 9 below.)

Other countries developed their own socialist parties with slightly differing characteristics, depending on the social and economic conditions in each state. In Belgium, for example, a small, densely populated and highly industrialised country, a well-organised socialist party was able to make its influence directly felt by means of a number of political general strikes, a technique which was used effectively to win an extension of the franchise and eventually to achieve universal suffrage, and which indeed could still be successfully employed in 1950 to bring about the abdication of King Leopold III.

In most of the countries of Western Europe by 1900 social democracy was a recognised movement within the state, acting within a constitutional framework of a kind that in differing degrees gave the socialist parties the opportunity both to spread their views and to influence the political, social and economic developments of their respective countries. However, in states where basic constitutional and political liberties did not exist or were severely restricted, the labour movement necessarily faced other problems and its organisation had to take other forms from that of the mass political party or the legal trade unions. In this as in so many other ways Spain and Russia stood outside the general lines of European development. The case of Spain is of interest because it is here that the anarchist tradition found its deepest roots and exercised its widest influence, while in Russia the history of the revolutionary movements before the First World War leads directly into the history of the Revolution of 1917 and the subsequent development of communism.

Spain, since the failure of the republic set up after the revolution of 1868 and the subsequent restoration of the Bourbon monarchy, seemed almost ungovernable. Agrarian discontent, the intrigues of the extreme conservative supporters of the rival Carlist line of the House of Bourbon, a parliamentary regime which did not attempt to deal with the fundamental problems of the country – all these were exacerbated by the defeat of Spain by the United States in 1898 and the loss of her remaining Caribbean and Pacific colonies. Even more than in Italy regional differences and local loyalties weakened the control of the central government. In Catalonia, industrially the most advanced part of the country, a strong federalist movement worked for autonomy and self-government and provided a tradition within which the anarchist demand for decentralisation and local independence of all central government found a ready hearing. In the Basque country a strongly conservative and devoutly Catholic peasantry clung to their hopes that the traditional rights of their province would be restored to them.

In the 1870s the ideas of Bakunin had been brought to Spain, and although soon afterwards Marx's emissaries attempted to win the Spanish sections of the International for Marxist orthodoxy, the result was permanently to divide the Spanish working-class movement. Spain was indeed the only country in Europe where Bakunin's ideas took deep root and continued to dominate a large and important section of the Spanish workers. While the miners and steel-workers of Asturias or of Bilbao responded to the orthodox Marxist teaching about the role of the industrial proletariat in the inevitable triumph of the revolution and accepted the disciplined organisation of the socialist party, to the landless labourers of Andalusia and even to many of the textile workers of Catalonia, with their desire for regional independence and a proud tradition of technical skill and of self-improvement, Marxist ideas offered little. The anarchist movement, on the other hand, succeeded in uniting the most advanced industrial workers with the most backward rural proletariat in a common belief that only a radical and total transformation of society could solve their problems and improve their lot.

It is comparatively easy to see how the Andalusian agricultural labourers, without land of their own, working irregularly and for miserable wages on the vast under-cultivated estates of the south, liable to die of starvation in a bad year and without any hope of improving their condition by legal and political means, responded at once to the millenarian appeal of the anarchist agitators who promised a new world once the landlords had been overthrown by a violent revolution. It is harder to explain why the small peasant or landless labourer in other parts of Europe – in southern Italy or Sicily for example – did not do the same. Perhaps the tradition of ideological extremism in Spanish history provides part of the explanation, so that the violent anti-clericalism of the Spanish anarchists, for instance, expressing itself from time to time in the burning of churches or the sacking of convents, is a counterpart to the particular fanaticism with which the Spanish Church from the days of the Inquisition on had regarded its opponents.

Among the industrial workers, especially in Catalonia, the ideas of anarchism inspired many dedicated organisers and agitators, as well as much confused, verbose and unrealistic oratory. The total rejection of the existing order, the ideal of workers' control of the factories and the hope of independence from any central government, were eagerly accepted by people who still had memories of the days when they had been self-reliant artisans and who now faced, or so it seemed, ruthless employers backed by the forces of a hostile state. It was often the purely destructive side of the doctrine that was emphasised, and during the 1880s and 1890s in Spain as elsewhere anarchists expressed their hatred of society in a series of violent actions – bombs in theatres or in religious processions, and in 1897 the assassination of the Prime Minister, Canovas del Castillo. By the turn of the century, however, although there were spontaneous outbreaks of violent rioting as in the 'Tragic Week' in Barcelona in 1909, when the population protested against the call-up of reservists for an unsuccessful colonial war in Morocco, many anarchists in Spain, as in France, realised that violent gestures – 'propaganda by the deed' as it was called – could only lead to police repression and persecution, so that gradually they turned to more effectively organised action through the labour unions. Anarcho-syndicalism became, to an even greater extent than in France or Italy, the means by which the Spanish working class expressed its deep suspicion of political activity and its belief in direct action to achieve its ends in a situation where the possibilities of reform by legal means seemed remote, and Spanish working-class history is characterised by a series of bitter strikes often accompanied by violence, until in 1936 with the outbreak of the civil war the moment for the revolution seemed to have come.

Nineteenth-century Russia, like Spain, was a country in which the chances of social reform by legal means seemed small and in which hopes of change were repeatedly disappointed. The reforms of Tsar Alexander II had solved few problems and created new ones, and after his assassination in 1881 by a group of young men and women convinced that an act of supreme self-immolation and violence would release the forces for good inherent in Russian society, his successor Alexander III started a reign of black reaction and almost unbroken repression. The hopes aroused by the reforms of the 1860s were dead, and the sometimes naive expectations of those intellectuals of the 1870s, who thought that by 'going to the people' and preaching to the peasants Russian society could be rapidly transformed, were shown to be vain. Yet, as Bakunin had seen, the Russian peasantry was potentially the most revolutionary element in Europe, and the Populists of the 1870s and the Social Revolutionaries in the early years of the twentieth century were right in recognising this: hunger for land and a desire for some kind of economic security were powerful motives for revolt in Russia, as in the south of Spain. At the same time, however, during the last twenty years of the nineteenth century, the industrialisation of Russia was proceeding fast and a new and potentially revolutionary urban proletariat was coming into being.

Throughout the nineteenth century the Russian intelligentsia – the Russian word has become generally used to describe a self-conscious class of intellectuals aware of a particular political or social mission – had been eager to adopt new ideas from the West. It is typical of this enthusiasm that Russian was the first foreign language into which Karl Marx's *Capital* was translated. But, although Marx in the years immediately before his death in 1883 was studying Russian problems carefully and considering the possibilities for revolution in Russia, Marxism as a doctrine, asserting as it did that the revolution would come through the development of a class-conscious proletariat in the advanced industrial countries, did not at first sight seem particularly appropriate to the Russian situation, where industrialisation was still very far behind Western Europe and the proletariat only beginning to emerge as a social force. Nevertheless, a group of intellectuals headed by G.V. Plekhanov, P.B. Axelrod and Vera Zasulich – the latter one of the heroines of the revolutionary movement who had made a sensational attempt on the life of the St Petersburg police chief – attempted to form a social democratic party on the Western European model.

Such an enterprise was extremely difficult, especially in the atmosphere of repression which followed the assassination of Alexander II, and Plekhanov and his associates were obliged to run their party from outside Russia. (Plekhanov, for example, left Russia in 1880 and only returned in 1918 after the Revolution.) Thus the great debate about the applicability to Russia of Marx's analysis was conducted in Zurich or Geneva or Brussels or London as much as in Russia itself. Plekhanov maintained that the proletarian revolution in Russia could only take place after the bourgeois revolution; Russia, that is to say, must pass from feudalism to capitalism before it would be ready for socialism. This doctrine, however, left room for a great deal of argument about tactics. What should the attitude of the social democrats be towards the peasants? What view should they take of the attempts of some of the more progressive administrators in Russia, such as Count Witte, to introduce regulations improving conditions in factories, which might make the workers less revolutionary and more contented with their lot? How far should they collaborate with the liberals or with other revolutionary groups? These debates transferred to the Russian context the discussions about revisionism and reformism with which the socialist parties of Western Europe were preoccupied.

During the 1890s the influence of the *émigré* socialist leaders was necessarily limited by the difficulty of communicating with potential supporters inside Russia and the ever growing problems of maintaining any continuous organisation in the face of a vigilant and efficient secret police. Nevertheless the socialists were able to make converts among the younger generation of intellectuals and to win over from the Populists people who preferred the intellectual rigour of Marxism to the eclectic and often sentimental ideas of the Populist tradition. Such a convert was the young Lenin. The son of a schoolmaster and educational administrator, Vladimir Ilitch Ulyanov (he used the pseudonym Lenin permanently from about 1901) was born in 1870. When Lenin was seventeen his elder brother was executed for taking part in a plot to assassinate the Tsar, Alexander III, and he himself was expelled from the university as a result. He rapidly turned himself into a dedicated professional revolutionary, though rejecting his brother's belief in individual terrorism and becoming a convinced and learned Marxist. He was soon in trouble with the authorities and after a period of exile in Siberia left Russia in 1900, returning for some months after the Revolution of 1905 and then finally in April 1917.

Thus Lenin's initial influence on the development of Russian socialism was in the sectarian discussions of the *émigrés*, and it was in this period that he developed some of his characteristic beliefs about the nature and methods of revolution and ideas about tactics which he continued to apply for the rest of his career. To the orthodox Marxism of Plekhanov and the other Russian socialist intellectuals he added the belief, derived partly from the veteran French revolutionary Auguste Blanqui and partly from one of the Russian Populist conspirators of the 1870s, P. N. Tkachev, that revolution must be the work of dedicated professionals, willing to give up everything – family, friends, conventional morality or personal satisfaction – for the cause. Revolution, though it would be made by the proletarian masses, would not come spontaneously; it was the revolutionary elite in the socialist party which would direct the workers' efforts, and it was the party which would take decisions on their behalf.

Lenin made his reputation as a polemicist by his attacks on those members of the socialist parties who believed that their efforts should be concentrated on achieving immediate practical gains for the working classes. At the same time he was demonstrating his belief in the necessity of a strictly disciplined party by splitting his party rather than accept any compromise with his opponents. A small number of convinced and undeviating adherents was always in Lenin's view of more practical value than an amorphous body of followers with confused and contradictory ideas.

It was in pursuit of these ideas and tactics that Lenin carried out his most famous splitting operation when in 1903 he forced a division of the Russian Social Democratic Party into two groups, known from the Russian words for minority and majority as Mensheviks and Bolsheviks, with Lenin's followers, the Bolsheviks, temporarily the more numerous. Although the two factions were able to collaborate on certain issues, their differences were never healed, with the Mensheviks representing orthodox social democracy on the German model, insisting on the necessity of working for the bourgeois capitalist revolution before going on to the next stage, and preserving the scruples of a liberal and humanitarian system of ethical values in the methods they pursued, while the Bolsheviks stood for total ruthlessness in the pursuit of revolutionary ends and were ready to use any revolutionary situation to turn the bourgeois revolution immediately into a proletarian one.

The subsequent importance of Lenin and the momentous consequences to the world of the success of Bolshevik doctrine and tactics should not however make one forget that at the beginning of the twentieth century the Bolsheviks were only a small faction in the international socialist movement and, although Lenin was making a reputation for himself in international socialist circles as a formidable theoretician, his influence especially inside Russia was still very small. At the same time the industrial development of Russia was creating a potentially revolutionary proletariat alongside a potentially revolutionary peasantry. In 1896 and 1897 spontaneous strikes in the factories of St Petersburg showed the strength of the new working class, even if the workers were not allowed by the authorities to organise trade unions until 1906. The secret police developed new and surprising methods in an attempt to control this activity and developed workers' movements under police direction and supervision, in the hope of turning the energies of the proletariat into harmless activities or at least activities which the police could control. These tactics and the penetration of genuinely revolutionary organisations by police agents (one of them became a member of the central committee of the Bolshevik Party) did not, however, succeed in controlling the growing unrest of the working class, and indeed the boundary between 'police socialism' and a real subversive movement was often hard to define: thus it was a demonstration led by one of the police's unwitting tools, the Orthodox priest Father Gapon, which marked the beginning of the Revolution of 1905.

The events of 1905 in Russia showed that a combination of war-weariness after the disastrous defeat by the Japanese in the Far East, peasant risings, which had already occurred in 1902 and which broke out again in February 1905, and proletarian unrest in the cities could produce a revolutionary situation in which the government was forced to make concessions. A constitution was introduced and a parliament (the state *Duma*) set up – even if it was elected on a restricted franchise and although its powers were soon curtailed. As a result not only was there a freedom of debate unknown before and renewed discussion about the possibility of rapid change in Russia even after the authorities had succeeded in restoring order and repressing the active revolutionary movements of the year 1905 itself, but also a fresh point was given to the arguments about participation or non-participation in parliamentary life, which the socialists in the West had been discussing for some years but which only now were of practical relevance to the Russian Social Democrats.

Above all, however, the Revolution of 1905 and its comparative failure led all those who opposed the tsarist regime to reflect on the nature of revolution in Russia and to speculate on the form it should take. Thus the Social Revolutionaries were confirmed in their belief that it was the peasants who would provide the true insurrectionary force in Russia. The Mensheviks, noting the concessions made to liberal opinion in the new constitution and in the summoning of the Duma, felt as strongly as ever that in Russia a bourgeois liberal revolution must be the next historical stage and that this must precede a socialist proletarian revolution. Lenin, on the other hand, drew his own lessons from the events of 1905. It was, he wrote later, 'the great rehearsal';[7] and although he himself had played little part in the revolution (he returned from exile in November 1905, living an underground existence from the middle of 1906 until he returned to exile in Geneva in January 1908), he used his observations to develop his own theories. He believed even more strongly than before in the necessity of an efficient and dedicated revolutionary organisation; he realised that the revolutionary impulses of the peasants would soon be exhausted once they had possession of the land and that they would have to be forced into the next stage of revolution against their will, and he agreed with Lev Trotsky (L.D. Bronstein) who had played a leading part in the St Petersburg Soviet of Workers' Deputies which had shown itself for a few brief months to be an effective form of revolutionary administration, that the revolution must be 'permanent' and that its leaders must always be pressing on to the next phase until success was finally achieved and the revolution of the proletariat accomplished.

The Russian Revolution of 1905 was the most impressive revolutionary outbreak in Europe since the Paris Commune, and it naturally made an enormous impression on the international socialist movement. For those who had taken part such as Rosa Luxemburg, one of the most forceful and eloquent of the left-wing intellectuals of Lenin's generation who had hurried back from Germany to her native Poland to plunge into revolutionary activity as well as into a controversy as to whether the Polish national revolution for independence from Russia should take precedence over the social revolution – the orderly bourgeois habits and the decorous parliamentary activity of, for example, the German Social Democrats seemed far removed from the revolutionary reality they had just experienced. This, and also the growing international tension in Europe in the first decade of the twentieth century, gave a new urgency to the debates on socialist tactics in the international socialist congresses which had been meeting regularly since 1889.

One of the fundamental beliefs of Marx and his followers was that socialism must be an international movement. Since all history was, according to Marx, the history of class struggle, class divisions and the class war were more important than national divisions and national wars. A worker had more in common with his fellow workers in another country than he did with the capitalists in his own. In 1889 a new Socialist International was founded – the Second International, in succession to the First International, Marx's International Working Men's Association which had been formally dissolved in 1876. As the strength of the European socialist parties increased, so the hopes grew that the International might be able to coordinate their efforts and provide them with common tactics and policies. In 1900 an International Socialist Bureau was set up in Brussels, and many socialists hoped that it would serve as a sort of general staff for the international revolution.

In the event the International Socialist Bureau tended to be little more than a secretariat responsible for the practical planning and organisation of international socialist congresses. However, in some ways, the International had considerable apparent successes. During the 1890s its congresses had successfully maintained the doctrine that socialist action must be political action, and thus had excluded the anarchists with their distrust of politics and their faith in direct violence. The International had provided a forum for discussion of the revisionist controversy and at its congress at Amsterdam in 1904 it had had one of its most notable successes when it laid down that the conflicting branches of the French socialist party should unite on the basis of a refusal to ally with bourgeois parties or to participate in governments, a decision that was loyally carried out by Jaurès and his followers, even though they had grave doubts about the validity of the principle underlying it. It was a success which was not repeated, for the International was unable to prevent the Czech socialists in the Austro-Hungarian Empire from breaking with their German colleagues on straight national grounds, thus demonstrating that in an age of growing nationalist emotion national ties were, in spite of Marxist teaching, stronger than class solidarity. Nor did the International Socialist Bureau succeed in overcoming the doctrinal differences between the various sections of the Russian social democrats; and the unification of the Russian party was still on the agenda of the international congress which was planned for the summer of 1914 and cancelled because of the outbreak of war.

From the spring of 1905 when a German challenge to French influence in Morocco started talk for the first time for nearly twenty years of a Franco-German war, socialists of all countries began to be increasingly aware of the growing dangers on the international scene. Germany's naval expansion and rivalry with Britain, France's desire to recover Alsace–Lorraine or to complete her North African empire by the acquisition of Morocco, Austrian fears of Russian ambitions in the Balkans and Russian hopes of compensation elsewhere for their humiliating defeat by the Japanese, all seemed potential sources of danger and called for some sort of common action by socialists to prevent war. None of the activities of the International aroused greater hopes nor ended in greater disappointment. While there were people on the Left in nearly all socialist parties ready to advocate that any declaration of war should be met by a general strike in each of the countries involved, so that mobilisation would be impossible, the more experienced leaders, especially in the German Social Democratic Party, realised that this was impracticable, and that even the best organised socialist party would not be strong enough to challenge the whole power of the State which, it was thought, in these circumstances would be used against them. Consequently, although right up to the outbreak of war in 1914 – and notably at a moving special congress of the International at Basle in 1912 – socialists reiterated

75

their determination to avoid war, they were somewhat vague about exactly how they were going to be able to do this. Jaurès placed his hopes in the traditional liberal methods of peace-keeping and called for disarmament and arbitration. He opposed military increases and led an active though unsuccessful campaign in 1913 against the French government's move to extend the period of conscription from two years to three; and he worked out an elaborate scheme for substituting citizens' militia for a standing army – a system which the Swiss had shown to be practicable in a small country but which is less appropriate to a large one. What is significant is that Jaurès in common with nearly all other socialists did envisage circumstances in which a war of national defence would be necessary and justified, however critical he might be of existing French defence policy. Similarly in the case of Germany both Engels and Bebel had declared that war to defend Germany against invasion by Tsarist Russia would be justified.

Thus, when the International at its congress at Stuttgart in 1907 tried to formulate a resolution laying down its policy in the event of war, it is not surprising that they produced a rather vague and in some ways inconsistent document which claimed that war was inherent in the capitalist system and would only be abolished when capitalism itself had been destroyed, but in the meantime, 'it is the duty of the working class . . . fortified by the unifying activity of the International Bureau, to do everything to prevent the outbreak of war by whatever means seem to them most effective'. The resolution however never states what these means might be. Those people on the Left such as Lenin and Rosa Luxemburg who had seen how the strains of military defeat had contributed to the revolutionary situation in Russia in 1905 succeeded in adding to the resolution a call to use 'the violent economic and political crisis brought about by the war to rouse the people, and thereby to hasten the abolition of capitalist class rule'.[8] It was a policy which Lenin consistently advocated until he was finally successful in 1917 in putting it into practice.

It is very easy to point out the inconsistencies of the international socialist position with regard to war (as with regard to much else), just as with our knowledge of how quickly international socialist solidarity collapsed in 1914 (see pp. 187–9 below) it is easy to deride socialist optimism and even to question the sincerity of some of the socialist leaders. This would be a mistake. The international socialist movement in the years before the First World War was imposing enough to alarm governments. Just as in nearly every country the existence of a socialist party seemed to offer a standing challenge to the established order of society, so the existence of the International seemed to many governments to be a dangerous threat to national defence and the successful prosecution of a war. The French government had a plan to arrest a large number of known socialist agitators on the outbreak of war, while in German court and military circles there was much talk of abolishing universal suffrage and reviving anti-socialist legislation in order to deal with a party which seemed to many members of the ruling class to consist of potential traitors. Above all the socialist movement, as it gained in strength and, in many countries, in parliamentary influence, provided the growing industrial proletariat with a faith and a hope – a faith that history was on their side and a hope of a new society in which the exploitation of one class by another would come to an end and the workers of the world unite in a new order of peace and justice.

4

IMPERIALISM

By the end of the nineteenth century a new balance of power in Europe had resulted from the unification of Germany and her growing industrial strength. A new concept of society and of the role of the State was modifying the social and political structure of the industrial countries of Europe and challenging the belief in the principles of *laissez-faire* and of free trade. But the development that had the profoundest historical effect was the expansion of Europe overseas. This led to new imperialist rivalries among the great powers and to the belief that the balance of power had to be regarded as a world-wide question and not one limited to Europe alone. It opened the countries of Africa and Asia to European influence on a far greater scale than ever before, giving their populations a taste of the evils as well as the benefits of European technology, European administrative methods and European ideas. The map of Africa was divided up as a result of bargains among the colonising powers to suit their administrative or diplomatic convenience, so that in the twentieth century these boundaries often became quite illogically the boundaries of independent states, corresponding to no ethnic or economic reality. The effects of this movement on the peoples of Africa and Asia have been well summed up by the English political thinker Leonard Woolf:[1]

European civilisation, with its ideas of economic competition, energy, practical efficiency, exploitation, patriotism, power and nationalism descended upon Asia and Africa. But with it it also carried, involuntarily perhaps, another set of ideas which it had inherited from the French Revolution and the eighteenth-century forerunners of the French Revolution. These were the ideas of democracy, liberty, fraternity, equality, humanitarianism. They have had a profound effect upon the later history of Imperialism, for they have led to the revolt of the subject peoples against it.

The influence was not however all one-way. Through the imperialist experience the countries of Europe were brought into contact as never before with primitive and exotic cultures, and these in turn had a profound effect on European sensibility. By the early twentieth century the art of Africa for example was contributing to the revolution in European painting inaugurated

78

by Pablo Picasso around 1907; and already some fifteen years earlier Paul Gauguin had settled in the French colony of Tahiti, finding in the South Seas his main inspiration in the last years of his life. The sounds of oriental music – heard at the great Paris International Exhibition of 1889 – were making their way into the work of composers such as Claude Debussy. At the same time the science of anthropology was developing rapidly as colonisation made the observation of unfamiliar societies both practically easier and increasingly important for governments and administrators, so that the study of little-known and remote peoples was contributing to the development of relativist ethical theories and to the questioning of established moral and social values characteristic of the *fin de siècle*. (See chapter 5 below.)

This movement of imperialist expansion has been explained in a number of different ways; and perhaps no single explanation is sufficient to account for developments which differed widely in different parts of the world. The most comprehensive explanation is that which attributes the imperialist movement to economic pressures. This view was developed by a number of critics of imperialism in the early years of the century, notably by an Englishman, J.A.Hobson, and by some socialist thinkers in Germany and Austria, but it was given its most popular and influential form in a pamphlet written by Lenin in 1916: *Imperialism, the Highest Stage of Capitalism*. Although like nearly all Lenin's works this was written as a political pamphlet in the course of day-to-day controversy, it nevertheless provided a simple all-embracing theoretical explanation of imperialism which has continued to be the basis of the communist analysis of the economic relations between advanced industrialised states and undeveloped societies, and of the 'neo-colonialism' which, on this view, is still practised even after former colonies have become politically independent. According to Lenin, with the industrial development of Europe and the concentration of capital in fewer and fewer hands through the organisation of trusts and cartels and through the increasingly important role of the banks in financing industrial and commercial enterprises of all kinds, financiers were finding it ever more difficult to invest their money profitably. The European market was saturated, and consequently it became essential to find new fields of investment overseas. This need, according to Lenin, forced the European powers to divide the world between them in a struggle for new industrial markets and new areas in which to invest, and this struggle led in many cases to the direct annexation of territory as the only means of securing these investments once they had been made. The result was that the rivalry between the powers increased, so that in turn imperialism necessarily led to war.

Although no single general theory accounts for each specific case of imperialist expansion and although economic factors alone are not sufficient to explain each instance, nevertheless it is certain that economic pressure groups – whether financiers seeking new fields for investment or merchants seeking new outlets for their goods and new sources of raw materials – played a considerable part in persuading the governments of Europe to embark on colonial expansion. On the other hand economic interest did not always involve direct political control: Great Britain for instance had considerable investments in Argentina and, although Lenin described it as a semi-colony, nevertheless its political situation was very different from that of a true colonial territory. Moreover in general even for the imperialist countries investments in other industrialised areas were more important than investment in the colonies. British investment in North America was far greater than that in Africa, for example, while French investments in Russia alone · were over twice as large as those in the French colonies.

There were, however, a number of other motives in addition to economic ones which contributed to the imperialist movement. An urge for scientific discovery and for the exploration of unknown territory helped to open up Africa. The desire of Christian missionaries to convert the heathen led to the establishment of centres of European influence in remote parts of the world. All these motives merged into each other and into less reputable ones. Rivalry between Catholic and Protestant missionaries could easily develop, for example, into rivalry between the French and the British governments; and it was the murder of two German Jesuit missionaries in China in 1897 which provided the German government with the excuse for the seizure of the port of Kiao-Chow. Trade, missionary activity and exploration were inextricably involved with each other. The Scottish merchants who founded the Imperial British East Africa Company were as concerned with the spread of the gospel as with establishing trading posts. 'Christianity, commerce, civilisation,' according to the great explorer Livingstone, 'went hand in hand.'[2] In France the president of the French Geographical Society made the point equally clearly in a speech in 1874:[3]

Abstract science, gentlemen, does not suffice for humanity. Science is only really fruitful when it is an instrument of progress and production. It is not just in the interest of curiosity that exploration and geographical discoveries have been made. The discovery of America, the persevering explorations of the interior of Africa . . . have had besides a scientific end, a political and commercial object.

Even the most barefaced colonial exploitation presented itself in scientific or humanitarian guise: King Leopold II of the Belgians, whose Congo Free State was notorious for its brutal administration and its bad treatment of the African population, had taken care to label his original enterprise a 'Comité d'Etudes du Haut Congo', and to proclaim his disinterested scientific and philanthropic intentions.

Once the imperialist movement had started, it generated its own momentum. Governments occupied areas in order to stop other governments from moving in; the strategic needs of existing colonies demanded the safe-guarding of their boundaries and of the routes to them, so that the imperialist powers felt obliged to acquire yet more territory. Moreover questions of prestige played a large part; and it was generally accepted, often without much analysis, that, in the words of the French statesman Léon Gambetta, 'to remain a great nation or to become one, you must colonise'.[4]

In addition to the new colonial gains of the late nineteenth century many European countries held overseas territories acquired in earlier centuries. Empires once great still survived in diminished form: Portugal held (and indeed continues to hold after the withdrawal of the other European powers from nearly all of Africa) important areas in West and East Africa, which Britain and Germany both hoped to acquire if, as seemed likely in the 1890s, Portugal fell into such financial disarray that she would be obliged to dispose of her colonies as security for loans to her government. Spain, although she lost most of her remaining empire after her defeat by the United States in 1898 – a bitter blow to Spanish pride and the source of a protracted crisis of conscience among Spanish intellectuals – when Cuba became independent and the Philippines passed under American control, still kept part of Morocco (a position of some strategic importance) and small territories elsewhere. The Netherlands had until after the Second World War a vast and rich empire in South-East Asia, which assured the prosperity of this small state as well as providing a career for many Dutchmen.

However it was Britain which had the largest empire acquired in earlier periods, and the possession of this empire largely determined the nature of late nineteenth-century imperialism in England. On the one hand, in Canada, Australia and New Zealand, Britain had colonies populated almost exclusively by people of European stock; and by the end of the nineteenth century these had acquired virtual self-government. On the other hand, in India Britain ruled an enormous, variegated and densely populated empire, whose inhabitants differed in religion, language and cultural tradition from each other, and still more from their British rulers.

The existence of the self-governing colonies with their British population (though of course there was a substantial French minority in Canada) in-spired many Englishmen with a vision of a world-wide English-speaking federation linked by a common belief in parliamentary government and by ties of mutual economic interest. In practice, however, discussions on the creation of a more closely linked imperial federation – an idea with which Joseph Chamberlain, British secretary of state for the colonies from 1895 to 1903, was particularly associated – came to nothing. The colonial leaders were too conscious of their recently gained self-government and too sus-picious of anything that looked like the reestablishment of central control from Westminster to accept the idea of an imperial parliament, while the belief in free trade was still strong enough to prevent the adoption of a preferential tariff for trade within the empire and the erection of tariff barriers against the rest of the world. Throughout the first half of the twentieth century however many British politicians, administrators and publicists continued to look for a form of association which would adapt the old empire to new political concepts. After the First World War, when important military assistance was provided to Britain by the colonies, the idea of a British Commonwealth was developed (and finally given formal legal expression in the Statute of Westminster of 1931), a free association of independent states linked by a common loyalty to the Crown. This comparatively loose link, though satisfying an emotional need at a time when many people felt that British power was declining, and providing convenient machinery for the discussion and coordination of foreign policy, was much weaker than the imperialists at the turn of the century hoped and expected, but the existence of Commonwealth ties, however tenuous, was a consistent factor in British policy until the 1960s, making for a reluctance on the part of British governments to involve themselves wholeheartedly in Europe in the years immediately after the Second World War.

The possession of India raised different problems for Britain. Whereas the questions arising between the British government and Australia, New Zealand or Canada were constitutional and economic, or naval and military, the administration of India both posed vast technical problems and raised fundamental questions about the right of one people to rule another and about the purpose of such rule. At the end of the nineteenth century such doubts had however not gone very far. The British administrators in India were mostly efficient, just, dedicated and high-minded, but they remained a caste apart from the society over which they ruled. It was only gradually that the British nerve failed and that British liberals, instead of attacking particular instances of bad government in India, attacked Britain's right to be there at all. (For this gradual change of mood it is worth comparing Rudyard Kipling's stories of the 1890s with E.M.Forster's *A Passage to India* published in 1924.) For generations India provided a training ground for the British army as well as supporting a separately administered Indian army, while the Indian civil service offered a career to many of the ablest graduates of Oxford and Cambridge. There were few middle-class families in Britain which did not have some contact with the Indian Empire through a son in the Indian administration or a cousin in the army.

In addition to this, British trade with India and British investment in India gave the British a real reason for staying there. (It has been estimated that India took over 40 per cent of the cotton goods exported from Lancashire in the last decades of the nineteenth century, before industrialisation in India itself made it a major competitor in the field of textiles.) This profound commitment to India, and the fact that the need to secure the routes to India and to safeguard its frontiers had become an unquestioned axiom of British foreign policy, necessarily had a great influence on British imperialist expansion in other parts of the world during the 1880s and 1890s. Thus, for example, the construction of the Suez Canal and the opening of a shorter sea route to India after 1869 made Egypt seem an area of vital importance to Britain; and, if the occupation by Britain of Egypt in 1882 was due in part to a desire to protect the interest of British investors in Egypt itself, its retention was due to the need to control a vital section of the route to India. And once in Egypt the British felt the need to expand in Central and East Africa because of their preoccupations about the security of Egypt and especially of the Upper Nile, control of which by a rival power was thought to threaten the water supply on which the whole of Egyptian economic life depended.

Here again imperialism developed its own impetus. The possession by Britain of an existing empire and especially of India made many British politicians, administrators and soldiers anxious to prevent expansion by other European powers into areas adjacent to British territory or on the routes to British possessions – even though some statesmen, like Lord Salisbury, remained sceptical about the necessity of doing so: 'I would not be too much impressed by what the soldiers tell you about the strategic importance of these places,' he wrote as Prime Minister to the British representative in Egypt in 1892. 'If they were allowed full scope they would insist on the importance of garrisoning the moon in order to protect us from Mars.'[5] It was not only the need to protect existing colonies that led to expansion into new territory. The activities of merchants often forced occasionally reluctant governments to take over new responsibilities. Trading companies such as the Royal Niger Company in West Africa or the Imperial British East Africa Company in Uganda found themselves in situations which they could not handle on their own – wars with local tribes which were too big for them, or the rivalry of other Europeans (as in the case of the British and French on the Niger) – and they were often able to mobilise public opinion at home which would force the government to act and to take over direct responsibility for the territory in which the companies were operating. In Germany Bismarck, himself, as he protested, '*kein Kolonial-mensch*', found that by the mild encouragement he gave in 1884 and 1885 to colonialist merchants and explorers in Africa, in order to win votes and perhaps to make sure that German economic interests were not in any way neglected, he had created a powerful pressure group which he and his successors could not ignore.

Piecemeal and for a variety of reasons the British increased their empire vastly between 1880 and 1905, so that at the end of the process the population of the British colonies was estimated to be over 345,000,000, at a time when the United Kingdom itself had some 40,500,000 inhabitants. Imperialism was a popular cause in England in the 1890s. Some people have attributed this to a sense that Britain's industrial position was declining with the rise in power and productive capacity of Germany and the United States. It is true that the commercial rivalry between Britain and Germany was in the 1890s a topic for propagandists in Britain, and that German salesmen were operating effectively in areas, such as the Middle East, in which the British had had hitherto an unchallenged commercial lead. Moreover, rightly or wrongly, many Englishmen believed that colonial possessions would bring direct economic benefits in the form of cheap food, while the fact that Britain's rivals, especially Russia and France, were protectionist led to a fear that British trade would be excluded from areas under their control.

This sense that Britain's position in the world was being challenged is not only apparent in the 'scramble for Africa', where British territorial colonial gains were most extensive. It also underlay British policy in China, where Britain had been by far the most influential and important trading power since she had forced the Chinese in two wars earlier in the century to open their ports to foreign traders. By the 1890s however the emergence of Japan as an efficient Westernised power and her defeat of China in 1895 changed the situation. By intervening to save the integrity of the Chinese Empire in the face of Japanese demands, France, Germany and Russia staked their claim to a say in China's future; and this intervention was followed by a race for concessions and spheres of influence in which each of the European great powers played a part, so that Britain's commercial and naval pre-eminence in the Far East was challenged, especially by Russia, since Russia's eastward expansion overland across Siberia and into central Asia, helped by the construction of the Trans-Siberian railway (finally completed in 1902) was safe from interference by the British navy. Fear of Russian activities in the Far East was now added to the traditional British fear of the Russian threat to India, at least until the Japanese victory in the Russo-Japanese war of 1904-5 called a halt to Russian expansion into North China and Korea.

Britain's world-wide interest and world-wide claims, boosted by the new cheap popular press and slogans like 'the Empire on which the sun never sets', found their most striking symbolic expression in Queen Victoria's Diamond Jubilee celebrations in 1897 when, in the words of the Duke of Argyll, 'we could not help remembering that no Sovereign since the fall of Rome could muster subjects from so many and so distant countries all over the world'.[6] A less favourable observer, Beatrice Webb, complained of 'Imperialism in the air - all classes drunk with sightseeing and hysterical loyalty'.[7]

However, this mood of national self-congratulation did not last long. Within three years Britain was engaged in a hard and bitter war in South Africa against the Boers, the descendants of Dutch settlers in the Transvaal and Orange Free State whose independence had been recognised by the

British in 1881 and 1884 after a first military encounter, and who were trying to assert their right to limit the activities of people from outside their territory in exploiting the rich gold and diamond mines, and thus upsetting the social balance of the small, conservative farmer republics. Although the British won the war and forced the Boer republics into a Union of South Africa, the war had been longer and tougher than had been expected, and it did much to change the popular mood in Britain. As Sir Edward Grey, the foreign secretary of the Liberal government which came to power late in 1905, wrote:[8]

> Before the Boer war, we were spoiling for a fight. We were ready to fight France about Siam, Germany about the Kruger telegram,* and Russia about any thing. Any Government here, during the last ten years of last century, could have had war by lifting a finger. The people would have shouted for it. They had a craving for *greed* excitement, and a rush of blood to the head. Now, this generation has had enough excitement, and has lost a little blood, and is sane and normal.

Although public enthusiasm for the British Empire remained for many years and a jingoistic nationalism revived from time to time – notably at the outbreak of the First World War – the period of the most strident popular imperialism was already past by the first years of the twentieth century.

Although British imperialism was the most notable example of the phenomenon, both because of the extent of territory acquired and because of the popular enthusiasm aroused, all the great powers of Europe were affected by the imperialist movement, with the exception of Austria–Hungary which was for the most part too preoccupied with the conflict of nationalities within its own frontiers to look outside (though even here, there were a few politicians and bureaucrats who thought wistfully of colonial gains in the Middle East as a means of reasserting the monarchy's position in the world).

During the period after 1870 France extended her North African empire, where Algeria had already attracted a number of French settlers, by the establishment of a protectorate over Tunisia in 1881, and later over Morocco in 1912, using in the latter case the pretext that disturbances on the Algerian border necessitated French action in Morocco so as to keep order. Meanwhile France was also acquiring a large empire in the Far East and in Africa. In the Far East from 1858, when the French had invaded Annam, they had taken over a number of states whose existing structure was too weak to resist European penetration – Annam, Cochin-China and Tongking (the three provinces which now compose Viet-Nam) were grouped together with Cambodia and called French Indo-China in 1887, and the protectorate of

---

* This was a telegram sent by Emperor Wilhelm II to President Kruger of the Transvaal in 1896 congratulating him on having repelled a raid by a small irregular force from Cape Colony under Dr Jameson.

Laos was added six years later. In the 1880s the French were actively encouraged in their colonial ventures by Bismarck, who hoped that overseas expansion would direct French popular attention away from the lost provinces of Alsace and Lorraine. Indeed, whereas for Britain the maintenance of a world-wide role was the main function of her foreign policy, the French were torn between a desire for empire and the desire for revenge in Europe for the defeat of 1870 and for the loss of French territory. Thus, for example, the defeat of a French army in Indo-China in 1885 led to the fall of the government of Jules Ferry and an outcry that colonial adventures distracted France from her true task. As one nationalist publicist put it, 'I have lost two children and you offer me twenty servants.'[9] However, in spite of setbacks and in spite of rivalry with Britain (which had annexed Burma in 1886) – a rivalry which enabled Thailand (Siam) to survive as an independent buffer state – the French Empire in the Far East provided substantial economic gains, even if these gains were limited to a comparatively few bankers and trading companies. Together with the Dutch East Indies and the British territories in Malaysia, French Indo-China produced a considerable proportion of the world's rubber supply; investment in such developments as railway construction yielded a high rate of interest, so that French bankers at home were directly involved in the development of France's empire in the Far East. Above all, however, French rule over an ancient and civilised people in Indo-China did much to keep alive France's belief in herself as a great power which had successfully recovered from the humiliation of 1870, and the colonies provided for the French army a field on which military glory could still be won and an opportunity for ambitious officers to make a successful career of a kind difficult to achieve at home in peace-time.

The French share in the scramble for Africa was also large, even if much of the territory she conquered consisted of what Lord Salisbury referred to once as 'light soil' – the sands of the Sahara – and offered limited attractions to French investors. If the dream of British imperialists in Africa such as Cecil Rhodes was to establish a direct link from the Cape to Cairo running through British territory all the way, so the French had hopes of a link across Central Africa joining their new colonies in West Africa with their base on the Red Sea at Djibuti. Throughout the 1890s this Anglo-French rivalry in Central Africa was a central theme in the diplomatic relations between the two countries, with the French trying to extract concessions and favourable commercial and frontier agreements from the British, and the British trying to maintain their position and to keep as much of Africa as possible open to British trade and influence. It came to a head in 1898 with a direct confrontation at Fashoda on the Upper Nile. A French expedition sent across Africa to stake a claim to the territory came face to face with a British force which had just succeeded in reconquering the Sudan from the followers of the Muslim religious leader, the Mahdi, and the French were forced to realise that to oppose Britain in Africa was beyond their powers, unless they had the support of Germany in Europe, a support whose price was the renunciation for good of Alsace–Lorraine; and this was a price no French government could afford to pay. Although the French public felt bitter about British colonial successes and although the French press conducted a violent campaign against Britain at the time of the South African War, it is perhaps true to say that consistent and continuous colonial enthusiasm was less widespread in France than in Britain. In all the imperialist countries there were important pressure groups anxious to maintain popular support, but in France, although such groups with a direct economic, administrative or military interest in the colonies influenced the government at certain moments, they very rarely had mass backing, and investment in the colonies was far less popular among the French middle class than say investment in loans to Russia. It was only in Algeria, conquered by France in the 1830s and 1840s, that there was a large population of French settlers, and under the Third Republic this was constitutionally part of metropolitan France rather than a colony.

Yet in one way, French imperialism had a more marked effect both on its subjects and on the mother country than British. Whereas the British were content to administer their colonies, either directly through British officials or indirectly through local rulers with British advisers (as in northern Nigeria or in the princely states of India), with the avowed goal in the former case of eventually preparing the subject peoples for self-government, the French were far more ready to assimilate their colonial peoples into French society and culture. French colonialism was based on an assumption that French subjects in Africa or Asia could be turned into Frenchmen and that this should satisfy their ambitions. (It used to be said that African children, who learnt from the same textbooks as French children, could be heard solemnly repeating in class that their Gaulish ancestors had blue eyes and long fair hair.) This was as much an illusion as the British belief that the inhabitants of the colonies could be gradually and gratefully trained for limited self-government. In both cases the experience of foreign rule, methods and ideas contributed to the movement for national independence in the colonies, but it is arguable that the French left a deeper cultural mark on their former subjects than the British ever did.

Colonisation was not necessarily the result of expansion overseas. The most successful colonising power, in the sense that the empire has lasted and that there has never been a process of decolonisation, was Russia. We have seen how throughout the nineteenth century Russia was expanding eastwards into central Asia and Siberia, bringing under Russian rule the Moslem and pagan tribes who inhabited these vast and potentially rich areas. During the 1880s and 1890s the administration was reorganised and, with the construction of the Trans-Siberian Railway, migration into Siberia was encouraged, reaching

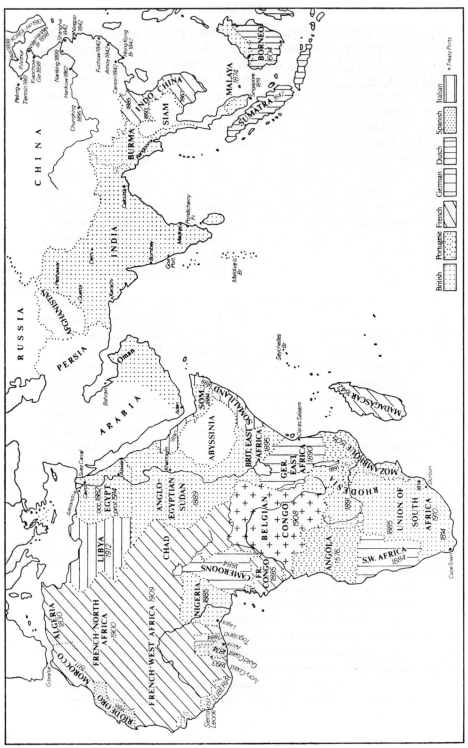

The European Empires c. 1900

Legend: British · Portugese · French · German · Dutch · Spanish · Italian · • Treaty Ports

CHINA
RUSSIA
Peking
Trentsin 1861
Kiachow Ger1898
KOREA Jap 1910
Port Arthur
Wei Hai Wei Br 1898
Shanghai 1842
Ningpo Br 1842
Nanking 1899
Hankow 1899
Chungking 1895
Fuchow 1842
Amoy 1842
Canton 1842
Hong Kong Br 1842
INDO-CHINA 1885
BURMA 1885
SIAM
1893
1863
MALAYA 1874
Singapore 1819
SUMATRA 1647
BORNEO 1604

AFGHANISTAN
Peshawar
Quetta
Karachi
INDIA
Bombay
Calcutta
Madras
Pondicherry Fr.
Goa Port.
Maldive Is. Br

PERSIA
Oman
ARABIA
Bahrain
Aden
SOM.
SOMALILAND
Seychelles Br

RUSSIA
Suez Canal
Alexandria
Cairo
EGYPT occ.1882 prot.1914
Aswan
Khartum
ANGLO-EGYPTIAN SUDAN 1899
ABYSSINIA
1896
BRIT. EAST AFRICA 1895
GER. EAST AFRICA 1890
Dares Salaam
1891
MOZAMBIQUE 1505
1891
RHODESIA 1889
MADAGASCAR 1642

MOROCCO 1911
RIO DE ORO 1886
ALGERIA 1830
Gibraltar
FRENCH NORTH AFRICA 1900
LIBYA 1912
FRENCH WEST AFRICA 1909
CHAD
FR. CONGO 1885
CAMEROONS 1884
NIGERIA 1885
BELGIAN CONGO 1908
ANGOLA 1576
S.W. AFRICA 1884
UNION OF SOUTH AFRICA 1910
Durban
Cape Town
1814
1885
1874

Sierra Leone 1787
LIBERIA
Ivory Coast 1893
Gold Coast 1874
Togoland 1884
Accra
Lagos

its peak in the years 1907-9 when over half a million settlers a year moved in, building a rough pioneering society not unlike the American West in the early days and developing a vigorous textile industry as well as producing large quantities of wheat. There were, moreover, among the soldiers, administrators and businessmen with economic interests in the Russian Far East, some who hoped to extend Russian influence still further and to move into Korea and Manchuria, where there were important sources of raw materials – timber and minerals – as well, it was thought, as a growing market for manufactured goods. In 1897 Russia had occupied Port Arthur, a base on the coast of North China, thus obtaining a port on the Pacific which, unlike the Siberian port of Vladivostok, was free from ice all the year round and which would, it was hoped, both enable Russia's considerable naval strength to be brought to bear in the Far East and provide a new terminus for the Trans-Siberian Railway. At the same time the influence of the group in favour of expansion, even at the risk of war with Japan, was growing. These ambitions led in 1904 to the outbreak of the Russo-Japanese War, fought in effect for the control of Korea, a country which the Japanese regarded as essential for their national security. Russia's defeat by Japan was an unexpected disaster for the Tsarist government, and put an end to Russian hopes of an even greater Far Eastern empire as well as bringing to a head all the currents of unrest which culminated in the 1905 Revolution.

Imperialism in Russia not only took the form of the colonisation of Siberia and of expansion in the Far East leading to the clash with Japan. It also found expression in an intensive programme for the Russification of the non-Russian peoples of the empire. This was particularly resented by the Poles, Ukrainians and Finns, but it also affected the Moslem Tartar peoples on the Volga and in the Crimea as well as the Christian Armenians in the Caucasus, while even the Germans in the Baltic provinces, the source of many of the most loyal and efficient bureaucrats in the empire, had their German university of Dorpat closed and were obliged to accept the replacement of German by Russian as the language of the courts of justice. With the exception of a brief period between the two world wars, the majority of the inhabitants of these provinces, the Latvians, Lithuanians and Esthonians, had to be content with the alternative and sometimes even simultaneous suppression of their national identity by Germans and Russians.

Britain, France and Russia in their different ways possessed vast empires which brought them considerable economic benefits even if these were not always as great as had been hoped. The other great powers which had imperialist aspirations, Germany and Italy, show how far the possession of colonies had become a matter of national prestige rather than a matter of national interest or of economic advantage. In both cases the achievement of national unity had left the next generation anxious for something more, for a new national mission and a new source of national pride. In the international atmosphere of the 1880s and 1890s such an ambition could only be satisfied by the acquisition of colonies – 'a necessity of modern life',[10] as the Italian Prime Minister Crispi called them. The Italians had at least one good ground for wanting colonies. Italy, and especially the south, was very overpopulated and more and more Italians were forced to emigrate each year, the number rising to 873,000 in 1913 – some to seek temporary work elsewhere in Europe, others to settle permanently or for long periods in South America and, increasingly in the years before 1914, in the United States. Thus the idea of obtaining an empire in North Africa (and Tunisia is less than 100 miles from Sicily) was an attractive one, both because it would provide territory in which Europeans could settle, as the French were demonstrating in Algeria, and because it would fulfil the dream of founding a new Roman Empire in lands which had been one of the richest provinces of ancient Rome. It was therefore a bitter disappointment when in 1881 the French, encouraged by Bismarck, obtained a protectorate over Tunisia. For the next fifteen years, therefore, Italian foreign policy was largely dictated by jealousy of France. The Italians built a substantial navy; they conducted a tariff war against France; but in spite of this, and in spite of their Triple Alliance with Germany and Austria–Hungary concluded in 1882 and renewed regularly over the next thirty years, which provided some comfort to their national pride by giving Italy a recognised status as a great power, they were not successful in gaining any foothold across the Mediterranean until 1911 when they were able to seize Libya.

The first African territory Italy acquired was on the Red Sea in 1882. Once installed there, the Italians felt their prestige was involved, and a policy of 'renunciation' would have proved fatal to any government proposing it, even in the face of considerable military difficulties. The alternative to withdrawal was expansion, and in 1885 they occupied Massawa, after the murder of an Italian explorer. By 1890 the Italians were in possession of the colony they named Eritrea (emphasising their historical links with ancient Rome by taking the Latin name for the Red Sea), and had established a protectorate over part of Somaliland. In the course of these developments they became involved with the ancient and somewhat decrepit Christian empire of Ethiopia. At first Emperor Menelik, anxious to strengthen his precarious hold on his throne, was prepared for cooperation and gave concessions to the Italians, but in 1893 he denounced his treaty with them; and once more Italian national sentiment demanded advance rather than retreat. With patriotic references to Garibaldi's campaigns (both Crispi, the prime minister, and the governor of Eritrea had been comrades in arms of Garibaldi in 1860) and claiming that they had 'renewed in Africa the splendour of Garibaldi's victories',[11] the Italian army became more and more involved, and early in 1896 suffered an unexpected and humiliating defeat at the hands of the Ethiopians at Adowa, leaving nearly two thousand Italian prisoners in Menelik's hands.

The disaster at Adowa not only led to the fall of Crispi's government and to a prolonged political and social crisis in Italy. It also led to a short-lived revulsion against colonial enterprises and to a long-term desire among Italian nationalists to wipe out the shame of the Ethiopian catastrophe. Thus a comparatively pointless colonial expedition turned into a potent nationalist myth, so that Adowa was not forgotten, and the dream of revenge and of refounding an Italian empire in Ethiopia remained alive, to contribute to the eclectic programme of Italian Fascism and to inspire Mussolini's attack on Ethiopia in 1935.

In the case of Germany the desire for a colonial empire was one aspect of a deep sense of uneasiness and dissatisfaction about Germany's place in the world at the end of the nineteenth century. Bismarck, although he had occasionally encouraged the colonialist lobby for his own domestic or diplomatic ends, was fundamentally uninterested in colonial expansion. His policy remained firmly centred in Europe: 'Here lies Russia, and there lies France, and we are in the middle. That is my map of Africa',[12] he once said. After his dismissal in March 1890 by the young Emperor Wilhelm II, however, many forces in Germany were making for a more adventurous policy. *Weltpolitik* became one of the catchwords of the new reign as *Realpolitik* had been in Bismarck's day. The actual colonies obtained by Germany in South-West Africa, Tanganyika and the Pacific were never very important or economically rewarding, but the possession of colonies seemed to many Germans the symbol of having achieved the status of a world power. For this reason the acquisition of colonies was closely linked in German minds with the construction of a large German navy. This was a view whole-heartedly adopted by the Kaiser himself. In 1894 he had read the important work of the American strategic thinker Alfred Thayer Mahan on the *Influence of Sea-Power on History* published four years earlier and from it he, like many of his generation, acquired a belief in the overwhelming importance of sea power for the growth and success of nations in peace and war.

Weltpolitik meant for Germans in the 1890s the invention of a new world mission for Germany worthy of her industrial, technological, cultural and military strength. It was an ideal which attracted the middle-class supporters of the National Liberal Party, whose fathers had worked for German unification and who were themselves looking for a new objective for their German national enthusiasm; and it was an ideal which important pressure groups were prepared to pay large sums to popularise. Thus the manufacturers of the steel required to build the ships for the new German battle fleet and the mine-owners who produced the coal to fuel it paid for the flood of pamphlets and propaganda of all kinds put out by the Navy League to arouse popular support for the idea of a large German navy. In 1897 the German admiralty, under Admiral Tirpitz, embarked on an ambitious naval programme and, three years later a further naval expansion was undertaken. The consequences, both domestic and foreign, were serious. The cost of naval armaments had mainly to be met by increased government borrowing and from increased contributions from the financial resources available to the individual states of the empire for local purposes. (Even during the First World War the German government was unwilling to increase direct taxation, while the whole influence of the Prussian landowning class was thrown against any substantial land or inheritance tax.) Thus by 1914 the German government faced a number of unsolved financial and fiscal problems.

At the same time, the construction of a large German navy made the British suspicious, since it was felt in England that the purpose of the German fleet could only be to challenge British naval superiority, a superiority which most British politicians regarded as a vital element in Britain's security and prosperity. Although Britain and Germany could reach a settlement on particular issues and, for example, resolve their specific rivalry in the Middle East, where an agreement on the proposed railway from Constantinople to Baghdad was ready for signature when war broke out in 1914, their general distrust of each other arising from the naval rivalry and the armaments race made any recognition of a real community of interests impossible to achieve.

The building of the German navy and the support for it from many sections of German society, not only those powerful ones with a direct economic interest in naval armaments, was a more potent manifestation of the prevailing imperialism than the actual development of such colonial territories as Germany was able to acquire. For many Germans, anxious to find a new role for their country and disappointed that the most attractive potential colonies were already occupied mainly, it seemed to them, by Britain, a powerful navy was the one means available of readjusting the world balance of power in Germany's interest. Thus the German navy on this view was not so much intended as a means for the direct seizure of colonies but rather as a means of tipping the balance of power in Germany's favour and of breaking Britain's world-wide predominance. These rather vague ideas were held in a crude and simple form by the Kaiser and Tirpitz; but they were also developed with greater subtlety and depth by a number of publicists and historians, whether they wrote in terms of the balance of power or whether they were dreaming of a German economic sphere in central Europe developing alongside an expanding German influence outside Europe.

The development of colonial and imperialist ambitions by the major states meant that European diplomacy was now concerned with a wider area than ever before. Although Europe was still the centre of the international stage, the stage itself was a much larger one; and with the emergence of the United

States and Japan as important naval powers with growing interests in the Pacific, new factors had appeared which were to affect the world balance of power profoundly and to exercise a determining influence on the history of international relations in the twentieth century.

The critics of imperialism in the years before 1914 predicted that colonial rivalries and the struggle for new markets and fields of investment would lead inevitably to war. In fact the war, when it came, was fought primarily for European interests and European goals, with the hope of colonial gains playing only an incidental part. However, there were three ways in which the imperialist movement directly affected the relations between the European states in the years before 1914 and contributed to the atmosphere which made war possible. Firstly, the international alignments adopted over colonial questions often cut across the pattern of international relations that had emerged in Europe itself in the years after the Franco-Prussian War. Secondly, specific agreements on particular colonial questions sometimes led to a more general *entente*, as in the case of Britain's settlement of outstanding colonial disputes with France and Russia. And third and perhaps most important, the colonial rivalries and the arms race which accompanied them (especially in the case of Britain and Germany) affected the whole of international life, encouraging doctrines of racial superiority and giving support, or so it seemed, to the crude evolutionary theories which interpreted the relations between states in terms of the struggle for survival, by then widely accepted as governing the world of nature.

In the years between 1870 and 1890 it was German foreign policy which dominated the international scene, and it was a policy intended to serve purely European ends. With the achievement of German unification under Prussian leadership, the aim of Bismarck's diplomacy was to maintain Germany's position unchanged. To achieve this Bismarck needed to ensure that France remained isolated and thus unable to think in terms of revenge for 1870 and of a war for the recovery of Alsace–Lorraine. If Germany were involved in hostilities with another European power, there was always a danger that France would side with Germany's opponent. In particular, should Austria–Hungary and Russia clash as a result of their rivalry in the Balkans, and should Germany then be obliged to take sides with one of them, there was a real possibility that France would come in on the other side. Consequently one of Bismarck's chief objectives was to avoid having to make a choice between Austria–Hungary and Russia, and to maintain a stable situation in south-east Europe which would make such a choice unnecessary.

This had been the motive of Bismarck's diplomacy before and during the Congress of Berlin of 1878. It had led him to sign the Dual Alliance with Austria–Hungary in 1879, partly because if Austria–Hungary were formally Germany's ally it would be easier for Germany to influence her foreign policy. At the same time Bismarck was anxious to keep on good terms with

Russia, first by trying to form a League of the Three Emperors of Germany, Austria–Hungary and Russia, ostensibly to demonstrate monarchical solidarity in the face of a threat of revolution, and then, when the crisis over Bulgaria in 1885–6 had shown how unstable the situation in the Balkans still was, by a direct secret agreement with Russia in 1887 (later known as the 'Reinsurance Treaty'), which would at least 'keep the line open to St Petersburg', as the current diplomatic phrase went, and in the event of another Balkan crisis give time for negotiation before committing Germany to one side or the other. In addition Bismarck had tried to ensure the stability of Europe by bringing Italy into the Triple Alliance with Germany and Austria–Hungary in 1882, and by making an alliance with Roumania in 1883. In 1887 he succeeded in persuading Britain to express a cautious interest in maintaining the *status quo* in the eastern Mediterranean by making an agreement with Austria–Hungary and Italy.

Many of these agreements remained secret, wholly or in part, and although their general lines were mostly known, there was always a suspicion that there was more to them than met the eye, either in the form of military commitments or of proposals for territorial changes. Thus, while the complex diplomatic system which Bismarck created did for the time being serve its purpose in maintaining the equilibrium of Europe and the security of Germany, it also gave radicals in all countries renewed cause for attacking secret diplomacy and an international system in which questions involving peace and war and the fate of millions were settled behind closed doors and without public discussion. Although Bismarck's system temporarily made for stability in Europe, it also contributed by its methods of secrecy to an increasing suspicion between the governments of Europe.

Bismarck's fall in 1890, the result as much of personal antagonism between the aged statesman and the young Emperor Wilhelm II and of disagreement between the Chancellor and the Emperor about how best to deal with the growing strength of socialism in Germany as of differences about foreign policy, nevertheless led to important changes in the international situation. Bismarck's Reinsurance Treaty with Russia was not renewed, though the Russians were willing to do so. In spite of all the differences of political system between the Third Republic and tsarist autocracy, then in one of its most repressive phases, France and Russia were growing closer together. The Russians were, with the start of the Trans-Siberian Railway, embarking on a new stage of their expansion into Asia and they needed security in Europe. They also needed foreign capital to help this and other projects for industrialising and modernising Russia. In fact in 1887 Bismarck, partly perhaps as a result of a characteristic lack of understanding of the links between economics and diplomacy, and partly as a result of temporary annoyance with the Russians because of a recently imposed restriction on the holding of land by foreigners which affected many prominent Germans, had forbidden the floating of Russian loans on the Berlin stock market. The result was that the Russians turned to France, so that over the next years many milliards of francs were invested by Frenchmen in Russian bonds, much of them by small savers who therefore acquired a direct interest in Franco-Russian relations and in Russian internal stability – later an important factor in French attitudes to the Bolshevik Revolution.

There were therefore good objective grounds for a closer relationship between Russia and France, especially as this would give France a sense of security by suggesting to Germany a potential threat of the war on two fronts which Germany was desperately anxious to avoid. In 1890 and 1891 courtesies were exchanged between the two countries, of which the one which attracted most public attention was the Tsar's salute as the *Marseillaise*, with all its revolutionary associations, was played during a visit of the French fleet to Russia. In August 1891 secret letters were exchanged between the two governments allowing rather vaguely for common action in the case of a threat of war, and a year later this was followed by a military agreement, finally ratified at the end of 1893. With a Franco-Russian alliance apparently confronting the Triple Alliance of Germany, Austria–Hungary and Italy, many of the gains for Germany of Bismarck's diplomacy had been lost.

In fact, however, the overwhelming interest of the European powers during the 1890s in imperialist expansion meant that the attention of their governments was concentrated on overseas developments, and European problems temporarily seemed less important. Germany's ambitions to be a world power were contrary to the principles of Bismarckian foreign policy, which had always aimed at identifiable ends and limited objectives whereas under Wilhelm II German aims were often vague and uncertain at the same time as being grandiose and ambitious. Overseas expansion brought all the European powers into more direct competition with Britain than had been the case when they had been primarily involved with European questions alone. France and Britain were rivals in Africa and in Siam. Russia appeared to be challenging British pre-eminence in the Far East. To Germany, looking round for 'a place in the sun' in the colonial field, Britain seemed to block the way to expansion in every part of the world.

A major challenge to Britain's position in the Far East came when France, Germany and Russia, in an alignment which cut across their pattern of alliances in Europe, combined to intervene in the name of the preservation of Chinese integrity at the end of the Sino-Japanese War, thus making the Chinese question an international one and putting an end to Britain's leading position there. In this case the French after some hesitation were prepared to collaborate with the Germans in spite of all their prejudices against them, both because they hoped to further their own interests in China and because they were anxious to oblige their new allies, the Russians. In general indeed, when it came to joint action in the imperial field to safeguard the European position against local challenges, the powers were prepared for the moment to forget their differences. When the Boxer Rising in China (a nationalist movement directed against the influence of the Europeans in China) in 1900 threatened to lead to the expulsion of foreigners, all the European powers (as well as the Japanese) contributed contingents to suppress it, and the French even agreed that their troops should serve under a German general.

The intervention by the powers to limit Japanese gains after China's defeat in the war of 1895 was followed by an attempt by the European powers to secure zones of influence in China in which their trade would enjoy preferential treatment and to acquire bases on the coast to back up their claims: thus, after the Germans had seized Kiao-Chow and the Russians in turn had obtained Port Arthur, the British government felt obliged to take Wei-hai-wei (a port which the German admiralty had already considered and rejected) as a 'cartographical consolation', to use Lord Salisbury's term.

The British were therefore no longer in an unchallenged position in China. Other European powers now had opportunities to trade and to make territorial gains there and they were able to enjoy the advantages won by the British some decades before of exemption from ordinary Chinese law and of trial in special courts, an inequality especially resented by the Chinese. However, the British saw the biggest threat to their position in the spread of Russian influence in the north of China and by the end of 1897 were anxious for local diplomatic support against Russia, since they were unsuccessful in attempts to reach agreement with her. Their first idea, when it became clear that no direct agreement with Russia was possible, was to come to an arrangement with Germany. Germany was not at this time a serious rival to Britain in the colonial field; her naval building had only just begun and it was some five years before the British admiralty began to be worried about it. As recently as 1890 the British had concluded an amicable agreement with Germany by which Britain had given Germany the tiny North Sea island of Heligoland in return for the rich East African island of Zanzibar. Although there were moments of ill-feeling, as over the German sympathy for the Boers in South Africa, there were no major issues outstanding between the two countries and no reason, it seemed to the British government, why they should not collaborate in the Far East.

There were other grounds, however, which led British statesmen, notably Joseph Chamberlain, the Colonial Secretary, to see in Germany a 'natural ally' for Britain at a moment when some British leaders saw in British isolation a danger to Britain's world position now that the network of alliances among the European powers had been tightly woven. Chamberlain was convinced, as he said in a speech in 1899, that[13]

At bottom the character . . . of the Teutonic race differs very slightly indeed from the character of the Anglo-Saxon . . . We find our system of justice, we find our literature, we find the very base and foundation on which our language is established, the same in the two countries, and if the union between England and America is a powerful factor in the cause of peace, a new Triple Alliance between the Teutonic race and the two great branches of the Anglo-Saxon race would be a still more potent influence in the future of the world.

However mistaken the premises of such an argument, its racialist overtones were common to many British imperialists. It is perhaps worth noting, for example, that Cecil Rhodes, who made a fortune in South Africa, became Prime Minister of the Cape Colony and was responsible for British expansion into the country which bears his name, when he endowed his famous scholarships at Oxford University intended them for German students as well as for Americans and citizens of the white British colonies.

Although the Kaiser, whose attitude to England and to his English relatives (he was the grandson of Queen Victoria) varied from sentimental friendship to jealous hostility, favoured an English alliance, his ministers and the permanent officials at the German Foreign Ministry were in no hurry. They were not particularly interested in helping Britain out of her difficulties in the Far East unless in return the British were prepared to cooperate in Europe, either by joining the Triple Alliance or at least by promising benevolent neutrality in a war of Germany and Austria–Hungary against Russia and France. They believed that time was on their side and that Britain's rivalry with France and Russia in the colonial field would eventually force Britain into an alliance on Germany's terms. Consequently the attempts made in 1898 and again in 1901 to negotiate an Anglo-German alliance came to nothing, the Germans wanting a general commitment which the British were not prepared to give and the British hoping for local support in the Far East which the Germans thought would embroil them with the Russians unnecessarily, leaving them, as they never tired of repeating, 'to pull the chestnuts out of the fire' for England. In the event, the British found what they wanted in the alliance with Japan which they signed early in 1902 and which, or so it seemed at the time, had no implications for Britain outside the Far East.

The failure to achieve an Anglo-German alliance at the beginning of the twentieth century has been regarded by some historians, especially in Germany, as a disastrously lost opportunity which might have prevented the First World War. In practice, however, the abortive negotiations had little chance of success at a moment when the British still were more conscious of their world-wide interests than of their involvement in Europe, and when the Germans were confident that their tactics of waiting till Britain's international position weakened further would bring them an English alliance on Germany's terms. The most successful international negotiations are those about detailed and specific points. Between Britain and Germany at this time there were no specific points in dispute and therefore nothing on which to base a limited detailed agreement. In the years after 1901 when the German naval programme was fully under way, there was a specific point at issue –

It was just that such large imperialistic power.

Britain generally had

the question of naval disarmament; but on this point neither side was prepared to make any serious concessions to the other. As long as the British wanted limited support outside Europe to protect their imperialist interests, and as long as the Germans wanted a British commitment in Europe that would maintain German security while Germany pursued her vague plans of *Weltpolitik*, it is hard to see how any agreement would have been possible.

The extent to which specific agreements about colonial differences could lead to more general cooperation within Europe is illustrated by the British *Entente Cordiale* with France in 1904 and by the Anglo-Russian agreement of 1907. The Fashoda crisis of 1898 had shown that the French were not strong enough to challenge Britain's position in Africa if the British were determined to maintain it. Moreover, the crisis had also shown that France's ally Russia was reluctant to give France any immediate and positive help outside Europe. The agreement over the boundaries of the Sudan which ended the crisis meant that the French had to give up hope of threatening the British position in Egypt by pressure from the Upper Nile. On the other hand, they still had considerable influence in Egypt itself, since each of the main European powers had a vote on the *Caisse de la Dette* which had been set up at the time of the occupation of Egypt to regulate the Egyptian finances in the interest of the European investors. Any major change in the economic organisation of Egypt therefore needed the agreement of the powers represented on the *Caisse* and in particular of France. By 1902 Lord Cromer, the British representative in Egypt, was ready with a far-reaching plan of financial reform, and this would in any case sooner or later have involved negotiations with the French.

At the same time, as it happened, the colonial lobby in France with which Delcassé, the Foreign Minister, had close connections, was anxious to round off France's North African empire by the acquisition of Morocco, a move which would require the consent of Britain, who had an interest in trade with Morocco and, more important, a concern with Morocco's strategic position at the entrance to the Mediterranean. It was on the basis of these respective aims that negotiations between Britain and France were started in 1903. After months of intricate discussions – a model of diplomatic bargaining which can be followed in detail in the published volumes of British and French documents on foreign policy – agreement was finally reached in April 1904 in a treaty which in effect gave Britain a free hand in Egypt, and promised British support for a French move into Morocco, while clearing up in addition a number of long-disputed points such as the question of fishing rights off the Newfoundland coast and the spheres of interest of the two countries in Asia.

On the face of it this was simply a wide settlement of colonial disputes, conducted in an atmosphere of new cordiality, of which the famous visit of King Edward VII to Paris in 1903 was the symbol rather than the cause; and it is uncertain whether either government at the time thought more of the agreement than this. However it soon became apparent that the *Entente Cordiale* had an effect on the relations between the European powers in general as well as in the sphere of British and French imperialist policies. In March 1905 the German government precipitated a crisis when the Kaiser landed at the Moroccan port of Tangier and declared that Germany would safeguard her interests in Morocco and that she considered the Sultan as an independent sovereign. This attempt to assert Germany's interests in one of the few potentially profitable African territories which were still independent, and to split the solidarity of the recent Anglo-French *Entente*, failed badly.

Although the Germans succeeded in creating a critical situation in which war between France and Germany once more seemed a possibility and although the French cabinet was sufficiently alarmed to force the resignation of Delcassé, who was held responsible for the crisis, in fact the result was a closer collaboration between France and Britain both before and during the conference on Moroccan affairs which met at Algeciras in January 1906. At the conference it was Germany, not France, which was isolated, with Austria–Hungary alone of the powers supporting Germany's proposals for Moroccan reform and for the supervision of Moroccan administration, while even more important there had been in the preceding months very tentative, very unofficial and very non-committal talks between the British and French general staffs about joint measures to be taken in the event of war with Germany. Within two years of the signing of the Anglo-French agreement it had become clear that the new Liberal government in Britain was just as anxious to collaborate with the French as its Conservative predecessors who had negotiated the agreement, and that the signature of what had seemed to be a limited treaty dealing with colonial questions in fact had a deep significance for the relations of the European powers with each other and for the balance of power in Europe.

The new friendship between France and Britain was also tested during 1904 and 1905 by the war between France's ally Russia and Britain's ally Japan; and the Germans used the opportunity to put forward proposals for a continental league of Germany, France and Russia directed at Britain. Here again German attempts to divide France and Britain, arising from the belief held by the German foreign ministry that the *Entente* could not really be serious, came to nothing, largely because Delcassé was now committed to collaboration with Britain. It was his mediation that helped to resolve a major crisis between England and Russia after the Russian fleet, early in its voyage round the world which ended in total defeat by the Japanese, had fired on some British fishing boats in the Dogger Bank area in the North Sea, apparently mistaking them for Japanese submarines.

By 1906, therefore, the *Entente* between Britain and France had been strengthened rather than weakened, basically because after the settlement of their outstanding colonial disputes each country became increasingly preoccupied with the situation in Europe. The Moroccan crisis of 1905–6 had not only revealed Germany's diplomatic isolation; it had also revived the idea that a war between France and Germany was probable. Such a war would be fought in Europe and would be fought essentially for European rather than imperialist aims. (Indeed the crisis over Morocco was followed by a period during which French and German mining firms collaborated, with the encouragement of their respective governments, in an attempt to prospect and exploit the resources of Morocco.) By this time, the British were beginning to regard the German naval programme as a serious threat; in 1903 the government decided to construct a naval base at Rosyth in Scotland to counter the German foundation of a North Sea fleet, and the fear of the establishment by Germany of a base on the Atlantic coast of Morocco largely accounts for the wholeheartedness of British support for France in 1905 and 1906. Although there were many people in Britain who could not believe that Germany was a real danger to Britain's position in the world, others, including some members of the Liberal government and a number of senior officials in the Foreign Office, were beginning to see that this was so, and that consequently the close links with France must be maintained.

The defeat of Russia by Japan also had the effect of turning Russia away from plans of expansion in the Far East, as well as removing the immediate Russian threat to British interests in China. In the circumstances it seemed reasonable for Britain and Russia to try to reach a settlement of outstanding questions arising out of their imperial rivalries in Asia. This agreement, which the French were naturally anxious to encourage, took a long time to negotiate. The British Liberal government was worried about the instability of the Russian system as demonstrated by the 1905 Revolution, and many of its radical supporters were bitterly opposed to an agreement with the tsarist government which might improve its credit abroad and help to strengthen it at home. Military men on both sides were urging the civilians not to make concessions, since both the government of India and the Russian general staff were worried at the possibility of losing influence in Persia, one of the main areas under discussion. However, the agreement was finally signed in April 1907. It provided for the neutralisation of Tibet and the withdrawal of the British military mission there, while the Russians recognised that Afghanistan fell within the British sphere. Persia was maintained as an independent state but it was divided into Russian and British zones of influence with a neutral zone in between.

Although Russia did not give up her interest in central Asia or her attempt to improve her position in Persia, the agreement of 1907 removed some of the immediate causes of friction between Britain and Russia. It also held out to the Russians the hope that Britain might not oppose their aims in Europe at a time when, searching for advantages to compensate for the humiliating defeat in the Far East, the Russian government had revived its ambitions in the Balkans and its hopes of controlling the exit from the Black Sea through the Bosphorus and Dardanelles. Although relations between Britain and Russia never became as close as those between Britain and France, the ending of the old hostility between them can be seen as yet another sign of the way in which agreements in the imperial sphere reflected a growing preoccupation by the great powers with the affairs of Europe. The Germans suspected, wrongly, a deliberate plan by Britain to encircle and isolate her, and the feeling that Europe was dividing into two armed camps was inescapable. At a moment when Europe was at the height of its influence in the world, the disruptive forces within it were leading to what some historians have seen as the first round of a disastrous European civil war.

The critics of the prevailing imperialism at the end of the nineteenth century based their attacks on various grounds: humanitarians were outraged by the exploitation of Africans in the Belgian Congo, by the brutality with which the Germans repressed the rebellion in South-West Africa in 1904 or by the 'methods of barbarism', as a leading British Liberal statesman put it, which the British used to combat guerrillas in the South African War by rounding up the scattered farmers of the *veld* into 'concentration camps' – a phrase to acquire even more sinister implications later in the twentieth century.

A more fundamental theoretical criticism of imperialism and of its effects on society as a whole was developed by writers anxious to trace the links between imperialist expansion and the internal social and economic structure of the European states. The most important of these were two socialist thinkers, the Austrian economist Rudolf Hilferding and Rosa Luxemburg, who, as we have seen, was, by the early years of the twentieth century, already an important and influential figure on the Left of the German Social Democratic Party. They believed, as J. A. Hobson did and as Lenin was to repeat in his pamphlet on imperialism in 1916, that imperialism was an inevitable product of the economic pressures of capitalism and of the need to find new outlets for capital investment; but they also suggested that the violence and injustice involved in colonial rule was making the liberal ideology of an earlier generation of free-traders out of date, so that imperialism was not simply the activity of overseas expansion, but rather an all-pervasive phenomenon affecting almost all branches of society.

The imperialism of the period 1880–1914 was one aspect of a revolution which was challenging the ideas of an earlier generation. Just as the virtues of free trade were being questioned and the necessity of state intervention in many fields was becoming accepted, so the relations between states and the motives for their policies were now based on fresh assumptions about the nature of man and society, assumptions which affected the internal politics of many states as well as their external relations. While it is possible to account for each specific act of imperialism in particular terms – economic hopes, national prestige, strategic necessities – a number of general assumptions underlay the whole imperialist movement. These included the belief in a national mission and the often genuine, sometimes hypocritical, belief in the duty of the advanced peoples to bring civilisation and good administration to the backward ones, to bear, in the most famous phrase of all the British imperialist slogans, 'the white man's burden'.* However the most profound groups of ideas inspiring the concept of imperialism were those which can be roughly classified as 'social Darwinism', and which saw the relations between states as a perpetual struggle for survival in which some races were regarded as 'superior' to others in an evolutionary process in which the strongest had constantly to assert themselves.

Charles Darwin, the English naturalist whose books *On the Origin of Species*, published in 1859, and *The Descent of Man*, which followed in 1871, launched controversies which affected many branches of European thought, had not himself devoted much attention to any social implications his ideas might have had, and his remarks about the place of war in society for example are often contradictory. In working out his theory of natural selection, he was primarily concerned to show that in the natural world one species evolved from and often replaced another in a continuous process of evolution, and thus to refute the doctrine that everything in the world as it now exists derived from a single simultaneous act of creation. His views had of course a profound influence on the natural sciences, especially on biology, but they had also played a crucial part in the mounting confrontation between science and religion which shook the consciences of many intellectuals in the mid-nineteenth century, especially in the Protestant countries where a belief in the validity of the individual decision and in the right of each conscience to choose freely for itself existed side by side with a belief in the divine literal inspiration of the scriptures.

By the 1890s this conflict was abating, with the methods and conclusions of natural science becoming widely accepted (see chapter 6 below) and theo-

---

* Rudyard Kipling's poem *The White Man's Burden* (*The Five Nations*, London, 1903, p. 79) is an exhortation to the Americans to take up their imperial responsibilities. Its first verse runs:—

> Take up the White Man's Burden—
> Send forth the best ye breed—
> Go bind your sons to exile
> To serve your captives' need;
> To wait in heavy harness,
> On fluttered folk and wild—
> Your new-caught sullen peoples,
> Half-devil and half-child.

It is worth noting that the general tone of the poem is pessimistic: the colonial administrator is there 'to seek another's profit and work another's gain', and his reward is 'the blame of those ye better, the hate of those ye guard'.

logical doctrines adapted so as to allow at least some place for the established truths of science. The ideas of Darwin, however, and of some of his contemporaries such as the English philosopher Herbert Spencer, who first seems to have used the phrase 'survival of the fittest', were rapidly applied to questions far removed from the immediate scientific ones with which Darwin himself had been concerned. As in the case of Marx (a thinker whose admiration for Darwin was such that he had offered – without success – to dedicate the first English edition of *Capital* to him), the popularised versions of Darwin's teaching inspired much of which the author might well not have approved, and spread ideas not to be found in the original, at least in the crude form in which they were later propagated. The element of Darwinism which appeared most applicable to the development of society was the belief that the excess of population over the means of support necessitated a constant struggle for survival in which it was the strongest or the 'fittest' who won. From this it was easy for some social thinkers to give a moral content to the notion of the fittest, so that the species or races which did survive were those morally entitled to do so. *Darwin ≠ Marx*

The doctrine of natural selection could, therefore, very easily become associated with another train of thought developed by the French writer, Count Joseph-Arthur Gobineau, who published an *Essay on the Inequality of Human Races* in 1853. Gobineau insisted that the most important factor in development was race; and that those races which remained superior were those which kept their racial purity intact. Of these, according to Gobineau, it was the Aryan race which had survived best, but he was very pessimistic about the future and believed that racial purity was impossible to preserve in the nineteenth century, and that consequently the outlook even for the Aryans was one of decline. Gobineau's large and sombre work, with its appearance of being a serious work of ethnographic science, had more influence in Germany than in France. His theories were first taken up by the great composer Richard Wagner and his circle; and after Wagner's death in 1883 they were kept alive by his widow and friends. It was indeed Wagner's English-born admirer and son-in-law Houston Stewart Chamberlain who contributed to carrying some of these ideas a stage further in his book *The Foundations of the Nineteenth Century*, written in German and published in 1899.

This immense, turgid, repetitive book which now seems almost unreadable, had a considerable success in Germany over a long period, and Hitler himself admired the author sufficiently to visit him on his deathbed in 1927. With an accumulation of historical, theological and ethnographical detail, H.S. Chamberlain saw human development as dominated by the necessity to preserve the essential character of each race. The races which had survived were those which had successfully done this, like the Germanic race and the Jews. (It is not easy to follow who counted as Germanic; sometimes Chamberlain is realistic enough to see from how many different stocks the nineteenth-century Germans derived and he refers to them as Slavo-Celto-Germanic; often he seems to mean just the north Europeans in general.) One of the themes of his work is the contrast and conflict between these two peoples, and for this reason he produced an elaborate proof that Jesus was not a Jew. The book's message was the necessity of preserving the Germanic values intact at a time when Europeans were spreading all over the world, since it was Germanic blood alone which made Europe an organic unity and this was now threatened with dilution from many sources. For H. S. Chamberlain the doctrine of a master race which has developed its qualities in the struggle for existence and improved them by a process of natural selection is coupled with the belief that such a master race has its own specific mission. At a moment when Germans were looking for a new purpose in the world and a new national cause to provide the younger generation with the same inspiration that the struggle for national unification had given their fathers, it is easy to see how doctrines of racial superiority could reinforce pseudo-Darwinian beliefs about the necessity for Germany of 'a place in the sun'.

If racial theories were most widely accepted in Germany, they were not a negligible factor elsewhere. 'What is Empire but the predominance of Race?'[14] Lord Rosebery (a former British Prime Minister) demanded in 1900; and we have seen how Joseph Chamberlain (no relation of H. S. Chamberlain) and Cecil Rhodes dreamed of an alliance between Britain and the USA, based on the solidarity of the superior Anglo-Saxon races, and desired some association with Germany on the assumption that there was some racial affinity between Teutons and Anglo-Saxons; and among other leading British imperialists Lord Milner was not alone in believing that 'Stronger, more primordial than ... material ties is the bond of common blood, a common language, common history and traditions.'[15] The belief, even when it was not worked out in any theoretical way, that the white races were superior to the black or yellow was a basic assumption of imperialism. Even though some of the imperialist powers believed that with time the subject peoples could be educated up to the level of their rulers, in practice this belief was only applied to a very small elite, and even then – as in the case of the British in India – with considerable social and practical reservations. Underlying all imperialist activity, whatever detailed form it took and whatever its immediate causes, was a belief in the necessity of a struggle for survival among the powers, a conflict between living and dying nations; and in this struggle an appeal to a belief in the natural superiority of a particular race often played a part.

There was, however, a negative as well as a positive side to the racialist and pseudo-evolutionary assumptions of imperialism. Side by side with the enormous self-confidence of the European peoples setting out to divide the world between them and to impose their will on subject races, there existed a growing anxiety that the position of the ruling races might itself be challenged, not only by the other European states which they recognised as equals, but by the peoples inside or outside their own borders whom they had taken for granted were their inferiors. It is interesting in this connection to see how many writers in the 1890s began to be afraid of what became known as 'the Yellow Peril' (a phrase taken up enthusiastically by the German Kaiser, with his usual gift for reflecting and expressing what many of his subjects were thinking). The fear that the Chinese, already an important mercantile community all over south-east Asia – and sometimes significantly referred to by Europeans as 'the Jews of Asia' – might compete successfully with European trade, was coupled after the resounding defeat of Russia by Japan in the war of 1904–5 by an anxiety about what might happen if the peoples of the East became as efficient industrially and militarily as the Western nations. For the moment, in the years before 1914, these fears, though widely expressed, were not yet very serious, although later in the century both the commercial and the military threat to the European position in Asia were to become real. What is significant is that the very same ideological assumptions which gave the imperialist movement its strength – a belief in the inequality of races and in the struggle for survival – could also lead people to question their own position, to have grave doubts about their own future and even to predict 'The decline of the West' (the title of a famous book by Oswald Spengler, which was published in 1918. See p. 482 below).

This association of racialist theories with a neurotic fear of an alien people is nowhere more clearly seen than in the growth of anti-Semitism, which was already a notable phenomenon of the last two decades of the nineteenth century, even though it did not reach its ghastly climax until the Germans' attempt to exterminate the European Jews during the Second World War. Since the French Revolution most of the countries of Europe had removed the legal disabilities and inequalities from which the Jewish communities had suffered since the Middle Ages. The Jews, that is to say, were now legally on the same footing as other citizens, in so far as they now had the right to vote, to stand for election, to move freely, to adopt any profession. Only in Russia were nearly all the Jews still obliged to live in certain districts and subjected to increasing rather than diminishing legal and administrative difficulties in such matters as their right to choose a profession. However the emancipation of the Jews had brought its own problems. Although many Jews were anxious to assimilate into the societies in which they lived and were even prepared if necessary formally to become Christians, and although the Jews, like members of other religious faiths, were affected by the ideas of scientific free thought and of agnosticism prevalent in the second half of the nineteenth century, most of them still belonged to a separate, identifiable community with their own religion, customs and in many cases language. (The Jews used

Hebrew for religious purposes; most of the Jews of Eastern Europe spoke Yiddish – a dialect of German.)

The difficulty for the Jews was how to make their recently conceded civil rights a reality and how to overcome the centuries-old prejudice which had emphasised their separateness from the people among whom they lived and which in the nineteenth century was taking new forms. While the old Christian hostility towards the Jews as the people responsible for the crucifixon of Jesus was still to be found among some Roman Catholics, particularly the Jesuits, and in the Russian Orthodox Church, new grievances against the Jews were invented, arising out of the circumstances of industrialised, capitalist society and out of that very freedom of movement which the emancipation seemed to offer the Jews. Because in the Middle Ages Christians had been forbidden to lend money at interest, the Jews had been among the great money-lenders of Europe. By the nineteenth century the rich Jews of Frankfurt, Vienna, Paris or London, headed by the most famous and most successful of all Jewish dynasties, the Rothschilds, were closely associated with the expanding banks of Europe, while the Jewish pedlar and small money-lender in the rural areas of Hesse in Germany or of Galicia, the Polish province of Austria–Hungary, continued to perform their traditional function.

Much of the anti-Semitism which developed in the 1880s and 1890s therefore had economic grounds. The German Social Democrat leader, August Bebel, once called anti-Semitism '*Der Sozialismus des dummen Kerls*' (fools' socialism), and it was very easy for an attack on the power of high finance and on the big banks to turn into an attack on those Jews who formed a readily identifiable section of the capitalist class. In other sectors of economic life the Jews again provided a scapegoat: in Vienna, for example, Jewish tailors who had moved in from the villages of Galicia were prepared to work for lower wages than the Viennese craftsmen, and were held responsible for unemployment when times were bad. In many rural areas the farmers and landowners who had borrowed money from the local Jewish money-lender hated him when he pressed for payment in a year when the crops had failed.

However, a hatred of Jewish capitalists, or direct economic competition between Jew and gentile in the cities, or the rural anti-Semitism based on fear of the money-lender among debt-ridden peasants, were not the only bases for anti-Semitism. Economic anti-Semitism, mistaken and regrettable though it was, has at least an apparently rational explanation. Harder to understand were those forms of hatred and fear of the Jews which did not arise from day-to-day contact but which were sometimes experienced by people who had scarcely ever seen a Jew. In France, for example, where the Jewish community was only some 80,000 strong and where in the secular and liberal atmosphere of the Third Republic the Jews were to a large extent successfully assimilated, there was, from the 1880s onwards a vigorous

popular anti-Semitic movement, with its own widely read press and literature. This was originally largely the work of one publicist, Edouard Drumont,
who used the indignation caused in 1882 by the failure of a bank, the *Union
Générale*, widely but wrongly believed to be owned by Jews, to start a successful anti-Jewish agitation. Drumont in his writings, of which the most
notorious was *La France Juive*, a work which sold over 100,000 copies on its
publication in 1886, combined several of the themes common to anti-
Semitic writers of every country. Drumont had a hatred of modern urban life
and he wrote sentimental stories about old France, a France whose values
were, he alleged, being undermined by the influence of Jews everywhere in
French life.

Drumont's propaganda about the Jewish conspiracy was given a new lease
of life by a financial scandal in 1891. The famous engineer Ferdinand de
Lesseps, whose great achievement had been the construction of the Suez
Canal a quarter of a century earlier, had, in his old age, launched a scheme for
a canal across the isthmus of Panama. This had met with all sorts of unexpected difficulties, and its supporters were threatened with the loss of all
their money, totalling some $300,000,000. The promoters therefore, who
included two Jews, Baron Joseph Reinach and Dr Cornelius Herz, did their
best to cover up the impending failure by seeking for support from prominent politicians; and in 1888 the government had authorised a state loan to
the project. This however failed to prevent the bankruptcy of the company.
In the search for a scapegoat, the shareholders accused a number of members
of parliament of corruption, and it was easy for Drumont and his associates
to allege that it was the Jews who were behind the fiasco; and he was able to
win a wide circulation for his anti-Semitic periodical, *La Libre Parole*.

A few years later the Dreyfus affair (see also pp. 64–5 above) gave yet
another opportunity for renewed anti-Semitism in France, since the agitation
against Dreyfus and those who were demanding a revision of his condemnation for espionage was easily turned into an attack on Dreyfus' Jewish
origins – he was one of the few Jews on the General Staff – and the zeal of
his supporters was quickly attributed to a Jewish conspiracy. The Dreyfus
case indeed united all those who believed that the authority of the State, as
represented by the officers who had prepared the case against Dreyfus and
the court martial which had condemned him, should not be questioned, even
when its decisions were unjust. They were people whose intense nationalism
led them to demand that anyone of alien origin should be prohibited from
holding public office – and this included the Jews first and foremost. To
them it was a case of 'on the one side true France and the army, on the other
the republic and the Jews'.[16]

The emotions of the Dreyfus controversy forced many Frenchmen to
reformulate their political beliefs and to take sides for or against the liberal,
lay republic. On the republican side there was a movement to support the

government of Waldeck-Rousseau, which was committed to safeguarding the constitution and to reopening the Dreyfus case: and it was this movement that succeeded – partly because the Right, though vociferous, made no attempt to overthrow the regime and limited themselves to meaningless gestures, as when one of them struck the President of the Republic's hat off at a race meeting. However, among the right-wing nationalists and conservatives the Dreyfus affair did lead directly to the foundation of a new radical royalist group, the *Action Française*, which was to have a continuous existence until the Second World War and which, even if it never had the mass support for which its leaders hoped, nevertheless provided a consistent and well-publicised ideology for the anti-republic right, in which anti-Semitism was a prominent element.

The most important figure in constructing this ideology was Charles Maurras, who formulated at the time of the Dreyfus case ideas which he held consistently throughout a long life so that, when at the age of seventy-seven he was condemned in 1945 for having supported the Vichy regime (which owed much to his ideas), he is said to have exclaimed, 'It is Dreyfus' revenge.' Maurras not only rejected parliamentary democracy and called for a system of representation on a corporate or professional basis within the framework of a restored monarchy; he was also obsessed by the danger to French security of the elements in France who were not in his view wholly committed to France – the 'four confederate states', as he called them, the freemasons, the Protestants, the Jews and the *métèques*, a word he invented to include anyone else of foreign origin living in France. These people were to be excluded from French public life, which was to be restricted to those with at least three generations of French ancestors.

The other spokesman of this new nationalism – though he claimed to be republican rather than royalist, and did not agree with the *Action Française* in its total rejection of the whole of French history since 1789 – was Maurice Barrès, a gifted novelist and critic, who broke with most of his friends in the advanced literary circles of Paris at the time of the Dreyfus case. For Barrès the Jews were almost automatically excluded from French life, since nationality was a question of 'the land and the dead', a result of generations living on and being buried in the soil of France. Just as Maurras regarded the presence of the Jews as a threat to French security, so Barrès regarded them, and especially their participation in the Dreyfus agitation, as a threat to the social solidarity of France – a solidarity which in his view was always more important than the achievement of justice in an individual case.

Yet, for all the virulence of Drumont's pamphleteering and the intelligence and eloquence of nationalist rhetoricians like Maurras and Barrès, anti-Semitism in France did not, at least until the Vichy regime in the Second World War, deeply affect the life of the Jews in France. Jews were successful in politics and the administration, even if there was always considerable prejudice against them in the army and the diplomatic service. Anti-Semitism often tended to be regarded as 'an affair of the clubs and the racecourses', to quote a phrase of Léon Blum's. Blum himself indeed was not uncharacteristic of the assimilated French Jews. At the time of the Dreyfus case, he was a young man just making a reputation for himself as a critic and writer. Later he went into politics and became the leader of the Socialist Party after the First World War and Prime Minister of the Popular Front government in 1936. He made a successful career, that is to say, in spite of recurrent taunts from the Right urging him to 'go back to Jerusalem' and he thought of himself as identified with France – 'A French Jew', as he put it towards the end of his life, after the grim experiences of the Second World War, 'of a long line of French ancestors, speaking only the language of my country, mainly nourished by its culture refusing to leave at a moment when I faced the greatest dangers'.[17]

Such a career would have been impossible in Germany or in Austria-Hungary where anti-Semitism developed much further both as an ideology and as a political movement, while it was in Russia from 1881 on that the Jews were not only exposed to discrimination and denied civil rights but were periodically subject to physical violence. From 1880 there developed in the German-speaking world an anti-Semitic movement with a profuse literature attacking the Jews from many different standpoints. In Berlin the Protestant Christian Social movement, led by the court chaplain Adolf Stöcker, linked anti-Semitism with a puritanical attack on the more ostentatious and flamboyant elements in the new German capitalist class, while in Vienna the Catholic Christian Social movement under the reforming mayor Karl Lueger also combined genuine efforts at social welfare with an appeal to the anti-Jewish prejudices of the Viennese lower middle class anxious at what they believed to be an economic threat from their Jewish rivals.

These were primarily practical movements exploiting long-standing feelings against the stereotyped Jewish financier or money-lender, and neither Lueger nor Stöcker were particularly concerned with ideological anti-Semitism. (Lueger indeed took a pragmatic line: when criticised for receiving Jews in his home, he replied, 'I decide who is a Jew.') Others, however, produced pseudo-scientific works stressing the total difference between Jew and German or between Aryan and Semite, with the implication that the Jews were a foreign body that must be rooted out of the German *Volk*. These ideas formed an important part of the anti-liberal nationalist thinking in Germany at the end of the nineteenth century so that from this time on it went without saying that any nationalist movement in Germany was to a greater or lesser extent anti-Semitic in content. (See pp. 151–4 below.)

It was this assumption that anti-Semitism was an intrinsic part of almost any right-wing or nationalist party in Germany that made the formation of a separate specifically anti-Semitic political party virtually unnecessary. A party was formed on this basis and had twenty-five deputies in the Reichstag by 1907, but its direct influence was by then already declining so that the socialist leader Bebel could confidently assert in 1906: 'It is a consoling thought that it has no prospect of ever becoming a decisive influence in political and social life in Germany.'[18] Unfortunately, it would be truer to say that the party never became a decisive influence just because its doctrines had become absorbed into the presuppositions of a number of other parties and groups. In Austria, too, the anti-Semitic movement merged into other German nationalist groups: the party founded by Georg von Schönerer, one of the most fanatical anti-Semites in Austria (though he was also almost equally anti-Catholic), found its strength among the Germans of Bohemia and combined anti-Semitism with an equally racialist hatred and fear of the Slavs in general and of the Czechs in particular.

In France anti-Semitism had made few inroads on the actual exercise of their civic rights by the Jews. In Germany and Austria Jews laboured constantly under a sense of humiliation and discrimination; although in Germany Jewish financiers and industrialists were occasionally received at court by Wilhelm II, even the most successful of them could not forget for long that they were regarded as belonging to an inferior race. 'There comes a painful moment in the life of every young German Jew,' the industrialist Walther Rathenau, one of the most prominent of them wrote, 'which he remembers all his life: when he fully realises for the first time that he has come into the world as a second-class citizen, and that no virtue and no merit can free him from this situation.'[19]

However it was in Russia that in the years before the First World War anti-Semitism often took the form of physical violence. Here some five million Jews – about one-fifth of the total Jewish population of the world – lived in restricted areas in western Russia, the so-called 'Pale of Settlement'; and from 1882 onwards there were recurrent *pogroms* against them. In one of the worst, at Kishinev in 1903, 45 Jews were killed, 400 injured and 1,300 houses and shops destroyed. These attacks were deliberately organised sometimes by the police, anxious to direct discontent with the tsarist regime on to another target, sometimes by private individuals. Moreover it was in Russia that some of the crudest popular anti-Semitic literature originated – again some of it inspired by the police – which included the notorious *Protocols of the Elders of Zion*, a document purporting to give first-hand evidence of the existence of a Jewish world-conspiracy, soon translated and disseminated widely in what Norman Cohn has called the 'subterranean world where pathological fantasies disguised as ideas are churned out by crooks and half-educated fanatics for the benefit of the ignorant and superstitious'.[20] Most sinister of all it was in one of the Russian nationalist anti-Semitic groups, the Union of the Russian People founded in 1905, that the idea of the actual physical extermination of the Jews was launched, an idea which was also shared by a few pathological fanatics in Vienna in the years from 1909 to 1913 when the young Adolf Hitler was living there as an unsuccessful house-painter with frustrated artistic ambitions.

The Jews themselves tried various answers to the apparently growing threat of anti-Semitism in Europe. Many, especially among the most wealthy and successful, hoped to become assimilated into the classes among whom they lived. Very many – especially from Russia, where their material conditions of life grew ever more precarious – emigrated, to the East End of London or to the United States, often taking with them utopian revolutionary ideas bred out of their desperation. Some on the other hand drew different conclusions from their experiences, and believed that in an age of growing nationalism the only hope for the Jews lay in asserting their own national identity and in establishing their own national state. This idea had been first propounded in the 1860s by the German Jewish socialist and associate of Karl Marx, Moses Hess, but had had little immediate influence. Subsequently the first wave of *pogroms* in Russia in 1882 led a Russian Jew, Leon Pinsker, to advocate the 'self-emancipation' of the Jews and gave new impetus to the movement for establishing Jewish agricultural settlements in Palestine. However the creator of the Zionist movement as an effective political organisation, which was finally to succeed half a century later in creating the state of Israel, was a Viennese journalist and playwright, Theodor Herzl, who without apparently knowing of Pinsker's writings published his pamphlet *The Jewish State* in 1896, at a time when his experiences as a journalist in Paris during the Dreyfus trial had reinforced his fears of a general wave of anti-Jewish sentiment in Europe. Although Herzl died in 1904 aged only forty-four, he succeeded in establishing a Zionist organisation committed to the establishment of an autonomous Jewish state in Palestine and, in spite of opposition from many Jews who thought that such a plan would mean an end to the possibility of assimilation, he succeeded in making contact with the German, British and Turkish governments in the hope of enlisting their support, as well as explaining his views to the Pope, who received them coolly, and to the King of Italy. While not immediately successful in obtaining concessions from the Turks or the backing of any of the great powers (though the British government offered the Jews territory for settlement in East Africa), the Zionist Congress which Herzl founded continued to develop its influence, and during the First World War its leader Dr Chaim Weizmann was able to secure from the British Foreign Secretary Arthur Balfour the promise that the Jews should be given a 'national home' in Palestine.

It was the racial presuppositions behind the imperialist movement that intensified the growth of anti-Semitism, so that it was not surprising that Herzl and the Zionists responded in racial and national terms with a plan for a return to Palestine, which would give the Jews roots as deep and as ancient as those which Barrès praised in the French people. Equally, at a time when the acquisition of territory outside Europe was a principal concern for European states, it was natural that Herzl should turn to the great powers in the hope of securing their help in obtaining territorial concessions in Turkey. For better or for worse Herzl had linked the destinies of the Zionist movement with those of the imperialist powers; and after he failed to obtain the support he had hoped for from the Kaiser, he turned to Britain: 'England, the free and Mighty England,' as he put it, 'whose vision embraces the seven seas, will understand us and our aspirations.'[21] It is a sign of the extent to which colonialist and nationalist visions had affected European thought and action that even the answer of the persecuted should be couched in the same language as that of the imperialist.

5

LIBERALISM AND ITS ENEMIES

By the beginning of the twentieth century many of the political, social and intellectual movements which were to transform Europe over the next fifty years had already been launched. Moreover each movement provoked a corresponding reaction. The imperialist movement discussed in the last chapter not only produced the developments in the colonies which were to lead to the establishment of new independent states half a century later; it also led to a movement of radical criticism in the imperialist countries themselves, a movement which both contributed to the revolutionary forces of the twentieth century in Europe and also helped to prepare the way for decolonisation by destroying confidence in the Europeans' right to rule 'backward' peoples. The socialist movement obliged governments to take social legislation seriously; but it also provoked a renewed fear of revolution which resulted in new counter-revolutionary and anti-socialist ideologies. The widespread belief that scientific progress would solve almost all problems and that the methods of the natural sciences could be applied to the study of history or of society or of literature gave rise, in reaction, to a new emphasis on the irrational element in man and on the importance of the instinctive and subconscious emotions. As industrial and technical advance transformed the environment, so people reacted against industrialism and sought ways to regain contact with what seemed a more natural and simpler way of life.

These contrasts and conflicts made the period from 1890 until the outbreak of the First World War one of the most interesting and creative in the whole history of European civilisation. But it would be wrong to see this period wholly in terms of the new revolutionary social and intellectual forces which were to shape consciousness and society[1] in the twentieth century. In politics the demands for universal suffrage and a representative government were becoming increasingly successful, so that the liberal ideas which had been revolutionary in the previous generation were now becoming political orthodoxy and were affecting even the conservative empires of Germany and Austria–Hungary. In Russia the Revolution of 1905 led to the establishment for the first time of a national parliament and to a semblance of constitutionalism. The acceptance of the forms of parliamentary government in Italy or Spain seemed to mark a victory for liberal principles, even if their obvious inadequacy in practice to deal with the real problems of these countries contributed to the development of criticisms of parliamentary government from Right and Left alike.

Britain and France provided successful examples of parliamentary democracy in action. In both countries there was a wide electorate and in both countries the executive was unmistakably responsible to parliament. In practice, however, parliamentary government worked rather differently in the two countries. In Britain two parties contested with each other for a majority in the House of Commons, members of which were elected by a straight majority in what were with a few exceptions single-member constituencies. Although other parties – the Irish and after 1900 the Labour Representation Committee, which became the Labour Party in 1906 – won some seats and might, in circumstances such as those after 1910 when neither the Liberal nor the Conservative Party had an overall majority in parliament, exercise considerable pressure, for the most part the British system tended to give a substantial majority to one or other of the two major parties. The prime minister and government, therefore, were usually assured of the support in the House of Commons necessary to enable them to carry out their policies. A general election had to be held by law once every seven years till 1911 and once every five years after that, so that, even if a government decided to dissolve parliament before it was obliged to do so, it was nevertheless assured of office for a period of several years, unless the party in power was threatened by an internal split (the case of the Conservative Party in 1905, divided between supporters of free trade and advocates of a protective tariff) or when, as in the case of the Liberals in 1910, they felt that their majority was not large enough to enable them to introduce controversial legislation without a further appeal to the electorate.

The British electoral system and the existence of only two major parties thus enabled the executive to retain its hold over the legislature as long as the government leaders maintained control over their own party. There was accordingly an increasing emphasis on party solidarity and party organisation, both in order to maintain support in the House of Commons and in order to appeal effectively to the new mass electorate. Although the discipline of the parties in Britain and the efficiency of their electoral organisation was at the beginning of the twentieth century still very weak compared to what it was to become fifty years later, it was already strong enough for some observers to complain of the tyranny of the masses and the dangers of ruthless professional political machines and pressure groups managing elections and parliaments. (A notable example of this kind of thinking was a study of British and American party politics, *Democracy and the Organisation of*

Political Parties, by a French political scientist, Moritz Ostrogorsky, published in 1903.)

In France on the other hand whatever criticism could be made of the parliamentary life of the Third Republic, it could not be said that party discipline or party organisation were in danger of becoming too strong. The legislature was supreme and, whereas in England the parliamentary defeat of a government normally led to a general election, thus obliging members of Parliament to reflect before casting a vote against the government and endangering their own seats, in the French Chamber of Deputies governments could be overthrown by a chance vote on deputies who perhaps hoped they might themselves be represented in the government which would result from the ensuing reshuffle. (See p. 13 above.) If the Chamber of Deputies could be said accurately to represent the people, then the sovereignty of the people could be said to be ensured by the sovereignty of parliament over a succession of governments. In practice however the continuity of government in France was assured by the fact that many of the same politicians contrived to serve in successive governments, so that the same names recur in various ministerial roles, as well as by the existence of an efficient centralised professional administrative service. While politicians on the Right called for a strong government, they were not in fact able to overthrow a system which seemed to satisfy the desire of Frenchmen to be free of government interference, especially in matters of taxation, and to see their local interests safeguarded by the political bargaining of their representatives in Paris. Neither General Boulanger in 1887, who seemed briefly to be the heir of the Bonapartist tradition of strong leadership, nor those conservatives who used the Dreyfus affair as an opportunity to attack the republican constitution were able to overcome the vested interests which the Third Republic had now created for itself, so that the outcome of the Dreyfus crisis was a 'government of republican solidarity' affirming its belief in the republican constitution and in such radical causes as the disestablishment of the Roman Catholic Church in France. In fact, very few Frenchmen wanted strong government. The provincial politicians who formed the core of the parties of the Centre were content with verbal appeals to the revolutionary tradition and to republican loyalty, while supporting social and economic policies which did not touch their pockets or those of their constituents.

This preference for a weak, approachable government based on a series of bargains between solid middle-class politicians even found a theoretical spokesman, in the person of the political journalist Alain (the pseudonym of a high-school teacher, E.A.Chartier). In a series of short articles over twenty years starting in 1906 Alain repeated a few simple propositions which expressed the unspoken beliefs of millions of provincial French electors. All government, he believed, is likely to turn into a tyranny unless it is subjected to constant criticism and control by the electors, who can only retain their liberty by being extremely suspicious of all acts of the executive. The means by which this control is to be exercised is by direct pressure on individual deputies. The Radical prime minister Emile Combes, who was responsible for carrying through the disestablishment of the Church in 1905, once exhorted the deputies to 'think of their electoral districts' ('*Regardez vos circonscriptions!*'). This in Alain's view was what members of parliament should be doing all the time; and anything which interfered with this direct contact – a strong party machine or a too powerful bureaucracy – must be avoided if liberty was to be preserved.

This essentially negative attitude towards government presupposed a stable society to offset the political instability which fear of strong government tended to produce; and at least until the First World War and indeed in some respects until the Second World War, it seemed to give Frenchmen what they wanted. The republic had survived the demands for strong government made by the Right at the time of the Dreyfus case; and the effect of that crisis had been to inaugurate a period of government in which the Radical-Socialist Party, whose presuppositions Alain was in fact expressing, became the essential element in a series of governments which introduced measures of mild social reform while not interfering with the economic interests of their electors. The Dreyfus case had provided an example of the way in which French public opinion could genuinely make itself felt so as to expose injustice and to right wrongs, although it was a movement outside parliament and largely independent of the established political parties which had successfully reopened the case of Dreyfus and led to a revision of the verdict against him, as well as showing the strength of moderate republican sentiment in the country.

The power of moderate opinion in the French provinces, in addition to expressing itself through the electoral system of single-member constituencies and a double ballot, which favoured bargains and compromises (see p. 13 above), was also built into the constitution, since the upper house of parliament, the senate, was elected indirectly by electoral colleges composed of the members of the local government councils and of representatives of each *commune* (the smallest unit in the administrative system). Although the system had been reformed in 1882, when life senators had been abolished and the composition of the electoral colleges changed so as to weaken the influence of the smallest villages, it was still weighted against the larger cities, and consolidated the political strength of the medium-sized provincial towns. During the whole life of the Third Republic the senate, in addition to providing safe seats for a number of important ministerial figures, was a consistently conservative element in the political system, particularly where economic and fiscal measures were concerned. And it is perhaps a measure of the satisfaction felt with the constitutional arrangements of the Third Republic that demands for any further reform of the senate after 1882 were slow to come and never very important.

This was not the case in Britain where the powers of the upper house o parliament, the House of Lords, became a major political issue in the first years of the twentieth century, and where the existence of a chamber composed of members of a hereditary aristocracy seemed a direct challenge to the principles of liberalism and of a constitution based on universal suffrage. There were already clashes between the predominantly conservative House of Lords and the Liberal government in office between 1892 and 1896; and Gladstone himself, in his last parliamentary speech before his retirement in 1894 at the age of eighty-five, said that 'Differences of prepossession, differences of mental habit and differences of fundamental tendency, between the House of Lords and the House of Commons, appear to have reached a development in the present year such as to create a state of things of which we are compelled to say that, in our judgment, it cannot continue.'[2] It was however not until the Liberals won a large majority in the election of 1906 and undertook extensive measures of social reform that the crisis came to a head. In the following years a series of clashes between the two Houses culminated in 1909 with the rejection by the House of Lords of the budget for that year which contained provisions, perhaps more of symbolic than of practical importance, for a tax on land values to be levied on the sale of property. This seemed a direct threat to a large section of influential Conservative supporters, already complaining about the 'death duties', the inheritance tax introduced by the previous Liberal government, and about the compulsory schemes for social insurance recently set up by Asquith's administration. It was an issue on which the Conservatives were prepared to fight a constitutional battle, and it seemed to the Liberals, and especially to the Welsh radical Lloyd George who as Chancellor of the Exchequer was responsible for the budget, an excellent opportunity to launch a campaign against inherited property and privilege. After two general elections in the same year (1910) and the obtaining by Asquith of a promise from the new king, George v, to create new members of the House of Lords if necessary, so as to give the government a majority in the upper house favourable to their proposals for constitutional reform, the Lords gave way; and in 1911 the Parliament Act severely limited the powers of the Lords, removing their absolute veto on legislation passed by the Commons and curtailing their powers to delay it. On many subsequent occasions there has been talk of reducing the powers of the Lords still further and indeed of abolishing them altogether, but even after the Second World War the Labour Party's reforms were limited to shortening the period of delay which the Lords could impose on legislation and to the creation of a category of life peers in addition to, but not instead of, the hereditary ones. Since 1911 the issue has not been one which has aroused much public interest or passion; and the abandonment, largely as the result of apathy, of proposals of reform in 1969 suggests that English people no longer regard the existence of the House of Lords or even of a hereditary peerage as a serious infringement of the principles of universal suffrage and parliamentary democracy.

On the other hand devotion to the principles of universal suffrage inspired an effective and to the Liberal government disturbing movement in Britain in the years before 1914. Whereas in France the demand for votes for women (not in fact granted until after the Second World War) remained largely an academic question, in Britain some members of the Womens' Social and Political Union, founded in 1903, decided by 1912 to resort to direct action – bomb attacks, hunger strikes, interruption of political meetings, demonstrations on public occasions (as when a lady threw herself in front of the King's horse during the Derby, the most popular and famous race of the season). These tactics, familiar enough in the Europe of the 1960s, were a deep shock to the still very conventional society of liberal England, and the largely middle-class organisers of the 'suffragettes' at least made votes for women into a live political issue, even if the Liberal Party for a number of reasons was unwilling to take up their cause. It took the experiences of 1914 to 1918 to make the movement a successful one; the contributions of women to the war effort and their obvious ability to do jobs hitherto regarded as men's work made a telling argument. It remains an open question whether the final achievement of votes for women in 1918 would have been as successful if it had not been for the notoriety won by the militant agitation of the suffragettes before the war.

France and Britain provided effective examples of the workings of constitutional democracy based on universal male suffrage; and the movement towards the extension of the right to vote was also a major political issue in the smaller democracies of Europe. In Belgium, and in Norway and Sweden, constitutional change and the achievement of an efficient democratic system was bound up with their own internal national problems. Belgium in 1870 was about equally divided into French- and Flemish-speaking groups; but over the next thirty years not only was the Flemish section of the population increasing more rapidly than the French, but also Flemish was being revived as a language of the educated classes: in 1883 instruction in Flemish was made obligatory in the schools of the Flemish areas, and by 1898 all acts of the legislature were published in both Flemish and French. The balance between the two nationalities remained one of the fundamental long-term problems of the Belgian state, and later in the twentieth century seemed to threaten its very existence. However, in spite of these potential strains, Belgium was a prosperous constitutional state in which by the end of the nineteenth century rapid industrial development had produced a substantial and well-organised labour movement. It was the workers' organisations, both socialist and Catholic, in revolt against the conservatism of the Catholic politicians who held power for much of the period, which led the movement for an extension of the franchise by means of a series of effective general strikes, so that in 1895 the principle was conceded (although some people – property-owners, fathers of families and university graduates – were granted extra votes); and at the moment of the German invasion in 1914 a further reform was under consideration.

Sweden and Norway had been united under a common king in 1815, but the Norwegians remained conscious of their own historical and national traditions. They differed from the Swedes in their language and to a large extent in their economic interests, as Swedish industry developed during the last quarter of the nineteenth century, and the Swedes wanted a protective tariff, while the Norwegians remained in favour of free trade. Both countries had a vigorous parliamentary life; and when from the 1880s onwards the differences between them became serious enough to endanger the union, it was in the two parliaments and in public discussions in the press and among intellectuals that these questions were raised. The issue on which the breach finally came was a demand by the Norwegians to assert their independence in external relations through the appointment of Norwegian consuls abroad (a matter of more than symbolic concern to a nation that had the third largest merchant navy in the world) instead of being represented by Swedes. The final crisis finally came in 1905; and although on both sides there had earlier been talk of the use of force – by Norway to win total independence and by Sweden to maintain the Union – in fact the separation was achieved by peaceful means, and the democratic constitutions of both countries were strengthened by the experience. After a decisive vote in Norway in favour of a monarchy rather than a republic, the crown was offered to a Danish prince, and the establishment of independence was followed by the introduction of universal suffrage; indeed Norway was one of the few countries which gave some women the right to vote. In Sweden too the political crisis which ended the Union was followed by an extension of the franchise; and universal male suffrage was introduced in 1909.

The apparently successful working of parliamentary democracy in Britain, France and the smaller countries of northern Europe, and the widespread belief that this form of political organisation was the key to moral, social and economic progress, made liberals and socialists in those countries which did not yet have effective representative government all the more eager for it. In Germany, where, as we have seen, Bismarck to his subsequent regret had for his own purposes introduced universal suffrage in elections to the Reichstag, many of the individual states of the empire, and notably Prussia, still had a restricted franchise; and the question of reform of the Prussian electoral system had become by the beginning of the twentieth century a central issue in German internal politics, though it was only in the last weeks of the empire's existence that in October 1918 the Prussian electoral law was finally revised and universal suffrage introduced. In addition to the restrictions imposed by the electoral laws of many of the individual states, the working of democracy in Germany was hampered by the fact that the chief executive authority of the empire, the Imperial Chancellor (who was in practice also Prime Minister of Prussia), was not responsible to the imperial parliament and could not be overthrown by it. When a chancellor was dismissed or obliged to resign, it was because he had lost the confidence of the Emperor rather than that of parliament. The Chancellor needed to keep a majority in the Reichstag it is true, since this was the body which enacted laws and voted the budget, but its lack of ultimate direct control of the executive necessarily weakened its role. In this system the parties tended to become pressure groups representing particular social and economic interests. Since neither the Chancellor nor the secretaries of state were normally chosen from among members of the Reichstag, parliamentary life, instead of being based on a struggle for political power and executive responsibility, became mainly concerned with bargaining about tariffs and fiscal arrangements, with securing privileges for the producers of one commodity rather than those of another, or for one social group at the expense of another. It could of course be said that this is what parliamentary politics are about anywhere; but whereas in France and in Britain the members of parliament were liable, if they overthrew a government, to find themselves responsible for running the country themselves, in Germany the prize of political power was denied to the parliamentary politicians, so that parliamentary life often seemed to lie outside the sphere in which the real decisions were made. Instead the Chancellor and the state secretaries were responsible only to the Emperor, and ultimately it was he alone who could coordinate and control the policies of his advisers – and this was something which Kaiser Wilhelm II notably failed to do. There is a famous story that in the international crisis of July 1914 the Austro-Hungarian Foreign Minister, on receiving two contradictory messages from the German government, one from the Chief of the General Staff and one from the Chancellor, threw up his hands and exclaimed, '*Wer regiert, Moltke oder Bethmann?*' ('Who rules, Moltke or Bethmann?')[3] Who actually ruled in Berlin? It was a question to which it is hard to give an answer; but it was certainly not the elected members of parliament.

It was of course in the two great autocratic empires of Eastern Europe, Austria–Hungary and Russia, that any liberalisation of the constitution by means of an extension of the franchise and the introduction of a truly representative parliament was bound to have the most profound effect. The Compromise of 1867 between the Emperor Franz Joseph and the Hungarian leaders had given the Hungarians control over the internal arrangements of Hungary, with a parliament controlled by the Magyar aristocracy and gentry, in which the non-Magyar races, or for that matter the Hungarian peasants, were not represented. In the Austrian half of the monarchy, although the predominance of the Germans in the *Reichsrath* (parliament) was maintained, the other nationalities were nevertheless sufficiently represented to be able to pursue at least a policy of parliamentary obstruction, bringing business to a standstill on numerous occasions by banging on their desks and shouting in protest against, for example, the creation of a Slovene high school in a town in the province of Styria or the renaming of a Bohemian railway station. These tactics had less importance than they might have had, however, since the Reichsrath itself had little power and as in Germany the true authority was independent of parliament and the ministers and officers responsible to the Emperor alone.

The functioning of the Austro-Hungarian monarchy depended on the Hungarians being left free in their half of the monarchy to govern the other nationalities and to insist on the adoption of the Magyar language as a necessary condition of any career in the government, while in the Austrian provinces the government relied on a cumbrous but dedicated bureaucracy in a policy of balancing the demands of the various national groups against each other, keeping the nationalities in, to use a much-quoted phrase of the time, 'a balanced state of mutual dissatisfaction'. At the beginning of the twentieth century the various tensions inside the monarchy were increasing. Relations between Czechs and Germans in Bohemia were growing worse, with the emergence of a radical anti-Slav (and anti-Semitic) movement among the Germans, and the various compromises between the two nationalities which were suggested from time to time all proved unworkable in practice. Of more immediate importance, however, was a crisis between the Hungarians and the Emperor serious enough for foreign observers to talk about the possible break-up of the monarchy.

The immediate cause of the crisis was a dispute between the Crown and the Hungarian government about control of the army – together with foreign relations the one area of government still treated as common to both parts of the Dual Monarchy. After disputes about increasing the annual intake of conscripts, and demands from the Hungarians for the use of Magyar rather than German as the language of command in Hungarian units, and for other measures emphasising Hungary's military independence, the Hungarian government resigned in May 1903 and produced a constitutional deadlock and a crisis which it took three years to resolve. As part of the compromise which was eventually reached, Franz Joseph insisted on the introduction of a bill to extend the franchise in Hungary. This was a new version of an old method, by which the Emperor hoped to use the threat of enfranchising the non-Magyar nationalities to bring pressure to bear on the Hungarian parliament. In the event successive Hungarian governments were able to delay and postpone this measure, so that up to the end of the monarchy's existence in 1918 the Hungarian parliament remained almost exclusively in the hands of the Magyar aristocracy and gentry.

If universal suffrage was a measure which the Emperor was prepared to use in an attempt to gain his own ends in Hungary, in the Austrian half of the monarchy it was introduced in 1907, partly as a result of pressure and demonstrations in Vienna and other cities by the growing Social Democratic Party, partly because it was hard for the Austrian government to refuse a measure which the Emperor was pressing on the Hungarians and partly because of the impression made on Franz Joseph by the 1905 Revolution in Russia. The result, in spite of attempts to draw the boundaries of constituencies so as to favour Germans at the expense of the other nationalities, was to produce a body probably more representative than any so far seen in Austrian constitutional history. And even if the Reichsrath itself was not able to increase its control over the executive power, the new possibilities of discussion provided by a broadly based elected assembly increased the public awareness of the monarchy's national problems – and perhaps served to increase the sense that these might be insoluble.

The acceptance of a degree of liberalism in the constitutional development of Austria–Hungary showed how far the principles of representative government were penetrating; and the lesson was even more strikingly demonstrated by the Russian Revolution of 1905 which, even if it fell far short of the achievements for which liberals and revolutionaries of all shades in Russia hoped, nevertheless produced an atmosphere in which Russian problems were the subject of new and intense discussion and in which fundamental criticisms of Russian government and society could make themselves heard. The revolution began, in an atmosphere of dissatisfaction and revolt resulting from the defeats by Japan in the Far-Eastern War, with the shooting by troops of a large number of peaceful demonstrators presenting a petition to the Tsar. Strikes by workers and the establishment of the St Petersburg Workers' Council - the Soviet - were accompanied by peasant revolts and by mutinies in the army and navy. (One of these, the seizure by the sailors of the battleship *Potemkin*, was to be turned into a potent revolutionary symbol twenty years later in one of the most famous films of the Soviet director, S. Eisenstein.) The middle classes and the more enlightened members of the aristocracy attempted to extend their influence in local government, and demanded parliamentary representation. Faced by these manifold threats to the regime, the Tsar was obliged to grant a constitution – a reform from above, like the emancipation of the serfs some fifty years earlier – designed to ward off worse upheavals. The new parliament (the State Duma) which assembled early in 1906, even though elected on the basis of limited suffrage, contained a majority of liberals and reformers committed to fundamental changes, and in particular to land reform. However it soon became clear that the Tsar and his personal advisers were not prepared to go any further along the liberal and constitutional path or to pay much attention to the Duma and to the widespread demands for radical change which it represented. Parliament was dissolved in July 1906; a fresh Duma elected in February 1907, although its right wing was stronger than previously, still contained a strong reforming element and still refused to support the ministers nominated by the Tsar. Accordingly this parliament was in turn dissolved, the electoral law revoked and a third Duma elected by a very much restricted electorate. Although by this means the conservatives and centre groups were strengthened and the revolutionaries once more driven underground or into exile, the very existence of a constitution and a parliament in a country which had hitherto been a complete autocracy was in itself a far-reaching change. Russian political life could never be the same again, and the possibility of a peaceful transformation of the tsarist autocracy into a more liberal form of government could, in spite of the setbacks experienced by the first two Dumas and the opposition of the Tsar himself, eventually be envisaged.

The success of parliamentary democracy in Britain, France and the small states of northern Europe depended on two things – a consensus of opinion in favour of the existing constitutional system, and a governing class which was sufficiently elastic to absorb new elements and thus convince the industrial workers that their interests were to some extent represented at the governmental level. In France the Dreyfus crisis had revealed how deep and widespread support for the republican constitution in fact was, and it was not until the 1930s that the system again came under serious attack. In Britain the appearance in parliament of the Labour Party and the adoption by the Liberal government of a programme of genuinely radical social reform showed that the constitution was sufficiently flexible to resist the assault made on it by the exponents of direct action in the trade union movement, in the women's suffrage organisations or among the Ulster Unionists opposing home rule for Ireland and the Irish nationalists fighting for it.

It was in those countries which had on paper apparently real democratic parliamentary systems but in which the system was obviously not working, because of uneven economic development and the lack of any common interests between the various classes, that the most profound criticisms of the liberal state came to be made. In Spain, as we have seen (see pp. 69-70 above) the anarchist movement was more effective than anywhere else in Europe, and the anarchists' complete rejection of political action and their belief that elections and parliamentary government were just a sham masking the determination of the ruling classes to retain their position and privileges undiminished seemed to be partially justified by the experience of parliamentary government in Spain. However it was in Italy that the weaknesses of the liberal system were most apparent and that criticisms of them were most clearly expressed, both in theory and in practice. The success after the First World War of the Fascist movement in Italy – the first appearance of a political system which was to challenge the assumptions of liberal democracy throughout Europe – had its foundations in the experiences of Italy at the end of the nineteenth and beginning of the twentieth centuries.

The unification of Italy had been a cause which won the sympathy of liberals all over Europe; and the popular basis of the new regime had been, or so it seemed, demonstrated by the plebiscites in 1860, 1866 and 1870 in which all adult male Italians had been entitled to vote and which had ratified each stage in the formation of the Italian kingdom. However once the new state was in being its governments did not have a comparable popular base. Although a law of 1882 substantially widened the franchise, it still left the majority of Italians without a vote – and to them must be added those Roman Catholics who abstained on principle from exercising their right to vote in a state to which they remained unreconciled. One of the qualifications to vote was ability to read and write, and although by 1912, when universal male suffrage was finally introduced, the number of electors had risen to three million – partly no doubt as a result of the spread of literacy – illiteracy remained a major obstacle to the working of Italian democracy. Moreover the combination until 1912 of a property qualification and a literacy qualification for the right to vote meant that the electors were fewest in the south of Italy and Sicily, where the population was poor and backward, so that the southern constituencies were easily manipulated by politicians in their own interests.

For several years after 1876, when Agostino Depretis became prime minister, an attempt was made (see p. 8 above) to lower the temperature of politics and to find some common ground between the parties, but the system of *trasformismo* only succeeded in convincing many Italians that parliamentary politics consisted of a series of cynical bargains within a narrow clique without much regard for the interests of the country as a whole. By the 1890s there were more specific grounds for attacking the parliamentary system. Between 1889 and 1893 a series of bank failures had led to accusations of corruption against leading politicians. In 1893 there was a peasant rising in Sicily, caused largely by rising taxation and increased rents at a time of economic difficulty. This movement led to bloody clashes with the police, and was only finally suppressed when the new government of Crispi reluctantly introduced martial law. Although Crispi managed to survive this crisis as well as the bitter accusations against his private morals made by his opponents, the disastrous Ethiopian campaign finally led to his fall (see p. 91 above), and started a prolonged crisis in which the future of parliamentary government in Italy seemed to be at stake. A bad harvest in 1897 brought the threat of famine to many areas; and the growing socialist party, some of whose members had already been active in the Sicilian revolt and of whom many were committed to the tactics of direct action, was able to start effective demonstrations. All over Italy, but especially in the south, there were violent disturbances, culminating in May 1898 in Milan, where for several days a truly revolutionary situation seemed to exist, with the erection of barricades and open hostilities between demonstrators and the army.

The government fell as a result of these troubles; and the ministries which followed tried in vain to carry through parliament a coercion bill to deal with the widespread public disorder. The sessions of parliament became increasingly chaotic as the parties of the Left adopted tactics of obstruction and filibustering; and finally 160 deputies on the Left refused to take part in the proceedings any more and walked out of the chamber. However the Government, headed by a distinguished general and former war minister, Luigi Pelloux, failed either to obtain the suspension of the absent deputies or the sanction of the judiciary for government by decree, and decided to dissolve parliament. The election which followed led to a majority for the parties of the Left and to Pelloux's resignation.

The fact that Pelloux and his supporters had refrained from acting unconstitutionally and that the elections of 1900 seemed to have justified the policies of his opponents, the moderate Left, might suggest that, like the French, in this period undergoing a comparable constitutional crisis as a result of the Dreyfus affair, Italians were reasserting their belief in the sovereignty of parliament and in the liberal constitution. To some extent this was true. Although a decade of disorder culminated in July 1900 with the assassination of King Umberto by an anarchist (sent for the purpose by a group of Italian immigrants from Paterson, New Jersey), in fact the new century began in an atmosphere of comparative political calm and of economic recovery. Under the leadership of Giovanni Giolitti, Prime Minister almost continuously from 1903 to 1914, a real attempt was made to introduce a spirit of compromise and of practical reform into parliamentary politics.

Giolitti's achievements are still very much a matter of controversy. To some historians he seems a statesman who was making a determined effort by means of pragmatic policies and moderate reform to steer a course, as he put it, between revolution and reaction, and to give liberal democracy time in which to strike real roots in Italy. To his critics, on the other hand, *Giolittismo* was simply an equally cynical version of the *trasformismo* of Depretis twenty-five years earlier, a system of government based on bargaining between selfish politicians and pressure groups, and upon the skilful electoral management of constituencies in which – especially in the south where Giolitti's main support lay – a small number of ignorant and venal electors could be easily managed by the government in power. The era of Giolitti was ended by the First World War which transformed Italian politics, as it did the politics of every European state, so that it is impossible to say how Giolitti's career might have been assessed if it had not been for the war and for the subsequent success of Fascism in Italy. What is true however is that, although between 1900 and 1914 liberal democracy in Italy seemed to be more firmly established and to be functioning more efficiently than it had ten years earlier, the criticisms of the parliamentary system continued, and the attacks on liberalism persisted, so as to contribute to the climate in which in the immediate post-war period the rise of Fascism was possible.

The attacks on the liberal state in Italy came from three directions. First, the growing working-class movement was increasingly conscious of the gap between the political ideals of equality and liberty in which the liberals professed to believe, and the practical experience of economic inequality and of the lack of freedom to choose his own way of life which was all too apparent to the worker in the growing industries of northern Italy, and still more to the landless agricultural labourer in the south. Secondly, many Italians, in spite of the setback to Italian imperialist ambitions in Ethiopia, still dreamed of a new Roman Empire and of a rejuvenated Italy no longer living on the relics of a proud past, a museum to be visited by respectful but patronising foreign tourists, but rather a country in which the greatness of Italy's past would dictate Italy's future, in a community of the living and the dead similar to that which Barrès was advocating for France. Closely linked with this trend in Italian nationalism was a demand for the modernisation of Italy by people who claimed to despise Italy's past and to believe in a new, industrialised, mechanised twentieth-century future. Finally, some Italian social scientists and political thinkers produced some of the most perceptive theoretical criticisms of liberal democracy to be found anywhere in Europe at the beginning of the twentieth century. All three of these movements had their parallels elsewhere in Europe, but it is in Italy that they can be observed most clearly and in their most extreme form.

The Italian socialist movement was subject to the same strains and divisions as the other socialist parties of Europe. It contained reformists, prepared to cooperate with Giolitti and the liberals; and some of these left the socialist party in 1911 to form a separate political group. There were also a large number of orthodox Marxists who believed in political action but who eschewed any collaboration with bourgeois parties. But in a situation in which, as Giolitti himself realised, 'the upward movement of the popular class is accelerating day by day',[4] there were in the Italian trade union movement a growing number of people attracted by syndicalist ideals of direct action. As one of their leaders remarked after a general strike in 1904, 'Five minutes of direct action were worth as many years of parliamentary chatter.'[5] Thus although the revolutionary situation of the late 1890s was kept under control, industrial unrest and political demonstrations in Italy were marked by a degree of violence and direct revolutionary action which both left its mark on the consciousness of the Italian Left (where the idea of direct action was enthusiastically adopted by the young socialist schoolmaster and journalist Benito Mussolini), and confirmed the Right in a belief that revolution might not be far off. There were, for example, dramatic demonstrations against the war of 1911 in which the Italians, in their search for a North African empire, conquered Tripolitania and Libya from the Turks; and in June 1914 the

'Red Week' of strikes and demonstrations gave the false impression that revolution was imminent (see p. 68 above).

The same readiness to go out on the streets and to settle political issues by direct action could be found among some of the nationalists. One group led by Enrico Corradini linked the aims and methods of the syndicalists to the nationalist cause. Just as internal politics could be interpreted in terms of the class struggle, so international politics could be interpreted in the same way: Italy accordingly, in her struggle for colonies and for recognition as a great power, was a 'proletarian nation', a champion of the have-nots against the haves, and a country in which the social unrest behind the syndicalist movement was only to be removed by a programme of nationalist expansion. Another movement which adopted similar tactics of direct action and displayed a similar taste for violence was that of the Futurists, a group of middle-class writers and artists, whose main importance was in connection with the artistic developments of the period to which they made a more significant and positive contribution than they did to politics. (See p. 162 below.) The Futurists became adept at the tactics of the café brawl and the direct assault on the sensibilities of the bourgeoisie; they were equally critical of socialism – 'that ignoble exaltation of the rights of the belly' – as of 'timid clerical conservatism symbolised by the bedroom slippers and the hot water bottle'.[6] They wanted a modern, dynamic industrialised Italy; and above all they were ready to exalt war as 'the only cure for the world' (*guerra – sola igiene del mondo*), a war which would demonstrate and encourage the heroic virtues of the youth of the new Italy. Thus among nationalists of very different trends in Italy there was a common contempt for liberal democracy as practised by Giolitti, and a willingness to resort to direct action and, in the words of the philosopher and historian Benedetto Croce, a close and anxious observer of these phenomena, a 'determination to go down into the streets, to impose their own opinions, to stop the mouths of those who disagree'.[7] Therefore, for all the apparent success of Giolitti's regime and in spite of the absence in the period 1900–14 of sensational political crises such as had disturbed the previous decade, liberal democracy in Italy was nevertheless confronted by a wide range of vigorous and active critics willing to go to almost any extreme to express their ideas and to further their politics.

At the intellectual and theoretical level, too, there were in Italy political thinkers and conservative politicians ready to base a general criticism of parliamentary democracy on their observation of the Italian situation. Two of these critics, Gaetano Mosca and Vilfredo Pareto, won an international reputation, and their ideas provide concepts helpful in the analysis of the Fascist movement, which came to power in Italy partly as a result of the defects in Italian democracy which they had observed and on which they had based some of their conclusions. Mosca, a Sicilian born in 1858 and who lived almost till the end of Mussolini's dictatorship (he died in 1941), had observed Italian parliamentarians at close quarters, since he had been editor of the Journal of the Chamber of Deputies (the Italian equivalent of *Hansard* or the *Congressional Record*), became a deputy in 1908 and, after a period as an under-secretary in the government during the war, ended up as a senator, in which capacity he had the courage to make a notable speech opposing Mussolini in 1925. Mosca's criticism of democracy therefore, which was first formulated in his youth, become mellower with time. Moreover, the motive which led him to criticise the parliamentary system was the same which led him to oppose Mussolini – a concern for individual liberty. In some respects, therefore, his criticisms echo those of earlier critics who had attacked democracy in the name of liberty and human dignity, notably Alexis de Tocqueville and John Stuart Mill, but they gain extra point from being written in the age of universal suffrage – the introduction of which in 1912 in Italy Mosca strongly opposed – and from Mosca's practical experience of the workings of day-to-day parliamentary life.

Mosca, whose most important work *Elementi di Scienza Politica* (known in its English translation as *The Ruling Class*) was first published in 1896 and then reprinted in a revised edition just after Mussolini's accession to power, taught that in any society the ruling class – the people who take political decisions and the people who execute them – are necessarily always a minority of the population. The best governments – and this was less and less the case with Italy – were those where this ruling class was recruited from people with common moral beliefs and with sufficient economic independence to ensure their unselfish detachment. To Mosca as to many Italian politicians, including Giolitti himself, it was in England that parliamentary democracy was most successful, because it had developed gradually and because the country had been sufficiently stable for a long enough period to allow the ruling class to expand itself without revolution and without losing its internal cohesion. The delicately balanced system which Mosca wanted – in which the bureaucracy was supervised and controlled by an enlightened deliberative assembly – was threatened by the introduction of universal suffrage because then the representatives were increasingly concerned with getting themselves elected. The member of parliament imposed himself, that is to say, on the people who believed that he was in fact representing them. To do this parliamentary candidates were increasingly obliged to pander to the electors by promising all sorts of things they could not provide and arousing hopes they could not possibly fulfil. The result was a steady decline in the standard of public life and increasing corruption in every branch of it, since the duty and the interest of the ruling class became more and more opposed to each other.

Mosca was worried, too, at the extent to which both in France and Italy the government was controlled by parliament. When parliament is sovereign, then 'the irresponsible and anonymous tyranny of the elements which win elections and speak in the name of the people weighs on the whole of the judicial and administrative machine',[8] and there is no independence left at any point in the machinery of government. It was a common complaint against the working of Italian political institutions; and indeed Mosca was echoing a fear which Crispi had expressed in 1887 that 'parliament should become a tyrant and the cabinet its slave'.[9] In his disapproval of the parliamentary bargaining on which Italian governments were based, and in his distrust of the methods of political parties in their organisation and electioneering, Mosca resembled another political scientist whom he much admired, Robert Michels. Michels was a German who lived much of his life in Italy and Switzerland and who described what he called 'the iron law of oligarchy' by which power in political parties – and he had in mind especially the German Social Democratic Party to which he had originally belonged – inevitably became concentrated in the hands of a few experienced professionals for whom the maintenance of the party's electoral position and organisation became more important than the policies it was supposed to serve. Many of the criticisms of the working of democracy before 1914 developed by Mosca or by Michels are perhaps still apt today, especially when we study the political institutions of some of the new states outside Europe. But for all his awareness of the difficulty of balancing freedom and organisation, individual liberty and effective government, Mosca remained a liberal at heart in his concern for personal independence and dignity; and it was his tragedy that the weaknesses of the system which he analysed led to its being replaced by one in which the qualities he valued were even less in evidence.

Pareto, although he was equally shocked by the pettiness and corruption involved as he thought in the working of democracy and by the loss of dignity caused by taking part in electoral proceedings – he wrote with disgust that in England parliamentary candidates 'were not ashamed to send out their wives and daughters to canvass voters'[10] – was less concerned with moral values than with the problem of the winning and retention of power so as to maintain society in a constant state of equilibrium. Pareto was not himself directly involved in day-to-day political life (except for one unsuccessful attempt when still quite young to get himself elected to parliament) and indeed he lived most of his somewhat lonely and unhappy life in academic detachment in Switzerland, where he occupied a Chair at the University of Lausanne. He was born in 1848, the son of a liberal aristocrat from Genoa; and it could be said that the relationship between liberalism and aristocracy dominated his later thought. He became a distinguished theoretical economist; but it is in his sociological writings, culminating in the enormous *Trattato di Sociologia Generale* (called in its English translation *The Mind and Society*) published during the First World War, that his most original and influential ideas were developed. Pareto regarded himself as an objective social scientist, concerned to analyse society rather than to prescribe for it. His work is often highly abstract in style, and he constantly uses tables, graphs and algebraical formulae to illustrate his points. Yet behind the cool scientific style, the detached refusal to be taken in by the deceptions which men, consciously and unconsciously, use to mask the real motives for their social and political actions, one gets glimpses of a temperament fascinated by the violence and the cruelty of the natural world and of much of human history.

Much of the *Trattato* is devoted to an elaborate attempt to classify the psychological factors making for different kinds of social action, and to describe systematically the links between logical and non-logical behaviour. Although this attempt at a descriptive catalogue of social psychology is often interesting and original, and although Pareto's insistence on the role of unconscious urges underlying human actions and his analysis of the devious ways in which we provide rational explanations of them are at points strikingly similar to the ideas which Freud was developing at the same time, apparently quite unknown to Pareto, the aspect of Pareto's sociology which made him both an effective critic of the liberal state and a prophet of the practice of totalitarian governments later in the twentieth century was his account of the formation and the role of political elites. 'This phenomenon of new elites,' he wrote 'which through an incessant movement of circulation, rise up from the lower strata of society, mount up to the higher strata, flourish there, and then fall into decadence, are annihilated or disappear – this is one of the motive forces of history and it is essential to give it its due weight if we are to understand great social movements.'[11]

In the liberal politics of contemporary Europe and especially of France and Italy Pareto thought he could observe an elite in decline. The ruling class was not only failing to ensure its own renovation by constantly recruiting and assimilating new members; it was failing to distinguish between its own true interests and the phrases with which these were disguised and justified. The maintenance of society in a state of equilibrium is not achieved by any single political or economic formula. Measures which at first lead to the circulation of elites, to the introduction of new blood into the ruling class, may subsequently lead to immobility and decadence. For instance the abandonment of free trade and the introduction of a protective tariff on industrial products had in Pareto's view given the opportunity to what he calls 'speculators', men of commercial shrewdness and cunning for whom the making of money is the prime motive, to influence the government and persuade the state to help them, as Pareto says, looking back to the Italy of the 1880s and 1890s, by 'protective tariffs, railway deals, government contracts in which the state was robbed right and left, banking irregularities that were later exposed'.[12] At the same time, as Pareto pointed out elsewhere, State intervention was interfering with the process of natural selection, and artificially preserving the weakest members of society instead of cultivating the virile virtues required for the state to survive. For this both the false idealism of humanitarian reformers and the actual working of the democratic system were responsible: 'Going along to the polling station to vote is a very easy business, and if by so doing one can procure food and shelter, then everybody – especially the unfit, the incompetent and the idle – will rush to do it.'[13]

It is this cynicism about the accepted values of liberal society, the belief that all expressions of humanitarian idealism or of utopian socialism are simply a justification of actions which are fundamentally selfish, that makes Pareto a disturbing critic of liberalism. At the same time his insistence on toughness and virility if a ruling elite is to survive, and his emphasis on the necessity for a government to use force if required (he was for example very scornful of the British government's failure to keep the suffragettes in prison when they went on hunger strike), make Pareto a forerunner of much in the theory and practice of twentieth-century Fascism. Indeed Mussolini recognised the fact not only by claiming that he himself had attended Pareto's lectures at Lausanne in his youth, but also in the appointment of Pareto as senator in 1923, shortly before his death. Pareto divided ruling classes into lions, who ruled by force, and foxes, who ruled by cunning; and the coming to power of the Fascists seemed a clear instance of the lions replacing the foxes and of the defeat of a demagogic plutocracy by people who knew how to use force, though it was perhaps as well for Pareto's relations with the Italian government that he did not live long enough to turn the scorn of his icy intellect on to the bombast and emptiness of Mussolini's political ideas, and to observe in European Fascism the typical development he had observed in previous regimes relying chiefly on physical force, which 'tended to degenerate into government by armed mobs'.[14]

Mosca and Pareto used their scientific analysis of society as a means of questioning the liberal assumptions which in the years before the First World War seemed to be gaining ground everywhere in Europe and to be finding expression in the spread of universal suffrage and parliamentary government. In fact, however, in addition to these direct attacks on liberalism as a political doctrine, the presuppositions of many members of the previous generation, their confidence in man's progress and in human reason, were being questioned in a number of different ways. The great social thinkers of the early and mid-nineteenth century – Saint-Simon, Comte, Marx – had all accepted, however great their differences, that history was moving forward, and that, either by slow evolution or by a revolutionary jump, the lot of man would be improved. As the English positivist sociologist Herbert Spencer put it in his *Social Statics*, first published in 1851, 'Progress is not an accident but a necessity. Surely must evil and immorality disappear; surely must men become perfect.'[15] While this underlying confidence was perhaps not finally lost in Europe until the middle of the twentieth century, there were already in its first decade a number of thinkers in various fields who were suggesting a different conclusion.

Pareto's immense theoretical analysis of society, though in some ways the most ambitious and the most complete work of abstract sociological thinking in the early years of the twentieth century, was only one – and in the long run not the most influential – of several attempts to give the study of social change a new basis. These new ideas which were to become the foundation of many of our beliefs later in the twentieth century came not only from the sociologists and anthropologists explicitly setting out to analyse and explain the nature of human society, but also from psychologists, historians, philosophers and indeed physicists, whose views in a popularised form often gave an impression quite different from the highly technical theoretical significance which their authors originally intended them to have.

Auguste Comte, Herbert Spencer and Karl Marx himself had all believed that sociological analysis was a necessary preliminary to social change. The new generation of sociological thinkers were concerned to show that society was more complex and the causes of change deeper and more mysterious than hitherto believed. Georges Sorel, as we have seen in an earlier chapter (see pp. 66–7 above), criticised Marxist social democracy for its failure to come to terms with the nature and necessity of violence, and had stressed the role of irrational belief – the 'myth' - in bringing about revolutions. Pareto, too, had been concerned to show that many actions for which logical explanations were given were in fact the result of non-logical emotional and psychological urges (called by him by the rather obscure name of 'residues'). By the beginning of the twentieth century sociologists and political scientists were spreading the idea that political behaviour was often based on irrational and emotional assumptions. Thus the French writer Gustave Le Bon, in his *Psychologie des Foules* (1895) – a book admired incidentally by Adolf Hitler – analysed, although rather superficially, the behaviour of crowds and of the new mass electorate created by the introduction of universal suffrage. Le Bon was a somewhat pessimistic conservative, but his preoccupation with the irrational springs of mass political action was shared by an English political scientist with socialist sympathies, Graham Wallas, who in his books *Human Nature and Politics* (1908) and *The Great Society* (1914) drew attention to the necessity of reckoning with man's irrational side in any political planning.

The more men studied society, the more complex the motives for social change seemed to be, and the more precarious the balance of the liberal political system of Western Europe. Marx had taught that ideologies and philosophies, legal systems and religious beliefs were all part of a 'superstructure' conditioned by the underlying economic realities. By the end of the nineteenth century, however, some thinkers began to reassert the importance of religious belief as a motive for social action. In the 1890s a young German professor of economics, Max Weber, began to turn his attention to sociology and in particular to the relationship between religious beliefs and the economic structure of society. Max Weber is a thinker whom it is even harder than most to evaluate in a short space. He was one of the most original thinkers of his generation; and his work has influenced profoundly that of nearly all subsequent sociologists. On the other hand when he died in 1920 at the age of fifty-six his great work of synthesis which would have set out a whole methodology for the social sciences was still incomplete; and his working life had been interrupted by severe bouts of neurotic illness (the worst of which left him unable to work or even to read for four years, and forced him in 1903 to give up his university chair), so that his writings consist of a series of massive fragments rather than forming a single whole. The first and most influential of his studies in the sociology of religion was published as a series of essays in 1904–5. This work, *The Protestant Ethic and the Spirit of Capitalism*, set out to show that it was the values inculcated in many parts of Europe by Calvinist puritanism that established the moral attitudes which made possible the emergence of capitalism. The values prized by the puritans, dedication to work, dislike of luxury and of ostentatious extravagance were favourable to the amassing of capital, and these values and the attitudes underlying them survived in man's minds when the original religious impetus behind them had disappeared. Much of Max Weber's work was in fact an implicit criticism of Marx and of the materialist conception of history. It suggested a different relationship between ideology and economic life and like the work of several of Weber's contemporaries laid stress on the importance of irrational motives and the unconscious survival of past beliefs. 'The many old gods robbed of their magic, and thus in the form of impersonal forces, have risen from their graves and strive for power over our life,'[16] he wrote. What is impressive about Max Weber – in addition to the vast historical sweep of his learning, which places twentieth-century European civilisation against the perspective of other cultures with other values – is the struggle to achieve a detached view of the nature of social change and to systematise the immense complexity of human society without losing sight of that complexity. Weber was anxious to combine the scientific approach of the sociologist with the imaginative insights of the historian, and he realised that while the sociologist could establish what he called 'ideal types' of rational behaviour, human beings rarely if ever conformed to these.

Max Weber himself was passionately interested in contemporary German politics, although it was only in the last years of his life during the First World War and the German Revolution that he became actively involved in political affairs. He was constantly concerned with the tensions in German society and with the need to solve the problem of integrating the industrial workers into a national community. In a world of struggle, he believed, national communities must inevitably strive for power if they were to survive; and throughout Weber's writing there is a pessimistic belief that this might well lead to a disastrous war. At the same time social and political forms must adapt themselves to new circumstances. In the case of Germany this meant a strengthening of the industrial and professional middle class and its assumption of political responsibility in place of the old feudal aristocracy. Democracy was not for Weber an axiomatic end in itself, but rather one way of ensuring the selection of political leaders. Bismarck, for all his great services to Germany, had failed to provide a political education for Germany; and an effort would have to be made to give Germany the political leadership which was, as it seemed to Max Weber as to many others of his generation, patently lacking in the system of government under Kaiser Wilhelm II.

Thus Weber was not surprised by the war and the German Revolution of 1918, and in the last years of his life he found himself forced by the logic of his attitude to play a political role. He was involved in November 1918 in the foundation of the German Democratic Party, an attempt to provide a new political framework for the German liberal middle classes, though he was increasingly depressed about what was happening in Germany. His last great unfinished work, *The Theory of Social and Economic Organisation*, is full of an awareness of the precariousness of political systems, and in particular of the dangers of the growth of bureaucratisation – 'the inescapable shadow of advancing mass democracy'. The only way to guard against this was by a combination of parliamentary control with dynamic political leadership. It was in this connection that he developed – and successfully urged in the debates on the new German constitution – a theory of plebiscitarian democracy which would allow for the rise to power of what he called the 'charismatic' leader – a man with the power to fascinate, enthral and inspire his fellow-countrymen. Weber perhaps failed to see what this might lead to; and he did not live to witness the rise of Fascism in Europe which his own sociological categories have helped us to understand.

Max Weber is of interest and importance, not only because he was one of the founders of a new science of society, but also because he embodied in himself so many of the problems and contradictions of his generation – in his sense that European society was in a period of crisis, and in his underlying pessimism about the outcome, in his awareness of the strong irrational forces which might sweep away the precarious foundations of Western civilisation and above all in his desire to establish a dispassionate scientific study of man's development, in which value judgements would have no part and which by its very relativism prepared the way for a new irrationalism, the analysis of which has been made easier for us by the intellectual models which Max Weber provided.

In a sense the same is true of another of the founders of modern sociology, the Frenchman Emile Durkheim. Although Durkheim was concerned to establish a methodology for the study of society which would be genuinely scientific (in for example his *Rules of Sociological Method* published in 1895), and although he was insistent throughout his work on the necessity of ridding social thought of metaphysical presuppositions and of assembling and analysing empirical evidence, he emphasised the importance of studying societies as wholes which can not be described simply in terms of a collection of individuals. He stressed the need for a comparative study of society, and although firmly and successfully rooted in the France of his day, he was always aware of the fragility of the social structure of contemporary Europe. Whereas the earlier social thinkers such as Herbert Spencer had seen in the society in which they lived the highest point yet reached in social evolution, and had implied that future development would be along much the same lines, Durkheim and his followers drew attention to the variety and relativity of social organisations and suggested that the liberal society of Western Europe was not necessarily the form towards which all social development was inevitably moving.

Durkheim, in his study of *Suicide*, published in 1897, also drew attention to some of the weaknesses characteristic of contemporary industrial society. As a result of the rapid pace of economic change and of the prevalence of *laissez-faire* doctrines which accompanied it, society was no longer performing its role of restraining the individual and of marking clear limits to what he might hope to attain in life. One of the causes of the increase in the suicide rate which Durkheim had established was, he believed, the fact that men's desires were now unlimited, and that what they wanted was often unattainable, so that they felt continuously frustrated and thwarted. In more stable societies the social system had been strong enough to force men to link their desires to objectives which they might reasonably hope to achieve: but in European society at the end of the nineteenth century a state of what Durkheim called *dérèglement* or *anomie* prevailed, a lack of acknowledged rules for social behaviour and a breakdown of the categories of social organisation, so that men no longer knew where they stood. The nature of the society was such as to encourage ever growing dreams of material well-being and riches; and these were in the nature of things by no means all capable of fulfilment. 'The appetites which industry brings into play', Durkheim wrote, 'find themselves freed of all constraining authority. This apotheosis of material well-being, by, so to speak, sanctifying them, has placed economic appetites above every human law.'[17]

Although Durkheim's doctrine of *anomie* implies a direct attack on the liberal economic doctrines of capitalist industrialist society, he was not totally pessimistic about the future, as some of his contemporaries among the social scientists were. If his account of the strains imposed on the individual by the development of large-scale industry has something in common with Marx's description of the 'alienation' of the industrial worker in capitalist society, Durkheim's insistence on the possibility of adapting men's desires to what they might reasonably expect, and his belief that men could be brought to face the reality of their situation and to abandon fantasy in formulating their wishes, bring him close to Freud. For all his realisation of the dangers of the situation produced by the economic, social and political developments of the nineteenth century and of the weaknesses of the conventional liberal solutions for dealing with them, Durkheim remained a believer in reason and in progress; and indeed he explicitly stated that the motive for his socio-logical writing was 'his desire to contribute to the moral constitution of the Third Republic'.[18]

Durkheim's work and that of his colleagues associated with the French periodical *L'Année Sociologique* had considerable influence on another field of study which in the long run was to contribute to ending European confidence in the inevitability of progress and in the universal applicability of Western liberal values and methods. This was the study of anthropology. The development in the mid-nineteenth century of the study of primitive societies had been one of the results of the breakdown of the universal acceptance of Christianity and the consequent increase of interest in other religions and in the myths and legends common to all faiths, as well as what had hitherto been regarded as the blind superstition of backward peoples who had not yet seen the light of Christian doctrine. 'Instead of passing over as of no account or else regarding as purely mischievous, the superstitions of primitive man,' Herbert Spencer had written, 'we must inquire what part they play in social evolution.'[19] And much of the study of primitive societies had been undertaken in the hope that they would throw light on earlier stages in the evolution of contemporary European man. By the beginning of the twentieth century however – partly because of a few investigators who had used the opportunities provided by the spread of colonial rule for the study of 'backward' peoples and partly because of the influence of American anthropologists who had begun serious fieldwork on the Indian societies of North America – the evolutionist presuppositions were being discarded and, while some anthropologists such as Sir James Frazer in *The Golden Bough* (published in 1922, but the fruit of some thirty years work) were trying to establish what there was in common between the beliefs and practices of widely separated societies, others especially in Britain were beginning to produce detailed studies based on extensive fieldwork, from which new principles of classification and new tools for analysis were to emerge. While the French school of anthropologists were elaborating new theories about the structure of thought in primitive societies, which showed that instinctive mental operations could be as efficient and as complicated as those based on rational analysis on the European model, the Anglo-Saxons showed by their detailed practical work that the structure of primitive societies was often as elaborate and as well-adapted to the needs of their members as the methods of organisation of 'advanced' Western communities. Anthropological studies, that is to say, by showing that there was no need to assume that all societies were bound by the laws of nature to evolve in the same direction, were suggesting that the civilisation established in Europe on the basis of liberal principles and industrial technology was only one of many possible alternative ways of organising society, even though Europe's technological strength seemed to be enabling it increasingly to impose European values on other peoples and areas. Here ultimately was another underlying cause for the loss of nerve among Europeans which was to become apparent after the First World War; and the social sciences, by providing the tools for the analysis of contemporary social structure and of established political, economic and social ideas, were contributing to the change which was to come over Europe's position in the world in the first half of the twentieth century.

The middle of the nineteenth century had not only seen the development of political liberalism; it had also been a period when there seemed to be no limits to the applicability of the methods of the natural sciences to all problems. During the century this movement had resulted in the attempt, especially in Germany, to reconcile religion and science by applying the criteria of rational scholarship to the study of the Bible and to the evidence of the gospels, thus marking a new development in Protestant theology. Similarly the French philosopher, critic and historian Hippolyte Taine, who died in 1893, had believed that all historical change could be explained in precise scientific terms and the study of history pursued according to the experimental methods followed in the natural sciences, in which hypotheses were tested by reference to the facts. Literature, art, even ethics, could, Taine and many others of his generation believed, all be studied in the same manner. Ideas of this kind both in France and in Germany had led to a new interest in precise historical scholarship based on detailed work in the archives and to a cult of detachment and impartial accuracy in historical writing, summed up in the famous phrase of the great German historian Leopold von Ranke who died in 1886 at the age of ninety-one, that history should be written 'as it actually was' ('*wie es eigentlich gewesen*').

But by the end of the nineteenth century this kind of certainty too was being challenged and the same emphasis on the irrational and on the importance of instinctive reactions which we have noted in the sociological writers of the period, began to be applied to other branches of thought. In 1893, for example, the twenty-nine-year-old Italian philosopher Benedetto Croce published an essay on *History Subsumed Under the Concept of Art*, the first of a long series of books in which he was to develop a philosophy of history in opposition to the prevalent belief in the painstaking accumulation of detailed facts which, it was hoped, could be assembled into an objective picture of the past. 'All history is the history of thought,' he wrote later: the facts with which the historian deals vibrate in his mind: and in writing history he is in some sense analysing himself and increasing his own self-knowledge. Our understanding of past events and actions depends on the degree to which we can recreate the thought of the participants by an imaginative effort to identify ourselves with them. Croce, who remained one of the dominant intellectual influences in Italy until after the Second World War, was thinking along similar lines to a number of German historians and philosophers in his emphasis on the necessity for imaginative recreation in historical writing. This kind of attack on the positivist historians had important consequences, even if they were not always what Croce had originally intended. For, once it is accepted that it is impossible to achieve objective truth in our statements about the past, it is hard to avoid the conclusion that our view of history is inevitably conditioned by our present circumstances. Our historical writing is thus necessarily the product of our own epoch, and however much historical imagination and sympathy, or however much detailed scholarship we display in our attempt to recreate the thought processes of past generations, we are bound to be limited by our own beliefs, preoccupations and emotions. Historical objectivity, therefore, is, on this view, a chimera; and each generation of men will need to rewrite history for themselves. Thus it seems to follow from Croce's views and from those of some of the German philosophers of history, such as Wilhelm Dilthey that historical truth is always relative, and the final, certain, objective answers, which the positivist historians believed to be within their grasp, would for ever elude them.

This revolt against the apparent certainties of the previous generation, and the feeling that reality was not susceptible of a cut-and-dried final analysis is a significant aspect of nearly all branches of thought at the end of the nineteenth century and in the early years of the twentieth. In philosophy, for example, the Frenchman Henri Bergson in a number of books, starting with the *Essai sur les données immédiates de la conscience* published in 1889 when he was thirty years old, started from a study of perception and from the work of contemporary neurologists and psychologists (including the American William James), who had been concerned with the mechanics by which we acquire our knowledge of the external world. He criticised a mechanistic view of our mental processes and stressed the role of time and of memory in building up our picture of the world. 'All division of matter into independent bodies with absolutely determined outlines is an artificial division,' he wrote in *Matter and Memory* (1900).[20] Reality could not be broken up and dissected into a series of separate hard facts, but rather experience was a continuous process of constant change, in which the dimension of time is as important as that of space. 'There is one reality, at least,' he wrote in his *Introduction to Metaphysics*, published in 1903, 'which we all seize from within, by intuition and not by simple analysis. It is our own personality in its flowing through time – our self that endures.'[21]

Bergson's influence, especially in France but also in Italy (though less in Germany or England), was greater perhaps than that of many more profound thinkers, in part because of the elegance and clarity of his style (his lectures at the Collège de France became fashionable Parisian entertainment). But it is partly also because his insistence on the importance of instinct and on the necessity of viewing reality as a continuum which we approach from many different directions summed up what many of his contemporaries felt, especially in the artistic field, whether or not they were directly influenced by Bergson's own teaching. Marcel Proust for instance (who had attended Bergson's lectures while a student and who was indeed a cousin of the philosopher's wife), began work on his great novel *A la recherche du temps perdu* in the summer of 1905. In this work he set out to record the flow of time in the individual consciousness and to show how time modifies all men and all situations as they become inextricably involved in a web of memories and associations, so that we cannot understand anything if we try to isolate it in one moment of time without simultaneously trying to see it as it is changed and modified by time's inexorable flow. One of the first English critics, when the first volume of Proust's novel was published in 1913, summed up his achievement with a specific reference to Bergson and wrote of Proust's 'images in which matter and memory are subtly combined in a warm flood of life revived, without the intervention of the understanding'.[22]

If Bergson and Proust were concerned to introduce and to emphasise a new conception of time, some of the visual artists in the period immediately before the First World War were equally concerned to introduce a new concept of space and to break down in another way the preconceptions with which men had looked at the outside world. In fact European art had been going through a series of revolutions ever since the painting of Claude Monet, *Impression, Sunrise* (1872 – in the Musée Marmottan, Paris) had given a name to the Impressionist movement, and since the first Impressionist Exhibition in Paris in 1874 had shocked the French public with a new conception, based in part at least on new scientific theories about light and colour, of how to depict the natural world. The development which began by challenging the conventions used in the depiction of nature ended by questioning the value of depicting the world in a naturalistic way and by 1914 some artists were, by painting totally abstract works, denying the value of depicting the external world at all. In part this was due to a reaction against the spread of photography. Whereas in the early years after the invention of photography the photographer had seemed to provide a new standard of realism which painters felt obliged to try to attain, by the last quarter of the nineteenth century artists began to feel that there was no need for them to do what photography could do as well or better. A painter such as Edgar Degas was able to use the instantaneous images of photography to give a new vividness and tension to his pictures of race-horses or ballet dancers, but in the process he was moving away from the realism conventionally regarded as photographic. While the great generation of Impressionists – Claude Monet,

Pierre Renoir, Camille Pissarro – continued into the twentieth century to paint marvellous landscapes, still lives and figure pieces, with all the assurance of their new technical discoveries, the Post-Impressionist painters, such as Paul Gauguin, Vincent Van Gogh or Paul Cézanne, seemed to be searching behind the surface images for some sort of inner formal structure or emotional meaning in the figures and landscapes which they painted; and by the beginning of the twentieth century the revolt against naturalism in art was in full swing – in the fierce colours of the painters known as the *Fauves*, Henri Matisse, André Derain and Maurice Vlaminck, or in the paintings of Germans such as Ernst Ludwig Kirchner and other artists in the group called *Die Brücke* (the Bridge), who used violent distortions and wild coloristic schemes to express the complexity of their inner emotions and their reactions to the world around them. The artistic movement which went furthest in the direction of revising the conventional conception of space was that of the Cubists. Just as Proust in his novel had tried to break down the accepted notion of time and to build up his picture of the world by looking at his characters from many different temporal viewpoints, so Pablo Picasso, Georges Braque and their associates in Paris from 1907 onwards were producing paintings which set out to depict objects from a number of simultaneous viewpoints in space, and were inaugurating a revolution in European art as profound as any previously experienced.

In this search for new ways of analysing society and the individual and for new ways of looking at and describing or depicting the external world, which is characteristic of the period around the turn of the century, perhaps the theory which has had the profoundest effect on the consciousness of Europeans and which was to lead to some of the most fundamental questioning of old-established beliefs and was to affect deeply moral codes and ethical behaviour was that of the Viennese psychologist Sigmund Freud. Freud's doctrines are so well known and, often in a garbled and misunderstood form, have become so much part of the familiar stock of our knowledge and opinions in the middle of the twentieth century that there is no need to describe his ideas at length; and, indeed no summary can do justice to the subtlety of his thought and the elegance of his style. Freud started as a doctor interested in nervous diseases – and he studied some of the same reports of physical disabilities and derangement of the senses as Bergson had done, in particular the work of the great French physician Jean Martin Charcot, who had done pioneering work on the relation between mind and body since the 1870s. However, in his investigations Freud soon began to go much further in formulating a general theory of the origins of neuroses and of the structure of the self than any of his contemporaries had done. In 1900 he published his *Interpretation of Dreams* and although the book only sold six hundred copies over eight years his ideas rapidly became known, first among professional psychiatrists and then to a wider public. Freud himself, when developing the theory and practice of psycho-analysis, was primarily concerned with its clinical application in the treatment of neurosis and it was only later in his life that – in books such as *The Future of an Illusion* (1927) and *Civilisation and its Discontents* (1929) – he became interested in following up the wider social and philosophical implications of his work. Nevertheless Freud's work had from the start important consequences for social theory and not only transformed our understanding of human nature but also implied a picture of man in society.

Many thinkers at the end of the nineteenth and the beginning of the twentieth century had stressed the importance of understanding the instinctual side of man's nature and had suggested that the emotions and unconscious urges were more important than rational thought in providing the key to men's actions. It was Freud, however, who first provided a detailed theoretical hypothesis about the role of the subconscious and the ways in which it influences behaviour. What shocked Freud's contemporaries was of course the extent to which he equated the promptings of the subconscious with the sexual urge, which he regarded as the fundamental driving force in human nature. Indeed, two of his most prominent early followers, Alfred Adler and C.G.Jung, soon broke with him because they could not wholly accept this aspect of Freud's teaching: Adler virtually discarded the subconscious and stressed that the need to overcome a sense of inferiority in society was the basic explanation of much human behaviour, and tried to link psycho-analysis to an optimistic and perhaps somewhat simple-minded belief in the possibility of establishing a socialist society which would make the adaptation of men to social life comparatively easy. Jung, in the course of a long life, became increasingly interested in the exploration of the possibility of describing a collective subconscious and in analysing the symbolic content of the myths which had haunted mankind since primitive times, and came to accept the therapeutic value of religious belief and the role of irrational faith in giving society its coherence.

Freud's account of the unconscious mind and his demonstration of the mechanism by which men rationalise their unconscious motives and fears by means of an elaborate system of symbols gave a new dimension to our awareness and understanding of human nature. For writers and artists it suggested a new area of exploration which they were to investigate over the decades after the work of Freud became more widely known. For the ordinary man, Freud's teaching made possible a franker discussion of sexual activities and problems than ever before, and this gradually led to a revision among the educated classes of Europe of much of the hitherto accepted moral code. It is worth noting that Max Weber was already worried by this aspect of the consequences of Freud's teaching in 1907 and in a controversy with one of Freud's followers expressed his anxiety at the consequences which might follow if Freud's theories were applied outside the consulting room and so break down the precarious moral balance of society.

But Freud's work had other implications too. He was one of the few great thinkers who consistently rejected metaphysics and who did not preach any all-embracing solution for the ills of mankind. The process of psycho-analysis, by making an individual face squarely even the most unpleasant facts about his own past, aimed at making life bearable for him, at enabling him to adjust to the demands and strains of his daily existence, no more. Some people – including some of Freud's own followers – found this bleak and pessimistic view of the world and of society too limited; and the social implications of Freud's doctrines seem to be acceptance of the existing order and of the truth about oneself. We must by an effort of introspection find the way of adapting ourselves to the world in which we live rather than changing it. By adjusting to himself, man would adjust to society. To this extent Freud for all his insistence on the importance of instinct and in spite of his discovery of the role of the unconscious in our lives, remained a rationalist who had no sympathy with the exploitation of the dark forces of the twentieth century, on which he himself had thrown so much light.

The contrast between the detached scientific aims of thinkers such as Durkheim or Freud and the dark instinctive forces which they analysed and to which their work drew attention is one of the most notable features of the intellectual climate of Europe before 1914. Just as the political freedom of the liberal state produced critics who reacted against the parliamentary system as such, so too the broadening of scientific enquiry to include new subjects of investigation and to suggest a new range of explanations for human behaviour led to a reaction against that very scientific temperament and scientific method which had made these discoveries possible. At the same time spreading industrialisation and continuous technological advance, while increasing the material choices and widening the kinds of experience open to the people of Europe, led, as the next chapter will attempt to show, to a reaction, similar and closely related to the one just discussed, against the whole structure and presuppositions of industrial and mechanised society.

6

THE INDUSTRIAL SOCIETY
AND ITS CRITICS

By the beginning of the twentieth century there were few parts of Europe which had not been affected by the industrial revolution; and indeed those countries where industry had developed early in the nineteenth century were now experiencing changes in the type and the organisation of industry which were to have profound consequences. While the older established industries continued to be of major importance – coal for example remained the most important source of energy and still continues to be so – the new industries, chemical, electrical and mechanical, led to the development of new techniques of organisation and management as well as resulting in products which affected the quality of life all over Europe.

Yet, while new consumer goods and services were becoming ever more widely available – bicycles, sewing-machines, typewriters, telephones – and while by the early 1900s the rich were owning automobiles (the British government presented one as a princely gift to the Amir of Afghanistan in 1904), it seemed to many people that this intensified industrialisation and technological progress had been achieved at the cost of increasing dehumanisation. Mass production for a growing mass market and the need to cut costs and maintain profits in an increasingly competitive international economic system led to the use of new machines and new techniques of management. New factories were constructed and laid out so as to save labour and to rationalise and standardise production. At the same time the methods of scientific management pioneered in America by Frederick W. Taylor (and often called in Europe 'Taylorism') were increasingly adopted in European factories, resulting, as David S. Landes puts it, in 'the conversion of the operative into an automaton to match and keep pace with his equipment'.[1]

In many of these new developments Germany took the lead. It was in Germany that the links between technical scientific education and industrial expansion became closest, so that the German universities and *Technische Hochschulen* (Institutes of Technology) became models for institutions of higher education in other countries, especially in the United States, and it has been pointed out that the pace of technological and educational development in Germany had so far outstripped that of Britain that in 1913 Germany had nearly 60,000 university students while the British total was 9,000. And at a more humble level it has been estimated that by 1900 only 0.05 per cent of Germans were illiterate, whereas the figure was 1 per cent for England and 4 per cent for France. In Germany too the centralisation of financial control over industry had gone further than anywhere else in Europe, so that Germany seemed to be the classic land of the cartel and of massive industrial trusts. The pace of industrialisation and the centralisation of German economic life had led, as we have seen in chapter 3, to the equally rapid development of a powerful, well-organised and disciplined socialist party, so that it seemed plausible to argue that it was in Germany that the revolution of the proletariat against the capitalist system, as foreseen by Marx, was most likely to occur.

In fact, all over Europe, the period between 1900 and 1914 was one of increasing labour unrest. This was probably due to a decline in real wages, following the prolonged period of rising wages and falling prices in the last quarter of the nineteenth century. Moreover, even if the condition of the working class in many parts of Europe had improved enormously since 1870, the condition of the rich had improved still more, so that the contrast between the ostentatious luxury of many of the rich and the circumstances under which the workers were mostly living was more striking than ever before. The glitter of the Paris of 'la belle époque', the heavy and leaden grandeur of for example the Villa Hügel near Essen, the residence of the German armaments king Krupp, the vulgar opulence of much upper-class life in Edwardian England gave new point to the revolutionary criticisms of society. The American sociologist Thorstein Veblen in his *Theory of the Leisure Class* (1899) coined the phrase 'conspicuous waste' to describe the behaviour of the new rich, and in his *Imperial Germany and the Industrial Revolution* (1915) showed how the inequality of incomes and the new extravagance of the German capitalist class had begun to undermine the loyalty and industry of the German workers, so that they were becoming, he thought, like their English counterparts who according to Veblen 'had no whole-hearted interest in the efficiency of the work done, but rather in what can be got in terms of price'. On the other hand Veblen goes on,[2]

The employer had none but a humanitarian – said to be quite secondary – interest in the well-being or even in the continued efficiency of the workmen. From which follow on the one hand inhibiting trades-union rules, strikes, lockouts . . . and on the other hand an exploitation of the human raw material of industry . . . in the way of over-work, under-pay, unsafe and unwholesome conditions, and so forth.

In the decade before the First World War the trade unions in Western Europe were increasingly well-organised to make good their claims. In Britain a notable growth in membership of the trade unions was accompanied by a series of dramatic strikes – in 1911 by the seamen and dockers, by a national rail strike and by a series of strikes in the coal mines – which seemed to justify the belief in direct industrial action which some of the new union leaders advocated. In France, although the organised unions were numerically much less strong than in Britain or Germany, their leaders were, as we have seen (see pp. 66–7 above), exceedingly militant; and in 1909 and 1910 the public employees in the post offices and on the railways organised nation-wide strikes, which the government used troops to break. These confrontations between organised labour and the forces of the State convinced many people that the problems of industrial society were still far from a solution; and that the solution when it did come might be a revolutionary one.

This was particularly the case in Germany. The Social Democratic Party's steady growth had been temporarily checked in the elections of 1907, partly as a result of the internal divisions aroused by the revisionist controversy (see pp. 61–2 above) and partly because the government, by fighting the election on issues of foreign and colonial policy, showed how much support nationalist slogans and patriotic programmes could win from the electorate. However, in the next few years, the trade unions strengthened their organisation, while the radicals on the Left, impressed by the Russian experiences of 1905, were increasingly active in their agitation for a revolutionary solution. The success of the Social Democrats in the 1912 Reichstag elections confirmed the fears of some of the ruling class that the danger of revolution was imminent, so that in the Crown Prince's circle there was talk of an anti-socialist coup and the establishment of military rule. Yet in fact, when confronted by the massive machinery of the Wilhelmine state, many workers felt frustrated and powerless. The years from 1912 to 1914 were a time of rising prices and rising unemployment, and the clashes between strikers and the authorities grew in intensity. Troops were used against strikers in the Ruhr in 1912 and a strike in the Hamburg shipyards ended in a lock-out from which only the workers suffered. If the official party leaders still maintained a belief in the possibility of obtaining improvements within the existing State pending the inevitable triumph of the revolution in the future, many Germans both inside the socialist party and outside it were more and more worried by the gap which seemed to divide the workers and especially the socialist workers from the German national community.

Criticism of the industrial society was not limited to socialist and working-class circles and, just as a generation before Bismarck had sponsored a system of social insurance in an attempt to keep the industrial workers quiet, so there were now businessmen anxious, from a mixture of idealism and self-interest, to lessen social tensions and to ease class conflicts. One of the most interesting and perceptive of these was the German industrialist and financier Walther Rathenau, the chairman of the great electricity combine the AEG

(*Allgemeine Elektrizität Gesellschaft* – the German General Electric Company), a man at the centre of a network of financial and industrial undertakings who was also a social theorist. Rathenau shocked many of his colleagues by publishing a series of books and articles calling for a redistribution of incomes, a curb on consumption and the abolition of inherited wealth, so as to make it easier for a worker to rise into the ranks of the managerial classes. Power would lie with an aristocracy of merit made up of managers who had made their own way in a world cleared of hereditary privileges. Industry would be organised in vast cartels working according to an overall economic plan in which industrialists would cooperate with the government in determining goals and priorities, much as in fact happened in Nazi Germany. Profits, instead of being wasted on frivolous consumer goods (Rathenau was particularly bitter about the fashion industry), would be ploughed back into technological improvements or used to finance research and educational foundations. The problems which the French social thinker Henri de Saint-Simon had foreseen a century earlier were now real enough: how to use the benefits of machines and of mass production without destroying the quality of life, and how to use and distribute the vast resources which the industrial revolution had opened up without replacing old social injustices by new ones. Rathenau's solutions were not adopted by his contemporaries, and although his ideas aroused some interest abroad, especially in Scandinavia, his fellow industrialists in Germany mostly saw him only as a traitor to his class, while to the socialists and trade unionists, whom he despised, he seemed just to be making hypocritical suggestions to help the perpetuation of the capitalist order. Nevertheless Rathenau's analysis of German society was accurate enough:[3]

It will be difficult for future writers of German history [he wrote] to understand how, in our time, two class systems could penetrate each other; the first is a survival of the feudal system, the second the capitalist class system, a phenomenon produced by mechanisation itself. But it will strike him as even odder that the newly arisen capitalist class had first of all to contribute to the strengthening of the feudal order.

Moreover, as the leading figure in a vast financial and industrial empire, Rathenau foresaw many of the ways in which the capitalist system was developing, so that his writings suggest a view of economic organisation not unlike that of some of the economic and social analysts of the 1960s. He understood the way in which technological change necessarily alters the structure of social and economic life, and he saw the problem posed for the State by the emergence of huge industrial cartels, conducting their own policies, their own international relations and their own economic plans. Above all Walther Rathenau, himself trained as an electrical engineer, was aware of the powerful and contradictory effects of mechanisation, which he called 'one of the great movements of history, comparable to the introduction of agriculture in prehistoric times, or the great discoveries of primitive times – weapons, fire and clothing'.[4]

The problem of man's relation to the machine had been acute since the beginning of the nineteenth century, but by 1900 the pace of technological development, the new methods of industrial management and the ever increasing complexity of economic organisation had forced people to look more critically at industrial society than ever before. While the benefits of machinery were clear enough, and while the standard of living even of most of the poorest classes had risen, it was also clear that mechanisation tended to dehumanise labour, to alienate the worker from his task by reducing man himself to an element in the mechanical process, as well as destroying the environment, polluting the atmosphere and making, or so it seemed, an unbridgeable gap between town and country. Many people were becoming aware of the price which was being paid for the advantages of mechanisation and industrialisation, and by the 1890s in all the industrial countries of Europe social thinkers and reformers were increasingly concerned with the problem.

Some thinkers made an attempt to make the best of both worlds, to bridge the gap between town and country, to retain some of the advantages of mechanisation without losing the virtues of a simpler, more rural life. The anarchist thinker Prince Peter Kropotkin, who was impressed by the potentialities of machines for relieving men of tedious or unpleasant tasks, dreamed of factories surrounded by fields and market gardens, in which the benefits of industry could be combined with those of agriculture. More practically, in Britain philanthropic industrialists such as W.H.Lever, the founder of the important British chemical firm later known as Unilever, and the Quaker chocolate manufacturer George Cadbury worked with architects and town-planners to produce 'model villages' at Port Sunlight, near Liverpool (1888), and Bournville near Birmingham (1895), in which the workers were given decent houses and gardens and the possibility of a communal life (based incidentally on a strict teetotalism). In 1898 Ebenezer Howard, a self-taught social reformer and planner, launched a movement for the construction of 'garden cities' in his book *Tomorrow – a Peaceful Path to Real Reform*. This had considerable success, though more as a middle-class movement than one of direct benefit to industrial workers, and led to the foundation of a number of garden cities, of which the first was at Letchworth. The movement had a certain effect outside England too: a *città giardino* was founded near Milan and in France a campaign was launched in favour of the *ville jardin*.

These were movements which in England were the result of several decades of discussion and of practical work to improve the quality of life in an industrial society, going back to the writings of John Ruskin (who died in 1900 but whose most influential work was done before 1870) and above all of William Morris. It was Morris who, already a well-known writer and artist, brought to the English socialist movement, with which he became actively involved in 1883, a message, both utopian and practical, of revolt against industrial society in the hope of achieving a richer life for the workers. Morris's vision was based on the idealised view of the mediaeval past, and his social views sprang from a hatred of the machine and of machine-made products. While one cannot help admiring his uncompromising and robust vision, and sympathise with many of his causes (his last public appearance shortly before he died in 1896 was at a meeting of the Society for Checking the Abuses of Public Advertising), his rejection of the contemporary world and of what most of his contemporaries regarded as progress necessarily limited his influence. In his imaginary utopian vision of the future as sketched in *News from Nowhere* (1890–1), as well as in his more directly political writings, Morris was reluctantly prepared to envisage the use of machines for a few tasks (though without specifying very clearly which ones) but on the whole his solutions implied a return to a completely pre-industrial society. Consequently his influence was ultimately more in the field of design than in that of social organisation. In his insistence on hand-made products, on individual craftsmanship and on mediaeval models, Morris created a movement for the reform of the decorative and applied arts which had wide repercussions both in England and on the Continent.

For a time at the end of the nineteenth century English architects, designers and town-planners were among the most influential in Europe. British artists set an example followed elsewhere, and influenced many aspects of the international movement known in France and Belgium as *art nouveau* or in Germany and Austria as *Jugendstil*. While some of the enthusiasm of Ruskin, Morris and their followers for the Middle Ages had led to the adoption of unnecessary and elaborate decoration – so that the houses in Letchworth or in Hampstead Garden Suburb were given fake half-timbered exteriors in imitation of certain mediaeval or Tudor village styles – much of Morris's own work in the design of wallpapers or fabrics or furniture emphasised the use of a natural flowing line and of simple forms. While *art nouveau*, as it developed, was to create its own elaboration and proliferation of forms, with convoluted patterns of whirling plants, at the beginning it was a movement which aimed at clearing away some of the clutter of mid-nineteenth century ornamentation and bringing a new simplicity of design into everyday objects, including the everyday objects of the machine age. (Among the most famous public use of *art nouveau* forms were Hector Guimard's designs for the Paris *métro* stations built around 1900.)

The movements to recover lost craftsmanship, to simplify life, to go 'back to the land' in an attempt to escape from the evils of industrial society were one aspect of the revolt against political and economic liberalism which had, it seemed, produced the abuses of industrialism and the injustices of a *laissez-faire* society. They were movements which could lead, as in the case of William Morris, to a kind of socialism, a demand for planning and co-operation in order to avoid the effects of unrestrained economic competition and of increasing mechanisation. They could lead, as with some anarchists and some adherents of the garden city schemes, to a belief in free associations of individuals organised on a communal basis, deliberately reducing their physical requirements by becoming vegetarians or by giving up alcohol. The most famous as well as the most radical of all the reformers who at the end of the nineteenth century preached a total rejection of modern society and the need for a complete moral transformation, was the great Russian novelist Leo Tolstoy. After becoming one of the best-known writers in Europe with the publication of *War and Peace* (1869) and *Anna Karenina* (1873), Tolstoy had by 1879 at the age of fifty-one become convinced that the life he had been leading hitherto was totally wrong, and that the only hope for himself and indeed for all mankind was the literal adoption by each individual of Christ's teaching, and especially of the precepts in the Sermon on the Mount, as a basis for everyday life. In a series of books and essays, of which the most notable is *What then must we do?* (1886), and in his last novel *Resurrection* (1899), Tolstoy developed a few basic moral principles. He attacked the shams and inequalities of contemporary European society, and especially those of the upper-class Russia to which he belonged, and he called for a return to the basic essentials of life: 'to procure my own food, clothing, heating and dwelling, and in doing this to serve others'.[5] Men must learn to live by their own hands, without the need of exploiting the labour of others, and they must learn to do without the luxuries and complications of urban civilisation. Land-holding must be reformed, so that everyone could ensure his own subsistence. (Tolstoy was an enthusiastic propagandist for the ideas of the American Henry George, who hoped that the introduction of a single tax on land values would both ensure equitable distribution of agricultural land and free the State from dependence on any other form of revenue.) Above all, these goals could only be obtained by an act of will on the part of every individual, who must be willing to dispense with the shams and deceptions of so-called civilisation and return to the simplicities of rural life and to the basic truths of the Christian gospels. This moral regeneration involved the renunciation of all force. Tolstoy had the utmost respect for those members of extreme Christian sects in Russia (such as the *Doukhobors*) who refused military service, and he was bitterly outspoken in his condemnation of the Russo-Japanese War. But there was no branch of living to which Tolstoy did not apply his ruthless moral logic. Not only did he condemn smoking, the drinking of alcohol and the eating of meat, he also criticised the prevailing European concept of art, condemning Shakespeare and Wagner alike, and calling for a direct and simple communication between the artist and the ordinary man – and especially the Russian peasant in whom Tolstoy, like Bakunin, saw a residue of primitive goodness which might serve as the basis for a new moral order – and for the linking of art to the promulgation of moral and religious truths.

It was not surprising that these views, propagated by one of the most famous living Russians, aroused the anger of the Russian authorities. Tolstoy was expelled from the Russian Orthodox Church, and, although too eminent to be arrested or prosecuted, he was subject to censorship and to increasing difficulties in the publication of his later work, while all kind of personal pressure was put on him to keep silence. In fact the old man's efforts to carry out his precepts in his own life were as impressive as his work. Living like a peasant on his own estate, working as a shoemaker in the winter evenings, he both set an example and posed a dilemma, for his new way of life fitted in badly with that of his wife and led to agonising tensions and sufferings both for him and for her, so that at the last in 1910, old and ill, he tried finally to escape from the remaining fetters of his family and past, and left home, to die exhausted a few weeks later.

It is hard to estimate the extent of Tolstoy's influence, but it went far beyond the several short-lived communities which were founded in Europe and America to put his ideas into practice. The Indian leader Gandhi corresponded with Tolstoy and absorbed much of his teaching into his own subsequent beliefs. For intellectuals all over Europe the example of Tolstoy remained a profoundly disturbing challenge, while in Russia many of his ideas became part of radical social thinking and were in turn transmitted by Russian *émigrés* into other quite different contexts, such as the *kibbutz* movement in Israel. His consistent opposition to the methods of tsarist rule made him a hero to the younger generation in Russia after the Revolution of 1905. When he died, the students in the universities of St Petersburg and Moscow organised in his memory demonstrations against capital punishment, one of the causes about which he had felt most strongly. When these were banned by the authorities, the students went on strike for a whole term, effectively linking up Tolstoy's own beliefs with a new revolutionary awareness among the young in Russia. Tolstoy was an extreme example of the reaction against European society at the end of the nineteenth century, but his very extremism emphasises the importance and the nature of the movement as a whole.

Reaction against mechanisation and against industrial society could take the form of Tolstoy's total rejection of all contemporary values. It could in other cases involve an attempt literally to bring more light into the lives of the workers, but it could also lead to a reaction not only against the industrial environment but against all the scientific and rationalist assumptions on which contemporary European society was increasingly coming to be based. The slogan 'Back to the Land' could easily be converted into an appeal to '*Blut und Boden*', to the dark forces in the blood and the black mysteries of the soil. This was particularly true in Germany where, in addition to publicists who put forward these views on ideological grounds, there was a power-ful pressure group, the Agrarian League (*Bund der Landwirte*), anxious to preserve the economic and social position of the German landowner and farmer, and to keep the preponderance of the country over the town by stressing the importance of the land for the conservation of German society and the maintenance of the true German tradition. It is worth, for instance, comparing the book by Ebenezer Howard on garden cities with a pamphlet published two years earlier in Germany (apparently unknown to Howard) by Theodor Fritsch, *Die Stadt der Zukunft* (The City of the Future). The solutions proposed in each case were not dissimilar – new forms of communal ownership of land that would allow each citizen a patch of garden and some direct contact with the soil and the joys of nature. But the tone is very different. Howard wastes little time on the ideological preconceptions of his proposals, and instead is soon involved in a detailed discussion of their practical financial and administrative aspects. For Fritsch, on the other hand, town-planning was an instrument of moral and ideological renewal, part of a scheme to purify Germany and to purge it of alien elements. Fritsch was a publisher who had already begun to specialise in anti-Semitic literature, and for him the dream of a pre-industrial society was linked with all sorts of idea about racial purity. Fritsch's plans for garden cities did not get very far; but his racialist books, and those by his associates which his firm published, pro-vided a repertoire of anti-Jewish ideas and propaganda for many years to come. Fritsch indeed lived just long enough to see the rise to power of the Nazis, who were quite ready to recognise what they owed to his doctrines.

There were many other writers in Germany who had considerable in-fluence and who had pretensions to link the reaction against industrial society with the cult of the *Volk*, the unsullied national stock. Just as Houston Stewart Chamberlain (see pp. 103-4 above) had given his racialist doctrines an appearance of scientific validity, so other writers linked them up with general ideas of social and cultural rejuvenation. They were writers who in Fritz Stern's phrase combined 'cultural criticism with extreme nationalism [and] maintained that the character of modern liberal society was alien to the spirit and traditions of their peoples'.[6] This was by no means only a German phenomenon: we have seen something of the same criticisms in the ideas of Maurice Barrès in France; but it was in Germany that such beliefs were most widespread and contributed most deeply to the unspoken assumptions of a whole generation; and it was in Germany that such beliefs had the most striking and disastrous political consequences.

One of the most famous books of cultural and social criticism to emerge from this current of thought was *Rembrandt als Erzieher* (Rembrandt as Educator), published anonymously in 1890 and written by Julius Langbehn. This was his only substantial book; its immediate enormous success was not epeated, and Langbehn himself died in 1907 in largely self-imposed obscurity. He had claimed that 'To lead men back to natural spontaneity and simplicity, away from the artificial and the artful, that is my true vocation.'[7] His book remained one of the texts which provided ideas and arguments for all those many Germans who were looking for a way out of the drabness of urban society and for a new sense of national identity.

Among the seminal works which shaped the presuppositions with which the Germans entered the First World War and later came to accept National Socialism, *Rembrandt as Educator* occupies a strange position. Langbehn did not worry about theoretical consistency, so that his teaching on the one hand emphasised the necessity and the value of German national feeling and on the other hand stressed the need for individual freedom and expression, for the assertion of the independence of the artist in the face of the trammels of bourgeois society and the restraints of a conventional educational system. Although Langbehn's anti-Semitism was as virulent as that of any of his contemporaries, it was not, as in the case of some of them, the central theme in his writing. For him the Jew – and he meant the assimilated Jew and not the member of the traditional Jewish orthodox community – above all represented the materialist, scientific modern spirit against which he was in revolt. His anti-Semitism, like that of many social critics of the time both in Germany and in France, was part of his hatred of the city, in Langbehn's case especially Berlin. In contrast to the city it was in the countryside that the true values of the German people were to be found in life and in art: 'The new German art will base itself on the peasantry, that is on the *Volksthum* in its best and simplest sense.'[8] One of his few close friends was the Bavarian painter Wilhelm Leibl, whose reputation largely rested on his representation of realistic scenes from peasant life. Rembrandt was chosen as the central figure of the book because his art seemed to Langbehn to reveal the depth and seriousness of the unadulterated German soul. (He took it for granted that Rembrandt counted as German because in his view it was in *Niederdeutschland*, north-west Germany and the Low Countries, that the true German traditions were best preserved.) The rambling, repetitive book ranges from a discussion of Rembrandt himself, through Shakespeare, also regarded by Langbehn as a *Niederdeutscher*, Goethe, Bismarck, Wagner, to hypnotism and phrenology and back again, from classical antiquity to contemporary German politics. The themes which recur again and again are the possibility of a national regeneration for Germany based on the values simultaneously of the peasant and the aristocrat in a society in which spirit (*Geist*) and the land (*Boden*) are intimately linked: 'the nearer the culture of the spirit and of the soil are to each other, the better for both of them; land and people, body and soul belong together.'[9] Prophets are more important than professors, and 'the instincts of a people are cleverer than the sayings of its sages'.[10] Specialisation and academic learning are the death of true culture, just as academic medicine is the enemy of true health. The rejuvenated

Germany, in which the various German tribes (*Stämme*), including it seems the Scandinavians as well as the Dutch and even the Venetians, will each contribute their own specific qualities, will inevitably dominate Europe; and its virtues will be so apparent that other peoples will gladly accept this domination.

These are ideas which were quickly taken up by Langbehn's contemporaries. There are echoes of them in the hermetic lyric poetry of Stefan George. Walther Rathenau, who began his active career soon after the publication of *Rembrandt*, follows Langbehn in his contrast between the simple profundity of Rembrandt and what he considered the shallow mechanistic art of Zola or Manet, the one typical of the 'kingdom of the soul', the other of worldly materialism.

It was to the young that Langbehn looked for the regeneration of society and the revival of the true German spirit. He writes enthusiastically of a generation of broad-shouldered blond young men, and he praises physical education and cleanliness at the expense of academic study, for which he has nothing but contempt, even in the hands of such great scholars as the historians Ranke and Mommsen. 'If there were instead of the 50,000 bars in Prussia today, 50,000 public bathing establishments, the physical, spiritual, and even moral health of every citizen would be better than it now is.'[11] Langbehn himself made no attempt to found any sort of organisation and in practice had only one single devoted disciple, but the spirit of his teaching found expression in one of the most significant developments in Germany at the turn of the century, the growth of the youth movements. Between 1890 and the First World War educational and social reformers all over Europe were concerned with developing new, freer methods of teaching and learning and were trying to give opportunities for young people in the urban areas to escape from their often depressing surroundings. At the same time there was a growing awareness of the problems of adolescence, an awareness exemplified in Frank Wedekind's play *Frühlings Erwachen* (Spring's Awakening, 1891) or in the Austrian Robert Musil's novel *Die Verwirrungen des Zöglings Torless* (Young Torless, 1906). Many people, including the young themselves, began to think of youth as a class apart. The words of one German educational reformer in 1913 sum up a whole new attitude towards the young which still remains very familiar sixty years later:[12]

Youth, up to now only an appendage of the older generation, excluded from public life and forced into a passive role, begins to become conscious of itself. It is trying to create a life for itself independent of the laws of convention. It is striving for a way of life which corresponds to the nature of youth, but which will also make it possible for youth to take itself and its activity seriously and to take its place in general cultural activity.

These ideas found a particular resonance in Germany at a time when, as we have seen, there was widespread anxiety about Germany's place in the world and her political future. Some people reacted by adopting a violent and intense nationalism; others sought to turn away from politics and to seek a solution in the development of the free individual and in the simplicities of nature. Both trends could be found in the youth movements which were being founded from 1901 onwards (the first and most famous being the *Wandervögel*), and which by 1913 at a great outdoor meeting which celebrated the centenary of the German victory over Napoleon's armies at Leipzig – a great event in the German national and liberal tradition – were combined in a loose association of Free German Youth. It has been estimated that the strength of these movements was never more than sixty thousand; and this membership was predominantly middle-class.[13] The success of the movement was greatest in the Protestant areas of Germany, since the Catholic Church preferred to organise its younger members in purely confessional groups, whereas in France it was the Church which was almost alone in attempting to found any sort of youth movement. Nevertheless the influence of the ethos of the Free German Youth was profound, and very many of the intellectual leaders of the next generation were formed by it. The movement was a reaction against the stuffiness of bourgeois society, and it was characteristic that its members developed their own style of unconventional dress. It was also a reaction against the conservative philistinism of the older student organisations, with their emphasis on drinking and duelling, and one of the features of many of the groups was an insistence on sexual restraint (though others were more concerned to assert their abandonment of bourgeois conventions by insisting on the right to free love), as well as on the renunciation of alcohol and the consumption of 'natural' vegetarian food. Above all, the movement was a reaction against the city, and its most typical activity was the long expedition into the forests and the mountains.

At the same time, for all its revolt against existing society and its explicit assertion of its non-political nature, the German youth movement was imbued with a mystical nationalism, a belief in a purified and rejuvenated Germany, a nation in touch with its ancient roots in German soil, preserving its own traditions untainted by decadent foreign influences. Some of the groups banned Jews openly; and there was a widespread feeling that, as one of the leaders said, 'there are certain imponderabilia that remain strange to the average Jew who lacks a certain freshness and simplicity'.[14]

The youth movement, like the related movements elsewhere to take people 'back to the land' and to revive forgotten arts and crafts, was simultaneously liberal and reactionary and, in its inception in Germany, anti-political. However, the political parties, impressed by its success, began to realise the potentialities of a youth movement organised on a political basis. In particular, the German Social Democratic Party attempted to provide for the working class a youth movement which would give young workers an opportunity for sport and recreation while filling some of the gaps in their education which had ended at the age of fourteen, and at the same time instilling into them socialist principles. This movement, started in 1905 by a young socialist politician from Baden, Ludwig Frank, had considerable success, and its newspaper reached a circulation of 100,000, though, as might be expected, many of its members were often too radical for the taste of the party leadership. The idea had already been adopted by socialists elsewhere, in Austria, Belgium and Switzerland, and in 1907 the first international socialist youth conference was held. In England the enterprising socialist journalist and follower of William Morris, Robert Blatchford, had already in 1894 had the idea of sponsoring cycling clubs for the young readers of his popular paper *The Clarion* and of his well-known book *Merrie England*, which had set out to give a more attractive picture of the collectivist future than some of the rather puritanical early British socialists, with their roots in non-conformist Protestantism, were prepared to envisage.

It was in Germany, however, that the youth movement had most effect. The particular circumstances of German society, confronted with very rapid industrialisation and with political frustration and uncertainty, gave the movement a dynamism and importance it did not have elsewhere. In France, where urbanisation had been much less intense than in Germany and England, the demand for organised expeditions into the country was less strong, and many city and town dwellers still had direct links with the countryside. Even in France, however, attempts were made to introduce sport and gymnastics into the curriculum of the State schools, though without much success. However the Baron Pierre de Coubertin, the active inspirer of one of these movements, who claimed '*Je rebronzerai une jeunesse seule et confinée, son corps et son caractère, par le sport, ses risques et même ses excès*' ('I will bronze again our lonely and confined youth, its body and its character, by sport, its risks and even its excesses'),[15] at least succeeded in organising the first Olympic Games, and thus starting a famous series of international sporting encounters which some people have seen as improving international relations, others as worsening them.

In Britain sport and tough physical exercise were an integral part of the 'public school system', the misleading name given to the private secondary schools for the education of the middle classes, the number of which had increased substantially during the second half of the nineteenth century. Nevertheless, the strains and losses of the South African War had made the British extremely aware of the relative decline of their power. This led to a renewed insistence on the potential strength of the British Empire (an annual Empire Day was proposed in 1904 and officially introduced in 1916) as well as to demands for conscription and to the foundation of organisations with such names as the Duty and Discipline Movement or the National Service League. Another form which this anxiety took was an almost neurotic concern with national physique; and it was certainly true that the health and size of members of the urban working classes compared very badly with those of the other classes of English society. The point was not lost on the Germans either; and the German ambassador noted after the funeral procession of Queen Victoria in January 1901, at a moment when the military escort had to be provided from such troops as were not committed to the war in South Africa: 'The military ranks stretched for miles. A muster of troops morally degraded, idiots, undersized and pitiable beings, the dregs of the population. With astonishment and dismay we beheld yesterday that the English have reached the end of their military capacity.'[16] In 1907, however, a serious attempt was made to provide for all classes opportunities for organised outdoor activities and for experience of the countryside when General Sir Robert Baden-Powell, a soldier who had studied irregular warfare against the Zulus and Ashanti in Africa and who had become a national hero as the commander of the town of Mafeking during its long siege in the South African War, started the Boy Scouts. A comparison of Baden-Powell's *Scouting for Boys* (1908) with any of the texts of the German youth movement tells one something about the differences between British and German society and ideology on the eve of the First World War.

The German youth movements had strong emotional and sentimental overtones; their purpose was to restore a sense of *Volksgemeinschaft*, of membership of a national community, a state with a life and morality of its own, and to give young Germans new roots in the countryside and in the past of their country. The tone of Baden-Powell's work is much more one of breezy practicality. Its subtitle is *A Handbook of Instruction in Good Citizenship*. Its main concern is to teach handicraft and personal hygiene, woodcraft and natural history, methods of rescue from drowning or from runaway horses, and to give urban boys (and girls, for in 1909 the Girl Guide movement was founded as a counterpart to the Boy Scouts) a sense of the adventure of outdoor life. There is, it is true, an undertone of militarism – 'Every boy should prepare himself, by learning how to shoot and to drill, to take his share in the defence of the (British) Empire if it should ever be attacked'[17] – and there is an unquestioning assumption of British superiority, though at the same time an assumption of lurking dangers which mysteriously threatened Britain's greatness. Yet the presuppositions on which the code is based are those of the old liberal society, self-help, self-reliance and self-improvement: 'Work for the good of the State or of the business in which you may be employed, and you will find that as you succeed in doing this you will be getting all the promotion and all the success that you want.'[18] For all the insular and imperialist spirit behind *Scouting for Boys*, it is easy to see how these principles could be adapted to countries other than Britain, while the practical methods of training and organising young people provided an example easily followed elsewhere, so that the Boy Scouts and Girl Guides had a rapid success, and the movement soon became an international one, a last tribute, as it were, to the old Mazzinian ideal that by serving the interests of each nation the interests of Europe as a whole were being equally furthered.

These movements to get away from the city and back to the healthy country air, or in some cases to the roots of national culture, had many by-products. Just as a hundred years earlier the first awakening of national consciousness among many of the peoples of Europe had led to the collection of folk-songs and folk-tales, so now at the beginning of the twentieth century there was a new interest in popular arts, whether this took the form of a revival of peasant crafts or the scholarly recording of vanishing folk-music. It was traditional songs which the Boy Scouts or the *Wandervögel* sang. And, at a more sophisticated level, composers were finding in folk-music new melodic inspiration and new harmonic idioms. In Hungary Béla Bartók published in 1906 his first collection of Hungarian popular songs, and the Spaniard Manuel de Falla brought out his *Seven Spanish Popular Songs* in 1912. In both cases and especially that of Bartók, whose study of the folk-music of south-east Europe was both scholarly and extensive, these national melodies were to become the foundation of an individual and national style, and for Bartók the starting-point for a series of bold, experimental compositions which made him one of the most interesting composers of the first half of the twentieth century. If the mild echoes of long-forgotten country songs in the work of English composers such as Frederick Delius and Ralph Vaughan Williams were less revolutionary, this may in part have been due to the fact that industrialisation and the changes in the English countryside had made the folk-song already a dying tradition, whereas in Spain or in Hungary it was still very much a living one.

The most sensational impact of material derived from folk-song was made on sophisticated European audiences by the early ballet scores of the young Russian composer Igor Stravinsky, *The Firebird* (1910), *Petrouchka* (1911) and above all *The Rite of Spring* (1913) – a score which after sixty years has still not lost its power to shock. These were written for the Russian Ballet which the impresario Serge Diaghilev first brought to Western Europe in 1909, and which seemed, in its use of the dance, in its combination of exotic colours, its costumes based on peasant designs and its exploitation of folk mythology, to provide a new type of advanced artistic and theatrical experience. In Stravinsky's music folk-song was used as a means of conveying a primitive rhythmic intensity, and the composer was hailed by advanced artists all over Europe as having introduced a new element into European music, while his more conservative listeners reacted, as their parents had done to the works of Richard Wagner, by predicting the end of civilised harmony.

The fact that the rediscovery of folk-song could, on the one hand, symbolise for the youth movements a return to a purer pre-industrial world and, on the other hand, be used by advanced composers such as Stravinsky to produce results of the utmost sophistication which shocked the conservatives, is yet another example of the ambivalence which is inherent in many of the developments we have been discussing. Many of them had results which were simultaneously 'progressive' and 'reactionary'. The desire for the primitive in art could represent a desire for lost innocence; but it could also be seen as a desire for a new range of expression and for a new violent experience.

Technological progress had resulted in a number of movements in reaction against it, but these did not stop European society on the eve of the First World War from being increasingly conditioned by the new machines and the new scientific discoveries. Moreover there were many people who were ready to welcome these developments and to be enthusiastic over such achievements as the first aeroplane-crossing of the English Channel in 1909 by the Frenchman Louis Blériot, six years after the Americans Wilbur and Orville Wright had made the first petrol-driven aeroplane-flight. In 1901 the Italian Guglielmo Marconi had demonstrated the possibility of sending wireless messages across the Atlantic; by 1912 the British postmaster-general was signing a contract with the Marconi company for the development of radio links within the British Empire (and incidentally causing a political scandal when it was alleged that ministers, including Lloyd George, had been speculating in the company's shares). The discoveries which had fired the imagination of the science fiction writers of the older generation, such as Jules Verne who died in 1905 and who had foreseen the circling of the moon by men in a space craft, were coming closer to reality, and among the new generation of novelists the Englishman H.G.Wells was exploring, in *The Island of Dr Moreau* (1896) and *The Food of the Gods* (1904), the possibility of inducing biological changes in man and animals, and, in *The War of the Worlds* (1898) and *The First Men on the Moon* (1901), the consequences of space travel, which the new technology seemed to be bringing within reach. These early scientific romances of the young Wells emphasise the possible horror of the future and were much more pessimistic than some of his later speculations about a new rational scientific society run by a new race of technical managers.

The prospect of air travel (and, it soon appeared, of air warfare) and of radio communications made the world seem smaller and Europe's dominance in it all the more secure as long as Europe retained the monopoly of these discoveries. But at the same time the work of theoretical scientists was suggesting new dimensions to men's thought, new concepts of distance and space and new ideas about the nature of matter. In 1899 a German scientist, Max Planck, put forward a new theory suggesting that radiation, which had been intensively studied during the previous decade – a study which had led in 1895 to the discovery of X-rays – might act in discontinuing bursts and not as a continuous and predictable stream. And in 1905 another young German physicist, Albert Einstein, first stated his specific theory of relativity, and formulated it in its final general form ten years later. By using complicated astronomical observations and advanced mathematical calculations, Einstein developed a theory which suggested that measurements of energy and mass were inextricable from questions of speed and movement and that, in a universe which might be for ever expanding, no observation from a single fixed point could be relied on to tell the whole truth. Matter, it seemed to result from these discoveries, was far more unstable than had been hitherto believed; scientific truth was less universal than generally supposed. Although theories of this kind, involving highly technical mathematical operations, were harder for the layman to understand than the simpler certainties of Newtonian physics which they seemed to be replacing, they gradually began to influence the moral and metaphysical outlook of educated Europeans so that, often in inaccurate and misunderstood forms, the notion of relativity, of the quantum leap or of the expanding universe had within a few years created a new world picture and suggested new technological advances which contributed to the sense of intellectual excitement and of ever widening possibilities created by the inventors and the engineers.

For the moment those who were prepared to make the most of the new technology had plenty of immediate spheres of activity which affected the ordinary man more directly than the speculations of the theoretical physicists. While disgust with the city was, as we have seen, the emotion which lay behind many of the movements to go back to the land or to revive forgotten arts and crafts, pride in the city led others to devise new methods of construction and to envisage new forms of city life. As might be expected the people who were most eager to exploit technological advance so as to improve the quality of urban life were those most directly involved in the application of technological discoveries, and especially the architects. As one English architect put it in 1905, architecture must be based on the 'unchallenged acceptance of modern materials and modern conditions'.[19] All over Europe there were architects anxious to put this principle into practice, and in some places public authorities prepared to give them the opportunity of doing so. From the mid-nineteenth century onwards the use of iron for building, often in conjunction with glass, had given Europe its characteristic urban monuments: the Crystal Palace, for example, built for the Great Exhibition in London in 1851, and the Eiffel Tower, which was the centrepiece of the Paris Exhibition of 1889. (It was not surprising that the Eiffel Tower was a particular object of loathing for the French anti-Semitic writer Edouard Drumont (see p. 107 above), symbolising all that he hated about the city; and it is tempting to relate his dislike of its bold, thrusting form to his exaggerated fears about the threat to French girls from the sexual potency of the Jews.)

By the end of the nineteenth century the use of new materials – steel and reinforced concrete – began to be combined with a new aesthetic. Steel framed buildings were being constructed in America from 1890 onwards; reinforced concrete began to be widely used from around 1904; and the plainness of these materials led to a belief that they must be allowed to speak for themselves without unnecessary decoration or ornament. In the work of the Glasgow architect Charles Rennie Mackintosh, who by 1900 had achieved an international reputation, the forms of *art nouveau* (see p. 148 above) decoration are combined with a new simplicity and toughness of architectural design. In France Tony Garnier, who believed that 'In architecture, truth is the result of calculations made to satisfy known necessities with known materials',[20] began in 1906 a long association with the city of Lyons under its young mayor Edouard Herriot, and planned a wide range of public buildings in which the new functionalism and the demands for a neo-classical simplicity were combined. In Vienna Adolf Loos attacked unnecessary ornament and praised the plumber as 'the quartermaster of culture',[21] building in the first decade of the new century houses and shops which look forward to the style of twenty or thirty years later, by which time Loos' influence had become widespread.

It was, however, in Germany that the exploitation of new materials and the development of what was to become the 'international style' of architecture later in the twentieth century were carried furthest in the years before 1914 (or at least furthest in Europe, for many of these technical and stylistic innovations had been influenced by developments in the United States). The trend in Germany was encouraged by some measure of official support. The rulers of a few of the smaller states had enlightened tastes: the Grand Duke Ernst Ludwig of Hesse patronised young and advanced artists and architects, and in 1900 gave them a chance to display their work in an exhibition at Darmstadt, just as Duke Georg of Saxe-Meiningen had supported the advanced theatre and sponsored in 1886 the first public performance in Germany of Ibsen's *Ghosts* when it was banned elsewhere. More important, in Prussia, the largest and most important of the German states, an official of the board of trade, Hermann Muthesius, gave active support to a group of designers who in 1907 founded the *Deutsche Werkbund*, dedicated to the principle of what was called the *'neue Sachlichkeit'* (the new functionalism or realism). The influence of the *Werkbund* was to contribute notably to changing the face of German cities and revolutionising the design of industrial buildings, but it is worth noting that Muthesius also acknowledged his debt to Langbehn's *Rembrandt as Educator* 'which recalled to the mind of Germany the importance of artistic as against scientific culture'[22] – a good example of the ambiguity and all-pervasiveness of Langbehn's influence. The aim of the movement was to prove that the new technological methods and materials could produce a valid art for the new industrial age. This ideal was summed up in 1913 by a young architect who was to become one of the key figures in creating the architectural style of the twentieth century, Walther Gropius:[23]

Compared to other European countries, Germany has a clear lead in the aesthetics of factory building. But in the motherland of industry, in America, there exist great factory buildings whose majesty outdoes even the best German work of this order. The grain silos of Canada and South America, the coal bunkers of the leading railroads and the newest work halls of the North American industrial trusts can bear comparison, in their overwhelming monumental power, with the buildings of ancient Egypt.

Gropius himself put his ideas into practice in the famous factory he built with Adolf Meyer between 1911 and 1913 at Alfeld-an-der-Leine, near Hanover, for the Fagus shoe-last makers, and other German firms, among them the *Stahlwerksverband* and Rathenau's AEG, were employing advanced architects, including the influential Peter Behrens, to build them new factories and office blocks. While on the one hand the official German taste, as represented by the artistic views of Wilhelm II and his court, was intolerably heavy, pretentious and sentimental, it was nevertheless in Germany that what Nikolaus Pevsner has called the pioneers of modern design found the biggest opportunity to put their ideas into practice; and it was to Germany that many of the revolutionary architects and designers of the next generation such as the young Swiss Charles Edouard Jeanneret, later known as Le Corbusier, came to study.

If the new architectural ideas and the development of a new aesthetic of functionalism were beginning by 1914 to change the appearance of some of the cities and factories of Europe, the excitement of the new discoveries – motor-cars, aeroplanes, radio, the cinema – was also creating a new romanticism about the machine and about the glitter, glamour and pace of city life. Already as early as 1877 Claude Monet had seen in the clouds of steam from the locomotives and the shafts of light through the glass roof of the Gare St Lazare in Paris a subject for a painting as valid as the changing light on the façade of the cathedral of Notre Dame which he painted later; and Camille Pissarro and others had seen the railway as an integral part of the nineteenth-century landscape. By the beginning of the twentieth century however there were artists beginning to adopt an even more positive attitude to the new mechanised urban environment. The older generation of writers concerned with exploring the splendours and miseries of city life, and in particular Emile Zola, who died in 1902, had used a new and, as it appeared to many of his contemporaries, extremely shocking naturalism to depict the realities of the city. For Zola the novel was as powerful a weapon of social criticism as it had been for Charles Dickens half a century before. Yet for all his indictment of the existing system and for all the horror and squalor of some of the scenes Zola depicts, there emerges from his work an epic sense of the scale and grandeur of much of modern life, so that to many people in the next generation he seemed to be the poet as much as the critic of urban life.

Life in the city was inevitably a theme for writers and painters by the beginning of the twentieth century, and the relation of man to machines was becoming part of the subject matter of art. The famous Italian writer Gabriele d'Annunzio, who always had a shrewd instinct for whatever was up to date, had already in 1910 made the hero of his novel *Forse che si, forse che no* (Perhaps or Perhaps Not) an aviator, perhaps the first to appear in realistic rather than in science fiction. Artists were using new, advanced styles to convey the twentieth-century scene. The German Expressionist painter Ernst Ludwig Kirchner, in a series of street scenes from 1907, was depicting the sadness and the excitement of the city, while in France during 1911 and 1912 Robert Delaunay and Fernand Léger were using the Cubist techniques they had learnt from Picasso and Braque of breaking up space and depicting objects from several simultaneous viewpoints, to convey the dynamism of urban life.

It was however in Italy and in Russia, both countries where industrialisation and the use of machines had developed much later than in France or Germany, that a new and strident aesthetic doctrine was promulgated, calling for the recognition of the machine as a central part of human existence. In 1909 the Italian writer F.T.Marinetti published his *Futurist Manifesto*, in which he declared that 'the splendour of the world has been enriched by a new beauty, the beauty of speed' and asserted that 'A racing automobile . . . is more beautiful than the Victory of Samothrace.'[24] We have seen in the previous chapter how the disgust which Marinetti and his friends felt for the stagnant state of Italian society and its obsession with the past fitted into the climate of opinion in Italy before 1914 and contributed to the atmosphere in which Italian Fascism was to come into being. In art their influence was more widespread and less harmful. They suggested new ways of conveying the excitement of speed and the pace and dynamism of the city, and they began a new movement for the incorporation of mechanical elements into art. Marinetti visited Russia and found that his ideas were eagerly taken up by advanced artists there who were concerned with inventing new modes of revolutionary expression and who became for a brief period after 1917, before the Bolshevik authorities changed their mind about the nature of art, almost the official artists of the Russian Revolution. Both in France and Germany and even (in the work of Wyndham Lewis and the Vorticist group) in England the Futurists contributed new ideas about how to incorporate the machine and the twentieth-century city into the framework of European art. For all their violence, their praise of war and their hysterical Italian nationalism the Futurists also drew attention to some of the positive aspects of the machine age, and suggested an alternative attitude to that of the followers of William Morris and all who saw hope for the future only in a rejection of all technological progress and in a return to a pre-industrial era.

In trying to assess the effect of ideas on political and social behaviour and to reconstruct the climate of opinion in Europe on the eve of the First World War, it is important to distinguish between the new and revolutionary theories, such as those of Freud and Einstein, which were as yet only known to a few people, and which did not have their full impact till a quarter of a century later, and the ideas, mostly originating a generation earlier, which had become commonplace and a part of the outlook of ordinary educated people. And perhaps too behind this is yet another level of belief, into which even the new ideas of a hundred years before had scarcely penetrated. Most of the peasants of Europe, in spite of the spread of compulsory education, the construction of railways and the invention of the bicycle, still accepted without question the beliefs of their Church and the stability of the existing social order unless, as happened in Spain in 1892 and 1903, in Sicily in 1893 and in Russia in 1905, economic conditions became so intolerable that the peasants burst out in a largely undirected wave of revolt.

At the level of the sophisticated and educated people from whom the political, industrial and intellectual leaders of Europe were drawn, the gap between the *avant-garde* and the average man was considerable. Although the British Conservative prime minister A. J. Balfour, or the Liberal war minister R. B. Haldane, might claim some knowledge of German philosophy, and the French prime minister Georges Clemenceau be on friendly terms with Monet and Debussy, most of the members of the ruling classes of Europe before 1914 were acting on ideas and assumptions formulated twenty or thirty years before, and took little interest in advanced ideas and advanced artistic developments. Although in Vienna philosophers were developing theories about the nature of mathematics, the structure of language and the relationship of words to objects which were to change our ideas about the philosophical nature of truth, and although Freud was exploring the subconscious mind, while the young composer Arnold Schoenberg was destroying traditional tonality and constructing a new musical language, they achieved little public recognition, and none of their spirit of innovation filtered through to the officials who administered the creaking bureaucracy which held the heterogeneous Austro-Hungarian state together. In France Picasso and Braque were destroying the traditional concept of space as effectively as Schoenberg that of tonality, and inaugurating the greatest revolution in European painting since the Renaissance; but it would be fanciful to suggest that this somehow reflected the coming break-up of bourgeois society; and the tastes of political circles in the Third Republic were more accurately reflected by those parliamentarians who in 1912 protested in the Chamber of Deputies against the Cubist painters having their work shown in the officially recognised *Salon*. At many levels the assumptions of an older generation were being undermined, but many of those whose values and views of human nature and the external world were being threatened remained uneasily oblivious of the threat.

Yet, if we look at the prevailing assumptions of the rulers of Europe in 1914 as well as of those who protested against them, we can find some currents of opinion deriving from thinkers active some forty or fifty years before. We have seen how Darwinian ideas had a great influence on the ideology of imperialism at the end of the nineteenth century, but it is important to realise how literally the doctrine of the struggle for existence and of the survival of the fittest was taken by the majority of the leaders of Europe in the years preceding the First World War. The Austro-Hungarian chief of staff for example, Franz Baron Conrad von Hoetzendorff, wrote in his memoirs after the war:[25]

Philanthropic religions, moral teachings and philosophical doctrines may certainly sometimes serve to weaken mankind's struggle for existence in its crudest form, but they will *never* succeed in removing it as a driving motive of the world ... It is in accordance with this great principle that the catastrophe of the world war came about as the result of the motive forces in the lives of states and peoples, like a thunderstorm which must by its nature discharge itself.

Seen against this sort of ideological background, Conrad's insistence on the need for a preventive war in order to preserve the Austro-Hungarian monarchy becomes comprehensible.

We have seen too how these views were not limited to military figures, and that Max Weber (see pp. 132–4 above) for example was deeply concerned with the international struggle for survival. Again Kurt Riezler, the personal assistant and confidant of the German chancellor Theobald von Bethmann-Hollweg, wrote in 1914: 'Eternal and absolute enmity is fundamentally inherent in relations between peoples; and the hostility which we observe everywhere ... is not the result of a perversion of human nature but is the essence of the world and the source of life itself.'[26] When the English statesman Lord Milner died in 1925, a *Credo* was found among his papers containing the significant statement that 'A Nationalist believes that this is the law of human progress, that the competition between nations each seeking its maximum development, is the Divine Order of the World, the law of life and progress.'[27]

If assumptions based on a misconception of Darwin's theories conditioned the outlook on international relations, and in some cases on the relations between classes, of the rulers of Europe before 1914, the assumptions of many of those who were critical of existing society and who were looking for new possibilities for self-expression were also based on the writings of the previous generation. One of the authors whose ideas percolated far beyond the people who had read his plays, let alone seen a performance of any of them, was the Norwegian dramatist Henrik Ibsen. Ibsen died in 1906 aged seventy-eight but his plays had already begun to appear in the 1860s. Together with Zola, whom he did not appreciate ('Zola goes down into the sewer to take a bath; I, in order to cleanse it,' he once said),[28] he was regarded as one of the most shocking, disruptive and morally subversive writers of his age. In England for example (where Karl Marx's daughter Eleanor had been one of his earliest admirers and propagandists), *Ghosts*, although written in 1881, did not receive a commercial performance* – and a scandalised reception – till July 1914.

So many of the ideas which Ibsen expressed in his plays have been commonplaces in European society for some fifty years now and so many of the causes he advocated have triumphed that, although his plays still have an unfailing impact in the theatre, it is hard to recreate the atmosphere in which his name represented to the young all that was most independent, emancipated and unconventional. But plays such as *A Doll's House* (1879) and *Ghosts* (1881), *Rosmersholm* (1886) or *Hedda Gabler* (1890) exposed the hypocrisies of bourgeois life and the dark passions and self-deceit which lay behind the stuffy conventional forms of behaviour, while the call for the emancipation of women and for a wife's right to order her own life found many willing hearers. It was these plays that made Ibsen's reputation as a moral reformer, even if some of the more poetical earlier plays, *Brand* (1866) and *Peer Gynt* (1867), and the works of the very end of his life, *The Master Builder* (1894) or the mysterious *When We Dead Awaken* (1900), convey a more subtle message about the need for every man to follow his own conscience and values, and about the danger of self-deception which inevitably accompanies this. Ibsen remained obsessed with his native Norway, its limitations and its problems, even though he spent most of his life abroad in Italy and in Germany (where his work was first successful), but, as George Bernard Shaw, himself one of Ibsen's most influential admirers and by 1914 also a successful dramatist concerned with using the drama for advancing radical causes, wrote 'Ibsen's intensely Norwegian plays exactly fitted every middle and professional class suburb in Europe.'[29]

However, perhaps the most all-pervasive influence on all those who in 1914 were revolting against accepted ideas and current doctrines was Friedrich Nietzsche. Nietzsche's books were written between 1872 and 1889, when he became incurably insane. He had been comparatively little read during his creative period; but by the time of his death in 1900 he was already a figure of European importance, whose teachings were being quoted, misquoted and interpreted in a number of different ways. In the years before 1914 no one with any intellectual pretensions was ignorant of his work, and

---

* There had been one performance in London in 1891 and three in 1897 – the year of Queen Victoria's Jubilee – which gave rise to the curious rumour that the play had actually been seen by the Queen herself.

during the war the pocket edition of *Thus Spake Zarathustra*, perhaps his most famous work, the first parts of which were published in 1883 and which had then scarcely sold at all, was a best-seller. When the war broke out Nietzsche's teachings were, in the Anglo-Saxon countries at least, vaguely held responsible for it. At the same time it was to Nietzsche that many young radicals all over Europe looked in their search for arguments and slogans with which to attack the established order. Mussolini, for example, was writing in 1908: 'To understand Nietzsche we must envisage a new race of "free spirits", strengthened in war, in solitude, in great danger.'[30] And Gavrilo Princip, the young Serb nationalist revolutionary whose assassination of the heir to the Austro-Hungarian throne on 28 June 1914 led to the crisis which brought about the First World War, was fond of reciting Nietzsche's short poem *Ecce Homo*, with its lines 'Insatiable as flame, I burn and consume myself.'[31]

Nietzsche's writings had an explosive effect on a whole generation; and he is one of those thinkers, like Jean-Jacques Rousseau, whom the reader can interpret in a number of different ways, according to his own predilections and interests. Nietzsche had begun his career as a classical scholar, and was appointed professor of Greek at the University of Basle in 1869 when he was still only twenty-five years old. He remained an academic for ten years – although an unorthodox one – and had, after his health broke down, lived as a freelance writer, moving in search of health and sunshine from Switzerland to the Riviera and back again. The period at Basle brought him one of the major experiences of his life, his friendship (later to turn to bitter enmity) with the great composer Richard Wagner, at that time living in Switzerland on the Lake of Lucerne. Nietzsche shared with Wagner an admiration for the philosophy of Arthur Schopenhauer (1788–1860), and both men took from Schopenhauer a belief in a blind force driving men forward to their destiny. Schopenhauer himself had believed, following the thinkers of the Orient, that the only way to escape from this blind striving was by a contemplative withdrawal from life. Nietzsche on the other hand implied that by a great effort man could transcend his destiny and shape life and the world anew for himself, while Wagner in his music dramas *The Flying Dutchman* (1843), *Tristan and Isolde* (1865) and *The Ring of the Nibelungs* (first performed between 1869 and 1876), suggested that such redemption would come through a self-immolating love; (in Wagner's last work, *Parsifal*, first produced in 1882, a year before his death, the same basic idea was given Christian overtones).

After leaving Basle in 1879 Nietzsche felt himself increasingly alienated from Bismarck's Germany. In his earlier writings he had had great hopes that Germany was on the threshold of a renaissance and that there would be in Germany a rebirth of the Hellenic world. This was linked with his friendship with Wagner and his belief (shared by Wagner himself) that the composer's work would contribute to this rebirth. But after 1875 Nietzsche had quarrelled with Wagner and become disgusted with what he repeatedly called Wagnerism and the coarsening and loutishness that had taken possession of Germany since the founding of the Reich. For the rest of his life he was increasingly lonely, in spite of the devotion of a few close friends and the appreciation of one or two discerning critics such as Taine and the Danish writer Georg Brandes. In a series of books, of which *Thus Spake Zarathustra* was to be the most influential, Nietzsche called for a new morality, a new attitude to life and what he called a 'revaluation of all values' (*Umwertung aller Werte*). This could only be achieved by exposing the false values of existing society and by questioning the existing system at all points; and sometimes Nietzsche envisaged that such a process would have to be carried out by a new race of 'supermen' (*Ubermenschen*) free from sentimental inhibitions and prepared without scruple to use violence in the building of a new, nobler world.

Any short summary of Nietzsche's views inevitably does him an injustice. It ignores not only the trenchancy and humorous irony with which he attacked the stuffiness and complacency of late-nineteenth century bourgeois society, but also the poetic insights and the lyrical and gentle aspects of his work – his longing for a fresh innocence of vision and for a freer life in which each individual could develop in his own way. Yet to stress the violent and even racialist aspects to be found in Nietzsche's work is nevertheless not entirely unfair. It was his attack on liberal sentimentalism and on a hollow belief in progress that attracted the generation which, all over Europe, seized on his writings around the turn of the century; while his emphasis on the purifying virtues of violence accounts in part for the enthusiasm with which the outbreak of war was greeted by many intellectuals in nearly all the belligerent countries. The racialist ideas – the concept of the superman and the notorious praise of the 'blond beast' – were deliberately emphasised by Nietzsche's sister and literary executor Elizabeth Förster-Nietzsche, who indeed suppressed parts of his work if they conflicted with the extreme nationalist views of herself and her husband. Nietzsche's sister, like Wagner's widow, lived long enough to receive personally the tributes of Adolf Hitler, and Nietzsche was claimed by the Nazis, and accused by their enemies, as a forerunner of the Nationalist Socialist movement in Germany.

Yet Nietzsche's appeal in the first years of the twentieth century was not just to fanatical nationalists and to those people who were looking forward to war or who, like Georges Sorel, were praising the virtues of violence. Nietzsche's poetical language and mystical insights found echoes in the lyric poetry of Rainer Maria Rilke and other writers of the period; but above all his message of revolt against bourgeois values, his call for a new individualist morality in which each person would carry out the command *Werde, was du bist* (Become what you are) appealed to the younger generation all over

Europe, so that there were few *avant-garde* movements – whether it was that of the Serb students of the Young Bosnia group, planning the murder of the Archduke Franz Ferdinand, or the anarchist intellectuals in Paris asserting the right of the individual to live freely in a free society, or the Italian Futurists with their strident demands for a new form of art which would express a fresh vision of movement, sound and light, or the German youth movements, seeking escape from industrial society in the forests or on the seashore – which did not in one form or another derive from Nietzsche. In his unfinished notes Nietzsche wrote, 'What I am doing is to recount the history of the next two centuries. I am describing what is coming, what can no longer come in any other form: the rise of nihilism.'[32] It is in his writings that we must seek some of the keys to understanding not only the presuppositions of the Europe of 1914, but also what has happened in Europe in the twentieth century.

7

THE COMING OF THE FIRST WORLD WAR

At the end of the First World War the victorious Allies insisted on including in the peace treaty a clause by which Germany accepted responsibility 'for causing all the loss and damage to which the Allied and Associated Governments and their nationals have been subjected as a consequence of the war imposed on them by Germany and her Allies'.[1] This simple explanation that the war was the direct result of German policies and German ambitions has been the centre of controversies about the origins of the war ever since. It has led to a detailed examination of the diplomatic archives to support or refute the view that Germany was responsible and has made the question of German 'war guilt' the main theme of innumerable political and historiographical discussions. The issue was given new life by the Second World War, which led to a fresh study of German foreign policy to examine the question whether there was a continuity between the aims attributed to Germany in the First World War and Hitler's goals in the Second World War.

The discussion in the preceding chapters of the period between 1870 and 1914 will have suggested that any single explanation for the outbreak of war is likely to be too simple. While in the final crisis of July 1914 the German government acted in a way that made war more likely, the enthusiasm with which war was greeted by large sections of opinion in all the belligerent countries and the assumption by each of the governments concerned that their vital national interests were at stake were the result of an accumulation of factors – intellectual, social, economic, and even psychological, as well as political and diplomatic – which all contributed to the situation in 1914 and which can be illustrated in the events of the last weeks before the outbreak of war.

While some people have argued – and it was a popular view in the period between the wars – that the war was the result of the 'old diplomacy' and of an alliance system based on secret agreements, others, and especially some of the leading German historians since the Second World War, have seen in the war a half-conscious or in some cases deliberate attempt by governments

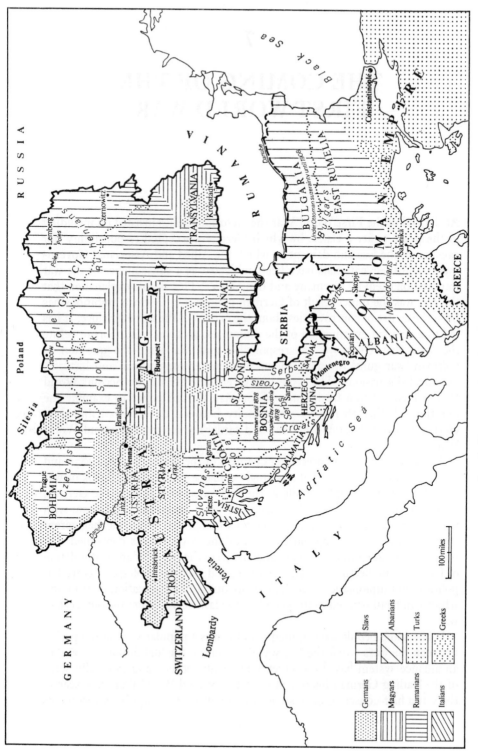

Austria-Hungary and the Ottoman Empire

to distract attention from insoluble domestic problems by means of an active foreign policy and an appeal to national solidarity in time of war. For Marxists the war was inherent in the nature of capitalism; the forces which drove states to expand overseas were in this view leading inevitably to a clash in which the great international cartels would no longer be able to agree on a peaceful division of the under-developed world and would force governments into war for their own economic interests. Other writers have concentrated attention on the implications of strategic decisions and on the influence of for example the naval rivalry between Germany and Britain in creating international tension, or on the effects of the German decision finally taken in 1907 that, in order to defeat the French army before turning to fight the Russians on the Eastern Front, it would be necessary to violate the neutrality of Belgium, and thus run the risk of bringing Britain into the war as a guarantor of Belgian neutrality under the treaty of 1839.

In the years between the first Moroccan crisis of 1905-6 (see pp. 99-100 above) and the final *débâcle* of 1914 there was much talk of war all over Europe, and some talk of ways to avoid it. There were a number of issues over which it was felt war might break out. In 1905 the German Emperor's bid to assert German influence in Morocco had, as we have seen, led to a threat of war between France and Germany and, although this was followed by a period of cooperation between German and French industrialists involved in the exploitation of Moroccan mineral resources, in 1911 the Germans made a second bid to demonstrate their interest. They sent a warship, the *Panther*, to the Moroccan Atlantic port of Agadir, ostensibly to protect German residents against internal disorders in Morocco, but in fact in the hope of blackmailing the French into giving up some of France's colonial possessions elsewhere in Africa in return for the recognition of France's interest in Morocco. Once again there seemed to be a danger of war, and once again the result was to link Britain and France more closely to each other. While for Germany pressure on France might seem a means of extorting colonial concessions and enhancing Germany's status as a world power, for France the underlying quarrel with Germany was over the provinces lost in 1870 and, though the French were not willing to provoke a war over Alsace-Lorraine, it was always taken for granted that if there were to be a war with Germany the recovery of the lost provinces would be the principal war aim.

During these years some efforts were made in France to strengthen the French army and to improve its political position. The Dreyfus case had, it seemed, alienated the army from the republic, while during the ministry of Emile Combes from 1902 to 1905, when the government was primarily engaged in separating the Church from the French state, relations between army and government were worsened still further when it was discovered that the War Minister was using those officers who were freemasons, and thus considered to be reliable republicans, to report on the religious and political beliefs of their military colleagues. Political considerations continued to affect military appointments well into the First World War. Georges Clemenceau, a former radical and passionate Dreyfusard, but an equally passionate French patriot, who was Prime Minister from 1906 to 1909, was exceptional when he showed himself unprejudiced in using talented officers, as in his appointment of Ferdinand Foch – whose brother was a Jesuit and whose own Catholic convictions were well known, so that he had already had his promotion delayed – to the influential post of commandant of the *Ecole de Guerre*. The French army leaders were anxious to meet German military increases by making a larger number of reinforcements available at the outbreak of war, especially as they were committed to a tactical doctrine of immediate all-out offensives in the initial campaign which might be expected to have a high casualty rate. In 1913 a bill was passed in the Chamber, in the face of bitter opposition from Jean Jaurès and the socialists, extending the period of conscription from two years to three.

The strength of France's military position against Germany lay in the fact that she was allied to Russia, and thus Germany was liable to be faced by a war on two fronts if the terms of the alliance came into action, while for Russia the advantage of the alliance seemed to be that Germany might be deterred by fear of France from intervening if Russia became involved in war as a result of her ambitions to extend her influence southwards into the Balkans and to Constantinople. The French alliance had, it was believed, given Russia security in Europe while she was occupied with expansion in the Far East in the period before the Russo-Japanese War. After the disastrous defeat and the bitter experiences of 1905 there were many Russians, and especially the Foreign Minister Alexander Isvolsky, who hoped to restore the prestige of Russia by gains in Europe. Once the Russian interest in the Balkans and the Straits revived, there was a danger of a confrontation with Germany's ally Austria–Hungary, whose own internal difficulties were involving her more and more in what was happening in the Balkans.

In 1908 there was a *coup d'état* in Turkey by a body of officers, popularly known as the Young Turks, who came to power with a programme of modernisation and reorganisation of the decrepit Ottoman Empire. Their attempt to reassert sovereignty over areas which had in practice been long lost to Turkish control – Bulgaria, which had been an independent principality nominally under Turkish suzerainty since 1878, and Bosnia and Herzegovina which had been occupied and administered by Austria–Hungary also since 1878 – at once led to a strong reaction. The Prince of Bulgaria proclaimed himself King on 5 October 1908, and on the next day the Austro-Hungarian government formally annexed the provinces of Bosnia and Herzegovina, a step on which they had decided two months earlier, soon after the *coup* in Constantinople. The Russian Foreign Minister had originally agreed to the Austrian move on the understanding that in return the Austro-Hungarian government would support a Russian demand for the opening of the Bosphorus and Dardanelles to Russian warships (while keeping to the existing arrangement which obliged Turkey to close them to the ships of all other powers) – an old ambition of successive Russian governments. In practice, however, the Austrians acted while Isvolsky was still travelling round Europe trying to persuade the other powers to support him, and he claimed that he had been personally betrayed by the Austrian Foreign Minister Count Aehrenthal.

A bitter diplomatic struggle followed, with the Russians urging the summoning of an international conference of the signatories of the 1878 Berlin treaty which had originally authorised the occupation – but not the annexation – of the two provinces by Austria. The German government came to Austria's support and, after what some people regarded as a veiled threat of war, forced the Russian government to give way and to acquiesce in the Austrian action. The crisis showed how easily the rivalry between Russia and Austria in the Balkans could become of European concern; and it also marked a stage in Germany's commitment to Austria–Hungary, since the Kaiser declared rather tactlessly that he had stood by the Austrian Emperor 'in shining armour' while the German chief of staff Helmuth von Moltke (the nephew and namesake of the architect of the German military victories of 1866 and 1870), assured his Austro-Hungarian colleague General Franz Conrad von Hoetzendorff, 'The moment Russia mobilises, Germany will also mobilise.'[2] This remained an unfulfilled promise on this occasion, for the Russians were not yet sufficiently recovered from their defeat in the Far East to be able to mobilise in support of their ambitions in the Balkans; but there were some people in Austria, and notably Conrad himself, who felt that Austria had been given a blank cheque by Germany for her future policy in the south-east.

The Bosnian crisis of 1908–9 showed how easily the instability of the Balkans could upset the equilibrium of all Europe, but it also showed clearly that the conception of the Austro-Hungarian dynastic multinational state went against the desires and supposed interests of the smaller national groups. The greater part of the population of Bosnia was Slav, and over the border in Serbia the military clique who controlled the government was determined that if there were to be any change in the status of the province, Serbia ought to acquire it. Inside Bosnia a group of young and fanatical revolutionaries in the Young Bosnia movement were increasingly active in planning terrorist activities against the Austrians, and they undoubtedly found considerable support in Serbian government circles. At the same time, the Austro-Hungarian government was in a difficult position. It was faced with growing national self-confidence among many of the subject nationalities; in particular the Czechs were very well organised, and all attempts to reach a compromise between Czechs and Germans in the province of Bohemia repeatedly broke down, as neither group was prepared to accept the domination of the other. The Czech problem, although some influential Czech and Slovak leaders had contacts with the Russian government, remained an internal one without international ramifications. The southern Slav problem on the other hand, posed as it was by the demands of the Croats and Slovenes for autonomy, and of the Serbs for union with Serbia, at once involved the Serbian kingdom, and thus Russia, the self-appointed protector of the Slav population of south-east Europe.

Two courses were open to the Austro-Hungarian government: they might attempt to crush Serbia and to bring all the Serbs under direct Austro-Hungarian control or they might hope, while leaving her independent, to reduce Serbia to the status of a vassal state, as she had been in effect in the 1880s or early 1890s, and thus limit the extent of Russian interference in the Balkans, and counter the attraction of Serbia for the southern Slavs inside the monarchy. There were people in 1908 ready to try the first course, but, as Aehrenthal, the Austro-Hungarian foreign minister, ruefully remarked, 'The idea of absorbing Serbia in the monarchy or partitioning her between Austria–Hungary, Bulgaria and Roumania proved on closer consideration for the moment not practicable.'[3] The second course proved equally difficult to follow. The Habsburg government had failed to arouse any sympathy or support among the population of Bosnia–Herzegovina, while its relations with the Croats and Serbs in Croatia (a province of the Hungarian half of the monarchy) grew worse after a notorious trial at Zagreb in 1909 in which some fifty people were accused of conspiracy on the basis of vague and trumped-up evidence, involving forged documents supplied by the government to the eminent historian Heinrich Friedjung and used by him in an article accusing leading Croats and Serbs of treason. Although the Croats were Catholic and the Serbs Orthodox, a common hatred of Austria–Hungary was drawing them closer together and the extremist movement in Bosnia included young men from both nationalities and religions as well as Muslim descendants of the inhabitants of Bosnia who had been converted under Turkish rule.

The growing demand for national self-determination in the Balkans had two targets, Austria–Hungary and Turkey, for in Macedonia and Thrace many thousands of Serbs and Bulgarians, as well as Greeks, were still living under Turkish rule. While relations between the Bulgarian and Serbian governments were bad, since both claimed that if Macedonia were freed from the Turks it should be theirs on ethnic grounds, they nevertheless succeeded, helped by skilful Russian diplomatic mediation, in forgetting for the moment their differences in the face of common enemies. In March 1912 a treaty, largely aimed at countering alleged Austro-Hungarian designs, was signed between Serbia and Bulgaria, and three months later one between

Bulgaria and Greece, on the basis of a common enmity with Turkey, although both claimed the port of Salonika and parts of the province of Thrace, should the Turks give them up. Taking advantage of Turkey's defeat by Italy and the loss of Libya, Tripoli and the Dodecanese (see p. 90 above), the new Balkan League attacked Turkey and succeeded in driving the Turks out of Salonika, which the Greeks occupied one day before the Bulgarians arrived, and eventually out of Thrace. For the Serbs, who had a notable military success against the Turkish army and who hoped for parts of Albania and Macedonia, the first round was over, and as the Serbian prime minister Pašić said, 'We must now prepare for the second, against Austria.'[4]

By May 1913 with the signature of the Treaty of London between the Balkan League states and the Turks, Turkish rule in Europe was ended except in Constantinople itself and in the eastern part of Thrace. But within a month the victorious allies were quarrelling over the spoils, and the Second Balkan War was fought by Bulgaria against Greece and Serbia, with the Bulgars losing part of Macedonia to Serbia and much of Thrace to Greece, while the Roumanians, who had remained neutral in the First Balkan War because they had no direct demands on Turkey, took the opportunity to seize from Bulgaria the disputed border province of the Dobrudja.

The implications of the Balkan Wars were considerable. These small states showed themselves unwilling to fit into the patterns devised for them by the great powers, for the rivalry between Bulgaria and Serbia made nonsense of the Russian aim to weld them into a block against Austrian penetration of the Balkans. Their military capacity was greater than had been supposed – and journalists, as well as the Italian Futurist chief Marinetti, had hurried to the siege of Adrianople to obtain their first sight of twentieth-century European warfare, while military experts observed the effects of heavy artillery. But above all the success of the Balkan states, and even their own internecine rivalry, showed that the day of the multinational empires was finally passing. Ottoman rule in south-east Europe was at an end. How long could that of Austria–Hungary survive? Although the Austrians succeeded in limiting some of the Serbian gains and persuaded the other powers to agree to establish an independent Albania to limit Serbian expansion southwards, it was clear that a crisis between the Habsburg government and the southern Slavs could not long be delayed. Such a crisis would not only involve the southern Slavs but also their protector, Russia. As the German Chief of Staff wrote to the Austrian General Conrad in February 1913, 'A European war must come sooner or later in which ultimately the struggle will be one between Germany and Slavism . . . but the aggression must come from the Slavs.'[5]

There had been talk of war between France and Germany in 1905 and 1911 and even, unrealistically but symptomatically, in 1908 when the French arrested some German deserters from the French Foreign Legion who had taken refuge in the German consulate at Casablanca. There had been talk of war between Germany's ally Austria–Hungary and France's ally Russia in 1908, while by 1913 the prediction 'There'll be trouble in the Balkans in the Spring' had become a common joke in the London music halls. In addition to these two possibilities of war, between France and Germany and between Austria–Hungary and Russia, there was also a third, that between England and Germany as a result of their naval rivalry, a threat which some observers, including the French socialist leader Jean Jaurès, regarded as the gravest of them all.

The creation of the German navy was, as shown in chapter 4, an aspect both of Germany's vaguely formulated desire to be a 'world power' and of the internal situation in the German Empire. There were powerful economic pressure groups which stood to gain from naval expansion and there were many people who saw in the creation of an overseas fleet and a German colonial empire a new mission for Germany which would give a new purpose to the German state and to German society now that German unification had been achieved and now that Germany was among the most powerful military and industrial countries in the world. The creation of a large ocean-going fleet was bound to arouse the suspicions of Britain; and Admiral Tirpitz in his naval planning as chief of the German Admiralty always had Britain in mind. He had both to ensure enough political support for his plans to enable the naval programme to be carried out and continued over a long period of years without interference from the Reichstag, and also to convince Britain that her world predominance would be in danger unless she was prepared to make some sort of political agreement with Germany. The exact aims of German policy were never precisely formulated, and this was one of the most dangerous features of the situation – but there were hopes that Britain might agree to remain neutral in a European war and that she might be willing to give Germany some colonial territory. (Indeed in 1913 there were serious negotiations about the possibility of dividing the Portuguese colonies between Britain and Germany.)

The British government however was clear that, anxious though they were for an agreement which would enable them to cut the growing heavy expenditure on naval building, a large German navy would be a constant threat to Britain's freedom of action and even a danger to Britain's existence. As Sir Edward Grey wrote to King Edward VII in 1908, 'We have to take into account not only the German navy but also . . . the German army . . . There is no corresponding risk of this kind to Germany, for however superior our fleet was, no naval victory in the world could bring us closer to Berlin.'[6] And Winston Churchill, who had originally been critical of British naval building because of the money it took away from social welfare schemes, on becoming First Lord of the Admiralty in 1911 became an ardent advocate of a strong fleet. In March 1913 he said, 'I must explicitly repudiate the suggestion that Great Britain can ever allow another naval power to approach her so nearly as to deflect or to restrict her political action by purely naval pressure. Such a situation would unquestionably lead to war.'[7]

From 1906 onwards, when the British started to build the *Dreadnought*, a battleship with more and larger guns and greater speed than any so far constructed, and when the Germans followed with an accelerated programme of new large ships, it was clear that each country was arming with only the other in mind. While German army officers were talking about the coming inevitable conflict between Germans and Slavs, German naval officers were looking to the day when their strength would be matched against Britain in a final bid for world power. On the British side, and among many of the German civilian leaders, there was a belief that the conflict might still be avoided. Even if Sir John Fisher, the truculent First Sea Lord (the chief naval representative on the Board of Admiralty presided over by the civilian First Lord of the Admiralty), talked at moments of striking at the German fleet before it was completed – and rumours that '*Der Fischer kommt*' ('Fisher is coming') kept children in the German naval base at Kiel away from school on one day in 1907 – there were some people in the British foreign office for whom Russia remained a potential enemy, in spite of the Anglo-Russian agreement of 1907 (see p. 100 above), and who saw in Russia's rapid recovery from the collapse of 1904–5 a potential threat to the balance of power as great as that of Germany. In Persia and in the Far East Russia still seemed a rival to Britain, and her potential military strength was revealed by the fact that in December 1913 the Russian government planned to increase the army by 500,000 men – more than the total peace-time size of the Austro-Hungarian army. For all the talk of the danger of war with Germany few people in the ruling circles of Britain saw it as inevitable, but the naval armaments race was creating an atmosphere in which, should there be a threat of a European war arising from other causes, it might be increasingly difficult for Britain to keep out.

The Anglo-German naval rivalry had also had the effect of encouraging practical cooperation between Britain and France. The first Moroccan crisis in 1905–6 had given rise to the first tentative staff talks between the two countries, and in 1912 after the second Moroccan crisis an informal agreement was reached by which the French fleet would be concentrated in the Mediterranean to offset the Austro-Hungarian and Italian navies, while the British would be responsible for preventing the Germans from attacking the north coast of France. Although this agreement was hedged about with all sorts of provisos, since Grey could hardly commit the British government to future action without the consent of parliament and of his own Liberal Party, the 1912 agreement served as a basis for British naval planning, and Grey himself at least seems to have regarded it as a binding moral commitment to France; and, when war did break out, he was to be bitterly criticised for it by radicals within his own party. 'By some hidden contract,' the influential liberal newspaper *The Manchester Guardian* wrote, 'England has been technically committed behind her back to the ruinous madness of a share in the violent gamble of a war between two militarist leagues on the continent.'[8]

This view that the existence of the European alliance system had caused the war became a popular one after 1918, when liberals all over Europe hoped that the principles advocated by President Wilson would be a basis for a new international order and that the foundation of the League of Nations would inaugurate a period of open diplomacy and democratic control of foreign policy, though it was never quite clear what this would mean in practice. In fact, however, the alliance system before 1914 worked when the alliances corresponded to strategic and political needs, and failed to influence policy when these common interests were not present. Thus the Franco-Russian alliance made obvious sense as long as both countries had reason to fear Germany; but it had become clear that it would not work outside Europe; Russia had shown no interest in France's African interests at the time of the Fashoda crisis, and during the war in the Far East France had worked to reconcile her ally Russia and her new friend England, and did not commit herself wholeheartedly to support of Russia. The German–Austrian alliance made sense as long as the German government believed that Austria–Hungary must be preserved in order to maintain the balance of military and political power in central and eastern Europe; and, indeed, as the Germans began to be haunted by the fear of encirclement, especially after the Anglo-Russian agreement of 1907, Austria–Hungary appeared to be the Germans' only reliable friend, who must be supported at all costs. For the Austro-Hungarian government, however sensitive it was to what sometimes seemed the heavy-handed and patronising attitude of the Germans towards them, German support was the one means by which they might hope to deal with the southern Slav problem without Russian interference.

The Anglo-French agreement of 1904 had originally and deliberately not been more than the settlement of outstanding disputes between the two countries, but each crisis provoked by Germany's growing strength and increasing diplomatic, military and naval activity had forced Britain and France into closer cooperation, however much, for internal political reasons the British government asserted that it was not in any way bound to come to the assistance of France. Grey had seen as early as 1906 that mutual reliance as a result of informal contacts could be morally as binding as a formal treaty of alliance: 'If there is war between France and Germany, it will be very difficult for us to keep out of it. The *Entente* and still more the constant and emphatic demonstrations of affection (official, naval, political, commercial, municipal and in the Press) have created in France a belief that we shall support them in war.'[9] Relations between Britain and Russia, on the other hand, never became as close, and it was only in June 1914 that there were tentative and inconclusive contacts between the British and Russian naval chiefs – though even these were sufficient, when reported to the Germans, to increase German fears of encirclement and to convince some of the German leaders that they must act quickly to break out of the iron ring which they believed to be closing around them.

On the other hand the existence of a formal alliance was not sufficient to produce joint action where there seemed in any given situation to be few common interests between the powers concerned. Although Italy renewed the Triple Alliance with Germany and Austria–Hungary in 1912, she had improved her relations with France, and had been willing to work with Russia in order to promote her own ambitions in the Balkans – where the Albanian coast was of obvious strategic interest to her. In 1909 the Tsar had paid a visit to the King of Italy and had ostentatiously taken an inconvenient and roundabout route so as to avoid crossing Austro-Hungarian territory. The Italian nationalists were eager to complete the unification of Italy by bringing in the inhabitants of the 'unredeemed' areas (*Italia Irredenta*) of the Trentino and Trieste, where Italians were still living under Austrian rule, while the existence of a small Italian minority along the Dalmatian coast also turned Italian attention to the eastern shore of the Adriatic. The Austrian government had failed to win the support of more than a few of the Italian minority. It was characteristic of the Austrian dilemma that, even when they were willing to make concessions to the nationalities, it proved impossible in practice to do so: there had long been talk of founding an Italian university in Austria, but when it came to choosing a site, it proved impossible to find one. The obvious place was Trieste, but this would at once become the centre of Italian nationalist and irredentist feeling, while the Italian law faculty at Innsbruck had had to be closed after fights between Italians and Germans. The creation of a new university was bound to lead other nationalities to demand a similar one for themselves and an Italian university, wherever it was, would at once lead the Slovenes to call for a Slovene one at Ljubljana. In spite of the alliance Italian–Austrian relations could never be very cordial, and were always liable to be upset by for example what seemed to be callous Austrian press comment on the catastrophic earthquake in the Messina area in 1909 ('A favourable factor in our calculations', one Austrian journal described it). It was therefore not surprising that Italy refused to join her allies at the outbreak of war and shortly afterwards proclaimed that she was following a policy of '*sacro egoismo*'.

The same sort of situation made nonsense of Roumania's alliance with Germany and Austria–Hungary. Although the King was a member of the House of Hohenzollern and had much sympathy with his kinsman the German Emperor, the liberal politicians looked to France for their cultural and political ideas, and they were only too ready to remind the Roumanian people that some three million Roumanians were living under Hungarian rule over the mountains, in the province of Transylvania and elsewhere in the Hungarian kingdom. The Austro-Hungarian minister in Bucharest repeatedly reminded his government of the necessity for the Hungarians to make some sort of gesture to the Roumanian population of Hungary if the alliance were to survive, but his pleas were not listened to by a Hungarian regime committed to a policy of ruthless Magyarisation, which gave the subject peoples equal rights only if they gave up their own national identity, learnt the Magyar language and assimilated totally into the Hungarian national group.

For all the talk of war and in some quarters at least a belief that it was not only inevitable but also desirable, the international crises before July 1914 had in fact not led to violent conflict. What were the differences in the situation in July 1914 which this time brought about a war which many people had been expecting for the past nine years? The Moroccan crises had involved France and Germany but Russia had no interest in France's African ambitions and no objection to Germany developing an African empire on her own. The Bosnian crisis of 1908 had been resolved because the Russians knew that they were not yet militarily strong enough to stand up to an insistent German demand that they should drop their opposition to the Austro-Hungarian annexation of the provinces of Bosnia and Herzegovina. In the Balkan Wars the interests of the small states had sometimes been in conflict with those of the great powers, and none of the powers was prepared to go to war for the selfish interests of any one Balkan state as against its neighbours. It was this situation which had given Sir Edward Grey the opportunity to call a conference of ambassadors in London which had been successful in preventing the spread of the Balkan Wars and in limiting the results of Austria's attempts to prevent Serbia from gaining too much territory. It was a hope that a similar conference might find a way out of the Austro-Serbian conflict in July 1914 which underlay Grey's diplomacy in the final crisis; and it was the refusal of the other powers, especially Germany and Austria, to accept a genuine mediation which made Grey's efforts fail.

The July crisis of 1914 on the other hand not only rapidly involved all the potential sources of conflict among the great powers – Austro-Russian rivalry in the Balkans, Franco-German mutual resentment and distrust, the Anglo-German naval rivalry – but it came at a moment which for a number of reasons seemed, especially to the Germans, one at which the chances of success were greatest. In fact however the crisis developed slowly and it was not until 23 July that it started to escalate into a major European war. On 28 June 1914 the Archduke Franz Ferdinand, heir to the throne of Austria–Hungary, was assassinated in Sarajevo, the capital of Bosnia, where he had gone for army manoeuvres, by a group of young terrorists who had shortly before crossed over the border from Serbia with the connivance of some Serbian officials. The assassination was incidentally successful almost by accident: a first attempt in the morning had failed, though wounding one of the Archduke's aides, and it was only because the Archduke wanted to visit him in hospital, and stopped his car for a moment to change the route, that Gavrilo Princip, one of the conspirators, who by then believed that the whole enterprise had failed, suddenly found himself with the opportunity, as the car happened to draw up alongside him, to carry out his mission; and he shot both the Archduke and his wife.

The assassination of royal personages had not been uncommon during the previous years: the Empress of Austria had been murdered in 1898, the King of Italy in 1900 and the King of Portugal in 1908, to say nothing of President McKinley, who was assassinated in 1901; and once the immediate shock was over, most Europeans went off on their summer holiday unaware of the crisis that was impending. In France the papers were devoting most of their attention to the trial of Madame Caillaux, the wife of a prominent politician and former Prime Minister, who had shot a leading newspaper editor because of what he had been printing about her husband. And in Britain, as we shall see, the growing threat of civil war in Ireland was the main preoccupation of the public and the press. The diplomats were concerned about the arrangements for the establishment of the new state of Albania and the installation of its new ruler, a minor German prince. Actually, however, the Austro-Hungarian government had soon decided that the assassination, and the apparent complicity of the Serbian authorities, showed the necessity for reducing Serbia to the status of an Austrian satellite. In the deliberations which followed the assassination Stephen Tisza, the Hungarian Prime Minister, a Calvinist with a strong sense of moral responsibility for his decisions, made two conditions before agreeing to a tough line against Serbia: first that the monarchy should not actually take over any more Slav inhabitants, and second that a promise of German support must be secured before any action was taken.

When on 5 July the Germans received the Austrian request for backing, they decided that they must support Austria and that here was an opportunity for strengthening the international and domestic position of their only reliable ally, at a time when they were increasingly aware of their own international isolation. Once this decision had been taken, the German government – or at least the Kaiser, Jagow, the State Secretary in the Foreign Ministry, and Moltke, the Chief of Staff – were repeatedly urging Austria to act speedily and were impatient at the delay in opening the next stage of the crisis. After overcoming further hesitations on the part of the Hungarian Prime Minister, the Austro-Hungarian government decided on 14 July to send an ultimatum to Serbia so harsh that acceptance of its terms would achieve the goal of reducing Serbia to a client state; and, if it were rejected, then the Austrians would have the excuse to crush Serbia by military action. The text of the ultimatum was finally agreed on 19 July, and it was delivered on 23 July: the Serbian government was told to forbid activities against Austria on Serbian territory, to ban one of the main Serb nationalist organisations, *Narodna Odbrana*, and – a direct threat to Serbia's independence – to allow Austrian officials to take part in the enquiry into the assassination of the Archduke. The delay between Franz Ferdinand's murder and the despatch of the ultimatum not only served to lull suspicions about the forthcoming action, but also gave time to bring in the harvest before mobilisation.

Thus until 23 July, although rumours had spread that Austria's terms to Serbia were going to be tough, and although the German ambassador in London had hinted to Grey on his return from Berlin on 6 July that there might be serious trouble coming, there were few signs that there was about to be a major crisis which would not be limited to Austria and Serbia alone. It was the publication of the ultimatum that made everyone realise the gravity of the situation. Austria–Hungary had decided that the assassination gave her the best opportunity to deal with the Serbian question, and rightly or wrongly felt that a reduction of Serbian influence was a question of life or death for the monarchy if it was to deal with the problem of the nationalities at all. The German government had decided that Germany had a vital interest in strengthening Austria–Hungary by backing her in a radical and possibly violent solution of the southern Slav question. Each hoped that the promise of German support would have the effect, as it had in the Bosnian crisis of 1908–9, of frightening the Russians and allowing Austria–Hungary to deal with the Serbs on her own. At the same time, assuming, as most of the German leaders did, that a European war was bound to come sooner or later, then even if the present conflict were not localised, it seemed that this was as good a moment for running the risk of war as any. By 1916 the military strength of Russia would be still greater, and the Anglo-Russian naval conversations might have led to a close cooperation between the two fleets; the reorganisation of the French army as a result of the extension of the period of conscription from two to three years was not yet complete; and with England faced with a major crisis in Ireland, it seemed to the Germans unlikely that she would be inclined to intervene in a European war.

When on 24 July the Russian Foreign Minister Sazonov learnt the terms of the Austro-Hungarian ultimatum, he exclaimed, '*C'est la guerre euro-péenne.*'[10] And on the next day the Tsar received a formal appeal for help from the Serbs. It so happened that the Russian government had just received an official visit, planned some time before, from the French President Raymond Poincaré and the Prime Minister René Viviani, who had left St Petersburg to return to Paris by sea on 23 July. (They did not reach home until 30 July, and during these days, when radio communication with ships at sea was still unreliable, the French government was left without leadership.) We do not know exactly what had passed at these meetings, but the visit certainly looked like a vote of confidence in the solidarity of the Franco-Russian alliance, and it must have been a potent factor in the minds of the Russian leaders when responding to the Serbs' appeal on 25 July which, as the Prince Regent of Serbia wrote to the Tsar, 'we confidently hope will find an echo in your generous Slav heart'.[11] The Serbs might have felt some doubt as to what the Russian reply would be, for both in 1909 after the annexation of Bosnia and in 1913 after the Balkan Wars Russia had under pressure from Germany acquiesced in Austrian policy, and had obliged the Serbs to give up their hopes of Bosnia and then to abandon their intentions of winning a port on the Adriatic. But in fact it was just these two previous episodes which made the Russians determined to act now; and even before the Serbs' formal appeal for help, a decision to mobilise part of the Russian army had been taken, though not yet put into effect. While the sentimental appeal to Slav solidarity was not without effect on some groups and individuals in Russia, and while the German attempt in the previous year to establish a permanent military mission at Constantinople had renewed suspicions of German intentions in south-east Europe, there were other influential leaders who would have preferred an alignment with imperial Germany rather than with republican France. Nevertheless in the circumstances of July 1914, although Sazonov and the Tsar hoped that it might be possible either to prevent Austria from crushing Serbia by a threat of force, or to persuade Germany to restrain her ally and produce some acceptable compromise, they were equally prepared if necessary to go to war, since it was felt that a failure to back Serbia this time would mean the abandonment of Russia's claim to influence in the Balkans and the acceptance of German preponderance in the area, with Russia's position as a great power, laboriously regained over the years since 1905, in danger of being lost for many years to come. It was with these considerations in mind that the Tsar ordered mobilisation. Originally he and his civilian advisers had hoped to mobilise on the Austro-Hungarian frontier alone, in an attempt to show that they had no quarrel with Germany, but the military leaders explained that this was not possible, since the mobilisation had long been planned to take place along the whole frontier of Russia and could not on technical grounds be changed.

It has sometimes been argued that the Russian decision to mobilise, finally carried out on 30 July, was the crucial moment that led to general war, and that if it had been delayed further (it had already been postponed by twenty-four hours) it might have been possible to reach a diplomatic solution. This is unlikely. While the Serbs had shown themselves willing to discuss the terms of the ultimatum and to agree to many of them, they were not prepared to give the total uncritical acceptance within forty-eight hours which the Austrians demanded, although they knew that their immediate military prospects were bleak, exhausted as the small country was after the efforts of the two Balkan Wars. Even without the assurance of Russian help they were going to have to fight; the Austrians had mobilised against them and were actually at war by the time the Russians carried out their mobilisation, and it looks as if, sure of German backing, the Austrians were determined on a violent solution, whatever the Russians did.

Sir Edward Grey had tried hard to find a diplomatic solution which would localise the war, even if localisation in fact meant leaving the Austrians a free hand to deal with Serbia as they pleased. But his well-meaning attempts broke down because of the determination of Austria–Hungary and Germany to pursue the course on which they had decided and to allow no discussion of the terms to be imposed on Serbia. The main result of Grey's diplomacy was to leave Europe uncertain what Britain's intentions were, since as long as there seemed to be a remote chance of a diplomatic solution, he was reluctant to give any positive answer in reply to the increasingly insistent requests from France and Russia for British support, for fear of encouraging them to show themselves intransigent in negotiation. And, indeed, it is unlikely that he could have carried his own government colleagues with him if he had given an unequivocal promise to France and Russia in the early stages of the crisis. He has often been criticised for his hesitation and for not making Britain's position clearer, but even if he had been in a position to do so, it is uncertain whether it would have made much difference. Although Bethmann-Hollweg, the German Chancellor, had hoped that there might be a way of keeping Britain out of a European war, the military and naval leaders had always assumed that she might come in, and had laid their plans accordingly. The one attempt which the Germans made late on 29 July to secure British neutrality in the event, by then increasingly likely, of a war between Germany and France, by promising to make no territorial demands on France after the war, was greeted by a senior Foreign Office official with the words 'The only comment that can be made on these astounding proposals is that they reflect discredit on the statesman who makes them.'[12]

Once the Russians had mobilised on 31 July, the military machine took over from the diplomats. Just as the Russian mobilisation plans required a simultaneous mobilisation along both the Austro-Hungarian and German frontiers, so the German plan drawn up in its final form in 1907 by Count Schlieffen, the then Chief of Staff, required that Germany must attack France in order to knock out the French army before turning to face Russia. It was, that is to say, impossible from a military point of view, whatever the diplomatic situation, for Germany to fight Russia without simultaneously going to war with France. When, in a moment of clarity and anxiety, the Kaiser asked if it would not be possible to act against Russia alone, he was told by his military advisers that it was out of the question to undo the plans elaborated over many years, and that instead of an army ready for war he would have a mass of armed men with no food. Bethmann-Hollweg had long been anxious that the first move in a war should come from the Russians, both because of the possible effect this might have on Britain's attitude, and still more because the German public, including the Social Democrats, would be strongly behind a war in which Tsarist Russia could be represented as the aggressor. Once Russia had mobilised however, the German government was free to escalate the crisis further. The first stage of mobilisation (the state of 'imminent danger of war') was ordered as soon as the reports of Russia's mobilisation were received on 31 July and later that day Bethmann telegraphed an ultimatum to St Petersburg and Paris calling on Russia to suspend all warlike measures within twelve hours and on France to promise within eighteen hours to remain neutral and to hand over her fortresses of Toul and Verdun as a guarantee. On the next day Germany was at war with Russia and French general mobilisation had been ordered. On 2 August the Germans demanded from the Belgians the right to send troops through the country as part of the campaign against France. The Belgians refused, and the Germans invaded the country all the same. By 3 August the war in the West had begun.

The attitude of England had been uncertain up to the last minute. Grey had made genuine efforts to mediate, but had met with no response, especially from the Germans. While he and Asquith, the Prime Minister, were convinced that Britain could not remain neutral, other members of the government, led by Lloyd George, the Chancellor of the Exchequer, as well as influential figures in the business world such as Lord Rothschild, were convinced that for Britain to be involved in a continental war would be contrary both to the traditions of British liberalism and to Britain's worldwide financial and commercial interests. It was only over the weekend of 1-3 August that in Lloyd George's words, and not without effect on his own position, 'the war had leapt into popularity between Saturday and Monday',[13] with great demonstrations in London in favour of war. In fact the range of choices open to the British government had narrowed with each day of the crisis and they were reacting to events rather than influencing them. By 3 August Lloyd George and all but a few less influential members of the government had accepted that Britain would have to join France and Russia. The feeling of obligation to France, anxiety about the safety of the English Channel and the fear that, if Germany were victorious while Britain stayed out, Britain would sooner or later have to confront alone a vastly strengthened Germany, all seemed to leave Britain with no choice. The decision to intervene was taken even before the German refusal to respect Belgian neutrality and Belgium's appeal to Britain under the terms of the treaty of 1839, which guaranteed Belgian neutrality, and the validity of which had been reasserted by the Gladstone government at the time of the Franco-Prussian War of 1870; but it was the invasion of Belgium which provided the legal basis for

British intervention. On 3 August the British despatched an ultimatum to Germany calling for the evacuation of Belgium, and when this expired without reply on 4 August, Britain and Germany were at war.

As the crisis developed, opposition to the idea of war dwindled, and war was accepted by the citizens of each country not only as a necessity forced on them against their will, but also as a moment of emotional release and of warm-hearted national solidarity. This was all the more surprising because all over Europe the socialist parties had for years been asserting their opposition to war and their determination to prevent it, while in liberal circles it was widely believed that the economic and commercial links between the nations of Europe were now so close that it was inconceivable that they should be broken by a war which, it was thought, would be fatal to the whole structure of international trade and credit. At the same time it was hoped that governments, realising where their own interests lay, would be ready to submit their disputes to arbitration.

In 1907 there had been an international congress at The Hague to discuss disarmament and arbitration, and although it achieved very little except to propose the establishment of an international court (finally set up in 1920), it had demonstrated that governments, however cynically, must act as if they took these possibilities seriously. Thus, while on the one hand fears of war had been growing, on the other hand reaction against war and the belief that it was out of the question had also been spreading. This current of opinion was summed up in 1911 by the Belgian socialist leader, Emile Vandervelde, as follows: 'There are in Europe at present too many pacifist forces, starting with the Jewish capitalists who give financial support to many governments, through to the socialists who are firmly resolved to prevent mobilisation of the nations and in the event of defeat to spring at the throats of their rulers.'[14]

The belief that the economic fabric of international life was too closely knit to allow war to break out found expression in the final crisis of July 1914. In Britain Lloyd George, as Chancellor of the Exchequer responsible for economic policy, was well aware of anti-war opinion in the City of London, and this contributed to his initial opposition to British intervention. As late as 31 July Grey told the French Ambassador, who was pressing for a clear statement of British intentions, 'The commercial and financial situation was extremely serious, there was danger of a complete collapse that would involve us and everyone in ruin; and it was possible that our standing aside might be the only means of preventing a complete collapse of European credit in which we should be involved.'[15] In Germany while many industrialists had a direct interest in naval construction and in the arms industry, and were dreaming of an expanded zone of German economic predominance in Europe and an expanded colonial empire overseas, even if this involved a risk of war, others felt that their own economic interests were bound up with the maintenance of peaceful international trade, and the chairman of the Hamburg-America steamship line, Albert Ballin, a personal friend of the Kaiser, was particularly active in the final crisis in trying to find a peaceful way out in conjunction with the British financier Sir Ernest Cassel.

Both in France and in Germany the threat of socialist opposition to the war had been taken seriously. The French trade union movement, the *Confédération Générale du Travail*, had often reiterated its intention of staging a general strike in the event of war, and this policy had been accepted by Jean Jaurès, the leader of the Socialist Party, at the Socialist party congress early in July. Although the police reports on the socialist attitude suggested that their views were not to be taken too seriously – and indeed there were no practical preparations by the unions for the general strike against war – the Ministry of the Interior had prepared a list (the notorious *Carnet B*) of militant union leaders who were to be immediately arrested in the event of mobilisation. In Germany while the Social Democrats had rejected the idea of the general strike, they were committed by many statements and congress resolutions to opposing war by all means in their power, and they had repeatedly asserted their solidarity with the French working class and their determination to prevent a war between France and Germany. On the other hand a war against Russia was something which the German Social Democrats from the time of Marx onwards had always been prepared to envisage. For them tsarist rule was the epitome of tyranny; and, whatever the faults of the German state, its rule was preferable to that of the Russians, while the German socialists felt an invasion of Germany by the Cossack hordes would put an end to the effective organisation which the socialists had laboriously built up over the previous twenty-five years. They remained, in effect, governed by the principle which their revered leader August Bebel had laid down in 1891: 'The soil of Germany, the German fatherland, belongs to us the masses as much and more than to the others. If Russia, the champion of terror and barbarism were to attack Germany to break and destroy it . . . we are as much concerned as those who stand at the head of Germany.'[16] For this reason Bethmann-Hollweg, the Imperial Chancellor, had realised that it was most important to give the impression that the war was a result of Russian aggression and to play down the fact that at the same time Germany was attacking France and violating Belgian neutrality.

When the crisis started, the International Socialist Bureau, the executive organ of the Socialist International, was busy preparing for the international socialist congress due to be held in Vienna in September, and an emergency meeting of the socialist leaders was summoned at Brussels on 29 July. That they still did not wholly realise the gravity of the situation is shown by the fact that, while they recognised that with war between Austria–Hungary and Serbia already declared on the previous day it would not be possible to hold their congress in Vienna, they were nevertheless going ahead with plans for it to meet in Paris early in August. Although Victor Adler, the Austrian socialist leader, gave the impression of a sick and broken man when, true to a principle he had enunciated some years earlier that it was better to be wrong with the working-class masses than right against them, he had admitted that his party was powerless to influence events, and that the workers in Vienna were enthusiastically anti-Serbian, there was still a hope that somehow things would turn out all right and that, as Jaurès put it, '*Les choses ne peuvent ne pas s'arranger*'[17] (It's impossible that things should not turn out all right). The socialist leaders parted after expressions of solidarity and of their intention to continue to work for peace, but with no practical plan of action, while Jaurès in particular had made it quite clear that he in no way held the French government responsible for the worsening situation.

In both France and Germany the critical test of the socialists' attitude was their action in parliament. Would they refuse to vote for the emergency credits required for the war, as Bebel and Liebknecht had done in 1870, or would they respond to the mood of patriotic solidarity and show their support for the war by voting the credits? In France there was little doubt: Jaurès had already shown his support for the government's general position, though this did not save him from being assassinated immediately after his return from Brussels by a young nationalist fanatic who believed him to be selling out to the Germans. The Prime Minister spoke at Jaurès' funeral and the President of the Republic sent warm condolences to his widow, and it was in this mood of national reconciliation that the war began. The syndicalists had obeyed their mobilisation orders without a murmur, and the government had already felt confident enough on 30 July to revoke the orders to arrest the militants listed on *Carnet B*. Within a month of the outbreak of war two socialists, including the Marxist leader Jules Guesde, had joined a government of 'sacred union' (*Union Sacrée*), pledged to defend the fatherland against the invaders, and the government had the support of the old revolutionary and protagonist of the general strike against war, Edouard Vaillant.

The German parliamentary party had hesitated a little longer and, uncertain what the attitude of the authorities was going to be towards them, had taken the precaution of sending two of the senior members of the executive to Zurich with the party funds, in case they were going to be prevented from operating on German soil as in Bismarck's day. However, the authorities were anxious for socialist support and were soon convinced that they had nothing to fear. The parliamentary group, after hours of agonised debate and after sending an emissary to Paris to see if there was any last minute chance of common action with the French, decided that they would support the government; and on 4 August their votes went unanimously in support of the war credits, with even those members such as Hugo Haase, the leader of the parliamentary party, who had opposed the decision voting with his majority in order to preserve party unity.

The action of the French and German socialists in giving their support to the war was only one example of the almost unanimous solidarity shown by the citizens of all the belligerent countries, and it was only exceptional because of the sincerity and frequency of their earlier expressions of their devotion to the cause of international proletarian solidarity. For the French the defence of the soil of France and the institutions of the republic against the German invaders was in the tradition of the Revolution and of the republican attitude in 1870-1, while the belief that the French state and the French constitution, for all their shortcomings, were worth preserving had already been demonstrated by Jaurès and many other socialists at the time of the Dreyfus affair. Equally for the German Social Democrats the war was primarily one to defend Germany against the reactionary armies of Russian autocracy, and this too was in keeping with their pronouncements over many years. A few British voices were raised on the Left, in the Labour Party and among radical liberals, criticising the decision to go to war, and two members of the government resigned, but they represented only a small minority. In Russia the social democratic members of the Duma abstained from voting for the war credits, and five Bolshevik members were arrested for calling the tsarist government the real enemy, but some of the most celebrated political exiles, including the anarchist Kropotkin and the socialist theorist Plekhanov, expressed their support for the British and French, and consequently for the Russian cause. Lenin, who was in Austria when war broke out and who was able with the help of the Austrian Social Democratic Party to make his way to Switzerland, where he remained till 1917, was almost alone in denouncing both the war and the bankruptcy of the Second International and in calling for an immediate revolution and for the formation of a new socialist international organisation to further this purpose.

In Germany the Social Democrats and the liberals had united behind the Kaiser in support of the *Burgfrieden*, the solemn civil truce between the parties in time of national peril. In France there was a brief moment of solidarity and respite from parliamentary quarrels behind the idea of the *Union Sacrée*. In Britain, although the Conservative Party remained officially in opposition and did not join a coalition with the Liberals till May 1915, the outbreak of war led to a temporary cessation of political controversy. As Asquith, the Prime Minister, put it at the height of the July crisis, 'It is the most dangerous situation of the last fifty years. It may incidentally have the effect of throwing into the background the lurid pictures of civil war in Ulster.'[18] Most of the belligerent countries faced long-term political problems from which the war seemed to provide a temporary relief. But it was in Britain that on the eve of the war the situation seemed most acute. The Liberal Party, dependent since 1910 for their parliamentary majority on the support of the Irish Nationalist Party, had finally been obliged to act on the Irish question, and to carry out the pledge to grant Home Rule to Ireland which had been an important item in the party programme since Gladstone's day. However, the proposed establishment of a parliament in Dublin with wide powers of self-government for the whole of Ireland now met with violent opposition from the northern province of Ulster, which had grown in economic strength and self-confidence with the development of the ship-building and other industry in Belfast and had also grown in political awareness since Gladstone's day.

The majority of the inhabitants of Ulster were Protestant Presbyterians and bitterly resented the prospect of being subject to rule from Dublin, since the vast majority in the other provinces were Catholics and any all-Irish parliament was certain to be overwhelmingly Catholic in membership. With the direct encouragement of the Conservative Party (the official title of which was the Conservative and Unionist Party since Joseph Chamberlain had split the Liberal Party over Gladstone's home-rule proposals in 1886 and later led his followers into the Conservative Party), the Ulster Unionists prepared to defend themselves against separation from Britain under the slogan launched by Lord Randolph Churchill in the 1880s, 'Ulster will fight and Ulster will be right.' They were busily arming themselves, while the Nationalists in the South of Ireland were equally active in preparing for what looked increasingly like an impending civil war; and the British government had been forced to face the unpleasant fact that many of the officers in the British garrison in Ireland would refuse to carry out orders to use force against the Protestant Ulstermen to make them accept the new constitutional proposals. The crisis in Ireland, though long developing, had come to a head simultaneously with the international crisis; and when the London *Times* headed a leading article on 3 July 'Efforts for Peace', it was to Ireland that it was referring. A conference of the leaders of all the parties called by the King had broken down on 24 July; and two days later there was shooting in Dublin, after a load of arms was seized as it was landed. The crisis was unsolved when overtaken by the greater European drama; and it was with some relief that all the political parties in Britain agreed to drop the issue for the duration of the war. It was not until Easter 1916 and a brief unsuccessful nationalist rising in Dublin that the question became a critical one again.

Whereas the British government had not entered the war in order to escape from the insoluble national and religious feuds which it faced in Northern Ireland, the Austro-Hungarian government had provoked war with Serbia and run the risk of a European war because it believed that a blow against the southern Slavs might enable it to cope with their infinitely more numerous and complicated national problems. The surprising thing is that for a moment at the outbreak of war it looked as though the gamble might succeed. The army was one of the genuinely multinational institutions of the monarchy (the murdered Archduke Franz Ferdinand, who had been Inspector General of the army and had the reputation of being a bad linguist, spoke seven out of the monarchy's ten languages).[19] The mobilisation had taken place without serious incidents, and there still seemed to be reserves of loyalty to the aged Emperor Franz Joseph, and even, especially in Vienna, positive enthusiasm for the war. At the same time the governments both of Austria and Hungary were taking no chances and preparing to act against subversion and unrest: large areas of country near the battle zones were placed under direct military rule; many civil rights, including trial by jury, were suspended. In Austria a special 'war supervisory office' was given wide powers to override the civilian authorities, while in Hungary, although the supremacy of parliament and of the civil power were maintained, the civilian government was just as tough and ruthless in dealing with the nationalities as any military command could be. While a few of the most radical leaders of the subject nations went abroad to work for Austria's defeat – notably Thomas Masaryk, the leader of the small group of Czechs and Slovaks who had come to believe in the necessity of total independence for a new Czechoslovak state, and the Croats Trumbič and Supilo, who were working for the creation of a new southern Slav kingdom of Serbs, Croats and Slovenes – the majority of Czech, Croat and other non-German or non-Magyar politicians still believed that their future lay within some form of Austrian state, and they hoped at least to be able to use the present crisis as a means of winning autonomy. The Poles had always felt more positively in favour of the monarchy than most of the other nationalities, and they hoped that a victorious war against Russia would liberate the Poles under Russian rule and prepare the way for some sort of new autonomous Polish state.

It was the Czechs who were the first to break the front of patriotic solidarity among the nationalities. Although they had reluctantly obeyed their call-up orders, the Czechs felt little enthusiasm for the war, and in April 1915, the 28th Regiment, largely recruited from Prague, surrendered *en masse* to the Russians rather than continue fighting. It is still arguable whether this action was simply the result of war-weariness and bloody-mindedness among the Czech soldiers (a mood very well caught in Jaroslav Hašek's novel *The Good Soldier Schweik*, still uncompleted when the author died in 1923), or whether it was a more positive gesture of national hostility to Austrian rule. The government reacted strongly; two leading deputies were arrested and sentenced to death – though the sentences were not carried out; the more conservative Czech politicians reiterated their loyalty; and the more radical leaders were arrested or went into exile. Nevertheless the long and fruitless bargaining about a possible form of government which would maintain the historical integrity of the province of Bohemia and at the same time do justice to the claims of both Czech and Germans, continued almost down to the end of the war, and the Austrian government resisted pressure from the army to put Bohemia and Moravia under military rule. Although there were further Czech desertions, so that the Czech Legion fighting with the Russian army eventually totalled three thousand men, and literary and other demonstrations of opposition in Prague and other Czech cities, the reaction of the Czechs until the very end of the monarchy was one of sullen non-cooperation rather than of active resistance or revolt.

The other nationalities did not seriously endanger the security or integrity of the monarchy until the last stages of the war; and the most sensational protest against the regime was an individual act by a Social Democrat, Friedrich Adler (named incidentally after Friedrich Nietzsche), the nervous and studious son of the party's revered leader Victor Adler. In October 1916 Friedrich Adler shot the Austrian Prime Minister dead as he sat at lunch in a restaurant, as a protest against the fact that parliament had not met since 1914 and that no regular channels of opposition to the government were open; and his subsequent trial gave him an excellent opportunity for making his view known. (It is a sign of the comparative mildness of Habsburg rule that Friedrich Adler's death sentence was commuted, and he was able to emerge from prison safe and sound, to become the first Foreign Minister of the new Austrian Republic in 1918, and to have a long and active career in the international socialist movement between the wars.)

Although in 1914 the Austro-Hungarians were forced out of much of Galicia and had to call for German support, which enabled them to recover the lost territory in 1915, they had defeated the Serbs by 1915, and fought a long campaign on the Italian border, and in October 1917 they scored a notable victory over the Italians. Their military record over at least the first three years of war was such as to suggest that the claims that the army embodied what was most loyal to the Habsburgs had something to support them. Although we now tend to say that the outbreak of war doomed the Austro-Hungarian monarchy, this was by no means the general impression that would have struck an observer in Vienna in August 1914 or even a year later. A few people had, it is true, realised how precarious the structure was: 'How often do I ask myself whether it is really worth our while to attach ourselves to this state which is creaking in every joint and to take so much trouble to drag it forward',[20] the German Ambassador in Vienna wrote shortly before the outbreak of war. Yet the momentum – or the inertia? – of the bureaucracy and the army proved strong enough to carry the monarchy through the first two years of war; and it was only with the death of Franz Joseph in November 1916 aged eighty-six, after reigning through so many vicissitudes for sixty-eight years, that, with the removal of this potent symbol of continuity, the internal stresses of the monarchy, exacerbated by war, really began to be apparent.

In Russia too, at least among the minority for whose views we have any evidence, the outbreak of war seemed to call out reserves of patriotic loyalty and enthusiasm for the Slav cause. The Duma met briefly to vote the war credits, and again for a very short session in February 1915, but in its subsequent sessions the original enthusiasm of its members was giving way to bitter criticism of the way in which the government was running the war. The very cumbrousness and limitations of the Russian bureaucratic and military machine also meant that many functions connected with the supply of the armies, and especially with the evacuation and medical care of the wounded, were in practice taken over by voluntary organisations such as the Red Cross or by the committees which were immediately set up at the beginning of the war by the municipalities and the local representative assemblies, the *zemstva*. While these developments gave more scope for local initiative and for wider participation in administrative affairs than had been possible in peacetime, the voluntary effort to fill gaps in the machinery for the running of the war created bodies which themselves later became centres of criticism and opposition to the government. While the size of the Russian army was enormous – it is estimated that by the end of 1914 there were over six-and-a-half million men under arms – neither the transport nor the armament production were sufficient to make the most of this mass of manpower. Nevertheless, although within a few weeks of the outbreak of war the Russian armies had been defeated by the Germans in East Prussia, they had been successful against the Austrians in invading Galicia, and in spite of being driven out the following year they remained capable of mounting a major offensive as late as June 1916. The Russians, like the Austrians, hoped to have something to offer their Polish subjects, but although the Polish leaders in the Duma at first supported the Russian war effort, other Poles had crossed into Austria and were fighting in a Polish Legion on the side of the central powers, while the politicians from Russian Poland placed their hopes increasingly in persuading the British and French to insist with their Russian allies that Poland should be granted a genuine measure of independence.

The illusions with which the First World War began all stemmed from the belief that the war would be short. When the French soldiers chalked *A Berlin* on the railway wagons taking them to the front, or when the British said, 'It'll all be over by Christmas', or when the German Crown Prince summoned his compatriots to a 'bright and jolly war' (*'Auf zu einem frisch-fröhlichen Krieg!'*), they all assumed that a comparatively short campaign, such as that of 1866 or 1870, would suffice to decide the issue, and that the peace would bring them tangible and visible gains, after which life would go on much as before. Very few people realised the effort and the suffering likely to be involved. Although Sir Edward Grey, looking out of the windows of the Foreign Office on the evening of 3 August, remarked, 'The lamps are going out all over Europe: we shall not see them lit again in our lifetime,'[21] for many Europeans the moment was an exhilarating one, 'great and unforgettable', as Walther Rathenau recalled. 'It was the ringing opening chord for an immortal song of sacrifice, loyalty and heroism.'[22] And even a German prone to pessimism, General von Falkenhayn, the Prussian War Minister, shortly to become Chief of the General Staff, was sufficiently impressed by the grandeur of events to exclaim on 4 August, 'Even if we end in ruin, it was beautiful.'[23]

Intellectuals hurried to place their talents at the disposal of their governments: while the great German historian Friedrich Meinecke described the outbreak of war as 'One of the great moments of my life, which suddenly filled my soul with the deepest confidence in our people and the profoundest joy',[24] a group of Oxford historians published a pamphlet (which Meinecke then joined other German academics to answer) explaining why Britain was at war, and declaring 'Military anarchism shall be destroyed if England, France and Russia can destroy it.'[25] The eminent and aged French historian Ernest Lavisse expressed his joy that 'he was not dead before having seen this war'.[26] The radical and iconoclastic French novelist Anatole France recalled later with embarrassment that he 'had gone as far as to make little speeches to the soldiers living and dead, which I regret as the worst action of my life',[27] and the philosopher Bergson sounded a note only too familiar on both sides when he declared that the struggle was one 'of civilisation against barbarism'.[28] Poets such as the young English writer Rupert Brooke celebrated the new mood in indifferent but much admired verse:[29]

> Honour has come back, as a king, to earth
> And paid his subjects with a royal wage;
> And nobleness walks in our ways again;
> And we are come into our heritage.

These hopes were soon to be disappointed; and many poets and intellectuals were before long criticising the war and seeking for ways to end it or to limit its disastrous consequences by planning for the time when it would be over. If we try to account for the widespread optimism and enthusiasm with which the war was initially greeted by many people in all the belligerent countries, we have to look at many of the factors described in the preceding chapters – the belief that the doctrine of the survival of the fittest could be applied to international relations, so that war seemed to be the supreme test of a nation's right to survive; the belief, stemming from Nietzsche, that only by a supreme shock and effort could the limitations of bourgeois life be transcended and its essence transmuted into something nobler. Or again, even if the governments of Europe did not deliberately envisage war as a way out of their internal political difficulties, the fact remains that war briefly produced a sense of national solidarity in which bitter political quarrels were forgotten: Irish Catholics and Ulster Protestants could agree to shelve their differences 'for the duration', as the phrase went; right-wing Catholics and socialist free-thinkers who had not spoken for years shook hands with each other in the French Chamber of Deputies, and the Kaiser gave a warm greeting to a gentleman whom he mistakenly supposed to be the Social Democratic leader Scheidemann. In Germany in particular the war seemed to create a new sense of solidarity, of belonging to a *Volksgemeinschaft* such as a generation of social critics had been longing for, a national community in which class antagonisms were transcended and in which the Germans felt rightly or wrongly a sense of mission and of purpose which had been lacking since the 1860s and early 1870s.

But perhaps in addition to the illusion that the war would be a short one, the illusion which received the most bitter blow, even though it was to be revived hopefully by President Wilson in 1918, was the belief that international relations could be conducted on a rational basis in which the interests of the various nations could be made to harmonise with each other without the need of an armed conflict. It was this illusion that had governed Grey's diplomacy and his attempt to mediate between the continental powers in the last days of July 1914; and it was a similar belief that inspired the leaders of the Second International when they came to Brussels in the hope of finding a way to demonstrate that the international solidarity of the European working class was stronger than the division between their capitalist rulers. The ideological assumptions on which European liberalism had rested were already breaking down before 1914. The war was going to hasten this process in the field of practical politics and everyday social and economic life. The war destroyed the political, economic, social and territorial structure of the old Europe and neither conservatism nor liberalism nor even socialism were ever going to be the same again. From the standpoint of sixty years later there is all too much truth in the prophecy made by Jean Jaurès in 1905: 'From a European war a revolution may spring up and the ruling classes would do well to think of this. But it may also result, over a long period, in crises of counter-revolution, of furious reaction, of exasperated nationalism, of stifling dictatorships, of monstrous militarism, a long chain of retrograde violence.'[30]

8

THE EUROPEAN CRISIS, 1914-18

At the beginning of September 1914 the Germans were still confident of victory, even though their initial campaign against France had not gone entirely according to the plan which General von Schlieffen had laid down seven years earlier. This was because his successor Moltke had lost his nerve at the height of the battle and had felt himself obliged to check the advance of his right wing which was supposed to move west of Paris, for fear of his advancing armies losing touch with each other. He also decided to despatch two corps to the hard-pressed Eastern Front (though they arrived too late to affect the battle there). As a result the French were able to stop the German advance at the battle of the Marne from 9 to 12 September. Over the next weeks the war changed its character. Instead of a war of movement, in which there was hope of a quick decision, the armies on the Western Front were by mid-November at a standstill, digging themselves into a line of trenches stretching continuously from the English Channel to the Swiss frontier. By the end of the year it was clear that the war was going to be a long one and that its result would depend as much on economic strength as on military action. The generals on both sides put their faith in amassing sufficient men and munitions to be able to break the deadlock, and in the meantime hoped to wear down the enemy's strength and his reserves of men and munitions by a series of smaller actions which would nibble away, as General Joffre, the French commander put it, at their resources. The numerous attempts made to mount attacks on the Western Front only ended in heavy casualties, often with no more than a few hundred yards of shell-pitted muddy ground to show for it, and even when the generals were more ambitious, as in the German attack on Verdun in February 1916, it was the defenders who won a negative advantage in the long-drawn-out battle, and the French defence of Verdun could be reckoned as a victory, even though their losses were as great as those of the attackers.

The belligerent governments found themselves obliged to take control of the economic life of their countries on an unprecedented scale, in order to provide the munitions and manpower needed for these costly battles and also to organise their stocks of vital raw materials which each side was trying to deny to the other by means of a naval blockade. These measures had profound effects on the nature of European society. The methods needed to mobilise resources for a prolonged and exhausting war necessarily meant the final abandonment of many of the old liberal ideas about *laissez-faire* and even individual rights, while wartime organisation together with the experience of the trenches led to new social problems and a new social consciousness. As after the Napoleonic Wars, so after the First World War, the old order was never completely restored however much many people tried. Some of the changes would doubtless have come about eventually in any case: we have seen already how far collectivist ideas of the State and militant attacks on liberal society had developed before 1914. But the war, as Lenin wrote from his Swiss exile early in 1917, was 'a mighty accelerator of events',[1] and its social, political, economic and psychological results were even more lasting than the immense physical damage which it inflicted on Europe.

The German government on the outbreak of war at once gave the local army commanders extensive powers over the civil administration. It soon became clear, however, that this would not be adequate to procure the raw materials needed by the army. Accordingly, within a few weeks Walther Rathenau was put in change of the provision of strategic raw materials, and at his instigation special State corporations were set up to deal in certain commodities required for the war effort, and to establish priorities among the various consumers of materials in short supply. This was an early example of State intervention into economic organisation which spread as the war went on. (By 1917 there was even a State company dealing in *Sauerkraut*.) In Germany, especially in the so-called Hindenburg programme of October 1916, ambitious plans were put into operation for the 'total mobilisation' of reserves, for the transfer of machinery from the less vital industries to those essential for war production and for the ruthless shutting-down of factories which did not directly contribute to the war effort. The effect of these measures in Germany was not only to set a precedent for the cooperation between the State and big business in running the economy – a precedent which was to be followed in the Nazi period and in the Second World War. It also resulted in an increase of the already existing trend towards the concentration of big business, with the development of large cartels at the expense of the smaller firms.

The mobilisation of Germany's resources for total war revealed again, just as pre-war German politics had done, the conflicting interest groups which dominated German society. While the big industrialists were anxious to use the opportunity to consolidate their power and, in addition to taking advantage of the profits to be made from war contracts, to prepare for post-war production and for the resumption of their export trade as well as the exploitation of the new industrial and commercial resources which were hoped for from the territorial gains Germany was expected to win at the end of the war, the military administrators at the Prussian War Ministry wanted to maintain good relations with the trade unions and to keep the cooperation of such labour as was available for war industries. The Social Democrats and many of the liberals in the Reichstag were often pleasantly surprised at this attitude. One trade union newspaper wrote at the beginning of 1916.[2]

The military dictatorship has in many cases shown more understanding for the needs of the people than the bureaucracy. It is more competent in mass supply and requisitioning and knows also how to evaluate the conditions for the successful conduct of the war . . . better than the civil administrative people, for whom the landowner and the commercial councillors are still individuals to be regarded more highly than the average man of the people. ['Commercial Councillor' was a title given in Germany to senior financiers, industrialists and businessmen.]

This mood of cooperation in the spirit of the *Burgfrieden* of 1914 did not last. By the end of 1916 the High Command, determined to limit the power of parliament, to discipline the workers and to introduce a ruthless compulsory direction of labour, had removed those officers and civilians who had been following policies of conciliation and cooperation with the Social Democrats, and had taken into the hands of the General Staff many of the powers previously exercised by the Prussian War Ministry. Committed to a policy of total mobilisation in order to achieve their goal of total victory to be followed by extensive annexations in west and east – an aim with which most of the big industrialists sympathised – they established a dictatorship in which they attempted, not always successfully, to organise the resources of Germany for a final effort which would bring them victory in 1918.

The French economy suffered particularly from the fact that the initial German invasion, even though it had been checked, still left the Germans in occupation of about 6 per cent of French territory, an area in north-east France which included most of the French resources of iron, much of the textile industry and over half of the coal, which the Germans were now able to exploit for their own purposes. The industrial losses were not limited to the occupied area, since much of the actual fighting zone was necessarily unproductive for the duration of the war and some time after it. The war therefore forced the French not only to increase their imports from their allies, but also to reorganise and modernise their industry with the help of State advances of capital, and it was the First World War which really completed the industrial revolution in France and led to a big expansion of French heavy industry, and to a considerable improvement in technology.

The effects of mobilisation in France were first felt in the countryside; and throughout the war agricultural production remained much lower than before. Of nearly three million men mobilised in 1914 41 per cent were peasants, the biggest single group among the soldiers. Moreover the agricultural areas in the zones occupied by the Germans had been important sources of wheat supply, so that this increased the problem of feeding France in war-time. The army was reluctant to release many men for agriculture and the peasant farms of France had to struggle on as best they could with the labour of women and children and some foreign immigrants, but the result was a chronic shortage of grain and sugar as well as of cattle. By the last months of the war almost all food was supposed to be rationed; and in the cities three meatless days a week were ordered. Yet, as both some of the soldiers and the more militant workers noticed, there still seemed to be black-market supplies for the rich who scarcely appeared to be suffering from the war.

As new factories were set up away from the front, a new industrial labour force created and existing plants expanded, so too there was a movement of popu-lation, especially as refugees from the occupied areas had to be found homes. (The number of workers in the military arsenals rose from 50,000 at the start of the war to 1,600,000 by the end.)[3] Women not only had to take over much of the men's work on the farms; as elsewhere they also went into industry in increasing numbers and worked at jobs where they had not been seen before. 'If the women working in the factories stopped for twenty minutes,' General Joffre once remarked, 'France would lose the war.'[4]

The fact that the front was on French soil not only made the contrast between the war zones and the rest of the country all the more striking, it also meant that the army controlled a large part of France – the 'zones of the army' from which they did their best to exclude civilian politicians. This resulted in a long struggle between parliament and the army, with deputies who had been mobilised returning to Paris from the front to make their criticisms, and with the military committee of the Chamber claiming its right to investigate the production of munitions and the system of supplying the armies. The army, indeed, would have preferred to keep arms production under its own control and to use military labour in military arsenals and workshops where possible. This system was not geared to a long war and as parliament reasserted itself – and in the first months of the war the govern-ment had virtually handed over to the army by leaving for Bordeaux, when it was feared that Paris might fall to the Germans, and remained there from the beginning of September 1914 till early December – so, especially as pro-duction had to be increased beyond the capacity of the purely military establishments, civilian control of production was reestablished and a number of under-secretaries were attached to the War Ministry to supervise various aspects of the war economy.

The Italians, when they entered the war, were also faced with the problem of industrial weakness and an almost total lack of the essential raw materials, especially coal. The war therefore helped to some extent to modernise the Italian economy. Industrial capacity was increased and big steps were taken in the development of hydro-electric power. The State control which this involved also led to much corruption and to accusations of profiteering out of the war and of unfair decisions to grant State help, so that these economic interventions by the State, while they helped certain sectors of Italian industry, also contributed to the suspicion with which parliamentary government was regarded by a number of Italians.

The British government soon found itself having to cope with shortages of munitions and shortages of men. Lloyd George was put in charge of munitions production in June 1915 and made a reputation as a statesman determined to carry on the war vigorously; and, even if his methods were infuriating to more orthodox administrators, he at least showed a talent for improvisation and for infusing a sense of urgency into the government and industrial system. A breach was made in the British liberal tradition in May 1916, when compulsory military service was finally introduced after it had become clear that voluntary schemes were not enough and that the complicated system introduced by Lord Derby, the Secretary of State for War, in November 1915, whereby men 'voluntarily' enlisted – often under heavy social pressure – for service when required, had only produced half the number of men expected. The labour shortage had another important social consequence. Women began to do men's work, in the factories and offices and behind the lines at the front, and the movement for women's rights which had caused so much political trouble before the war had now assumed a practical form which removed it from controversy and left women at the end of the war several stages further on the road towards total equality with men.

If women had to be accorded a new equality, especially in Britain, as a result of their part in the war effort, the same was even more true of organised labour in nearly all the belligerent countries. To mobilise manpower, increase industrial output or to lengthen working hours at a time when unemployment had almost disappeared, the cooperation of the trade union movement was essential. This was not only obtained by the presence of socialists in the governments of Britain and France during part of the war; it also resulted from day-to-day collaboration with union leaders, and it necessarily had an effect on their attitude to the government as well as on the government's attitude towards them. The Secretary-General of the French *Confédération Générale de Travail*, the militant syndicalist leader Léon Jouhaux, summed up this new attitude when he said, 'We must give up the policy of fist-shaking in order to adopt one of being present in the affairs of the nation . . . We want to be everywhere where the workers' interests are being discussed.'[5] The result was that by the end of the war the trade unions had an enormously enhanced position, and their situation was much stronger, whether they were collaborating with the government, as during much of the war, or whether they were opposing government policy, as they were all over Europe as soon as the war ended. Everywhere they emerged from the war numerically stronger, better organised and more self-confident, so that when the war was over the European trade union movement entered on a new phase in its history.

It was not sufficient to organise industry or to mobilise manpower in order to carry a modern state through a long war. The war also had to be paid for, and the methods adopted in the different countries had profound effects on the post-war international situation. The most obvious method, and one to which all the belligerent countries resorted, was to borrow money, either abroad or internally. Foreign loans came mostly from allies and were utilised partly to pay for imports from those allies. By the end of the war there was an intricate structure of inter-allied debts to be paid off, with Britain, France and their allies especially indebted to the United States, so that the international financial situation immediately after the war was dominated by demands for payment and attempts to raise money for this purpose. At the start of the war it was possible to borrow money almost more easily than in time of peace since people were prepared, in the first rush of patriotic enthusiasm, to subscribe to loans or pay higher taxes more readily than before the war, when finding money for the arms programmes had been a major financial problem, especially for Germany. But money had eventually to be found to pay off the war loans to which citizens had patriotically subscribed in wartime, repayment of which they expected in time of peace. This too was to complicate the post-war financial situation both in Germany and France, for governments were forced either to borrow more money in order to pay off their previous debts, or else to issue more paper money for the purpose, and thus hasten the process of inflation already begun during the war. There were considerable rises in indirect taxation though, as consumption went down during the war, these did not bring in so much money as they might have done. In England Lloyd George declared, 'We are fighting Germany, Austria and Drink'[6] and the King set an example, perhaps not very widely followed (certainly not by Asquith, the Prime Minister), of giving up alcohol for the duration of the war, and in Russia the sale of alcohol was prohibited. England was the only country to attempt to meet part of the cost of the war by a large increase in direct taxation. Here the income tax was raised to a new level and the principle accepted which has been a basic part of British public finance ever since that a high rate of income tax was a legitimate way of paying for the running of the country and of redistributing the nation's wealth.

In practice the problems facing all the major countries engaged in the war were similar, but the solutions found varied with the political and social traditions and circumstances in each case. All the countries at war experienced a manpower shortage, and a consequent struggle between the army and industry for such labour as was available, and this in turn, as prices rose and food as well as men grew scarcer, increased the bargaining power of the trade unions which were the official spokesmen of the organised working class.

Both sides suffered from the other's attempts at blockade. Both sides needed enormous quantities of explosives for the mutual slaughter on the Western Front. As raw materials became scarce a system of controlled priorities had to be established, so that the enterprises engaged in war production were favoured and other firms forced to stop production, and this everywhere led to charges of favouritism and corruption, and to the attacks on the 'profiteers' who were making money out of the war. At the same time high prices and shortages led, in spite of the introduction of rationing, to an active black market and to renewed criticisms of hoarders and profiteers. Soldiers looked enviously at the industrial workers who had been allowed to continue to work at home, and the gap between the front and the civilian world grew greater. The solidarity with which the war had originally been greeted had by 1916, as the situation grew worse, given way to recriminations between rival interest groups.

While the generals were still trying to break through the enemy's lines on the Western Front and were devising new weapons which it was hoped would achieve this end – poison gas was first used by the Germans against the Russians in January 1915, but unsuccessfully, and on the Western Front with better results three months later, and the first British tanks went into action in September 1916 – the politicians were looking for ways to open up new theatres of war and to tip the balance by bringing in new allies and new resources of manpower. In October 1914 Turkey joined the war on the German side, and this had the effect of reopening the whole Balkan question and arousing new ambitions among the smaller states of south-east Europe. The British at this stage hoped that the Bulgarians might be tempted to join the Allies (it has become customary to refer to Britain, France and their allies as 'the Allies', and the German–Austrian group as 'the Central Powers'), in spite of the fact that their differences with Serbia over their rival claims in Macedonia still seemed insuperable. Partly to convince the Bulgarians of the seriousness of British intentions and partly in the hope of opening up a new front, marching on Constantinople and driving the Turks out of the war, the British government after much argument sent an expedition to the Gallipoli peninsula, at the western entrance of the Dardanelles, but this in fact achieved nothing and had to be withdrawn at the end of 1915. The effect on Bulgaria therefore was the opposite from what had been intended, and she signed an alliance with Germany and Turkey in September 1915, following this within a few weeks with an attack on Serbia.

By this time the Serbs had been virtually knocked out of the war; on 9 October 1915 the Germans and Austrians occupied Belgrade, and the Serbian army was in full flight across the mountains of Albania. Nor had the Allies been more successful in bringing Greece into the war. The liberal Prime Minister Eleutherios Venizelos was anxious to come in on the side of the

British and French, and it was agreed that the British and French should send an army to Salonika, from which base it was hoped to strike into the Balkans. But this project too came to very little and a new government in Athens, although unable to force the Allies to withdraw from Greek soil at Salonika, was openly pro-German in its sympathies; it was not until 1917, after what was virtually a civil war in Greece, that a *coup d'état* succeeded in bringing Greece into the war on the side of Britain and France. By the end of 1915 Germany and Austria seemed to have the advantage in south-east Europe, with Bulgaria and Turkey on their side and with the remnants of the Serbian army eventually withdrawn to the protection of the Allied bridgehead at Salonika, and with neither Greece nor Roumania yet in the war on the Allied side.

The neutral country from which most was immediately hoped at the start of the war was Italy, the one great power of Europe which had kept out of war in August 1914. Although bound by an alliance to Germany and Austria, the Italians remained neutral at the outset of the war because the terms of the alliance did not automatically operate except when their allies were attacked: and in this case, of course, it was the Germans who had declared war on France and Russia, while Austria had not even informed the Italians of the ultimatum to Serbia. Italian opinion was deeply divided. The attractions of neutrality were considerable, and the choice was not so much between entering the war on one side or another, but rather between trying to make the Austrians pay a substantial price for Italian neutrality and trying to extract from the Allies promises of gains after the war in return for fighting on their side. Although there was considerable sympathy for Germany and Austria in conservative and Catholic circles, and a general belief among industrialists and businessmen that Germany would win, and although some of the extreme nationalists were anxious to go to war for its own sake regardless of which side it was on, the general hostility to Austria was such, and the feeling about *Italia Irredenta* so strong, that no government could have carried the country into war on the Austrian side. During the first months of the war the Italian government was being wooed by both sides. Italian aims were clear enough: they wanted to win from Austria the South Tirol, Trieste and the surrounding province of Istria and a substantial part of the Dalmatian coast. On the other hand for Austria–Hungary these demands were so large that it was hard to conceive a government which was still undefeated in the war agreeing to them, especially as a concession to the principle of nationalism in the case of the Italian subjects of the monarchy would establish a most dangerous precedent, which might be invoked by other nationalities such as the Roumanians. For the Allies however it was comparatively easy to offer Italy large areas of enemy territory after the end of the war – but until they won the war they would not have the territory to dispose of.

The Italians were therefore faced with a gambler's choice: they might negotiate with the Germans, who sent the former chancellor von Bülow to Rome as a special envoy to try and win over the Italian government, and settle for such terms as Germany might persuade a still undefeated Austria–Hungary to concede – or they might join Britain and France on the assumption that they would win the war and therefore be in a position to enforce Italy's maximum terms on a defeated Austria. By the time the Austrians were ready to talk of serious concessions – the Italian-speaking parts of the Trentino, though not Trieste nor any of Dalmatia – the Italian price had gone up and they were demanding the immediate cession of Austrian territory without even waiting till the end of the war, something to which the Austrians were hardly likely to agree. In April the Italian government decided to sign the secret treaty of London with Britain, France and Russia; and on 23 May 1915 they entered the war.

The decision was not taken without a considerable internal struggle. While the government under Antonio Salandra, in office at the outbreak of war, was committed to neutrality, which it was hoped would assure for the Italians not only the obvious economic rewards of staying out of the war but also a substantial price for continuing non-belligerency, there soon grew up a vocal opposition in favour of intervention on the Allied side. Its support was very mixed. There were many intellectuals whose political sympathies lay with the liberal democracies of France and Britain and who stressed their cultural ties with Paris and their political links with London. A group of liberal volunteers under Garibaldi's grandson went off to fight on the Western Front with the French Foreign Legion. There were extreme nationalists who believed that Italy's position in the world could only be secured by means of a victorious war, and they were naturally joined in demanding a war against Austria by anyone who had ties with the Italians still under Austrian rule.

During the autumn of 1914 the campaign for intervention was already under way when it was joined by a demagogue and journalist of considerable gifts, Benito Mussolini. Mussolini had made his way from school-teaching into journalism and he had been an active and radical member of the Italian Socialist Party, and at the outbreak of the war was the editor of the party's official newspaper, *Avanti!*. The Italian socialists were committed to the policy of neutrality, and their leaders could feel some satisfaction in August 1914 that theirs was one of the few socialist parties in Europe which had remained true to their principles and consistently opposed war, whether it was the Italian invasion of Tripoli or the European war which was now beginning. During the first months of the war some of the socialist leaders were working actively though unsuccessfully with the Swiss Social Democrats in trying to reestablish some links between the socialists in the neutral countries and, if possible, between the socialists in the countries at war. Mussolini however was too dynamic and belligerent by temperament to appreciate such patient diplomatic efforts. It was the active revolutionary side of socialism that had attracted him, and his socialist ideas were linked with Nietzschean notions of a new race of supermen emerging from war, and with Georges Sorel's conception of violence as a moral end in itself. Already on 6 August 1914 he was writing, 'Perhaps this war will, with its blood, set the wheels in motion,'[7] and during the early months of the war he was becoming increasingly restless. In November he broke with the Socialist Party and appeared as the editor of a new newspaper, the *Popolo d'Italia*, dedicated to the cause of active intervention on the Allied side and financed it was rumoured by funds supplied by the French Embassy though in fact these do not seem to have been forthcoming for several months. During the winter of 1914–15 the campaign for intervention became more violent, and Mussolini had the support of the Futurist leader Marinetti and other extreme nationalists in demonstrations against individuals or bodies, such as the Socialist Party, who supported neutrality.

Yet many parliamentarians and business men were dubious. They remained convinced of German strength and were worried that Italy might be sacrificing a smaller substance for a larger shadow. At the same time opinion had veered with the course of the war: the British expedition to the Dardanelles had not created the new situation in the Balkans which had been expected, and in the spring of 1915 the Germans and Austrians seemed to have recovered the initiative on the Eastern Front. The deputies in the Italian Chamber were reluctant to follow the mood of the increasingly active interventionist organisations outside parliament, and many of them had been shocked by the violence and direct action which had accompanied some of the interventionist demonstrations. Mussolini, who in the previous August had been urging revolution if the government went to war, now talked of revolution if they did not do so. As a result Salandra, who with his colleagues had decided on war, felt obliged to resign because he was uncertain of a clear parliamentary majority. It was the intervention of the King which resolved the crisis, as he refused to accept Salandra's resignation, and the deputies were now impressed by the extent to which opinion outside parliament still seemed in favour of war, so that when parliament met again there was in fact a large majority for the government and for the decision to go to war. The Italian entry into the war, unlike that of other countries, had been the result of careful calculation and long-drawn-out negotiations. But it had also caused a political crisis, and the way in which it was resolved, by royal intervention supported by demonstrations on the streets, suggested that the critics of parliamentary institutions in Italy had much evidence to support their views.

The secret promises made by the Allies to Italy of large areas of Austrian territory showed how the military deadlock and the lengthening of the war had resulted in the search for new allies, and therefore had also resulted in the formulation of new war aims. At the start of the war Britain and France were committed to demanding the liberation of Belgium and the return of Alsace-Lorraine to France, with a rather vaguer intention of saving small states such as Serbia from being swallowed up by more powerful neighbours. Once Turkey joined the war the way was open to speculation about a possible peace at Turkey's expense, and the British, hoping to use the opportunity permanently to annex Egypt which was still under a shadowy Turkish suzerainty, were quite ready to promise the Russians that they should have Constantinople and the Straits after the war in return for Russian recognition of the British position in Egypt. A secret agreement to this effect was signed in March 1915 – possibly hastened on by rumours that the Russians were considering a separate peace with Germany. The Russians, too, were heavily involved in the negotiations with Italy, since they felt obliged to stand up for the Serbian claims to the Dalmatian coast which the Italians coveted and where indeed the Slav majority far outnumbered the small Italian minority. The strategic and historic claims of one allied state went against the ethnic claim of another so that the reconciliation of the demands proved impossible and only showed how precarious was the community of interests which bound them together in war.

On the German side the prospect of a quick victory which still seemed to exist in September 1914, before the consequences of the battle of the Marne became apparent, led the government to draw up plans for a post-war settlement. Although the deadlock which had set in by October 1914 meant that they had to be put aside for the moment, so that the government expressly discouraged any public discussion of war aims, nevertheless the 'September programme' of 1914 remained throughout the war a set of goals which the Germans hoped to be able to realise in any peace settlement. These war aims included in the west further territorial annexations from France, so as to round off the industrial zone in Lorraine which the Germans had acquired in 1870 by the addition of the important mineral resources of the districts of Briey and Longwy, as well as the occupation of the Channel coast from Dunkirk to Boulogne, and permanent control of Belgium's foreign relations, together with the occupation of Liège and Verviers. In the east the German frontier would be extended and thus, with Austria–Hungary closely linked with Germany, a vast zone of economic control in central Europe would be created. These were ideas that appealed to the military leaders and also to the industrialists who wished to expand their sources of raw materials and to be at the centre of a large trading area in central Europe – an idea given more popular currency with the publication in 1915 of a book called *Mitteleuropa* by a well-known publicist and social reformer, Friedrich Naumann.

The war-aims programme of September 1914 was only discovered in the German archives after the Second World War, and was published in 1961.[8] Its publication at once gave rise to a discussion of the relation of these war aims, put forward within six weeks of the start of the war, to German policy immediately before the outbreak of war. These were certainly goals which many influential people in pre-war Germany would have liked to achieve; and the September programme itself was very similar to a draft which Walther Rathenau had submitted to the Chancellor not long before. These ideas were being widely discussed in the years before 1914 and it is not surprising to find them embodied in a policy-planning document as soon as war had begun and while an early victory still seemed to be in sight. But it would perhaps be a mistake to conclude, as some historians do, that it was to achieve these aims that Germany actually went to war, and that these were long-premeditated goals which the German government was prepared to go to war to attain. Still, once the war had started, the ideas were there to be formulated, and although, as the fortunes of war changed, the aims in the September programme were modified or expanded by various of the leaders of the German army and government, the basic German objectives remained much the same throughout the war; and so long as there was any chance of attaining them through military victory, their existence made a negotiated peace impossible.

As the war continued and as the casualties rose, without the campaigns of 1915 and 1916 bringing a decision any nearer, there began to be discussions of the possibility of a negotiated peace. At the same time, both sides were aware of the necessity of justifying the rising slaughter – the battle of the Somme in late summer of 1916 had cost the Allies some 600,000 casualties and the Germans about 750,000. It became increasingly necessary for governments to explain why they felt the war must go on and what they were hoping to achieve. At the same time the attitude of the last remaining powerful neutral, the United States, became of crucial importance to the nature and course of the European war. At the end of 1916 President Woodrow Wilson, newly elected to a second term of office, invited the belligerents to state their war aims, in the hope that this would serve as a basis for mediation. The attempt was unsuccessful, as was a comparable one by the Pope in August 1917. Any statement of war aims only served to show how far apart the objectives of the rival powers were. While the Germans did not answer Wilson directly and implied that they would be satisfied with the gains they had already achieved, the Allies not only declared that they were fighting for the restoration of Belgium, Serbia and the territories occupied by the German and Austrian armies, but also stressed that they wished to see the independence of the Slavs, Italians and others under Habsburg rule, and 'the freeing' of the populations subject to the bloody tyranny of the Turks'.[9] In the circumstances, these were propaganda statements aimed at American opinion rather than an expression of actual possibilities, but they serve to show how far discussion of war aims had moved since 1914.

The Germans at the end of 1916 placed their hopes in ending the war by means of the naval blockade of Britain. It had early become apparent that the naval war for which Britain and Germany had prepared so desperately before

1914 was not going to be the kind of naval war which in fact was fought. There was only one indecisive encounter between the great battle fleets – the battle of Jutland in the North Sea in May 1916 – and this was never repeated, as neither side was willing again to risk losing their big battleships, and many of the larger ships spent the rest of the war in harbour at Kiel or at Scapa Flow. The war at sea became increasingly a war of submarines and destroyers, a war, that is to say, aimed at enforcing a mutual blockade, interrupting commerce and destroying merchant shipping. Admiral Tirpitz decided during 1915 that the way to defeat Britain was by ruthless use of submarines (the *Unterseebooten* or U-boats) to destroy not only British ships but also neutral ships bringing supplies to Britain. He had however failed to persuade Bethmann-Hollweg to authorise the unrestricted submarine campaign, because Bethmann realised that such a course would at once turn neutral opinion, and especially that of the United States, against Germany. As a result Tirpitz resigned in March 1916, but the General Staff continued to press for the adoption of the submarine weapon against all ships bound for England.

Up to this point the United States had been more indignant at the British insistence on stopping and searching neutral ships and confiscating cargoes destined for ports from which they might reach Germany than they were at the German blockade methods. Bethmann and more moderate opinion in Germany were in favour of retaining this advantage, and against a course which might not only antagonise the American government and people but even bring America into the war. However by late 1916 the influence of the German High Command was growing fast, and that of the civilian members of the government weakening accordingly. In August 1916 General Paul von Hindenburg, who had been in command on the Eastern Front and had won the decisive battle of Tannenberg which drove the Russians out of East Prussia in August 1914, became Chief of the General Staff, with his inseparable adviser General Erich von Ludendorff as First Quartermaster General, in which capacity Ludendorff quickly established a firm personal control over the civilian war effort. And, in October 1916 the Reichstag, in an effort to strengthen its own power, passed a resolution that the Imperial Chancellor, though solely responsible to the Reichstag for political decisions in connection with the war, 'in taking these decisions . . . must rely on the views of the Supreme Command', and it added, 'If it is decided to initiate a ruthless submarine campaign, the Imperial Chancellor can be certain of the support of the Reichstag.'[10] By Christmas Hindenburg was determined to use this new support against the Chancellor and, after he had declared that 'a ruthless submarine campaign is the only means of carrying the war to a rapid conclusion',[11] it was decided on 9 January 1917 to begin unrestricted submarine warfare.

The consequences of this decision were enormous. The German military and naval authorities were confident that the new strategy would defeat England in six months and that therefore, even if America were to come into the war, the war would be over before United States aid could be effective. The gamble very nearly paid off: by April the British government was forced to face the prospect of starvation, with only six weeks' supply of grain in the country. The government ceased to publish the figures of shipping sunk, and began to question whether it would be possible to continue the war at all after November 1917. The situation was saved largely by the development of new naval tactics for the organising of merchant ships in convoys – a course only adopted by the senior admirals with extreme reluctance – and the sinkings began to diminish. In the meantime, however, on 7 April 1917 the United States had taken the fateful step of declaring war on Germany. Although the immediate reasons for America's entry into the war were ones of practical self-interest – the danger posed to American trade by the German submarine campaign and the threat from German intrigues across the border in Mexico, where the Germans were offering the Mexican government an alliance in the event of war with the United States and holding out hopes of the return to Mexico of Texas, Arizona and New Mexico – the American declaration of war not only potentially changed the balance of power in Europe, it also transformed the scope and nature of the war, and suggested that its purposes far transcended what were thought of in America as the selfish ends for which the European powers were originally fighting.

In his message to Congress on the outbreak of war, Wilson declared that this was a war 'for democracy, for the right of those who submit to authority to have a voice in their own governments, for the rights and liberties of small nations, for a universal dominion of rights by such a concert of free peoples as shall bring peace and safety to all nations and make the world itself at last free'.[12] This was very different language and a very different style from anything that had so far been heard from European statesmen; and in fact the idea of turning the war into a crusade for democracy and a new international order was more common in opposition circles in Britain than among members of the British and French governments. Wilson had been indirectly in touch with some of the radical thinkers about international relations in Britain, and they continued to have an influence on his thought about war aims and a post-war settlement, sometimes to the embarrassment of the British and French governments. Although now, with our experience of the failure of the 1919 settlement and a more cynical attitude towards the expression of high ideals by American presidents engaged in wars, Wilson's rhetoric sometimes seems empty and hypocritical, to the Europe of 1917 America's entry into the war seemed to offer new hope, not just of victory, but of a victory of a kind that might 'make the world safe for democracy' and justify in part the terrible loss of life that seemed till then likely to have occurred in vain.

By the beginning of 1917, after two and a half years of inconclusive fighting, all the European belligerents were faced with internal crises; and it is in this year that the debate about war aims became inextricably involved with a general discussion about the nature of post-war society. To understand the post-war political pattern of Europe we must look at the opposition to the war, which was growing in strength during 1917. In the parliamentary democracies, Britain and France, this uneasiness expressed itself in the form of political instability; in Germany it led to the emergence of what was in effect a military dictatorship; in Russia it led to revolution.

During the summer and autumn of 1916 there was a widespread feeling in Britain that Asquith as Prime Minister was not pursuing the war with sufficient vigour, and an internal government crisis, the result of personal intrigues and political ambitions as well as concern for the prosecution of the war, led to Asquith's resignation in December 1916 and his replacement as Prime Minister by Lloyd George. In practice, although Lloyd George was able to strengthen the central direction of the war, by establishing a small war cabinet responsible for overall strategic and economic planning, to extend economic controls and in effect to kill the old liberalism, his power over events was limited by the extent to which Britain was committed to the war in the west and to using all her resources on the Western Front. Lloyd George quarrelled with the military leaders and made some changes in the senior posts, but was unable to take the drastic step of removing General Sir Douglas Haig from command of the forces in France, or to change the army's mind about the correctness of the strategy which they were determined to pursue. The contempt of the generals for the politicians and the divisions between the long-suffering soldiers in the trenches and the staff officers behind the lines or the civilians at home were becoming more marked, but only military success could change the situation. Military success depended on the generals and not on the politicians; and the generals still believed in wearing down the enemy's resistance and reserves by attacking his trenches on the Western Front. The introduction of conscription in May of 1916 had at least removed some of the inequalities between British citizens, and it also did away with some of the more hypocritical displays of war hysteria, the empty rhetoric of the recruiting speeches or the gesture of those young ladies who presented white feathers on the streets to men of military age not in uniform. Conscription also showed that there was some degree of total opposition to war. This had long been an integral part of the British radical tradition and of some of the non-conformist Protestant sects. Elaborate provisions were made by the government for the exemption from conscription of people who could prove a 'conscientious objection' to military service. The treatment of pacifists was often harsh and unjust, but the recognition of the category at all was a sign of how far moral and religious objections to war were rooted in the English liberal tradition; and in no other belligerent country in Europe were such scruples even recognised as providing a valid reason for refusing military service, and perhaps as a result in other countries opposition to the war took a more uncompromising and revolutionary form.

In some intellectual and middle-class circles in Britain there was growing opposition to the war and increasing discussion of what a world at peace might look like. The radical Union of Democratic Control provided a steady criticism of the government and of war-time political solidarity. Other bodies opposed conscription and gave help and encouragement to those who were objecting to military service. A few of the leading writers in Britain made their position quite clear. The philosopher Bertrand Russell wrote and spoke against the war, was prosecuted and imprisoned, and dismissed from his fellowship at Trinity College, Cambridge; many of the members of the so-called Bloomsbury group (see p. 320 below), were either, like the critic Lytton Strachey, conscientious objectors, or, like Leonard Woolf, active in the critical discussion of war aims and conditions of peace. In Switzerland Romain Rolland, one of the very first French intellectuals to criticise the policies which had led to war and question the excesses of war-time propaganda and the breaking of the ties that linked the intellectuals of Europe to each other, tried to make contact with writers in Germany and Austria such as Stefan Zweig, who was given leave by the Austrian government to go to Zurich for the first performance in 1917 of his ponderous, elaborate, symbolical pacifist play *Jeremias*.

Switzerland became a refuge for all those who, for whatever reason, wanted to avoid or escape the war. In the cafés of Zurich, often unknown to each other, revolutionary exiles, among them Lenin, could be seen along with revolutionaries in another sense, such as the Irish writer James Joyce. The Lorrainer Iwan Goll, born in France but brought up as a German, whose *Requiem für die Gefallenen in Europa* (Requiem for the fallen in Europe, 1917) was one of the most outspoken pieces of German anti-war literature, was a student in Lausanne at the outbreak of the war and remained in Switzerland where he became a friend of Joyce as well as of Rolland and Zweig. The German novelist Hermann Hesse, because of his pacifist views, spent the war in Switzerland and remained there for the rest of his life. It was in Switzerland, too, that some artists and writers founded a movement which went further than any other in asserting that the total madness of the war and of the society which produced it could only be countered by a total rejection of all existing values and by the exposure of the absurdity both of life and art. The Dada movement, started in Zurich in 1916, became the most radical artistic movement yet seen in its denial of the value of art itself: and it has continued in one form or another to inspire movements of artists against art throughout the rest of the twentieth century. Throughout the war Switzerland, although sympathies varied to some extent with the language of the cantons, remained a genuinely neutral haven in a divided Europe; her press gave almost the only dispassionate account of the war and her cities provided a meeting place, not only for the intellectuals of Europe, but also for all the spies and political go-betweens who were operating in the margin of the political and military operations of the belligerent governments. All these activities increased in the spring of 1917, as the military situation for both sides grew more difficult and when America's entry into the war and the Russian Revolution gave new focuses for all those who opposed the war or demanded a clear formulation of war aims.

The British and French governments placed great hopes in the plans for an offensive on the Western Front in the spring of 1917 put forward by the French General Robert Nivelle, who convinced his own government, and to an even greater extent Lloyd George, that he possessed the secret of the successful breakthrough which had so far eluded the allied commanders. For Lloyd George a quick success in the west would not only consolidate his own political position, but it would also resolve his conflict with the British generals and open up new possibilities of prosecuting the war in other theatres and of bringing it to a speedy end. But Nivelle's self-confidence, which had led the Allied governments to entrust him with the preparation of the new offensive, turned out to be misplaced. The offensive was launched, but it failed to make the spectacular gains which had been hoped of it. Over the next months both the French and British armies, at the cost of very heavy casualties, tried to revive the momentum of the offensive. The French advance had clearly failed by the end of April 1917 and had not won any decisive advantage. The French armies began to mutiny; and when the British tried in the summer and autumn to resume the attack, allegedly to take the strain from the French and in a vain hope of reaching the German U-boat bases on the Belgian coast, they only became involved in a series of costly and profitless encounters – to the most notorious of which the village of Passchendaele gave its name, and which became symbolic of the whole futility of the slaughter, mud and hopeless horror of the Western Front – a mood caught in verse by the young soldier poet Siegfried Sassoon, one of several who were beginning to express the reaction against the political and strategic ineptness which seemed to be sending tens of thousands of young men to unnecessary and pointless destruction:[13]

> Squire nagged and bullied till I went to fight
> (Under Lord Derby's scheme). I died in Hell –
> (They called it Passchendaele) . . .

> Two bleeding years I fought in France for squire;
> I suffered anguish that he never guessed;
> Once I came home on leave, and then went west
> What greater glory can a man desire?

[For Lord Derby's scheme, see p. 200 above.]

One result of the campaigns of 1917 was to produce increasing signs of revulsion against the war, both political and literary. While the British poets at the front, such as Siegfried Sassoon or Wilfred Owen, expressed a tragic and hopeless resentment at the unsought fate which cut the man in the trenches off from a normal human life, in Germany and Austria some of the writers and artists who had at first welcomed the excitement and the sense of comradeship which the war produced also now began to turn against it. As early as May 1915 the painter Max Beckmann was writing, 'For the first time I have had enough'[14]; and by 1917 there were a number of plays, poems and novels openly criticising the war – though often war in general rather than this particular war. The German writers mostly wrote in highly general and symbolical terms compared to the specific references to the actual horrors of the present war to be found in the English poets and in for example the bitterly realistic and brutal account of life in the trenches, *Le Feu* (Under Fire), which the French writer Henri Barbusse had begun to publish in serial form in 1916 and which, after it had appeared in book form in 1917, sold 230,000 copies by the end of the war. The intensity with which many Germans had welcomed the outbreak of war was only equalled by the intensity with which some of them now preached a wholesale new order for mankind. Fritz von Unruh, for instance, had in his pre-war writings glorified the Prussian spirit and the desire for self-sacrifice, but after a few months of the war he was already revolting against the system and calling, in *Ein Geschlecht* (A Clan), for a mystical affirmation of life and joy in the face of the nihilism of war. Others like the young dramatist Ernst Toller and the poet Johannes R.Becher soon combined their literary protest with more active involvement in the revolutionary political movements which became of increasing importance from 1917 on.

When one considers the boredom, discomfort and fear of the soldiers' life on the Western Front, in the bleak plains of Eastern Europe or in the rigours of the Alpine climate, it is perhaps surprising that there was not more protest, whether expressed symbolically in literature or openly in mutiny – as was the case in the French army for a few weeks in 1917. There was, in fact, almost till the end of the war, alongside the poetry or drama which revolted against its horrors, a literature of acceptance, of stoicism or of making the most of such happiness as could still be found. This mood is evoked in English by the poet Robert Graves in his autobiography *Goodbye to All That*, looking back on the war in 1929. And both the half-Polish French writer Guillaume Apollinaire, to whom the war and military service suddenly gave a sense of being rooted in French life which he had hitherto lacked, and the Italian Giuseppe Ungaretti combined an imaginative but accurate record of the sights and sound of war with an intense awareness of their own personal lives, which transcended the nightmare around them. As Ungaretti put it, crouched all night beside a corpse he wrote 'letters full of love ... *Non sono mai stato tanto attaccato alla vita* [I have never been so attached to life].'[15]

For the French the failure of the Nivelle offensive resulted in a prolonged political crisis and a collapse of morale which nearly proved fatal. Until March 1917 the French government, although there had been changes of prime minister and rows about military appointments and the relations between the generals and the civilians, had nevertheless been comparatively stable, and the principle of the *Union Sacrée* and of a broad representation of all the parties had been maintained. However, in March 1917, as a result of the alleged 'insults to parliament' offered by the war minister, General Lyautey, a well-known colonial administrator, the government fell; and this time the official representatives of the Socialist Party did not join the reconstituted ministry, which soon had to face the consequences of the failure of General Nivelle's offensive. The most immediate task was to restore morale among the soldiers at the front, who had simply refused to obey orders to return to the trenches to risk death in what they saw were pointless attacks, or who were protesting against lack of leave and lack of rest. Although there were suggestions that the mutinies were the result of political agitation and of the activity of revolutionary agents, there is no reason to attribute them to anything more than a natural reaction of the hard-pressed soldiers in a desperate situation, even if sometimes they shouted revolutionary slogans or sang the *Internationale*.[16] The task of giving back to the army a degree of self-confidence fell to General Philippe Pétain; and by improving conditions and providing adequate rest and reliefs for the troops at the front and then using them for small, carefully prepared and successful operations, he saved the French army from collapse. At the same time he acquired a popular paternal image and a reputation for good sense and comparative clemency, which was not forgotten by those who brought him to power twenty-three years later at a moment of even worse peril for France.

However, the government was attacked both by the extreme Right and by the formidable and experienced political leader Georges Clemenceau for its failure to prosecute the war more vigorously, while at the same time the Socialists were criticising the government both for the useless bloodshed of Nivelle's offensive, for its lack of clear war aims and for punishing the mutineers at all. It was a dark moment for the French. In addition to their military failure the Russian Revolution of February 1917 – the consequences of which are discussed below (pp. 220–30) – threatened to lead to the end of the war on the Eastern Front and to expose the French and British in the west to the whole strength of the German army before the resources of the United States could be brought to bear in Europe. At the same time conventional politics in France, and many of the political leaders of the Third Republic, were discredited by a series of scandals: a patriotic propaganda paper which had at one time been financed by the Ministry of the Interior was subsequently alleged to have been paid by the Germans to publish anti-British articles, and when the editor was found dead, the Right declared that he had been murdered to keep his mouth shut: a Radical deputy could give no clear account of a package of Swiss banknotes found in his locker in the Chamber: a lady named Mata Hari was suspected of seducing prominent persons to extract secrets from them and was executed, as was an Egyptian adventurer, Bolo Pasha, known to have received German money and to be on friendly terms with leading Frenchmen. The result was that the Minister of the Interior, Louis Malvy, was accused of negligence and was forced to resign, and the government had to be remodelled. Then further scandals were brought up against Malvy, in an atmosphere of gloom and suspicion, and a deputy from the *Action Française* accused him of having betrayed military secrets to the enemy and so contributing to the French military failures. Although Malvy was cleared by a military committee of enquiry, he was later arraigned before the Senate sitting as a High Court, and was sentenced to five years' banishment for negligence. Rumours of this kind continued to spread: in January 1918 the Radical Socialist leader and former prime minister, Caillaux, who was rumoured to be planning a *coup d'état* in order to make peace, was arrested on charges of 'intelligence with the enemy' and it took two years before he was finally cleared.

By November 1917 therefore, with the military situation even worse because of the defeat of the Italians at the battle of Caporetto in the previous month, with food becoming short and in a general atmosphere of suspicion and recrimination, the government, the third to fall in eight months, had been defeated in the Chamber on a trivial issue. There were only two possible solutions: either Joseph Caillaux would come to power and attempt to negotiate peace, or Georges Clemenceau would form a government committed to war to the end. The President of the Republic, Raymond Poincaré, convinced that the war must be fought vigorously, had no choice but to ask his personal enemy, Georges Clemenceau (who had once said that he had the soul of a rabbit in the skin of a drum)[17] to form a government because it was clear that he alone of the leading political figures had the energy and determination to carry on the war in the face of defeatism among the politicians and the growing opposition of the organised working class. And in cooperation with Marshal Foch Clemenceau succeeded in restoring some sort of confidence in the government and the army leadership. By governing almost single-handed, for he deliberately surrounded himself by nonentities – he once described his ministers as 'the geese who saved the Capitol' and complained that his Finance Minister was 'the only Jew I have ever met who knows nothing about finance'[18] – he established a sort of stern Jacobin dictatorship which enabled France to survive the strains of 1918 and to emerge victorious.

Although it seemed in 1917 that the Germans were in sight of victory and Britain and France on the verge of defeat, yet the situation inside Germany was also critical during that year, for all the hopes that Russia might drop out of the war and Britain be starved into surrender by the U-boat campaign. The success of the High Command in pushing through the policy of unrestricted submarine warfare in the face of the Chancellor's opposition, and the growing control exercised by Hindenburg and Ludendorff over all aspects of the German economy, left the politicians in the Reichstag disappointed and dissatisfied, and made the position of the Chancellor, Bethmann-Hollweg, very difficult. At the same time the British blockade of Germany was making its effect: food was short, rationing had been introduced and a major strike among the metal workers in April 1917 showed that the internal situation was by no means stable. Moreover, the solidarity which the parties had shown at the outbreak of the war was beginning to break down. As early as December 1914 a single deputy on the left wing of the Social Democratic Party, Karl Liebknecht (the son of Wilhelm Liebknecht, one of the party's founders), voted against the renewal of the war credits; and a year later twenty deputies voted against, while a number abstained. In March 1916 the leader of the socialist parliamentary group, Hugo Haase, came out in opposition to the war, and this led to a split in the party. A breach in the *Burgfrieden* could not be prevented. In April 1917 the dissident group, now openly opposed to the war and calling for a 'peace without annexations and indemnities', formed itself into a separate party, the Independent Social Democratic Party (*Unabhängige Sozialdemokratische Partei Deutschlands*, USPD).

In the Reichstag the liberals and the Catholic Centre Party as well as the Social Democrats, worried over the decline of their influence, were anxious at least to have promises of domestic and constitutional reform after the war. As a report to the government put it, 'the Majority Socialists consider it absolutely necessary to give rights at the moment when so little bread can be given'.[19] At the same time the example of what had happened in Russia with the overthrow of the Tsar in February 1917 seemed to give a new meaning to the demands for change in Germany. The Kaiser declared in April 1917 that he was prepared to consider constitutional changes – the main demand was for the introduction of universal suffrage in the state of Prussia – and although the Prussian conservatives were strong enough to block any immediate reform, a commission was appointed in May 1917 to discuss the question. While the National Liberals could unite on the need for constitutional reform, they were divided on the question of war aims, with some of their most influential members such as Gustav Stresemann prepared to support the programme of annexations in west and east to which the High Command was committed. However by July 1917 when it was clear that the U-boat campaign had not defeated England in six months, that the Russians had not yet left the war and even looked like mounting an offensive in Galicia, and that in spite of the French failures the Germans had not broken through in the west either, a number of Reichstag members, led by the Centre party's leader Matthias Erzberger, began to express themselves in favour of a negotiated peace. This led Ludendorff to call for the appointment of a new imperial chancellor who would be a more reliable spokesman for the Supreme Command in the Reichstag than the unfortunate Bethmann appeared to be. On 8 July, two days after Erzberger had made a speech calling for a negoti- ated peace because a decisive military victory no longer seemed likely, Bethmann was forced to resign, since Ludendorff had declared that he would go if Bethmann did not. He was succeeded by an insignificant Prussian official, Georg Michaelis, who Ludendorff hoped would simply make sure that the Reichstag would obey the wishes of the General Staff. In practice he proved unable to do this: and on 19 July the Reichstag passed by a sub- stantial majority a resolution which stated, 'Germany resorted to arms in order to defend her freedom and independence and the integrity of her territorial possessions. The Reichstag strives for a peace of understanding and the permanent reconciliation of peoples. Forced territorial acquisitions and political, economic and financial oppression are irreconcilable with such a peace.'[20]

This raised hopes that there might now be a basis for a negotiated peace – though it made no mention of Alsace-Lorraine, which the French expected to recover outright and which even the German Independent Social Demo- crats only thought should be the object of a plebiscite after the war. Other people were putting forward similar views – the Pope in August, and in England in November Lord Lansdowne, a respected Conservative statesman who had been Foreign Secretary at the time of the signature of the Anglo- French *Entente* in 1904; but the Pope was not listened to and opinion in British ruling circles was so strongly against Lansdowne that *The Times* refused to print his letter setting out his views, for fear that any public discussion of peace might weaken the will to continue the war. Above all, however, there was no chance that the German Supreme Command would be prepared to drop its programme of annexations to please the Reichstag. In practice, although the Reichstag succeeded in forcing Michaelis's resigna- tion after he had tried to pass a law making the Independent Socialist Party illegal, these apparent victories for a moderate majority of liberals, Social Democrats and the Centre Party only served to mark the impotence of the Reichstag. By the beginning of 1918 it was quite clear that, for all its show of independence in the summer and autumn of 1917, the Reichstag was as powerless as it had ever been, and that Hindenburg and Ludendorff were the real rulers of Germany, committed more tenaciously than ever to a pro- gramme of extensive annexations at the expense of France and Belgium in the West and Russia and Roumania (which had joined the war on the Allied side in August 1916) in the East.

The weakness in the German position in 1917 lay not only in the incipient opposition in the Reichstag and in growing labour unrest, but also in the situation of her ally Austria–Hungary. The death of Franz Joseph in November 1916, and the accession of his great-nephew the young Emperor Karl, opened up the final crisis of the monarchy, and the remaining two years of its existence were filled with growing tensions, both economic and political. The war had revealed how wide the gap was between the two halves of the monarchy, and the Hungarian government had used the opportunity provided by the war to act in almost total independence of Vienna, so that the future of the *Ausgleich* (the Compromise between the Hungarians and the emperor originally reached in 1867 and renewed every ten years since and due to come up for renewal in 1917) looked uncertain. It was at the economic level that Austrian dependence on Hungary was most apparent. Vienna and the Austrian provinces relied on Hungary for their grain supply. In peacetime, if the harvest was bad, this could be supplemented by maize and rye from Russia and Roumania, but in the war, with the British blockade becoming increasingly effective, the Austrian half of the monarchy became almost totally dependent on Hungary for its needs, and the Hungarian government showed itself quite impervious to requests to release more grain, except when it itself needed industrial products from Austria. The Austrian government had introduced economic controls and food rationing very early in the war, but the centralised administration and the complex bureaucratic machinery was breaking down, caught in the conflicting interests of the various provincial administrations. By the beginning of 1917 food was short and of bad quality, the black market was active everywhere and the complaints of the people were mounting. (The Viennese satirist Karl Kraus, in his magazine, *Die Fackel* (The Torch) and in his long dramatic composition *Die letzten Tage der Menschheit* (The Last Days of Mankind, 1922) caught unforgettably the conflicting voices of all classes of Austrian society – cynical, desperate, hypocritically patriotic or good-naturedly grumbling.)

Emperor Karl and his advisers, believing that it would not be possible for the monarchy to hold out through another year of war, decided early in 1917 to explore the possibilities of a separate peace, and, through his brother-in-law, Prince Sixte of Bourbon-Parme, an officer in the Belgian army, he approached the French government, offering to make some concessions to Italy and to press the Germans to return Alsace-Lorraine to France. These secret negotiations, although they appealed to the ever hopeful Lloyd George, did not come to anything. The French were sceptical, and were not even certain that they wanted a separate peace which would probably bring Italy out of the war as well as Austria; and the Italians soon made it clear that they were not interested in peace with Austria on any terms which the Emperor might conceivably be willing to accept. Above all however it was the extent to which Austria was now bound to Germany that made Karl's diplomacy unrealistic. Germany would never have allowed Austria to drop out; and any peace would have to be a general one and not a separate one. The Emperor at

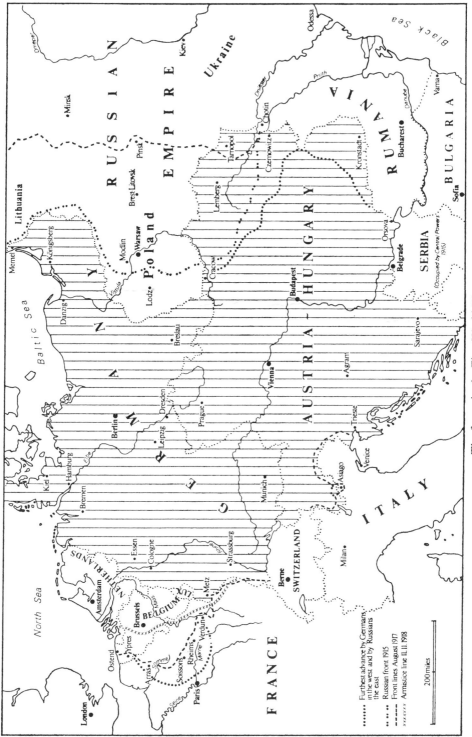

The fronts in the First World War

Furthest advance by Germans,
in the west and by Russians
the east
Russian front 1915
Front lines August 1917
Armistice line 11.11.1918

200 miles

one point suggested that, if the Germans would consider giving up Alsace-Lorraine, he would compensate them by giving them Austrian Silesia; and this proposal shows that he was thinking in terms of eighteenth-century dynastic diplomacy rather than of the realities of international life in the twentieth century. Although later in 1917 and early 1918 various further contacts were established between Austria and the Allies, none of them met with any more success. Austria was bound to the German war machine whether the Austrian Emperor liked it or not, and the only effect of his well-intentioned efforts was, when in 1918 Clemenceau published Karl's original proposals, to increase suspicion and dislike between the Austrians and the German High Command.

The new Emperor was no more successful in his search for internal peace. In May 1917, with the recent overthrow of the Russian Tsar very much in everybody's mind, the Austrian parliament met for the first time since March 1914. The parliament had been prorogued three years before because of the persistent obstruction of the nationalities, and especially of the Czechs, and by 1917 the situation had got worse rather than better. Each of the nationalities was now solely concerned with saving itself from the general wreck which they all saw coming. Czech, Yugoslav and Polish *émigrés* were actively trying to persuade the Allied governments to recognise their claims; and any re-modelling of the monarchy along the mildly federal lines which the Emperor had in mind was by now irrelevant – even if the Hungarian government had been prepared to make any concessions to their nationalities parallel to those contemplated in Vienna. The German nationalists in Austria saw their future as lying in closer links with the German Empire and in an alliance with the Hungarians in which both master races would, as the Hungarians had already done, impose their will on the subject peoples, and these ideas fitted in with some of the proposals for a German-dominated *Mitteleuropa* which had already been discussed in Germany. Politically, economically and militarily it became increasingly clear that Germany would have to take over more and more responsibility for her ally, and that Emperor Karl's hopes of independent action at home and abroad were vain.

Between the autumn of 1916 and the end of 1917 all the belligerent countries of Europe experienced internal crises and serious political upheavals, but in no country were the changes so profound or the results so far-reaching as in the case of Russia. The factors which everywhere underlay the European crisis were present in Russia – war-weariness, food shortages, rising prices, demands for more efficient conduct of the war and for better conditions for the troops – but they were exacerbated by the nature of Russian institutions and by the personality and beliefs of Nicholas II. The Tsar was an autocrat: that is to say that he believed himself to have a divine mission to rule as an absolute sovereign without sharing his power with anyone, and without admitting that the ministers could be responsible to anybody but himself. On the other hand he had been reluctantly obliged after the Revolution of 1905 to allow the formation of a representative parliament, the Duma, even though he and his advisers had taken care that it should have very little power and that it should be based on an exceedingly narrow franchise. Again, as we have seen, in order to meet the demands of war-time administration and supply, a number of voluntary bodies had been set up in 1914 and, as the war went on, these not only assumed more importance but also formed central committees, notably a central war industries committee on which a few workers were allowed to sit and the chairman of which was A. I. Guchkov, a prominent liberal politician and former president of the Duma, who had been an outspoken critic of the regime and who was particularly disliked by the Tsar personally. Thus, although all power theoretically still rested with the Tsar, there were by 1916 several bodies involved in the conduct of the war which were increasingly critical of the way it was being run.

The meetings of the Duma in 1915 and in February 1916 (when the Tsar himself opened the session in a conciliatory gesture that does not seem to have had much effect) showed that, as in Germany, a liberal parliamentary block was emerging which was deeply critical of the monarch and his advisers. The difference was that in the case of Russia there was no equivalent to Hindenburg and Ludendorff to assume dictatorial powers on behalf of the High Command. In fact, in an attempt to quell criticism of the generals and of the Commander in Chief, the Grand Duke Nicholas Nicholaievich, the Tsar decided in September 1915 to take command personally. From then on he was mostly at the front, leaving behind ministers, whom he changed frequently ('All these changes make my head go round,' he wrote to his wife in September 1916),[21] and more important his fanatically autocratic and bigoted consort, the Tsaritsa Alexandra. She showered him with recommendations and advice, much of it received from the sinister Rasputin, a sectarian monk who had become a favourite of the court because he seemed to have occult healing powers which enabled him to help the Tsar's young son and heir, who was afflicted with haemophilia and whose life was endangered by every bruise or scratch. The ministers and many members of the Duma asked the Tsar not to take over the command of the armies personally at a moment when the campaign had been going extremely badly: in 1915 the Russians had been forced to withdraw from Galicia and the other areas occupied in the previous year, and the precedent they quoted of the retreat before Napoleon in 1812 and the subsequent victorious advance did not seem a very convincing one. Although in 1916 General Bruslov was able to inflict a substantial defeat on the Austrians, who had moved troops to the Italian front, the morale of the army seems never to have wholly recovered from the experiences of 1915, and the offensive of 1916, although successful in taking some 450,000 prisoners and advancing into Austrian territory, placed renewed strains on the creaking machinery of supply and medical care.

The demands which the army made on the overworked railway system were disrupting the supply of food to the cities, the population of which had grown considerably since the war began, so that, as everywhere in Europe, prices were rising, such peasants as were left on the land were hoarding food to sell on the black market and supplies of consumer goods were becoming scarce. By the autumn of 1916 reports from the police and the army were almost unanimous in their anxiety about the weakening of military discipline and about the growing complaints by both soldiers and civilians against the war and against the government. As in France after the defeats of 1917, rumours of treachery in high places spread; and the Empress, partly German and partly English, who, whatever her other personal and political faults, was fanatically loyal to her husband and his country, was nevertheless accused of helping the Germans. It was in this atmosphere that a group of conservatives attempted to clear the air and save the reputation of the Tsar by the brutal murder of Rasputin in December 1916; but the removal of one bad counsellor from the imperial circle was no longer enough to save the dynasty.

By the beginning of the New Year it was clear that the mounting discontent was coming into the open. The Duma became the symbol of the possibility of a more liberal regime, although its members were following events rather than guiding them, and it served as the focus of demands for reform. But the really important events were happening outside parliament – on the streets, where hundreds of thousands of workers were spontaneously expressing their sense of grievance and hardship by means of political strikes, in the villages, where, as a police report put it, 'there is a marked increase in hostile feelings among the peasants not only against the Government, but also against all other social groups such as industrial workers, government officials, the clergy, etc.'[22], and in the army, where discipline was breaking down and where patriotic appeals of the kind that might have worked in 1914 were now greeted with the utmost cynicism. If food and peace could only be obtained by a revolution, there was at home and at the front a vast mass of Russians ready to support one.

When the Duma met at the end of February,* and was soon afterwards prorogued by the government, there were widespread strikes in Petrograd,† and desertions from the front were mounting. The leaders of the Duma who formed a committee to take control of the situation soon found that their deliberations were liable to be swamped by crowds of soldiers and workmen who themselves organised a rival centre of power, the Petrograd Soviet of

* Until 1918 the Russians used a different calendar from the rest of Europe: here the dates are given in the old style, since the revolution is usually known as the February Revolution, although by Western reckoning it occurred in March, just as the Bolshevik revolution later in the year is known as the October Revolution, although the Western calendar would place it in November.

† After the outbreak of the war the name St. Petersburg was changed to Petrograd, the Russian equivalent of the older German name.

Soldiers' and Workers' Deputies. For a few days the Tsar's government, the Duma committee and the Soviet existed side by side, but the government failed to prevent the spread of the strike movement and there were signs of mutiny in the Petrograd garrison. On 8 March there was a vast workers' demonstration and even some of the army commanders themselves had to admit that they had lost control of the situation. By 15 March a provisional government was formed by the Duma with the backing of the Soviet; and late that evening the Tsar, who was on his way back from his headquarters but unable to reach Petrograd because the revolutionaries controlled the railway lines, was compelled to abdicate.

The effects of these sudden events were felt throughout Europe. For liberals in France and Britain the overthrow of the tsarist autocracy was welcome in itself, but also because it made Russia seem a more respectable ally and improved the chances, it was believed, of a just peace. For the Americans it made entry into the war easier by removing, in Secretary of State Lansing's words, 'the one objection to affirming that the European war was a war between Democracy and Absolutism; that the only hope of a permanent peace between all nations depended upon the establishment of democratic institutions throughout the world'.[23] The spontaneous popular movement which had so rapidly and with such unexpected ease swept away the Romanov dynasty wanted peace above everything, and this was coupled in the minds of the peasants (and those whom Lenin called 'peasants dressed in soldiers' uniforms'),[24] with the hope that the revolution would bring them possession of the land. The satisfaction of these two demands was the main problem which faced the provisional government; and its failure to bring an end to the war or to introduce a large-scale land reform contributed to its weakness and downfall.

The provisional government was under considerable pressure from Russia's allies to remain in the war; but it soon became clear that the difficulties which had hampered the war effort before the revolution were quite unchanged by it. Indeed the situation had deteriorated: the breakdown of administration, transport and supplies which had been one of the causes of the revolution was made worse by the rapid crumbling of the substructure of government which followed the change of regime. In the army itself discipline had collapsed; and one of the first acts of the revolutionary soldiers in the Petrograd Soviet was to insist on the issue of an order ('Order no. 1') abolishing badges of rank and establishing political committees inside each army unit. While the members of the provisional government under Prince Lvov were uttering impeccable liberal sentiments, the large middle class, which a liberal revolution presupposes, just did not exist in Russia. The liberal politicians were trying to make a revolution in a vacuum in which they had to create, not only their political support, but also an administrative and economic base from which to work. It was for this reason that the existence of the Soviets, of which the Petrograd Soviet was the most important, was very significant. The Soviets had been formed spontaneously in a number of cities; originally known as workers' councils, they soon took the name 'workers' and soldiers' councils', and were dominated by the two parties representing the industrial proletariat and the peasant soldiers – the Menshevik Social Democrats and the Social Revolutionaries. Not only was the Petrograd Soviet a rival executive body to the provisional government, but the Soviets in the cities were often the only effective administrative organ to be found. With the collapse of the ordinary forms of government the Soviets were in a position of being the only body which could organise and distribute supplies and perform the day-to-day functions of public administration. The existence of the 'dual system' meant that it was hard for the provisional government to act without the Soviets' support, and consequently they had to establish an agreed policy with them. This also, on the personal level, gave great importance to the one man who from the start was both a member of the government and of the Petrograd Soviet – the radical lawyer and Minister of Justice Alexander Kerensky.

As far as the question of the war was concerned, a temporary compromise was reached. The alternative to seeking a negotiated peace seemed to be an immediate cease-fire which would leave all Russia exposed to a German advance; and it was only the Bolsheviks who were prepared to envisage this, and even they were not unanimous about it until Lenin had returned to Russia early in April and was able to establish his personal domination over the party. Any attempt on the other hand to persuade the Allies to consider starting peace negotiations implied a continuing Russian war effort until the negotiations were complete. For the moment, the provisional government was able to agree with the Soviet that Russian policy should aim at a peace without annexations and indemnities. The effect of this statement, coming as it did so soon after America's entry into the war, was to open, on a wide international scale, a debate about war aims and the possibilities of a negotiated peace: and we have already seen how the formula found an echo in the German Reichstag's peace resolution in July 1917. The open appeal for a just peace by one of the leading powers engaged in the war gave new hope to the minority groups which had ever since 1915 been pressing for an end to the war, and who had themselves launched the phrase 'a peace without annexations and indemnities'. The Russian Revolution and the appeal for a just peace turned what had been a small minority into an important pressure group in every country of Europe.

In September 1915 a small group of socialists had met, at the initiative of members of the Swiss socialist party, at Zimmerwald in Switzerland. It was the first direct contact between socialists of opposing countries since the start of the war. They were in many ways unrepresentative, since the majority of their colleagues at home were still committed to supporting the war.

Moreover in war-time it was hard to obtain a passport to visit a neutral country: many of those who attended were already in Switzerland as exiles, such as Lenin and Zinoviev: others, including the leader of the French *Syndicat des Métaux* (Metal Workers' Union), Alphonse Merrheim, had crossed the frontier clandestinely. Yet the Zimmerwald congress is significant not only because it marked, on however small a scale, the emergence of a new international movement on the Left, but also because it revealed three lines of policy which were to lead to the development of three groups in the socialist movement over the next few years. On the one hand there were the representatives of the German Independent Socialists and the French syndicalist Merrheim, for whom the immediate and pressing need was an end to the war. On the other extreme there was Lenin, who called for the immediate conversion of the war into a civil war and preached a policy which was to become known as 'revolutionary defeatism', a policy of courting defeat in order to hasten the revolution. At the same time Lenin had launched, at the outbreak of the war, a call for the foundation of a new Third International, to replace the old Second International which he felt had totally failed in the crisis of 1914. In between were those who still believed that the war could be used for revolution, but who were reluctant to support a complete breach with the past and the old International, and who believed, as the Menshevik Martov did, that in some countries, and notably Russia, there must first be a bourgeois revolution and a negotiated peace before moving on to the next stage – the revolution of the proletariat. The difference between the two extremes was well expressed by Merrheim when he recalled that he had said at Zimmerwald, 'I did not come here to create a Third International. I came here to make the cry of my anguished conscience heard by the proletariat of all lands, that they might rise internationally in a common action against war. As for the mass strike, ah, Comrade Lenin, I do not even know if it will be possible for me to return to France to say what happened here at Zimmerwald.'[25] Six months later a further meeting was held in Switzerland, at Kienthal, and the same divisions revealed themselves, with Lenin and his supporters remaining in a minority.

The movement against the war was by 1916 a substantial one, both in France and Germany. In Germany the Social Democratic Party was splitting (see p. 216 above), and in April 1917, again under the direct impact of the events in Russia, the minority formed themselves into the Independent Social Democratic Party. On the left of this party there were other more directly revolutionary groups, one of which, the Spartacus group (called after the famous slave revolutionary of Roman times), was led by the indefatigable Rosa Luxemburg and by Karl Liebknecht, the first of the German socialist deputies in the Reichstag to protest against the war. Both of them spent much of the war in prison, though they were able nonetheless to circulate a number of revolutionary pamphlets, but neither of them was able to go to the meet-

Lenin for a civil war

ings at Zimmerwald and Kienthal. In certain industries the shop stewards were active revolutionaries and hoped to use the general working-class discontent with shortages and rising prices, such as expressed themselves in the Berlin strikes in April 1917, for revolutionary ends, though it was not until the last weeks of the war that they finally succeeded in doing so.

In France it was in the rural areas away from the battle zone that the first expressions of pacifist feeling appeared in local branches of the Socialist Party: people from the north who had been forced to leave their homes by the German invasion were, it seems, more bellicose. The movement became more important when it won the support of the *Syndicat des Métaux* and its leader Alphonse Merrheim, and when large numbers of socialists in Paris and the suburbs began to listen to revolutionary critics of the war such as Jean Longuet (a grandson of Karl Marx and a godson of Clemenceau) and the rising young syndicalist lawyer and advocate of the general strike, Pierre Laval, not yet the opportunist politician of the Right he was to be twenty years later. Advocating the acceptance of peace offers from whatever quarter they came, the *'minoritaires'* at the CGT congress in August 1915 produced the slogan 'This war is not our war'; and it was in this spirit that Merrheim went to Zimmerwald, and Laval to Kienthal. The movement continued to grow in strength, and in December 1915 Longuet and Laval succeeded in winning a majority of the important socialist *Fédération de la Seine* – which included the Paris region – for their views.

The Russian Revolution, and above all the call for a peace without annexations and indemnities, at last seemed to give all the various movements to end the war a practical focus. The first to realise this were the socialists. The socialist parties in the neutral countries now felt that there was a chance of reconstructing the links between the members of the Second International and of using this as a move towards the public discussion of war aims and of a negotiated peace. Accordingly they planned, for June 1917, an international socialist congress to be held at Stockholm. This at once put the governments of the belligerent states in a difficult position. They believed that, at a time when they were all facing internal difficulties and growing criticism, any discussion of war aims and a possible negotiated peace might weaken still further the will to continue fighting. On the other hand it was clear that the Russian government was anxious to pursue the idea of the Stockholm congress as a hopeful way of moving towards peace and of appeasing the Russian public. The socialist members of the British and French governments, Arthur Henderson and Albert Thomas, were sent on a mission to Russia to encourage the provisional government to continue the war; and Henderson returned convinced that the plans for the Stockholm meeting must go forward and that the British and French should allow representatives of their socialist parties to attend.

However neither the British and French nor the German governments were prepared to consider this, so that the conference ended by being simply a series of visits to Stockholm by representatives of socialist parties to discuss the situation with the Scandinavian and Dutch organisers. Henderson resigned from the British government in protest; on the other hand the Seamen's Union, still a firmly patriotic body, refused to allow the pacifist socialist leader, Ramsay Macdonald, to board the ship that was to take him to Stockholm. In France, although the socialists asked whether: 'the means of restoring hope to the troops and confidence to the working population would not be found in the political conduct of the war. Whether you like it or not, Stockholm is the pole star.'[26] The government, including Albert Thomas, who had been the only socialist willing to continue to serve in it when the other socialists withdrew, and who was being talked of in some circles as a possible prime minister, was adamant in its refusal to grant passports to any socialists to go to Stockholm. The German government acted in the same way: and the gap between the majority socialists who continued, with whatever misgivings, to support the war and the independents, now in open opposition, grew unbridgeable. None of the governments except the Russians had shown any enthusiasm for the Stockholm proposal, and even President Wilson came out firmly against it.

This did not help the Russian government to escape from its contradictions. It is true that they had declared for a peace without annexations and indemnities and had dismissed their foreign minister Miliukov because he suggested that the acquisition of Constantinople might still be a Russian war aim. Again, some sympathisers with the Zimmerwald movement had joined the government in May 1917, but this did not prevent it ordering a brief, unsuccessful offensive in June, after which the exhaustion of the Russian army was only too apparent, while in July the Black Sea fleet was in a state of mutiny. The government, in fact, continued to be, as Prince Lvov had written in April, 'tossed about like debris on a stormy sea' [27] There is a famous story that at the first All-Russian Congress of Soviets in early June - a congress dominated by Social Revolutionaries and Mensheviks, with Lenin and the Bolsheviks very much in the minority – a Menshevik minister said: 'At the present moment there is no political party which would say: "Give the power into our hands, go away, we will take your place." There is no such party in Russia.' And Lenin from his seat in the hall called out 'There is!'[28] In April, when he returned from Switzerland, Lenin was only the representative of a minority who, even within the Zimmerwald movement, had been unable to convert the other minority socialists to his view of the necessity of turning the war into a civil war and making an immediate revolution. Within seven months he had put his programme into action and had made a successful, if still precarious, revolution. His success has been variously explained by historians. Some see it as the result of Lenin's gifts of revolutionary agitation and organisation and of his conception of the role of the party in the revolution. Others explain it in terms of the weakness of the provisional government and of the lack of a middle class in Russia which could make the bourgeois revolution which Lenin's Menshevik opponents regarded as the necessary next stage in Russia's historical development. All these factors played a part in the outcome; yet again and again one is struck by the very small margin by which Lenin succeeded, and for some time the making and pursuing of the revolution was far from being the inevitable march forward that it has sometimes tended to seem in retrospect.

Although there were among the members of the provisional government men who were both intelligent and disinterested, none of them, and this was particularly true of Alexander Kerensky, who took over as prime minister from Prince Lvov in July, had the will-power and determination of Lenin, nor the backing of a disciplined and ruthless party like the Bolsheviks; and it is arguable that only a total ruthlessness could have achieved anything in the face of the vast problem facing any Russian government in 1917 – how to end the war, how to introduce land reform, how to reestablish some form of administrative and economic life in the face of the breakdown of the transport and supply system and of a rapid inflation of the currency. Lenin did not solve the problems: he either ignored them or made them worse, and used the opportunity presented by the complete breakdown of the administrative and governmental machine to construct a new and revolutionary one.

Lenin's return from Switzerland to Russia had been facilitated by the German government who helped make the technical arrangements for his journey, well knowing that, whatever else he did or did not do when he got to Russia, he was bound to cause trouble to the Russian government and weaken the Russian will to continue the war. The Germans had indeed for some months been spending a small part of their secret service budget on subsidies to the Bolsheviks, a comparatively minor sector in a wider plan to spread subversion among their enemies, whether by bribing the French press or by encouraging nationalist movements in Ireland, India or the Caucasus. Communists have denied the existence of these payments and refused to accept the evidence showing that they were made: but it could be argued that accepting German money for ends which in the long run no German government could approve was merely a sign of Lenin's shrewd realism.

As soon as Lenin arrived at the Finland Station in Petrograd on 3 April 1917, he made the extent of his revolutionary ambitions clear: 'Any day,' he is reported to have said to the crowds outside, 'if not today or tomorrow, the crash of the whole of European imperialism may come. The Russian revolution, made by you, has begun and it has opened a new epoch. Hail the world-wide socialist revolution!'[29] He was quick to assert his authority over the Bolshevik Party, among whose leaders in Petrograd were the young Molotov, and Stalin, who had recently returned from exile in Siberia, and to impose the discipline which was an essential part of his revolutionary method; and he was quick to see that the Soviets could be used as a means of revolution. Although the Bolsheviks were in a minority in the Soviets, Lenin launched the slogan 'All Power to the Soviets!' because he believed that they offered the best weapon for making it impossible for the provisional government to rule and to carry out the bourgeois revolution which the Mensheviks demanded. A month after Lenin, Trotsky, who had spent most of the war in Paris and the past few months in New York, also returned to Petrograd, and, as the leader of the St Petersburg Soviet in the 1905 Revolution, at once assumed an important role in the movement. He was a member of a small internationalist group of socialists, neither Bolshevik nor Menshevik, and in the past his relations with Lenin had been variable. Now, however, he realised that his conception of revolution and that of Lenin were similar, so that within the next months he decided to join the Bolshevik Party and brought to it a genius for agitation and for revolutionary improvisation in the military and administrative fields.

The month of July, when Trotsky finally joined the Bolsheviks, marked a crisis for them and ended in Trotsky's arrest and in Lenin's flight. There were four days of apparently spontaneous demonstrations on the streets, for which the government held the Bolsheviks responsible, although in fact Lenin, while making no concealment of his willingness to overthrow the government by force, did not think that the moment had yet come for it. The party newspaper was banned, and the party leaders arrested or driven into hiding. Lenin was able to escape to Finland and to live quietly there for the next few weeks. There he characteristically occupied himself with writing a theoretical analysis of the situation and a theoretical justification for his own position in a pamphlet called *State and Revolution*, which is one of his most important and revealing works.

State and Revolution is an argument in favour of the necessity of violent revolution, since this is the only way by which the proletariat can destroy the bourgeois state and overcome the opposition of the former exploiting class. It is based on a close analysis of certain texts of Marx and Engels in an attempt to show that this is what they consistently believed, and it is in particular concerned with what Engels in fact meant by his famous phrase 'the withering away of the state'. The pamphlet is directed against the Mensheviks' support for the provisional government in the hope that this could be replaced without a revolution, and their belief that socialism would evolve without anyone doing anything about it, but it also dismisses in passing the anarchist view that it will be sufficient to abolish the bourgeois state for the ideal society to follow automatically. The way between these two extremes lay, Lenin thought, in the 'Dictatorship of the Proletariat'. Even if, once communism is completely established and classes abolished, the state will eventually wither away, there must still be an intermediate period when the proletariat will 'need the state to overcome the resistance of the exploiters'.

'The proletariat needs state power, the centralised organisation of force,' Lenin goes on, 'both for the purpose of crushing the existence of the exploiters and for the purpose of *guiding* the great mass of the population – the peasants, the petty-bourgeoisie, the semi-proletarians – in the work of organising socialist economy.'[30] For Lenin – and how wrong he was proved within a few years of his death, and even in his own lifetime – the machinery for this operation would not need to be very severe: it is 'a matter comparatively so easy, simple and natural that it will cost far less bloodshed than the suppression of the risings of slaves, serfs and wage labourers, and will cost mankind far less'.[31]

The essence of the argument is that the aim of the revolution must not be, as the Mensheviks and Social Revolutionaries at this period believed, the capture of the state by democratic means so that the machinery of government could be used peacefully to build socialism, but rather the total destruction of the existing state machinery in order to build a new revolutionary system which will enable the exercise of the dictatorship of the proletariat in what Lenin regarded as the transition stage between socialism and communism. This is the last theoretical work which Lenin was to write before himself wielding the power of the state, and it brings out two contradictory elements in his thought, the belief in the necessity of force and of violent coercion, and the faith in the ultimate result which would lead to the end of the class system and the withering away of the state – elements indeed so contradictory that some writers have doubted the sincerity of Lenin's belief in the second of them. It is a doubt impossible to resolve. The manuscript was broken off, unfinished, when Lenin left Finland to return to the revolutionary struggle. As he said six months later (and it is a sentiment that makes him more like Bakunin than like Marx) 'It is more pleasant to go through "the experience of the revolution" [which was to have been the title of the next chapter of *State and Revolution*] than to write about it.'[32]

By September 1917, after a failed attempt at a military *Putsch* by a right-wing general, L.G.Kornilov, Lenin and some of the Bolshevik leaders were themselves ready for the seizure of power by force. They now had a majority in the Petrograd and Moscow Soviets – though not in the Soviet movement in general – and, after Trotsky's release from prison, he became chairman of the Petrograd Soviet, and was active in making practical preparations for the insurrection. Lenin, first impatiently sending messages from his hiding-place in Finland, and then coming in disguise to Petrograd, set out to convince the other Bolshevik leaders that the time had come to make the revolution. He was especially opposed by Zinoviev and Kamenev, who believed that no action should be taken, at least until after the next All-Russian Congress of Soviets due to meet at the end of October. Lenin made no secret of his views, and they aroused alarm not only in the ranks of the provisional government, but also among the other left-wing parties, who believed that an insurrection was bound to fail, that it would prepare the way for a new, more successful right-wing coup such as that which Kornilov had attempted and that it would put an end to what little resistance to the Germans Russia was still able to offer. The decision to make the revolution was taken by 9 October, and the Petrograd Soviet under Trotsky went ahead with making the military plans. Although the insurrection was expected, the government proved powerless to stop it. In the night of 24-25 October the main government buildings were seized, and Kerensky found that none of the troops in Petrograd would support him. The sailors too were mostly staunch revolutionaries, and the cruiser *Aurora* sailed up the river Neva with its guns trained on the government headquarters in the Winter Palace. Most of the members of the government were arrested, though Kerensky escaped and left in an unsuccessful attempt to rally troops to crush the revolution – the first step on a long journey which was to end with him nearly fifty years later preparing for publication, in an American academic setting, the documents concerning his brief period of office, if not of power.

When the All-Russian Congress of Soviets assembled on the evening of 25 October, Lenin was able to report that power was now in their hands. They were by no means all prepared to accept it. The situation was still extremely confused, and the Bolshevik methods were criticised by both Mensheviks and Social Revolutionaries. However, by the end of the meeting the Congress resolved 'to take power into its own hands' and on the next day set up a Council of Peoples' Commissars, composed of Bolsheviks. It remained to be seen how far the Bolshevik power was firmly based, in the face of the criticisms of the other revolutionary parties, who still believed that the way to revolution was through the election of a Constituent Assembly and the establishment of a new democratic constitution; and, on the other side, in the face of the efforts of the survivors of the provisional government and of people to the right of them to rally support in the provinces in order to crush the revolution. The struggle inherent in the existence of dual power still had to be decided, no longer between the Soviets and the government, but between the Soviets and the Constituent Assembly, which finally, after being postponed for a month, met in January 1918. The Bolsheviks allowed the elections to be held, but they soon showed that they were quite ready to deal with awkward opposition: one of the Social Revolutionary leaders was arrested, and the principal liberal party, the Cadets, was declared 'an enemy of the people'. When the Assembly met, it was nevertheless quite clear that the Bolsheviks, with about a quarter of the seats, were still in a minority. Just as Lenin had not concealed his intentions of making the armed insurrection in October, so now in January he made no secret of his intention to ignore the Constituent Assembly if it did not agree to vote itself out of existence – and this, even though the Social Revolutionaries had split, it was not prepared to do. After hours of discussion Lenin sent word to the commander of

231

Constituent Assembly - Lenin el
wipe it out.

the guard on the Tauride Palace where the sessions were being held, to close the meeting. A sailor thereupon went up to the chairman, put his hand on his shoulder and said, 'I have instructions to inform you that all those present should leave the hall because the guard is tired.'[33] In an atmosphere of total confusion the assembly adjourned, and when they tried to reenter the building, they found soldiers at the door to keep them out. Shortly afterwards the assembly was formally dissolved by the executive committee of the Soviets, and the third All-Russian Congress of Soviets adopted by a large majority a Declaration of Rights of the Toiling and Exploited Peoples, which the Constituent Assembly had refused to pass, and which among other things proclaimed Russia to be 'a Republic of Soviets of Workers', Soldiers' and Peasants' Deputies'.

Lenin always believed that the communist revolution must be an international one. He had consistently called for the establishment of a Third International to coordinate revolutionary activity, and one of the arguments he had used in October 1917 in favour of an immediate armed uprising was that the revolution was near in Germany and in the other advanced countries in the West. In this he was mistaken: although the Independent Socialists in Germany were in open opposition to the war, although there had been some signs of mutiny in the German navy in the summer of 1917, and although there were in existence in Germany small groups of real revolutionaries such as the Spartacus League, the government and High Command were able – in spite of severe mass strikes in January 1918 – to keep control until after the military defeat of the German armies in September 1918. In France the strict measures which the Clemenceau government introduced to check defeatism and increase the war effort had their effect, although the government failed to grant the army's demand for the arrest of Merrheim, because of the anger it would have aroused even among those trade unionists who supported the war. From March 1918 onwards the renewed German offensive in the west made it clear how dangerous the situation of France was and evoked a last upsurge of French solidarity and patriotism in the defence of the soil of France.

Perhaps the country which looked like fulfilling Lenin's hopes and prophecies first was Italy. In August 1917 a delegation from the Petrograd Soviet had visited Turin, where the workers in the automobile industry turned the occasion into a large-scale demonstration against the war, to the accompaniment of cries of 'Viva Lenin!'. The Austrians were able, with the collapse of the Russian armies, to transfer troops to the Italian front: and in October 1917 they inflicted a massive defeat on the Italians at the battle of Caporetto. Yet in Italy, as in France, military defeat and national danger briefly united the country. The military crisis was resolved, largely through British and French help, and the campaign was resumed. A new government was formed and, again with Allied help, a new effort at economic organisation was made, so that the country and government just survived the last months of the war. The result however was a growth of extremism on both sides. While the nationalists, eager to wipe out the shame of Caporetto, were praising the military virtues and the aggressive spirit of the elite troops, the *Arditi*, in the working class the revolutionary fire continued to smoulder and the movement of revolt continued to gain support. As elsewhere in Europe, a confrontation was being prepared which was to dominate the period immediately after the end of the war.

While hoping for revolution in the West, the Bolshevik leaders were determined to do what the provisional government had failed to do and to make peace – at any price, as it turned out. At the same time they believed that they could exploit the general movement in favour of a definition of war aims which the February revolution had evoked, by denouncing the policies of the belligerent governments and by appealing to the war-weariness of the peoples of Europe. The first thing which the new government did on the assumption of power was to issue a decree proposing 'to all warring peoples and their governments to begin at once negotiations leading to a just demo-cratic peace'.[34] And Trotsky, on becoming Peoples' Commissar for Foreign Affairs, had followed this up by publishing the secret treaties which had been made by the tsarist government, including the agreement promising Constan-tinople to Russia and the secret treaty of London which had brought Italy into the war. This caused some embarrassment, for although the general terms of these agreements were known, their publication seemed to con rm all the suspicions which radicals had long felt about secret diplomacy.

The immediate effect was to contribute to the growing demand on the Allied side for a full statement of war aims. For the British, Lloyd George made a speech to the trade unions on 5 January 1918, in which, without going into details, he asserted that 'Government with the consent of the governed must be the basis of any territorial settlement in this war',[35] though at the same time denying any intention of breaking up Austria–Hungary. But it was President Wilson especially who felt he must make his position clear. He had maintained from the moment of America's entry into the war that the people of the United States were fighting for something grander and more universal than what he believed to be the selfish aims of the European powers; he had insisted that the United States was a power associated with, but not allied to, Britain and France; he did not want to have anything to do with the Allies' earlier commitments, to the extent of apparently suppressing from his memory the fact that he had been told the terms of the secret treaty of London by the British Foreign Secretary within a few weeks of America's declaration of war. Moreover he still believed that it might be possible to keep Russia in the war by taking at face value the call for a clarification of war aims, and he hoped that his words would reach the Russian people and help them decide to resist the German demands. On 8 January 1918, with these and other considerations in mind, President Wilson laid down fourteen points which he regarded as a basis for a future peace, and which constituted at once the broadest and the most specific statement of war aims yet to be issued on the Allied side.

The Fourteen Points are a mixture of general principles and specific recommendations and they assumed enormous importance later on, when they became the basis of discussion for the actual peace terms to be imposed on Germany. What they represented at the start of 1918 however was, it seemed, a real concession to the ideals of liberals everywhere and a real response to the demand for a peace without annexations and indemnities. They were held to herald a new era in international relations, since they specifically rejected the kind of secret negotiations which Trotsky's publication of the treaties had revealed. The President called, in the first of the Fourteen Points, for 'Open convenants of peace openly arrived at, after which there shall be no private international understandings of any kind, but diplomacy shall proceed always frankly and in the public view.' And he went on to appeal for freedom of the seas and of trade, for disarmament, and for the adjustment of colonial claims, where 'the interests of the populations concerned *must* have equal weight with the equitable claims of the government whose title is to be determined'. These general principles were followed by specific recommendations: Russia must have 'an unhampered and unembarrassed opportunity for the independent determination of her own political development ... under institutions of her own choosing'; Belgium must be evacuated and Alsace–Lorraine restored to France; the Balkan states must have their relations with one another 'determined by friendly counsel along historically established lines of allegiance and nationality'; and the peoples of Austrian–Hungary 'should be accorded the freest opportunity of autonomous development', as should the non-Turkish nationalities of the Ottoman Empire. There was to be an independent Polish state composed of 'territories inhabited by indisputedly Polish populations which should be assured a free and secure access to the sea'. Finally a general association of nations should be established to safeguard the political independence and territorial integrity of great and small states alike.[36]

This ambitious programme dominated the discussions about international relations in Europe for many years; and its underlying principles, such as the self-determination of nations and the freedom of peoples to choose their own institutions, became phrases which every political leader used, often cynically, for the next half-century. It aroused hopes which could not be fulfilled; but for the moment in January 1918 it seemed to be a real promise of a new order in Europe and to many people a new incentive to face the hardship and horror of yet another year of war in the hope of a better future.

It was in respect of Russia that it became clear just how complicated the situation was, and how hard it would be to develop Europe according to the principles prescribed by Wilson. The Soviet government had followed up the decree calling for a general peace with the signature of an armistice with Germany, and with negotiations for peace at the German headquarters at Brest-Litovsk. The Russian delegates, headed by Trotsky, dragged out the negotiations as long as they could, still hopeful that, with the help of propaganda among the soldiers, the revolution in Germany and Austria might break out. The terms proposed were extremely harsh – in addition to taking the Baltic provinces and Russian Poland away from Russia, the Germans proposed to set up a puppet state in the Ukraine and thus deprive Russia of a very large area of productive land. The Russians had no choice but to accept. Trotsky made a dramatic gesture and simply announced that Russia would stop the war but would not sign the peace, and withdrew with his delegation, saying that there would be a state of 'no war, no peace'. But, with the German armies prepared to advance further into Russia, Lenin decided that, at whatever sacrifice, Russia must gain a breathing space to concentrate on the immediate internal problems which had to be faced. On 3 March the treaty was signed at Brest-Litovsk and ratified by the Russian government on 29 March, after bitter complaints from the Social Revolutionaries and some Bolsheviks about the extent of the sacrifice of Russian soil involved: but, as Lenin put it in a resolution to the Bolshevik party congress, 'In view of the fact that we have no army, that our troops at the front are in a most demoralised condition, and that we must make use of every possible breathing-space to retard imperialist attacks on the Soviet Socialist Republic, the Congress resolves to accept the most onerous and humiliating peace treaty.'[37]

The Germans had won the war in the east, and the terms of the treaty of Brest-Litovsk satisfied the most demanding annexationists. It even looked as though, with the promise of food supplies from the Ukraine, the Austrians might still be rescued from collapse. For the Allies, the formal withdrawal of Russia from the war was not unexpected, but the harshness of the treaty and the extent of the German annexations, which were emphasised again in the terms of the treaty which the Roumanians – their position made untenable by the collapse of the Russian armies – were forced to sign in May 1918, served to stiffen the will to resist and fight on, since the Russian experience made it clear what kind of terms Germany was likely to demand if victorious in the West. Moreover the fate which had befallen the Bolshevik republic and the rebuff to socialist hopes of a new kind of revolutionary peace made even some of the extreme Left more hesitant in their opposition to the war.

However, if the Germans had won the war in the East, they had still to win it in the West, and from November 1917, when it was clear that Germany would be able to move troops from Russia to France, Ludendorff had been planning a vast offensive for the spring of 1918. He realised that it was essential for Germany to win the war before American strength had been fully mobilised; and he was aware of how desperate the German supply situation was as a result of the British blockade. During that bleak winter food and clothing were short, and the strikes in Berlin in January 1918 were indicative that, even if they as yet lacked effective political direction, the German workers were becoming increasingly restless and discontented. Time was not on Germany's side; a short-term preponderance in manpower on the Western Front was.

Accordingly on 21 March 1918 the carefully prepared and overwhelming German attack was launched against the British sector of the front. It came at a time when there was considerable difference of opinion among the Allied generals about the proper strategy to follow, when they were still thinking of hanging on grimly till the campaign of 1919 when perhaps the Americans might tip the balance. In the atmosphere of crisis caused by the German attack, it was agreed that the French General Foch should be Commander in Chief of all the Allied armies, with Pétain and Haig, the generals in command of the French and British forces coming under him. This was in part the result of Lloyd George's desire to weaken the political and strategic influence of the British generals, but it perhaps helped to coordinate the French and British efforts at a crucial moment, even if it did not remove the differences between the commanders.

Pétain was aware of French weakness and wanted above all to reduce the initial shock to the Allied armies by giving ground if necessary and meeting the German blow later. Foch on the other hand was an advocate of standing firm and of using every opportunity for a counter-offensive. Haig was worried that his reserves might be taken away to help the French, and that the French would not come to the support of the British if required. General Pershing, the American commander, was determined to play an independent role and to take over his own section of the front. Yet somehow in spite of these differences, or with each approach contributing something different at different stages of the campaign, the Allies managed to survive. They were obliged, in the face of a series of German attacks, to give up more ground than at any time since 1914. By the beginning of June the Germans were on the Marne, and Paris, which had been under attack from the air and from the enormous new cannon known as Big Bertha (after Frau Bertha Krupp von Bohlen, the heiress to the Krupp armament empire), seemed to be in danger. But at this point Ludendorff realised that he was coming to the end of his resources, and although he tried one last offensive in July, he was unable to strike the finishing blow on which he had counted. His gamble had failed to come off. On 18 July the Allies counter-attacked and were able to take the Germans by surprise, using tanks effectively and decisively. Foch was at last able to see his great dream of a general offensive realised, and the Germans began to withdraw.

Already in June Kühlmann, the German State Secretary in the Foreign Ministry had declared that 'An absolute end to the war can hardly be expected through purely military decisions alone, unaccompanied by diplomatic negotiations', [38] but he had not been heeded, and the general staff had forced his resignation. By August the German army was still hoping, in spite of its retreat, to stabilise the front and be in a stronger bargaining position, even though Ludendorff himself now seems to have been extremely pessimistic and to have suffered some sort of nervous collapse. He had no further reserves of men, while the Americans now successfully attacking on their sector were a clear sign that the Allies could hope for fresh support in campaigns to come. A serious epidemic of a virulent strain of influenza was sweeping across Europe and was to kill many thousands of people, but the impact was, as it happened, felt in the German army more quickly than on the Allied side. It became harder and harder, however much the German High Command tried to do so, to maintain that the Germans were still within sight of victory; and by the beginning of September it was plain that Germany's allies were in an even worse plight. On 14 September the Austrian Emperor was openly exploring the possibilities of peace; on 27 September Bulgaria asked for an armistice. In these last weeks of the war the Allied army of French, British, Italians, Serbs and Greeks, which had been sitting at Salonika since 1915 waiting for the opportunity of opening up a Balkan front, but always starved of men and munitions because of the priority given to the Western Front, was at last able to contribute to the victory.

On 28 September Ludendorff decided that, if the German army was to be preserved and to be available for dealing with any threat of revolution inside Germany, there must be an immediate armistice. But first he insisted that there must be a new government to take the responsibility for this humiliating step, so as to leave the army, he hoped, with the reputation that it had not been defeated in battle but rather 'stabbed in the back' by the civilians. 'I have asked His Majesty', he declared, 'to bring those circles into the government to whom we mainly owe it that we are in this position. We will therefore now see these gentlemen assume ministerial posts. They are now to make the peace which *must* now be made. They shall now eat the soup they have brewed for us [*Sie sollen die Suppe jetzt essen, die sie uns eingebrockt haben*].'[39] The same sentiment was expressed more conventionally by the Kaiser, who issued a decree saying, 'I wish that the German people should cooperate more actively than before in the determination of the fate of the Fatherland. It is therefore my will that men who have the confidence of the people should have a broad share in the rights and duties of government.'[40] A new government was formed under Prince Max of Baden, a member of the ruling family of one of the most liberal German states and a former president of its parliament, who had been actively engaged during the war in organising the German Red Cross. Two members of the Social Democratic Party joined the new cabinet. The German Revolution had begun; and on 3 October 1918 the Germans asked for an armistice.

With the request for an armistice the process of making peace had started, even though it was over a month before the terms of the armistice were finally agreed; and the war came to an end on 11 November 1918. During these weeks the first stages of the German Revolution were taking place, the Habsburg monarchy was breaking up from within and the future territorial arrangements of east and south-east Europe were to a large extent being determined. The great European crisis inaugurated by the Russian Revolution was entering into a new phase.

9

REVOLUTION AND COUNTER-REVOLUTION

When the fighting on the Western Front stopped at 11 am on 11 November 1918, the victorious powers did not yet count the cost of their victory and the defeated did not yet believe the extent of their defeat. Although the war was apparently at an end, yet fighting was still going on in several parts of Europe: in Russia, where anti-Bolshevik forces were trying to establish alternative governments, and where nationalist movements in the Ukraine and in the Baltic territories were trying to set up independent states: in central and south-eastern Europe, where the nationalities recently freed from Habsburg rule were fighting over the inheritance. The Allied blockade of Germany and Austria was maintained until June 1919, and added to the humiliations, fears and hardships of a dismal winter in Berlin and Vienna. The economic life of Europe was dislocated as it had not been for centuries and, as hasty preparations were being made for a peace conference in Paris, the governments of Europe were anxiously coping with the upsurge of revolutionary feeling, unleashed in 1917 and only kept in check as long as the war was actually going on. The fear of revolution was never far from the minds of the rulers even of the victorious countries such as Britain and France, whose political systems seemed to have emerged intact from the war.

There seemed to be good grounds for these fears. Between October 1918 and the spring of 1919 revolutions broke out in Germany, Austria and Hungary, and in the expectation that these would spread, the Third International, for which Lenin had been calling since 1914, was founded in Moscow in March 1919. The whole of central Europe was in a state both of economic collapse and political instability. The Austro-Hungarian army had demobilised itself with surprising smoothness, and the railway system somehow continued to function; but the authority of the Emperor and his government over the peoples of the monarchy had vanished. In Prague a new independent Czechoslovak state was proclaimed and rapidly established itself; Croats and Slovenes declared their solidarity with the Serbs in a new southern Slav kingdom soon to be known as Yugoslavia; the Poles in Galicia united with their compatriots in what had been Russian and Prussian

239

Poland to form a new Polish republic; the Roumanians hastened to claim the Hungarian province of Transylvania. But the frontiers, form of government and above all the economic basis for these new successor states still had to be established. At the same time Britain and France faced economic difficulties and labour unrest as a result of the switch from war to peace and the demobilisation of their vast armies.

But it was in defeated Germany that the hopes of revolution seemed brightest and the dangers to the old order greatest. When Prince Max of Baden was asked to form his government at the beginning of October 1918, the situation was already desperate. The leaders of the Social Democratic Party who were about to join the government heard on 2 October 1918 how hopeless the military and economic situation was; and 'Ebert went as white as death and could not utter a word; Stresemann looked as if he had been shot.'[1] For months the German public had believed the army's promises that victory was within sight; and it took even the leaders a long time to realise how little room for manoeuvre they had in the armistice negotiations. A few people talked of continuing the war and of resisting the Allies with a popular uprising, and even Ludendorff, who not long before had insisted on an immediate armistice, now demanded that the war should be resumed in the hope of being in a better position to bargain with the Allies. It was too late; the food shortage, the influenza epidemic and the deep pessimism among the civilians as the truth became known, made any further resistance impracticable. Such active steps as the Germans were able to take only made things worse: the submarine warfare continued, and on 11 October a passenger liner was sunk, killing a large number of women and children, some of them American, and this, reinforced by British and French suspicions of Germany, led Wilson to formulate his position more sharply.

The Germans had asked for an armistice that would lead to peace negotiations on the basis of Wilson's Fourteen Points. This had been accepted, with some hesitation, and also perhaps some cynicism, by the French, and by the British only after the point demanding the freedom of the seas (which the British thought might prevent them imposing a blockade in a future war) had been withdrawn. By the middle of October 1918, however, it was clear that the victorious powers were going to demand internal changes in Germany; and they themselves hastened on the German Revolution. The American attacks on the Kaiser and on the German military leaders became stronger; and by 23 October Wilson was insisting, 'If the Government of the United States must deal with the military masters and the monarchical autocrats now ... it must demand not peace negotiations but surrender.'[2] It soon became clear that the introduction of a government responsible to the Reichstag and a promise of a reform of the Prussian franchise would not satisfy the President and the Allies. First Ludendorff and then the Kaiser himself had to go. Ludendorff resigned on 26 October 1918; it took a little

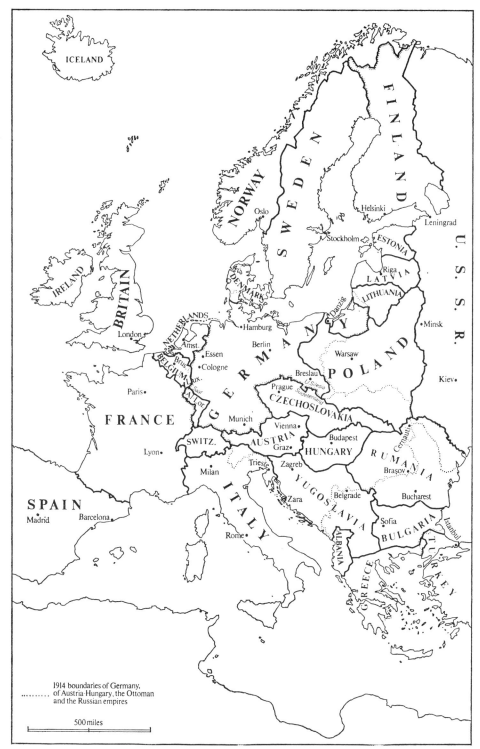

The peace settlement of 1919

longer to get rid of Wilhelm II. Not that there were many people who positively wanted a republic. Prince Max felt bound to the Kaiser by family and class ties and even Friedrich Ebert, the Social Democratic leader, was worried that a change of regime might lead to chaos and revolution. On the other hand, the American government had made it clear that the Kaiser was an obstacle to peace, and inside Germany the Independent Socialists and the Spartacists were demonstrating against him and agitating for his abdication. The Kaiser left Berlin for the army headquarters, hoping to find support there, but he was told, 'The army will march home in good order under its leaders and commanding generals, but not at the order of Your Majesty, as it no longer stands behind Your Majesty.'[3] One of the officers who had been consulted summed up the mood of the soldiers, which was that of much of the country, by saying 'The troops don't have anything against the Kaiser; he is actually quite without interest to them; they only have one wish, to go home as soon as possible.'[4] As Walther Rathenau remarked a few months later, 'A general strike by a defeated army is called the German revolution.'[5] On 10 November the Kaiser left for the Netherlands, where he lived in exile long enough to see, not without some misgivings, the German army occupy that country in 1940.

On 9 November Prince Max had resigned and Ebert became head of the government. The Social Democrats had decided two days before that the Kaiser's abdication was the only way to obtain peace and to deal with the spontaneous revolutionary outbreaks which, starting with a revolt among the sailors of the fleet at Kiel, had spread widely over the country. The socialist attitude was summed up by Ebert in words for which he has since been much criticised by the Left: 'If the Kaiser does not abdicate, social revolution is inevitable. I do not want it; I hate it like sin.'[6] On 9 November it looked as though, whatever Ebert wanted or did not want, the social revolution was coming. On that day there was a general strike in Berlin and many soldiers of the reserve army were in open revolt. Workers' and Soldiers' Councils were being set up in many parts of Germany, and the Russian example was in everybody's mind. Ebert still wanted to have a constituent assembly before declaring Germany a republic; but his colleague Scheidemann decided that an immediate decision was necessary and, interrupting his lunch, proclaimed the republic to the crowds outside the Reichstag building. It was still not clear what sort of republic it would be; and two hours later at the Berlin *Schloss*, Karl Liebknecht, the Spartacist leader, proclaimed another kind – a 'free, socialist Republic'.

The next months decided which kind of republic it was going to be and ended in the defeat of the revolutionaries. This was partly due to the divisions between the Independent Socialists and the Spartacists (who became the Communist Party of Germany – KPD – on 1 January 1919), and partly to the effectiveness with which the majority socialists in the government suppressed

Social revolution
in Germany

the attempts at making an uprising. But the chief reason was that the old organs of administration remained intact and the revolutionaries never succeeded in getting control of them, even though they had imposed a socialist government. Whereas in Russia the soviets had largely taken over the running of the country even before the October Revolution, because the governmental and administrative machine had broken down, in Germany the Workers' and Soldiers' Councils often had nothing else to do except literally to put rubber stamps on instructions issued by the appropriate regular authority. The Independent Socialists joined the government on an equal footing with the majority socialists at the start of the revolution, but they resigned late in December 1918, after a row about the suppression of a sailors' revolt in Berlin. Yet they did not really have any immediate alternative policy between that of the majority socialists in the government and the revolutionaries outside. The Communists too, as the Bolsheviks in Russia had been, were in a minority in the Congress of Workers' and Soldiers' Councils, which in December 1918 decided by a large majority to support the elections to a constituent assembly, and unlike the Bolsheviks the German Communists were unable to prevent the assembly from functioning and producing a new constitution.

The result was that the government's authority was never really challenged on the Left, although for three months there were repeated demonstrations, especially in Berlin. Rosa Luxemburg, with Karl Liebknecht the uncontested leader of the revolutionary Left, had always believed that the revolution, when it came, would be the result of a spontaneous rising of the workers. In contrast to Lenin she believed that the Communist Party should not push the workers forward into revolution faster than they would go of their own accord, and in the winter of 1918–19 it became clear that, whatever demonstrations and strikes the Communists and the revolutionary shop-stewards were able to stir up, the mass of the workers were not behind the movement. The Communists remained a small minority party, without the organisation to take over a mass movement, even if it had existed, and without Lenin's conviction that a minority party could all the same seize and hold power. Rosa Luxemburg was caught in the contradictions of her own doctrine. By waiting till there was a spontaneous drive towards revolution among the masses, she was unable to influence the immediate course of events which were shaping the new Germany; and she herself was a victim of an action of which she theoretically disapproved for, early in January 1919 as a protest against the government's dismissal of the Independent Socialist police chief in Berlin, all the left-wing groups started demonstrations in Berlin. These continued for several days with decreasing success (there is a limit to the number of times people will respond to appeals to go out on the street and demonstrate, especially in the middle of the Berlin winter), and the government was able to suppress the disturbances. In spite of all the signs that the revolutionary impetus was flagging, the Communists persisted in trying to turn the riots into an armed uprising. This was quite unsuccessful: Rosa Luxemburg and Karl Liebknecht were arrested; and on 15 January 1919 they were removed from prison and brutally murdered. There were other attempts at Communist risings over the next months, in Bremen and in Brunswick, and there was a general strike in Berlin in March, while in Munich, as we shall see, a Soviet government was even set up for a few weeks. Up to 1923 the German Communist leaders never wholly abandoned their hopes of making the revolution, yet, in retrospect, the failure in January 1919 seems decisive.

Later in January the Constituent Assembly was elected and the Social Democrats emerged as the biggest single party. In August the Assembly passed a new constitution which, drafted by a leading political scientist, seemed to offer the most up-to-date guarantees for a liberal constitutional development. But in fact, if the social revolution had failed in Germany, the liberal revolution did not succeed either. The Weimar Republic, as it is known from the name of the city, full of memories of Goethe and German humanism, where the Constituent Assembly met, was to be confronted with exceptional perils and difficulties, but some of these were inherent in the nature of its origins. The republic derived from a civilian government which the General Staff had insisted in forming so as to relieve the army of the responsibility for making an armistice. From its inception it bore the burden of the defeat. The Kaiser had abdicated as much under foreign pressure as from any demand in Germany, and the government which Ebert and Scheidemann formed had come into power because there was apparently no alternative, rather than as a result of any positive enthusiasm. Once in power the Social Democrats, following the line from which they had never deviated during the war, saw themselves as patriotic Germans trying to save what could be saved in the defeat of their country and trying to mitigate as far as possible the hardships which all Germans were facing. When Ebert expressed his hatred of social revolution, he was worried about the breakdown of orderly administration which this would involve, the disruption of transport and food supplies and the dangers of making an already bad situation even worse. At the same time he hoped, and in this he had been confirmed by the British Admiral Beatty's refusal to treat with the Sailors' Councils about the surrender of the German fleet, that the Allies would be more impressed by a moderate government than by an extreme revolutionary one, and would therefore be likely to grant better terms.

The weakness of the socialist position was that they had no means of carrying out their policies except through the old and deeply conservative bureaucracy, just as they had no means of restoring order except with the help of the old and deeply conservative army. At the very start of the new regime, Ebert had been in touch with General Groener, Ludendorff's successor at the army headquarters, who had stated unequivocally that 'the army puts itself at the disposal of the government, that in return for this the Field-Marshal [Hindenburg] and the officer corps expect the support of the government in the maintenance of order and discipline in the army. The officer corps expected the government to fight against Bolshevism and was ready for the struggle.'[6] And some four weeks later, when the troops made their formal entry into Berlin, Ebert, who himself had lost two sons in the war, said 'I salute you who return unvanquished from the field of battle',[7] and thereby contributed to the myth that the army had been 'stabbed in the back' rather than defeated by the enemy. When faced with the disturbances in Berlin in January 1919, Noske, the socialist minister of the interior, carried these policies a step further, and used the irregular paramilitary organisations formed out of ex-members of the army (and known as the *Freikorps*) to put down the Communists, so that he seemed to condone the murder of Rosa Luxemburg and Karl Liebknecht at their hands. The gulf between the majority Social Democrats and the Communists was from then on unbridgeable.

The government's deliberate refusal to make any fundamental changes in the personnel of the army, judiciary or bureaucracy, in the interest of keeping the administration running with as little disruption as possible, may have had a short-term justification and saved the Germans from having an even worse winter than they did, or even, as some have claimed, saved the country from civil war. It meant, however, that a large body of people concerned with carrying out political decisions under the new republic had no enthusiasm for, and in many cases a deep hostility towards, the new regime. At the same time the Left – Independent Socialists and Communists – was also now alienated from much that the new regime represented. It was said that the Third Republic in France was the regime which divided Frenchmen least. Perhaps, from the start, the Weimar Republic was the regime that divided Germans most.

In Moscow (which had become the capital of Soviet Russia early in 1918, in place of Petrograd, later called Leningrad) the Bolshevik leaders were still at the beginning of 1919 desperately looking for signs that the European revolution was about to break out. The hopes of a German revolution had not yet materialised. In December 1918 the German socialist government had refused permission for a strong Soviet delegation to attend the congress of the German workers' and soldiers' councils; in January 1919 came the suppression of the Communist rising in Berlin and the murder of Karl Liebknecht and Rosa Luxemburg. However the situation in central Europe was still so disturbed that it was not unreasonable for Lenin to continue to hope for revolution and for the Western governments to be very much afraid of it. Lenin, and indeed other Soviet leaders after him, believed that the revolution in Russia could only survive if there were also revolutions in the industrially more advanced countries of the West. He believed too that the capitalist states could not for long tolerate the existence of a socialist state in Russia, and that sooner or later they would band together in an attempt to defeat the revolution. At the beginning of 1919 it looked as if these fears were justified.

The Allied governments had been ill-informed about what was going on in Russia; they were apprehensive about the nature and aims of the Bolsheviks; they were anxious while the war was still going on that the Germans should not capture stocks of war material that had been supplied by them to the Russians. The British were worried by Turkish gains at Russia's expense, and by a possible threat to their own interests in Persia and on the Indian frontier, and already in December 1917 had despatched a military mission to Transcaucasia. In the East the Japanese were showing signs of wanting to profit from the confusion to establish themselves on the Siberian seaboard. By the end of the summer of 1918 the British, French, Americans and Japanese all had troops in various parts of Russia. There were a number of anti-Bolshevik groups vying for Allied and American support, and holding out promises of reestablishing some sort of front against the Germans as well as providing a more acceptable alternative to Bolshevik government. During 1918 the British, French and Americans gradually found themselves committed to an ill-organised intervention in Russia and to contributing rather ineffectually to a Russian civil war.

Thus, in Siberia, in the extreme north-west of Russia and in the south, the British, French, Americans and Japanese were giving support to the Russian generals who had succeeded in raising counter-revolutionary armies, while in the Baltic provinces bands of German soldiers, ignoring the armistice and the end of the war, were still fighting the Bolsheviks. The Allied intervention, which had begun as an attempt to prevent supplies from falling into German hands and to encourage the Russians to resist the Germans, had now turned into an open attempt to overthrow the Bolshevik government, and to open participation in the Russian civil war. It was a policy only reluctantly supported by the Americans and it deeply divided the British government. The French were perhaps the most resolutely anti-Bolshevik, at least in words, partly because one of the first acts of the revolutionary regime in Russia had been to repudiate the debts incurred by the tsarist government, so that very many Frenchmen who had invested in Russian bonds were suddenly faced with serious losses, and formed themselves into a politically influential pressure group. In fact, the intervention in Russia was a complete failure: the soldiers wanted to go home; the White Russian counter-revolutionaries turned out to be brutal or incompetent or both, and the various liberal and socialist groups which had supported the provisional government were unable to agree with the White generals or with each other.

By the end of 1919 it had become clear that intervention had failed, and the decision had been taken to withdraw American and Allied troops. The threat to the Soviet regime was not finally removed till October 1920 however, for in April of that year, while the flames of civil war were still flickering, the Poles, hoping to detach the Ukraine and Byelorussia from the Soviet Union and to link them with Poland, and encouraged with supplies and advice from the French, invaded Russia. It was a sign of the efficiency with which Trotsky had constructed the Red army from nothing that the Russians were able to drive the Poles back and advance nearly to Warsaw, until they were checked by the Polish army, advised by the French general Weygand who had been hastily despatched for fear that the revolutionary armies might be about to sweep across Europe. With the signature of a treaty with Poland however, and the establishment of Russia's western frontier, although it did not contain the Polish territory for which the Russians had hoped at the height of the Red army's advance, the threats to the Soviet regime seemed for a time to have lifted.

In pursuit of the great goal of the European revolution, the Soviet government, at its moment of greatest isolation in January 1919, issued invitations to a meeting in Moscow to found a Third International; and the founding congress of the Communist International (Comintern) was held early in March. It was still very hard for people from outside to travel to Russia; and difficulties of transport and the problem of obtaining passports and crossing frontiers prevented the congress from being very representative. The majority of delegates came from among those foreigners already in Russia, mostly prisoners of war who had adopted communism and not yet returned to their own countries. One of those who did manage to arrive from outside was a German Communist who caused some embarrassment by announcing that his party considered the foundation of a Third International to be premature. However, he abstained from voting against a resolution establishing the new body; an executive committee (EKKI) was set up and a number of proclamations issued. Within a few weeks it looked as though the establishment of a Communist International might not after all be premature. On 21 March a Soviet regime was set up in Hungary, and early in April Bavaria was proclaimed a Soviet Republic. The alarm of the statesmen at the Paris peace conference was expressed in a diary entry by President Wilson's personal adviser Colonel House: 'Bolshevism is gaining ground everywhere . . . We are sitting on an open powder magazine and some day a spark may ignite it.'[8]

The circumstances in which these two revolutions took place, however, made them short-lived. In Hungary in the turbulent days at the end of October 1918, when the Habsburg Empire was falling apart and when the *Ausgleich* between Austria and Hungary had already been denounced, an idealistic and liberal member of the high aristocracy, Count Michael Károlyi, had been brought to power in Budapest. Károlyi's support was never very broadly based and was limited to some of the students and intellectuals, some of the middle class of Budapest and the other large cities, a very few of his fellow members of the old ruling class, and a small socialist party. During the next few months and indeed from the very first day of his rule, when he was shocked by the brutal murder of his predecessor, the war-time premier Stephen Tisza, the unfortunate Michael Károlyi was forced to see how far from reality were his dreams of a liberal, peaceful Hungary forming part of a Danubian federation under the benevolent auspices of President Wilson. The former subject nationalities, Slovaks, Roumanians, Croats and Serbs, broke away to join new or enlarged national states, whose armies marched in to claim territories which the Hungarians still maintained were theirs. The government depended for such mass support as it had on those industrial workers whom the Social Democrats were able to organise.

In November 1918 a Communist party was founded, under the leadership of a tough, skilful and energetic ex-journalist, Béla Kun. Kun had just returned from Russia where, like many of the other Hungarian Communist leaders, he had been a prisoner of war and become a convert to Bolshevism; and he had himself played some part in the revolution. Once back in Hungary Béla Kun, on true Leninist lines, set out to split the Social Democratic Party and to attack the Károlyi government which the socialists supported. In the desperate situation of the winter of 1918–19, when the Hungarian workers and small peasants were short of food and threatened by external enemies on all sides, he succeeded in winning a certain amount of support. Károlyi was faced both by this agitation on the Left and by the hostility of the Right, as well as by demands from the Allies for Hungarian withdrawal from Transylvania, the province claimed by the Roumanians on ethnic grounds. In February 1919 there were riots in Budapest and, as in the events of July 1917 in Russia, the Social Democrats who dominated the government decided to arrest the Communist leaders. However, widespread agitation against the government continued, and some of the socialists were beginning to criticise Károlyi for not taking equally vigorous steps against right-wing conspirators (including Károlyi's own brother) who were trying to overthrow the government. As the disorders in the streets of Budapest grew worse, some of the socialists began negotiating with Kun in prison, and when Károlyi was faced with renewed Allied demands for withdrawal from further territory, he resigned on 21 March 1919, handing over power to, as he put it, 'the Hungarian proletariat', which in practice meant Béla Kun and the other imprisoned Communist leaders.

In spite of extensive use of terror Béla Kun was no more successful in governing Hungary or in saving Hungarian territory than Károlyi had been. The course which Károlyi had chosen had failed; but so did that followed by his revolutionary opponents. Béla Kun himself expressed the dilemma when he wrote, 'To those who say that the dictatorship of the proletariat in

Hungary is but sheer gambling on the coming of the world revolution, I have only this to ask: Which is the game of chance – to place ourselves firmly behind the international revolution of the proletariat or to lay the country's future on the altar of Wilsonian pacifism?'[9] Each gamble turned out to be equally unrealistic. The revolutionary regime was dependent on the trade unions for the provision of soldiers for the Red army, and although these succeeded in reoccupying much of Slovakia and imposing a temporary Soviet regime there, the government was faced with the impossible task of fighting not only the Czechs but also the Roumanians and finally the Yugoslavs as well. By July it was clear that the government was breaking up into a number of increasingly bitter and opposed factions. On 1 August 1919 the Soviet government resigned, and Béla Kun acknowledged defeat, saying, 'The proletariat of Hungary betrayed not their leaders but themselves. After a most careful weighing of facts ... I have been forced to come to this cold and sobering conclusion: the dictatorship of the proletariat has been defeated economically, militarily and politically.'[10]

Béla Kun fled to Vienna and later to Moscow, where he played an important part in the international communist movement until he was liquidated by Stalin. Others of his colleagues also remained active and influential in exile, the Marxist philosopher and critic Georg Lukács, the economist Varga, and Mátyas Rákosi, who became the Stalinist leader of the new Hungarian communist regime after the Second World War.

The Bavarian Soviet Republic had an even shorter life, and it was an episode that was at the same time tragic and also a little ludicrous. At the end of the war there were many people in Munich who felt that Bavaria had been linked to Prussia long enough and who were anxious for some form of Bavarian autonomy. The revolution in Bavaria had followed a pattern of its own independently of the revolution in Berlin, and the King of Bavaria had abdicated a day earlier than the Kaiser. The revolution was led by an Independent Socialist intellectual who had been an active opponent of the war, Kurt Eisner. The new government was faced both by left-wing revolutionaries demanding more power for the workers', soldiers' and peasants' councils, and on the Right by the conservatives who were calling simultaneously for Bavarian autonomy and for an end to socialism. On 21 February 1919 Eisner was killed by a nationalist aristocrat, at a moment when he was in any case faced with the prospect of defeat in the newly elected constituent assembly, and had already written out his resignation. Almost immediately after, Eisner's leading Social Democrat colleague was badly wounded by a member of the extreme Left. A period of total confusion followed: the Munich Workers' and Soldiers' Council decided, against the opposition of the Communists, to proclaim an independent socialist republic; the regular government under a majority socialist fled from the city. For a week early in April Munich was in the hands of a soviet run by a group of intellectual anarchists, among them the literary critic and anarchist Gustav Landauer and the young Expressionist writer Ernst Toller, whose autobiography, *Eine Jugend in Deutschland* (1933), admirably evokes the atmosphere of this venture into politics by members of Munich's left-wing artistic Bohemia. Faced with this ready-made revolution, the Communists took over. It was too late. By 1 May on orders from Berlin the army intervened, and after a few hours' fighting the revolution was over and the majority socialist government restored to power.

The revolutions in Hungary and Bavaria had been welcomed by the Bolsheviks as a sign that the insurrection was spreading throughout Europe. This belief was shared by their opponents, with the result that both these revolutions inspired a serious counter-revolutionary movement. In Hungary Admiral Horthy was proclaimed regent (for the absent king, the ex-emperor Karl, who did not however receive any support when he later made two visits to Hungary in the hope of recovering his crown), and introduced a period of strong authoritarian government in which the old ruling class was restored to power, and set out, by means of a period of repression and terror, to eradicate all signs of the socialist and communist revolution. In Bavaria the army and conservative leaders made Munich into a centre of opposition to the republican government in Berlin and a place in which every sort of counter-revolutionary plot could be hatched and every right-wing fantasy acted out.

The failure of the attempts at Communist revolution in Germany, in Hungary and in Austria (where the Communist agitation between April and June 1919 was checked without difficulty by the effective Social Democratic government which had come to power in November 1918, on the departure of the Emperor), suggested that the European revolution was not going to take place as soon as Lenin had originally expected and hoped. Nevertheless, while all over Europe conservatives were increasingly worried about the threat of revolution and were taking steps to resist it, the mass movements in favour of revolutionary change continued to grow in activity, and in some cases in numerical strength. What was not yet clear was what the relationship of these mass parties would be to the Communists and to the newly formed Communist International. In Germany the Independent Socialist Party was in opposition to the government but was not yet an actively revolutionary party. It was however able to profit by the fact that the majority Social Democrats had been in office during the hard and humiliating months of 1919 when the German government was faced with the Allies' peace terms and obliged in June to sign the Treaty of Versailles. (See chapter 10 below.) In the elections of June 1920 the right-wing parties increased their strength considerably, but so did the Independent Socialists on the Left, while the Social Democrats and the moderate parties of the Centre, which had been involved in responsibility for the Weimar constitution and for the peace treaty, suffered large losses. The republic had nevertheless survived a right-wing attempt, by a general whom the government had dismissed and a retired civil servant called Kapp, to seize power in March 1920 with the support of one of the *Freikorps*. The Kapp *Putsch* failed partly because the regular army refused to back it, but also because it was met by an effective general strike organised by the trade unions in support of the government. At the same time, however, the Communists, after some initial hesitation, decided to support the Independent Socialists and the Social Democrats in their resistance to this threat to the republic. While there was much discussion about the doctrinal correctness of this policy, there is no doubt that it gave the Communists new hope of mass action, and it was endorsed by Lenin, who was quite ready to see the Communist parties of the West become mass parties provided that they remained disciplined and under Comintern control.

In the summer of 1920, too, the hopes of revolution revived again. Not only did the Kapp *Putsch* in Germany seem to the Communist leaders, with their almost astrological faith in historical parallels, to be the 'German Kornilov affair' (see p. 230 above) which would soon be followed by 'the German October Revolution', but, more practically, the Soviet success in the war against the Poles seemed to offer hope of direct Russian aid to the revolutionary movements of Europe. And even when this hope proved illusory, with the withdrawal of the Red army in front of Warsaw, the Polish war nevertheless demonstrated that the revolutionary regime in Russia was infinitely more solidly established than it had been a year earlier. One of the results was to strengthen the position of the Comintern and to make it look like a body which every truly revolutionary group should try to join. Its attractions were the greater because of the failure of the Social Democrats to recreate anything more than a shadow of the old Second International, which to many socialists seemed an out-of-date and discredited organisation. At the same time an attempt made by the Swiss and the Austrian socialist parties – and the Austrian party was a vigorous and active one which included some able theorists and also showed itself effective in practice when it took over the municipal government of Vienna – to found yet another international body came to nothing. The parties of the Left with any revolutionary pretensions were faced with the choice of whether or not they should join the Comintern.

The second congress of the Comintern met in Moscow in July 1920 and, although some of the British socialists who had visited Russia two months earlier had been shocked by the lack of organisation in the Comintern headquarters, the congress was certainly more impressive than the founding congress of the previous year. The delegates were far more representative and there were also a number of observers from those parties which were still hesitating whether to join. At the congress the executive committee of Comintern set out firmly to establish itself as the general staff of the revolution. Lenin had always believed that it is better to split a party in the interest of maintaining discipline rather than to preserve unity on the basis of equivocation and compromise. In pursuance of this principle one of the main results of the Comintern congress was the publication of twenty-one conditions to which parties applying for membership would have to conform. The intention was that adherence to the Comintern should mark a complete breach, not only with reformist social democracy, but also with those elements in the international socialist movement, such as many members of the German Independent Socialist party and of the Austrian and Swiss parties, who were still looking for a basis of compromise between Communists and Social Democrats. In particular all responsible positions in the working-class movement must be filled wherever possible by Communist party members, and any members of parliament in the party must 'subordinate their entire activity to the interests of genuinely revolutionary propaganda and agitation'. Moreover, the discipline of member parties must be rigidly maintained on the principle of what was called democratic centralism: 'In the present epoch of acute civil war the communist party will be able to fulfil its duty only if its organisation is as centralised as possible, if iron discipline prevails and if the party centre, upheld by the confidence of the party membership, has strength and authority and is equipped with the most comprehensive powers.' Periodical purges of the membership must be carried out. Every party 'is obliged to give unconditional support to any Soviet republic in its struggle against counter-revolutionary forces'. All decisions of Comintern congresses and of the executive committee were to be binding on member parties. Finally any member who rejected these conditions must be expelled.[11]

These were tough demands, aimed at bringing into the Communist movement a disciplined mass following, especially from those socialist parties which had shown themselves already inclined to break with the old order and the old International. They were particularly addressed to the German Independent Socialists and to the French and Italian socialist parties, and in each case they provoked a split. The German Independents, with nearly five million votes in the elections of June 1920 (as compared with the Communist vote of less than half a million), were now a serious force which, it was hoped, might soon make the German revolution, though they were as deeply divided in tactics and tendencies as they had ever been. At a special party congress at Halle in October 1920, which Zinoviev attended as representative of the Comintern, the debates were about the fundamental problems of what constituted a revolutionary situation and whether one existed in Germany, whether the revolution must be the result, as Rosa Luxemburg had believed, of a spontaneous movement among the masses, or whether the role of the party was to drive them forward into revolution in spite of themselves. Although some speakers expressed apprehension at the extent to which the Twenty-one Conditions involved the surrender of the right to decide about purely German circumstances, the belief in imminent revolution was so strong, and the appeal of the Communist International and its emissaries so great, that the congress voted by a substantial majority to accept the Twenty-one Conditions and to join the Comintern. The German Communist Party had suddenly become a mass party instead of an insignificant and divided minority and, although the members unable to accept the congress decision mostly went back to the Social Democratic Party and gave it a small increase in support, the new party was able to win over three and a half million votes in the next elections in May 1924.

The divisions in the socialist movement over the question of support for the war were transformed after the armistice into divisions about the nature of the Bolshevik regime in Russia and about the right way to make a revolution at home. As a result a mass Communist party emerged in Germany by the end of 1920, and within the next few months similar parties were created in several other countries of Western Europe. The working-class movement was permanently divided, notably in France and Italy, where the divisions remain today, while in Germany the rivalry and bitterness between Communists and Social Democrats not only weakened the Weimar Republic, but also contributed to the establishment after the Second World War of two rival German states, based on rival conceptions of society, one liberal and democratic with a strong social democratic party cooperating in the working of a parliamentary constitution, and the other communist and authoritarian, governed by a centralised party dictatorship.

At the same time, just as the growth of mass social democratic parties at the end of the nineteenth century led to a conservative reaction against the liberal constitutions and the universal suffrage which had enabled the socialists to win votes, so in the early 1920s the appearance of mass parties openly dedicated to the cause of revolution contributed, especially in Italy and then in Germany, to the growth of mass movements of an anti-communist nature which eventually established the Fascist and National Socialist dictatorships.

However for the many people who feared the revolution the first place to look for security was in a conservative reconstruction of the old state. It was only when this failed that they turned, half in spite of themselves, to the new mass counter-revolutionary movements. This can be illustrated by comparing the situation in France and in Italy during the immediate post-war years. In both countries the socialist parties split and communist parties emerged, generating a fear of revolution, but in France the old order survived, whereas in Italy it gave way to a new Fascist dictatorship. During the final months of the war, as we have seen, the French government succeeded in keeping the support of most of the French people; the small minority of militant syndicalists who attempted to organise strikes in the spring of 1918 were not very successful, and the movement was suppressed without difficulty. However, the moment the armistice was signed, the submerged or suppressed conflicts broke out again. Once the appeal to solidarity in face of the invader was no longer relevant, the syndicalists and socialists returned to the slogans of the class war.

There was a big rush to join the trade unions and the socialist party in the months after the armistice, and the general effect was to strengthen the radical wing, so that those who had been '*minoritaires*' during the war looked like winning a majority for a development in a radical and revolutionary direction. There were many immediate grievances to encourage revolt: delays in demobilisation, inflation, the rise in the cost of living, the persistence of war-time controls, the continued imprisonment of some of the militant activists and the intervention in the Russian civil war – which led to serious mutinies in the French fleet in the Black Sea in April 1919 – but above all there was the feeling that now there was an opportunity for revolutionary change, and that the syndicalist tactics of direct action practised before 1914 might be used effectively to disrupt French society and to win justice for the French working class. In the early summer of 1919, and again early in 1920, there were widespread strikes and clashes with the police. In 1920 a big strike on the railways, where the physical and nervous strains of the war had been particularly great and where there was a long tradition of effective syndicalist organisation, nearly led to a general strike.

However, the confrontation between unions and employers on this occasion revealed the strength of the French employers in what one of them called a 'civilian battle of the Marne'.[12] With the help of volunteers – and the students of one state technical college tried to persuade the authorities to suspend classes so that they could go out and break the strike – with the support of the government and by means of reprisals against the strikers, they succeeded in overcoming the *élan révolutionnaire* of the members of the unions. The fact was, and its realisation caused disappointment, recrimination and division in the French working-class movement, that there was not a revolutionary situation in France and no amount of *élan révolutionnaire* could create one. The point had been brought home in the parliamentary elections of November 1919, when the socialists had not been at all successful in winning seats under a new electoral law based on a modified form of proportional representation, and a strongly conservative Chamber had been elected.

The socialists seem to have been least unsuccessful in those constituencies where their left wing was strongest, and many people believed that both the electoral setback in 1919 and the defeat of the strikers in 1920 were the result of too little militancy and too little revolutionary spirit among some of the party and union leaders. It was in this mood of division and controversy that the question of French adherence to the Third International was raised. The first group in France to take the name of Communist Party had in fact been composed of left-wing syndicalists, who were largely anarchists attracted by the idea of the soviets as a basis for a new social organisation, but the prospects of a serious and effective Communist Party in France, as in Germany, depended not on small splinter groups, but rather on how far the CGT and the Socialist Party were prepared to adhere to the Comintern and accept its discipline. In February 1920 the Socialist Party congress agreed to enter into negotiations with the Third International with a view to joining, though some of those who accepted were doubtful whether there would ever be any agreement on the terms, while a minority had wanted to apply immediately and unconditionally for membership. Consequently in June 1920 two leading members of the party, the Secretary-General, L. O. Frossard (who was to become the first Secretary-General of the Communist Party and then move rapidly away from it, ending up as a minister in the Vichy government in the Second World War), and the editor of *L'Humanité*, Marcel Cachin, who became a staunch and lifelong member of the Communist Party and an active senator until his death in 1958, went to Moscow to discover what the possibilities of adherence to the Comintern were. While there, they became convinced of the necessity of joining, though it is not entirely easy to see why. On arrival they had been coldly received by the Bolshevik leaders, who had expected them to announce that the French party would apply unconditionally and immediately for membership of the Comintern. They had been shocked by the terrible economic difficulties resulting from the revolution. They were subjected to a disagreeable cross-examination by the Comintern leaders assembled in the second congress, which they had been allowed to attend. Yet they were impressed by the conviction and the achievement of the revolutionary leaders, and they ended up by applying personally for membership of the Third International and accepting the Twenty-one Conditions, before returning to France to put them before the Socialist Party congress at Tours in December 1920.

Their report was an important element in the final decision. At Tours, as in the German Independent Socialists' congress two months earlier, the debate ranged over the whole of the party's traditions, principles and aims. There were a number of nuances among the supporters and opponents of the motion to apply for membership of the Comintern, but the final vote gave a big majority in favour of accepting the Twenty-one Conditions and of joining. In the debates the spokesmen of the orthodox socialist tradition, and especially Léon Blum who, after making a reputation as a man of letters and as a lawyer, found himself, in the vacuum left by Jaurès's death, one of the party leaders, pointed out the dangers inherent in the centralised discipline demanded by the Twenty-one Conditions and in the use of terror as a means of government by the Bolshevik leaders. The majority who, taking over the party machinery and the party newspaper, constituted themselves into the French Communist Party, were more optimistic; and doubtless many of them believed, as one syndicalist who visited Russia in July 1920 said, that in France '*La révolution se ferait tout autrement*.'[13] Certainly several of them, including Frossard and Merrheim, left the party quite soon, when it became clear that the Twenty-one Conditions meant what they said.

Lenin had foreseen quite clearly the problems that would confront – and still confront – a French Communist Party: 'The transformation of the old type of European parliamentary party, reformist in practice and lightly tinted with a revolutionary shade, into a new type of party truly revolutionary and truly communist, is an extraordinary difficult thing. It is certainly in France that this difficulty appears most clearly.'[14] In practice the initial success of the Communists in drawing mass support from the Socialists did not last long, and throughout the 1920s their strength fluctuated. Although during the period of the Popular Front in the 1930s, and during and after the Second World War, they grew much stronger and the Socialist Party began to lose support, they have never solved the problems which Lenin perceived, nor the additional ones posed by the subjection of a large national communist party to the dictates of Moscow. This was in part due to the traditions which Lenin indicated, but also to the ambivalent relations in France between the Communist Party and the syndicalist movement. While many members of the CGT were revolutionary, and sympathised with the Communists for that reason, they had always insisted on the autonomy of the trade union movement and on the priority of industrial over political action. The subordination in Russia of the unions to the party was so apparent that only a minority of French syndicalists were prepared to commit themselves to Communist leadership. In 1921 this minority split off to form the CGTU (*Confédération Générale de Travail Unifiée*) – a misleading title since its creation marked a schism rather than a union – but even some of the leaders of this movement were soon in trouble with Moscow, although the group continued in existence until, in the enthusiasm for the Popular Front, it was able to reunite the two wings of the movement in 1935. (See pp. 350–351 below.)

For the French Socialists too, as the chances of reunion, on which many of them had still placed their hopes, receded, the situation remained difficult and paradoxical. Although an important parliamentary party, the Socialists persisted until 1936 in their old tactics of refusing office in a non-socialist government, while Léon Blum, the undisputed leader of the revived party after the split, elaborated a subtle justification for this line by drawing a distinction between the conquest of power – the revolution – and the exercise of power within a capitalist society, the latter only being permissible in moments of extreme crisis. Albert Thomas, the right-wing Socialist who left political life in 1920 on becoming the first director of the newly established

International Labour Organisation, said that there was no middle road between liberal democracy and Communism: 'Either Wilson or Lenin. Either the democracy of the French Revolution, reinforced by the struggles of a whole century or else the primitive, incoherent, brutal forms of Russian fanaticism. We have to choose.' On this Léon Blum commented, 'I choose neither Wilson nor Lenin. I choose Jaurès.'[15]

The search for a third way intermediate between liberal capitalism and Communism preoccupied the European Left for the next half-century and continues to do so. In the meantime the split in the French working-class movement and the consolidation of a wholly constitutional and parliamentary Socialist Party contributed to the survival of the old institutions of the Third Republic, and Léon Blum never regretted this, any more than Ebert regretted his support for the constituent assembly and the Weimar constitution. In fact, the power of the French bourgeoisie seemed to have been confirmed, and France in the 1920s, for all the economic and social changes and the psychological damage caused by the war, remained at least till the 1930s politically little different in structure from what it had been before the war. The rulers of the Third Republic, faced with the threat of revolution, had succeeded to a large extent in a conservative reconstruction of the old state and had found that the old constitutional methods had been adequate for their purpose, without as yet adopting the new radical counter-revolutionary methods to which the Italian middle class had recourse in these years and which the German middle classes were also to adopt ten years later.

It was indeed in Italy in 1919 and 1920 that the hopes of creating a mass Communist party seemed brightest, and the possibility of a revolution appeared to be a real one. 'In Italy,' the leaders of the Comintern declared in August 1920, 'there are at hand the most important conditions for a genuinely popular, great proletarian revolution.'[16] Yet by 1923 the Italian socialist movement had split into a number of mutually hostile groups, a powerful counter-revolutionary movement had come to power, and within three years Mussolini had established a complete dictatorship. The tensions in Italian politics and society and the criticisms of parliamentary democracy which had already been there before 1914 (see chapter 5 above) were all made more acute by the divisions caused by the war and the disillusionments provoked by the peace. The economic situation was particularly bad in the months immediately after the armistice, as Italy's allies cut down on the supplies of coal and other raw materials with which they had kept the Italian war effort going, and were no longer able to give Italy the loans which had been available during the war. The Socialist Party, which had maintained its disapproval of the war, carried that disapproval over to the unfortunate veterans who were now being demobilised, and renewed their reputation of being 'anti-national' at a moment when a hysterical nationalist movement was developing out of the disappointment that Italy's territorial gains from the war were not as great as had been hoped. The division of 1914 between interventionists and non-interventionists was being revived in a new and more virulent form.

The parliament elected in 1913 was not renewed till November 1919; and even then many of the older politicians seemed out of touch with the new aspirations and hopes which led people to think that 1919 was the beginning of a new era – a frame of mind so widespread that it was even given a name, *Dicianovismo* (the Italian for nineteen being *dicianove*), recalling the similar hopes of the movements which had welcomed the twentieth century with titles such as Futurism and 'Twentieth-centuryism' (*Novecentismo*). Even the Catholic Church in Italy was affected by the new mood, and the Vatican, for the first time since the foundation of the Italian kingdom, authorised the creation of a Catholic political party, the Popular Party, which gave expression to a real desire for social reform and which, for a brief period, seemed to provide a focus for the demands of the peasants, for whom there was no place in a largely Marxist socialist party, and who were desperately hoping for land reform, even in some areas forcibly occupying the land themselves. Revolutionaries in Italy, socialist, syndicalist or anarchist, suddenly became aware of the similarities with the situation in Russia in 1917, where the revolution arose out of a combination of peasant unrest and proletarian agitation. During 1919, in addition to the agrarian disturbances, there were very widespread industrial strikes and many clashes with the police. Membership of the trade unions rose rapidly, as it had in France. The Socialist Party was in a militant mood, though deeply divided about doctrine and tactics, and there seemed to be good hopes of its being able to use the growing unrest and social ferment to create a genuinely revolutionary mass movement, hopes which were symbolised by the party's decision, taken immediately after the formation of the Comintern and confirmed by a party congress in October 1919, to join the Third International, and by the talk of its leader Giacinto Menotti Serrati becoming 'the Italian Lenin'.

The revolutionary wave reached its peak in the summer of 1920, when the metal-workers' union – here, as in France, one of the most militant – started a series of strikes, especially in the Fiat works in Turin, a city where there was a vigorous group of left-wing Marxist intellectuals of whom the young Antonio Gramsci became the most famous. The strikes spread to other centres in north Italy, and when the owners of a large Milan automobile factory threatened a lock-out, the workers retaliated by occupying the plant. These 'sit-in' tactics were widely adopted in many places in north Italy, and the employers were obliged to seek an agreement which gave the strikers many of the practical concessions which they had demanded. Yet what in purely trade union terms was a notable, though short-lived victory, was a political defeat. The occupation of the factories in north Italy did not lead to the seizure of power because the movement lacked a base outside the area affected and because it lacked the organisation to link up with the other centres of dissatisfaction and with the peasant movement. Gramsci and his friends in Turin were still without the national prestige of the older socialist leaders, and these, even when not avowedly reformist, did not take the lead in the revolutionary movement, but preferred to wait for what they regarded as the inevitable collapse of capitalism. In May 1920 Gramsci had summed up the situation quite rightly when he wrote, 'The present phase of the class struggle in Italy is the phase that precedes either the conquest of political power by the revolutionary proletariat . . . or a tremendous reaction by the capitalists and the governing caste.'[17] The strength of this reaction soon became apparent. Earlier in 1920 the Italian industrialists had organised themselves into a powerful pressure group, the Confederation of Industry (*Confindustria*) and were increasingly determined, especially after the occupation of the factories, to break the workers' movement and to remove what they believed to be the threat of Bolshevik revolution. As one of the leading industrialists put it, 'The future belongs to the organised classes';[18] and the industrialists were to show themselves better at organising themselves to protect their class interests than the workers were. They found a willing ally in Mussolini who, after his newly founded Fascist movement had had very little success in the elections of November 1919, was adding an appeal to the fears of the rich and respectable to his original exploitation of the feelings of extreme nationalism and disillusionment among ex-soldiers. From the late summer of 1920 he was organising his Fascist squads of toughs into a force that systematically attacked Socialist Party offices and Socialist Party members in many areas of north Italy. The counter-revolutionary forces would perhaps have been strong enough to defeat the socialists in any case, at a time when the parliamentary leaders were unable to give the country any stable government and when the Socialists were uncertain whether they really wanted reform or revolution, but the task of the counter-revolution was certainly helped by the divisions in the socialist movement.

While the Italian Socialist Party had enthusiastically joined the Third International very early on, its leaders only became aware of the implications in the summer of 1920 after the publication of the Twenty-one Conditions. The party leader Serrati, though much given to revolutionary Marxist rhetoric, was anxious to preserve the unity of the party, and especially to keep within its ranks some of the most respected of its leaders who were by now reformists – notably Filippo Turati, who had been mentioned by name in the Twenty-one Conditions as someone who must be expelled. The party congress at Leghorn in January 1921 was therefore devoted, on Comintern instructions, to 'rectifying the line of the Party and of purging it and its parliamentary group of non-Communist elements'. The result was that the party split, just as the German Independents and the French Socialist Party had done, but in this case those who had reservations about accepting the Comintern's conditions were in a majority, and the left wing marched out to another hall to turn themselves into the founding congress of the Italian Communist Party. This was a disappointment for those who had hoped that a disciplined mass revolutionary party would emerge, and that the Communists would win the mass support of the Italian working-class electorate: in the elections of May 1921 the Socialists won over a million and a half votes, whereas the Communists only had about 304,000.

Nor did the Leghorn congress mark the end of the divisions. In the Communist Party there were deep doctrinal and tactical divisions between Gramsci and the Neapolitan engineer Amedeo Bordiga, who had been the other notable leader of the revolutionary left in 1919–20, and had been unremittingly hostile to participation in elections and having anything to do with the bourgeois state. (He was also one of the few people prepared to stand up to the Comintern leaders and to refuse to follow every twist and turn of Comintern policy.) The Socialist Party finally expelled Turati and the other parliamentary reformists, who formed yet another socialist group, the United Socialist Party. (As in the case of the French trade unions, the use of the word united was a sure sign of schism.) The 'Maximalists' – Serrati's party from which by 1921 the right and left wings had both broken away – continued to maintain that theirs was a revolutionary party and, even in the growing crisis of the whole Italian political system caused by the rise of Fascism and the growing paralysis of parliament and administration in the face of it, were under no circumstances prepared to collaborate with bourgeois parties. Even the reformists, Turati and his friends, only decided that they were willing to do so when it was too late to help the government. The Socialists dismissed the Fascist threat as a quarrel between rival factions of the bourgeoisie from which the proletariat could remain aloof: on the day after Mussolini became Prime Minister at the end of October 1922, the Fascists who had broken into the office of the Socialist newspaper *Avanti* found an editorial already set up which made just this point. The paper was allowed to continue publication.[19] It was not until 1926 that Mussolini finally abolished the opposition parties and established a total dictatorship (see p. 268 below) although the Communists had been much persecuted by the police before this and had already started a semi-clandestine organisation; but from early 1921 onwards they were increasingly powerless to affect what was happening or ultimately to prevent the establishment of Fascist rule.

The passing of the revolutionary wave in Italy by the end of 1920 in fact marked the end of a phase in the development of the international communist movement and its significance was emphasised by a disastrous attempt at insurrection made by the German Communists in March 1921 after the police had moved in to disarm strikers in central Germany. Between the spring of 1919 and the spring of 1921 the situation both in Europe and in Russia had changed profoundly, as Trotsky was forced to admit when he told the third Comintern congress in June 1921: 'Now for the first time we see and feel that we are not so immediately near to the goal, to the conquest of power, to the world revolution. At that time, in 1919, we said to ourselves: "It is a question of months." Now we say: "It is perhaps a question of years." '[20]

Two main factors had contributed to this change. In Russia itself, while the immediate threat to the regime had been removed and the civil war was at an end, there was a desperate need for a breathing space, for a period of relaxation after the rigours of 'war communism', which would check the growing criticism inside the party. This led in March 1921 to the announcement of what became known as NEP, the New Economic Policy, and at the same time to a more uncompromising line against criticism inside the Communist Party and opposition from outside it. A dramatic rising by the sailors of the fleet at Kronstadt in March 1921 gave point to the criticisms that the party leadership had been too rigorous and harsh in ignoring the needs and demands of the peasants and of the common people as a whole. Lenin's determination to crush opposition – and the Kronstadt rising had been put down with great ruthlessness – was coupled with the attempt in the NEP to recover the support of the peasants, exhausted by three years of forced requisitioning. The NEP permitted a limited amount of private trading in the hope of reviving the economic life of the country and of giving some satisfaction to the needs of ordinary people for some private property and a few consumer goods.

At the same time as economic conditions and internal unrest dictated the introduction of the NEP as a means of obtaining a breathing space, it had become clear too that outside Russia not only was the European revolution no longer imminent, but also the mass revolutionary parties which had seemed to be emerging in Germany, France and Italy had less solid support than had been expected. This not only led to a change of tactics in Comintern so as to win mass backing by an attempt at collaboration between Communists and Socialists, but also, and in the long run this was more important, to the adoption by Lenin and the Soviet leadership of the policy of using normal diplomatic methods to keep the capitalist world divided, while at the same time building up national Communist parties to serve the needs not only of revolution but also of Russian foreign policy.

The end of the war with Poland in 1920 led to a settlement of Russia's western frontiers, and the Soviet government had also accepted the independence of the small states on her borders, Finland, Latvia, Lithuania and Esthonia. As early as the beginning of 1920 the Russians had been trying to establish trade relations with the West, and especially with Britain; in March 1921 after protracted negotiations and many delays a formal trade agreement between the two countries was signed. While several countries refused to recognise the Soviet Republic (the United States did not do so until 1933), relations were nevertheless being gradually restored with the outside world, so as to open, as Lenin put it, 'one window after another',[21] however great the mutual suspicions which remained. In 1922 the Russian government took its biggest step yet out of isolation; it received an invitation to the international economic conference at Genoa and used the opportunity to sign the treaty of Rapallo with Germany (see p. 283 below), intended, so far as Russia was concerned, to prevent the establishment of a European bloc of capitalist states by encouraging the continuation of the division between defeated Germany and her conquerors.

In the last year and a half of Lenin's life (he died in January 1924 after some months of illness), his short-term hopes of world revolution had been disappointed, but nevertheless the revolution in Russia had been successful in surviving the civil war and establishing the new regime. The Communist Party's hold on power was unchallenged: its methods and organisation were becoming increasingly those of a bureaucratic system; all potential opponents from outside the party ranks had been removed; the Mensheviks either went abroad into exile or stayed in Russia and accepted the regime, and the leaders of the Social Revolutionaries were brought to trial in June 1922 – one of the earliest acts to draw the attention of socialists and radicals outside Russia to the realities of the Soviet system. Although the slogan of 'Socialism in one Country' was not in fact adopted until December 1924, it was being practised by the end of 1922.

The fear of revolution and the success of the Bolsheviks in winning and retaining power in Russia provoked counter-revolutionary reactions all over Europe, and continued to do so even when the immediate threat of the European revolution had disappeared. In some countries this fear simply made the government take a tough stand against the trade unions and, as in Britain for example, where the unions had talked of calling a general strike against intervention in Russia, make secret plans for military action in the case of industrial unrest. The Communist threat became part of the stock-in-trade of the conservatives and provided the old ruling class with ready-made opponents and ready-made slogans. Just as during the war both sides had been prepared to make up and to spread atrocity stories about each other, so now reports of Bolshevik atrocities were common, some of them true – and the brutal murder of the Tsar and his family had been an early example – but very many of them as absurd as those which were told in 1919 of the establishment of 'commissariats of free love' and of 'the nationalisation of women'. Again, to take a more serious example of the political use which could be made of anti-communist propaganda, the publication in England of a letter (later found to be a forgery) from the Comintern leader Zinoviev to the British Communist Party calling on them to foment violent revolution, made a convenient electioneering issue for the Conservatives in 1924 and helped to overthrow the first tentative Labour Party government, since it was always easy, however misleading, to accuse social democrats of undue softness towards Moscow.

More serious and more important, however, were the counter-revolutionary parties which became a danger not just to revolutionaries but to the whole system of liberal and parliamentary government. It is these radical but backward-looking mass movements which became a new feature in Europe between the end of the First and the end of the Second World War. They embodied in effective political form the attacks on liberal democracy and the rejection of rationalism which had in the years before the war been theoretical and intellectual rather than practical. It was the experience of the war and its aftermath which gave the revolt against reason and the repudiation of liberalism mass support. And, although in many parts of Europe the same symptoms could be seen, it was in Italy and Germany, where views of this kind had already been fashionable before the war, that Fascism and National Socialism became the archetypes of a new form of dictatorship which used all the technical means of mass propaganda and mass oppression available in the twentieth century to achieve almost total control over nearly all aspects of public and private life. Bolshevism provided a ready-made enemy for these movements. Alarm at the Communist doctrine of world revolution combined with the economic difficulties and uncertainties resulting from the war and the apparent inability of parliamentary institutions to deal with them, to drive many members of the middle classes into supporting movements which would protect them against revolution as well as, they hoped, bringing them economic security and the satisfaction of belonging to a great nation. Fascism of some kind or another might well have developed in the circumstances of post-war Europe even without the fear of Communism; but that fear played a large part in determining the actual form which European Fascist movements took, and contributed to a large extent to their success, especially among the *bien pensant*, who might otherwise have been frightened off by the excess and manifest absurdity of much of Fascist and National Socialist doctrine and practice.

It was in Italy that a movement of this kind first appeared; and it was in Italy that the word Fascism originated. The Italian word *fascio* had long been used to describe small groups committed to revolutionary or dynamic action, and had been used, for example, by the Sicilian revolutionaries of the 1890s as well as by Mussolini himself in his interventionist campaign in 1914–15. It means literally 'bundle', and has the connotation of a bundle of sticks which, each fragile in itself, become strong when tightly bound together, and it was possible, later in the development of the Italian Fascist movement, to turn it into a symbol of authority and dignity – the *fasces* or bundles of rods borne by certain officials in ancient Rome.

Italian Fascism was a movement which contained many elements in addition to the fear of revolution, although this played a very important part in its growth between 1919 and 1922. Since it was the first movement of its kind to win power in Europe, and since its name was then used to describe a wide range of more or less similar (and sometimes dissimilar) movements in other countries, it is important to see what its ingredients were in the early stages, just as it is important to see what were the specific elements which, after the establishment of the dictatorship, made up the Fascist system of government (see chapter 12 below). It is also important to distinguish which aspects of Fascism were the products of a particularly Italian situation and which are more general symptoms of a wider European malaise. Many of its components existed in Italy before 1914 – a vigorous critique of liberal institutions and values, an intense feeling of national pride and a desire to gratify this by making Italy a great military and imperial power, a belief in direct action as a means of attaining political and ideological goals (see pp. 127, 205 above); and these trends had been accentuated by the experiences of the war. However two new factors had arisen since the war: first the nationalist propaganda now had a new form and a new audience, and second there was available in Mussolini an extremely skilful demagogue and politician who succeeded in fusing these various elements into an effective mass movement, and in linking to it the industrialists, businessmen and landowners who were afraid of revolution, and also those members of the middle classes whose desire for law and order was apparently satisfied by the brutality of the Fascist *squadre*.

The Italian nationalists had gone through some intense experiences in the course of the war: the campaign for intervention, culminating in the 'radiant May' of 1915, the bitter humiliation of the defeat at Caporetto and the eventual exhilaration of victory. Above all there was the hope of winning not only the South Tyrol and Trieste, but also much of Dalmatia, to say nothing of the possibility of gains in the Middle East at the expense of the Ottoman Empire. The soldiers who came home from the war were anxious to see and taste the fruits of victory, and wanted, in addition to social reform, the visible satisfaction of their national pride. In 1919 these desires found their symbolic expression in the city of Fiume. This port on the Adriatic had until 1918 been part of Hungary, and its economic links were with central Europe. It had a mixed population, Italian and southern Slav, while the surrounding countryside was almost entirely Slav. It did not form part of the territory promised to Italy under the Treaty of London, and in 1919 it was claimed by the new Kingdom of Yugoslavia. Even in the areas already promised to Italy by the Allies there were many districts where the principle of self-determination had been sacrificed to other considerations: in the South Tyrol (or Alto Adige as the Italians called it) 230,000 German Austrians were to come under Italian rule in order to provide Italy with a strategic frontier on the Brenner Pass. President Wilson, who disapproved of the Treaty of London, was certainly not prepared to allow Italy to take territory beyond what she had already been promised by France and Britain. During the long negotiations relations between Wilson and Orlando, the Italian Prime Minister, grew increasingly bad and, after Wilson had issued an appeal to the Italian people over the head of their representatives at the peace conference, the Italian delegation walked out. The excitement in Italy was intense; the government fell; there were brawls between Italian and French soldiers in the garrison which occupied Fiume pending a decision on its future. Then, after weeks of riots and strikes, on 12 September 1919 the Italian writer Gabriele d'Annunzio entered Fiume at the head of a legion of volunteers and soldiers who had disobeyed their officers in order to support this nationalist demonstration.

D'Annunzio, at this time a man of fifty-six, had an international reputation as a poet, novelist and dramatist, as a writer of highly coloured *fin-de-siècle* verse and prose, an explorer of exotic sensations and a man who had always made his private life into public drama. He had been associated with Mussolini in the interventionist campaign in the winter of 1914 and, although officially too old for military service, he had demonstrated his patriotism and bravado, and shown himself at home in the new machine age, by flying an aeroplane on missions over Austria and scattering propaganda leaflets over the enemy capital. Once in Fiume, where his legion was soon increased by volunteers from all over Italy, he gave full play to his genius for self-dramatisation and to the rhetorical imagery of his Italian style, devising a constitution for the city which claimed to be a revival of the Italian mediaeval communes, based on guilds to which its citizens were expected to belong, grouped according to their professional activity. For some fifteen months, until he was finally evicted by a reluctant and embarrassed Italian government, which had signed an agreement with the Yugoslavs setting up Fiume as a 'free city' between the two countries, D'Annunzio kept court as dictator of the city, organising vast parades of his followers, who greeted his appearances on the balcony of his palace with wild war-cries of *Eia, Eia, Alala* or with *Giovanezza*, the song of the *Arditi*, the elite troops of the war, which later became the Fascist anthem. (In 1924 a fresh agreement gave the city of Fiume to Italy and the rest of the territory to Yugoslavia; Italy renounced her claims on Dalmatia. After the Second World War Fiume became part of Yugoslavia under its Slav name of Rijeka.)

The whole episode seems in some ways almost comical, the acting out of the fantasies of a self-dramatising international star, but it showed just how deep were the emotions which nationalism in Italy could arouse; the withdrawal from Fiume was regarded as a betrayal by many Italians and added to the general sense of frustration and humiliation. Moreover the Fiume adventure demonstrated that, just as in domestic politics Mussolini's followers were prepared to take matters into their own hands regardless of the law, as when they sacked the offices of the Socialist daily *Avanti* in Milan in April 1919, so the extreme Italian nationalists were prepared, on the international plane, to take direct action in defiance of the decisions of the peace conference and of their own government. Above all, the whole style of D'Annunzio's operations – the mass meetings, the cult of the Leader, the hysterical oratory, the bodyguards – suggested a new and dramatic way of running a political movement, which was to become the formula for both the Fascist and the Nazi parties. The lessons of D'Annunzio's venture were certainly not lost on Mussolini, who had hastened to assure D'Annunzio of his backing, but who had watched his popular success with a certain jealousy. They were both appealing to many of the same sources of support, especially ex-soldiers disillusioned with the workings of the peace conference or of parliament, for whom the end of the war meant boredom and the loss of the admiration to which they felt they were entitled.

Mussolini had been invalided out of the army in 1917 and had returned to his journalistic work. At the end of the war, with some of his old companions from the interventionist campaign, he had founded the so-called *Fasci Italiani di Combattimento* (Italian combat action groups). From the start Fascism was an eclectic movement and in its early days in 1919 it attracted a number of people who later broke with it, including some, such as the great conductor Arturo Toscanini, who soon became its most determined opponents. It appealed to the radical mood of 1919 with a mixture of intense nationalism, anti-parliamentarism, anti-socialism and anti-clericalism; it had a syndicalist wing which hoped to link the ideas of social reform with those of nationalism; and above all it offered a prospect of dynamic action and movement, in contrast to what seemed the stagnation of parliamentary politics. Marinetti and the Futurists were enthusiastic supporters.

But the total lack of success of the Fascist candidates, including Marinetti and Toscanini, in the parliamentary elections of November 1919 forced Mussolini to think again about the structure and tactics of his movement. He made it more respectable: he dropped the violent anti-clericalism which had been a feature of his early programme, and thus took the first step which was to lead eventually to the Lateran Treaty of 1929, by which the Fascist government settled the old quarrel between the Italian state and the Pope, and by which the Vatican became an independent sovereign state. But if Mussolini was trying to win support from Catholic conservatives by abandoning his anti-clericalism, at the same time he was giving a free hand to the local bosses and leaders of the Fascist squads. During the next two years they effectively terrorised their opponents, especially the Socialists, in many areas of northern Italy, both in the towns and countryside. Individuals were beaten up or forcibly dosed with castor oil; offices and printing shops were ransacked or destroyed, while the authorities, and especially the police, for the most part looked on with some sympathy.

266

In the parliamentary elections of 1921 Mussolini's supporters won thirty-five seats, after a campaign fought in coalition with nationalists and right-wing liberals under the leadership of the aged Giolitti, with a programme combining anti-socialism with nationalist attacks on his predecessor who had 'renounced' Fiume. He believed that Fascism could be tamed and controlled so as to serve his own political fortunes, although Mussolini did not conceal his contempt for the parliamentary game, and talked of 'settling accounts with the liberal state'.[22] Still Mussolini's entry into parliament had made him respectable, and he continued to act like a bourgeois politician, turning the Fascist movement into a regular political party and making not very successful attempts to curb the violence of the *squadre* and the open illegality of the local Fascist bosses, and even negotiating with the Socialists for a truce which neither side took very seriously. Giolitti was, however, unable to keep his majority together and retired in June 1921, a month after the elections. His successors found themselves increasingly unable to govern a country which was deeply divided and which seemed to be on the brink of civil war, and in which in many cases the officials just did not carry out the government's instructions. The hopes of the government enforcing an end to violence faded away.

The Fascist squads, impatient with the impotent governments in Rome and with Mussolini's attempts to restrain them in the interests of his new-found parliamentary respectability, increased their activity, while Mussolini began to be spoken of as a possible prime minister who now had the support of many landowners and industrialists as well as that of former followers of D'Annunzio, and of some of the Catholics in the disintegrating Popular Party. His opponents were divided: the majority of the Socialists, the largest single group in parliament, refused to collaborate with any other party, while not many of the Liberals realised what the Fascist threat in fact meant; and in any case the state of the parliamentary system in Italy was such that few people outside parliament felt much enthusiasm for it. The economic situation was going from bad to worse: there had been bank failures; there was growing unemployment and increasing inflation to add to the sense of crisis and desperation. It is arguable whether, even if there had been a strong government, it would have been able to deal with the Fascist lawlessness. Both the army and the police had many Fascist sympathisers in their ranks, although in the summer of 1921 there were at least two occasions on which local police fought and dispersed Fascist bands. The attitude of the army depended in part on that of the King; and by the late summer of 1922 with much of the north of Italy totally controlled by the Fascists it became clear that only a last effort to uphold the constitutional order would stop Mussolini from seizing power if he were not granted it. A suggestion was made that the King should declare martial law and use the army to restore order. It seemed at first that he was willing to grant the Prime Minister's request, but his advisers were deeply divided; and when it came to the point the King changed his mind, and refused to exercise any initiative.

On the night of 29 October 1922, while his supporters were massing for a 'March on Rome' and for a *coup d'état* if necessary, Mussolini took the train to Rome and was duly and constitutionally asked to form a government, while regular troops, in a last show of authority, held up the advance of the Fascist forces so that, when they did arrive in Rome, it was to celebrate Mussolini's appointment as Prime Minister rather than to bring him forcibly to power. For the next two and a half years Mussolini retained some semblance of constitutional legality, and his government was ostensibly a coalition with some of the members of the old political parties. During this period the *squadre* – now called the Militia – continued their activities. The secret police began to make life difficult for the socialist and communist opposition. A new electoral law was passed which worked heavily in the Fascists' favour and made them much the largest party in parliament after the elections of 1924. There was one last moment in 1924 when an attempt was made to reassert constitutional rights and to remove Mussolini from office, after one of the most outspoken opponents of the regime, the reformist socialist deputy Giacomo Matteotti, had been kidnapped and brutally murdered by Fascist thugs organised by the director of Mussolini's press office, many of whose illegal activities were known to Mussolini and actively encouraged by him. For a short time the shock and anger caused by this crime shook Mussolini's personal position. The Liberal and Socialist opposition withdrew from parliament and met separately without the Fascists, but once again they failed to find a coherent plan to defeat Mussolini, and once again the King refused to take any initiative. When Giovanni Amendola, the parliamentary leader of the opposition, published the evidence of Mussolini's knowledge of some of the acts of violence (though not apparently this one) organised in his own secretariat, Mussolini acted to silence his opponents, using his militia to arrest many members of the opposition, increasing the censorship, removing unreliable officials from office and thus demonstrating that the opposition, caught in their own loyalty to constitutional proceedings, were unable to stop him doing whatever he wanted to do. In November 1926 the opposition deputies were finally and formally deprived of their parliamentary seats and the last vestiges of the constitution disappeared. Italy became a one-party dictatorship. Mussolini had demonstrated what he once called '*La nostra feroce voluntà totalitaria*'[23] ('Our fierce totalitarian will'), and started to carry out his intention of 'making the nation Fascist' ('*Fascistizzare la nazione*').[24] He had given two sinister words to the twentieth-century political vocabulary, Fascism and Totalitarianism.

In Italy the counter-revolutionary movement had turned into a totalitarian dictatorship. There were a number of features peculiar to the Italian situation which helped this process: the disrepute in which parliament was held by many Italians, the divisions in the Italian working-class movement, which made nonsense of their rhetoric suggesting that revolution was near, the particular emotional quality of Italian nationalism. But there are nevertheless some aspects of the rise of Fascism in Italy which have much in common with counter-revolutionary movements elsewhere, and especially in Germany during these years. Later of course Hitler was to profit from Mussolini's example, and his own rise to power in the period 1930–3 has striking similarities in its combination of constitutional legality and public violence, and in his use of the conservatives who thought they could themselves use him.

The people who joined the *Freikorps* in Germany were very similar in origin and temperament to the Italian Fascist *squadristi* – demobilised soldiers with a taste for violence, some of whom nourished a romantic memory of the solidarity with war-time comrades in the trenches as well as deep feelings of national humiliation and frustration. The various Free Corps and similar organisations which flourished in Germany in the early 1920s committed many of the same crimes as the Fascists in Italy. Although they were not as systematically organised for political purposes, their violence was even greater, and included the murder of political opponents whom they accused of betraying the German people – Karl Liebknecht and Rosa Luxemburg, Mathias Erzberger, the Centre Party leader who had actually signed the armistice, Walther Rathenau, who became Foreign Minister in 1921 and who signed the Treaty of Rapallo with Soviet Russia the following year. And in each case the German courts were for the most part reluctant to impose other than very mild penalties on people convicted for crimes of this kind.

It was in Munich, with its direct experience of the brief Soviet republic in 1919 that these counter-revolutionary movements flourished most. Small groups of ex-servicemen tried to keep alive the mystical sense of union which they claimed existed between former *Frontkämpfer*. The irrational *völkisch* movements of the pre-war days (see pp. 150–5 above) all flourished in an atmosphere in which Bavaria was believed to represent a more wholesome German society than that embodied by the socialists in Berlin and by the rational attempt in the Weimar constitution to introduce a genuinely liberal system. Others tried to win working-class support for anti-socialist programmes; and all of them were imbued with a hysterical anti-Semitism which gave fresh currency to the old Russian forgery, the *Protocols of the Elders of Zion* (see p. 110 above). It was into this world that a young Austrian serving as a corporal in the German army, Adolf Hitler, drifted in April 1919, at the height of the revolutionary disturbances. The first political association which he joined was the German Workers' Party dedicated to the principles of 'national socialism', a true German socialism which was contrasted with Jewish Marxism or Russian Bolshevism.

The racial element in these German counter-revolutionary movements was much stronger than in Italy. They had inherited the ideas of the pre-war *völkisch* movements, and anti-Semitism was a central part of their ideology – an aspect almost entirely lacking in Italy where there was anyway only a very small Jewish community, long established and deeply rooted in Italian society. On the other hand the movement in both countries had certain common theoretical ideas on which their criticism of the liberal, parliamentary state was based. There was much rhetoric about the evils of the principle of representation based on one man, one vote, and both in Italy and Germany theories of the corporate state were elaborated, in which individuals would have no right of representation as such but only as members of professional groups, 'corporations' uniting people in their social function instead of in a purely mechanical and mathematical way. This had been the basis of D'Annunzio's curious Charter which he had promulgated for Fiume, but it was an idea with a long history in German political thinking, where it had been part of the idealised neo-mediaevalism of the German romantic movement, and it had also figured in much nineteenth-century Catholic political philosophy (see p. 44 above).

In Germany criticism of parliamentary democracy was based on the belief that the Weimar constitution had been the product of defeat and of alien influences and that it was somehow part of the dictated terms imposed on Germany by her enemies. The new constitution, many German conservatives argued, was a mechanical device which would strangle the free expression of the true German spirit. After the Nazis came to power the Weimar period was frequently referred to in their language as the *Systemzeit*, the time of the system, a system, it was suggested, imposed from outside and with no spontaneous national roots in the German soul and the German soil. Throughout the 1920s these ideas were repeated again and again in German books and periodicals which stressed the difference between the German political tradition and those of Britain and France: and now these were no longer academic philosophical doctrines, but ideas which were leading to direct and violent attacks on the Weimar constitution, or at least to a passive refusal to try and make it work, just as in Italy the intellectual criticisms of liberalism made by Mosca or Pareto provided an intellectual justification for standing aside during the crisis of the liberal system after 1919.

What the German counter-revolutionary movements lacked in 1923 was the widespread mass support which Mussolini had succeeded in winning for Fascism and the political organisation he had been able to give to it. The groundswell of opinion was present in Germany; it still had to find effective political expression. And in the meantime from 1924 onwards the Weimar Republic appeared to have achieved a degree of economic recovery and political stability which might, it seemed, after all give it a chance of survival such as parliamentary government in Italy perhaps had never had. Although in the period from 1920 to 1923 circumstances in Italy and Germany were in many ways similar, the totalitarian counter-revolution in Germany was not immediately successful and it was ten years before National Socialism finally triumphed over the German Republic, years which to begin with seemed full of hope and in which both Germany and Europe appeared to have recovered a measure of prosperity and stability.

THE SEARCH FOR
STABILITY

The war which ended in November 1918 was a European war; and the peace settlement of 1919 was a European peace. Although, as Lloyd George put it, 'it is not one continent that is engaged – every continent is affected',[1] the war outside Europe had been an extension overseas of European rivalries. The world empire which some of the rulers both of Britain and Germany hoped to create as a result of the war would have been an empire based on Europe, an extension into the world beyond of the struggle for mastery in Europe. We are now accustomed to call the war the 'First World War', but for the generation just demobilised it was simply the 'Great War', a war fought, whatever the propaganda about its being a war to end war, to determine the balance of power in Europe. The men who made the peace found themselves primarily concerned with European frontiers and European security arrangements. In the disillusionment which quickly followed the peace it was hard for a generation which had been through the war and which had suffered huge material losses – something over seven million men were killed – and still greater spiritual wounds, to think otherwise, or to realise that the war had had profound effects on the world outside Europe, and that it had changed for ever the relations of Europe with that world.

The reasons for this concentration on Europe, and for the persistence of the belief that it was Europe alone which mattered in world politics, lay both in the attitudes of the ruling classes of Europe and in the particular international political circumstances of 1919. During the half-century before 1914 European supremacy in the world had been absolutely taken for granted. European technology, European ideas and European systems of government were confidently believed to be the best in the world; and it was to Europe that leaders in the world outside looked for the methods by which they hoped to end European domination. Before 1914 the ruling classes of the great European imperialist powers had assumed without question their right to govern others in the interests of progress and enlightened administration, and most even of their radical and socialist critics had attacked the methods of colonial rule rather than its existence. A few anthropologists had suggested that cultures based on values and ideas totally different from those of Europe might be equally valid; a few painters and musicians had turned to the art of Africa and Asia in a search for new modes of expression (see pp. 78-9 above). But in general the men who led Europe into and through the war had not yet lost their belief in their right to rule other peoples.

Throughout the period between the wars this complacency was increasingly threatened by nationalist unrest among Arabs or Indians for example or by the emergence of a new regime in China, dedicated, as that of Japan had been fifty years earlier, to the destruction of the 'unequal treaties' which placed Asian people in a position of legal and economic inferiority to Europeans. At the same time the Soviet leaders were not only claiming that they had made Moscow the centre of the European revolutionary movement but also that they were at the head of the world revolution. There was now a European power openly dedicated to the end of European rule abroad, whatever Russia might be doing in her own Asiatic provinces; and the revolutionary leaders of Asia, if not yet of Africa, were in the 1920s turning to Moscow for revolutionary training, guidance and support. Hitherto the European powers had from time to time tried to weaken the imperial position of a rival state in the interests of their own policies and ambitions – as the British had incited the Arabs to revolt against the Turks, or the Germans encouraged revolutionary movements in the Caucasus against the Russians or in Ireland and India against Britain, in the First World War. Now there was a European power openly dedicated to the goal of ending colonial rule as such; and this was yet another reason for the hatred felt for the Bolsheviks in countries which still possessed large overseas empires, such as Britain, France or the Netherlands.

The confidence in the European powers' right to dispose of non-European peoples meant that at the peace conference problems outside Europe were of secondary importance and were still thought of in European terms. The world outside Europe, or at least most of Asia and Africa, still seemed to be the arena for a struggle for control between European countries, so that for example the problems of the Middle East were considered in terms of Anglo-French rivalry rather than in terms of the interests of Arabs or Kurds or Turks or Greeks or Jews. It was not until after the Second World War that European confidence in the right to rule was finally shattered, and that the methods necessary to maintain control in the face of fanatical and dedicated nationalist movements became increasingly unacceptable to wide sections of the European public – as indeed the British were already finding out in Ireland in the period immediately after 1919.

However, there were more immediate political reasons why between the wars Europeans remained preoccupied with the relations between the European states. Even though the significance of the international Communist movement for Asia and Africa was beginning to be apparent, the threat of revolution in Europe concentrated the immediate attention of the old ruling classes on domestic politics and on the necessity of reasserting their power, either by strengthening their existing constitutional control as in France or Britain or, where this was not possible, by turning to the new radical counter-revolutionary movements. Yet, although the danger of revolution, in the worsening economic climate of the months immediately after the end of the war, was never far from the minds of the politicians of Europe, they also had the immediate task of making peace with Germany, of drawing up a new territorial settlement to deal with the situation created by the disappearance of the Austro-Hungarian Empire, and of constructing a new international system by means of the League of Nations, as promised by Wilson and as expected by liberal opinion everywhere. In facing these tasks they were immediately confronted with a conflict of principles and policies between the European Allies, Britain and France, and the government of the United States, a conflict embodied in the leaders of the three countries who attended the peace conference which opened in Paris on 18 January 1919.

Georges Clemenceau, the French Prime Minister, who had been mayor of Montmartre in 1870 and remembered vividly that other German invasion, Raymond Poincaré, the President of the Republic, a lawyer from Lorraine with close family links with the province annexed in 1870, and Ferdinand Foch, the Commander in Chief, conscious of how narrow had been the margin by which the French had survived and repulsed the German attack in 1918, were all in varying ways determined to make a peace which, whatever else it did, would guarantee French security by keeping Germany as weak as possible, militarily, economically and territorially. In Britain Lloyd George, who had divided the Liberal Party by his breach with Asquith in 1916 and who in November 1918 fought a very successful election in alliance with his Conservative coalition partners, had promised the electorate – which had responded enthusiastically to slogans such as 'Squeeze Germany till the pips squeak' and 'Hang the Kaiser' – that Germany would be made to pay for the war both materially and morally; and a vociferous section of parliamentary opinion in London was determined to make him fulfil these promises. On the other hand President Woodrow Wilson had, from the moment of America's entry into the war, stressed the importance of a just peace and of using the opportunity to create a new international order based on the League of Nations, the establishment of which he was determined to make an integral part of the peace settlement. He came to Europe in person to head the American delegation to the peace conference – an unprecedented step for a head of state, and one which inaugurated, for better or for worse, a new era of 'summit diplomacy' – and the warmth of the popular welcome which he received in Britain, France and Italy convinced him that he embodied the hopes of the world for a new and better era in international relations.

The Germans had accepted the armistice on the assumption that the peace settlement would be based on Wilson's Fourteen Points and the additional general principles which he had stated in subsequent speeches. But when it came to apply them in practice to the details of the peace treaty with Germany, a number of difficulties and anomalies appeared. These arose partly from the differences in the policies and aims of America and the European Allies, and in part from the nature of Wilson's own points and principles. For the French there were three main ways in which they hoped to maintain their security against Germany and make up for the demographic inferiority of which they were constantly aware. They wanted to reduce Germany's potential military strength by control of the west bank of the Rhine, if possible by means of territorial annexation or the creation of an independent buffer state; they wanted the permanent disarmament of Germany; and they wanted to make Germany pay for the entire cost of the war to France, both in order to restore the devastated areas of France and also to restore French finances, which were for some years conducted in the expectation, disappointed as it turned out, that 'L'Allemagne paiera.' But there was also a feeling that heavy reparations, by depressing the German economy, would help to keep Germany weak. This was in contrast to the British attitude since the British, once the first wave of post-war vindictiveness had given way to more rational considerations, came to realise that a degree of German recovery was important for British trade and for the restoration of Britain's own economic health.

During the war, while nearly all Frenchmen accepted without question that the unconditional return of Alsace–Lorraine was France's primary war aim, some went further and hoped for territorial gains on the left bank of the Rhine. This was the view of many big industrialists, who particularly wanted the Saar basin to round off the Lorraine coal- and steel-producing area, just as their German equivalents were hoping to make further annexations from France for similar reasons. It was shared by right-wing nationalist publicists, such as Charles Maurras and Maurice Barrès, and by many military men. In early 1917, a few weeks before the February Revolution in Russia, the French government obtained the agreement of the Russians to their plans for annexations on the Rhine, in return for giving the Russians a free hand in the settlement of their western frontier with the Polish provinces of Germany and Austria. The agreement lapsed with the fall of the Tsar; and its publication by the provisional government caused the French some embarrassment. In the changed and chastened mood of late 1917 and 1918 the French government said no more about these plans, and it was only at the Peace Conference that they were revived.

Wilson and Lloyd George had the greatest difficulty in persuading the French to give up their plans for annexation of the left bank of the Rhine; and, indeed, it was not until 1923 that the French finally lost hope of stimulating a separatist movement in the Rhineland which might produce a buffer state between France and Germany. Wilson opposed the demand for annexation both as a violation of the principle that, as he had put it, 'peoples and provinces are not to be bartered about from sovereignty to sovereignty as if they were mere chattels and pawns in a game',[2] and also because it would add an element of instability to the European settlement, just as the German annexation of Alsace–Lorraine had done after 1870. Lloyd George, once the conference had started, was trying to extract himself from the more extreme positions which he had taken up in his election campaign, and he was worried that, if the peace terms were too hard, the German government might fall and thus increase the danger of revolution in Germany and the spread of Russian influence. 'France,' he said, 'was most afraid of the Teuton', but his view was that the Teuton was largely done for. The nation he feared was the Slavs.[3] Under pressure from Britain and America the French were reluctantly forced to accept what was to them an unsatisfactory compromise: the Rhineland should remain German, but both banks should be permanently demilitarised so that the Germans would not have the right to station troops or build fortifications there; the area, as well as bridgeheads over the Rhine, should be occupied by Allied troops for fifteen years; the French would have the right to administer the Saar basin and to use the mines for a period of twenty-five years, after which the future of the region should be decided by a plebiscite (which in fact in 1935 restored the Saarland to Germany by an overwhelming majority and provided Hitler with one of his first triumphs in foreign policy). In return for these concessions, which to the French leaders seemed considerable, Britain and the United States promised that they would sign with France a treaty of military guarantee which would bring France immediate military help if she were attacked by Germany.

On the disarmament of Germany it was easier to obtain agreement: but here again the policy was based on contradictory assumptions. Germany was to be limited to a long-term army of 100,000 men; conscription was to be abolished; certain weapons – tanks and military aircraft for example – were to be forbidden. The French assumed that these provisions would be permanent and would ensure French military superiority for years to come. For Wilson, however, and indeed for all those who took the Covenant of the League of Nations seriously, the time would soon come when each country would have disarmed down to Germany's level, by carrying out Article 8 of the League Covenant which laid down that all nations should reduce their armaments to the lowest level consistent with their national security. With such differences of approach and such vagueness in the language of the Covenant, it is not surprising that hardly any progress was made over the question of disarmament, although disarmament proposals and conferences occupied a great deal of time in the Foreign Ministries of Europe and filled many sessions at Geneva, until the idea was finally killed with Hitler's advent to power in 1933.

The question of what reparations Germany should pay was a complicated and controversial one, and again revealed the difference of assumptions between the Allied governments. Almost everyone agreed that Germany should pay something towards the cost of making good the physical damage done in Belgium and France, and even some Germans – Walther Rathenau for instance and some of the Social Democrats – were prepared in principle to accept this. The problem was how much they should pay; and the whole question was given a new dimension by the insertion in the peace treaty of the notorious 'war guilt clause' as a means of providing a legal basis for the demand for reparations. This obliged the Germans to accept responsibility for starting the war, and to acknowledge that the loss and damage for which recompense was now sought was the consequence of a war 'imposed' by Germany. The emotional effect of the reparations issue was thus as great and as important as the financial one. Not only did the war guilt clause make no distinction between the Kaiser's government and that of the new republic, which was expressly charged with the responsibility for its predecessor's policies, but it also suggested that a degree of moral blame attached to Germany from which, by implication, her opponents were free. This moral aspect provided a powerful argument for the very many Germans who, from the moment the treaty was signed at Versailles in June 1919, were attacking it as a '*Diktat*', a dictated peace imposed on the Germans instead of one freely negotiated on the basis of the Fourteen Points, which is what they claimed to have expected. The difference in the peace negotiations between victors and vanquished was stressed by the fact that the German delegation was kept virtually under house arrest and was given no chance to discuss the terms of the treaty with the Allied representatives, but only to submit their comments in writing. As Clemenceau, the President of the peace conference, said: '*L'heure du lourd règlement des comptes est venue.*' Germany's guilt was assumed; and, in spite of the fact that the Covenant of the League of Nations was an integral part of the peace treaty, the emphasis was not on making a new start, but rather on the stern exaction of moral and material penalties.

As far as the practical rendering of the reparations account was concerned, the problem was to find a sum which would both satisfy the Allies' demands and be within Germany's capacity to pay. For this reason the exact figure was not settled at the peace conference but was left over to protracted subsequent negotiations, ending in 1921 with the announcement to the Germans of a vast but somewhat arbitrary figure which they were expected to raise somehow. For the next five years the reparations question was to have a disastrous effect on the economic life and on the international relations of Europe.

A further major grievance for Germany arose from the territorial settlement on her eastern borders; and here the difficulty of applying the Fourteen Points in practice became a source of bitterness. President Wilson had specifically stated that a Polish state would be created 'with access to the sea'. The obvious point of access to the sea was the old Baltic city of Danzig; but this was a place whose population and culture were very largely German, while in the country surrounding it the Poles were in a majority, though with a substantial German minority. At the same time, the creation of what came to be known as the 'Polish corridor' cut off the German province of East Prussia from the rest of the German state. It was – and this was characteristic of all the attempts to redraw Europe's frontiers on the basis of national self-determination – impossible to recreate a Polish state within viable boundaries without leaving a German minority on the wrong side of the border, as well as driving a geographical wedge between indisputably German territories. Because the Germans had come to regard themselves as racially and culturally superior to the Poles and had, in the years before the war, been trying systematically to strengthen the German presence in the Polish provinces of Prussia, the resentment caused by the loss of territory to Poland and by the existence of the Polish corridor went very deep. Lloyd George, in his belated attempts to mitigate the harshness of the terms offered to Germany, did succeed in making Danzig an autonomous free city under the auspices of the League of Nations, but this satisfied neither Germans nor Poles and in fact ruined Danzig, since the Poles constructed a new port of their own across the bay and took much of the trade away from the older city. If the loss of the corridor was primarily of emotional importance, though the area had considerable agricultural value, Upper Silesia, the other region which was contested between Germany and Poland, had been one of the main industrial centres of the German Empire; and here again the final settlement of the frontier in 1921 after a plebiscite – another concession to Lloyd George's desire to avoid the irrevocable – only served to leave both sides dissatisfied (the German Reichstag was draped with black on the day the convention with Poland was signed), and to show how great the problems were in any attempt to divide on ethnic lines an area which was an economic unity.

To the German resentment at the settlement of the border with Poland was added the conviction that the principle of self-determination had been deliberately abandoned in the refusal to allow the German-speaking provinces of the vanished Austro-Hungarian monarchy to unite with Germany. Two main groups of people were involved: in Bohemia about three million Germans now became citizens of the new Czechoslovak Republic, which claimed the historic boundaries of the old kingdom of Bohemia and the maintenance of the old Austrian frontier, which would give a strategic border to the new State. To the south the old crownlands of the House of Habsburg now became the new Republic of Austria, consisting of the great city of Vienna, cut off from most of the vast empire of which it had once been the capital, and a few rural and mountainous provinces. In the case of Czechoslovakia it was once again impossible to devise a frontier which would satisfy conflicting ethnic, economic, strategic and historic claims. Someone was bound to be left with a sense of grievance and in the atmosphere of 1919 it is not surprising that the victorious powers should prefer this to be the Germans and Austrians rather than the Czechs, who by the end of the war had come to be accepted as allies. In the case of the Austrian Republic however there was a considerable majority in favour of union with Germany: this was geographically feasible and on the principle of self-determination there should have been no objection. But here again, the French argument against increasing German territory and population at the moment of Germany's defeat proved stronger; and an explicit ban on the union of Austria with Germany was included in the final peace treaties with both countries.

(The treaties of peace with the different belligerent countries were as follows: Versailles with Germany, Saint-Germain with Austria, Trianon with Hungary, Neuilly with Bulgaria. The Treaty of Sèvres with Turkey never came into operation, and was replaced by the Treaty of Lausanne in 1923. The Germans used to refer disdainfully to the original group of treaties as the 'suburban treaties' [*Vorortsverträge*] from their places of signature.)

Wilson had accepted, often with obvious reluctance, the many points at which the treaties did not seem to accord with the principles on which he believed the peace should be based, in the hope that, when the League of Nations came into being at the beginning of 1920, it would provide the machinery for revision of the peace settlement and for the righting of the wrongs committed in the bitter international atmosphere of 1919. He had, for instance, at many points yielded to the Italian demands in the hope of winning their support for the League. He had insisted that the Covenant should be an integral part of the Treaty of Versailles, so as to oblige all the states involved in the war with Germany to subscribe to it. Before leaving Paris he seemed to be increasingly disillusioned at what had gone on there and increasingly convinced that the League offered the only hope for a just peace. Yet his own domestic position in the United States rendered all these hopes vain, and on his return from Europe he was forced to realise the strength of the opposition which had grown up against him personally, against his policies and against the idea of a United States involvement in Europe and in particular in the League of Nations. From November 1919 to March 1920 an unsuccessful struggle, in which the President himself could play only a limited part as he had suffered a stroke while on a speaking tour to win popular support for his foreign policy, was waged in the United States congress for the ratification of the Treaty of Versailles, as first the section dealing with the League and then the treaty as a whole were rejected by the Senate.

This not only had the result that America never became a member of the League, but it also meant that the treaty guaranteeing military assistance to France, which had been the price of French renunciation of the Rhineland, also never came into effect; and, in the absence of America, Britain too did not ratify it. The League of Nations had originally been conceived by President Wilson, and by such statesmen in Britain and France as had shared his enthusiasm for it, as a world organisation, and it did indeed in the 1920s occupy itself to some extent and with some success with non-European problems. However, the American retreat into isolation after the collapse and defeat of Wilson and the election in 1920 of the Republican Warren G. Harding deprived the League of a whole extra-European dimension, and left it in the hands of the European great powers, especially of France and Britain, preoccupied above all with the establishment of a stable system of security in Europe. At the same time the conception of the purpose which the League was to serve had been changed. Wilson had hoped that it would provide machinery for improving and revising the peace settlement. The French, on the other hand, came to regard it increasingly as a means for upholding the peace treaties and for preventing their revision. And, betrayed, as many Frenchmen felt, by the Anglo-Saxons and by the lapsing of the promised guarantee against a German attack, they tended to base their foreign policy on a stubborn search for their own security and on a rigid insistence that Germany should fulfil every article of the Treaty of Versailles. The question of relations between France and Germany therefore became of paramount importance to the stability of Europe, and had profound effects on the internal development of both countries.

Criticism of the peace settlement began before it was even completed. The German resentment is understandable enough, and at first the German government resigned rather than sign the Treaty of Versailles. Yet there was no alternative: and, after Hindenburg had reported that military resistance was impossible, a new government (a coalition between the Social Democrats and the Centre Party) was formed which was prepared to sign. The treaty was accepted by the German parliament by 237 to 138 votes – the strong minority representing the important body of German opinion which never accepted the treaty, or indeed the republic which they held responsible for it. The aim of every subsequent German government was to revise the treaty, to delay its execution or to find ways of getting round its provisions. For the time being there was not much that could be done about the frontiers: but there were still the questions of disarmament and of reparations to be settled. The French were jealously watching any military move made by the Germans: when, after the Kapp *Putsch* (see p. 251 above), the German government sent troops into the demilitarised zone to put down a threatened Communist rising, the French at once occupied the cities of Frankfurt and

Darmstadt in retaliation. In January 1921 the Allies issued the German government with an ultimatum and finally forced them, ostensibly at least, to reduce their forces to the numbers stipulated in the treaty, increasing German resentment that no other country showed any signs of carrying out the obligation to disarm imposed by the League Covenant.

But, although the disarmament section of the Treaty of Versailles appeared to have been fulfilled by the Germans, there was still room for manoeuvre. The very fact that Germany now had a small professional army instead of a large one based on an annual intake of conscripts, was put to good use, and the 100,000-man army became a cadre of highly trained men each capable of performing the tasks of the ranks above him, and thus available to serve as a nucleus for rapid expansion once the restrictions on the German army could be removed. The Treaty of Rapallo with the Soviet Republic in 1922 (see p. 262 above and p. 283 below) not only showed that the Germans still had some diplomatic freedom of action, but was also accompanied by secret military agreements by which the Germans established factories in Russia for the manufacture of poison gas and were entitled to send officers to train with the Red army in the use of weapons forbidden to Germany under the peace treaty. By the mid-1920s the German High Command had succeeded, with the connivance of successive governments, in building up a system of secret rearmament by which apparently peaceful factories turned out components which could be used for weapons and apparently peaceful social groups carried on clandestine military training – activities subsidised by nationalist businessmen, such as the press and film magnate Alfred Hugenberg, or by the filtering through of government loans intended for welfare purposes. Many of these activities did not escape the Allied control commission: but, as the memories of the war grew less vivid and the demand for the withdrawal of the occupation troops grew louder, there was increasingly little the Allies could do to stop secret rearmament; and a study of the Allied attempts to check the level of German armament in the 1920s suggests some of the difficulties in any scheme for enforcing disarmament by inspection and control in a sovereign state determined to evade its provisions.

However, it was the question of reparations which in fact caused the most serious crisis between France and Germany in the 1920s, as well as revealing divergences of policy between France and Britain, and in one way or another contributing to the economic difficulties of the countries involved. The reparations clauses of the Treaty of Versailles attracted immediate criticism, notably in the work of the young English economist, John Maynard Keynes, who resigned from the British delegation to the peace conference in order to publish in the summer of 1919 his brilliant and polemical account of the conference and his savage criticism of its result, *The Economic Consequences of the Peace* – a book which sold 148,000 copies in two years and started in Britain a widespread reaction against the peace treaty, producing a sense of guilt among many educated Englishmen which conditioned their attitude towards Germany until 1938. The reparations settlement has subsequently been strongly attacked by others; Winston Churchill, although a member of the British government which had signed the treaty, after the Second World War described the reparations clauses as 'malignant and silly to an extent that made them obviously futile'.[4] Controversy still continues as to whether the Germans might have made a greater effort to pay than they did, and as to the extent of the harm done to the German economy by such payments as they did make. It is at least certain that the enforcement of the reparations clauses did not give the Allies nearly as much money as they had hoped, and made any kind of stable international system in Europe impossible during the crucial five years immediately after the war, while contributing, for psychological as much as for economic reasons, to the weakening of the authority of the republican government in Germany.

The French attitude to the reparations question was a simple one. They needed the cash, and the deliveries of coal and timber which the Germans were required to supply, for the reconstruction of the areas devastated by the war and also for the restoration of their public finances. The British approach was more complicated. They had increased the total reparations bill by insisting that this should not include just payment for physical damage but also the cost of pensions arising from the war – for widows, for orphans, for the disabled. 'I could not face my people,' Lloyd George said characteristically, 'and say that human life was of less value than a chimney.'[5] The British too needed the money to help them pay the very large debt which was owing to the United States, where the new Republican administration was proving inflexible in its attitude to the inter-Allied debts. ('They hired the money, didn't they ?' President Harding is reported to have said.) On the other hand, by the end of 1921 they also hoped that it might be possible to propose a general moratorium on inter-Allied debts, but realised that some agreed settlement of the German reparations question would have to be reached first. They therefore had an interest in finding an arrangement which the Germans would accept and in trying to persuade the French to be less intransigent.

The Allies after much argument had finally agreed among themselves in January 1921 on the sum to be asked of the Germans; and they had forced the Germans, after the French had again moved troops into the unoccupied zone of Germany, to accept a slightly scaled-down version of the enormous figure in May 1921. By the end of the year however the Germans declared their inability to pay the annual instalment due and declared a moratorium. It is true that the German economic and financial situation was growing serious: budgets were unbalanced and inflation was growing worse. However, in May 1921 a new government, in which Walther Rathenau became Minister of Reconstruction and subsequently Foreign Minister, tried to find a fresh approach to the problem, and for the first time a German government showed some willingness to try to fulfil the treaty terms. For a short period it looked as though this might meet with some success. Briand, the new French Prime Minister, was more flexible in his approach than his predecessors, and Lloyd George revived the idea of a military guarantee to France in return for concessions on the reparations issue, thinking correctly that only a solution of the problem of French security against Germany could lead to any return of confidence or to any stability in Europe. However, Briand was unable to carry his colleagues in the government with him and was forced to resign. His place was taken in January 1922 by Raymond Poincaré who, after ending his term as President of the Republic, had returned to parliamentary politics as a Senator, and who now was insisting, with all his lawyer's tenacity, on the exact fulfilment by Germany of all the terms of the treaty. Any fresh approach to an agreed solution of the reparations question was thus ruled out, and the European economic conference at Genoa in April 1922, from which much had been hoped, achieved nothing, except to give the Russians the chance of signing the Treaty of Rapallo with Germany at a moment when Rathenau was totally discouraged by the failure of his overtures to Britain and France. The Treaty of Rapallo, proclaiming, as it did, German friendship for the Soviet Union, had more symbolic than practical importance, although it was followed, as we have seen, by secret agreements for limited military cooperation; but it represented a temporary success for those people in the German High Command and Foreign Ministry who believed that collaboration with Russia might restore to Germany some scope for diplomatic initiative. Two months later however, Rathenau paid for it with his life, and was murdered by a group of young nationalists who hated him as a Jew and who believed that he was preparing to hand Germany over to the Bolsheviks.

Although the shock of Rathenau's assassination brought the government of which he had been a member some short-lived support from everyone except the most intransigent nationalists, during the next months the situation in Germany continued to grow worse and inflation became catastrophic. The extent to which the financial situation was out of control is shown by the fact that in January 1921 one dollar was worth 15.5 marks; a year later it was worth 45.5 marks; in July 1922 118 marks, and then by December 1922 it had rushed up to 1,810 marks. A new government of businessmen and experts under Wilhelm Cuno, the Chairman of the Hamburg-America Steamship Line, failed to solve the problem, and the Germans were once again declared to be in default on their reparations payment to France.

This was a moment of considerable European tension and instability. Not only had Mussolini's march on Rome just taken place (see p. 268 above), but relations between France and Britain were worse than at any time between the wars because of disagreement about policy in the Middle East, where, as a result of Lloyd George's support for Greek claims in Asia Minor, Britain and France had been on the edge of war with Turkey, a war which had been averted only by French insistence on negotiating with the Turks and on persuading the British to give up their commitment to Greece. As a result, later in October 1922 Lloyd George had finally been forced to resign by his Conservative colleagues, who found themselves in increasing opposition to his policies, not only in the Middle East, but even more in Ireland where, at the end of the war, encouraged by the general talk of self-determination and its application in Europe, a full-scale rebellion had broken out. After two years of severe but unsuccessful repression, Lloyd George had decided to negotiate with the nationalist leaders, and had in December 1921 signed a treaty recognising an independent Irish Free State, an action for which most of his Conservative colleagues had never forgiven him. It was a year later when the accumulated strains of the post-war years were showing themselves in many parts of Europe, that the French government under Poincaré decided to take direct action against Germany over the question of reparations. If Germany would not deliver the coal and timber due to France under the treaty, then, Poincaré's argument ran, the French would go and fetch it themselves. On 11 January 1923 French and Belgian troops occupied the Ruhr basin, taking what Poincaré called 'productive pledges' (*gages productifs*) by seizing the mines with a view to ensuring their operation in the interests of France.

It was a policy which totally misfired. Not only did it make French relations with Britain even worse, it also completely failed in its purpose, leading to an inflation in France caused by the financial burden of maintaining troops in the Ruhr, and to a severe weakening of France's international credit. The consequences for Germany were even more disastrous.

The German reaction was one of passive resistance to the French; and this attitude was supported by almost the whole of German opinion. 'Only two people have been able to bring about German unity,' one American observer remarked, 'Bismarck and Poincaré.'[6] Even the German Communist Party, which began by being equally hostile to both the German and French governments, soon decided to support the campaign against the French, which fitted in very well with Moscow's policy of preventing any agreement between Germany and France. Adopting a line which became known as 'National Bolshevism', they supported passive resistance, and even claimed that a young member of the ultra-nationalist group, Schlageter, who was shot by the French for sabotage, and who later became one of the Nazis' heroes, was moving in the same direction as the Communists who, it was declared, were fighting 'for a freedom which is identified with the freedom of their whole people, with the freedom of all who work and suffer in Germany'.[7] But the cost of passive resistance was too heavy. After the stopping of production in the Ruhr and a prolonged and effective railway strike, the economic situation became desperate. The currency lost all value: printing presses could hardly keep pace with the fall in the value of paper money; handcarts were needed to carry enough money to pay even small accounts. Confidence in the German economy had collapsed totally, and with it confidence in the German state. The social consequences were disastrous. 'There are about Germany today as beggars,' Gustav Stresemann wrote four years later, 'many who have lost hundreds and thousands and millions in War Loan, mortgages, savings, bank deposits and government paper.'[8] A large section of the German middle class, already impoverished by economic developments since the war, now found themselves ruined. But if the economically weak grew weaker, many of the economically strong grew stronger. Anyone, such as the big bankers and industrialists, who could sell goods abroad or who had any foreign currency, could, with the expenditure of only a small fraction of their foreign holdings, liquidate all their debts inside Germany by paying them in nearly worthless paper money, or could use the opportunity to instal new equipment at very low cost. The tendency, already existing before 1914 and increased by the war, for the concentration and cartelisation of German financial and industrial life was carried a stage further by the inflation.

In August 1923 Cuno's government resigned, and he was succeeded by Gustav Stresemann, who was to control German foreign policy, first as Chancellor and then as Foreign Minister, until his death in 1929. He had been a member of the old National Liberal Party, and now was the head of a small party – the German Peoples' Party (*Deutsche Volkspartei*, DVP) – which had taken over many of the National Liberals' attitudes. He had been an annexationist during the war, but he was realistic enough to see that the only way to begin to build up Germany's strength and to restore her international position as a great power was to make some attempt to fulfil Germany's treaty obligations and to restore a measure of confidence between Germany and her former enemies, so that a beginning might be made with the revision of the treaty. A practitioner of *Realpolitik* in the Bismarck tradition, Stresemann saw that Germany's basic military weakness 'determined the limits, the nature and the methods of German foreign policy'.[9] The first major decision of his government, a broadly based coalition of the republican parties, was in September 1923 to call off passive resistance and to convey his willingness to open negotiations with the French. By now, however, he was confronted with a series of threats to the very existence of the German state. Apart from the necessity of stabilising the currency and restoring some sort of normal economic life, Stresemann faced two political challenges: in central Germany and Hamburg the Communists, in October 1923, made their last attempt to carry out the German revolution. In Bavaria in November Hitler made his first attempt at a *coup d'état*. In addition to these threats there was a less important attempt at a right-wing *Putsch* in the fortress of Küstrin, not far from Berlin, on 1 October, while the French were making unsuccessful attempts to encourage a separatist movement on the Rhine.

The German Communist Party changed its line as soon as Stresemann showed that he was ready to seek a settlement with France. The collaboration with other Germans and the National Bolshevik propaganda were abandoned, and the party resumed a policy of total hostility to the government. There were in any case good grounds for thinking that at last, in the late summer of 1923, a revolutionary situation was developing in Germany. The party's tactics were discussed at length by the German Communist leaders, who went to Moscow for meetings with the executive committee of the Comintern, and, against the advice of Heinrich Brandler, the leader of the KPD, it was finally decided to make an insurrection in Thuringia, where the Communists had agreed to join the Social Democratic state government. The rising on 21–2 October 1923 was a failure and was suppressed by the army, as was a simultaneous outbreak in Hamburg. The Communists lacked the resources, the arms and the preparation to stage a successful revolution as long as there was a regular army available to oppose them. Their last bid to make the German revolution failed, and with it the last prospects of a revolution in Europe. It was characteristic of the ruthlessness of Communist discipline that Brandler, who had advised against the rising, but who had nevertheless loyally carried out the Comintern instructions to attempt it, was removed from his post in disgrace and made a scapegoat for the failure.

In Munich the suppression of the Soviet Republic in 1919 had been followed by a brief period of Social Democratic government, but in 1920 this had been replaced by a deeply reactionary administration, when right-wing politicians and generals succeeded in making in Munich the kind of *coup* which Kapp had failed to make in Berlin. The state government in Munich looked with deep suspicion at the central government in Berlin and did nothing to check the various nationalist groups and right-wing conspiracies which flourished in the congenial atmosphere of Munich. One of these was the German Workers' Party, which Adolf Hitler joined in September 1919 and which he quickly succeeded in taking over for his own, as yet not fully worked out, purposes. In the autumn of 1920 it took the name National Socialist German Workers' Party (*Nationalsozialistische Deutsche Arbeiterpartei* – NSDAP, Nazi for short). In 1923 Hitler was thirty-four years old. He had acquired as a young man in Vienna the stock ideas of the radical Viennese anti-Semites in their most extreme form, as well as a violent hatred of the Slavs. At the same time he had watched with impotent admiration the effective political organisation of the Austrian Social Democrats, and the powerful demagogy of their opponent Karl Lueger, the Christian Social mayor of the city. He had served in the German army in the war, had been decorated and had risen to the modest rank of corporal, and at least, when he came to Munich, he had the status of the old *Frontkämpfer*, the front-line soldier who occupied such an important position in the *mystique* of the extreme nationalist movements in Germany, as in Italy. He was as yet a figure with no national reputation, but in Munich his talents as a political organiser and orator were beginning to be known. However there was in 1923 in Munich a far more famous figure symbolising Germany's national aspirations and the desire to return to an undefeated past. This was Field Marshal Ludendorff who would be, it was hoped, an attractive figurehead for the *coup* for which Hitler and his associates were working.

The actual *coup* of 8–9 November 1923 was intended to seize power in Munich with the tacit consent of the Bavarian government, and then to use Munich as a base from which to challenge the government in Berlin. National Socialism was so far a purely Bavarian movement and seemed very little different from the other right-wing groups in Munich. If it was to succeed at all at this stage it must first succeed in Bavaria. However, the attempt at a *coup* was a complete failure. In spite of the presence of Ludendorff in full Field Marshal's uniform, and the doubtful loyalty of many Bavarian soldiers and officers, the army fired on the Nazi column as it marched towards the centre of the city. One of its leaders, marching at Hitler's side, was killed, and the rest of the group dispersed or were arrested. Hitler himself was put on trial – and this helped his name to become nationally known. He was sentenced to imprisonment, a period which he used to work out his ideological position in his book *Mein Kampf* (My Struggle) and to reflect on what had gone wrong.

The reason why neither the Communist rising nor the Nazi *coup* had had any success in spite of the extreme precariousness of the situation of the German government and the chaos in the economy was that the army decided to support the government. 'Gentlemen,' General von Seeckt, the head of the army, told members of the government, 'none but I in Germany can make a *putsch* and I assure you I shall not make one.'[10] It was this that enabled Stresemann's government to survive; and it was due to Seeckt's realistic belief that in the long run the army stood to gain more from co-operating with the German state, however unsatisfactory it might be, than from working against it. By the end of 1923 the German state was, almost miraculously, intact, and its immediate opponents crushed. The price was an even closer dependence on the army leadership than had been the case in the early months of the republic, and the acceptance of the army as an autonomous body within Germany, a sort of state within the state, with whose activities the government would not interfere. In constitutional terms, Stresemann's success was due to his use of the article of the constitution (Article 48) which enabled the President to authorise the Chancellor to govern by decree in an emergency without consulting parliament. That an emergency existed in 1923 none can doubt; and Stresemann handled it with the utmost skill. But the precedent of governing by means of a combination of rule by decree and military action seemed a dangerous one to the Social Democrats, and they resigned from the government. The crisis showed how precarious the republic was; and Stresemann, however regrettable his dependence on the army and on the use of emergency provisions might have been, had at least won for it a breathing space and a chance for its constitution to start to function normally again. As the British Ambassador in Berlin wrote: 'Political leaders in Germany are not accustomed to receive much public laudation: those who have seen the country through these perils deserve more credit than is likely to be their portion.'[11]

While staving off the political threats, Stresemann's government had begun to tackle the economic situation. A new currency was issued in the middle of November 1923. The new money was allegedly based on the value of Germany's agricultural land, and, since currency stabilisation is always more of a psychological question than one of hard figures, this particular fiction went some way towards checking the inflation and restoring confidence in the value of money. It could only be a very short-term measure, but it was clear that German recovery was now in the interest of all Europe and could only be achieved by international action.

Poincaré himself faced an election in the spring of 1924 and in France too, as inflation grew serious and prices rose, he was greeted with shouts of '*Poincaré la faim*' and '*Poincaré la Ruhr*', and began to look for a way out which would enable him both to obtain some reparations payments, instead of none at all, and at the same time to withdraw the troops from the Ruhr without loss of prestige. The way out was provided by the appointment of an international commission of experts, headed by an American banker, Charles G. Dawes, to recommend a solution to the reparations deadlock. The Dawes committee reported in April 1924, and its recommendations were accepted, though with some reluctance, by both the French and the German governments. In both cases the nationalists complained that the interests of the country were being betrayed, but, whereas in Germany Stresemann's position had been made worse by a slight swing to the right in the elections of March 1924, the French elections in May led to the defeat of Poincaré and to a reaction against his policies, so that the new government under the Radical Edouard Herriot was more inclined to a flexible policy. Although the question of reparations had not lost its emotional power ('There are perhaps five hundred people in Germany who have read the experts' report,' Stresemann said, 'However, there are millions of Germans who know that other Germans languished in French prisons.'),[12] for the first time it was being discussed in practical terms and in relation to Germany's actual economic situation. The Dawes Plan was a temporary measure and laid down what should happen for the next five years, thus avoiding asking the French to accept formally any diminution of the total sum due. During this period Germany would pay annuities rising each year. But because this would only be possible if the German economy began to function again, it was agreed that very large loans from abroad should be made to Germany and that the whole arrangement should be formally guaranteed by a mortgage on the German railways and industrial installations.

The economic effect was remarkable. Confidence in the German economy revived, and the short-term loans raised abroad, especially in the United States, were very successful. Capital began to be available in Germany, much of which was used by state and municipal governments for ambitious programmes of public housing and public works. Unemployment figures fell. The currency was stabilised. In the years 1925 to 1929, however much the nationalists might complain about the 'enslavement' of Germany, there was a substantial improvement in Germany's economic position and, politically, some hope that the republic might after all have a chance to establish itself. In 1929 the solution of the reparations question was taken a stage further with a second expert plan, drawn up by a committee under the American Owen D. Young, which finally envisaged an eventual end to reparations – though not until 1988.

The political gains for Germany were also important, although they were never enough to satisfy Stresemann's nationalist opponents. By 1925 French troops were withdrawn from the Ruhr, and the acceptance of both the Dawes and the Young Plans was accompanied by the speeding up of the withdrawal of the Allied occupation troops from German soil: the last troops marched out in June 1930, five years earlier than laid down in the Treaty of Versailles. Germany was admitted to the League of Nations in 1926 as part of a general settlement of her position in Europe which, by the end of 1925, seemed to have provided a solution to the problem of French security. This was the result of genuine collaboration between the German, French and British governments during 1924 and 1925. Stresemann succeeded in establishing a measure of personal confidence between himself and Aristide Briand, who became French Foreign Minister in April 1925, and also with Austen Chamberlain, the Foreign Secretary in the British Conservative government which came to office in 1924; and they created an atmosphere in which Germany could once more feel herself an equal partner in the European security system. By the treaty of Locarno, signed in October 1925, the British and Italians guaranteed the frontiers of Belgium and France against German attack and the frontiers of Germany against a French attack, thus partially meeting what had been the principal French demand since the lapse of the treaty of guarantee promised in 1919, but at the same time giving the Germans some security against a repetition of an episode such as the Ruhr occupation. While the Germans recognised their western frontier as final and the return of Alsace–Lorraine to France as permanent, they were not prepared to make a similar gesture in the east; and the furthest they would go was to sign arbitration pacts with Poland and Czechoslovakia, which now had formal treaties of alliance with France and whose existence, as we shall see, depended on France's willingness to go to war to defend them. (See chapters 12 and 13.)

Stresemann, Briand and Chamberlain were awarded the Nobel Peace Prize for their work at Locarno, which did suggest new possibilities of collaboration for the revision of the peace treaties, and for the satisfaction of Germany's aims, both immediate and long-term, by peaceful negotiation. The Locarno agreements gave new hope that the League of Nations might assume the role which Wilson had expected of it and that, in spite of the bitterness of the post-war years, a new international order in Europe might be attainable. The Locarno treaties were criticised at the time on the grounds that they made one set of European frontiers seem more inviolable than others, and that a regional arrangement of this kind might weaken the force of the League of Nations' machinery for maintaining security. But attempts made to strengthen the League in the period before 1925 had in fact come to nothing, largely because of British reluctance to accept any general commitment to act in unspecified circumstances, whereas the Locarno agreements did have the effect of linking Britain to a European settlement, and went some way to restore French confidence in Britain's concern for European security. Yet, as many members of the French Right pointed out, the military provisions did not really satisfy France's needs: since Britain and Italy were now guaranteeing the frontiers of both France and Germany, it was clearly not feasible to make any precise military plans. The British General Staff could hardly have talks with the French about defending France against a German attack and then cross the Rhine to work out detailed plans with the *Reichswehr* on how to repulse a French advance into Germany. Still, in the climate of 1925 the Locarno treaties seemed to mark a turning-point between the years of war and the years of peace, and to justify Austen Chamberlain's belief that 'a great work of peace has been done. I believe it above all because of the spirit in which it was done and the spirit which it has engendered. It would not have been done unless all the governments, and I will add all the nations, had felt the need to start a new and better chapter of international relations.'[13]

If one tries to look at the European scene between 1925 and 1929 as it appeared at the time, and without the knowledge of what came after, there seemed to be some grounds for hope. A measure of economic recovery and a measure of international stability had been achieved in Western Europe. In Germany money and work were available once more. In France, after recurrent financial crises, the franc was finally stabilised in 1928 by a ministry under Poincaré, who returned to office for the last time in 1926 as head of a government of national union, which was able to win the confidence of French financial circles.

In Britain the Conservative Prime Minister Stanley Baldwin was trying to lower industrial tension and to restore some degree of consensus in the country. Although there were by 1925 signs of economic recovery and a drop in the number of unemployed, the British coal industry, which had benefited from the fall in production in the Silesian and Ruhr mining areas, was now faced in its export markets with Polish and German competition. It was one of Britain's oldest and also most old-fashioned industries; and the mine-owners were not only reluctant to spend money on modernising their plant and improving conditions, but were also proposing to reduce wages and to demand longer hours. The result was a coalminers' strike which in May 1926 developed, out of sympathy with the miners, into a general strike. Yet, although at one point in 1924 Zinoviev had said that the revolution in Britain might just as well come 'through the door of the unions as through the door of the Communist Party',[14] the general strike was far from revolutionary: in at least one place strikers played football against the police; and the trade union leaders discouraged any attempt by their more radical members in the provinces to turn the movement into a political one by taking over control of local administration. The failure of the strike not only confirmed the Labour Party and trade union leaders in their belief in peaceful and constitutional means; it also encouraged Baldwin in his not unsuccessful attempts to lower the political and industrial temperature, in spite of the rage of the Labour Party at legislation which made a future general strike illegal. The effects of the strike were not felt long and parliament was soon busying itself with a question which aroused heated controversy – the reform of the official prayer-book of the Anglican Church.

In spite of the general strike there was in these years a general recovery of nerve and of confidence in Britain. In 1925 Winston Churchill, the Chancellor of the Exchequer, took the decision to return to the gold standard, and this, to the economically uninitiated and even to some economists, seemed a sign of confidence in Britain's economic strength. Britain's position in the world seemed to be secure. Until 1932 defence planning was based each year on the assumption that Britain would not have to fight a major war in the next ten years. Her imperial position also seemed to be as strong as ever: in 1924 a great British Empire Exhibition in the London suburb of Wembley demonstrated that Britain's imperial pretensions were undiminished, and masked the fact that Britain's trade balance with the rest of the world, like that of other European countries, had declined as not only the United States and Japan, but also India and some of the countries of South America were capturing markets which before the war had been predominately British. The links between Britain and the Dominions were both strengthened and loosened by the constitutional developments, culminating in the Statute of Westminster in 1931, by which the Crown remained the sole tie between Britain and her now fully independent former colonies in Canada, Australia, New Zealand and South Africa, and there was much talk of the British

Empire giving way to a Commonwealth of free peoples with similar institutions and similar political beliefs. There were even cautious hopes that India too might in time follow a similar path. The nationalist Congress movement under Mahatma Gandhi was following a policy of passive resistance with increasing effect, so that even many Conservatives had become convinced of the necessity of some move towards Indian self-government; and Winston Churchill in the early 1930s quarrelled with the Conservative Party because of the concessions that his colleagues were prepared to make in India. British confidence in constitutional progress at home and abroad and in Britain's position in the world still remained high, and at least until 1931 few people questioned the economic and political assumptions and misconceptions on which it was based.

But if contemporary observers saw grounds for hope in Europe, and if the general relaxation of tension after the experiences of the war years and their aftermath led to a new search for pleasure and a new pursuit of fresh means of expression, a few people noticed some of the weaknesses in the system. In Germany, although Stresemann had succeeded in winning support for his policies, every step he took was criticised by the nationalists for whom the pace of treaty revision was never fast enough, and, although in 1929 a referendum against the Young Plan did not win a majority, there were other signs that many Germans still hankered after the old regime and after an international order in which Germany would be the dominant power. To people abroad, especially in France, this German nostalgia for an old regime and for vanished greatness was illustrated by the election in 1925 of the aged Field Marshal Hindenburg as President of the Republic on the death of the socialist Friedrich Ebert. Moreover, in Germany a stable government depended on the maintenance of a coalition between a number of parties. If the coalition broke up there was no alternative but to try and patch it up again in some form or another, since there was no real parliamentary opposition prepared to take office, because neither the nationalist Right nor the Communists on the Left had any interest in maintaining the existing constitutional system and seriously trying to make it work. Above all the stability of Germany depended on her economic recovery, and a few critics were aware of how precarious this was, dependent as it was on short term foreign loans, and on the creation of employment by means of public works which would be at the mercy of any withdrawal of foreign credits. The events of 1930–1 were to show how vulnerable the German economy was to developments outside.

In France, although the devastated areas had been restored and the franc finally stabilised, the pre-war structural weaknesses had been made worse by the war. The system of public finance failed to ensure that people paid their taxes, and any attempts made to reform it at once met with the opposition of the many supporters of the Radical Party, without whom government was almost impossible. The result was that there was never enough money for social welfare or social security schemes. French industrialists, with few exceptions, were unwilling to modernise their factories or to introduce new techniques. French generals, at a time when the leaders of the defeated German army were thinking about new tactics and new weapons, remained obstinately fixed on the experiences of the First World War, placing their hopes on a bigger and better war of attrition in the trenches, and confident that the creation of a strong system of fortifications on the eastern frontier, started in 1930 under the War Minister André Maginot, would serve to exhaust the German army. The political system still placed power in the hands of the provincial middle classes, who wanted as little change as possible in their world, and a government which would not bother them. The stability and recovery of France depended on there being no major shocks to the system, no sudden strains demanding strong and imaginative leadership.

Before the war France had looked to her alliance with Russia to keep the balance against Germany. Now this was no longer possible: Russia had been absent from the peace conference – '*Monde immense laissé en dehors du règlement, mystère et menace*' as a French statesman put it.[15] To the outside world Russia now represented a threat of subversion from within by means of the Western communist parties, and Russian diplomacy was aimed at keeping the capitalist world divided. The Russians were worried by the Locarno treaties, which seemed to put an end to the special relationship which they had established with Germany at Rapallo. However, the German army was anxious to continue using the military facilities offered by the Soviet Republic, and Stresemann, for all his hopes of the West, did not want to break off all links with Russia. An agreement was signed by which the Germans agreed that their joining the League of Nations would not mean that troops could be sent across Germany for an attack on the Soviet Union, and in the disarmament talks which continued through these years Russia and Germany were often pursuing similar policies aimed at preventing the negotiations from achieving any notable result.

However, Russia was at this period necessarily largely cut off from Europe, and her influence less than either before or since. These were the years of the bitter struggle for power between Stalin and Trotsky after Lenin's death, ending in the establishment of Stalin in undisputed control and Trotsky's exile, in Siberia from January 1928 to January 1929 and after that abroad. But they were also the years in which the Soviet government was preoccupied with the total reorganisation of the economy, a great internal upheaval ending with the inauguration of the first five-year plan of 1929, in which everything was sacrificed to the development of heavy industry on the one hand, and on the other to the ruthless collectivisation of agriculture. During this period of building 'Socialism in one country', foreign Communist parties were being turned into effective agents of Soviet policy, and purged and disciplined for this purpose. At the same time, recognising that the period down to 1928 was one of 'gradual and partial stabilisation of the capitalist system',[16] the emphasis was on the long-term building up of the Communist parties rather than on immediate action, and on creating a party which would be able to rival the social democrats and win away their mass support. The general effect of these moves was a diminution in revolutionary ardour and a concentration on the immediate tasks of organisation and discipline, so that, while Soviet Russia was temporarily turned away from Europe (though still very much involved in China), the European Communist parties were less of an active threat than they had seemed in the immediate post-war years, and the preoccupation with them and with the Soviet Republic on the part of the governments of the West was accordingly also somewhat less.

However, if Russia was not apparently as much of a threat to the stability of Europe as it had seemed a few years earlier, it was still not a state with which any European country (unless, like Germany, forced by circumstances to do so) was going to seek close relations. The result was that France, in her attempt to offset the recovery of Germany, economically, politically and above all demographically, looked to the divided and unstable lesser states of central and eastern Europe. At the same time the very principles which had sanctioned the creation of the new states necessarily prevented them from becoming part of a stable international system, and were to contribute much to the internecine rivalry which was to tear Europe apart in the Second World War.

Of all the liberal hopes of the nineteenth century, that which turned into the most bitter disappointment was the belief that national self-determination and international order were somehow necessarily connected with each other. Mazzini's doctrine that each nation could, by pursuing its own independence, contribute to the welfare of Europe as a whole was taken for granted by liberals of a later generation. And President Wilson himself, when he envisaged a new European order based on the principle of national self-determination, clearly believed that this would increase international stability as well as furthering the principles of natural justice. In fact of course the opposite turned out to be the case. In the confusion of eastern and central Europe it was scarcely feasible to draw clear ethnic frontiers which did not leave a minority on the wrong side of the border; and the successor states of the Habsburg monarchy were born with national problems which were as bitter, even if smaller in scale, as those of the Austro-Hungarian Empire which the new states replaced. Wilson and the other statesmen concerned with making the peace settlement and the founding of the League of Nations had hoped that there would be time and goodwill enough for these problems to be capable of solution. Elaborate provisions were made for the protection of minority rights under the auspices of the League. They were largely ignored.

And even those nationalities which had entered full of hope into the new states – Croats and Slovenes in Yugoslavia or Slovaks in Czechoslovakia – often found that they were unequal partners, without the same opportunities for jobs in the administration or for political influence as the dominant Serbs or Czechs.

Mazzini, the nineteenth-century liberals and President Wilson himself, also all assumed that there was some necessary connection between national self-determination and democratic institutions; and it was hoped that the new states which emerged from the peace settlement would function as liberal parliamentary democracies, and that political liberalisation would accompany national emancipation. Yet the circumstances in which these states came into being made the realisation of these hopes very difficult. None of them succeeded in solving their internal economic and political problems. There were a number of reasons for this. Their economic difficulties were considerable: most of them had little industry and were dependent on the markets of the more developed countries for the sale of their agricultural products. Each new frontier meant a new tariff barrier, and each country started its existence with a burden of debt caused by the very process of setting up the state or taking over new territories, or, in the case of the defeated countries, paying for the war fought by the governments they had replaced. Most of them had very little experience of the working of parliamentary government. Often minority problems were added to social and class differences. To these sources of internal and domestic instability the peace treaties had added another, the bitter sense of grievance which dominated the foreign policy of those countries, especially Hungary, which felt that in their case the principle of national self-determination had been vindictively ignored.

One of the new states, Austria, proved scarcely viable at all. It owed its existence, as we have seen, to the decision of the Allies that the German-speaking provinces of the Austro-Hungarian Empire should not be allowed to join Germany, and during the 1920s it was kept alive economically by large loans organised by the League of Nations. Vienna had lost its *raison d'être* as the capital of a large empire, and therefore many of its inhabitants had lost their occupation. There was a disproportion and a conflict of interests between the city, still very large, however much it had lost of its former importance and grandeur, and the provinces, a conflict reflected by the tension between the Social Democrats, who controlled Vienna, and the Christian Social Party, which dominated the rest of the country and which maintained a precarious majority in the federal parliament. These tensions erupted into riots and a general strike in 1927, and in 1934 led to the suppression of the socialists and to the end of parliamentary government. Austria was a case of a country used to a high standard of living, with a high standard of literacy and a tradition of disinterested bureaucracy, which was unable to cope with sudden impoverishment and with the conflict of interests between the city and the countryside. Many of the new countries however, peopled by a backward and impoverished peasantry, and lacking administrative experience, did not have the substructure or the political traditions to sustain a sophisticated parliamentary system of government. Poland, for example, was torn by personal feuds between the leaders who had succeeded in creating the state out of the provinces partitioned between Prussia, Russia and Austria since the end of the eighteenth century, each with its own administrative system. It was burdened by the expense of the war with Russia in 1920, and by the attempt to extend its boundaries at the expense of Lithuania. In fact, within a few years of the creation of the State and the establishment of its constitution, Poland was governed by a veiled dictatorship which, under Marshal Pilsudski until his death in 1935, and then under his successors, lasted until Poland's defeat and further temporary extinction in 1939.

In Yugoslavia tensions between Croats and Serbs and between the peasants and the middle classes of the towns made stable government and consistent policies difficult. And when in 1928 the leader of the Croat Peasant Party was assassinated in the parliament house itself, the deadlock between the nationalities and the futility of parliament seemed complete. The King declared a royal dictatorship, and although, after he too had been murdered in 1934, his successor made some gestures towards parliamentary government, the tensions in the country were never resolved and its problems were no nearer solution by the time of the German invasion in 1941. Bulgaria – not a new state, it is true, but one which had suffered territorial losses after fighting on the German side in the war – faced revolution in 1919 from a strong Communist Party and from a strong peasant party, and also ended up with a personal dictatorship by the King, after years of terrorism and violence in which the parliamentary system scarcely functioned at all. Roumania too, where, as we shall see in a later chapter, a powerful movement was created on the Fascist model, was from 1930 onwards ruled by its King in a ruthless and corrupt manner. In spite of some genuine attempts at reform and constitutional government in the 1920s, and in spite of the fact that the possession of oil wells made Roumania potentially richer than her neighbours in the Balkans, liberal institutions were not able to take root.

Many of these developments differed little in kind from the kind of politics practised in the independent states of south-east Europe before the war, where French or British constitutional models had served as a cover for the struggle for power within a small ruling clique. The victims were the peasants whose way of life changed little with the changes of regime or even when, as in the case of the inhabitants of Transylvania, they were transferred from one country to another. The instability of the governments of Eastern Europe contributed to the international instability in the area and made it hard for any grouping of these countries to provide France with a substitute for the pre-war Russian alliance. While some countries could combine diplomatically, as in the so-called 'Little *Entente*' of Czechoslovakia, Yugoslavia and Roumania, drawn together by a common fear of Hungary and Hungary's revisionist claims, others were irrevocably divided, so that, for example, Yugoslav disputes with Bulgaria prevented any cooperation between them, and the dream of a Balkan peasant federation, which the Bulgarian peasant leader Alexander Stamboulisky had proposed, remained far removed from reality.

The two strongest states in Eastern Europe were Poland and Czechoslovakia. The Poles, even if their internal regime was one of deep conservatism and narrow nationalism with a strong anti-Semitic flavour, were, by their geographical position and the very intensity of their nationalism, convinced that they were a European great power with an international role to play. This conviction arose from the fact that the refounding of the Polish state coincided with the eclipse of Germany in defeat and of Russia in revolution, so that the two powerful neighbour states, on whose tolerance the very existence of Poland depended, and which when in agreement, as in 1939 to 1941, were able to obliterate Poland from the map, were temporarily out of the reckoning. In the absence of a powerful Germany and a powerful Russia, Poland looked like a substantial military power.

Equally Czechoslovakia, the one successor state of the Habsburg monarchy with a comparatively high degree of industrialisation and with a vigorous, efficient and cultivated urban middle class, looked like being the one country in central Europe where liberal institutions might really flourish and which might become an element of stability in an unstable area. The founder of the state, and its President till his death in 1937, Thomas Masaryk, was a man of noble liberal ideas, practical statesmanship and democratic conviction; his Foreign Minister – and eventually his successor as president – Eduard Beneš was a skilled politician and diplomatist. The new state came into being with able leaders and some agreement that the parliamentary system must be made to work, and that the large estates had to be broken up and a land reform programme put into practice. Yet the country's problems were many. It was composed of several nationalities – Czechs, Slovaks, Germans, Ruthenes, Hungarians and Poles. The interests of the peasants were not always those of the factory-owners or industrial workers. While the majority of Czechs were Protestant, the majority of Slovaks were Catholic. The result was that there were a large number of small political parties, each representing different combinations of these sectional interests. Parliamentary government depended on the formation of coalitions in which the largest party, the Agrarians, tried to do something for everybody. The problem of producing an integrated Czechoslovak nation was not an easy one; and the Slovaks complained that the promises of autonomy made in 1918 were never fulfilled. The German minority was even harder to reconcile; and it was a sign of success of the Czechoslovak Republic that in 1926–7 both Slovaks and Germans agreed to enter the government. As in many parts of Europe, a moment of hope was soon obliterated by the consequences of the world economic crisis.

Yet, even if Czechoslovakia seemed to be the new state with the best hopes of fulfilling some of the liberal ideals of 1919, its international position was a vulnerable one. Although the Czech army was efficient, and although part of the state's heritage from Austria–Hungary was one of the leading armament firms in Europe, the Skoda company, the frontiers of Czechoslovakia were never accepted by her neighbours. A border dispute with Poland over the industrial area of Teschen ('How many Members have heard of Teschen? I do not mind saying I had never heard of it,' Lloyd George told the British parliament in 1919 and was much criticised for his frankness)[17] prevented the two countries from ever cooperating effectively to form a solid counterbalance to Germany. In the south the Hungarians were continually hoping for the break-up of the Czechoslovak state and for the recovery of the Slovak areas which they regarded as irrevocably part of the 'Lands of the Crown of St Stephen'. And even with the harmless and weak republic of Austria, dependent on the Czech mines for most of its coal supply, Czechoslovakia's relations were never very close or cordial.

It was in these circumstances of political instability and economic fragmentation in central and eastern Europe that the transformation of the doctrines of nationalism, from being part of the liberal scale of values, finally led to a set of political beliefs which were bound to destroy the foundations of liberal society. Once national claims had been accepted as the basis for the territorial settlement of 1919, those whose claims had not been satisfied were inevitably in opposition to those who had gained the territories to which they believed they were entitled. Europe was divided by the peace conference into those who wanted the peace settlement revised and those who wanted it upheld. On the one hand were not only Germany and Hungary, but also Italy, who still hoped to reverse the settlement with Yugoslavia; on the other hand France, Poland, Czechoslovakia, Yugoslavia and Roumania had a common interest in upholding the treaties. Any wholesale revision of the treaties, however, depended on the creation and maintenance of an atmosphere of mutual confidence, a condition almost inconceivable in the case of Czechoslovak relations with Hungary, where the assertion of the most extreme Hungarian claims had been almost the only positive act of the reactionary regime installed in 1919, and also on the creation of governments sufficiently stable to be able to consider concessions without immediately being overthrown by a hysterically nationalist opposition. In Eastern Europe in 1929 these conditions were far from being fulfilled. In the West Stresemann was placing his hopes in the establishment of sufficiently good relations with France and Britain to allow him to negotiate further revisions of the treaty. After achieving the reparations agreements and the end of military occupation, he hoped for changes in the eastern frontier, parity of armaments and, more remotely, a possible return of the German colonies and the *Anschluss* (union) with Austria. Although he had achieved some of his aims, his political support inside Germany was still uncertain; and he died in October 1929, almost exactly when the first signs appeared of the world economic crisis, the consequences of which for Europe were to be the disappearance of such stability as had been laboriously achieved since the end of the war, and the start of a period of growing bitterness, hostility and frustration.

THE NEW SPIRIT

It was not just in hastening revolutionary political developments that war proved to be a 'mighty accelerator'. Many of the intellectual and artistic movements which before 1914 had already been challenging and under-mining the assumptions of the previous generation were given fresh impetus by the experiences of the war; and some of them with the development of the new mass media – the cinema, the gramophone and the radio – began to reach a wider public. The political and social effects of the war were such that people, according to their personal and national circumstances, could on the one hand entertain wildly optimistic hopes that a new revolutionary era was beginning in which anything would be possible and in which new artistic techniques were to be linked to new concepts of man and society. On the other hand the sights and sounds of the new art and the new music seemed also to be symbolic of the violent disruption of an established order and established values – *Kulturbolschevismus*, as the Nazis called it – and provoked either a demand for a purge of society or else a pessimistic nostalgia for vanished certainties.

The loss of life and the demographic effects of the war seemed to con-firm both views of the future of Europe. Seven million men had been killed and millions more disabled, leaving both a sense of irrecoverable loss and an intense desire that such a disaster must never be allowed to strike Europe again and that a new international society must be erected to prevent it. In the winter of 1918–19 the influenza epidemic and the near-starvation in much of Russia and central Europe took up the toll where the war had ended. In fact, however, it seems probable that the deaths in the war merely accelerated or modified very temporarily demographic trends already in existence. The French population was, as we have seen, growing very slowly before 1914, and grew even more slowly between the wars, actually declining in the decade 1930–40. This intensified the labour shortage in France and provided the underlying assumptions of French strategic thought between the wars. In Germany on the other hand, where the population was rising fast before the war, it continued to grow in the inter-war period, even before incentives were offered by the Nazi government to encourage large families. At the same time there is evidence that in some of the more advanced countries of Europe, such as France and Britain, the deliberate practice of birth control and the availability of contraceptives (though the French government, in an attempt to raise the birth rate, forbade their sale) was making families smaller, so that there was sometimes a conflict between the interests of the family, anxious to maintain its standard of living by restricting the number of children, and that of the State, concerned for strategic and ideological reasons to increase the size of the population.

The study of population growth and fertility in Europe between the wars is an extremely complicated and technical one, but whatever the actual numerical effect of the losses in the First World War on population and birth rates, the psychological effect was not something which could be measured in statistical terms. The sense of loss had a profound effect on political attitudes. To the feeling that 'this must never be allowed to happen again' was added the belief that the elite of Europe had perished, and that sometimes the burden was almost too heavy for their successors to bear.

The experience of the trenches had left a deep mark on all those who survived; and the failure of some of them to find jobs in the post-war world added to the disillusionment which provided the impetus for radical movements both of the Right and the Left. While some men never referred to their experiences in the war and blotted out the memory as best they could, others, such as the popular German novelist Erich Maria Remarque, in his *All Quiet on the Western Front* (1929), with its title taken from the clichés of war-time communiqués, used their memories to write an indictment of war. There were, too, many who, as the war receded, looked back on the sense of comradeship and solidarity which they had felt in the trenches and seemed to have lost in civilian life. Many joined Old Comrades' Associations, *Ligues d'Anciens Combattants*, *Frontkämpferverbände*, in an attempt to recreate the atmosphere which set them apart from those who had not shared experiences which had been both searing and in a way uplifting. In Britain such organisations were benevolent associations for social and charitable purposes. Elsewhere they became powerful political pressure groups. In France they provided much of the membership of the *Croix de Feu* and other Fascist leagues which sprang up in the late 1920s and early 1930s. In Germany the *Stahlhelm* and other para-military organisations of ex-soldiers, and the spirit which they represented, as reflected in the work of many German writers, such as Ernst Jünger in his *Im Stahlengewittern* (Storm of Steel, 1920), became a formidable political force in the disturbances of the post-war years.

Many of the writers and artists who had reacted against the war, or who had, like the French painter Fernand Léger, learnt in the trenches a new respect for the dignity and suffering of the common soldier, were, when the war ended, drawn to political action or at least to a political commitment, often to the Communist Party. In France, Henri Barbusse (see p. 213 above) was perhaps the most prominent among the many writers who welcomed the Bolshevik Revolution, and he became an active propagandist for the revolutionary Left and for the French Communist Party after its foundation in 1920, finding in communism, as he put it, 'a practical application, in the conditions of contemporary social life, of the eternal truths of reason and conscience'.[1]

The relationship of most European writers to communism and to the Soviet Union was to be more complicated. This was because of the nature of the Soviet regime itself and the disappointment and disillusionment which many felt, first with the methods used by Lenin to enforce his conception of the dictatorship of the proletariat, and then, after Lenin's death, with the growing dictatorial power of Stalin. But for intellectuals and artists there was also, by the 1930s, the additional source of disquiet provided by the changes in cultural policy in Russia and by the increasingly narrow view of the nature of art taken by the Soviet authorities. Although among most intellectuals the extreme and widespread revulsion from the Soviet system only came later, as the nature of Stalinism became more widely known, there were, from the early days of the revolution, reports from people once sympathetic to it but now extremely critical. The anarchists, who had seen in the Soviet system a move towards decentralisation and the withering away of the State, were quickly disillusioned by episodes such as the suppression of the Kronstadt rising in 1921 (see p. 261 above) but, when they tried to tell sympathisers in the West what was happening, they found that lecture halls emptied fast. A few Western radicals were worried by the increasing use of terror and the ruthless elimination of all opponents. Thus Bertrand Russell, for example, who visited Russia in 1920 full of sympathy for the idea of a communist revolution, published on his return his *Practice and Theory of Bolshevism*, in spite of his fears that 'to say anything against Bolshevism was, of course, to play into the hands of reaction'[2]; and the book remains one of the most trenchant criticisms of Lenin's regime.

However, in the early years of the Russian Revolution for many writers and artists revolution in artistic style and revolution in politics were inextricably connected; and indeed the experience of artists in the Soviet Union appeared for a few years to demonstrate this connection in action. Throughout the nineteenth century the Russian intelligentsia had always been astonishingly quick to respond to new ideas from Western Europe; and in the years immediately before the Revolution there were groups of writers and painters in Russia who were in close touch with developments in France and Germany, with Cubism and Futurism and Expressionism, and who had also contributed to the impact which Diaghilev's Russian Ballet had made on the capitals of the West before 1914 (see p. 157 above). In the confused, turbulent years between 1917 and 1922, the advanced artists in Russia seemed to have come into their own. They had a patron in Anatoly Vasilievich Lunacharsky, the Commissar for Education and the Arts. Trotsky was intensely interested in literary and artistic matters and in the relation of art to society (his book *Literature and Revolution* was completed in 1923), and although he criticised the Futurists, and in particular the poet Vladimir Mayakovsky, he followed their work with interest. Above all he called for tolerance of all styles and for the liberation of art from party dogma. 'The field of art,' he wrote, 'is not one in which the party is called on to command.'[3] Lenin himself, although he did not share Trotsky's concern for cultural questions, was, it seems, genuinely fond of Lunacharsky personally and prepared to back him, so that he tolerated the activities even of the advanced artists whose work he himself disliked, and firmly disassociated himself from those members of the party who were preaching the need for a new 'proletarian culture' (*proletkult*) which would reject all previous art and all forms of expression, as well as all types of education, which did not serve the immediate revolutionary struggle.

Thus for a short time a number of artists and writers who were among the most original and radical in Europe thought of themselves as the 'artists of the revolution' and received some official recognition as such.[4] They designed political posters. They ran the theatres and made films. They organised 'agitation and instruction' (*agitprop*) trains to bring their work and ideas to soldiers and workers in remote provinces. They staged performances of street-theatre to commemorate the events of the revolution. They designed the monuments of the new regime (even if they did not always get built, though Lenin's Mausoleum in Moscow survives as a memorial to some of the architectural ideas of the early 1920s). They painted the trees outside the Kremlin in bright, indelible colours – much to Lenin's annoyance – to celebrate revolutionary festivals. There were many aspects and many conflicting theories in this movement, and it was divided and subdivided into many schools and groups. Two main trends emerge however, and each relates to important developments in European and American art since the early 1920s. On the one hand there was a belief that the purpose of art was to reveal the essence of things behind their appearances, to show men a world of symbols or colours behind the forms of the ordinary world or behind the words which expressed the experiences of ordinary life. For the painters, such as Kasimir Malevich or Vassily Kandinsky, this led not only to a great deal of highly mystical writing about their work, but also, and this is more important, to the production of totally abstract paintings, which they were among the first artists in Europe to execute. As Malevich, who called his new style 'Suprematism', put it in a comparatively lucid passage, 'By means of Suprematist philosophical colour-thought, it has become clear that the will can develop a creative system when the object has been dismissed by the artist as a painterly source.'[5]

In contrast to these abstract developments, other equally revolutionary artists were attacking the whole concept of traditional art from a different standpoint. The 'Constructivists', of whom Vladimir Tatlin and El Lissitzky were perhaps the most important, held beliefs which on the surface seemed to have more in common with orthodox Marxism than the 'Suprematist' doctrines of Malevich. Their aim was, as one of their manifestoes put it, 'Not to create abstract projects, but to take concrete problems as the point of departure in work, problems which are presented to us by the Communist way of life . . . The end has come to pure and applied art. A time of social expediency has begun. An object of only utilitarian significance will be introduced in a form acceptable to all.'[6] In practice, however, much Constructivist art was abstract. Many of the artists used images and ideas from both schools, and Lissitzky had been close to Malevich personally. The abstract sculptures and reliefs were made of industrial materials. They seemed to proclaim, as some of the pre-war works of Picasso and Braque had done, that art in future must be created out of the ordinary stuff of everyday life and take its place among the ordinary day-to-day objects around us instead of being given a special place on an easel or in a frame on a wall. At the same time, however, the Constructivists were interested in practical design. Their abstract patterns were applied to textiles; they produced chairs and teapots, stoves or clothes for workers. Many of their more ambitious projects were somewhat fanciful, such as Tatlin's famous design for a *Monument to the Third International* (1919–20), a vast leaning tower which was to contain government offices and revolving cylindrical assembly halls. ('Meetings need not take place in cylinders and cylinders need not really rotate,' Trotsky complained.)[7] But the ideas and the images of Constructivism were applied to many branches of practical activity. Typography and poster design, not only in Russia, were for example permanently affected by them. Moreover, the climate of experiment and the new revolutionary artistic theories emphasised the links between the various arts, so that Soviet theatre, under directors such as Vsevelod Meyerhold, became for a time one of the most influential and original in Europe, while Soviet cinema set new standards for documentary and historical films in the work of Dziga Vertov and Sergei Eisenstein.

The sense of liberation and of intense new experience which many artists and intellectuals felt in the first year or two of the revolution gave way to a mood of less exuberance if not of actual disillusionment. The most famous internationally of all Russian revolutionary writers of the older generation, Maxim Gorky, who had brought to Russian prose a new revolutionary realism, nevertheless criticised many aspects of the new regime. During much of the 1920s he lived abroad, although he was later reconciled and welcomed back as an honoured figure until his death in 1936. But the official encouragement which Lunacharsky and to some extent Trotsky had given to the most advanced experimentation was gradually abandoned.

The dilemma of the revolutionary writer in the Russia of the 1920s is clearly illustrated by the career of the poet Vladimir Mayakovsky. He was born in 1893 and grew up in the Caucasus, where his father was a forest ranger. His reaction against rural life as a very young man made him receptive to the message of Futurism: 'After seeing electricity, I lost interest in nature. Not up to date enough,' he wrote.[8] He shared the Futurists' rejection of the past: 'And why/not attack Pushkin/and other/generals of the classics ?'[9] He quickly identified himself with the revolution, but his violent and Bohemian temperament and the reaction against authority which made him a revolutionary both in politics and in literature fitted in badly with the growing demand for discipline after the first chaotic years of the revolution. However, he gave literary support to the regime with a long elegy on the death of Lenin and, on returning from a visit to the United States and France in a mood of disillusionment with the West, he wrote 'I want/a commisar/with a decree/to lean over the thought of the age . . . I want the factory committee/to lock/ my lips when the work is done./I want/the pen to be on a par/with the bayonet/and Stalin/to deliver/his Politbureau/reports/about verse in the making/as he would about pig iron/and the smelting of steel.'[10]

Yet his last works, *The Bedbug* (1929) and *The Bath House* (1930), are satirical plays which make fun of many aspects of the Soviet system. Both of these were failures when they were performed – *The Bedbug* in a Constructivist setting directed by Meyerhold, himself a victim of Stalin's purges in 1939. Mayakovsky, involved in artistic controversy and faced with hostile criticism, more and more depressed personally, and refused a visa to go to Paris to see the woman with whom he was in love, committed suicide in April 1930. It is said that 150,000 people viewed his body: and on his grave was laid – as it were a last tribute from the Russian Constructivists – a wreath made of hammers, fly-wheels and screws: 'an iron wreath to an iron poet.'[11] He remains a controversial figure (especially since he was later praised by Stalin and rehabilitated) both in his work and in the circumstances of his death; but his suicide seemed to symbolise the change which had taken place in Soviet cultural life, and from then on the party's control of art and literature made the work of any artist who was not prepared to subscribe to the doctrine of socialist realism more and more difficult. Although during the 1930s the importance of art as an adjunct to ideological propaganda was increasingly recognised, its organisation became correspondingly centralised and bureaucratised.

Those advanced artists who stayed in Russia after 1917 (and not all of them did – the composer Igor Stravinsky for example remaining abroad and spending his life in Switzerland, France and the United States), in the midst of the violence and confusion of the early months of the revolution and of the civil war, developed their ideas in isolation. By 1921, however, they began to be known outside Russia and to resume their contacts with Germany and France. In 1922, for example, Kandinsky accepted an invitation to go to Germany to take up a teaching post at the *Bauhaus* (see pp. 308–309 below) in Weimar, the most advanced school of architecture and design in Germany, and found there too an atmosphere in which revolutionary ideas about art and revolutionary ideas about society were inextricably linked.

Even before the war, largely under the influence of Nietzsche, a whole generation of writers and artists in Germany and Austria had been awaiting a violent change. The literary and artistic movement broadly known as Expressionism conveyed an atmosphere of unease, fear, guilt and foreboding in which the experiences of contemporary bourgeois life were transfused with a sense of dread. The novels and stories, many only published posthumously, which the young Prague author Franz Kafka was writing between 1912 and his death from tuberculosis in 1923, depict a society in which the every day routine of middle-class life is suddenly turned into a world of anxiety and horror, in which the protagonist suddenly wakes up to find that he has turned into a gigantic louse (*The Metamorphosis*), or is involved in endless shadowy legal proceedings (*The Trial*) or in a nightmare struggle with a mysterious bureaucracy (*The Castle*).

A similar world is evoked in a well-known Expressionist poem:*

> *Dem Bürger fliegt vom spitzen Kopf der Hut,*
> *In allen Lüften hallt es wie Geschrei.*
> *Dachdecker stürzen ab und gehn entzwei,*
> *Und an den Küsten – liest man – steigt die Flut.*
>
> *Der Sturm ist da, die wilden Meere hupfen*
> *An Land, um dicke Dämme zu zerdrucken.*
> *Die meisten Menschen haben einen Schnupfen.*
> *Die Eisenbahnen fallen von den Brücken.*

Several of the Expressionist poets had perished in the war: (one of the best of them, the Austrian Georg Trakl, killed himself in a military hospital in Cracow in November 1914). Some of them had seen in the war only destruc-

---

* The hat flies off the bourgeois's head/There is a sound like a cry in all the air./Tiles fall off and break in two,/And on the coasts, we read, the tide is rising./The storm has come, the wild seas cough on the land and crush the thick dykes./Most men have colds./The trains fall off the bridges.
Weltende (The End of the World) by Jakob van Hoddis, published in 1918. Van Hoddis was eventually one of the people who in 1942 were victims of the Nazi programme to eliminate the mentally sick. The poem was the opening poem in a very famous anthology edited by Kurt Pinthus and first published in 1919 with the title *Menscheitsdämmerung* (Twilight of Mankind). It is perhaps typical of the movement that the word *Dämmerung* can mean both the dusk of evening and the twilight before dawn.

tion and disaster; but others had hoped that the intense suffering would lead to a new social order and to the brotherhood of man. '*Der Mensch ist gut,*' proclaimed Leonhard Frank in the title of an Expressionist fantasy of 1917, in which the victims of the war – the widows, the disabled, the parents who have lost their sons – transcend the horrors and proclaim a new world. The collapse of 1918 and the German Revolution seemed to confirm all their prophecies. Germany faced total disaster and ruin, but also was given an opportunity to clear the ground and to build anew.

As in France, a number of German intellectuals committed themselves to the left-wing political groups and later to the German Communist Party. We have seen (p. 250 above) how the Expressionist playwright Ernst Toller and the anarchist literary critic Gustav Landauer played leading parts in the Bavarian Soviet Republic. At the same time other writers and artists – first during the war in Zurich, and in New York and then in Berlin, in Cologne and in Paris – had decided that their mission was to destroy all art and, by the elimination of what had previously been considered as culture, to prepare the way for a new social, intellectual and artistic order. This movement, known as Dada, in its determination to mock at everything which had hitherto been taken seriously and to deflate the pomposities of the bourgeois world, had obvious political implications; and in Germany some of its representatives were for a time involved in revolutionary politics by serving as cultural commissars with the workers' and soldiers' councils, or by using the new techniques of photomontage and juxtaposition of incongruous images for satirical political purposes. While in many cases, as in the case of the Frenchman Marcel Duchamp, who spent the war in New York and introduced some of these ideas there, and who was, perhaps, in purely artistic terms the most influential artist to be associated with the movement, this revolt remained on the margin of politics, its demonstration of the absurd pretensions of respectable society and its revelation of new levels of subconscious symbolism contributed to the intellectual climate of Europe immediately after the war. Within a few years it also led to another movement which had close links with political revolution and for a time with the Communist Party – Surrealism.

Just as within the Expressionist movement the events of the war and revolution could inspire extremes of optimism and pessimism, so too the reaction to the events of the time could lead on the one hand to a lurid and turgid style – as in some of Becher's poems – or on the other hand to a demand for objectivity and simplicity, for a style which would be terse, direct and compressed – as in much of the writing of the German poet and dramatist Bertolt Brecht. It was in architecture and the applied arts that this move towards the '*neue Sachlichkeit*' was most apparent, though often the philosophical presuppositions behind it were as mystical and as irrational as those inspiring the extremes of neo-romantic Expressionist art. In several German cities there were socialist municipal governments which, especially when loans from abroad became available under the Dawes Plan of 1924 (see pp.288-9 above), were ready to give advanced architects commissions for workers' housing developments or for public buildings. The centre and focus of this movement was provided by the *Bauhaus*, a school of architecture, painting and design, originally developed at Weimar and then, from 1925 when the local political climate had changed and the *Bauhaus* was accused of being a 'Spartacist Bolshevist institution', at Dessau, in the small state of Anhalt in central Germany.

The influence of the *Bauhaus* extended beyond Germany. When after 1933 many of its leading members, including Walther Gropius and Ludwig Mies van der Rohe, were forced into exile, they contributed to the growth of a genuinely 'international style' of architecture throughout the world. The *Bauhaus* set out to be much more than a school of architecture. It not only taught painting and the design of furniture and textiles; it also promulgated a message about society. It carried on the ideas of pre-war reformers in its demand for return to the work of the individual craftsman. 'Architects, sculptors, painters, we must all return to the crafts.'[12] But now the concept of craftsmanship included the use of the machine, and the aim was to be, in Gropius' words, the creation of 'a clear organic architecture, whose inner logic will be radiant and naked, unencumbered by lying façades and trickeries; we want an architecture adapted to our world of machines, radios and fast motor cars, an architecture whose function is clearly recognizable in the relation of its forms.'[13] Factories were to be, as Gropius maintained, the cathedrals of the future, and would be linked with a new, decentralised, almost anarchist social organisation that would ensure that the use of machinery did not dehumanise man or falsify the relationship of one man to another.

The *Bauhaus*, until it was forced to close by the Nazis, was a centre of controversy in Germany, and to nationalist right-wing critics of the Weimar Republic it appeared to symbolise everything they disliked, socially, politically and artistically. To others it seemed to embody new ideals and new hopes. It certainly served as a focus of attention for artists all over Europe, and some of the most distinguished painters, including Kandinsky and Paul Klee, were on its teaching staff, while the composers Béla Bartók and Igor Stravinsky were visiting lecturers. It had links with other groups and movements in Europe, such as that of the Dutch abstract artists, among them Piet Mondrian and Theo van Doesburg, associated with the periodical *De Stijl*, which they had founded in 1917, and with the architects and painters in France led by Le Corbusier and Amédée Ozenfant who in the early 1920s were proclaiming in the title of their review, '*L'Esprit Nouveau*', the new spirit in twentieth-century art.

It was in Weimar Germany that the links between advanced art and revolutionary or left-wing politics were closest, outside the Soviet Union in the first years of the revolution, and the all-embracing claims of some of the

Expressionist writers and other artists emphasised the social and philosophical relevance of their work. In a society in which the old ruling classes rejected the new order and were trying to maintain their own position, new currents in art could seem as revolutionary as new political ideas, as is shown by the continuous denigration of the *Bauhaus* and its work. Just as in the 1890s the revolt against industrial society, which had given rise to the youth movements – still a notable feature of life in Weimar Germany, but now often associated with rival political groups – had been ambiguous in its implications and had been both revolutionary and reactionary in its effects, so in the 1920s the political and social message of the advanced writers and artists was not always unequivocally clear.

It was not only that leading writers moved personally in different political directions: Gottfried Benn, for example, one of the most famous German poets of his generation, was for a short time before 1936 an enthusiastic sympathiser with the Nazis, but after a long period of silence retreated, in the last years before his death in 1956, into a private lyrical world of pure poetry. Another equally prominent younger contemporary, the Munich writer Johannes R.Becher, ended up as the President of the Academy of the East German Democratic Republic and the author of its national anthem. More important, however, was that many artists, such as for example the painter Emil Nolde, himself a member of the Nazi Party in his native Schleswig-Holstein, combined a technique which placed them firmly among advanced contemporary painters with an imagery and a philosophy which linked them to the *völkisch* nationalist political movements. Nolde was himself claimed by nationalist propagandists as a true German artist who used Nordic ornamentation from the German bronze age. However neither this nor the protection of Nazi chiefs such as Goebbels and Rosenberg could save his pictures from Hitler's stylistic prejudices, and his works were included in the notorious exhibition of 'degenerate art' at Munich in 1937 – an attempt to discredit the best German painters of the day, which in fact has only made their reputations the more secure. Even some of the more symbolist-minded members of the *Bauhaus* itself, whose political views could not have been more opposed to National Socialism and whose work and ideas the Nazis condemned, came in their language about the social significance of architecture near to that of Hitler himself. For the architect Bruno Taut, who had gone to Russia even before the Nazis came to power, in the mistaken belief that the Soviet Union would give him the opportunity for large-scale city-planning on Constructivist lines, buildings must be 'organisms . . . expressing the human community'.[14] Hitler felt something similar; and in *Mein Kampf* complained that modern cities lack the monuments which, in the cities of antiquity and the middle ages, 'were well suited to unite the individual inhabitant with his city in a way which today sometimes seems almost incomprehensible to us'.[15]

It is this intense feeling of ambiguity and contradiction which makes the culture of the Weimar Republic both fascinating and important to the history of twentieth-century Europe. The writer who perhaps best reflects it, in an indirect and detached way, is Thomas Mann, already a respected author in the 1920s and a member of the German literary establishment who had gone out of his way to defend German policy in the First World War. Throughout his work, but most obviously in his *Doctor Faustus* (1947) – an allegory, it would seem, of Germany's fate in the first half of the twentieth century – he was aware of the simultaneous existence of destructive anti-rationalist forces and of the attraction of clarity and reason. It was in Germany that the dark, destructive ideas, of which the Expressionist artists as well as the nationalist propagandists had a large stock, were carried further than anywhere else in Europe. On the other hand in the Weimar Republic humanitarian ideals and a kind of enlightened optimism, as well as a belief that social problems could be directly reflected in art, were combined with an intense response to all the most advanced ideas and styles of the day, and created a climate of intellectual excitement made all the more poignant to us by the darkness which within a few years overwhelmed it.

While half a century later the influence of what we now think of as the culture of the Weimar Republic, partly through its dissemination by the exiles from Nazi Germany, is still felt in Europe and America, its hold on the life of Germany during the brief period of the republic was always precarious. The left-wing critics of German society, or the architects and designers trying to put into practice a new vision of urban life in the machine age might occasionally find support and patronage from a local Social Democratic administration or from an enlightened rich man. They might collaborate with the Communist Party in the hope of bridging the gap between the intellectuals and the working class. For the most part however they were fighting not only the conservatism of the bureaucracy, the judiciary and the universities, most of whose members still clung to the values of the Wilhelmine era, but also a new radical nationalism. This was not just represented by the Nazis, but also by some thinkers and writers with more serious intellectual credentials, such as, for example, Arthur Moeller van den Bruck, the German translator of Dostoevsky, who turned from literary to social criticism. In his most famous book, *The Third Reich* (1923), he carried some of the ideas of the *völkisch* writers of the 1890s over into the crisis of the 1920s and called, in tones of deep pessimism, for a new organic, national, elitist German state. The problem facing the radicals was well summed up by Karl von Ossietzky, an indefatigable propagandist against militarism and a member of a group of writers whose review *Die Weltbühne* (The World Stage) waged a constant campaign against secret rearmament, judicial bias and administrative injustice and in favour of political honesty and of individual liberty at all levels and in every sphere of life. 'One hears people say,'

Ossietzky wrote in 1924, 'that this republic is without republicans. Unluckily, the situation is just the reverse: the republicans are without a republic.'[16]

In Germany it was the precariousness of the political system resulting from war and revolution which forced many intellectuals and artists to take up political positions and to attempt to relate their work to the problems of the day. In France on the other hand, although a few writers and painters had, in the reaction against the war and the apparently unshaken power of the old ruling class, joined the Communist Party in the early 1920s, in general immediate political considerations were pressing much less hard on artistic and intellectual life than they were in Germany. The Third Republic, even if it sometimes seemed a little absurd or unimpressive, and even if it could be denounced for its lack of social policies and for the air of mild corruption and connivance prevalent in what one critic called '*la République des Camarades*'[17], nevertheless gave, at least until 1934, an impression of political stability and more important remained a genuinely liberal society in which there was a great deal of individual liberty. Moreover the tradition of intellectual independence and the belief in 'art for art's sake' had been deeply rooted in France since the first half of the nineteenth century, and the feeling remained that art was still a self-justifying activity. In the 1920s Paris was still, as it had been during the nineteenth century, the artistic capital of Europe. Even during the war, although many of its leading artists were at the front, and many of the foreigners who had settled in Paris were temporarily away, there had been a vigorous intellectual and artistic life. It is true that the circumstances of the war and the intense patriotic feeling sometimes led to extremes of nationalism: the works of Wagner were banned (as they were also in Britain and the United States); the eminent musician Camille Saint-Saëns declared that he was ready to make the sacrifice because 'the works of Wagner were the means employed by Germany to conquer souls';[18] and the greatest French composer of his generation proudly signed his last works '*Claude Debussy, musicien français*'. But even during war-time, once the first danger of defeat and of the fall of Paris had passed, the theatres, galleries and concert halls of Paris still functioned, and, alongside much entertainment aimed at providing relaxation for soldiers on leave, experimental work, such as the ballet *Parade*, in which the young Jean Cocteau collaborated with Picasso and the composer Erik Satie, could still be produced.

Behind much that was chic, frivolous or ephemeral in the artistic life of Paris after the war, two important movements can be traced which were reflected in the applied arts and which affected the taste and some of the ideas of a whole generation. These were the developments roughly labelled as Neo-Classicism and Surrealism. In 1917, a year before his death, the poet

Guillaume Apollinaire, recently wounded and home from the front, gave a lecture in Paris on *The New Spirit and the Poets* in which he predicted both trends. On the one hand, he said, 'the new spirit whose coming we are witnessing seeks above all to preserve the classical heritage of solid good sense, sure critical principles, a comprehensive view of the world and the human soul, and a moral responsibility that tends towards austere expression, or rather towards containment of feelings.' Yet the new poets will also 'lead you alive and awake, into the nocturnal closed world of the dream, into worlds that throb ineffably above our heads, into those worlds both closer to us and remoter from us which gravitate around the same point in the infinite as the world we carry within us.'[19]

The writers, artists and musicians of the 1920s were developing both parts of this programme. In the figures of directly classical inspiration which appear in many of Picasso's canvases of the early 1920s, in Stravinsky's deliberate turning away from the primitive and violent rhythmical excitement of *Le Sacre du Printemps* and in his reworking of the music of eighteenth-century composers or in his cultivation of a deliberately austere and bare formal style, in the calm, intellectually controlled symbolism of the poems of Paul Valéry, there is a spirit of order and simplicity. But it was not only in a renewed awareness of the art of the classical world or of the music of the eighteenth century that the new spirit revealed itself. In their preoccupation with simple, functional forms and unromantic imagery, some other artists were drawn to and indeed inspired by the machine. Their art was to be an art of contemporary life, an art especially of the city. It was here that the artists in Paris approached most closely the ideas of the architects and designers of the *Bauhaus*, with whom they had many contacts; and one of the most influential architects of the century, Le Corbusier, was actively involved with the movement in France for a purer, more mathematical artistic style. From the late eighteenth century, French architects had dreamt of urban utopias, and it was in this tradition that in the early 1920s Le Corbusier, though as yet more active as a painter than an architect, was designing projects for a city to house three million people.

The disillusionment with the modern city, widespread fifty years later, had not yet set in. For the Russian Constructivists, as for Corbusier (who, after just failing to win the competition for the League of Nations building in Geneva, was commissioned in 1928 by the Soviet government to build a headquarters for the Central Union of Consumers' Societies), the city was still a means of providing its inhabitants with a richer, fuller and more exciting way of life than anything they had previously known. This idealised urban life would be based on the machine; and in the art and architecture of the early 1920s the machine is seen as something totally beneficent. Aeroplanes and racing motor-cars provided the artists with subject-matter: the products of their art often aspire to the status of machines, and Le Corbusier's famous phrase called a house 'a machine for living in'; the forms of machines dominate Fernand Léger's great paintings of the 1920s. This preoccupation with machines led to an interest in and sympathy for the workers who ran them, and this in turn, both in France and Germany brought a new interest in popular culture and a concern to bridge the gap between it and the art of an *avant-garde* elite.

Popular culture in Western Europe between the wars meant jazz; it meant the cinema; it meant sport. The arrival in Europe of American jazz to take its place not only as a popular form of dance music alongside the waltzes, polkas and quicksteps of the late nineteenth century, but also as a musical phenomenon taken seriously by composers and critics, had already begun before 1914; in 1895 Claude Debussy had admired American circus artists and the music which accompanied their acts, and he later evoked them in his piano pieces with titles such as *Golliwog's Cakewalk* (1909) and *Minstrels* (1910), (named after the black 'minstrel shows' which were a popular feature in the music-halls of London and Paris). In the years before the war 'jazz bands' playing 'ragtime' began to appear in Europe, while the rhythm of the South American tango invaded the ballrooms, and was, like the waltz a century before, denounced by conservatives as dangerously lascivious. By the 1920s the music of black America had become the staple dance music of much of Europe, with a whole popular culture growing up around famous band leaders; and even austere intellectuals, like the great abstract painter Piet Mondrian, foxtrotting to the phonograph alone in his Paris apartment, became fascinated by the blues or the charleston.

The cinema, developed both in America and Europe in the 1890s and spreading in the first decade of the century, had in the years immediately before the First World War established itself as a form of entertainment in the cities of Europe; and by the end of the war a few directors had begun to see that it had possibilities beyond the simple comic, sentimental or adventure stories which formed its staple content. In his 1917 lecture already referred to Guillaume Apollinaire called the cinema 'the cosmopolitan art *par excellence*'[20] and also 'the popular art *par excellence*', and looked forward to the day when it would serve as a sophisticated means of expression for artists. This it was of course already doing in the 1920s; and in Russia, in Germany and elsewhere it was providing a serious new medium of which both Constructivists and Expressionists were quick to take advantage. But it was as a popular art that it retained its hold and its economic basis, and the great stars, particularly of the American film industry at Hollywood – a Mary Pickford, a Rudolph Valentino or the incomparable Charlie Chaplin – fed the fantasies of two worlds, while the introduction in 1929 of the sound film flooded the world with a torrent of synthetic sound which has never ebbed.

It was in the 1920s too that some sports became, as horse-racing had long been, popular forms of entertainment for hundreds of thousands of people who did not necessarily play games themselves. For the artists, footballers provided a new subject matter; the French painter Robert Delaunay in 1912–13 evoked the speed and dexterity of *L'Equipe de Cardiff* (the Cardiff team), while the Swiss composer Arthur Honegger made Rugby the subject of a symphonic poem in 1928. Increasingly in the twentieth century organised sport, and especially association football played by professionals (given in Britain royal approval when King George V attended the Cup Final in 1923), became a mass entertainment, even a mass cult, so that the local team became the focus of fierce loyalties, and an international match an occasion for patriotic emotion which led some social thinkers to look to sport as a surrogate for war.

While some artists in the 1920s were searching for a new spirit by means of contact with popular art and working-class culture, the development of new mass cultural media and of new mass entertainment only served to emphasise the gap between popular taste and the art of the *avant-garde*, and it was, as we have seen, a debate which dominated artistic discussion in the Soviet Union until it led in the 1930s to the adoption of an official style lacking both the creative originality of the advanced work of the day and the genuine vitality of popular art. At the same time much of the Communist-inspired art of Western Europe tended to a dry didacticism. In contrast to these attempts to bridge the gap between the elite and the masses, between the artist and the worker in the name of Social Realism, one of the other great revolutionary artistic movements of the 1920s, Surrealism, suggested a different way of transforming art and life. In its exploration of what Apollinaire called 'interior universes' it hoped to shock the bourgeois world out of its complacency and thus, as the Surrealists thought, to serve the same ends as the political revolutionaries. For a short time the Surrealists were welcomed as allies by the Communists. As Lunacharsky put it, 'The surrealists have rightly understood that the task of all revolutionary intellectuals under a capitalist regime is to denounce bourgeois values. This effort deserves to be encouraged.'[21] But the contrast between the wild Bohemian iconoclasm of the Surrealists and the disciplined political effort demanded by the Communists was too great. The alliance did not last long; most of the French Surrealists who had first become involved in politics as a result of their participation in the campaign against the French government's colonial war in Morocco in 1925, and who went on to join the Communist Party, left it again within a few years, though some of them returned later under the impact of the Spanish Civil War or, like Paul Eluard, during the Second World War. For most of them it was the expulsion of Trotsky from the party which showed the gap between their position and that of Stalinist orthodoxy. Of the leading Surrealist writers only Louis Aragon continuously remained a loyal party member and transferred his allegiance wholly from Surrealism to communism.

The first Surrealist manifesto was issued in 1924 by André Breton, who became the doctrinaire theoretician of the movement; and it gave a dictionary definition of Surrealism: 'pure psychic automatism by which it is proposed to express either verbally or in writing or in every other way the real functioning of thought. Dictation by thought without the exercise of any control by reason and beyond any aesthetic or moral preoccupation.'[22] The aim of the Surrealists was to exploit the new world revealed by psycho-analysis and to base poetry and painting on the free association of the images thrown up by the artist's subconscious. Their methods included 'automatic writing' and the juxtaposition of random phrases gathered from the newspapers in an attempt to capture the spirit and the mood of dreams in which anything may happen and where no juxtapositions are too incongruous to be acceptable. In the works of the best of the Surrealist painters and poets, Max Ernst, Joan Miró, Paul Eluard or Louis Aragon for example, the effect could be haunting and shocking and suggest a new way of looking at the world. Although the Surrealists recognised their debt to Freud, the admiration was not wholly reciprocated: Freud wrote at the very end of his life that he 'had been inclined to regard the surrealists, who apparently have adopted me as their patron saint, as complete fools (let us say 95%, as with alcohol)', but then went on to say that a visit from the painter Salvador Dali 'with his candid fanatical eyes and his undeniable technical mastery' had changed his estimate.[23] Perhaps, although they did not say so, their imagery in effect owes more to the more romantic mythological vision of Jung than to the down-to-earth clarity of Freud. Yet the Surrealists – and especially the painters – helped to make the discoveries of psycho-analysis part of the accepted imagery of the twentieth century, and thus contributed to the popularising of the ideas of Freud and Jung which have so deeply affected the culture of our time.

In 1935 the German philosopher Karl Jaspers wrote, 'Quietly, something enormous had happened in the reality of western man: a destruction of old authority, a radical disillusionment in an overconfident reason, and a dissolution of bonds have made anything, absolutely anything, seem possible.'[24] In producing this change of outlook from the late nineteenth century onwards, it had not been the professional academic philosophers who had been the most influential, but rather the great original thinkers such as Marx, Nietzsche or Freud whose ideas touched man and society at many different points; and new disciplines such as sociology or anthropology had partly assumed the role hitherto reserved for philosophy. In the reaction against the vast idealist synthesis attempted by Hegel in the early nineteenth century, many of the professional philosophers had been more preoccupied with technical questions, important in themselves, but without great impact on the ideas of ordinary people.

Some philosophers were concerned with problems of perception and the theory of knowledge; others, of whom Bertrand Russell was one of the most famous, combined this with an investigation of the relationship between logic and mathematics and of the underlying structure of our reasoning processes. Bergson and Croce, who had in the early years of the century stressed the importance of instinct and imagination and of the ever changing position of man in the flux of time or in the historical process (see pp. 137-9 above), continued to develop their ideas and to influence writers and historians outside the ranks of the professional philosophers. Bergson died during the Second World War in Paris, having refused the offers of the German occupying authorities to dispense him from the disabilities imposed on people of Jewish origin; and he insisted, even though fatally ill, on registering as a Jew. Croce after at first giving limited approval to Fascism soon became an open critic and lived to see the fall of Mussolini and to become a respected sage in the new Italy, having retained his independence throughout the Fascist regime as a grand international figure whom even Mussolini did not dare to touch.

There were, however, two philosophical movements of the years between 1920 and 1950 which had a deep influence beyond strictly philosophical circles. One was Existentialism, the other the movement originally known as Logical Positivism. It is not possible here to give any adequate philosophical account of these complicated, subtle and variegated doctrines, but we can try to show in a crude way the impact which the exponents of these ideas have had on their non-philosophical contemporaries. The historians of Existentialism find its origins in the nineteenth century in the religious philosophy of the Danish thinker Sören Kierkegaard (1813–55), and they see relevant ideas in the work of Nietzsche and of Dostoevsky. In its twentieth-century form it was developed in Germany by Karl Jaspers and, in language of the utmost difficulty and obscurity, by Martin Heidegger. By the end of the Second World War it had been taken up and propagated by the distinguished French writer Jean-Paul Sartre. It is perhaps through Sartre that Existentialism has had its main popular impact because, although himself for many years a professional teacher of philosophy and the author of a large technical treatise *L'Etre et le Néant* (Being and Nothingness), he is also an excellent novelist and dramatist, in whose own imaginative writing as well as in that of another French author, Albert Camus, it is possible to find some of the ideas of Existentialism in a more digestible form than in the technical philosophical works of its other exponents. Indeed, as was also the case with Bergson, it is among creative artists that the impact of Existentialist philosophy has been greatest.

Underlying Existentialist thought are certain old philosophical problems: is there anything of which we can be certain? Or in the words of the question which Leibniz asked at the beginning of the eighteenth century, and which Heidegger calls the basic question of metaphysics, '*Pourquoi il y a plutôt quelque chose que rien?*' ('Why is there something rather than nothing?')[25]

According to Sartre we can be sure of nothing except of our own immediate actions and above all of the act of choice by which at every moment of our lives, we decide to do one thing rather than another. It is these decisions that determine what we are; but it is also these decisions that determine what the world is like. It follows, in Sartre's words, that 'I am responsible for myself and for all men, and I am creating a certain image of man as I would have him be. In fashioning myself, I fashion man.'²⁶ It is this burden of responsibility on the lonely individual that makes the concept of anxiety so central a one in Existentialist thinking, since man can never rid himself of the necessity of choice, because it is only in the act of decision that he can be aware of his own existence, and yet he can never be sure of the motives which lead him to choose one course rather than another, and never be certain that he is not acting out of what Sartre calls *mauvaise foi*, bad faith or self-deception.

The attraction of this bleak doctrine, with its emphasis on loneliness and anxiety, in a time of social fragmentation and political collapse is obvious enough; and Existentialist philosophy is largely concerned with the emotions which had, as we have seen, already filled the work of many of the Expressionist writers and painters. Sartre was himself a soldier and then a member of the Resistance in the Second World War, and it was in the climate of France during the war and the German occupation, when individual Frenchmen felt, more than ever before, cut off from each other, and each alone felt responsible for deciding what his conduct was to be, that this philosophy – so different from nearly all the traditional French systems of metaphysics and morals – spread widely in France. In fact it is a doctrine without particular political implications. Although it imposes on each man the responsibility for his choices, and therefore for the situations which are the results of his choices, it gives him no guidance how to choose. Sartre has remained a man of the Left: Martin Heidegger became Rector of his university under the Nazis and whatever his later views, proclaimed, 'Do not let dogmas or ideas be the rules of your being! The Führer himself alone is the present and future reality of Germany and its law.'²⁷

Existentialist philosophy, in its concern for the individual act of choice and for the problem of establishing a personal identity, is clearly a doctrine with implications for imaginative artists and for psychologists. Logical Positivism, or Linguistic Analysis as its later developments are generally called, began as an attempt to reformulate the relations of philosophers and natural scientists. In the work of Ludwig Wittgenstein, too idiosyncratic and original a philosopher to be assigned the label of any school of thought, this is developed into a study of the limits of language, and in his later work an examination of the various ways in which we use language for all our various purposes – as scientists, as commonsense men in the street, as moralists or theologians or aesthetic theorists. Although the movement originated in

Vienna in the early 1920s, its influence has been greatest in the English-speaking countries, where certain philosophers, notably C.K.Ogden and I.A.Richards, were already developing comparable ideas about language. Wittgenstein, who had been in contact with British philosophers since before the First World War, settled in Cambridge in 1929, while, after the advent of National Socialism, other leading members of the group were forced into exile; then in 1936 a young Oxford philosopher, A.J.Ayer, published in his *Language, Truth and Logic* a lucid and cogent account of the basic ideas of Logical Positivism and its links with the British Empiricist tradition which immediately made the ideas of the original 'Vienna Circle' and of the early Wittgenstein widely known in the English-speaking world.

The implications of this movement went beyond the particular problems in logic or the theory of knowledge to which these philosophers devoted most of their writings. The message which reached beyond the world of professional philosophers was one of total rejection of traditional metaphysics. In asserting that the only propositions which had any meaning at all were those which were empirically verifiable ('The meaning of a proposition is the method of its verification' became almost the slogan of the original 'Vienna Circle') and that statements about such topics as God or morality were, quite literally, nonsense, which could be uttered for their emotive value but not for their factual content, the Logical Positivists seemed to rule out any meaningful discussion of religion or morality. Although the philosophers themselves took care to explain that they were only concerned with the analysis of factual statements and not with the value or lack of value of emotive statements about God or ethics, the effect of their teaching was sometimes regarded as yet another blow at traditional concepts of morality, yet another step in the emancipation of man from outmoded forms and precepts, so that the result came surprisingly near to the Existentialist position summed up by Sartre, quoting Dostoevsky, 'If God did not exist, everything would be permitted.'[28]

As Linguistic Analysis developed, many of the cruder aspects of the original Logical Positivism were modified; and the careful study of the way in which words are used in various kinds of discourse and of the limits of language gave a stimulus not only to our understanding of the nature of argument but also to the scientific study of language as such. Ludwig Wittgenstein himself, who had been close to the original Vienna Circle but always somewhat apart from them, developed in his lifetime two different philosophical approaches. In his *Tractatus Logico-Philosophicus*, finished in 1918 and published in 1921, an impressive work of considerable difficulty, but also often of great literary beauty, he was concerned to explore the limits of language, the nature of logic and the relation of language to facts, but he did not rule out the validity of religion or ethics, and merely raised the question whether there was anything to be said about them. They could only be shown and not discussed.

'*Und wovon man nicht reden kann, darüber muss man schweigen*' ('And about that of which we cannot speak, we must be silent') is the famous last sentence of the book.

During the rest of his life (he died in 1951) Wittgenstein published very little and it was only after his death that his later ideas began to appear in print. This was partly the result of his increasing dislike of academic philosophy and of his practice of conducting philosophical discussion in an intensely personal way with a small group of disciples; it was partly because of his practice of withdrawing from intellectual life during certain periods of his career – between 1920 and 1926 he had taught in village schools in the country in Austria, and in the Second World War he left his Chair at Cambridge to become a hospital orderly; and this increased the legendary·quality which he and his work had acquired by the end of his life. Whereas the *Tractatus* had been a great work of systematic philosophy which, for all its revolutionary ideas, had many of the features of a traditional philosophical treatise, his later work – the *Philosophical Investigations* and the notebooks known as the *Blue and Brown Books* – suggested a totally new approach to the subject. Instead of erecting a system of philosophy and trying to establish a general theory of the limits of language, Wittgenstein was now immersed in the study of individual examples of linguistic usage, an infinitely patient and delicate analysis of the rules for the use of words in different contexts or in different kinds of discourse. Philosophy must start with the world as it is, and this means with language as it is. To understand the world we must pay scrupulous attention to the way in which we describe all aspects of it. Although Wittgenstein himself questioned the comparison that was sometimes made between his method and that of Freud, there is certainly something similar in his almost therapeutic attempt to clear up confusions by means of analysing the different layers of linguistic usage which make up our thought and our communication with each other, and in his insistence that it is in man himself and not in any outside power that the answers to man's problems must lie.

Wittgenstein's first contacts with the English-speaking world had been with the Cambridge philosophers Bertrand Russell and G.E.Moore. Russell was one of the few twentieth-century English philosophers with a reputation on the Continent; and although this was at first based on his original contributions to the study of logic and of the foundations of mathematics, it grew with his increasing involvement in public causes, and by the fact that he was a social and educational reformer as well as a pure philosopher. Until his death in 1970 at the age of ninety-seven, he remained one of the most outstanding and the most independent figures in British intellectual life, and never abandoned his rationalist hope that men could be saved from the effects of their folly, whether intellectual or political. He had opposed the First World War; and in extreme old age he was active in radical protests against nuclear weapons or against the war in Viet-Nam, a public figure with a world-wide and ever more controversial reputation.

Moore was much less widely known outside the circle of professional philosophers; but he left a certain mark on English thought and on English literature because of the influence of his ethical ideas, as expressed in his *Principia Ethica* of 1903, on a group of young intellectuals in Cambridge in the early days of the century, some of whom later went to live in the Bloomsbury district of London and became known by its name. The group included the economist John Maynard Keynes (see pp. 325-6 below), the novelists Virginia Woolf and E.M.Forster, and a number of critics and painters, including Roger Fry, who was responsible for the development rather belatedly in England of a taste for French Impressionist and Post-Impressionist art. The aspect of Moore's philosophy which attracted them was summed up by Keynes as follows:[29]

Nothing mattered except states of mind, our own and other people's of course, but chiefly our own ... They consisted of timeless, passionate states of contemplation and communion, largely unattached to 'before' and 'after' ... The appropriate subjects of passionate contemplation and communion were a beloved person, beauty and truth, and one's prime objects in life were love, the creation and enjoyment of aesthetic experience and the pursuit of knowledge.

This led in the novels of Virginia Woolf to a poetic attempt to recreate the states of mind of the characters, and in the art criticism of Roger Fry and Clive Bell, to a theory of aesthetic detachment which looked at works of art for their 'significant form' rather than for their content. These ideas were accompanied by a belief, exemplified in the novels of E.M.Forster, in the necessity of exact and honest analysis of one's own state of mind and an insistence on total sincerity and frankness in personal relations. It was a doctrine which, in the limited circle which it reached, contributed to the general reaction against hypocrisy and cant and to a new moral attitude in which each person bore the whole responsibility for his own behaviour; and it played some part in liberalising sexual attitudes in Britain. But to outsiders it could seem priggish, self-centred and limited by a shallow rationalism leaving out, as Keynes himself saw, 'whole categories of valuable emotions'.

This was certainly the view of many critics, and especially of D.H. Lawrence, whose own novels, with their call for the recognition and liberation of dark instinctive and sexual forces, express values wholly opposed to the rationalism and aestheticism of Bloomsbury. (It was in reply to a report of Lawrence's criticisms that Keynes wrote the essay on his early beliefs from which we have quoted.) It is indeed arguable that Lawrence's lyrical praise of sexual activity and the frank discussion of it in his work contributed more to the change of moral attitude in Britain than the dispassionate discussion of ethical values which the members of the Bloomsbury group took over from G.E.Moore. In any case, their influence was largely limited to England, and even D.H.Lawrence's call for the liberation of the dark forces in man and for a new awareness of the importance of sex was addressed primarily to English ears, even if, because of the British obscenity laws, books such as his *Lady Chatterley's Lover* (1928) as well as James Joyce's *Ulysses* (1922) had to be printed in Paris rather than in England. The novels of Virginia Woolf and E.M.Forster conveyed no public message and were comparatively little known outside the English-speaking world; and even the economic theories of Keynes were not widely discussed outside Britain and the United States until after the Second World War.

However, even if Britain remained somewhat outside the main currents of intellectual and artistic life of Europe, these movements – for frankness and sincerity in human relations, for a more liberal and open attitude to sex – were shared in different forms by many of the advanced societies of Europe in the 1920s, except in those countries where the Catholic Church was still strong enough to impose a rigorous traditional morality. The new morality was partly the result of the spread of psycho-analytical doctrines and of popular, if often erroneous, notions of Freud's teaching. But it has also been argued that it was the result of the war itself, of the loosening of family ties and the emancipation of women, of the awareness of the fragility of life induced by the war and of the general sense of liberation from old values which followed it. In Weimar Germany – or at least in Berlin and some of the larger cities – as conservatives everywhere were eager to note, there was an atmosphere of overt sexual tolerance such as had not been seen in Europe for many years. Alongside the serious research being done at for instance Dr Magnus Hirschfeld's 'Institute for Sexual Science', there were night-clubs and brothels catering for every taste, and an atmosphere of permissiveness mixed with desperation, which the young English writer Christopher Isherwood depicted with insight and sympathy in his early writings, *Mr Norris changes trains* (1935) and *Goodbye to Berlin* (1938). For many conservatives it seemed a sign of the decadence of European civilisation, and the 100,000 people who had bought copies of Oswald Spengler's famous pessimistic survey of world history *The Decline of the West*, in the years after its publication in 1919, felt that they had much evidence to justify the title. For the Communists, too, the search for pleasure could be seen as a symptom of the demoralisation of capitalist society and provide the material for, for example, the satirical musical plays *The Threepenny Opera* (1928) and *The Rise and Fall of the City of Mahagonny* (1930) in which Bertolt Brecht collaborated with the composer Kurt Weill.

The search for a new set of ethical values in a Europe from much of which both the old religious certainties and the optimistic belief in the benefits of science and of material progress had vanished had been a common literary theme since the end of the nineteenth century. Of the established writers of the 1920s it was perhaps André Gide who reflected most clearly some of the moral conflicts involved, and he provided throughout his life a continuous object of attack for Roman Catholic critics in France and beyond as his international influence and reputation grew. Gide, who was born in 1869 and began to publish in the 1890s, in his early writings *Les Nourritures Terrestres* (Fruits of the Earth, 1897) and *L'Immoraliste* (The Immoralist, 1902) had been one of the first authors to bring Nietzsche's message to France. All his life he was torn, and very consciously so, between his desire to act on Nietzsche's command *'Werde was Du bist'* ('Become what you are') – in his own case to come to terms with his homosexuality – and the need to carry out the scrupulous examination of conscience enjoined by the French Calvinist Church in which he grew up. In some of his novels, *La Porte Etroite* (Strait is the Gate, 1909) or *La Symphonie Pastorale* (Pastoral Symphony, 1919), he was analysing the vagaries of the Protestant conscience, and in others, of which the most famous was *Les Caves du Vatican* (The Vatican Cellars, 1914), a half-serious, half-comic account of the consequences of an *acte gratuit*, an arbitrary and unmotivated act of violence, or the later *Les Faux-Monnayeurs* (The Counterfeiters, 1926), he was concerned to examine the basis of moral decisions and to stress the relation between imagination and action and the difficulty of acting according to a consistent moral code and of adopting a logical and honest moral attitude in European society of the twentieth century. Throughout most of his life Gide kept a journal (partly published in 1939, with a further volume in 1954, three years after the author's death). It is a book which remains a fascinating source not only for Gide's own personal predicament and evasions, and for the intellectual life of his time, but also for the artistic and moral sensibilities of the enlightened bourgeoisie of twentieth-century Europe, from whom so many of the certainties of their fathers and grandfathers had been taken away.

In 1927 Gide's contemporary, Julien Benda, published his tract *Le Trahison des Clercs* (The Treason of the Intellectuals) in which, from a traditional French rationalist position, he attacked the abandonment of reason by so many of the philosophers, artists and writers of his day; and he castigated intellectuals, and especially the philosopher Bergson, for failing to realise the political implications of their ideas. Over the next twenty years many people were to come to the conclusion that he was right. Already, within a few years of the publication of his book, the basis of much of the European intellectual and artistic activity which has been discussed in this chapter was swept away, first by the economic crisis, which struck Europe in 1930 and made some people feel that any artistic or intellectual activity not rooted in social needs was a frivolous luxury which Europe could not afford. And secondly the establishment of National Socialism in Germany and the growth of the Stalinist terror in the Soviet Union put an end to the hopes of the 1920s and justified the worst fears expressed by the pessimists. 'The sky over Europe and the whole world,' André Gide noted in his diary of 8

February 1933, 'is so heavy with the storm; hearts are so full of hatred that sometimes I cannot help thinking that only a conflict between classes could put off the mortal conflict between nations.'[30] And in December 1933 the executive committee of the Communist International declared that 'the objective prerequisites for a revolutionary crisis have matured to such an extent that at the present time the world is closely approaching a new round of revolutions and wars'.[31]

FASCISM, COMMUNISM AND DEMOCRACY, 1929-37

At the end of October 1929 the New York stock market collapsed after a long and unprecedented speculative boom. This loss of nerve in the greatest and richest capitalist society in the world had both practical and symbolic effects far beyond the United States itself, and its consequences demonstrated the instability on which the European economic recovery had been based. There had been some signs of an impending recession even before the crash in America: prices of agricultural produce, the staple export of most of Eastern Europe, had been falling for about a year; some sensational financial scandals had ruined many investors and showed the dangers of the prevailing climate of over-speculation; the volume of American lending to Europe was contracting somewhat. None of these might have become serious if it had not been for the psychological shock of the crisis in the United States and the end of the American boom. The effects were rapidly felt in Europe. The fall in the prices of food and raw materials which hit the agricultural countries of eastern Europe was accompanied by a drop in the demand for the industrial exports of the more developed countries in western and northern Europe. Peasants were left without markets and industrial workers without employment. At the same time the shortage of money in the United States obliged many American investors to call in their short-term loans, so that those countries, and in particular Germany, whose recovery had been based on an influx of foreign capital, suddenly found themselves obliged to halt the construction of public works and housing projects and to dismiss workers, being unable to borrow more money elsewhere to meet their debts or continue their operations.

The disastrous fall in farm prices and the increasing industrial unemployment during 1930 led to a growing lack of confidence in the whole economic system. By 1931 there was a serious monetary crisis: the most important of the Austrian banks, the *Credit Anstalt*, failed in May 1931, and two months later the large German *Darmstädter und National Bank* went bankrupt. In September Britain abandoned the gold standard and devalued the pound, and this example was followed by a number of other countries. The experience of the inflation in the years immediately after the war had left an atmosphere of psychological insecurity, so that to people who had just succeeded in rebuilding some sort of life for themselves the prospect of another inflation was more than they could bear, and any alternative seemed preferable to facing once more the loss of their savings and the collapse of their standard of living. In Germany this helped the extreme parties which promised radical economic solutions. In France it made it politically impossible for the government to devalue the franc at a time when it might have been economically desirable to do so in order to keep the price of French exports competitive with those of countries which had devalued their currency. With unemployment mounting and confidence in the currency and the financial institutions of Europe ebbing fast, the orthodox response of governments was to adopt a policy of deflation, and to attempt to restore confidence by balancing budgets, exercising economy, cutting expenditure, reducing the wages of state employees and dismissing redundant workers. This had the effect of diminishing purchasing power still further and increasing unemployment still more.

The crisis, and especially the persistent unemployment, caused profound damage to the political and social structure of Europe, and it was only gradually that politicians, financiers and economists began to adopt a new approach to the problem of economic recessions. In practice the New Deal in the United States suggested that the way to deal with a bad recession was to create employment by means of public works and, by the expenditure of government money, to restore purchasing power and the demand for consumer goods. But the revolution in thinking induced by the experiences of 1929 to 1932 went much further than the pragmatic measures introduced by President F.D.Roosevelt and his advisers. New economic theories were developed and a new concept of the nature of capitalist society began to take shape.

The theoretical basis for the new economic practice was provided by the British economist John Maynard Keynes in his book *The General Theory of Employment, Interest and Money* first published in 1936. While Keynes' *General Theory* is a technical treatise explicitly addressed to other economists – and it gave the subject, as Weber had given sociology, new models and new concepts – its general implications are simple and of great importance. 'The outstanding faults of the economic society in which we live are its failure to provide for full employment and its arbitrary and inequitable distribution of wealth and incomes',[1] Keynes wrote: and he hoped that his work would contribute to remedying these defects. In its insistence on the problem of unemployment – the great social issue in Europe and North America in the 1930s – it showed that what had hitherto been regarded as insoluble could in fact be solved by government action. What Keynes suggested was not, as the Marxists, for whom Keynes had the profoundest contempt, proposed, an economic system that was a total alternative to capitalism, but rather a way of making capitalism work and of removing some of its more objectionable social and moral features.

Keynes seemed to offer a middle road between Marxist state socialism and Fascist authoritarian societies:[2]

The authoritarian state systems [he wrote in his conclusion] seem to solve the problem of unemployment at the expense of efficiency and of freedom. It is certain that the world will not much longer tolerate the unemployment which . . . is associated – and, in my opinion, rightly associated – with present-day capitalistic individualism. But it may be possible by a right analysis of the problem to cure the disease whilst preserving efficiency and freedom.

Keynes died in 1946, after playing an important part in British government financial policy and in setting up at the end of the war the international organisations for financial cooperation, and an international monetary system which lasted some twenty-five years, so he did not live to see the way in which the planned capitalism, for which he had provided a theoretical basis, became the accepted form of economic organisation in most of the developed countries of the West. 'Practical men' he had written, 'who believe themselves to be quite exempt from any intellectual influences, are usually the slaves of some defunct economist.'[3] Perhaps he was right: Keynes's doctrines have been accepted, even by those who do not agree with them all, as a basis for a new way of economic thinking and a new analysis of the nature of capitalist society, and have passed into the accepted ideas about the world of many people who have never read a word of his writings.

With an apparent major crisis in the world capitalist system offering new prospects of revolution, the attitude of the communist parties was clearly of great importance. In the summer of 1928, over a year before the onset of the depression, the Comintern held its sixth congress. It was an occasion when foreign communists were forced for the first time to realise the changes which had come over the Soviet leadership and Soviet society since Lenin's death. Russia was engaged in a monumental struggle to transform itself by a rapid increase in heavy industry and by the forced collectivisation of agriculture. Stalin had put an end to free discussion within the inner leadership of the Communist Party: Trotsky was in exile in Siberia (he was expelled from Russia itself in 1929) and Zinoviev, the leading figure in the Comintern since its foundation, had been forced to resign as chairman of its executive committee and was expelled from the party a year later. His role in the Comintern had been taken by Bukharin, who was himself already at odds with Stalin because of his opposition to the policy of industrialisation and of the repression of the richer peasants, the *kulaks*. There is some evidence that several foreign delegates felt uneasy in the atmosphere of suspicion and intrigue in Moscow, and realised that what happened in the Comintern was now less important to Stalin and the Soviet leaders than what was going on in the Russian party. The disagreements between Trotsky and Stalin and then between Stalin and Zinoviev, and, in his turn, Bukharin, were genuine disagreements about policy, about economic organisation, about the problem of increasing agricultural production, about the relative claims of heavy industry and agriculture. In Lenin's day these would have been hammered out among the party leaders and, although Lenin's position and personality were such that his views usually were finally accepted, people who had spoken and voted against him were not penalised. Now, however, the debate was not just about policy but about who should control the party; and Stalin had begun to establish himself as a total dictator whom nobody dared to oppose.

The savage denunciations of Trotsky and the absence of Zinoviev showed the leaders of the foreign communist parties which way developments in the Soviet Union were moving; but for most of them in 1928, with revolution in the West still far off, the predominance in the Communist International of the one country where there had been a successful revolution was still not questioned. Although some Western Communists complained that the Sixth Comintern Congress seemed aimless and badly organised, they nevertheless discussed a large number of very important questions. The Congress received a long and in many ways impressive report from Bukharin analysing 'the general crisis of capitalism', and passed a programme predicting that 'the capitalist system as a whole is approaching the final collapse'.[4] Within a little over a year, with the onset of the world economic crisis, it looked as though much in Bukharin's analysis was justified. The growing unemployment and the sense of desperation was driving many workers into support of parties offering extreme solutions especially in Germany where the Communist Party had by 1930 won more than four and a half million votes in the general election, (an increase of over 300 per cent on the 1928 results), though the success of the Nazis had been even more striking. While in Germany it was not unknown for individuals to pass from one of the extreme parties to the other, the official attitude of the Nazis to the Communists was one of total hostility; they were one of the list of enemies which National Socialism was pledged to destroy, and the two parties were united only in their common opposition to the existing system.

This opposition was however an important element in the communist analysis of Fascism, as stated in 1928 at the Comintern Congress, and as developed over the next five years. For the Communists, Fascism, first in Italy and now as it was developing in Germany, was yet another sign of the impending collapse of capitalism, a symptom of the divisions and contradictions within the capitalist world and of the desperate means used by the bourgeoisie to halt the revolution. It could, the Communists thought, only be a passing phase which would prepare the way for the coming of the revolution and for the dictatorship of the proletariat. It followed, on this argument, that the chief opponents of the revolution were not the Fascists, but rather those elements in the state which, by supporting moderate reform, might prolong the life of the capitalist system, and especially the Social Democrats (often called by the Communists, in the jargon of the period, 'social Fascists'). The result of the Communists' faulty analysis in 1928 was to make it impossible in the critical years 1930 to 1932 for the working class parties in Germany to combine to present a united front or to adopt common tactics against the Nazis. The communist analysis of the conditions which produce Fascism was perceptive enough: it laid stress on the impoverishment of many of the lower middle class and the presence of 'socially declassed elements'. It pointed out the particular nature of Fascist social demagogy ('Anti-semitism, occasional attacks on money capitalism, impatience with the parliamentary "talking-shop" ') and it even admitted that Fascism won over some of the working class, although, in the communist view, these were 'only the most backward strata'.[5] It was the extent and persistence of the threat which the Communists minimised; and it was to be an infinitely costly mistake both to the Soviet Union and to the Communist parties of Europe.

The economic crisis, as it grew in intensity throughout 1930 and 1931, affected nearly every country in Europe, and it not only raised doubts about the future of the whole capitalist system but also posed immediate political problems to the European governments. Of the major industrial countries, France was the least affected and Germany the most. France, in a strong position because she had accumulated one of the largest stocks of gold in the world, was to feel the effects of the crisis from 1934 on, when much of the rest of Europe seemed to be on the way to recovery. For the moment, as France depended less on foreign trade and on foreign capital than either Britain or Germany, the French were not only able to maintain the value of the franc (it was only late in 1936 that it was finally devalued), but were also in a position to use their holdings of gold at a time when other countries were anxious for loans to bolster failing banks and faltering currencies, to reinforce their foreign policy.

The French government, therefore, was able to block a proposal for tariff union between Germany and Austria in March 1931 – a desperate attempt to save the economic situation in both countries. They refused a loan to Germany unless Germany stopped construction of her new battleships – these were so-called 'pocket battleships' which by ingenious technical designing had increased armour and fire-power while complying with the restrictions imposed by the peace treaty – and committed herself to accepting the territorial boundaries of 1919. They were able to take a tough line in 1932 over questions of disarmament, and refused to make any concessions to the German position and the German demand for parity, at a moment when the German government desperately needed a foreign political success to help its increasingly weak internal position. At one point, however, the French were forced by the prevailing economic circumstances to abandon what had been a central part of their foreign policy since 1919. In June 1931 President Hoover proposed a year's moratorium on the payment of all reparations and inter-Allied debts; and a year later, at a conference at Lausanne, when it was quite clear that there could be no question of Germany's being able to continue reparations payments, the reparations clauses of the Treaty of Versailles were quietly abandoned, and to the annoyance of some Americans inter-Allied debts were also wiped out.

The most immediate problems arising from the economic crisis were those faced by the two countries in which at the beginning of 1930 socialists were in the government: Britain and Germany. In both cases the links between the socialist parties and the trade unions were close and the parties depended on the unions for their mass support, and, in the case of the British Labour Party, for a large portion of their funds. At a time of growing unemployment the unions were concerned with ensuring the livelihood of their members, many of whom had lost their jobs. They wanted to maintain a reasonable payment of relief to the unemployed, while the governments, in response to the advice of their experts calling on them to cut expenditure, were anxious to reduce the rapidly increasing bill for unemployment. The systems by which payments to the unemployed were financed and administered differed in the two countries, but the basic political problem was the same: socialists in government, under pressure from parliamentary critics and from their own economic advisers, felt themselves obliged to try to limit the amount paid to the unemployed and therefore inevitably risked losing the support of many of the trade union members and dividing the party.

In Britain the elections of 1929 had left the Labour Party as the biggest party in parliament, though it did not have an overall majority, and when its leader Ramsay Macdonald formed a government, he depended on the support of the now much diminished Liberal Party under Lloyd George (who was himself out of action because of illness during a crucial period of the crisis of 1931 and who never recovered his political position). In August 1931 however, when the members of the government were unable to agree on the economy measures to be adopted, Macdonald accepted a proposal to form an all-party coalition government. The effect was to divide the Labour Party into two; the majority which opposed the proposal for a coalition and the minority which supported it. The latter subsequently took the name of the National Labour Party and rallied to the 'national' government which Macdonald formed with Conservative backing. The result was profoundly to weaken the Labour Party for a decade, and to confirm in power (by a large majority in the elections of October 1931 and again in November 1935) a government in which the influence of Macdonald and of the former Labour ministers rapidly became less than that of the Conservatives, whose leader

Stanley Baldwin was deputy Prime Minister and succeeded Ramsay Macdonald on his retirement. The political effects of the depression in Britain were considerable: the experience of unemployment left a scar which is still sensitive in the 1970s, and the Labour Party was left with an ineradicable suspicion of coalition government in peace-time. But the British constitutional machinery survived, and helped a solution of the crisis, with the old ruling class obstinately and unrepentantly in control.

In Germany on the other hand the fall at the end of March 1930 of the coalition government, headed by the Social Democrat Hermann Müller, because the parties providing the government's parliamentary support could no longer agree, and because the trade unions and the majority of the Social Democratic party refused to support a deflationary programme involving cuts in unemployment pay, led to a prolonged crisis, which ended not only with the fall of the republican system but also with the triumph of Hitler and the National Socialists, a triumph which had more effect on the course of European history in the twentieth century than any other event except the Russian revolution.

The effects of the great depression were felt all over Europe: and some of the reactions to them were similar all over Europe. National feelings were intensified; trade barriers were raised (in Britain, where the doctrine of free trade had first been propounded and had lasted longest, a protectionist policy was finally adopted in 1931); class antagonisms were made worse and, as the fear of revolution revived, a frightened middle-class sought new and extreme ways of protecting its interests. In Germany two parties immediately gained supporters as a result of the crisis – the Communists and the National Socialists. The Nazi gains were phenomenal: in 1928 they had won under a million votes; in 1930 they had nearly six and a half million and became the second largest party in the Reichstag. The basic weakness of the Weimar Republic was thus accentuated. Ever since 1919 there had been a large section of German opinion which had never accepted the republic and which had little interest in its survival. From 1930 on there were two large parties openly aiming at the overthrow of 'the system'.

Moreover the break-up of Hermann Müller's government, a 'great coalition' of Social Democrats, Catholics and liberals, in the face of the worsening economic situation, made it very hard to constitute a parliamentary majority at all. The solution adopted by the new Chancellor, Heinrich Brüning of the Centre Party – an austere, devout Catholic, with a dislike of parliamentary government and a romantic attachment to the qualities of discipline and self-abnegation he had observed during his war service – was to use Article 48 of the constitution which allowed, in an emergency, for government by decree without parliamentary backing. For this Brüning needed the support of President Hindenburg, now eighty-two years old; and for the time being the

President, pleased with Brüning's record as a machine-gun officer in the war and with his respectful patriotism, was prepared to give him the necessary authority.

After parliament in July 1930 had refused to endorse either government by decree or Brüning's bleak deflationary proposals – an increased income tax, a reduction of officials' salaries, a tax on bachelors – the Chancellor dissolved the Reichstag. The elections, with the success of the Nazis at the expense of the other right-wing parties and of the liberals, did nothing to solve Brüning's problems, although the Centre Party, with its loyal Catholic vote, maintained its position. The Social Democrats in spite of some losses remained the largest party in parliament; their old supporters continued to vote for them, but it seems likely that they were failing to attract the younger members of a growing electorate. However, the most the Social Democrats were prepared to offer Brüning was a reluctant 'toleration', as they called it, of his policy of governing by decree. It was clear that, while the opponents of the republic were more vigorous than ever, its supporters were not very enthusiastic about its present government but were unable to suggest an alternative.

The need for strong government was clear enough: farmers were being ruined, or thought they were, by the fall in world agricultural prices; unemployment rose: there were 4,400,000 out of work at the end of 1931, 5,000,000 in September 1932 and 6,000,000 in the winter of 1932-3. In July 1931 came the disastrous failure of the Danat bank. The objective dangers from 1930 on were obvious, and even more all-pervading was the atmosphere of fear: for the workers, fear of unemployment; for the middle classes, fear of a renewed inflation and for the breakdown of law and order; for young people, fear of a future which seemed to have nothing to offer but frustration. These fears were not to be assuaged by Brüning's programme of vigorous deflation and financial stringency accompanied by plans to form a new *Wehrsportverband* (Military Sport Association) to attract the disoriented youth of the country away from the Hitler Youth and other anti-government movements. The success of Hitler and of the National Socialist Party came to a large extent from Hitler's ability to play on the fears felt by nearly all Germans, and to exploit what has been called the 'politics of anxiety'.[6]

The circumstances of Germany in the years 1930 to 1932 were such as to provide plenty of opportunities to any demagogue promising strong government and the end of unemployment. Hitler went much further than this. His rise was due to the extent to which he was able to persuade different sections of the population of Germany that he wanted what they wanted, and to the lack of any deep-rooted alternative tradition or of any strongly held constitutional bastion. But it was also due to Hitler's own peculiar political genius, not just as an orator and propagandist but as a skilful manipulator of men and events. Nazi propagandists (as for example in Leni Riefenstahl's great film record of the Nazis' rise to power, *The Triumph of the Will*, made in 1937) were subsequently concerned to show that Hitler's triumph was inevitable, but this is both to underestimate his own political and tactical skill as well as the perseverance and cleverness which he showed when, as at several times in his career, he was on the point of failure.

After the fiasco of the Munich *Putsch* in 1923, Hitler might have been quickly forgotten and dismissed as yet another of the political cranks in the extreme nationalist underworld of Munich. In fact however he used his period of imprisonment – thirteen months under comparatively easy conditions – to write his autobiography and summarise his views in *Mein Kampf* and, as soon as he came out of prison, now describing himself as 'writer' instead of 'painter', he began to rebuild his political career on a new basis. Some historians, and many of Hitler's contemporaries, put off by the turgid and pretentious style, the repetitions and confusions and the total lack of originality of the ideas, have dismissed *Mein Kampf* as mere day-dreams, the expression, in A.J.P.Taylor's words, of 'dogmas which echo the conversation of any Austrian café or German beer house'.[7] This is to underestimate both Hitler and his book. *Mein Kampf* contains all of Hitler's beliefs, most of his programme and much of his character.

Mein Kampf is partly a rather misleading autobiography, partly a repetition of all the commonplaces of the *völkisch* ideas of the previous twenty-five years (see pp. 150–5 above), partly a political programme and partly a handbook for political action. Its ideas are based on a crude social Darwinism, a struggle for survival in which the criterion of fitness is racial purity. There is a hysterical insistence throughout on the danger from the Jews, and a clear link in Hitler's mind with the Jews as a sexual threat to the Germans; and this in turn is linked to a neurotic fear of syphilis and to denunciations of prostitution. 'A state which, in the epoch of race poisoning,' the book concludes, 'dedicates itself to the cherishing of its best racial elements, must some day be master of the world.'[8] But mixed in with all this rubbish Hitler has some shrewd things to say about the value and use of propaganda. He had been impressed by British propaganda during the First World War, and he praises the demagogic quality of Lloyd George's speeches and leadership, just as he was ready to learn lessons in organisation from the Roman Catholic Church or from the Austrian Social Democratic Party. For all his harping on the virtues of the undefiled German stock and the natural superiority of the German people, his contempt for humanity is enormous: 'The greater the mass [propaganda] is intended to reach, the lower its purely intellectual level will have to be.'[9] The masses can be manipulated and mobilised to serve the leader's ends or, as Hitler himself put it, 'I fanaticised the masses to make them tools of my policy.'[10] In *Mein Kampf* Hitler, apart from the insistence on the Jewish danger, the international Jewish conspiracy and the Jewish infection of healthy Aryan society, outlined what his policy was to be – total control of education, sterilisation of the unfit, conversion of trade unions into

332

'organs for representing occupational interests' which will 'increase the security of the national economy'[11] – this meant in practice the end of the unions' role in negotiating better conditions for the workers. Hitler was equally explicit in spelling out his foreign political goals – the reversal of the Treaty of Versailles, of course, and rearmament, but also much more besides: 'to ensure for the German people the land and soil to which they are entitled on this earth.'[12] This, Hitler goes on to explain, means expansion eastwards and the securing of German *Lebensraum* (living space) in Russia. It was a goal which Hitler never abandoned and which, together with his determination to solve the Jewish question and to eliminate the Jews from German life by means not yet specified at the time of the writing of *Mein Kampf*, dominated all his policies.

Yet while one can extract from *Mein Kampf* Hitler's political programme, it is the tone of the book which is important for the understanding of the nature of National Socialism. The hysteria, the bombast, the coarse Macchiavellism and above all the paranoid hatred and fear of the Jews make it extremely disagreeable to read, but it is a book which nevertheless gives the reader a real insight into Hitler's mind and into the fantasies which he was about to turn into reality. One can only agree with Hermann Rauschning, one of Hitler's supporters who later turned into a bitter critic, when he wrote, 'No enemy could wish for the German people a greater humiliation than that they should accept and believe this philosophy of life.'[13]

When Hitler came out of prison in December 1924, he had learnt from the failure of the Munich *coup* the lesson that to achieve power he was going to have to build up a party organisation and to give the National Socialist Party a broader base, both geographically and socially, than it had had in Munich. Just as Mussolini had learnt from his failure in the elections of 1919 that to win power he must gain the support of the prosperous and successful, so Hitler began to present himself in a guise which might appeal to respectable businessmen with nationalist leanings, making studiously moderate speeches in areas of Germany far from Munich, such as Hamburg, persuading a few – not yet many – industrialists to contribute to the party funds, showing himself willing to collaborate with the Nationalist Party, in the hope that its leader Hugenberg would think the Nazis allies worth subsidising. Until the depression brought the Nazis mass support, progress was slow: but at least by 1928 the party, though still weak, was part of the national political scene, with some of its prominent leaders – Goebbels, Goering, but not Hitler himself, who had not sought election – in the Reichstag.

The extension of the party's activities had its own dangers for Hitler, who was determined that his control of the party should not be weakened and that the '*Führerprinzip*', the leadership principle, which he regarded as an essential foundation for political organisation, should be maintained. The leaders of the movement in the north, the brothers Gregor and Otto Strasser, did in fact provide the one serious threat to Hitler's leadership, the more so because they stressed the radical content in the Nazi programme and questioned the deliberate moderation with which Hitler was hoping to attract respectable conservative backing. Hitler had however succeeded in asserting his authority over the party and over its paramilitary element, the Storm Troopers (*Sturmabteilung*, SA), and some of Strasser's supporters, notably the young journalist Joseph Goebbels, seeing which way things were going, transferred their loyalty to Hitler. Although Gregor Strasser remained a prominent party member till 1932, Hitler's control was not seriously challenged again.

Once the depression had hit Germany, Hitler's careful construction of a party machine began to pay off. He was able to offer something to almost every class and group in Germany. In a country where national feeling was deep and included many shades of opinion, from the liberals' desire to right the wrongs of the peace settlement to the *völkisch* mystical belief in Germany's world mission and the innate superiority of the Teutonic race, Hitler's reiterated denunciations of the Treaty of Versailles, his evocation of the virtues of the *Frontsoldat*, his promise to restore Germany's military greatness, all found a widespread echo. While to the more conservative and respectable nationalists he appeared to want what they did, and to be able to bring them mass support for their programme, it was just because Hitler seemed more vigorous and far-reaching in his demands than the orthodox conservative nationalists around Hugenberg that he was able to attract that mass support. Equally, in their social programme the Nazis offered something for everybody, and could vary the emphasis to suit each particular audience. To a middle class nervous about its economic security, Hitler offered an ideology based on saving the 'little man': the small shopkeeper would be protected against the competition of the large department stores, the independent craftsman would be guaranteed a future for his work. The bourgeoisie, shocked by what they regarded as the immorality of Berlin night life and the permissiveness of some of the young people, welcomed a programme which stated that woman's place was in the home, cooking for her husband and raising his children. They shared Hitler's *petit bourgeois* aesthetic tastes and were glad to echo his view expressed in *Mein Kampf* that 'If the age of Pericles seems embodied in the Parthenon, the Bolshevistic present is embodied in a cubist monstrosity.'[14] At the same time Nazi success in the rural areas was ensured by the doctrine of 'Blood and Soil' (*Blut und Boden*), and by the Nazis' praise of the virtues of the German farmer and the promise of a central place in the Nazi new order, and more practically by hopes of state support and subsidies in a time of falling prices.

Each section of the German population listened to the particular message in this conglomerate programme which appealed to it, and ignored or dismissed the rest. People who were attracted by, say, Hitler's promises to restore Germany's national greatness but shocked by the violence of his language, and indeed the actual violence of his followers on the streets, or felt that his attacks on the Jews went too far, consoled themselves by thinking that these were the passing features of a young political movement, or that by supporting the Nazi Party they would be able to control Hitler and curb the more extravagant actions of his lieutenants. Although the Nazis as a political party never won an overall majority of the German electorate, they reflected so many of the fears and prejudices of the German public that they could be sure of the tacit support which was granted to them almost till the end of the Third Reich.

During the period between the elections of November 1930 and Hitler's nomination as Chancellor in January 1933 Hitler needed to keep up the momentum which the electoral success had given the movement. He had to keep and increase his mass support, while at the same time demonstrating the weakness of the regime by sending his Storm Troopers on to the streets to beat up their opponents and show where the true power in the country lay. This meant steering a careful course between legality and illegality. Hitler believed that he could come to power by legal means, but that the illegal activities of the SA could help to break down the existing system and make his assumption of power seem inevitable. Such tactics needed careful timing. As one of Hitler's party leaders put it, 'The NSDAP will not let the German people rest till we have obtained power.'[15] But there were financial and psychological limits to the length of time such a pitch of agitation could be maintained; and on at least two occasions in 1932 the Nazi leaders were worried. In January 1932 Hitler, in a famous speech to the leaders of German industry in the Düsseldorf *Industrieklub* secured the support of many of them, but by the end of the year, with, as we shall see, some signs that the mass support for the Nazis was falling off, Hitler was again facing a shortage of money and again had to be rescued by a pact with a leading banker. A movement such as the National Socialist Party had to give the impression of a continuous move forward, of a constant dynamism, if it was to succeed. Any loss of impetus, any anti-climax, and it might lose the struggle. As Goebbels put it in April 1932, when the party seemed to be going from strength to strength, 'Something must happen now. We *must* shortly come to power, otherwise our victory will be a Pyrrhic one.'[16]

The political opportunities for maintaining this dynamism in 1931 and 1932 were considerable. In the elections in the individual German states in the summer and autumn of 1931 the Nazis had done very well, and in the spring of 1932 President Hindenburg's term of office came to an end and there had to be elections for a new President. The eighty-four-year-old field marshal was persuaded to stand again; and it was a sign of how weak the republic had become that this aged figure, unrepentantly surviving from the old imperial Germany and who had been in 1925 the candidate of the conservative forces, now became the one hope of the republican parties. The other main candidates were Adolf Hitler and the Communist leader Ernst Thälmann. (The nationalists put up a candidate of their own, but his lack of success showed the extent to which Hitler had taken over the supporters of the older nationalist parties.) Hindenburg was reelected, but Hitler had won nearly thirty-seven per cent of the votes and was now offering an open challenge to the republican system.

Hindenburg's reelection had seemed indispensable for the survival of the Brüning government, but in May 1932 Brüning was dropped by the President and his advisers. Left without the President's support and unpopular in the country, Brüning resigned. Yet the actual issue over which he, and a few weeks before him his War Minister General Groener, had been obliged to give way, was the one measure which might have done more than anything to save the republic – the banning of the SA. General von Schleicher, the political brain behind the army, decided, on the other hand, that the army could do a deal with the Nazis, and with their support abolish parliament and establish an authoritarian state under army leadership. As a political front for their operation, a so-called 'cabinet of barons' was formed under Franz von Papen, a Catholic aristocrat whom the French Ambassador described as enjoying 'the peculiarity of being taken seriously by neither his friends nor his enemies'.[17] But he was a friend of the President's son and a favourite of Hindenburg himself, so Schleicher thought he might serve his purpose. Hitler had promised his support to the new government in return for new elections and for the repeal of the ban on the SA, which was allowed to function again from the middle of June 1932, about a month before the elections, which were consequently fought in a growing atmosphere of terrorism and disorder. The Nazis emerged as the largest party in parliament, with 230 seats and 37.4 per cent of the votes. The liberal groups and moderate conservatives had almost disappeared, and the nationalists had also lost votes and seats. With 89 Communist members, ready if necessary to combine with the Nazis to make parliamentary government impossible, the defence of the republic lay in the hands of the 133 Social Democrats and the 90 deputies of the Centre Party and their other Catholic allies.

But in practice parliament was no longer in control; the votes cast in the election had a symbolic rather than a practical value, and marked another stage in the collapse of the republic. Hindenburg, however, still refused to appoint Hitler Chancellor; the old man liked, as he once put it, 'a cabinet of my friends',[18] and regarded Hitler as a vulgar upstart corporal; Papen again formed a government. He quickly demonstrated the weakness of the republican opposition by dismissing the Social Democratic government of the state of Prussia – a weak minority government reflecting the deadlock between the parties in the state Diet. While declaring that they would only yield to force, the Social Democratic ministers were obliged to leave their offices when a lieutenant and five policemen appeared to remove them. The failure to resist Papen's *coup* illustrates the basic weakness of the Social Democrats in meeting threats to the republican constitution. In March 1920 they had helped to defeat the Kapp *Putsch* by calling a general strike, but in the desperate economic situation of 1932 a political strike seemed to the trade union leaders to have no chance of success. Above all the Social Democrat leaders were the prisoners of their own concept of constitutional legality: they would only yield to force, but they would not make any serious effort to take the initiative by organising the resistance to force by force. They had organised a uniformed defence force, the *Reichsbanner*, but this was unarmed, out of a creditable respect for the law, and its leaders uncertain of the role they were meant to play. Since the Reichstag no longer had any control over the government, the socialists found themselves, both at the time of the Papen *coup* in Prussia and at the moment of Hitler's final seizure of power in March 1933, left with no option but to accept defeat with such dignity as they could.

Papen had no real basis of support except that provided by the backing of Schleicher and the army, while, although after the elections of July 1932 Hitler seemed to be in sight of obtaining power, he still had not in fact won it. The next months were filled with complicated intrigues to try and escape from this dilemma. After a total defeat in the Reichstag, Papen decided to try another general election, which was held on 6 November 1932. The results were surprising, and suggested that after all Hitler might not be invincible and that the Nazi movement might be fatally losing momentum. Although still the largest party in parliament, the Nazis had lost two million votes. However, the gains had not gone to the republican parties: the Social Democrats had lost some votes and seats, and, while the Centre Party had held their own, the conservatives and nationalists had won back some votes. Most significant of all perhaps was an appreciable gain (2 per cent more votes and 11 more seats, making a total of 100) for the Communists. But, even assuming that Hitler was not as irresistible as his own propaganda had made him out to be, there was still no real alternative. A parliamentary majority would have to include the Nazis and Hitler was not prepared to settle for anything less than the Chancellorship. Equally, the Nazis and Communists together, with just over 50 per cent of the seats in the Reichstag, could make any republican parliamentary solution impossible. The immediate victim was Papen, who now had virtually no support and, in the gap left by his resignation, Schleicher emerged from the background to take office himself, hoping that, by offering a post to Gregor Strasser, he would win some Nazis for his vague notions of social reform and thus split the Nazi Party.

Schleicher was Chancellor from 2 December 1932 till 30 January 1933, without a parliamentary majority, without any support in the country and with only a vestige of a programme. Hitler prevented a split in the Nazi Party, from which Gregor Strasser was expelled. At the beginning of the New

Year Hitler had a private meeting with Papen, and over the next weeks the possibility of a coalition between Hitler and the right-wing nationalists began to emerge, the result as much of Papen's desire to revenge himself for what he thought of as Schleicher's betrayal as of any long-term view of the situation. But for Hitler the alliance with Papen and the conservatives was important. Papen still had enough credit with President Hindenburg, whose physical powers were fading fast, to persuade him to accept the idea of Hitler as Chancellor, and by the end of the month the President had come round to the idea of a Hitler–Papen–Hugenberg government. On 30 January 1933 Hitler, the leader of the largest party in parliament, was constitutionally appointed Chancellor and head of a coalition government by the President of the Republic. Hitler's long flirtation with constitutional legality had at last brought its rewards. The Nazi revolution, however, had still to be made.

The new government contained only three Nazi ministers, and its formation could therefore be represented as a success for Papen and Hugenberg; but for the Nazi rank and file the emergence of their Führer as Chancellor was a clear sign of victory. Hitler went through the motions of attempting to obtain a parliamentary majority by negotiating with the Centre Party for their support, and when these negotiations broke down, as Hitler apparently intended that they should, the Reichstag was dissolved and new elections ordered. It was the election campaign that first showed that it was the Nazis rather than their coalition partners who called the tune. With the SA triumphantly clearing the streets of socialists and communists, with Goebbels using the state radio for a demonstration of his supreme skill as an organiser of propaganda, it required courage to stand against the tide, and it is a tribute to the loyalty of the Social Democratic Party's supporters that they turned out to vote in numbers almost as large as those of the previous year. Then on the night of 27 February 1932 there occurred an incident which gave the Nazis just the dramatic issue they needed to provide a climax for their electoral campaign and an excuse for acting against their opponents; the Reichstag building in Berlin burnt down. The causes of the fire are still uncertain. The Nazis at once attributed it to the communists (though it is hard to see what they stood to gain by such an act), but there soon were rumours, with evidence to support them, that it was the work of Nazi *provocateurs* out to provide an excuse for the suppression of the Communist party and for declaring an emergency. More recently it has been suggested that the young, mentally disturbed Dutch revolutionary found on the premises and immediately arrested, and whose political links, such as they were, were with anarchist and Trotskyist groups rather than with the Communist Party, had in fact made the fire all by himself. But whoever started the fire, it was the Nazis who gained from it, and the last week of the election campaign was passed in an atmosphere of growing hysteria, in which an emergency law severely restricted the activities of the opposition, and in which the Nazis were able to present themselves as the saviours of Germany from the Red peril. The result was a big increase in their vote and a big loss in that of the communists.

Yet even in what, given the circumstances of the campaign, could scarcely be described as a free election, the Nazis still did not have an overall majority. With 43.9 per cent of the votes they still needed the support of their nationalist allies. In fact however the exact figures of the election result were less important than the fact that the government was already going far towards suppressing constitutional liberties, and that these moves were overwhelmingly endorsed by the Reichstag. On 21 March in a solemn ceremony in the Garrison Church at Potsdam, a shrine of the Prussian military tradition and the burial place of Frederick the Great, in the presence of Hindenburg, the senior army officers, the ex-Crown Prince (who was seated behind a chair left vacant for his exiled father) and the newly elected members of the Reichstag without the Social Democrats and Communists, the new parliament was formally opened in an atmosphere of nationalist fervour full of overtones of the old imperial Germany. Although it was devised and stage-managed by Goebbels and his staff, it seemed still to assert the solidarity of Hitler with the old nationalist world and the old nationalist heritage. Two days later in Berlin the Reichstag, from which all the Communist deputies had been excluded, full of the brown uniforms of the Nazis and with SA men filling the galleries and corridors of the opera house which replaced the burnt-out parliament building, passed by 441 votes to 94 an Enabling Law giving full powers to the government. This perhaps gave a fairer picture of the support the Nazis could command than the number of votes actually cast for the party in the elections. Only the Social Democrats, in a final act of dignified defiance, faithful to the last to the Weimar constitution, voted against it. The Centre Party had come out in support of the government, though Brüning, the last parliamentary chancellor of the republic, is said to have left the chamber before the vote.

Over the next two years Hitler turned his government into a total dictatorship. His power was consolidated; his enemies were removed; education, culture, the Churches were all brought under control. The process known as *Gleichschaltung* (coordination) was applied, in theory and to a large extent in practice, to all aspects of German life. By the end of the summer of 1933 all political parties other than the NSDAP had been dissolved or voluntarily disbanded. The trade unions had been replaced by a government-run Labour Front. By the end of the year the unity of the party and the state had been proclaimed, and as a consequence the powers of self-government of the individual German states and of the municipalities were removed at the beginning of 1934. On 1 August 1934 Field Marshal Hindenburg died, and Hitler then assumed the office of Head of State as well as that of Chancellor. At the same time, the oath taken by members of the armed forces promised 'unconditional obedience to Adolf Hitler, Leader of the Reich and People'.[19]

A month before becoming Head of State Hitler had consolidated his alliance with the army leaders by agreeing that the army alone should have the right to bear arms in Germany. This meant checking the power of the SA and of its leader Ernst Röhm, who regarded the Storm Troops as the party's army and as destined to replace the old traditional military caste. In a series of swift, brutal murders on the night of 30 June 1934 Röhm and his leading associates were killed on Hitler's orders and thousands of other members of the SA also exterminated. For good measure Hitler took advantage of the general blood bath to remove others who might be potential rivals or who had crossed his path in the past, notably Gregor Strasser and General von Schleicher. Papen, the Vice-Chancellor, was arrested; he had, a few weeks before, at the prompting of his advisers, made a speech critical of some trends in the new regime and, although he himself was subsequently restored to favour and sent as special envoy to Austria, he never recovered his power and members of his staff were murdered unavenged. It was a sign of Hitler's stability, compared with that of Mussolini at the time of Matteotti's murder (see p. 268 above) that these acts of cold treachery raised little opposition, and even abroad hostile comment was soon over and forgotten.

After the abolition of the political parties and of the trade union movement, the army was one of the few remaining potential sources of opposition to Hitler's rule. Its loyalty was now assured by the suppression of the SA and by the start of a programme of rearmament. In 1938 Hitler dismissed a number of senior officers and replaced them by younger men whom he believed to be committed more whole-heartedly to his new order. Another possible focus of opposition was the Churches, but, although both Catholics and Protestants were as individuals to show courageous opposition to the Third Reich, especially in the later stages, they offered little opposition as collective organisations. Both the Churches were by tradition deeply conservative and in favour of strong government. Many Catholics had no great enthusiasm for parliamentary rule and some of them believed that government should be reorganised on a corporate basis, which is what in theory at least the Nazis were doing. The German Protestants had for the most part always been imbued with an intense and narrow German patriotism, and some of them had been closely linked with anti-Semitic movements and ideas. Still, a number of Protestants did show their disagreement with the official Protestant Church and formed the *Bekennende Kirche*, the Confessional Church, some of whose members reasserted a pietist tradition, stressing personal morality and individual responsibility. It was a creed held by some of the best theologians in Germany, and its leading exponents were among the bravest of the anti-Nazis – men such as Martin Niemoeller or Dietrich Bonhoeffer – yet by its very nature it was also one which precluded organised institutional resistance.

In September 1933 Hitler signed a Concordat with the Vatican; and, while the Church gave up its political, social and professional organisations, it was allowed to keep the right to run schools and to publish pastoral letters. Many of the bishops guarded these privileges carefully, and some of them occasionally spoke out against some of the barbarities practised by the regime, yet they, and still more the Vatican, which in its condemnation of Nazi Jewish policy was often more cautious than the more outspoken members of the German hierarchy, were above all anxious that the Church should survive as an organisation, and realised that any collective opposition might mean the prohibition of all the Church's activities. It was noticeable, indeed, that the issue by Pope Pius XI in 1937, two years before his death, of his encyclical to the Germans, *Mit brennender Sorge* (With burning anxiety), was followed by intensified persecution of individual Catholics. His successor Pius XII had been for a long time the Papal Nuncio in Germany and combined deep feelings for the Germans with a deep sense of the power of the National Socialist state, and none of his pronouncements attempted the open condemnation expressed by Pius XI. As in the case of the Protestants, a number of Catholic clergy showed that they were prepared to face martyrdom by asserting their Christian principles in the face of the crimes committed by the German government, but it was as individual rather than collective protests that these acts of Catholic resistance were important. The Churches in general did not, and perhaps could not, rise above the prejudices of most of their members, who had welcomed or accepted the rise of National Socialism, just as other Germans had done and for the same reasons.

The Nazis retained popular support not just because they had total control of the press and the radio or because they instituted an effective secret police (the *Geheime Staatspolizei*, Gestapo) and an efficient voluntary spy system through the Nazi party organisation. In the early years of Hitler's rule at least people really did believe that he was fulfilling his promises to give the Germans a better life and to restore Germany's power in the world. Unemployment was much reduced by public works, state and private building, and by the beginning of rearmament, as well as by a widespread industrial recovery. Private enterprise operated under the general direction of the State, so that the big industrialists were left undisturbed, and indeed their role was strengthened by the application to industry of the *Führerprinzip* which placed additional power in the bosses' hands. Government loans and tax concessions were given to industry to finance expansion. The basis for this economic recovery – in part the work of the President of the Reichsbank Hjalmar Schacht – was the isolation of the German economy from the rest of the world. The export of German money and the use of foreign currency were strictly controlled; great ingenuity was used to produce synthetic substitutes for essential materials which would otherwise have to be purchased abroad, and the aim of German economic development was declared to be autarky, a state of self-sufficiency which would both make Germany independent of the world economy, and at the same time prepare the country for war. Barter agreements were negotiated with the states of south-east Europe, so that Germany acquired their agricultural products in return for German industrial goods without having to spend precious foreign currency, and also incidentally gained political influence at the expense of France, who was in no position to reinforce her diplomatic ties with the Little *Entente* countries by purchasing the agricultural surpluses of, say, Yugoslavia.

Not all the promises in the Nazi social programme were kept: for all the talk of women's place being in the home, for example, the number of women workers in industry went up, even before the war; and for all the praise of the 'little men', large concerns continued to grow at the expense of small ones. However, in an atmosphere dominated by government propaganda on a scale never seen in Europe before, with a visible economic recovery and a strikingly successful foreign policy, most Germans were ready to overlook the failures of the regime to carry out all its commitments; and enough was done to make them believe that they really were at the beginning of a New Order.

If Hitler had not carried out the social revolution which some people had expected of him, one point in his programme was rapidly transformed into a horrifying reality – his 'solution' of the Jewish question. From the moment of Hitler's coming to power, action against the Jews began; it continued on an increasing scale until in 1942 Hitler ordered the 'final solution', the extermination of European Jewry, organised with terrible and matter-of-fact efficiency by Heinrich Himmler and his subordinates. In 1933 and 1934 there were boycotts of Jewish shops and businesses. The number of Jews admitted to the universities was first limited and then reduced to nil. Thousands of Jewish lawyers, doctors, civil servants, teachers, actors and musicians were removed from their professions in the first year of the regime. In 1935 the Nuremberg Laws, 'for the protection of German blood and German honour', were enacted, which made mixed marriages between Jews and non-Jews punishable by imprisonment, a penalty which in the war years was increased to one of death. As conditions for the Jews grew worse and more and more of them were forced to emigrate, so it became harder for them to take any money or possessions with them. The result was that pathetic cargoes of homeless and often penniless refugees arrived at the ports of the world, desperately seeking admission to countries reluctant to face the implications of this new mass problem at a time of unemployment and insecurity, when it looked as though other countries in Eastern Europe, especially Poland and Roumania, were prepared to follow the German example and to expel many more thousands of helpless Jews into a world not prepared to receive them.

'The victory of a party is a change of government. That of a *Weltanschauung* is a revolution,' Hitler said in March 1934.[20] By the outbreak of war in 1939 he had done much to carry through a revolution in this sense. Whether the Nazi beliefs should be dignified with the name of a *Weltanschauung* or an ideology is perhaps doubtful. They were rather a bunch of psychological attitudes and prejudices inherited from the nationalist writers and publicists of a previous generation and embodied in a political system dominated by Hitler's own personality and demagogic skill. However, the Nazi Party effectively controlled all aspects of German life. Press and radio were wholly in their hands, as was the educational system, while, out of school, boys and girls were recruited into the Nazi youth movements. In the universities, although a few scholars might take refuge in the more abstruse regions of pure science or of classical studies, Nazi ideas permeated what was taught. In a notorious ceremony on 10 May 1933, in the main squares of the cities of Germany and on university campuses throughout the land, the books of those authors disapproved of by the regime were formally thrown on to bonfires. The works of many of the best-known German and foreign writers were thenceforth banned from the Third Reich. Some of the most famous lyric poems in the language by the Jewish radical Heinrich Heine were now described as being by an anonymous author; a few years later the bust of the Jewish composer Felix Mendelssohn was removed from the Leipzig concert hall – against the opposition of the Mayor, Carl Goerdeler, later a central figure in the German resistance. And similar examples can be found in all branches of cultural life, which became dominated by a dreary and pretentious naturalism or by the hollow and grandiose style of the buildings which Hitler's architect Albert Speer was devising to feed Hitler's fantasy.

The basis of the organisation of the new totalitarian state was the *Führerprinzip*. This meant in practice that all decisions were ultimately liable to be taken by Hitler himself; but it also meant that the bosses of the various centralised corporate bodies in which the different professional and economic groups were organised, as well as the *Gauleiters*, the party officials in charge of each province, had considerable power which each was out to extend. Thus, for all the insistence on concentration, on *Gleichschaltung*, there was in the Nazi state considerable administrative overlapping and inefficiency and much personal rivalry among the party leaders, rivalry which could in many cases only be checked by the intervention of Hitler himself. At the same time those institutions of the old order which could serve the Nazi purpose continued to function. The civil service worked as loyally and efficiently as ever. Other institutions, such as the law courts, could be reformed or by-passed if they failed to serve the party's will. 'This is the last time a German court is going to declare someone innocent whom I have declared guilty,' Hitler exclaimed when the Protestant pastor Martin Niemoeller was acquitted by the courts. And indeed Niemoeller was soon rearrested and sent to a concentration camp where he survived until the German defeat in 1945.

343

Behind the new corporate organisations, the control of education and of the media of communication, the official culture, the mass rallies and the mass movements, lay the shadow of the terror and the fear of the concentration camp. People disappeared and were never heard of again, neighbours denounced each other; children informed on their parents. As time went on, and especially in the later years of the war, the terror increased, and the number of concentration camps to which people could be sent without trial in what was ironically called 'protective custody' grew. It was this that made any open opposition almost impossible and even any clandestine resistance very difficult. Most protests of necessity remained personal – a furtive act of friendship to a Jew, secret listening to foreign broadcasts, the passing on of a subversive joke or rumour. Some people adopted an attitude of 'inner emigration', an increasingly difficult attempt to withdraw into the world of private life and private values, in the hope that Hitler's boast that the Third Reich would last a thousand years would prove false, and that it might be possible to emerge with personal integrity and to contribute to the reconstruction of a decent German society. Above all, however, what made opposition or resistance hard was the knowledge that a majority of the German people had gone along with Hitler and had, if only for a time, wanted what he did; and even when some of them began to have doubts, by then the country was at war, and the appeal to national solidarity still strong so that it needed great courage and a lofty view of the nature of patriotism to commit what could easily seem an act of treachery.

Mussolini boasted that a party which governed a nation in a totalitarian manner was a new fact in history. In practice, perhaps, he never succeeded in governing Italy in quite so totalitarian a way as Hitler did Germany, and he himself, tyrannical, brutal and vain as he was, seemed somehow to remain on a human scale compared with Hitler. Mussolini was, however, anxious to suggest that Fascism was a universally applicable doctrine. 'Its ideas, doctrines and realisations', he wrote in his 'Fascist Catechism','are *universal* because it is in the position of saying to civilised people a word of truth without which there cannot be lasting peace in the world: therefore it is the sustainer and creator of a new civilisation'.[21] And, since the term 'fascist' has become widely used to describe many very different forms of political and social organisation and behaviour, it is worth looking at what Italian Fascism and German National Socialism had in common, and how far these features were shared by some of the other movements of the 1930s elsewhere in Europe which were to a greater or lesser extent modelled on them.

Most of the ideology of Fascism is as empty and bombastic as Mussolini's catechism quoted above; and in Mussolini's case definitions and philosophical descriptions of Fascism were thought up after he had come to power, in the mistaken hope that this would give his regime some intellectual respectability. However, there are a number of features which in combination made the Fascist movement and the Fascist state something different from anything seen in Europe before. We have seen how in Italy and Germany Fascism succeeded in an atmosphere of fear and revolution, in a time of economic instability and in a mood of frustrated nationalism (see Chapter 10 above). Fascism and National Socialism each had an eclectic appeal which could attract both conservatives and revolutionaries. In both Italy and Germany the Fascists claimed to be breaking down barriers between classes or between regions and to be creating a new sense of national community and solidarity.

The way in which this was expressed institutionally was supposed to be by means of the corporate state – though this was perhaps more of a sham façade than a real structure. It is an idea which has a respectable ancestry in European political thinking. On the one hand it derives from German idealist philosophy, and especially from Fichte and Hegel, from the belief that the State is more than the sum of its citizens and that it has an organic life of its own, with its own 'reason of state' which transcends individual morality. On the other hand it is based on a criticism of mechanical democracy and its demand for 'one man, one vote', and on the belief that it is only as part of a corporation which is an integral part of society that man has any political or social existence. The terminology of the corporate state was widely used in Fascist Italy and Nazi Germany, and professional or economic groupings were officially the basis for the state structure, though in practice they served as vehicles for the exercise of the Party's control or for the personal ambitions of their leaders. Nevertheless this aspect of totalitarianism has been much stressed; and some political scientists have made it the main theme of their analysis, stressing that the mass Fascist parties owed their success to the fact that they were, in Hannah Arendt's words, 'mass organisations of atomised isolated individuals',[22] which fulfilled a desire for solidarity on the part of men and women left solitary, uprooted and alienated from the mass industrial society of the twentieth century.

The sense in which Fascism and National Socialism were not ordinary political movements was emphasised by their leading spokesmen: 'Fascism is a religious conception in which man is seen in his immediate relationship with a superior law and with an objective will that transcends the particular individual and raises him to conscious membership of a spiritual society',[23] Mussolini wrote. And in Germany Alfred Rosenberg stated, 'This is the task of our century: out of a new myth of life to create a new type of man.'[24] This all-embracing claim and its application to every aspect of life helped to make opposition or resistance difficult or impossible; it also explains why in both Italy and Germany the Churches were objects of suspicion and surveillance which might be bought off, as the Catholic Church in Italy had been by the treaty of 1929, which left it in a very important position in the state, with control not only over much of the educational system but also of the laws affecting such matters as marriage and divorce, or else, as in Germany, could be threatened with persecution if it ventured outside its immediate sphere. Some people have maintained that the fact that the Church in Italy was accorded a prominent recognised status accounts for the fact that Italian Fascism was not quite as rigorous or as all-embracing as National Socialism was in Germany, just as the preservation of the monarchy in Italy left an alternative centre of constitutional power which could be and was brought into operation when it was decided to end Mussolini's rule.

Even when one has allowed for the social and economic situation which led to the rise of Fascism and National Socialism and for the psychological needs of men in industrial society, it still remains true that the main element in their ideology is a negative one. They drew their strength from the fact that they were always against someone – against the Reds, against the foreigners, against intellectuals, against the Jews (though in Italy this only came as a belated and half-hearted response to the German example and to German pressure). The very vagueness of their ideology both led to a restless striving after the unattainable – a new Roman Empire, a vast *Lebensraum* in the heart of the Eurasian land mass – but also to opportunism and to a fragmentation of leadership in which each party boss tried to build up his own personal empire at the expense of his rivals. It is for this reason that the personality of the Leader was of supreme importance, giving unity to the rival elements in the party and cohesion to the government. Since his will alone was law, it was on him that the whole state depended as long as he could enforce that will. '*Mussolini ha sempre ragione*' ('Mussolini is always right') was a slogan painted on walls all over Italy. A dictator's survival depends on maintaining the fiction that he is always right and a belief in the irreplaceable nature of the Leader. In the case of both Hitler and Mussolini it is doubtful whether their regimes were separable from their personalities, and whether even without military defeat the systems would have survived unchanged without them.

Italian Fascism and German National Socialism had close affinities with each other, even before the formal, but very personal, alliance between the Duce and the Führer in the Rome–Berlin axis of 1936 and the military 'Pact of Steel' of May 1939. Mussolini had, from the start of his own reign, followed the development of the nationalist Right in Germany and especially in Munich with great interest, and had had some indirect contact with Hitler in 1923. There were repeated, though never finally proven, rumours that Hitler in the early days of his movement had received financial help from Mussolini, and that this had played a part in Hitler's decision, from which he never departed, to renounce any German claims over the German-speaking inhabitants of the South Tirol. For Hitler, quite apart from the similarity of the external circumstances of their respective rise to power, Mussolini and the Fascist movement were an obvious model from which he undoubtedly learnt many lessons. After 1933, with the depression creating comparable social, political and economic problems in many parts of Europe, and with fascist governments firmly established in two of the greatest states, a number of movements which imitated Fascism and National Socialism came into being, and older anti-parliamentary movements, such as the *Action Française* took on overtly fascist characteristics, though the *Action Française* never won the mass support which was an essential element in fascist success.

Mussolini's example had been quickly noted in many countries of Europe; and movements were founded in the 1920s which combined aspects of Fascism – uniformed squads, a powerful leader – with older nationalist ideas and with the anti-liberal doctrines of writers such as Charles Maurras (see p. 108 above). In each case anti-communism was a central theme of their propaganda, often accompanied by anti-Semitism, and in each case the movement proclaimed its mission of national regeneration or national expansion, to make, for example, a Greater Finland, a Greater Roumania, a revived Hungary or a new independent Flemish state. However, although in some countries, notably in Hungary, Roumania, Finland and Belgium, these movements won considerable electoral support and, in some cases, political influence in the 1930s, it was not until the German conquest of Europe in the Second World War that some of them actually obtained power as the result of the direct influence of the German occupiers, except in Roumania where the Iron Guard movement played a large part in 1940 in overthrowing the royal dictatorship of King Carol and in the regime which followed his exile. These were movements which differed according to the circumstances of each country; and in many cases they were too torn by internal rivalries and intrigues to be effective. But they represented, as Fascism and National Socialism in Italy and Germany did, the mass of frustrations felt by many in an age of economic instability, nationalist excitement and fear of revolution. While in some cases (as in Hungary where one of the fascist movements based its strength on the landless agricultural proletariat), the fascists promised a social revolution and had some working-class support, for the most part their followers were students in search of excitement or middle-class people afraid for their social and economic security.

In many cases, too, the fascists were outflanked by the more orthodox conservative parties which in practice were their rivals; and some of these conservative regimes, in Austria, in Spain after the Civil War, in Portugal, in Hungary, were sufficiently authoritarian for them, both at the time and subsequently, to have been labelled 'fascist' by their opponents, although they lacked several of the characteristic features to be found in Germany or Italy. In Austria a local fascist movement, the *Heimwehr*, supported the attempts made by Engelbert Dollfuss and his successor Kurt von Schuschnigg between 1932 and 1938 to run a Catholic, corporate state in the face of a growing threat from the Nazis, who assassinated Dollfuss in 1934, and who were working for a union with National Socialist Germany. While features of this regime – the suppression, on the direct insistence of Mussolini, of the Social Democratic Party, the use of concentration camps for political opponents – were similar to fascist practice, its tone and style – Catholic, conservative, provincial and puritanical – were very different from the dynamic mass fervour of its Nazi rivals and even of its Italian patrons.

In Spain the economic difficulties and social unrest at the end of the First World War, when the commercial benefits of neutrality came to an end, led to talk, especially in anarchist circles, of a revolution like that in Russia. In fact, however, a military dictatorship was established by Miguel Primo de Rivera, whose aim, he said in language similar to that used by dictators in many parts of the world since, was 'to open a brief parenthesis in the constitutional life of Spain and to re-establish it as soon as the country offers us men uncontaminated with the vices of political organisation'.[25] This regime lasted till 1930, when Primo de Rivera was overthrown; soon afterwards the King was forced to leave the country and a republic was proclaimed. In this atmosphere of political instability and bitterness Primo de Rivera's son, José Antonio, founded one of several fascist-type movements, the *Falange*, complete with blue shirts and a fascist salute, and with direct contacts with Germany and Italy. José Antonio was arrested in 1936, and, after the outbreak of the Civil War, executed by the Republican government; the cult which followed his death suggests that he might have had a sufficiently charismatic personality to have led a successful fascist movement. As it was, however, within a year of the outbreak of the Spanish Civil War, the *Falange* was absorbed into the wider framework of General Franco's movement, deprived of its radical elements and incorporated as a comparatively minor partner in the conservative coalition on which Franco's authoritarian order came to be based.

While it was only in Germany and Italy that the fascist movements had sufficient mass support to bring them to power and to maintain their position, the parties modelled on them expressed the same frustrations and the same desires which made fascism a characteristic form of political organisation in Europe in the 1920s and 1930s. The challenge of the economic depression after 1930 made many people doubt whether the machinery of democracy and of parliamentary government were strong enough to take the measures needed to meet the crisis. In Britain, for example, an aristocratic member of the Labour Party, Sir Oswald Mosley, first formed a so-called New Party in association with other socialist intellectuals, notably the Marxist social theorist John Strachey, in the hope of introducing fresh ideas into British politics. But he quickly broke with his colleagues and founded the British Union of Fascists, a movement which slavishly imitated the Italian and

German models though fortunately without achieving their success. Other socialists elsewhere also moved towards a belief in more authoritarian means to solve Europe's economic and social problems. In Belgium, although there were active fascist movements both among the Flemish and the French-speaking populations, perhaps an even more significant development was that of the socialist leader Henri de Man, who produced a sort of New Deal for the Belgian economy, the *Plan de Travail*, and when he had been unable, as a minister in a national government formed in 1935, to put it into effect, became increasingly disillusioned with parliamentary politics, and even briefly welcomed Hitler's conquest of Belgium in 1940 as the sweeping away of an old corrupt world preparatory to making a new beginning in Europe. There were comparable developments among members of the French Socialist Party: some prominent members broke away to form a 'neo-socialist' group, and at least one of these, Marcel Déat, ended up as an active French fascist during the Second World War.

In the 1920s France had appeared to be the strongest power in Europe. By 1930 the French had largely repaired the physical destruction of industrial and agricultural resources caused by the war; and in the economic crisis of 1931 the franc remained firm when elsewhere currencies were being devalued and stocks of gold depleted. Yet within three years France faced a growing social and political crisis which in turn affected her foreign policy and contributed to her failure to maintain her international position established at such cost at the end of the First World War. This was partly due to the fact that by 1934 the French were feeling the effects of the economic crisis just when elsewhere the first signs of recovery were beginning to appear. Prices rose; unemployment increased; many people began to realise how backward France was in the structure of her economy and in the standard of her social services. French industry lacked the basis of mass production necessary for rapid expansion – a factor of particular importance in the French rearmament programme. The French peasant had been hit by the drop in world prices and by the over-production on a world scale of grain and wine.

In a mood of pessimism and self-doubt, confronted by the alarming spectacle of a resurgent Germany, new right-wing groups with names such as the *Croix de Feu*, *Solidarité Française* and *Jeunesses Patriotes* had been founded on the fascist model alongside the older *Action Française*, and were organising demonstrations against the parliamentary system and in favour of strong government. During 1933 political tension had been growing. There was a major financial scandal, the Stavisky affair, which had brought charges of corruption against members of the Chamber of Deputies, and especially against members of the Radical Socialist Party, an indispensable component of almost every government in the later years of the Third Republic. As the demand from the Right for a judicial enquiry into the scandals and for an effective purge of public life grew, it was the Radical Prime Minister Edouard Daladier who had to confront the rising storm. On 6 February 1934 there were large-scale demonstrations in Paris by the fascist organisations which were widely believed to be deliberately aiming at the overthrow of the republic. An ex-servicemens' demonstration in the Place de la Concorde developed into a full-scale riot, and the police were only with difficulty able to prevent the demonstrators from attacking the Chamber of Deputies. Daladier's government resigned and was replaced by a 'government of national unity' – a right of centre government under the former President of the Republic Gaston Doumergue, committed to a vague programme of reform and economic recovery and to the restoration of law and order.

It seems unlikely in fact that the riots of 6 February were part of a concerted attempt at a *coup d'état* by the fascist leagues; but the belief that this had been a real threat transformed and polarised French political life and increased the social tension. The immediate effect was to produce – as the Dreyfus case had done thirty-five years before – a rallying of the forces of the Left, who remained unimpressed by the pompously expressed good intentions of the Doumergue government. The first stage was a rapprochement between the Socialists and the Communists. During 1934, partly as a result of the example of the French Communist Party and partly because of Stalin's realisation that the Nazi revolution in Germany was going to last, the international communist movement launched the idea of a 'Popular Front' which should join communists, socialists and bourgeois liberals in a common effort to resist the spread of Fascism. There was much during the year 1934 to suggest that in many countries civil liberties and democratic institutions were being threatened: the Austrian socialist party was suppressed in February, after a day or two of armed resistance. Dollfuss in his turn was assassinated by the Nazis in Vienna in July, just after Hitler had, by the murder of Roehm, Schleicher and scores of others, revealed the degree of ruthlessness, treachery and brutality of which he was capable. For the next few years, it looked as if the people of Europe were taking sides for a vast struggle between democracy and dictatorship, fascism and communism, progress and reaction.

The move towards a Popular Front started in France, where many of the rank and file of both the Socialist and Communist Parties realised how dangerous the feuds between their two parties were, and remembered how this had contributed to Hitler's success in Germany. A pact of unity of action between the two parties was signed in July 1934. The Communists gave official approval to the new line at the Comintern World Congress in the summer of 1935. By the beginning of 1936 the parties in the Popular Front, Communists, Socialists and Radicals, had agreed on a somewhat vague programme, and on common tactics for the forthcoming general elections, and the Radicals had withdrawn their support from the government.

In the elections of May 1936 the Popular Front won an overwhelming victory, and the Socialist leader Léon Blum formed a government composed of Socialists and Radicals with the support, but not the participation, of the Communists. For a few weeks it looked as though a new era of social reform and economic recovery might be beginning. The workers celebrated th electoral victory with widespread 'sit-in' strikes, and hoped, by occupying the factories and even the Paris department stores, to force the pace of reform and to express, in Blum's words 'a feeling of impatience to see realised those reforms for which the electoral victory allows them to hope'.[26] And indeed the effect of the occupation of the factories and the strikes was to force immediate concessions from the employers, such as a rise in wages and the right to collective contracts about wages and conditions of work. This success was followed by legislation for social and economic reform – a forty-hour week, holidays with pay, a programme of public works, nationalisation of the arms industry, reform of the Bank of France. A long overdue effort to improve the condition of the French working class had been started.

Within a few months, however, it was obvious that the forces in France opposed to change were strong enough to stop any far-reaching reform programme. By the beginning of 1937 not only had the employers and industrialists recovered their nerve, but also Blum's own Radical colleagues were calling for a pause in reform and for more orthodox economic policies. Blum had been obliged to devalue the franc, and this had made him unpopular, without having any very marked effect on the economic recovery, while there were growing complaints about the cost of implementing his social reforms and French financiers were showing their mistrust of the government by moving capital abroad. In June 1937 the government was defeated in the Senate when it tried to impose a ban on the export of capital, and Blum was forced to resign as Prime Minister, even though a government based on a Socialist–Radical coalition lasted a few months more, until it was replaced by one without the Socialists under the Radical Edouard Daladier, supported by groups of the centre and moderate right.

Blum's failure was in part due to the opposition of the conservative financiers and economists and in part to the weakness of the executive in France, dependent as it was on a parliamentary majority made up of several parties which, whatever enthusiasm they may have felt for the idea of the Popular Front before coming to power, rapidly showed that they represented divergent interests. The Radicals, with their support coming largely from the provincial middle class, had quite different views about economic policy from the industrial workers who voted Communist or Socialist. The social, economic and governmental structure of France made any far-reaching reform difficult, but, in addition, the Popular Front government, within a few weeks of taking office, was confronted with a crisis in its foreign policy which further weakened its internal position. This was caused by the outbreak in July 1936 of the civil war in Spain.

Since the foundation of the Spanish Republic in 1931 the situation in Spain had been one of great tension and instability. The inherent problems of the Spanish state – rural underemployment, especially in the vast estates of the south, industrial under-development, separatism in Catalonia and in the Basque provinces – were exacerbated by the bitterness of the conservatives against a regime which they regarded as being in the hands of communists and freemasons, and at the other extreme by the fanaticism of the anarchists determined to wreck the bourgeois republic. The efforts of the first governments of the republic to introduce serious reforms, including autonomy for Catalonia, new freedom of action for the trade unions, or the separation of Church and State, only served to irritate the conservatives even more and to spur the anarchists on in their attempts at the real, total revolution. Conservative opposition expressed itself in an unsuccessful military *coup* in 1932. On the other side there were anarchist risings, notably one in 1933, which were suppressed with great ferocity. In the autumn of 1934, after elections at the end of 1933 had returned a conservative majority, the socialists made an unsuccessful attempt at revolution, especially in Barcelona and in the mining area of Asturias, where the movement was put down with considerable brutality by the government. After two years of weak conservative government, new elections were held in February 1936. There was a big swing to the Left, and the result was a victory for a Popular Front coalition similar to that which was to be successful in France three months later. In a mood of mutual suspicion, with the Left afraid of a right-wing *coup* and the Right convinced of the danger of imminent social revolution, a military rising in July 1936 under the leadership of General Francisco Franco, ostensibly to forestall a communist rising, rapidly turned into a general civil war.

Léon Blum's first reaction to the news from Spain was that the Popular Front government in France must supply the Spanish Popular Front with the arms necessary to maintain it in power, but under pressure both from his own Radical colleagues and from the British, he accepted the idea of an international agreement to prevent foreign intervention in the war. At the outset, indeed, the Spanish government believed that they could crush the rising provided Franco did not receive assistance from outside and, in order to avert a government crisis in France, Blum reluctantly agreed to sign the non-intervention agreement. Within weeks, however, it was plain that both Italy and Germany were giving substantial help to Franco, while the Soviet Union responded by sending supplies and advisers to the Republicans.

The intensification of the civil war in Spain by foreign intervention had political and emotional repercussions which affected all Europe. It was widely believed that the confrontation in Spain between Germany and Italy on the one hand and the Soviet Union on the other was the first round of a world-wide struggle between communism and fascism. Both Hitler and Stalin gave encouragement to this view by publicly basing their foreign

policy on ideological principles. In November 1936 the Germans signed an
Anti-Comintern Pact with the Japanese government, and Ribbentrop, the
Nazi leader who had negotiated the agreement, declared, 'Japan will never
permit any dissemination of Bolshevism in the Far East. Germany is creating
a bulwark against this pestilence in Central Europe. Finally, Italy, as the
Duce informs the world, will hoist the anti-Bolshevist banner in the south.'[27]
(Italy in fact made her formal adherence to the pact a year later.) The Russian
government had formally approved the policy of the Popular Front, and in
May 1935 had signed a treaty of mutual assistance with France, at the same
time instructing the French Communist Party to support the French rearmament of which till then they had been the most bitter opponents. This
was a part of Stalin's new policy of cooperating with capitalist states to resist
German fascism and of encouraging the communist parties of Europe to form
alliances with socialists and liberals in support of the new line in Soviet
foreign policy. In September 1934 the Soviet Union had joined the League
of Nations, and for the next four years the Russian representatives at Geneva
were vigorous advocates of a policy of 'collective security' to resist fascist
expansion. Once Stalin had decided that Germany was a greater threat to the
USSR than France or Britain, it was in accordance with the consistent logic of
Soviet foreign policy, based as it was on the principle of keeping the capitalist
world divided, that he should seek to work with the Western democracies
against Germany. At the same time the individual communist parties by
joining the Popular Front were able to ensure that their members came to
occupy controlling positions in the new organisations sponsored by it. In
France the divided trade unions were reunited, and in the new CGT Communists replaced syndicalists in a number of key positions.

In Spain, where at the outset of the Civil War, for all the talk of the
Bolshevist threat, the Communist Party had only been a very small section of
the Popular Front compared with the Anarchists, Socialists or Catalan
liberals, the Communists within a few months became the dominant influence in the Republican government, both because of their efficiency at
organising the military machinery needed to defend the republic – they were
largely responsible for the successful defence of Madrid in the autumn of
1936 which denied Franco immediate victory and meant that the war was to
be a long one – and because they were the channel through which material
aid from the Soviet Union reached the hard-pressed government. They were
able to use their position to liquidate their opponents: Trotskyist and other
non-Stalinist communist groups were dissolved, and the anarchists, who had
compromised with their principles sufficiently to enter the government in
November 1936, were defeated in Barcelona in May 1937, in a brief civil war
within the civil war, so that their influence was never as great again.

The effects of this polarisation, between the Popular Front on the one hand
and the anti-Comintern grouping centred on the fascist Rome–Berlin axis

(a phrase first used by Mussolini in November 1936) on the other, made the position of those who were not wholly in sympathy with either side a difficult one. The Pope for example in 1937, a few days after issuing the encyclical *Mit Brennender Sorge*, the most outspoken criticism of Nazi Germany ever made by the Vatican, published another encyclical, *Divini Redemptoris*, denouncing the 'pseudo-ideals' of communism.[28] In Britain a Conservative government with no liking for the Soviet Union hoped somehow to lessen the tension in Europe by trying rather unsuccessfully to make non-intervention in the Spanish war a reality, while in France Blum, bitterly criticised by the Right, some of whom went so far as to coin the slogan 'Better Hitler than Blum', was genuinely afraid that the civil war in Spain might set the example for a civil war in France. Both France and Britain were governed by men who remembered the horror of the First World War and who were appalled, as were the majority of their countrymen, by the thought of adopting any policy which might seem likely to provoke another war. And in both countries the deep pacifism of the labour movement and its equally deep suspicion of government intentions (even under the Blum government in France) were such that any government was seriously hampered politically and psychologically from carrying out an active foreign policy with its attendant risks of war. The dilemma of those who supported the idea of a Popular Front and of collective security was that while all of them wanted to resist fascism, many of them, committed to the principle of disarmament, were reluctant to abandon it and unwilling to support government plans to rearm.

Nevertheless the conflict in Spain suggested to many people that a new ideological battle had already begun and that the words of the *Internationale*, '*C'est la lutte finale; groupons-nous, et demain, L'Internationale sera le genre humain*', were about to come true. Volunteers from many countries in Europe and beyond – communists who had been forced into exile, intellectuals determined to show themselves capable of action, adventurers in search of excitement – joined the International Brigades which, under communist leadership, provided some of the most efficient military formations on the Republican side. The revolutions of the past were commemorated in the names of the battalions – the French *Commune de Paris* battalion, the American Abraham Lincoln and George Washington battalions or the Garibaldi brigade of anti-fascist Italians. In addition to organised support of Franco which the Italians and Germans were providing – whole units of the Italian army some 50,000 strong, and guns, planes and specialists from Germany – some volunteers with fascist or deep conservative sympathies fought for the insurgents, including a group of Irish fascists, French monarchists and White Russians.

The war in Spain accelerated the politicisation of intellectual and artistic life in Europe which had already begun under the pressure of the economic crisis, with its demonstration of the injustices of contemporary European society. The Spanish War was an issue which forced intellectuals and artists to define their political position, so that many even of the hitherto unpolitical found themselves attending anti-fascist meetings and joining anti-fascist organisations. Some writers, notably the French novelist André Malraux, an author always fascinated by the relation of the intellectual to the world of political action, fought in the war; and Malraux made it the subject of his novel *L'Espoir* (Days of Hope, 1937). The American Ernest Hemingway, long attracted by the violence and drama of Spanish life, was a war correspondent, and he too used his experiences in a vivid if often sentimental novel, *For Whom the Bell Tolls* (1940). Political analysts and social critics hurried to observe the scene or to participate in the fighting and produced some notable accounts of the war, especially George Orwell's *Homage to Catalonia* and the Austrian Franz Borkenau's *The Spanish Cockpit*. The young British poets W.H.Auden and Stephen Spender visited Spain and reflected the war in their poems; the communist writer John Cornford left his studies in Cambridge and was killed in the war, as was Julian Bell, Virginia Woolf's nephew, in revolt, perhaps, against the intellectual refinements and preoccupation with private life characteristic of the Bloomsbury group to which his parents belonged. For the Spaniards themselves a whole generation of artists and intellectuals was decimated by death or exile: the best-known Spanish poet of his day, Federico Garcia Lorca, was murdered by supporters of Franco in the early days of the war. And one of the most famous Spaniards outside Spain, the greatest artist of his generation, Pablo Picasso, commemorated, in perhaps the most important piece of public art of the twentieth century, the destruction by German bombers of the Basque city of Guernica.

Because the communist parties seemed to be the most effective and the most committed of the opponents of Franco, Hitler and Mussolini, many people joined them in the mid-1930s – even if later some of them bitterly regretted the step. Yet at this moment in 1936 and 1937, when the Soviet Union and the Comintern seemed to be taking the lead in the struggle against fascism in a more forthright way than the hesitant governments of the liberal democracies were prepared to do, Stalin was engaged in a ruthless purge of his party and setting in motion the machinery of a reign of terror which, it has been estimated, sent some eight million people to labour camps and condemned about a million to death.[29] It was not until after his death in 1953 that the scale of the purges became clear, when even the Soviet leaders themselves admitted something of what had happened.

To the outside world in the 1930s the sensational aspect of Stalin's policy was the series of trials of old Bolsheviks and military leaders, which started after the murder in December 1934 of Sergei Kirov, a member of the central committee of the party and of the Politburo and the head of the party in Leningrad. The Kirov murder, like the Reichstag fire in Germany in the previous year, provided an opportunity and excuse for removing a very large number of potential or suspected opponents; and, just as there is some evidence that the Nazis themselves burnt down the Reichstag building, so there is a strong suspicion that Stalin was responsible for Kirov's murder, thus removing by one blow a possible rival in the highest ranks of the party and providing the occasion for a massive purge. As a result of the murder an attack was launched on anyone suspected of 'terroristic activity' and in a series of trials first Zinoviev and Kamenev, and then many other old Bolsheviks including Bukharin, were accused of conspiracy and of complicity in Kirov's murder, as well as of association with Trotsky, an exile who had been expelled from France, expelled from Norway and who finally found a refuge in Mexico (where he was murdered in 1940 by an agent of the Soviet secret police). Then in 1937 a number of military leaders, including the Commander in Chief Marshal Tukhachevsky, were accused of espionage, of planning a *coup d'état* and of collaborating with Russia's enemies, Germany and Japan – a charge which had also been raised against some of the political victims of the purge and which may have been given some apparent foundation by evidence deliberately planted by the German secret police. It has been suggested that about half the total officer corps was purged, including ninety per cent of the generals.

There is still much that is obscure about what happened in the USSR in these years; and in the trials themselves the accused in many cases confessed in great detail and admitted the crimes with which they were charged. (A young Hungarian ex-communist, Arthur Koestler, in his novel *Darkness at Noon* published in 1940, attempted a fictional reconstruction of the psychological process which elicited these confessions.) In the atmosphere of Europe in the 1930s the trials confirmed the Right in their hatred and suspicion of the Soviet Union, while the purge of the Red army understandably made military leaders in France and Britain sceptical about Russia's value as a possible ally against Germany. On the Left, those critics who attacked Stalin's terror, or who like George Orwell experienced comparable methods employed by the Communists in Spain, were regarded as renegades or as traitors to the solidarity of the Popular Front. Writers such as André Gide, who, after expressing sympathy with the aims of the Russian revolution, now in his *Retour de l'USSR* (Back from the Soviet Union) written in 1936 expressed doubts about some aspects of the regime, were discounted or subjected to personal abuse.

In a situation where the USSR seemed to offer the best hope of saving Europe from fascism, many supporters of the Popular Front preferred to judge the Soviet Union by its new, apparently liberal constitution of 1936 rather than by the trials and the reports of the purges which filtered through to the West. Rather than heeding the critics, many people in Europe instead based their judgement on for example the massive volume of information and praise published in 1935 by the English Fabians Sidney and Beatrice Webb,

Soviet Russia: a New Civilisation? And it seems symbolic of the uncritical acceptance of the Soviet Union at its own valuation that, when it was reprinted two years later, the question mark in the title was omitted.

Since the Second World War, when the Soviet Union ceased to be an ally against National Socialism and seemed to be itself the main threat to liberal democracy in the West, many writers have stressed the similarities between the Soviet regime and the National Socialist and Fascist governments in Germany and Italy, and have suggested that totalitarianism is the characteristic form of political organisation in the twentieth century. And when one considers the purges in the Soviet Union in the 1930s, the deportation of whole peoples during the Second World War or the continuing use of concentration camps in Russia, the resemblances with Nazi Germany are obvious enough, just as there are many similarities in the techniques of indoctrination and control in all one-party states. As far as the machinery and methods of government are concerned, it is perhaps useful for the political scientist to analyse fascist and communist states in the same terms. For the historian, however, it is important to remember the ostensible ends which those states were intended to serve. For all Stalin's tyrannical hunger for power, for all the empty repetition of Marxist-Leninist jargon in the Soviet Union, for all the suffering caused by the rigours of the Soviet economic system, Marxism remains one of the great European political doctrines and deserves an intellectual respect which it is impossible to give to any form of fascist ideology. Moreover, in spite of the increasing disillusionment with the Soviet system which has been felt by a large section of the European Left since the end of the Second World War, and the feeling that a doctrine which aimed at the emancipation of man has in many cases led to a new enslavement, Marxist social philosophy has a positive message about the revolutionary transformation of society which was entirely lacking in the negative and contradictory slogans of fascism.

The immediate effect of the economic crisis in Europe was to increase domestic political and social tensions, to bring Hitler to power in Germany and to encourage the development of fascist movements elsewhere. It strengthened the feelings of discontent with the 1919 peace settlement which contributed to the rise of fascism, and which, even in countries that did not have avowedly fascist governments, prevented the achievement of any international stability in Europe during the 1930s. But the economic crisis was also a world crisis and so also brought important changes in Europe's relations with the rest of the world. In particular the disastrous results for the Japanese economy of the loss of her silk exports, and the undoubted hardship caused to Japanese peasants and small farmers, contributed to a new expansionist policy on the part of the Japanese army, which in 1931 sought both economic relief and national prestige in the invasion of the Chinese province of Manchuria. Japan's adoption of Western technology and her successful emergence as a great power, somewhat reluctantly accorded equality of status by the European nations, was perhaps the most important sign of the way in which Europe's position might be challenged. Japan's defeat of Russia in 1904–5 had had deep and long-term repercussions through Asia, and the lesson that an Asian state could challenge and defeat a European one was never forgotten. Japan had consolidated her international position by her participation on the Allied side in the First World War, by her position as a major naval power in the Pacific and more unexpectedly by her exemplary and conscientious performance of her duties as a member of the League of Nations in the 1920s. The superficial assimilation of Japan into Western international society, and the fact that not many people in Europe really understood the nature of Japanese government, made the shock caused by Japan's invasion of Manchuria all the greater.

China appealed to the League of Nations; a League commission of enquiry was constituted, but the members of the League failed to take any effective action to stop the invasion of Chinese territory. It was the first serious challenge to the whole League system, and the failure to meet it began a period of disillusionment with the League. It revealed how far Europe's preoccupations with its own economic and political difficulties prevented the European great powers, and especially Britain and France, from playing the role of world powers, since the French government was primarily preoccupied with developments in Germany and the question of disarmament and reparations, and Britain was in the midst of the financial crisis which ended in devaluation, and which also included as one of its consequences the reduction of expenditure on the British navy, and even a brief naval mutiny in protest against the cuts in pay.

In 1935 the authority of the League was damaged still further by the Italian decision to invade Ethiopia. This again was in part the consequence of the economic crisis, and partly the result of the built-in necessity for fascist systems to maintain their dynamism if they were to survive. Italy's economic position had always been precarious: the country lacked most of the vital raw materials, and although the fascist government had made some attempt to improve communications, increase hydro-electric power, reclaim waste land for agriculture and to make the country self-supporting by government regulations to save materials in short supply, the standard of living remained low even in times of comparative prosperity. At the same time for reasons of prestige Mussolini had encouraged the growth of the birth-rate; overpopulation seemed a genuine grievance justifying Italy's demand for colonies and for imperial expansion. In these circumstances the impact of the world economic crisis was bound to be disastrous: the price of wheat and of wine fell; and production of textiles dropped; unemployment rose sharply, reaching a peak in 1934. The much-acclaimed corporate system which had been thought of as a means of establishing social justice did not seem able to deal with the situation. Mussolini had now been in power for thirteen years, and there were signs not only of criticism of the regime – a criticism given point by Italy's economic difficulties – but also of a demand for something new and exciting, for a second wave of the Fascist revolution. In these circumstances Mussolini decided that a successful venture into imperialism and the extension of Italy's African empire might distract attention from domestic problems and renew the enthusiasm of his supporters, especially as Ethiopia, where Italy had suffered the humiliating and never forgotten defeat at Adowa in 1896, was a land which still had power to excite Italian nationalist ambitions.

Ethiopia was of no direct interest to the other European powers; and on purely economic and political grounds neither Britain nor France would have had any great objection to the Italians acquiring at least a predominant interest in the country. But Ethiopia was a member of the League of Nations: and Mussolini needed a more brilliant success than just the acquisition of economic rights or tacit control of a sphere of influence. The operation would only serve its purpose if it brought him spectacular military victory and obvious political gains. When therefore in September 1935, after a series of incidents on the border between Ethiopia and the Italian colony of Somaliland, the Italians invaded Ethiopia and the Emperor appealed to the League, a situation of considerable embarrassment was created for the British and French.

It was by now clear that Hitler was carrying out his programme of freeing Germany from the restrictions imposed by the treaty of Versailles: in March 1935 he announced that a German air force was in being and a week later he proclaimed the introduction of conscription. Germany had already left the League of Nations in October 1933. The natural reaction of the French government in the face of these changes in the balance of power in Europe was to look to Britain and Italy, her associates and indeed her guarantors under the Treaty of Locarno (see p. 359 above). The assassination of the Austrian Chancellor Dollfuss by the Nazis in 1934 had suggested that a German move against Austria was imminent; and the Italian government reacted with the gesture of sending troops to the Austrian frontier. Italy seemed therefore to have as much interest in resisting German expansion as Britain or France. In April 1935, the three governments had stated their determination to oppose 'by all practicable means any unilateral repudiation of treaties likely to endanger the peace of Europe'. For the French the value of this declaration was somewhat lessened by the announcement in June 1935 of an Anglo-German naval agreement, which seemed to confirm their worst doubts about Britain's reliability as an ally and to mark a breach in the anti-German front established two months earlier. Under the naval agreement Hitler in fact only promised not to build more ships than those he had already decided to construct in any case, since the navy had a comparatively low priority in his rearmament programme. But to the British Admiralty, increasingly preoccupied with the situation in the Far East and the naval threat from Japan, and apparently undisturbed by the psychological effect of the agreement on France, it seemed to provide a chance of avoiding a naval race with Germany such as had imposed so great a financial and political strain before 1914.

Hitler had begun his revision of the peace settlement, but it was not yet clear to the British and French governments how far he was prepared to go in his unilateral repudiation of its terms. Both countries had started programmes of rearmament to balance Hitler's open restoration of Germany's military and air strength. If they were seriously to resist further changes not only in the balance of power, but also in the territorial frontiers of Europe, they needed an effective system of alliances and of collective security, such as it had been hoped in the 1920s both the League and the Locarno Treaties might supply. Within six months of the Italian attack on Ethiopia the League was generally discredited as a means of keeping peace, and the Locarno system was in pieces.

In fact, as some critics had pointed out in 1925, these two systems tended to weaken rather than to strengthen each other. For the League to function as a guarantor of existing frontiers and a deterrent against aggression – and the governments of central Europe, and especially of Czechoslovakia, realised this was the best hope of securing their countries against a resurgent Germany and a Hungary determined to revise the 1919 frontiers – then France and Britain would have to take the lead, and be prepared to act in enforcing the provisions in the League Covenant for economic and military sanctions against an aggressor. In the circumstances of 1935, with most Europeans regarding Ethiopia as a remote and backward African state with which they were not directly concerned, support for the League against Italy had to be sought on the basis of a general belief in the principles of collective security embodied in the Covenant. Pierre Laval, the French Prime Minister, feared that the enforcement, on grounds of general principle, of the Covenant against Italy would cost France Italy's support against Germany and weaken if not destroy the Locarno system. He was therefore anxious to avoid any serious action against Italy. The British government, pressed by an active body of public opinion, at first took the lead in proposing the enforcement of the Covenant and the imposition of economic sanctions against the aggressor, but, from a general fear of war, from a perhaps exaggerated view of Italian naval strength in the Mediterranean and from a hope of still preserving some sort of links with Italy, pursued simultaneously with its advocacy of sanctions a policy of seeking agreement with Italy. Under the circumstances the economic sanctions, although enthusiastically voted by a large number of members of the League, particularly those with little or no trade with Italy, were not supported by any military threat; oil, the most essential commodity for Italy's war effort, was excluded from the list, and proposals to impose an oil embargo were repeatedly postponed. By pursuing two incompatible policies simultaneously Britain and France did not prevent Italy from conquering Ethiopia and did complete the alienation of Italy from their security system. After seeing what had happened first in Manchuria and then in Ethiopia, most people drew the conclusion that it was no longer much use placing their hopes in the League any more.

At the moment when hopes of using the League as a means of preserving the stability and balance of Europe in some sort of ordered international system were dwindling, the German government decided to break up the Locarno system. In March 1936, using as an excuse the fact that the French had just ratified their treaty with the Soviet Union, signed the previous May, the German army marched into the demilitarised zone on the west bank of the Rhine and denounced the Treaty of Locarno. The challenge to French security which her governments had feared ever since 1919, and which the Locarno agreements were meant to avoid, had now been made, and the French failed to react to it. The accumulated social and economic tensions which led to the rise of the Popular Front made a consistent foreign policy difficult. The government in March 1936, at the moment of the German occupation of the Rhineland, was a weak one, formed after the fall of Laval over his Ethiopian policy, and mainly concerned to carry on day-to-day administration until the elections in May. Its members were well aware that mobilisation to meet the German move might well cost them votes; and, with the British anxious to avoid a crisis and eager to take seriously Hitler's offers of a new international settlement, French ministers were ready enough to limit their protests to words. With the victory of the Popular Front in the election, and the outbreak of civil war in Spain in July, the internal situation in France seemed to fit into an international pattern, and talk of civil war there too did not seem wholly unrealistic.

The growth of fascist movements in many countries of Europe, the unresolved opposition between Right and Left in France and elsewhere in Europe, the sense, emphasised by the intervention of Germany and Italy and of the Soviet Union in the Spanish Civil War, that an international conflict between fascism and communism was impending, and above all the existence in Germany of a powerful and successful National Socialist government determined to destroy the precariously established post-war order in Europe, all created a new sense of urgency and crisis and a conviction that it was necessary to choose sides for the coming clash. Although in fact the conflict between Germany and Russia was not quite as near as it seemed to be in 1936 and 1937, a sense was growing that war between them was inevitable. Whatever the long-term dangers presented to Europe by the Soviet Union may or may not have been, in 1937 the threat seemed a remote one: that of German domination was becoming increasingly immediate and obvious.

13

HITLER'S WAR

Adolf Hitler had made his aims in foreign policy quite clear in *Mein Kampf*: but, just as each group inside Germany was attracted by those aspects of his domestic programme which appealed to them and ignored the rest, so foreign governments accepted at their face value Hitler's statements after he had come to power, and were reluctant to take seriously the vast plans of expansion and conquest sketched in his book. Yet for Hitler these extreme visions dictated his policy. His skilful day-to-day diplomacy and the opportunism of his short-term plans all served the extravagant ends that he had set for the German people in his Third Reich, which he once predicted would last a thousand years. (The First Reich was the mediaeval 'Holy Roman Empire of the German Nation'; the Second, that created by Bismarck in 1871.) His goals, that is to say, lay far beyond the revision of the 1919 peace settlement, which seemed to most of Europe, because indeed it was not unreasonable, to be what he was striving for in the 1930s. As long as Hitler's actions were limited to the restoration of Germany's armed forces, the remilitarisation of the Rhineland or even the alteration of Germany's eastern frontiers and the *Anschluss* with Austria, they seemed to be similar to the policies of Stresemann, though pursued more ruthlessly and from a position of greater strength. It was only during the Second World War that it became clear that Hitler had meant what he said in *Mein Kampf*.

Hitler's obsession with the question of race, which coloured every aspect of his programme, was coupled with his obsession with the need for *Lebensraum*, space into which the Germans could expand, and which would provide the master race with the raw materials and the manpower to support their domination over the rest of the world. This meant above all expansion eastward – to the grain of the Ukraine, to the mines of the Don basin or the oil of Roumania and the Caucasus. It meant expansion at the expense of the Slavs, who were to be kept for ever in a state of total inferiority. In Germany's attainment of the long-term aim of winning *Lebensraum* in the east, other powers could temporarily play a role as Germany's equals – England (about which Hitler, like the Emperor Wilhelm II, had ambivalent and contradictory emotions but which he believed to be succumbing rapidly to Jewish influence), Italy, Japan. The United States he consistently underestimated, partly because he regarded the country as increasingly decadent on account of its racial mixture and the power of the Jews. The important thing was for Germany to control what the German geographer Karl Haushofer, a man much admired by Hitler and the Nazis, and who had visited Hitler in prison while he was writing *Mein Kampf*, regarded as the 'heartland', the vast spaces of Russia, possession of which would lead to control of both Europe and Asia.

In the early days of Hitler's rule, however, it was easy to overlook that he had written, 'The boundaries of the year 1914 mean nothing at all for the German future.' A war just to restore them would, he thought, be hardly justified, whereas the achievement of true *Lebensraum* for the Germans, 'the land and soil to which they are entitled on this earth', would be an action which 'before God and our German posterity would make any sacrifice of blood seem justified . . . The soil in which some day German generations of peasants can beget powerful sons will sanction the investment of the sons of today, and will some day acquit the responsible statesmen of blood guilt and sacrifice of the people.'[1] The tone of Hitler's speeches on foreign policy after he had come to power was very different: he talked of peace; he signed a non-aggression pact with Poland in January 1934. And even each successive breach of the Treaty of Versailles and the denunciation of the Treaty of Locarno were followed by offers of a wider if vaguer international settlement.

Thus, as we have seen, the announcement of the existence of a German air force in March 1935, the introduction of conscription and the reoccupation of the demilitarised zone of the Rhineland in March 1936, each provoked alarm but no effective action on the part of Britain and France, and in each case the British government began to explore seriously the alternative proposals which Hitler offered. After March 1936 the French were to a large extent content to follow the British lead. The crisis had shown that they had no strategic plans for action against Germany other than to man their fortifications and wait for the German army to exhaust itself, as they hoped, in attacks on the Maginot line. This was a policy which required the mobilisation of French reservists, and there were no proposals for any more limited and immediate preventive action by the forces already available. Any government which proposed mobilisation in a situation in which French soil was not being directly attacked was bound to be unpopular; and in March 1936 a weak, caretaker government, awaiting the general election in April, did not take any initiative. Once the crisis was past, the French were in a more disadvantageous position than before, even on their own strategic assumptions. One of the consequences of the failure of the Locarno treaties was that the Belgian government withdrew from its association with France and returned to a policy of strict neutrality, so that there could be no

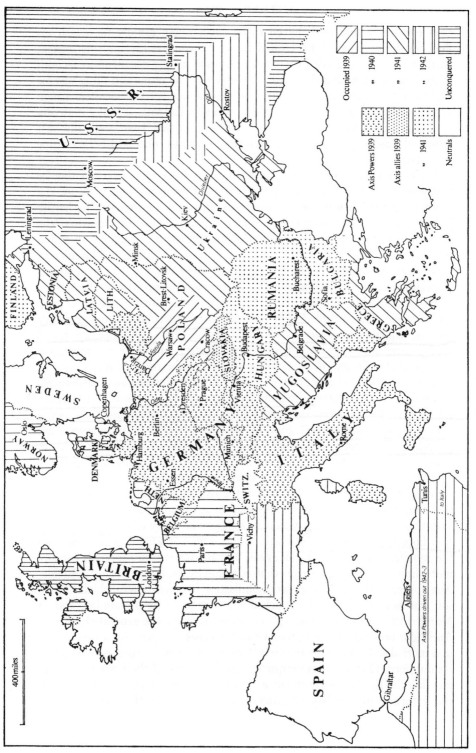

Europe in 1942

coordination between the French and Belgian defence plans, while the Franco-Belgian frontier remained unfortified, since the planned extension of the Maginot line to fill the gap was still uncompleted in 1940.

A few critics inside the French army, notably Colonel Charles de Gaulle, pointed out that a defensive strategy depended for its success on the availability of mobile reserves to counter a possible breakthrough by the enemy and to take the offensive when required. De Gaulle urged in vain an increase in the number of armoured divisions and the creation of a truly mechanised professional army such as the German army now was becoming. At the same time, although an effort was made, especially in the last year before the war, to increase the production of military aircraft, the output was never as rapid as the government hoped. Some politicians put the blame on the social legislation of the Popular Front government in 1936–7, but in fact the explanation lay rather in the structure of French industry, much of which had remained small-scale and unstandardised, and in the consequent difficulties of effective mass production. It was a technological lag, rather than labour troubles or the introduction of the forty-hour week, which was the main reason for France's failure to rearm sufficiently.

As long as German aims seemed reasonable – and to many British people the reoccupation of the Rhineland seemed to be a matter of the Germans, as the phrase went, 'going into their own back-garden' – the British and French hoped that agreed solutions could be found which would meet Germany's grievances, even if such solutions meant the end of the territorial settlement of 1919. When Neville Chamberlain became British Prime Minister on Baldwin's retirement in May 1937, he was determined to start direct negotiations with Germany, to find out just what Germany's demands were and to seek ways of meeting them. Accordingly in November 1937 he sent Lord Halifax, the Foreign Secretary and his closest colleague in the Cabinet, to visit Hitler in an attempt to discover what he really wanted and to start the process of what was called, using a word which had been popular in discussions of international relations in the 1920s, 'appeasement'.

Two weeks before Halifax's visit to Berchtesgaden, Hitler's mountain retreat in the Bavarian Alps, Hitler himself was considering what the next stages in his own plans might be. On 5 November 1937 at a meeting – the minutes of which, as kept by one of Hitler's military aides, Colonel Hossbach, have survived – Hitler outlined to the heads of the armed forces and to his Foreign Minister the aims of German policy and the possible courses it might follow. He had always believed that a war might be necessary to achieve his ends, and on this occasion he told his advisers that 'Germany's problems can only be solved by means of force.'[2] Nevertheless, he had also always believed that when war came it must be at a moment which he considered favourable. In 1936 Hitler had based his plans for rearmament on the assumption that it would take four years for the German army and air force to be ready, and that 1940 was the earliest date at which Germany ought to go to war. Till then Germany must seek what diplomatic advantages she could. Hitler realised the difficulties in the way of Germany's war preparations, especially the shortage of some essential raw materials which would in the event of a long war lay Germany open, as in the First World War, to the danger of a blockade. While the German government and German industry were developing synthetic substitutes for many commodities, and the German people were being told by Goering, the Commander in Chief of the air force and the head of the rearmament programme, that they must learn to prefer guns to butter, Hitler nevertheless was determined that the war when it came would be a short one. All his plans, at least until 1942, were based on a gamble that each of his goals could be obtained by means of a short *Blitzkrieg*, a lightning campaign which would bring swift victory in a few weeks. For this kind of war, while the production of certain weapons, tanks and aircraft for example was essential, total mobilisation of the economy, such as would be needed to face a prolonged war and a blockade, would not be necessary.

The meeting on 5 November 1937 was probably in part intended to reassure the service chiefs that Hitler would not risk war until German armaments were ready. (They had been extremely nervous about a possible French attack at the moment of the move into the Rhineland eighteen months earlier.) Without laying down a timetable Hitler envisaged war as coming not later than the period 1943 to 1945, after which the balance of forces would turn against Germany. What he did make clear was that in any case his next objectives were to be Austria and Czechoslovakia. The Commander in Chief, the War Minister and the Foreign Minister, all expressed some misgivings about Hitler's plans; and within a few months they were replaced by people with more confidence in the Führer: General von Brauchitsch became Commander in Chief instead of General Fritsch; Joachim von Ribbentrop succeeded Neurath as Foreign Minister, while Hitler himself took over the War Ministry from General Blomberg, having forced Blomberg and Fritsch to resign by criticisms and accusations reflecting on their sexual behaviour.

In fact events moved more quickly than Hitler had anticipated and within a few months, in March 1938, he was able to annex Austria. The *Anschluss* had always been one of his first aims. He himself had been born in Austria, and German nationalists in both countries had long felt that a great wrong had been done when in 1866 Bismarck had decided to create a united Germany without Austria, and that an even greater wrong had been done when the Allies refused to allow Austria to join the German Republic in 1919. The Austrian Nazis had attempted a *coup* with the assassination of Chancellor Dollfuss in July 1934, but they had been deeply divided on questions of tactics, and it is still argued by some that Hitler himself did not know of the plot, though this seems unlikely.[3] In any case, when it failed,

Hitler was quick to disown the conspirators and to turn to diplomatic methods of weakening the Austrian state. In July 1936 the new Austrian Chancellor, Kurt von Schuschnigg, signed a 'gentlemen's agreement' with Hitler, who agreed to respect Austrian independence, while Schuschnigg accepted that Austria was a 'German state' which would adopt a foreign policy in accordance with that of Germany. Hitler was hoping that internal pressures in Austria and the growing strength of the Nazi Party would lead to individual Nazi supporters entering the government, and that these would prepare the way for a peaceful union with Germany. In 1934 it had been Italian support for Austrian independence which seemed to be the main obstacle in Germany's way. After the Ethiopian affair and Italy's breach with Britain and France however, Mussolini was prepared to write off Austria in the interest of German friendship. By the beginning of 1938 therefore there was some hope, although Hitler was still perhaps not quite certain, that Italy would remain indifferent to Austria's fate.

Early in February 1938, after Schuschnigg had become increasingly worried by Nazi activity in Austria and the possibility of German intervention, Hitler decided to increase pressure on the Austrian government. He summoned Schuschnigg and told him he must include a Nazi nominee in his cabinet. This was reluctantly accepted, after Hitler had bullied Schuschnigg and hinted at military action if he refused. But when Schuschnigg returned to Vienna he decided to assert his, and Austria's, independence by announcing a plebiscite, in which the Austrians would be asked if they were in favour of 'a free and German, an independent and social, a Christian and united Austria'. It was a question so full of internal contradictions that anyone except totally committed Nazis could answer 'Yes' to it. Schuschnigg felt confident of a large majority, on some calculations as much as 70 per cent, and hoped that even the socialists, whose party had been suppressed four years before, would support him. It was Schuschnigg's initiative which forced Hitler to act. He had not intended to take military action against Austria and had thought that bullying and bluff would be sufficient to make the state disintegrate from within. Now, however, he had to do something to avoid a humiliating setback; and on 12 March 1938 an improvised and not very well executed invasion of Austria began.

Hitler had won his gamble. There was no Austrian resistance and on 14 March he himself entered Vienna in triumph. The process of *Gleichschaltung*, of turning Austria into a province of Germany and the former imperial city into a provincial capital, began. Soon afterwards a plebiscite was organised so effectively in both Germany and Austria as to give Hitler a vote of over 99 per cent. Abroad too there was no opposition. Hitler sent a special messenger to announce the news to Mussolini, and when the Duce 'accepted the whole thing in a very friendly manner', Hitler repeated again and again, 'I shall never forget this',[4] and showed his gratitude by quelling any movement by the Germans in the South Tirol in favour of the union with Germany. The British expressed concern, but it was clear that there was nothing they could do about it once the annexation had taken place, especially as their military advisers continually emphasized the dangers in the Far East and the impossibility of fighting both Germany and Japan. The French protested more strongly, but they were equally powerless. On the actual day of the German invasion France was without a government and Léon Blum, who formed a short-lived government on 13 March 1938, failed in his attempt to create a broadly based anti-fascist coalition, and was replaced by a government of the Centre and Right under Edouard Daladier.

The invasion of Austria was Hitler's first move outside German territory in defiance of the 1919 peace settlement. It increased the sense of crisis in Europe; but to Chamberlain and those who believed that an agreed settlement of German claims could still be reached, it was a sign that the policy of appeasement must be pressed all the more urgently. Everyone realised that a crisis over Czechoslovakia, now surrounded on three sides by German territory, could not be long delayed. The rest of Europe had not been bound by anything stronger than the Covenant of the League of Nations and the already tacitly abandoned Treaty of Versailles to do anything to preserve Austrian independence. Moreover, the Nazis were able to give the impression that they had entered Austria as liberators, and that the *Anschluss* was a great victory for the principle of self-determination. Czechoslovakia, on the other hand, had a firm treaty with France, which obliged France to come to her support if she were attacked.

The Germans in Czechoslovakia, some three million people, mostly living in the area adjacent to the German border known as the Sudetenland, had never been satisfied within the Czechoslovak state. Although in the comparative stability and prosperity of the late 1920s some of the German political parties, notably the Social Democrats, collaborated with the government, the depression of the early 1930s hit industries in the Sudetenland, and produced, as elsewhere in Europe, a climate in which it was easy for the Nazis to win support. The leader of the Sudeten German *Heimatfront*, Konrad Henlein, was an attractive personality – a fact which contributed to the sympathy which his demands aroused abroad, especially in England – and, with the rise of National Socialism in Germany, his party grew fast (but it was not actually called a National Socialist party). Although Henlein claimed to be ready to work within the framework of the Czechoslovak state, Hitler was, when the moment came for him to try and destroy Czechoslovakia, able to use an enthusiastic and well-organised body of support inside the Czech borders and the demands of the Sudeten Germans could be represented as a legitimate plea for self-determination, which it was hard for liberals abroad to oppose with a clear conscience.

The Czechoslovak state, although neither the Germans nor the Slovaks had been satisfied, had nevertheless shown itself to be considerably more stable and more genuinely democratic than any of its neighbours. Eduard Beneš, its President since the death in 1937 of the founder of the state, Thomas Masaryk, enjoyed a high international esteem. Czechoslovakia had an efficient modern army and a powerful system of fortifications on its western frontier, though this had now been outflanked by the German absorption of Austria. That the Czech government was prepared to defend itself if necessary was shown within two months of the German move into Austria. On the weekend of 20 May 1938 there were rumours that the Germans were planning an invasion of Czechoslovakia: units of the Czech army were mobilised but no invasion took place. We now know that Hitler did not intend to take military action at that moment, and the effect of the brief crisis was to confirm each of the governments concerned in their existing policies. Hitler, furious, it would seem, at being suspected of something he was not immediately proposing to do, decided to do it at once: a week after the Czech action, he amended his orders for operations against Czechoslovakia from 'It is not my intention to smash Czechoslovakia by military force in the near future' to 'It is my unalterable decision to smash Czechoslovakia by military force in the near future'.[5] For the French, Czechoslovakia's allies, the episode, while confirming their nervousness, seemed also to confirm their hopes that Hitler might after all be bluffing and that he could still be deterred by a show of decisive action. For the British the affair suggested that time was running out, and that the Czech government might be prepared to risk war and to provoke Hitler by its intransigence.

This was indeed the main difference between the French government's assessment of Hitler's intentions and that of the British. Daladier and Georges Bonnet, his Foreign Minister, still hoped it might be possible to outwit Hitler by diplomatic means, to call his bluff and make him willing to listen to reason. The British government, on the other hand, was convinced that Hitler meant business; that he was ready to risk war if he was thwarted and that therefore it was more urgent than ever to find out what his demands were and to try and meet them. The victim of both these policies was Czechoslovakia: the French had no effective military plans for coming to her assistance, while to the British she was, in Halifax's words, 'something you could not in fact protect and did not expect to restore',[6] and therefore certainly not worth a war.

During the summer of 1938 pressure on the Czech government increased. As Beneš, urged on by his allies, offered the Sudeten Germans ever wider measures of autonomy, Henlein was told by Hitler to demand still more concessions. The British government, with the very reluctant acquiescence of the Czechs, sent a mission under a distinguished elderly Liberal, Lord

Runciman, to recommend a solution. But even the further concessions suggested by Runciman were rapidly outdated. Throughout these weeks, Hitler was using all the resources at his command to build up a sense of crisis and of the intolerable wrongs which the Germans in Czechoslovakia were alleged to be suffering, while the Sudeten German Nazis were openly defying the Czech authorities and doing their best to produce a situation of chaos and disorder. To Chamberlain and many of the British it was unbelievable that Hitler should actually be ready to go to war when it was clear that so many of his ostensible demands could be met, and Chamberlain accordingly decided on a personal visit to Hitler to find out what it was he really wanted. On 15 September 1938 Chamberlain, making the first flight in his life, and carrying the umbrella which to many observers symbolised the peaceful bourgeois society which was now confronting National Socialism, went to Berchtesgaden.

He was sufficiently encouraged by his conversations to work out on his return a plan of concessions which the British and French were to persuade the Czech government to accept, and which involved the outright cession to Germany of most of the German-speaking areas. Although some Czechs talked of fighting to the last to defend their country, Beneš realised that he had no alternative but to accept. The fragility of his state was becoming increasingly apparent: not only were the Poles and the Hungarians agitating for territory which they thought had been wrongly taken from them at the peace conference, but the Slovaks too were always on the look out for any means of obtaining the autonomy of Slovakia. The only hope for Beneš was to end the crisis as quickly as possible, and – though it is probable that he did not have much confidence in the outcome – hope that his state could be consolidated without its German inhabitants and with the promise of a guarantee of its new frontiers by Britain and France.

However it soon became clear that Hitler would not be satisfied even with this solution. When Chamberlain paid his second visit to Germany and met Hitler at Godesberg in the Rhineland, Hitler insisted, not on an orderly transfer of the territory to be ceded, but on its immediate occupation by German troops. For a few days it looked as though war was inevitable and that the French, for all their lack of military plans, would have no option but to honour their commitment to Czechoslovakia. Although the British fleet was mobilised, Chamberlain, like most British people, still could hardly believe what was happening: 'How horrible, fantastic, incredible it is,' he said in a broadcast on 27 September 1938, 'that we should be digging trenches and trying on gas-masks here because of a quarrel in a far-away country between people of whom we know nothing. It seems still more impossible that a quarrel which has already been settled in principle should be the subject of war.'[7]

A face-saving solution was however found. Mussolini, who was at this point very anxious to avoid a European war for which Italy was not prepared either militarily or economically, and in which she could hardly hope to play a brilliant role, responded to a British plea to intervene with Hitler and persuaded him to postpone action while Chamberlain made a last effort to reach a peaceful way out. The result was a conference at Munich on 29 September, attended by Hitler, Mussolini, Chamberlain and Daladier – but not by the Czechs – which gave a little more international respectability to the satisfaction of Hitler's demands. Czech territory was to be occupied in stages and not all at once; there was to be an international commission to deal with disputes arising from the agreement; the new frontiers of the Czech state were to be internationally guaranteed. And Chamberlain believed – even if not for long – that he had achieved a great success when he and Hitler after the conference signed a paper stating Britain and Germany's intention never to go to war with one another again.

Peace had been saved; and the popular acclaim on their return from Munich to both Chamberlain and Daladier (who is said to have believed that the crowds at the airport had come to demonstrate against him rather than to welcome him) showed that the Munich policy, however humiliating it seemed for France and Britain, and however disastrous for Czechoslovakia, corresponded to the desire of the people of Europe for peace at almost any cost. The Munich crisis revealed much about the nature of international relations in Europe. It had been a crisis resolved by the four powers, Britain, France, Germany and Italy, who had forced their decision on a small state, Czechoslovakia. The Czechs, and especially Beneš, who resigned a few days after Munich and left the country, never forgot. If, after the Second World War and the recreation of their state from which in 1945 the German population was expelled wholesale, they placed little faith in the promises of the West and preferred, with disastrous results, to risk reliance on the Soviet Union, this is largely attributable to the memory of Munich.

The Russians did not forget either. They had been ignored by the other powers during the crisis. They were not invited to Munich. No notice was taken of the speeches which the Soviet Foreign Minister, Maxim Litvinov was making at Geneva in favour of collective security and a solid front against German aggression. Their policy in this crisis remains a subject of controversy. They had a treaty of mutual assistance with Czechoslovakia, dating from 1935; but this formally applied only if France had already come to the help of the Czechs. The internal situation in Czechoslovakia was unstable, and there is some reason to think that the Agrarian Party, a leading element in the coalition government, would have been extremely reluctant to accept Russian support and to see Russian forces on Czech territory. We do not know what support the Russians would have been in a position to give, even if they were willing, as Russian scholars claim, to go to war to save Czechoslovakia. They were in the throes of Stalin's purges; they were sending assistance to the Spanish Republic, even though now on a much reduced scale; they were involved in frontier fighting with the Japanese in Manchuria. It is arguable that they were no more ready for a European war in 1938 than the Western democracies. Moreover, Russian relations with Germany since 1933 had been somewhat equivocal. In spite of the suppression of the German Communist Party, in spite of the public gestures of ideological hostility on both sides, in spite of Russia's support for the League and her treaties with France and with Czechoslovakia, German–Russian diplomatic and commercial contacts had continued. Each needed to trade with the other; Russia produced certain raw materials, notably manganese, essential for German rearmament; the Soviet Union still needed technicians from abroad for the industrialisation programme. Thus the gulf between the two powers was perhaps never as great as it publicly appeared to be; and, at some time after Munich, Stalin, as we shall see, decided that it was worth bridging.

Some of the German generals had been worried at the risks Hitler had been running and talked of making a *coup* to remove him if he involved Germany in a war with France and Britain, and they had sent an emissary to London to make contact with the British government from whom he received rather a cool welcome. How far these officers would have gone and how successful they might have been remains a subject of speculation since the situation they envisaged never arose. The fact that Hitler's gamble succeeded to some extent reinforced confidence in his judgement, although a few officers and others continued to be nervous about his intentions and about the dangers to Germany of a war with France and Britain, and formed the nucleus of a continuing conservative secret opposition to Hitler. Hitler himself was somewhat disappointed even in his apparent triumph at Munich. He had hoped to achieve the total disruption of Czechoslovakia at one blow, and he was soon thinking of ways to achieve the final obliteration of the state. In the meantime neither France nor Britain took any positive steps for the implementation of their guarantee to Czechoslovakia, and Germany never gave the promised guarantee at all. With Hitler's backing the Poles and Hungarians obtained territorial concessions from the unfortunate Czech government; and Hitler encouraged the Hungarians to demand still more.

There has been much discussion about what might have happened if Britain and France had gone to war with Germany in 1938, but it is not possible to draw any conclusions from these hypothetical arguments about the capacity of the Czech army to resist a German attack or about the relative state of armaments of both sides. However it is certain that Britain, and to some extent France, used the year between Munich and the final outbreak of war to speed up their rearmament programme. Nevertheless, it is a mistake to think that awareness of deficiencies in British and French armaments played a large part in the decision to abandon Czechoslovakia in September 1938. Above all it was the result of an intense desire for peace, a deep horror aroused by memories of the First World War and a reluctance to believe that Hitler actually envisaged war as a means of attaining his ends. It seemed unthinkable that war could actually be willed by a statesman rather than come as the result of errors by diplomats and of the breakdown of a system of international relations. Although he pressed on with rearmament after Munich, Neville Chamberlain perhaps believed that he had obtained, as he put it, 'peace in our time'. Once the first feeling of relief had passed, however, many people were less confident, and a cold sense of apprehension settled over Europe for the winter.

In March 1939 Hitler showed his hand. Just as a year earlier internal developments in Austria had made him decide to carry out his intention of annexing the country, so now the activities of the Slovak nationalists and Hungarian attempts at further frontier revision gave Hitler the opportunity of doing what he had failed to achieve at the time of Munich. Using as an excuse the plea of the Slovaks for German assistance and the familiar protests from the Germans left inside Czechoslovakia against what they alleged to be the intolerable wrongs committed against them by the Czechs, Hitler sent his army into Prague on 15 March 1939. The Czechs, whose Prime Minister had been mercilessly bullied by Hitler personally, and who had been threatened with the destruction of Prague by aerial bombardment, did not offer any resistance. And because the crisis had begun with the Slovaks' demand for independence, the British and French governments were able to maintain that there was no question of the guarantee of the frontiers applying in these circumstances. Slovakia became an independent state: the Germans declared a 'Protectorate' over the Czech provinces of Bohemia and Moravia and placed them under direct German rule: the Hungarians occupied the province of Ruthenia. Hitler had finally shown beyond any doubt that he would not be bound by an international agreement and that he was prepared to attain his ends by any means. Although the speculation which had gone on through the winter as to what his next move might be had been temporarily answered, it was clear that Hitler would follow up the destruction of Czechoslovakia with another step towards achieving *Lebensraum* in the east. On 21 March he announced that he was taking over the district of Memel, on the borders of East Prussia and Lithuania, after the Lithuanians had willy-nilly accepted a German ultimatum. It now seemed almost certain that his next victim would be Poland.

The reaction in the rest of Europe to the occupation of Prague had been one of alarm and outrage. Even Mussolini was taken by surprise and was offended at having been given no prior warning of the move against Czechoslovakia. In fact he continued his own programme of aggressive expansion a few weeks later, and on Good Friday 1939 made the gesture of occupying the small independent state of Albania, although this had for a long time already been firmly under Italian influence. The result was to increase his dependence on the Germans, since the move aroused British and French suspicions that it might be followed by an attack on Greece. On 22 May 1939 Mussolini signed a full-scale alliance with Hitler.

For some months there had been discussions about turning the Anti-Comintern Pact into a tripartite alliance between Germany, Italy and Japan, a project about which Ribbentrop was particularly enthusiastic. As long as Mussolini thought he might still gain something by direct negotiations with France, he was not enthusiastic. Now that relations with France had deteriorated, however, and convinced that Germany was the strongest power in Europe, he was ready to sign, though on the mistaken assumption that there would be no war for three years. By this time the Japanese had decided not to proceed with the negotiations, and the result was the formal signature by Italy and Germany of the bipartite 'Pact of Steel'.

The British government, faced with a vigorous popular demand for an end to appeasement, answered Hitler's move against Czechoslovakia, after a short period of hesitation, with a grand diplomatic gesture intended to make plain British determination to resist further aggression and to demonstrate British commitment to Europe. On 31 March Chamberlain announced that Britain would give a military guarantee to Poland, and within two weeks guarantees were also offered to Roumania and to Greece. As a further demonstration of British seriousness, a limited measure of conscription was introduced.

The British guarantee to Poland marked a reversal of British policy. For twenty years successive British governments had refused to accept any special responsibility for the stability of Eastern Europe, and the British sacrifice of Czechoslovakia at Munich had been quite consistent with this policy. Now, however, the British government was publicly making a deliberate promise to involve Britain in fighting for the security of Poland and, through the guarantees to Roumania and Greece, to go to war in south-east Europe, though it was by no means clear how these promises could be implemented. Any effective action by Britain and France, who had confirmed her intention of standing by her existing treaty with Poland, depended on the attitude of Poland's eastern neighbour the Soviet Union, but, by the commitment to Poland, Britain's freedom of manoeuvre in her relations with Russia was strictly limited. Soon after the announcement of the British guarantee to Poland, the British and French started negotiations with the Russian government to try and establish a common front against Germany. The complicated diplomatic discussions which continued for some four months, the attempt to agree on a list of states to be guaranteed and on other details, had a certain unreality. It can be argued that they were conducted with a minimum of sincerity on both sides; and even if they were sincere, they now seem to us to have been doomed in advance.

The British and French governments had little confidence in Soviet military strength and considerable distrust of any close contact with the Soviet government, even if the Soviet leaders had been inclined to allow this. They – and especially the French – nevertheless believed that the appearance of a solid diplomatic front against Hitler might have the effect of deterring him. Stalin, on the other hand, wanted time and space. He needed time for Soviet internal reconstruction and rearmament, and he wanted to postpone a German attack on Russia for as long as he could. He needed space in order to keep the launching-point of such a German attack as far as possible from the heart of Russia: this goal could only be obtained by the stationing of Russian troops in Poland. The crux of the negotiations with Britain and France lay in the Soviet government's not unreasonable contention that to help Poland they would have to send troops over the Polish border, and in Poland's total refusal to let a single Russian soldier set foot on her soil, because the Poles felt (and this was not unreasonable either) that once there the Russians would never go away again.

The negotiations in Moscow dragged on through July and into August 1939, with military missions trying to work out the forms of joint action pending agreement on a wider political treaty. But at some point – the exact moment of the decision is still hard to determine – Stalin decided that his aims might best be served by a direct deal with Hitler. Some people have maintained that this was in Stalin's mind at least since Munich, and have seen a sign of this in his agreement to withdraw the International Brigades from Spain and in his reduction of aid to the Republican government, which was finally and totally defeated by Franco in March 1939. Others noted Stalin's speech of 10 March 1939, in which he warned the West against attempts to embroil Russia with Germany. Again the replacement of Litvinov by Molotov as Foreign Minister at the beginning of March seemed to symbolise a breach with the policy of collective security and collaboration with the West, with which Litvinov had been publicly associated. In any case the Germans were naturally very ready to take any steps which might prevent the possible *rapprochement* between the Soviet Union and Britain and France; and by the end of May they were sounding out the Soviet government about the possibility of political conversations. By mid-August the Russians, apparently convinced that negotiations with Britain and France were getting nowhere, were ready to turn to Germany. On 20 August Hitler asked Stalin to receive Ribbentrop; on 22 August Ribbentrop was in Moscow. On the next day a German–Soviet non-aggression pact was signed with a secret clause by which spheres of influence in Eastern Europe were defined, and which contained the sinister statement that 'the question of whether the interests of both parties make desirable the maintenance of an independent Polish state and how such a state should be bounded, can only be definitely determined in the course of further political developments'.[8]

Hitler had, soon after destroying Czechoslovak independence already decided to move against Poland at the end of the summer. The by now familiar process of creating a state of political tension in the free city of Danzig (where the Nazis were now in virtual control) and on the Polish borders was set in motion. Attempts were made to bully the Polish government into ceding territory and to agreeing to the incorporation of Danzig into the Reich. With the announcement of Ribbentrop's visit to Moscow and then of the signature of the Nazi–Soviet pact, Hitler hoped to demonstrate to the British and French the futility of their promises of help to Poland, and, on the day of Ribbentrop's departure to Russia, he told his army commanders to prepare to carry out the plans for an attack on Poland in four days time. Chamberlain, however, reiterated in categorical terms British support for Poland and sent a personal letter to Hitler in which he stated,[9]

It has been alleged that if His Majesty's Government had made their position more clear in 1914 the great catastrophe would have been avoided. Whether or not there is any force in this allegation, H.M. Government are resolved that on this occasion there shall be no such tragic misunderstanding. If the case shall arise, they are resolved, and prepared, to employ without delay all the forces at their command, and it is impossible to foresee the end of hostilities once engaged.

Hitler did in fact postpone the invasion of Poland in the hope that the British government might change its mind or even, as he expected at one moment, be overthrown in the House of Commons. But his overtures both official and unofficial did not come to anything. Early in the morning of 1 September 1939 the German attack on Poland began.

Although the French Foreign Minister Georges Bonnet was still hoping for some last-minute intervention by Mussolini which would provide a delay in which, as at Munich, some sort of agreed settlement might be patched up, this time there was no way out. The British government, pressed hard in the House of Commons and by public opinion outside, declared war on Germany on 3 September 1939, and the French, somewhat more hesitantly, followed the example a few hours later. For Mussolini, now formally allied to Hitler under the 'Pact of Steel', it was an embarrassing occasion. Italy was no more ready for war now than she had been before and, in spite of Mussolini's boasts about the state of the Italian forces with which he had tried to impress the Germans, he certainly did not want to go to war, and replied to Hitler's enquiries about Italy's position with an impossibly long list of raw materials which Germany would have to supply if Italy were to enter the war. Moreover, Mussolini had been bewildered and offended by the Nazi–Soviet agreement and its obvious discrepancy with the Anti-Comintern Pact and all Hitler's talk about a crusade against Bolshevism. He had rejected the attempts which the British had been making in the months before the war to detach him from Germany, but he was still not ready to go to war at Germany's side and continued to hope for an early peace. For the moment in September 1939 he had to be content with a rather ignominious non-belligerent status, as Hitler's armies swept on to a swift triumph in Poland.

More than fifty years after the outbreak of the First World War, we are still discussing the problems of war guilt and still have not produced a definite answer. We do not have the same difficulty in giving an answer to the question of who was responsible for the Second World War, or in finding plenty of evidence that it was Hitler who had deliberately unleashed the war in Europe, even if the immediate form which it took was not that which had been expected or even the only one which Hitler had envisaged. There has also been considerable discussion about the kind of war which Hitler was planning: and it is, as we have suggested, for a series of brief campaigns rather than for a prolonged total war that German economic and military preparations were intended. There is also argument about the responsibility of the other European powers, and especially Britain and France, for not preventing the war by stopping Hitler sooner; there are suggestions that the Poles talked, probably not very seriously, of a brief preventive war as early as 1933: we now know that the German army in March 1936 had instructions to make a fighting withdrawal if the French had moved against them in the Rhineland: perhaps at the time of Munich the generals would have overthrown Hitler if Britain and France had stood firm. All these speculations are inconclusive: an action against Germany in 1933 would have outraged liberal opinion all over Europe; a French humiliation of the Germans in 1936 might have united the Germans even more firmly behind Hitler and produced a surge of national emotion, as the occupation of the Ruhr had done in 1923; some people have expressed doubts about the seriousness of the generals' plots in 1938 and on their ability to execute them successfully. The fact which does remain is Hitler's unshakeable determination to achieve his ends by one means or another, and the total ruthlessness which he was prepared to use. 'Close your hearts to pity,' Hitler told his generals a few days before the Polish campaign began. 'Act brutally. Eighty million people must obtain what is their right. Their existence must be made secure. The strongest man is right.'[10]

Within a month the campaign in Poland was over. The Polish army had fought with great bravery, but it was out-manoeuvred and under-equipped. The bravado of its cavalry charges could not make up for the fact that they were conducted by men on horseback against tanks – even though these were not yet the heavily armoured vehicles which the Germans put into action later in the war. To complete the Poles' defeat, on 17 September 1939 Russian troops invaded eastern Poland. At the end of the short war the territory which had been German before 1918 was incorporated into Germany; the eastern provinces were taken over by the Russians, and the remainder of Poland was placed under direct German rule in what was called the 'General

Government of Poland'. In the division of the spoils an uneasy and suspicious truce was maintained between Russia and Germany, and the old lesson reiterated that in the event of a Russo-German agreement the existence of an independent Poland was hardly possible.

Stalin's determination to gain space on his western frontier was not yet fully satisfied. Agreements with the helpless Baltic states, Lithuania, Latvia and Esthonia, gave the Russians bases on their territory; and, in November 1939 the Soviet army, without any formal declaration of war, invaded Finland, claiming implausibly that they were establishing a new popular regime there. The Finnish resistance was stronger than anticipated, and the 'Winter War', in difficult terrain of forest, frozen lakes and marshes, dragged on for several months, arousing in Britain and France, as well as in Germany, renewed doubts about the efficiency of the Red army. At the same time the war in Finland suggested new ways in which the apparent deadlock of what was now beginning to be called the '*drôle de guerre*' or the 'phoney war' might be broken.

For France and Britain the war had not turned out quite as they had expected. The French, ensconced in the fortifications of the Maginot line – limiting their help to Poland to very tentative small-scale offensives against the German army in the west, and calling off the larger attack which was planned because, by the time mobilisation had proceeded far enough to allow it to be mounted, it was too late to affect events on the Polish front – waited throughout the winter, bombarded with German propaganda attacking the British as being responsible for the war and listening to the assurances put out by their own propaganda department under the direction of the dramatist Jean Giraudoux, which proclaimed, '*Nous vaincrons parce que nous sommes les plus forts*' – as, in purely numerical terms of the number of divisions they had mobilised, they in fact were. The British, expecting immediate devastating air attacks on London and the larger cities, and limiting their own air activity to the dropping of propaganda leaflets over Germany, had organised a large-scale evacuation of children to the countryside, with social consequences which were not without importance, as the common stock of experience widened and knowledge spread of how other sections of the population lived. Yet, although a black-out was imposed and gas-masks issued, and although a British army was sent to France, consisting of nearly all the regular army and a part of the volunteer reserve Territorial Army, little happened to make the British feel that they were really at war; and the winter of 1939–40 was in practice not so very different in Britain and France from the apprehensive winter of the previous year.

Hitler had in fact decided that his next move, preliminary to an attack on Russia, must be an assault in the west. His immediate plans for this were repeatedly postponed, because the generals were not ready or because the weather was unfavourable, but they were never abandoned. At the same time the rather vague offers of peace which Hitler made met with no response. While awaiting the expected German attack in the west, all hopes were placed in the long-term effects of the economic blockade imposed at the outbreak of the war, which the British estimated would last at least three years.

In the Allied blockade of Germany the question of the supply of iron ore from the north of Sweden, which reached Germany through Norway, had assumed considerable importance, and the British and French were convinced that if this could be stopped it might, in the words of a British Ministry of Economic Warfare memorandum, 'bring German industry to a standstill and would in any case have a profound effect on the duration of the war'.[11] The Russian attack on Finland and the unexpectedly successful resistance of the Finns seemed to provide the Allies with the opportunity both of establishing a foothold in the north of Scandinavia, and thus furthering their economic campaign, and also of helping a victim of aggression whose cause was popular in Britain and France among a public which was anxious that the governments should do something – it hardly mattered what – to give the impression that they were actually fighting a war. Consequently plans were made for the despatch of an Anglo-French expeditionary force to fight the Russians in Finland. It is a proposal which reads very oddly in the light of later events, but it was adopted with enthusiasm by the Allied governments, who were only prevented from putting it into operation by the fact that by the beginning of March 1940 Finnish resistance had finally reached its limits and the government had asked the Soviet Union for an armistice, which was followed by the cession to Russia of a substantial piece of Finnish territory.

By this time, however, even if they were not able to save Finland from defeat, the British and French were as convinced as ever of the need to prevent ore reaching Germany through Norway, and were planning the wholesale mining of Norwegian waters and the landing of troops at certain Norwegian ports. But in the meantime the Germans had decided to postpone the offensive in the west which they had been planning since the end of the Polish campaign, in order to forestall a British move into Norway. On 9 April 1940 the Germans occupied Denmark without resistance, and invaded Norway. The Norwegian army, taken by surprise, offered what resistance it could. The British and French embarked on a series of improvised operations, which failed, in spite of British naval superiority, to maintain a foothold in central Norway. An attempt to establish a base in the far north at Narvik, from which the Germans had been driven out, might conceivably have met with more success: but, while the western Allies were still reeling from the blows in Scandinavia, the long-awaited offensive in the west opened on 10 May, and soon obliged the British to withdraw their troops from Norway to meet this fresh crisis.

Although an attack in the west was expected, and, indeed, one of the bravest of the senior German intelligence officers opposed to Hitler had given information about it to the Belgians and Dutch, it nevertheless achieved complete surprise. This was partly due to the use of new methods: troops were landed from gliders and by parachute behind the Dutch defences and even directly on to the roof of one of the key Belgian fortified positions. But it was mainly due to the decision, for which Hitler himself was largely responsible, to make the main thrust against the French through the wooded hills and across the deep river valleys of the Ardennes, which the French believed to be impassable for tanks, instead of attacking through Belgium and Flanders as the French expected. The Germans had superior air power. They were able to use their planes against military and civilian targets. Rotterdam was bombed on 14 May 1940, the first example of the destruction of ancient and populous cities which was to be a feature of the war. Refugees were attacked on the roads and the movement of troops made harder, and the German dive-bombers attacked the troops themselves wherever they presented a target.

On paper the discrepancy between the two sides, except in the air, was not very great, but the French dispersed their tanks over the front and at no point were able to bring an effective mass of armour to bear in a counter-attack. The Germans on the other hand and especially General Guderian, a pioneer in the tactics of the new armoured warfare, realised the advantages of deep penetration by tanks, and pressed ahead far into French territory, creating alarm and confusion, and preventing the French High Command from forming a clear picture of the state of the battle. The French commanders were still working on the time-scale of the First World War, when the mounting of a counter-attack took weeks of preparation and when even the mobile battles of 1918 still moved at a comparatively slow pace. Again and again in May and June 1940 plans were made which in themselves might have been successful but which could not be put into operation until it was too late, and until the forces which were to carry them out were no longer in existence.

The French and British were also handicapped by the lack of previous consultation with the Dutch and Belgians, who hoped till the last that the observance of strict neutrality might save them. When the invasion started, they at once appealed for help, and French and British forces were sent to their assistance, a move inevitable on political grounds, but one which weakened the ability to meet the main German onslaught in France, and which, unable to reach the Dutch in time, only briefly delayed the Belgian defeat. The speed of the battle and the rapid German success put a great strain on relations between the Allies. The Netherlands were rapidly overrun and occupied, with the Queen and the government escaping to Britain. The Belgians were able to resist a few days longer, but when the military situation seemed hopeless and the possibility of holding out on Belgian soil had vanished, King Leopold III, without consulting the British and French, decided to surrender and, although the government left for London, the King himself chose to remain in Belgium under the German occupation and declared himself a prisoner of war. The British, when it became clear that the French plans for a counter-attack were not going to come to anything, and that the British army risked being surrounded and cut off, decided to concentrate on their last remaining port, Dunkirk, and to evacuate as many men as could be saved. This operation was in fact much more successful than had been expected: more than 200,000 British were saved and part of the encircled French army was also rescued. To the British this seemed a great victory snatched from the general catastrophe. To the French, however, conscious that it was French soldiers who had held up the German advance while the successful evacuation took place, and noting that some of the French rearguard had been left behind, the operation could easily be represented as further evidence for the belief that the British were ready to fight to the last Frenchman.

The occupation of the Netherlands was complete by 16 May; the Belgian army surrendered on 28 May; the evacuation from Dunkirk was finished by 3 June. The Germans themselves could hardly believe their own success. The campaign was Hitler's greatest gamble so far, and he was extremely nervous. On several occasions the German advance was held back by the High Command: early in the attack Guderian was temporarily stopped from pushing forward for fear of a French move to cut him off; and, for reasons which are still not fully clear, the German army did not press on and capture Dunkirk at a moment when the British and French probably could not have stopped it. Whatever the reasons, the Germans themselves were by no means convinced of the inevitability of their victory, and tended to over-estimate the threat of a counter-attack by the Allies. Even a minor success, such as that which the British tanks won at Arras on 21 May, was enough to alarm the Germans and make them pause. That the major counter-attack which the Germans expected never came was the result of wrong or slow decisions by the French command and of lack of liaison between the British and French armies, as well as of the inferiority of the Allies in the air, and of their failure to use effectively even such armour as they had.

But these purely military mistakes and failures were, as the German advance continued and the possibility of effective resistance in metropolitan France dwindled, soon merged in political decisions which determined the fate of France for the next four years and which left lasting effects on French life after the war. In both France and Britain the dissatisfaction with the 'phoney war' and the shock of the German attack on Norway had led to a governmental crisis. In March, with the failure of the hopes of sending an expeditionary force to Finland, Daladier had resigned, and Paul Reynaud succeeded him as Prime Minister, though Daladier remained Minister of Defence until the next government reorganisation in the midst of the battle of France. In Britain the invasion of Norway had led to the fall of Chamberlain on 10 May 1940 and the formation of a coalition government under Winston Churchill who, although as First Lord of the Admiralty in the previous ministry he had been responsible for some of the errors of the Norwegian campaign, was widely recognised as having the qualities of imaginative leadership required in this crisis, and who had gained the respect even of many members of the Labour Party for his uncompromising criticism of the policy of appeasement during and after the Munich crisis. The French government – and this added to the delay with which the military command reacted to the battle – replaced the Commander in Chief, General Gamelin, with General Weygand, a close associate of Foch at the end of the First World War, while Marshal Pétain, the defender of Verdun and the restorer of French military morale in 1917, was summoned from his post as Ambassador to Spain to take over the Ministry of Defence. It was these two men, one seventy-two years old and the other eighty-four, who were mainly responsible for the fateful decisions of June 1940.

The French army for the most part fought bravely, even though the odds were visibly turning against it. But German success was partly due to the way in which they were able to spread alarm among the civilian population, to block the roads with refugees and thus hamper military traffic, to create an atmosphere of invincibility in which no rumour was too absurd to be believed. During the Spanish Civil War General Franco had said that he had four columns besieging the city of Madrid, but that it would be the 'Fifth Column', his adherents inside the city, which would lead to its fall. During the catastrophe of 1940 it was easy to attribute defeat to the secret machinations of a fifth column of Nazi sympathisers, and German tactics encouraged these rumours. In the Netherlands German troops had dressed in Dutch uniforms and in France it was soon widely believed that German parachutists had descended dressed as nuns and in other equally elaborate and improbable disguises. The evidence suggests that the fear of the fifth column was much exaggerated, and that although Nazi sympathisers in the occupied countries later played an important part in assisting the German rulers, they contributed little to the initial German military victory. Indeed, the military success itself, and above all the bewildering speed of the advance across France, was enough to create a general sense of panic and to turn a military defeat into a national disaster, the loss of a battle into the rout of a proud people.

As the German tanks advanced, the French government moved from Paris to Tours, from Tours to Bordeaux. Winston Churchill, who paid three visits to France for consultations with the French leaders during the campaign, later recalled how depressed he had been on his last visit to Paris – when he had learnt the sad truth from General Gamelin that the French had no strategic reserve – to see from the windows of the French Foreign Ministry on the Quai d'Orsay aged clerks piling the archives on to bonfires in the courtyard to prevent them being captured by the Germans, whose arrival was believed to be even more imminent than it in fact was. Paul Reynaud continued to hope that the tide might yet turn. On several occasions he had appealed to President Roosevelt for American assistance; and Churchill believed that this was the only hope of strengthening the position of Reynaud and those members of the French government who were prepared to continue the war outside France if necessary, as against the increasingly influential group who wanted an immediate armistice. On 14 June, as the government was leaving for Bordeaux, Reynaud sent a desperate appeal to the President: 'The only chance of saving the French nation, vanguard of democracies, and through her to save England, by whose side France could then remain, with her powerful Navy, is to throw into the balance, this very day, the weight of American power.'[12] Although the President was personally committed to support of the Allies, and offered the French a substantial number of guns and aircraft, the dramatic gesture for which Reynaud was hoping was neither politically nor even constitutionally possible. It was to take many months of careful political manoeuvres for the President to be able to bring the United States near to entry into the war. For the moment there was not much that he and the growing number of Americans who were appalled by what was happening in Europe, could do to help, except to make plans for continued economic aid.

The British had only committed part of their available aircraft to the battle in France, and were, at a moment when the situation in France seemed hopeless and when the German air assault might be switched to Britain, reluctant to send any more planes to France. A French request for more air support was rejected on 3 June, a few days before the battle entered its final phase with the German advance around Paris (the city itself was occupied on 14 June). Although some further British and Canadian troops were sent to France, by 18 June these had all had to be withdrawn again. The refusal of British air support, like the evacuation of the British army from Dunkirk, seemed to the French a sign that Britain was not ready to make wholly common cause with her ally, and that for the British strictly national interests were being preferred to the necessity of saving France at all costs. To these criticisms British writers have replied that the situation in France was probably past saving anyway, and that it was the retention in Britain of her remaining air force squadrons that enabled her to survive the all-out German air attack after the fall of France. A last-minute gesture, originating with some of the French officials in London, notably Jean Monnet (after the war one of the most energetic proponents of the idea of a united Europe), was made by Churchill, when he offered a complete political union between the two countries, but this did not make any impact on French opinion or on a French government by then in the last stages of dissolution.

Once the outcome of the campaign in the west seemed certain, Mussolini finally decided to enter the war. On 10 June 1940 Italian troops attacked in the Alps and along the Riviera; and on this front the French defenders met with considerable success, rendered vain by the government's decision on the night of 16–17 June to ask the Germans for an armistice. The idea of surrender had been under discussion ever since the government had left Paris on 10 June, with Reynaud and some of the ministers determined to fight on, even if this meant leaving metropolitan France and continuing the war from French territory overseas. It was however the views of the respected military leaders, first Pétain and then Weygand, which persuaded the hesitant or uncommitted members of the government that there was no choice but to seek what terms the Germans were prepared to grant. The government arrived in Bordeaux on 14 June, and it was here that the decision was taken. By then opinion in political circles in favour of capitulation was growing; and Laval, out of office since the fall of his government in January 1936, appeared in Bordeaux to use all his political skill and powers of argument to build up a faction in favour of surrender. At first it was hoped that an armistice affecting only the forces in metropolitan France, might be possible, leaving the President of the Republic, Albert Lebrun (a man little fitted to be a national leader in an emergency), and the Presidents of the two chambers of Parliament, with such deputies as wished to join them, free to establish a new government in French North Africa, where there was still an intact army. This hope was soon shown to be vain. Pétain – who replaced Reynaud as Prime Minister once the decision to surrender had been taken – refused to consider it, and President Lebrun was persuaded to put off his journey. Although some deputies and members of the government got as far as embarking for North Africa, by the time they arrived at Casablanca they had come to be regarded as enemies of the state and were arrested on landing.

The German terms were received on 21 June: the northern half of France, as well as the Atlantic coast, was to be occupied by the Germans; the remainder of the country was to be unoccupied, and would thus give the French government the appearance of independence. The military clauses were harsh – demobilisation and disarmament of nearly the whole French army, while the fleet was to be disarmed under German and Italian supervision, though the Germans undertook not to make use of it themselves. One of the most vindictive and humiliating of the clauses was that which obliged the French to hand over to the Germans the refugees from Nazi Germany who had escaped to France. Pétain and the generals found these terms just acceptable and, as the Germans refused to discuss any substantial concessions, they had by now little choice. To the surprise of the French, the Italian terms, under pressure from Hitler, who was not particularly concerned with Italian gains and who was anxious for the armistice to be signed as soon as possible, were comparatively moderate, and the last obstacle which might have still provoked some of the senior French commanders, notably Admiral Darlan, the Commander in Chief of the navy, to resist, had been removed.

Hitler was determined to extract the greatest possible historical drama out of the signature of the armistice. The railway coach in which Foch had proudly received the German surrender in November 1918 was taken from its place in a museum and transported to the exact spot at which the previous armistice had been signed. Hitler was present in person, unable to conceal his delight at the scene; and on 22 June 1940 the armistice was signed. The eclipse of France seemed total. Yet the fact that part of her territory was left independent and that hopes were held out that the government might eventually return to Paris, that the French Empire was still intact and the fleet, even if it was to be disarmed, still in French hands, led some Frenchmen genuinely to believe that there was a chance that a regenerated France might still regain a place in a new order in Europe – 'It is in military defeat and internal troubles that other countries found strength to discover themselves and transform,'[13] Pétain declared. The feeling that Pétain alone could achieve this moral recovery was widespread; and in the confusion and distress of the summer of 1940 it was easy for Laval to muster enough parliamentary support when the deputies assembled at Vichy after the armistice, to persuade them to vote, on 10 July 1940, full powers to the aged Marshal. The Third Republic was at an end.

Other Frenchmen, though not very many of them as yet, were preparing to carry on the struggle. General Charles de Gaulle, known, and not, as far as his military colleagues were concerned, wholly favourably, for his views about armoured warfare, and who had been Under-Secretary for War in Reynaud's last reconstructed government, had succeeded in reaching London. There, in the first of the broadcasts with whose characteristic style the French people were to become very familiar over the next twenty-five years, this almost unknown voice announced, 'Whatever happens, the flame of French resistance must not and shall not die.'[14] With the establishment of Pétain's government at Vichy and that of de Gaulle's Committee of National Liberation in London, the two poles of collaboration and resistance between which French politics and society were to oscillate over the next years had been set up.

One last episode in the sad story of Anglo-French relations served to complete the breach between Britain and her former ally. The British government was extremely concerned about the future of the French fleet, and had little confidence in French ability to stop the Germans making use of it, at a moment when the safeguarding from German naval attack of Britain's supply lines to the United States and the Commonwealth was likely to determine the outcome of the war. On 3 July 1940 French ships in British ports were seized by the Royal Navy, and the largest part of the

French fleet, anchored at the base of Mers-el-Kebir in Algeria, was sunk or damaged by the British with the loss of some thirteen hundred French lives. It was an attack which some Frenchmen never forgot.

With the Germans in occupation of Norway, Denmark, the Netherlands, Luxemburg, Belgium and much of France, Britain's isolation seemed complete. It was more, too, than just military and political isolation. For the next five years, the experience of England was to be different from that of the rest of Europe, which shared the humiliation and oppression of German occupation, and which was torn by the moral problems of collaboration and resistance. While the experiences of 1940–5 in some ways bound the countries of Western Europe more closely together, they emphasised the differences between Britain and Europe, and British links with the United States and the Commonwealth.

After the surrender of France Hitler was confident that the British would come to terms with him. He had no direct ambitions as far as the British Empire was concerned, apart from the comparatively minor demand for the return of Germany's pre-1914 colonies, and he could not understand why the British would not accept the situation in Western Europe which he had created. The British, however, and especially Winston Churchill, whose personal leadership counted for much in the maintenance of British morale in these crucial months, were determined to go on fighting. As Churchill had put it in one of his most famous rhetorical speeches, before the final collapse of France,[15]

Even though large tracts of Europe and many old and famous states have fallen or may fall into the grip of the Gestapo and all the odious apparatus of Nazi rule, we shall not flag or fail. We shall go on to the end. We shall fight in France, we shall fight on the seas and oceans, we shall fight on the beaches, we shall fight on the landing grounds, we shall fight in the fields and in the streets, we shall fight in the hills; we shall never surrender, and even if, which I do not for a moment believe, this island or a large part of it were subjugated, and starving, then our Empire beyond the seas, armed and guarded by the British Fleet, would carry on the struggle, until, in God's good time, the new world, with all its power and might, steps forth to the rescue and liberation of the old.

By the middle of July 1940 Hitler had reluctantly realised that the British were not going to give up, and he told his staff to prepare for the invasion and conquest of Britain. The German naval staff were very conscious of the difficulties of transporting a large army across the Channel in the face of the British navy. It would, they believed, take at least until mid-September to assemble the shipping required. Hitler hoped that before launching the actual invasion it would be possible to defeat the British air force and win the kind of air superiority which the Germans had enjoyed in the Battle of France. Thus in early August the 'Battle of Britain' was launched. Over the next weeks the struggle in the air was closely fought. The Germans had more planes and more pilots; the British had the advantage of an efficient radar warning system, while they succeeded in raising the rate of aircraft production to a higher figure than that in Germany. Once it was clear that the RAF could not be destroyed, the Germans started the aerial bombardment of London on 7 September, ostensibly as a reprisal for a British raid on Berlin, but mainly because of the failure to beat the RAF in the daylight battles. The raids, with high explosive and incendiary bombs, became regular nightly features for months. At a time when civilians were joining the hastily improvised 'Home Guard' to supplement the regular army – alarmingly under-equipped as a result of the losses in France – and when the various air-raid rescue and fire services depended on civilian volunteers, the gap between soldiers and civilians which had been so notable a feature of the First World War vanished. The experience of 'the Blitz' not only provided the material for many a private epic of the war; it went some way towards breaking down the class barriers which until then were characteristic of British society.

As the air offensive failed to eliminate the RAF and give the Germans the air superiority which was the prerequisite of a successful invasion, Hitler decided to put off the attack which the British believed to be imminent. The preparations, after being postponed, were finally called off on 12 October, although it was not until the beginning of 1942 that the orders for the invasion were formally cancelled. The Battle of Britain had been lost by Germany but Hitler decided to pursue his war even though England had not been eliminated. Plans for the invasion of Russia were already in hand from August 1940, and it was to the execution of these that Hitler now turned.

With Hitler's victory in the west, the war necessarily ceased to be a European war and became a world war. As Hitler and Churchill both recognised, Britain's only hope of victory lay in an expansion of the war. 'Britain's hope lies in Russia and the U.S.A.,' Hitler is reported as saying at the end of July 1940. 'If Russia drops out of the picture, America too is lost for Britain because the elimination of Russia would greatly increase Japan's power in the Far East.'[16] At the same time, if a direct assault on Britain were not feasible, she might still be attacked in the Mediterranean and in the Middle East; and a successful campaign which would result in German preponderance in Egypt, Iraq, Iran and Turkey might in turn facilitate the attack on Russia. Moreover, the future of the French Empire became of increasing importance, both in the Middle East, where the French still controlled Syria and the Lebanon, and in Africa. An attempt by de Gaulle's Free French to seize Dakar in Senegal – a port occupying an important strategic position on the South Atlantic sea routes – failed, but nearly all the military authorities in French Equatorial Africa came out in support of de Gaulle's Committee of National Liberation and broke with Vichy. Although the majority of French colonial officials elsewhere remained warily loyal to Pétain's government, the possibility, which was later exploited, of using French North Africa as a jumping-off point for the reconquest of Europe was already being discussed. The strength of the loyalty to Vichy was however shown in the summer of 1941 when the British and Free French occupied Syria in the face of stiff French resistance and when, after the French surrender, only a very small proportion of the troops there joined de Gaulle's forces.

In the meantime Russia, Germany and Italy were all anxious to exploit the new European situation. Russia used the crisis of the summer of 1940 as an opportunity to incorporate the three Baltic states, Latvia, Lithuania and Esthonia, fully into the Soviet Union, and Roumania was bullied into handing over the provinces of Bessarabia and Northern Bukovina. Although the Soviet Union and Germany were still bound by their treaty of friendship, and although a new economic agreement was signed early in 1941, their mutual suspicions grew. The Germans sent troops to Finland; they gave a guarantee to Roumania and took control of the oil wells, and they were trying to treat the fascist regime of General Antonescu (see p. 347 above) as a puppet government. When Molotov visited Berlin in November 1940, the atmosphere was cold and distrustful. (It was during this visit, according to a story which Stalin later told Churchill, that Ribbentrop and his Russian visitors were forced into an air-raid shelter by a British attack, which did not stop Ribbentrop declaring that Britain was finished: Molotov is said to have replied 'If that is so, why are we in this shelter and whose are these bombs which fall ?')[17]

Hitler was not totally successful in getting his way in the Mediterranean. In spite of a friendly meeting with Pétain it was clear that any positive support for the German war effort from the Vichy government was not going to amount to much. Nor did General Franco, on whom Hitler was counting for an expedition to capture Gibraltar from the British, show much gratitude for the help which Hitler and Mussolini had given him in the civil war. After a meeting with Franco, Hitler told Mussolini that he would rather have two teeth out than go through it again. Franco, for all his protestations of solidarity with Germany and Italy, insisted that the price of his support would be economic aid far beyond the capacity of Germany to give. Mussolini, who had, as we have seen, failed to win anything spectacular from his belated attack on an already defeated France, had not renounced his Mediterranean ambitions; but an attack from Libya towards Egypt met with little success and was driven back by the British, so that within a few months the Italian troops in North Africa had to receive German help. Again, partly out of jealousy at Hitler's growing influence in the Balkans, Mussolini, without consulting the Germans, launched an attack on Greece at the end of October 1940. But here too the Greek resistance was too strong for the Italians, and German troops eventually had to take over the campaign.

On 5 December 1940 Hitler finally took the decision for which plans had been prepared over the previous five months, and issued his orders for the attack on Russia: 'The German army must be prepared to crush Soviet Russia in a quick campaign before the end of the war against England.'[18] Preparations were to be completed by the middle of May 1941. Over the next months Stalin, still anxious to gain time, went out of his way to appease Hitler: he raised no objection to the presence of German troops in Bulgaria in March 1941, in the course of the German attack on Greece; he refused to help Yugoslavia against Germany; he recognised the pro-German *coup* which had been carried out in Iraq; he discounted the warnings and precise information about the German attack which he received on several occasions from the British and Americans as well as from his own secret intelligence, being unduly suspicious, it seems, that the Western powers were trying to embroil him with the Germans. When the attack did finally come, it took both Stalin himself and the Red army by surprise.

First, however, Hitler had to clear up the situation in south-east Europe. The Italians had failed to conquer Greece; and in February 1941, when it was clear that a German attack through Bulgaria was impending, the British decided to send a force to help the Greeks, made up of troops now available as a result of the successful repulse of the Italians' attack on Egypt. This gamble at least suggested the possibility of reestablishing a foothold on the Continent of Europe and of countering German influence in the Balkans. In March 1941, after the Germans had persuaded the government of Yugoslavia to join them and to adhere to the Tripartite Pact of Germany, Italy and Japan (the final signature of which had been the great German diplomatic gesture of the autumn of 1940), a group of air force officers and others overthrew the government of the Regent Prince Paul, in the name of the young king Peter, and called for help from Britain. The Yugoslavs paid heavily for their courageous gesture of independence. Hitler, personally furious at the check to his plans, ordered an immediate onslaught on Yugoslavia. Belgrade was heavily bombed and the German tanks moved in. Within a few days the whole country was occupied. The Germans were equally successful in their attack on Greece. They drove out the British from the mainland, and captured Crete by a dashing airborne operation. By May 1941 the British in the Mediterranean were once more on the defensive. In order to fight the unsuccessful campaign in Greece and Crete they had been obliged to weaken their forces in North Africa, and from the end of March they were facing an attack not just by the Italians but by the German *Afrika Korps* under General Rommel. With the Germans stirring up anti-British feeling throughout the Arab world, the precariousness of Britain's position in the Middle East was still very apparent, and Hitler's victory in south-east Europe seemed as total as it had been in the west a year before.

Because of British intervention in Greece and for other reasons, Hitler decided to postpone the invasion of Russia by one month. Finally, however, in pursuit of the principal aim of Hitler's foreign policy, German troops attacked the Soviet Union early in the morning of 22 June 1941, on a broad front from the Baltic to Roumania. Hitler had believed that the initial campaign would beat the Red army in six weeks and that within six months the Soviet Union would be forced to surrender but, by the end of 1941, although the Germans had penetrated deep into Russia and had won fantastic initial successes, the Red army was still fighting and the Russian will to resist was unbroken, in spite of huge losses of men, equipment and territory. Leningrad was besieged; the Germans were almost in the suburbs of Moscow and the richest industrial regions of Russia had been occupied. Yet the Germans were suffering also because their advance had not been the total success for which they had hoped, and because of the unexpected toughness of the Russian resistance, the efficiency of some of their tanks and of the anti-aircraft defences of Moscow. The mud and then the snow of the Russian winter had come early and delayed the German forces, which had not the clothing or equipment to face a winter campaign in the Russian climate.

There has been much speculation whether it was the delay caused by the Balkan campaign which prevented the achievement of the final victory by the time of the onset of winter, and also about the importance of the fact that the Russians were able to transfer troops from Siberia when Stalin became convinced that the Japanese were not going to attack. Perhaps, however, even more fundamental was the basic German underestimation of Russia's resources and Russia's power, coupled with the uncertainty, after the successes of the first weeks of the campaign, as to whether it was more important to capture Moscow or to press on to occupy the Don industrial region and towards the oil of the Caucasus. From now on the responsibility for the decisions on the eastern front became increasingly Hitler's own, as the generals who questioned his strategic or tactical decisions were removed or forced to resign. By the end of 1941 it was clear that events, and not just on the Russian front, were getting out of his control. Instead of the series of short successful campaigns he had envisaged, he was from December 1941 involved in total war on a world scale.

The European states' failure to find political solutions to their domestic and international problems after 1918 had given Hitler the opportunities he needed to come to power and to launch his war in 1939. By 1941 the countries of Europe were mostly unable to affect the destiny of the Continent, and the decisions were being taken elsewhere, first in the gigantic battles in the heart of Russia, and then in Washington and in Tokyo. During the 1930s, as we have seen, the simultaneous challenge to the existing international order by both Germany and Japan had revealed how far the resources of the Western states were stretched. For the United States this had meant, down to 1940, at a time when the United States government was reluctant to have any foreign policy at all because of its concern with internal economic and social problems, a constant debate as to whether the Pacific or Europe was more vital to American interests. The fall of France and the isolation of Britain made this dilemma all the more acute. Britain was more than ever dependent on supplies from America, but the cutting-off of most of her normal trade made it very hard to pay for them. During the year after the French collapse President Roosevelt was finding a number of ways of meeting this problem – by the deal of 2 September 1940 by which Britain was to be supplied with some American destroyers in return for making available to the United States bases in the West Indies; by the Lend-Lease agreement of January 1941, by which the president assumed power to supply military equipment to Britain, if necessary without payment. Roosevelt was being pressed by some people to do more to help Britain, and by others to keep the United States out of war at all costs. At the same time the Americans were faced with the growing challenge of Japan in the Far East. The Japanese had profited from the war in Europe: they had persuaded the Vichy government first to give them bases in northern Indo-China and then in June 1941 they occupied the whole of Indo-China; they had hopes of obtaining important supplies of raw materials from the Netherlands East Indies; they were from the beginning of 1941 planning to attack the British base at Singapore. The elaborate negotiations between the United States and Japanese governments over the next months were conducted by Roosevelt in the hope of postponing the clash with Japan, since for him the war in Europe and Germany's defeat remained the first priority. By October 1941 it was clear that the negotiations were soon going to break down, though it was the Japanese, by their surprise attack on the United States fleet at Pearl Harbour on 7 December 1941, who took the initiative and started the war at a time of their own choosing. It was however Hitler who linked the war in the Far East with the war in Europe.

Although Japan had been an original member of the anti-Comintern pact (and the government was consequently disillusioned by the signature of the Nazi-Soviet agreement in 1939) and although she had signed the Tripartite Pact in September 1940, both Germany and Japan had pursued their policies independently of each other. The Germans had pressed the Japanese to attack Singapore in support of the German war with Britain. Then, after the invasion of Russia, they had urged the Japanese to occupy the Siberian port of Vladivostok. In neither case were the Japanese prepared to act unless it suited them, and they observed the non-aggression pact with the Soviet Union which they had signed in April 1941, because, after considerable debates inside the Japanese government, they had decided to strike south into the Pacific rather than west into Siberia. However, although, as Ribbentrop pointed out, Germany was only obliged under the Tripartite Pact to support Japan if she were attacked and not when, as Japan had done at Pearl Harbour, the Japanese started the war, Hitler nevertheless hastened to congratulate the Japanese on the attack at Pearl Harbour, and four days later he declared war on the United States.

In attacking the Soviet Union and in declaring war on the United States, Hitler made his two greatest mistakes. It is arguable that, if he had not taken the initiative in going to war with the United States, the American involvement in the Far East would have postponed United States commitment to the war in Europe and diminished aid to Britain. As it was, Germany's gratuitous declaration of war on America made it politically possible for President Roosevelt and his military advisers to make the defeat of Germany the first objective of American policy. Hitler's underestimation of American strength had consistently been even greater than his underestimation of Russian resources. He was now to pay for these errors.

In a more rational moment in 1940 Hitler had foreseen that the involvement of Russia and the United States in the war was the only way in which Britain could hope to win (see p. 387 above). Now, however, he was at his most apocalyptic when he spoke of a 'historic struggle which, for the next five hundred or a thousand years, will be described as decisive, not only for the history of Europe and indeed the whole world . . . A historical revision on a unique scale has been imposed on us by the Creator.'[19] What had started as a European war was now a world war, and it transformed the old Europe and its relations with the rest of the world irrevocably.

14

COLLABORATION, RESISTANCE AND LIBERATION

By the end of 1941 Europe, from the Pyrenees to the heart of European Russia and from the North Cape to Crete, was occupied by the Germans. Those countries not under Nazi rule, such as Hungary, Roumania and Bulgaria, were closely associated with Germany. Italy was Germany's partner; and Spain, although non-belligerent, was ideologically in sympathy with Nazi Germany and prepared to collaborate in many ways, such as providing facilities for German submarines in Spanish waters. The liberation of Europe now depended on outside moral and physical help, and above all on direct military action. Such action could eventually be taken by Britain, but only on a limited scale compared with the resources of manpower which the Russians could throw into the war, and the ever increasing material strength of the United States. It was this dependence on the world outside, and especially on the United States and the Soviet Union, which marked the final stage in the decline of European power in the world, because it inevitably gave the USA and the USSR a political and military foothold in Europe which they have not given up.

In fact, however, by the end of 1941 the limits of Hitler's conquests had already been reached. By the beginning of 1942, when he finally realised that his series of successful lightning wars would not bring him total victory, the Germans began planning for a long war; and this involved the ruthless exploitation of occupied Europe in the interests of sustaining the war in Russia. Within a year of the German declaration of war on the United States, there were signs that the German domination of Europe could not last. The Red army started successful counter-attacks in a number of sectors as early as December 1941, and a year later, in the weeks after 19 November 1942, the Russians won their greatest victory and one of the decisive battles of the war by counter-attacking at Stalingrad, forcing the retreat of the German army and obtaining the surrender of the German forces, including twenty-four generals, who had been cut off in the city. In October 1942 the British under General Montgomery began to drive back the German forces in the Libyan desert after winning the battle of El Alamein, and shortly afterwards

393

Allied troops under General Eisenhower landed at the other end of the North African coast, in Morocco and Algeria. It appeared that what Churchill, in a characteristic if perhaps misleading metaphor, called 'the soft underbelly of the Axis', the southern coast of Europe, was threatened with invasion; and the possibility of a successful landing on the Continent could now be envisaged. In the meantime however, for the peoples of Europe, the primary and immediate experience was that of German rule and of the problems of personal conduct which that experience imposed.

The methods of German rule in occupied Europe varied considerably. The most obvious difference was that between their conduct in Western and in Eastern Europe. In Hitler's vaguely formulated plans for a 'New Order in Europe', the role of Eastern Europe, and especially of Russia, was to provide areas of settlement for German (and honorary German, such as Danish, Swedish and Dutch) farmers, and thus to provide the food supply for a continent whose economy would be run by Germany, but in which there would be some independence for the advanced states of Western Europe, provided that they collaborated with German plans. It was this hope of a role in a new European order which led a few Belgians and Frenchmen who were not members of the local fascist groups to place some hope in the possibilities of collaboration with Germany; and it was the basis of the policy of Pierre Laval, Deputy Prime Minister in the Vichy government under Marshal Pétain from July to December 1940 and from April 1942 to August 1944, and of some of the other Vichy ministers, who hoped that by offers of concessions to the Germans they would win counter-concessions in return, and that the wily bargaining skill which had served Laval well in the politics of the Third Republic could be used in dealing with the Nazis. In the early stages of the occupation, with the members of the German army behaving in a comparatively correct way, and with Pétain personally treated with respect and courtesy by Hitler, this still seemed a possible course. Hitler, however, soon decided otherwise. 'It must be all the same to us if the renewal of economic life in France is prevented,' he said in September 1940. 'The French have lost the war and consequently they must pay for the damages... All concessions that we make to the French must be paid for dearly by means of deliveries from the unoccupied zone or the colonies.'[1] For the next four years the aim of German policy in France, apart from maintaining strategic control of the country, was to extract what they could from the French economy, in raw materials, industrial and agricultural goods and above all in labour, in the interests of the German war effort.

While the French had a comparatively privileged status in Hitler's Europe because at least they still had their own government with some degree of autonomy (although Alsace and Lorraine were annexed outright and became part of the Reich), other countries, whose legal governments had gone into exile, such as the Netherlands, Belgium or Norway, were placed under

German civilian commissars and were in effect under direct German rule. In theory the Nazis regarded the Norwegians, Dutch and Flemings as of German stock and therefore entitled to the honour of eventually forming part of the Third Reich. In practice, however, the Nazis never found enough local support to make these ideas seem plausible. Although in Norway they tried to use the Norwegian fascist party, the *Nasjonal Samling* (National Union) to run the administration for them, the experiment was not a success, since its leader Vidkun Quisling, whose name soon became a widely used and common synonym for 'traitor', commanded little Norwegian support and was not even very efficient at carrying out German orders. In the Netherlands the local fascist leader Anton Mussert was given no real power and, although a number of opportunists joined his movement in the hope of jobs, the majority of the population made it quite clear that they were going to have nothing to do with him, and that the Germans could hope for very little in the way of collaboration from them. The rival French fascist leaders – the ex-socialist Marcel Déat, the ex-communist Jacques Doriot and the nationalist thug with a good war record, Joseph Darnand – succeeded in recruiting paramilitary groups which were useful in assisting the Gestapo and in hunting down and eliminating Jews or members of the Resistance, and Darnand by the end of the war was Minister of the Interior and in charge of the repression of resistance. In general, however, these ideological collaborators fared little better than those who worked with the Germans for reasons of self-interest. Rejected by the majority of their countrymen, they were of only limited use to the Germans in whom they had placed their faith and whose defeat they ultimately shared. Some died fighting or killed themselves at the end of the war: some, notably Quisling and Darnand, stood trial after the liberation and were condemned to death: a few escaped to find refuge in Spain, as did the Belgian Rexist leader Léon Degrelle; some, such as Marcel Déat, just disappeared (ten years later Déat was reported to have died in a monastery in Italy).

The one aspect of German policy which at first attracted some ideological support was the attack on the Soviet Union. The war with Russia could be represented as a great crusade for Western civilisation, and volunteers from all Europe were encouraged to participate. General Franco, anxious to obtain military equipment from Germany and to show his solidarity with the dictators, declared that the campaign in Russia was 'the battle which Europe and Christianity have for so many years awaited',[2] and sent the volunteer Blue Division to fight on the Russian front. Among Hitler's other satellite allies, the Roumanians, whose dictator, Ion Antonescu, was one of the very few people whose advice in matters of strategy Hitler was prepared to listen to, embarked enthusiastically on the Russian war, but they were quickly disillusioned by the extent of their losses and by the feeling that their main enemies were still Hitler's other allies, the Hungarians, from whom they were hoping to recover those parts of the province of Transylvania which they had been obliged to hand over in 1940 on Hitler's orders, and who had only sent a small force to support the campaign in Russia.

Himmler, who wanted to use every opportunity of increasing his own influence and that of his ss forces at the expense of the army, extended membership of the *Waffen SS* (that section of the corps which served as front-line troops) to Scandinavians, Dutch, Belgians and French, and later to Ukrainians and to men from the Baltic states and even to Moslems from Bosnia. The military results were not always very successful; but by the end of the war foreigners formed a major proportion of the troops fighting with the ss division at the front, and the ss men from Western Europe, having no choice, fought bitterly to the last.

There were some Europeans who were prepared to collaborate with the Nazis on ideological grounds, or to join a crusade against Bolshevism, or to seek a career in what were thought to be the elite ranks of the *Waffen SS*. But the people in the occupied countries whose collaboration was most indispensable to the Germans were those who were prepared to work with them on the day-to-day tasks of administration and of industrial production. The Germans needed collaborators in the management of factories and on the boards of directors of economic undertakings; they needed the collaboration of the local police; many Germans, especially in Paris, were anxious to establish good relations with journalists, as well as with artists and intellectuals, and a few writers reciprocated. This type of collaboration was based on self-interest, ambition or vanity, and it depended on German successes. If, for example, a Belgian official was given the opportunity of a senior post at an earlier age than he would otherwise expect, or a French businessman could sell products to the Germans at a good profit, he was prepared to do this as long as the Germans seemed to be winning. Some were in any case too deeply involved with the Germans to be able to dissociate themselves from them in defeat, but many, as the tide turned, tried to reinsure by evading German demands or by giving help to the Resistance.

In the purges which followed the war many of these people were condemned to imprisonment and to other penalties, but thirty years later it is difficult to define the limits of collaboration, to decide what was voluntary and what involuntary, or where a wary attitude of waiting and seeing and looking after one's own interests ended and active assistance to the Germans began. It is easy to point to the ideological collaborators and to those who were wholly committed to the Germans, just as it is easy to recognise the '*résistants de la première heure*', the people who were actively involved in resistance from the start, or those who, in the countries of Europe where this was physically possible, joined guerrilla bands. In between lay the large mass of the population, anti-German by instinct and sympathy, but involved in working for a German-controlled political and economic system.

For most of the countries of Europe we still need the basic sociological investigations which would enable us to talk with confidence about the nuances and grades between the extremes of resistance and the extremes of collaboration, about the numbers involved, or the way in which people's opinions and actions changed and evolved as the war went on. The tendency at the end of the war was to brand as a collaborator not only anyone who had associated or cooperated with the Germans in any way, but also anyone whose conduct could be given a sinister interpretation by those, such as the communists, who had old scores to settle. All we can be sure of is the moral dilemma with which large numbers of people all over Europe – but especially in the West – were confronted in a situation in which, in Jean-Paul Sartre's words, 'because an all powerful police-force tried to force us to hold our tongues, every word took on the value of a declaration of principles'.[3]

It was the Russian campaign which revealed the hollowness of Nazi claims to be constructing a New Order in Europe, a concept which had led a few people in the defeated countries to believe that a sincere collaboration with the Germans might be possible and worth while. For some of them the attack on the Soviet Union also seemed to provide a cause in which they could collaborate. However the war in the East rapidly became simply the excuse for redoubled oppression and extortion in the rest of Europe, as the Germans exhausted the occupied countries to keep the campaign in Russia going. The methods used for this purpose brought recruits to the Resistance. At the same time it was in the doctrinaire refusal to regard the Slav peoples of Eastern Europe as anything other than racially subhuman helots that the failure of the New Order became most apparent.

When the German army began the invasion of Russia, German soldiers were welcomed in the border areas – the Baltic states and the Ukraine – as liberators, and there were some German officials and military commanders who were anxious to exploit this mood, while Goebbels saw the value for his propaganda of what seemed to be spontaneous anti-Bolshevism. But Hitler and Himmler were quick to forbid anything of the kind, and the occupation policy in Russia remained one of total oppression and exploitation. 'I have no interest at all in the fate of the Russians or the Czechs,' Heinrich Himmler, who as *Reichsführer SS* was responsible for the execution of these policies, declared. 'Whether they thrive or starve to death concerns me only from the point of view of our need of them as slave labour for our own civilisation [*Kultur*]; in all other respects I am totally indifferent.'[4] The result was two-fold: first the resistance of the Russians and the ferocity of the partisan war in the occupied territories was intensified, in the desperate knowledge that nothing could be worse than the results of surrender. Second, as some of the German leaders, including Himmler himself, came to realise when it was too late, the ruthlessness of the oppression and the death of millions of Soviet prisoners of war either by execution or by starvation deprived the German economy even of the forced labour which it had been intended that occupied Russia should provide.

The effects of Hitler's policies in the East were felt in their most horrifying and brutal form by the helpless Jewish populations, first of Eastern Europe, and then, as hundreds of thousands of Jews from Western Europe were deported to the East, by the whole of European Jewry. Hitler had for many years spoken of the expulsion of the Jews as a final aim; and in *Mein Kampf* there is a terrifying passage which shows how, early in Hitler's career, the possibility of reaching the 'final solution' of the Jewish question by means of extermination was already in his mind: 'If, at the beginning and during the war, someone had only subjected about twelve or fifteen thousand of these Hebrew enemies of the people to poison gas . . . then the sacrifice of millions at the front would not have been in vain.'[5] As the Nazi anti-Semitic policies increased in intensity in the 1930s, Hitler and his lieutenants became more than ever obsessed with the feeling that a war would give the opportunity for the final elimination of the Jews. 'Should the German Reich come into conflict at any time in the foreseeable future with a foreign power, the first thing we Germans would obviously think of would be our final reckoning with the Jews,'[6] Goering declared in November 1938, when the murder by a young Jew of a German diplomat in Paris gave an excuse for a fresh wave of anti-Jewish activity. The German conquest of Poland and part of Russia added a large Jewish population to those already under German control; and in dealing with them the form of the 'final solution' began to be worked out by Himmler and his staff. Very large numbers of Jews were shot out of hand, as the German armies advanced, by the special SS units detailed for the purpose and, after abandoning a plan for concentrating all the Jews in a ghetto in Madagascar where they might serve as a bargaining point in dealing with America, late in 1941 preparations were made for assembling all the Jews of Europe in the East, 'as a first stage'. By the beginning of 1942 the 'final solution' was under way. The efficient apparatus of German bureaucracy was set in motion to exterminate in gas chambers the remaining survivors of European Jewry, systematically rounded up for the purpose from the countries under Nazi rule and from the satellite states of Eastern Europe.

It is estimated that nearly six million Jews died at the hands of the Germans. There has since the end of the Second World War been much discussion about how this appalling action could have been possible, why there were no protests against it and, especially since the trial in Jerusalem in 1961 of Adolf Eichmann, one of the chief administrators of the extermination programme, why the Jews themselves passively accepted their fate without attempting to resist. Certainly the German authorities concerned had their misgivings, not on humanitarian grounds, but from fear of the public reaction should what they were doing become known. They devised elaborate cover stories to conceal the truth. That these stories were believed by the thousands of Germans who after the war said that they did not know what was going on, was perhaps the result of the natural instinct of anyone in a totalitarian society not to look for trouble, but it was also the result of anti-Semitic indoctrination over many years and of anti-Semitic assumptions which were widespread even before they were exploited by the Nazis. Many Germans and Austrians, as well as a large number of Poles and Roumanians, had long believed that there really was a 'Jewish problem' which needed solution; and many of them were quite prepared to think that deportation was the answer. Thus they were easily persuaded to accept the stories of Jewish 'resettlement' put about by the ss, and to close their ears to any rumours of the ghastly fate which was in fact prepared for the Jews.

There seem to have been few serious protests by the people actually involved in the carrying out of the extermination plans. The fanaticism with which the policy was carried through not only inhibited criticism but also made the operation into a doctrinal and ideological one in which there was no place either for humanitarian or for utilitarian considerations. While Himmler – a former chicken farmer and a vegetarian devotee of astrology and natural medicine – spoke of the German love of animals, and believed that the principles of animal breeding could be applied to the Germans and so strengthen their claim to be the master race, he also exhorted the ss to carry out the mass murders without flinching: 'To have come through this and to have remained decent [anständig] all the same ... this has made us hard. This is a never written and never to be written page of fame in our history.'[7] Such total ideological abandonment or perversion of the values of European liberal humanitarianism was accompanied by a similar disregard for the realities of economic life and of the needs of the German war effort: some of the rare protests raised inside the Nazi bureaucracy against the murder of the Jews came from those ss officials who were using Jewish forced labour in factories producing, for example, boots and belts for the army; and these objections Himmler impatiently brushed aside.

In Western Europe members of the Resistance succeeded in hiding and saving a few Jews, and in the Netherlands in February 1941 there was a mass strike in protest against the arrest of a number of young Jews, after some of them had organised groups to resist the anti-Semitic activities of the German occupiers. Although in Western Europe many Jews joined resistance movements and a few succeeded in surviving, such individual acts of opposition were extremely difficult, given the thoroughness with which the occupying authorities were carrying out Hitler's and Himmler's instructions. In the East there were risings in several of the concentration camps where Jews were assembled, ss guards were killed and a few prisoners escaped. In January 1943 the desperate and heroic revolt of the inhabitants of the Warsaw ghetto forced the Germans to move in tanks and artillery to suppress this final act of hopeless protest. For the most part, however, the Jews, battered by the unceasing anti-Semitic propaganda, knowing that they were inevitably destined for oppression in one form or another and in many cases unwilling to be a burden to their non-Jewish friends, were reluctant to believe the worst, and even appeared to accept the stories they were told about 'resettlement' or 'labour service'. There were many suicides: but for the most part the Jews, transported in conditions of intolerable squalor and humiliation, had little choice but to accept their fate.

The outside world, when it learnt what was happening, did little, and perhaps could do little. While the Allies, learning during 1943 from Polish resistance sources the truth about the camps in the East, used the information for their propaganda, they tended to believe that there was nothing they could immediately do, and that only victory could bring any relief to the Jews. Pope Pius XII was slow and somewhat devious in condemning what he undoubtedly knew about from the end of 1942, and he has been bitterly criticised since. In Hungary, although the government allowed the deportation of most of the Jews, the Regent, Admiral Horthy made some attempt to prevent the removal of part of the Jewish population of Budapest.

Controversy will continue as to whether more could have been done to save the Jews, as will discussion whether this episode holds a unique place among the horrors of Europe in the twentieth century, which include the indiscriminate bombing of cities, the Soviet purges or the systematic elimination of the Soviet government of groups and peoples believed to be hostile to the Soviet system. Yet the Nazi massacre of the Jews remains the most shocking of all, because of the way in which one of the most civilised nations in the world could combine efficient technological organisation of the means of destruction with a moral barbarism which had not been seen in Europe on such a wholesale scale for many centuries. The crazy and pointless ideology which made such action possible was based on no rational considerations and on none of the usual political calculations of profit and loss, but rather on a wild irrational urge to destroy regardless of the consequences, and illustrates what a disillusioned ex-Nazi once called the Nazi 'Revolution of Nihilism'[8] in its ultimate form.

There had been some form of resistance in all the occupied countries almost from the moment of the German invasion, even if this at first was limited to gestures of defiance, such as celebrating national anniversaries or refusing to speak to German soldiers. Individuals thought up their own personal protests: patriotic slogans were written on walls; the mayor of one French village stopped the clock on the Town Hall to show that he did not recognise 'les temps nouveaux'.[9] Others began to cut telephone wires or practise minor acts of sabotage. For the minority who were prepared to undertake active resistance, as well as for the majority who were content to sit out the occupation as best they could, the continuation of the war by Britain was enormously important. The British Broadcasting Corporation's programmes provided for many Europeans their only contact with the outside world, and the V for Victory slogan, expressed by the three long and one short sounds of the Morse code version of the letter V (and also, as was quickly discovered, by the opening phrase of Beethoven's fifth symphony), with which the BBC prefaced transmissions, served as a symbol of confidence during the dark days.

The invasion of the USSR not only increased the hopes of an ultimate German defeat, it also swung the communist parties of Europe on to the side of active resistance. Between the signature of the Nazi-Soviet pact in August 1939, and the German attack on Russia in June 1941, the official communist line had been that Britain was waging an imperialist war, and that the Soviet Union was therefore justified in making an agreement with Germany. In France the Communist Party, which had during the first few weeks in September 1939 still supported the war, was forced, not without some reluctance, to change its line to one of opposition, and lost some of its members as a result, as well as being declared illegal by the government; and the other communist parties were obliged willy-nilly to conform to the exigencies of Soviet foreign policy, dropping their anti-Nazi slogans and falling back on misleading historical parallels. This did not stop individual communists, even if they had formally accepted the official party line, from fighting bravely in 1940 or from joining in acts of resistance after the occupation. The French poet and novelist Louis Aragon, one of the Surrealists who had remained totally loyal to the Communist Party, was twice decorated for his services in the campaign of 1940. In the Netherlands communists were active in the protests against the anti-Semitic policies of the Germans in February 1941. The communists in their later writings have glossed over this ambiguous period and have denied that there was any resistance in Europe before they supported it. When after June 1941 their efforts could be turned officially to resistance, there is no doubt that they everywhere played a substantial part, and that years of clandestine opposition had provided an excellent training; but they were by no means the first and never the only resisters.

The German invasion of Russia had the immediate effect of turning the communists into members of the Resistance, but it also had long-term consequences which were important for the growing opposition in the occupied countries. In January 1942, faced with the prospect of a long war and of growing material support from America for Britain and Russia, the German government finally took the decision to mobilise for total war and to subordinate the whole of the European economy to Germany's needs. As the demand for labour in German industry grew, so workers in the occupied countries were conscripted in ever larger numbers for work in Germany and many young men preferred to go underground rather than to be rounded up for forced service in Germany. Such men and women often joined the guerrilla bands which began to form wherever there were mountains or forests in which they could assemble, and provided a new wave of recruits for the Resistance.

The scale and nature of the Resistance varied with the geographical and social structures of each country. In the plains of Russia or the mountains of Yugoslavia it was possible to organise a full-scale guerrilla war. In the Netherlands or Belgium on the other hand resistance was a question of underground organisation in a largely urban environment. The ways in which the Germans could be attacked were many, ranging from the publication and circulation of clandestine newspapers – an important element in giving a secret organisation a sense of political identity as well as in combatting the stifling hold of the occupiers on all the media of communication – to direct sabotage, and to the collection of military intelligence for transmission to the Allies. As time went on both the resistance movements themselves and the German organisations opposing them became more skilled and more sophisticated in their methods. Lessons about maintaining security and avoiding penetration by Gestapo agents were learnt in a hard school. Moreover, the more effective the Resistance became, the more brutal were the means used by the Germans against it, and especially their efforts to deprive it of the base of tacit popular support without which no resistance movement can hope to survive for long. Hostages were taken and executed: whole villages were wiped out or their population massacred. Lidice in Czechoslovakia and Oradour-sur-Glane in France became symbolic names on account of these reprisals; but each country has its own list of passive victims and martyrs.

If the Resistance was to be effective, relations with the outside world had to be maintained, both to coordinate its activities to fit in with Allied plans, and because it was from outside that the equipment for resistance – radio sets, explosives, fuses, weapons – could be obtained. Although there might be an occasional successful raid on a German depot to capture stores, and although, in those areas where communications with Allied territory were hardest, such as Czechoslovakia, members of the Resistance became expert in the chemistry of home-made explosives, making bombs in pudding basins in their kitchens out of materials bought from the chemist, the main source of supply was the British and later the Americans. Gradually methods were developed for delivering materials and men and women by parachute drops, and special squadrons of aircraft – never as many as the Resistance hoped – were allocated for this hazardous task. Routes in and out of occupied Europe were developed: training schools for members of the Resistance were set up in Britain and later in North Africa. Special networks in the Resistance helped escaped prisoners of war, and especially air force pilots, to return to Britain. There has been much discussion since the end of the war about the strategic value of all this activity and about the extent to which the sabotage activities of the Resistance seriously hampered the Germans. It is certain that in the last stages of the war, just before and after the Allied landings in northern France in the summer of 1944, the Resistance did much damage to German communications, and in other areas, such as Yugoslavia, they tied down troops who might have been used elsewhere. But perhaps the significance of the European Resistance lay not so much in its actual strategic or material achievements but rather in the psychological experience which it provided, the continuity it gave to national life and the basis which it offered for reconstruction after the war. Its importance was as much moral and political as it was military.

In the early stages of the occupation, a number of people succeeded in escaping from Europe and joining the exiled armies being built up in Britain. The Poles had been particularly intrepid in escaping from Poland and making their way to France, where a Polish army was formed, most of which escaped to England; and a surprising number of Poles continued to make the hazardous journey across occupied Europe and through a hostile Spain to join the Polish armies outside, so that in the case of the Poles the contacts between the army and exiled government outside and the 'Home Army', which formed one of the most effective resistance movements in Europe, were particularly close, in spite of the distance and difficulties. All the exiled governments in London were anxious to maintain their national armies, so as to stake a claim for a say in the post-war settlement, as well as to wipe out the memory of defeat by contributing to the common victory. Where there were legal governments established in London, while there might be friction with the British and Americans about particular operations or particular plans and while bad feeling could sometimes be caused unintentionally, as when a mistake in the British headquarters allowed the German security services to take over and run a whole network of the Dutch Resistance for nearly two years, their status was not for the moment in doubt.

In the case of the Free French however the situation was more complicated. The relations between Britain and America and occupied France were bound to be important, and it was in France that any invasion of the Continent would have to start. In the meantime support from Britain for the French Resistance was growing. At the same time, however, there were certain advantages in keeping some sort of links with the Vichy government. While secret contacts between Pétain and Churchill did not lead to much, President Roosevelt maintained diplomatic relations with the Vichy government until November 1942, in the hope of limiting French collaboration with the Germans. The relations between the British and United States governments and General de Gaulle, for whom President Roosevelt soon developed a deep personal dislike, were therefore complicated, and it was a long time before de Gaulle received full recognition from Washington and London. It was characteristic of de Gaulle that the less secure his own position was, the more vigorously he asserted his independence. Even though depending on Britain for all material support and for the technical means necessary to maintain contact with the Resistance in France, he was nevertheless determined to make it quite clear that he intended to keep French sovereignty intact and French authority, as represented by himself, unimpaired. The result was that there grew up a certain rivalry in London, if not in France itself, between those resistance networks organised directly by the British themselves and those organised by the Gaullist bureaux in London; and it is in these war-time days of uneasy cooperation and dependence that the explanation of much of de Gaulle's later attitude to Britain and the United States must be sought.

The crisis between the Allies and the Free French came late in 1942. For some months plans had been going ahead for an Anglo-American landing in North Africa. The main objective remained a direct assault on Hitler's forces by means of a landing in northern France. The Russians were pressing for a 'Second Front' which would relieve German pressure on their armies; and in May 1941 President Roosevelt had told Molotov that he hoped and expected that the creation of a Second Front would be possible in 1942. In fact, this proved not to be the case: as the difficulties of an opposed landing were investigated, it became clear that the invasion would need longer preparation, and a trial raid on Dieppe by Canadian forces in August 1942 confirmed these views. At the end of May 1942 the Germans attacked the British in Libya, and drove them back to the Egyptian frontier. It was not until General Montgomery's victory at the battle of El Alamein late in October 1942 that the campaign in the western desert turned in Britain's favour.

These factors all pointed to a landing in French North Africa as the main feature of Allied strategy in 1942, although it was only reluctantly and after prolonged discussions that the British and Americans could agree on this operation, which began with the establishment by the Americans of secret contacts with French military leaders in Morocco and Algeria. In April 1942 a senior French general, Henri Giraud, had escaped from a German prison and returned to France, where he refused German demands to return voluntarily to Germany and where he made contact with the American representatives at Vichy. To those Americans and British who were reluctant to give any further recognition to de Gaulle, Giraud seemed to provide a figurehead whom the officers in Morocco and Algeria might be prepared to recognise, since General Weygand had refused to accept this role. Accordingly plans were made to bring Giraud by submarine to North Africa as soon as the Allied landings took place. These landings, of which de Gaulle was not informed beforehand, took place on 8 November 1942, and were generally successful, though not everything went according to plan. Most of the French authorities in Morocco and Algeria had remained loyal to Pétain, although there was a small group of Gaullist resisters there, and although there was a rising in the city of Algiers itself, which was largely the work of Algerian Jews (the Arab population remaining largely indifferent to these events). Some of the senior officers were prepared to work with the Americans but not with the British, and were firm in their refusal to accept de Gaulle's leadership. And, just at the moment when it was intended that Giraud should appear and take command, Admiral Darlan, head of Pétain's government from the beginning of 1941 and still Commander in Chief of the Vichy armed forces, who happened to be in Algiers visiting his sick son, decided to support the Americans and rallied to the Allies.

Thus, while facing several days of serious fighting, because many units of the French army were not in fact ready to welcome the American forces as had been hoped, the American and British governments suddenly found it expedient to collaborate with a man who, for all members of the Resistance and all supporters of de Gaulle, was a traitor who had, it seemed, gone even further than Laval in working with the Germans, to whom he had made many concessions, including bases in the French colonies, without gaining anything substantial in return. He had never really believed that the Germans could be beaten or that the Americans would intervene effectively in the war, but now that he saw that they had, he decided that collaboration with them might after all be more useful than collaboration with the Germans. In spite of protests the Americans thought that Darlan might make their task easier and that because of his ambiguous relations with Pétain he might be able to bring them the support of local French officials and commanders, as in fact he did. However, his enigmatic career was cut short within a few weeks when he was murdered by a young man whom some Americans at once suspected of being a Gaullist agent, though he in fact seems to have acted on his own. The attempt to replace Darlan by Giraud, a man who, whatever his personal and military virtues, was lacking in political sense and experience, did not last long. After some months of uneasy cooperation between him and de Gaulle, the latter's position as sole Chairman of the French Committee of National Liberation was finally if reluctantly recognised by the end of 1943.

The effect of these events in France was profound. The Germans answered the Allied landings in North Africa by occupying most of the 'free zone' in the south, while the Italians moved into the remainder of the unoccupied area. The independence of the Vichy government was even more shadowy than before. On the other hand, the establishment of a Free French authority in Algiers gave a new impetus to the Resistance and provided a nucleus for the shaping of a new political authority for France. The whole North African episode, while bringing substantial military advantages to the Allies, also served to illustrate the complications of French politics and the division in French society which the experience of collaboration and resistance was bound to leave behind.

In other parts of Europe the hostility between resistance groups often became as acute as the hostility between the Resistance and the Germans. This was particularly the case in Greece and Yugoslavia, and was to have decisive effects on the post-war developments in these countries. In both cases the government-in-exile – that of King George of Greece in Cairo and that of King Peter of Yugoslavia in London – was a royalist one, largely conservative in its sympathies; and in both cases there were strong republican and communist groups in the resistance movement. In both countries, too, the main form which resistance took was the organisation of guerrilla bands in the mountains. The communist leaders were well aware of the possibilities which the Resistance offered for creating a revolutionary movement which might hope to seize power when the German occupation finally came to an end. At the same time, however, they were not able, at least until the very last stages of the war, to obtain any direct support from Russia, and if they were to acquire arms and supplies, these were going to have to come from the British, who had established military missions with the guerrillas in Yugoslavia from September 1941 and in Greece from October 1942.

In Greece the efforts of these missions were largely spent in trying to persuade the rival guerrilla groups to combine in attacking the Germans, and occasionally for brief periods they succeeded in doing so. As the war went on however, the Communist bands were more concerned to amass such supplies as they could obtain for use against their rivals after the war; and indeed at one moment, even during the war, there was a miniature civil war between Communists and their rivals, foreshadowing the major conflict which was to tear Greece apart between 1947 and 1949.

In Yugoslavia the first British mission to arrive found two rival resistance movements in being, and for some months it was extremely difficult, owing to bad communications and German counter-action, for the British government to form any clear picture of what was happening. One group, the Cetniks, led by Colonel Draza Mihailovič, later nominated Minister of War by the Yugoslav government in London, consisted of officers and men from the regular army, mostly Serbs who were determined to keep in being the nucleus of a national Serb force and who were, perhaps, as the Serb bands under the Turkish occupation had been, more concerned with survival than with attacking the enemy. The other group, the Partisans, led by the Secretary-General of the Yugoslav Communist Party, Josip Broz, known as Tito, saw themselves as a resistance movement embracing all the nationalities of Yugoslavia (Tito himself is a Croat), which would combine attacking the German and Italian occupying forces with the preparation of a new political and social order. As in Greece, the first hope of the British was to unify the rival factions in the interest of the Allied war effort, so as to interfere with German communications with North Africa and thus serve a direct strategic purpose. When it was clear that any unified resistance movement was as unattainable in Yugoslavia as it was in Greece, the British government decided to support the group which was most actively fighting the Germans. Since in many cases Mihailovič's forces had come to an understanding with the Italians and Germans that each would leave the other alone, British aid was withdrawn and switched to Tito. The vigorous prosecution of the war took precedence in the mind of the British government over all other political considerations, with the paradoxical result that Churchill, a romantic royalist whose government recognised that of King Peter, was committed to aiding Tito and the Communists, and thus undoubtedly contributed to Tito's final success in making the Yugoslav revolution and in abolishing the monarchy.

In one other even more important case, that of Italy, complex problems caused by the recognition of a transitional government and of its relations with a growing and active resistance movement created deep and lasting problems. In December 1942 the Allies had failed in their immediate objective of capturing Tunis and clearing the Germans and Italians out of the whole of North Africa, and the Axis Powers had sent strong reinforcements to Tunisia. It was only after five months of hard fighting that German and Italian forces in North Africa were forced to capitulate on 13 May 1943. Although not a victory on the scale of Stalingrad, this nevertheless enabled the British and Americans to capture a very large number of experienced and tough German and Italian troops, and showed that the Axis forces were no longer invincible but were now on the defensive.

For the Italians in particular the campaign had been a costly one in men, aircraft and shipping. But they had other reasons for anxiety as well. The African empire, the goal of Italian nationalists for more than sixty years, had been lost. They had been driven out of Libya and Tripoli, conquered in 1911; and the British had in the spring of 1941 expelled them from Ethiopia for the sake of which they had provoked an international crisis in 1935, and had restored the Emperor to his throne. On the Russian front, the Italian troops had suffered such losses that Mussolini was at the end of 1942 unsuccessfully urging Hitler to make a separate peace with the Soviet Union, while a few weeks later, the new Italian Chief of Staff, on assuming office, was pressing for the withdrawal of the Italian forces on the eastern front. Mussolini himself had been seriously ill in the autumn of 1942. (When the Japanese ambassador saw him in January 1942, all he could say, rather undiplomatically, was 'You, Duce, you worn out, very worn out, too worn out.')[10] This had led to much intrigue and speculation among the Fascist leaders. Feuds and cliques developed: the example of Darlan's change of sides was much quoted: there were rumours of overtures to the Allies.

However, Mussolini rallied sufficiently to assert his authority, and in February 1943 he dismissed several ministers and reconstructed his government. But the cracks in the structure of Fascist Italy were widening, now that it was clear that Mussolini's gamble on a short victorious war had failed. In

March 1943 there were impressive strikes in Turin and elsewhere in northern Italy, the result of economic hardship and war-weariness; and these gave the underground Communist Party a chance to show its strength and reminded the Fascists that they could no longer count on mass support. The old politicians of the pre-Fascist period began to meet secretly for discussions about the possibilities of a change of regime and of leaving the war; and they made contact with some of the officials at court and with others in the King's circle who were thinking on similar lines.

The crisis was precipitated in July 1943 by the Allied landings in Sicily. With the occupation of the whole of North Africa, the Germans were expecting an Allied landing somewhere in southern Europe – Sardinia, Sicily, the Balkans – but the actual attack in Sicily took them by surprise. The invasion of Sicily – an obvious next step from Tunisia – was originally regarded by the Allies as a subsidiary operation to improve communications in the Mediterranean and to maintain the pressure on Italy, while at the same time giving the Russians the impression that Britain and America were doing something. As it turned out, however, the operation was extremely successful. The Italian coastal troops surrendered or ran away at once. (Many of them were Sicilians who rightly thought that the best way to save their homes was not to fight.) The Allies moved cautiously, however, and German troops on the island put up a tough fight before finally being evacuated across the Straits of Messina, leaving the British and Americans in control of Sicily.

The successful invasion led to Mussolini's fall. With the will to continue the war rapidly dwindling among all sections of the Italian population, the only hope seemed to be either to extract Italy from the war by means of a separate peace, or else to look to the Germans to take over the defence of the country. While some among the Fascist leaders were prepared to draw even closer to Germany in the hope of saving the regime, a majority of them had now begun to think that their only hope of rescuing anything from the situation lay in getting rid of Mussolini and in trying to come to terms with the Americans and British. On 19 July 1943, nine days after the Allied landings, Mussolini had a rapid and rather inconclusive meeting with Hitler near Venice, at which Hitler boasted of the economic resources still available to the Axis in occupied Europe and spoke of mysterious secret weapons which would yet win the war. He discoursed on the strategic situation of Italy, but refused to supply more German aircraft, while the Duce could not apparently bring himself to tell the Führer just how desperate the situation was.

When he returned to Rome, which had in the meantime experienced a severe air raid, Mussolini had to face a discussion of the situation with his colleagues in the Fascist Grand Council, a formal body which had originally been the central committee of the Fascist Party and now was the supreme organ of the state, 'the unifying centre through which the antithesis between Party and government is rendered no longer possible',[11] as a leading Fascist put it. It was a body in which in theory the elder statesmen of the movement and the younger members of its ruling circles discussed and decided the great issues of the Party and the State. In fact, however, the meeting on the evening of 24 July 1943, and the events which followed it, showed how hollow the vaunted institutions of the Fascist state were, and how little control Mussolini now had over them.

During the ten hours of discussion Mussolini found that there was a majority on the Grand Council in favour of his removal – expressed formally as a recommendation that the King should take over supreme power. The various strands of the movement to overthrow Mussolini were coming together. The King had been told of the discussion in the Grand Council and was at last ready to listen to those of his personal advisers who wanted him to dismiss his Prime Minister. When the Duce arrived for his regular audience on 25 July, therefore, the King, in a few minutes of embarrassed conversation, asked him to resign. As he left the King's residence, an ambulance was waiting with an escort of military police, and Mussolini was taken, unresisting, into captivity.

There was remarkably little reaction from the Fascist Party or the militia; and Marshal Badoglio, who had been the Chief of the General Staff until his dismissal in December 1940, after the unsuccessful campaign in Greece, took over the government with little immediate visible change. He assured the Germans that he was continuing the war on their side, while at the same time sending a secret emissary to Lisbon to make contact with the Allies in order to negotiate an armistice. The armistice was signed on 3 September 1943. On the same day the British army in Sicily crossed the Straits of Messina to the mainland; and on 8 September an Anglo-American force landed in the Gulf of Salerno, just south of Naples. The end of Fascism and the elimination of Italy from the war had been achieved with apparent ease and speed, but the consequences were not so simple.

This was partly for military reasons. The Germans reacted quickly to the dismissal of Mussolini by taking over in northern Italy and reinforcing their armies there. When the armistice became known, they seized Rome, disarmed the Italian troops and took up strong positions to stop the Allied advance. The Allies failed to win their immediate objectives as quickly as they had hoped. It took them nearly a month to capture Naples and thus gain possession of a major port. By the end of the year they were still held up between Naples and Rome, and an attempt in January 1944 to break the deadlock by a new landing at Anzio, south of Rome, did not have much immediate success. It was not until June 1944 that Allied troops entered Rome, and it took another ten months of hard fighting before they reached the plains of north Italy, by which time the Germans were being defeated on the Russian and on the western fronts. The Allied High Command always regarded the needs of the Italian campaign as secondary to those of the main invasion in northern France, which at the end of 1943 had been finally fixed for the summer of 1944, and from this point of view the Italian campaign had served the purpose of tying down a substantial German force.

For the Italians the consequences of the slow Allied advance were grave. The King and the government were forced to leave Rome and take refuge with the Allied armies in the south. Their political position was ambiguous: although they were from October 1943 officially at war with Germany and recognised by the Allies as cobelligerents, the change from being treated as a defeated enemy to being treated as a near-ally was a slow one. In January 1943, at a meeting between Churchill and Roosevelt at Casablanca in Morocco, the British and Americans had committed themselves to the policy of demanding 'unconditional surrender' from Germany, Italy and Japan. It was a policy adopted in part because of the need to reassure the Russians that the delay in opening the Second Front was not due to a desire to make separate peace at their expense, and in part because Roosevelt and his advisers were very much aware of the difficulties in which Wilson had found himself in 1919 because of his prior commitment to the Fourteen Points (see chapter 10 above). The effect was however to reduce Allied freedom of political manoeuvre during the war. When the British and Americans landed in Italy, they originally intended to place the country under direct military government, and at first treated Badoglio and the King with considerable suspicion. However, as the cooperation of the Italian government proved useful, the Americans and British were gradually prepared to hand over more power to the Italians, though even so they were still subject to an Allied Control Commission, and Allied military government officials exercised direct control of local administration in the forward areas.

The delay in liberating the whole of Italy at first increased the political tensions in the country. There were virtually three rival authorities. There was a revived Fascist government in the north, headed by Mussolini himself, whom the Germans had, by a daring parachute raid, succeeded in rescuing from the mountain fortress in which he was imprisoned by the Badoglio government. This 'Republic of Salò' (named from the village on Lake Garda where Mussolini had his headquarters) was purely a satellite of the Germans, a refuge for those extreme Fascists who were unwilling or who had left it too late to change sides, a regime in which even Mussolini himself seemed to have little interest. On the other hand there was the King's government in the south, which hardly seemed convincingly anti-Fascist as long as it was headed by Badoglio, who had held high military office under Mussolini for many years, and owed allegiance to the same King who had summoned Mussolini to power in 1922 and had only dismissed him under extreme pressure of advice and events. Finally in the centres occupied by the Germans, in Rome and Florence and Milan, Committees of National Liberation set up by the Resistance commanded much support and were actively organising and conducting a vigorous fight against the Germans, so that by 1944 there was both an active underground movement in the cities and an active guerrilla movement in the mountains.

Even after the formation of a coalition government in April 1944 and the liberation of Rome in June, there were still tensions between the old politicians and the resistance leaders, many of whom were new men with new ideas. They included the Communists, who, like their comrades in Greece and Yugoslavia, regarded the resistance as a means of coming to power themselves and of making a social revolution. There were liberals, who, grouped in a movement which did not long survive the liberation, known as the *Partito d'Azione* (Action Party), tried to revive the pure republican idealism and the humane nationalism of the Mazzini tradition. Finally there were the Christian Democrats, some of whom, at least, were thinking of a Catholic social movement on the lines of the Popular Party which had flourished briefly after the First World War.

The government formed in April 1944 was a coalition of these parties, presided over by Badoglio until the liberation of Rome two months later, and then by an elderly survivor from pre-Fascist Italy, the ex-Socialist Ivanoë Bonomi. It was strengthened by the fact that the Communist leader Palmiro Togliatti, who had just returned from exile in Moscow, was prepared – to the chagrin of many members of the Resistance – to join, in spite of Badoglio's presence as Prime Minister and Victor Emanuel III as Head of State. This move towards a revival of the idea of a Popular Front, and towards the exercise of Communist influence within the administration as well as outside it in the Resistance, was confirmed by the Soviet recognition of the Italian government, a move followed without much enthusiasm by the British and Americans. The new government was a genuine coalition of anti-Fascists and included the Socialist leader Pietro Nenni as well as non-political figures such as the old philosopher Benedetto Croce. For all the differences between its components and the many unresolved problems which it faced, it seemed to offer a genuine and hopeful alternative to the Fascist regime. One consequence of its formation and of the negotiations which preceded it was that Victor Emanuel's days as King were numbered; and he agreed to withdraw in favour of his son Umberto, who was named Lieutenant General of the Kingdom, pending a referendum on the question of the monarchy to be held after the war was over.

The nature and political development of the resistance in each of the occupied countries of Europe, and the forms of collaboration – ranging from the full-scale collaboration of a government, as in France, through the non-cooperation, at times bordering on active resistance, of the Danish government, to the individual adoption of the German cause by a few opportunists or local fascists – left their mark on the situation in Europe at the end of the war. Political life depended almost everywhere on the relations between the various parties and groups which had cooperated in the Resistance and on their attitude to the representatives of an older political order, as well as to those who had collaborated. But the fate of Europe, which in 1940 had depended on German decisions, by 1945 depended on the relations between the great powers, and especially the United States and the Soviet Union, and it was by decisions taken by them in the course of the war that that fate was determined. At the same time the process of liberation also involved enormous material disruption caused by the war itself and the methods used in waging it.

During the First World War the aerial bombardment of cities, both by aeroplanes and by airships, had been used as a means of attacking enemy morale, and had suggested a new dimension to twentieth-century warfare in which civilians might be as much affected as soldiers at the front. In the years between the wars, much attention had been given to the development of bomber squadrons in the air forces of the great powers: and in the various discussions about disarmament no agreement was reached about the abolition of bomber aircraft, in part at least because they were used by the British and the French as a convenient means of controlling unrest in remote areas of their colonial empires. By the mid-1930s there was a widespread belief – expressed by Stanley Baldwin's famous remark in 1932, 'The bomber will always get through' – that this would be the decisive weapon in the next war. This belief was strengthened by the air raids, many by German planes and crews, in the Spanish Civil War, which demonstrated the effect which attack from the air could have on the civilian population in the cities.

In 1940 the Germans used mass air bombardment of towns as an important element in their attack in the west. Rotterdam had been the first city to be destroyed by this means, and by September 1940 the air raids on London and on other British cities had become a nightly occurrence which continued for several months on end. During the period when the British, carrying on the war almost alone, had no immediate prospect of attacking the Germans by means of a landing in Europe, it was natural that they should place great hopes in the possibility of winning the war by aerial bombing and by using bombers as a decisive weapon in the economic blockade of Germany. There were even senior officers in the RAF who believed that the war could be won by air power alone without the necessity of ground action, though this view was never shared by Churchill and the government. The result was much controversy about the best way to use the bomber. Some people argued that the accurate bombing of precise targets – factories making ball-bearings, for example – could cripple the German war effort. However, during much of the war German anti-aircraft defences on the ground and in the air made raids on precise targets extremely costly in machines and crews. Thus, alongside the use of precision bombing on specific targets, which continued until the end of the war, the alternative strategy of area bombing was increasingly accepted as a legitimate and valuable method of attack.

Area bombing, it was argued, would not only destroy industry and disrupt transport; it would also reduce the effectiveness of the German workers by making them homeless, and it would, it was hoped, ultimately destroy their will to continue the war. 'The aim of the bomber offensive,' the British Chiefs of Staff wrote in October 1942, 'is the progressive destruction and dislocation of the enemy's war industrial and economic system and the undermining of his morale to a point where his capacity for armed resistance is fatally weakened.'[12] These arguments proved in the event to be doubtful ones. While the bomber offensive caused much damage and disruption to the German economy, it did not cripple it, and it was only in the last months of the war, when the German army was already in retreat on the eastern front, in Italy, and in Western Europe, and when the Germans had finally lost command of the air, that German economic life began seriously to collapse. This was partly due to the ingenuity which the Germans, under the direction of Albert Speer, Hitler's former architect, whom he placed in charge of war production in 1942, showed in making good the effects of air raids, dealing with the homeless, dispersing industrial plant and in the later stages of the war building factories underground. Nor did the control of the population by the Nazi Party and the police weaken; and German morale did not break under the bombardment any more than British morale had in 1940.

The result of the bombing offensive by both sides was to destroy the cities of Europe, but especially of Germany, on a scale never seen before and to involve the civilian population in the direct experience of war to a greater extent than in any previous conflict. It is estimated that nearly half of the total of thirty million casualties in the war were civilians, though not all these were the result of aerial bombardment. As the technical means of aerial warfare grew more effective, with the development of radar devices for navigation and for aiming bombs, so the raids grew more deadly. From the spring of 1942 on, thousand-bomber flights took part in the attacks on the cities of Germany. Some of these raids resulted in disasters on a vast scale; according to British official historians, the raids on Hamburg at the end of July and the beginning of August 1943, in the worst of which a fire-storm caused people to die of asphyxiation in their shelters, meant that 'two-thirds as many people were killed by bombing in a single week as in the whole of Britain in the whole war'.[13] The most notorious and controversial of these massive attacks was that on Dresden in February 1945. The scale of the casualties, the total destruction of one of the most famous and beautiful cities in Europe and the fact that the attack took place at a time when the result of the campaign in Europe was no longer in doubt, have given the event a symbolic value in subsequent controversy and have raised all the arguments about the nature and justification of area bombing. In fact, the Dresden raid did not differ in kind from its predecessors elsewhere; it was the result of the Allied conviction that German morale was about to crack and it originated in a belief, already known to be mistaken before the bomber force set out, that an armoured division was passing through the city on the way to Hungary, so that the raid would demonstrate Anglo-American support for the Soviet Union. The whole debate has acquired significance because this was one of the worst air attacks experienced in Europe and because nearly six months later the dropping of an atom bomb on Hiroshima showed how the strategy of area bombing with a view to breaking civilian morale and destroying an enemy's capacity to resist, had now assumed new and even more horrifying proportions.

Both sides mobilised their scientific resources to produce new and better weapons during the war. On the Allied side the many other technical achievements have been overshadowed by the production of the atom bomb, which was ready for use just after the end of the war in Europe. From the beginning of the century, European scientists had been producing new theories about the nature and structure of the basic elements out of which the physical world is composed and had been challenging many of the assumptions of earlier physics. Einstein's theory of relativity had not only led to a scientific revolution; it had also seemed in the popular mind to confirm a widespread belief that nothing was certain any more, and its very name 'relativity' had been misinterpreted to apply to many aspects of life far removed from the realm of pure physics in which Einstein intended it to be used (see p. 159 above). Einstein's theories had been concerned with the categories of time and space and with the nature of the astronomical universe, and with the energy generated within the atom itself. Other revolutionary practical and theoretical thinkers at the beginning of the century, notably Ernest Rutherford and Max Planck, had been concentrating on the movement of atoms, the basic particles out of which, it was thought, matter was made up, and had shown that their behaviour was not as uniform or as predictable as had been supposed, and that they were to be analysed in terms of bursts of energy between their nucleus and the electrons which surrounded it. In the 1920s the most brilliant of the next generation of physicists, including the Dane Niels Bohr and the German Werner Heisenberg, were developing a new atomic theory concerned with the behaviour of the nuclear particles and electrons within the atom. By 1937 some scientists were considering what would happen if the nucleus could be split by external action, and by the time of the outbreak of war in 1939 the idea that the vast quantities of energy released in the process could be produced and controlled at will was becoming accepted by physicists, although they did not yet know how this was to be done in practice. The war itself provided the impetus for discovering the practical technical means of 'splitting the atom' and of harnessing a process which potentially had a greater explosive force than any bomb so far invented.

In its theoretical stages in peace-time the development of atomic physics had been an international undertaking, to which scientists of many nationalities had contributed by the free exchange and discussion of their hypotheses and experimental results. With the practical application of these ideas under the stimulus of war and the enforced break in the flow of international scientific information, the intellectual advantage now lay with the Allies, especially as many of the leading German, Austrian and Italian physicists had been driven into exile. They were later joined by others: two physicists from France succeeded in escaping in 1940 with the stock of 'heavy water', an essential ingregient in the atom-splitting process, which they had succeeded in making: in 1943 Niels Bohr was brought out of Denmark by the British, in cooperation with the Danish Resistance. First in Britain and Canada, and then in the United States, an international team of scientists was given every kind of official support in their search for a new atomic weapon. When the consequences of the construction and use of the atomic bomb became apparent in 1945, and after its effect on the post-war international situation had become clear, some of the participants had second thoughts about their role and the use to which their discoveries were being put, and the debate has still not ended. Although the results of their work were not directly experienced in Europe, its shadow has hung over the Continent ever since.

Work on the atom bomb in England and North America was in fact ahead of German developments in the same field, although the Allied experts did not realise this, and lived in fear that the Germans might solve the technical problems first. (One of the great acts of sabotage carried out by the Norwegian Resistance in 1943 was the serious damage of the plant producing heavy water for the German atomic programme.) The Germans, however, although Heisenberg and other eminent scientists were working on their atomic research programme, made their main effort in the last two years of the war, as far as weapons for mass destruction were concerned, in the development of pilotless aircraft and, more important, of rockets. (One of the most brilliant of their technologists, Wernher von Braun, later played an important role in the United States space programme.) Hitler, as the prospect of a German victory grew more remote, placed more and more hopes in his 'secret weapons' of which he boasted to Mussolini at their last meeting before the Italian surrender, and on which he was relying for a last-minute victory. By the summer of 1944 the first pilotless aircraft ('v1s') and, a few months later rockets ('v2s') were used against Britain, but the damage they did was comparatively small, although they caused some alarm at a moment when most British people were expecting an early end to the war. The RAF had concentrated much of its bombing effort in attacking rocket experimental stations, factories and launching pads, and the new weapons came into use too late to affect the assembling of troops and the other preparations for the Allied landing in Normandy, which finally took place on 6 June 1944.

The material cost of the liberation of Europe was bound to be high, just as the political and moral cost was. Even if, as many have argued, the policy of area bombing caused damage and casualties out of proportion to the results achieved (though this is almost impossible to calculate), attacks on precise targets could also harm civilians. Mistakes could be made, as when a lunatic asylum in Czechoslovakia was attacked in the belief that it was a factory. Housing in the area of industrial plants was often destroyed. In the great attack on German communications preceding the invasion, the towns of France and Belgium suffered to such an extent that Churchill was worried about the effect this might have on the welcome which the Allied armies would receive there when they arrived. When the Red army began its advance westward, through Poland and Hungary into Germany, Czechoslovakia and Austria, many cities which had already suffered aerial bombardment now became battlefields, as did the towns of western Germany in the last weeks of the war. The cities of the Ruhr and Cologne for example looked to the observer in April 1945 as though they were so totally destroyed that they could never be rebuilt, as though the ruins and rubble were on so vast a scale that they could never be cleared away. The physical reconstruction of the cities of Europe since 1945 remains one of the great technical, if not always one of the great aesthetic, achievements of the twentieth century.

The Anglo-American invasion of France at the beginning of June 1944, and the subsequent advance from the bridgehead, was followed in mid-August by the landing in the south of France of a force drawn from the armies in Italy. Paris was liberated after a rising by the resistance movements there on 24–6 August. By the middle of September all France except for Alsace and part of Lorraine had been freed; Strasbourg was taken two months later, though it was not until March 1945 that the rest of Alsace was cleared of troops. The liberation of Belgium was quickly achieved early in September, as the German armies withdrew for regrouping on German soil. At the same time, in the east, the Russians had advanced into Poland and the Baltic states, and Germany's satellites were crumbling under the military pressure. In August 1944 both Finland and Roumania asked for an armistice, while Bulgaria was occupied by the Red army in September. Yet in the autumn of 1944 victory was not quite as close as many people hoped and expected, and many Europeans suffered much from the delay.

Even in the face of the Russian advance and the successful Anglo-American invasion, Hitler still believed in some providential reversal of his fortunes – and, when President Roosevelt died suddenly on 12 April 1945, Hitler and Goebbels regarded this as a sign that the stars were working in their favour. Hitler hoped that it might still be possible to break the unity between Britain, the United States and the Soviet Union, and that, with the advance of the Russian armies westward, the Americans and British would inevitably break with Russia. ('The time will come when the tension between the Allies will become so great that the break will occur. All the coalitions have disintegrated in history sooner or later. The only thing is to wait for the right moment, no matter how hard it is,'[14] Hitler told some of his senior commanders at the end of August 1944.) He still believed in new and better secret weapons – and indeed one of these, a U-boat fitted with a new type of ventilation device, continued to alarm the British Admiralty right down to the last days of the war. Although the German economy was in a state of confusion, its transport system severely strained and increasingly short of oil as a result of the Allied bombing offensive, the Germans were still capable of counter-attacks. They took the Anglo-American armies completely by surprise with an attack in the Ardennes in December 1944, prompted by Hitler's hopes that if the western Allies were halted they might be willing to negotiate. In spite of its initial success, this attack was contained, but it had the effect of delaying the Allied advance to the Rhine. On the eastern front the German armies fought stubbornly, and as late as February and March 1945 they and the Hungarians could still mount a brief counter-attack in western Hungary.

The principal victims of this prolongation of the war into 1945 were not only the Germans themselves, as the destruction of their cities continued, but also those hundreds of thousands of Jews whose extermination continued methodically during these months, as did the execution of members of the Resistance and of the German opposition to Hitler, while in the concentration camps many of the prisoners who had escaped being killed now died of disease or starvation. In western Europe, the Dutch in particular suffered when the Allies failed, after their airborne landing at Arnhem in September 1944, to secure a crossing over the lower Rhine, and so could not complete the liberation of the Netherlands which would have been one of the results of success in this operation. The Dutch were therefore condemned to a hard and bitter winter, in which many people died of starvation and thousands were deported to Germany, before the German occupation army finally surrendered at the beginning of May 1945.

At their meeting at Casablanca in January 1943 (see p. 410 above), Churchill and Roosevelt had agreed that they would be satisfied with nothing short of 'unconditional surrender' by their enemies. It has sometimes been argued that this prolonged the war by strengthening the German will to resist: certainly Goebbels was able to make considerable use of it in his propaganda in the last months of the Third Reich. Hitler himself, however, at no point thought of surrender, but rather still expected the British or Americans to ask him for terms. The principle of unconditional surrender also prevented the British and Americans from making any contact with those

Germans who, especially after Stalingrad, were actively engaged in trying to remove Hitler. There had been talk of this among senior officers even before the war (see p. 372 above), but most of the critics had been silenced by Hitler's successes in 1940 and 1941. From 1942 however, as the campaign in the east began to go wrong, and as Hitler took over the complete strategic direction of the war himself and refused more and more to listen to professional military advice, a number of officers and others began to discuss ways of getting rid of him and of forming an alternative government. On several occasions they tried to start negotiations with British and American representatives about the peace terms which a new German government might expect, and each time the Allies refused to discuss the matter. Whether such discussion would have ever got very far is doubtful. The conspirators still hoped to retain most of the gains made by Hitler before the outbreak of war, and expected that Germany would keep, for example, the territory won from Czechoslovakia by the Munich agreement in 1938. In any case the British and Americans, partly because they knew how sensitive the Russians were to anything which sounded like negotiations for a separate peace, and partly because they believed that there was no point in making any commitments before the conspiracy had been successful and Hitler eliminated, were not interested in these hypothetical discussions, and stuck rigidly to the formula of unconditional surrender until that surrender actually took place in May 1945.

While lack of outside encouragement disappointed some of the conspirators against Hitler, they nevertheless continued with their plans. The German opposition was made up of a number of different groups: some were old opponents of the regime, including Social Democrats who had avoided or been released from concentration camps; a few were old Nazis who had realised that they were on the losing side. Many of them were upright Prussian conservatives, such as Karl Goerdeler, the former mayor of Leipzig, who was the political leader of the conspiracy. Others, several Catholic priests and Protestant pastors and the Prussian aristocrat Helmuth von Moltke among them, were mainly concerned with the moral evils of the Nazi system and with plans for the regeneration of Germany. The majority of the opposition however turned to active resistance only when it became clear that Hitler was both losing the war and committing crimes against humanity in the process. Not all of them were willing to remove Hitler by force; but a number of them, including a young staff officer with a brilliant war record, Colonel Klaus Schenk von Stauffenberg, who had grown up in the atmosphere of romantic conservatism in the circle of the poet Stefan George, decided that Hitler must be assassinated.

None of their several attempts succeeded. A bomb placed in Hitler's aircraft failed to explode; an occasion at which a young officer was ordered to show Hitler a new type of uniform and hoped to use the opportunity to blow up both the Führer and himself, was cancelled at the last minute. Finally on 20 July 1944 Stauffenberg himself succeeded in placing a briefcase containing a bomb under the table at which Hitler was presiding at a staff conference in his headquarters on the eastern front. The bomb exploded causing considerable damage, and Stauffenberg, who had slipped out shortly before and taken a plane to Berlin, believed that Hitler must have been killed. By a series of unlucky accidents, however, Hitler escaped with minor injuries. Meanwhile the plans for a military *coup* by those officers involved in the plot began to be put into operation, not only in Berlin, but also in Paris, Vienna and elsewhere. The repression was swift and brutal. Over the next months over five thousand people were executed: many others, including Field Marshal Rommel, committed suicide and only very few of the original plotters survived until the end of the Third Reich nine months later.

Although Hitler claimed that the plot was no more than the work of 'a very small clique of ambitious, unscrupulous, criminal and stupid officers',[15] the measures taken to root out opposition showed that he and Himmler believed it in fact to have been much more than this. The last months of the Nazi regime were filled with an atmosphere of suspicion and fear, as Hitler took his final revenge on the members of the German officer corps to whose cooperation he had owed his success, but whom he had always hated, and whose advice he now increasingly ignored. The majority of senior officers had not taken part in the plot, though some of them had an idea of what was going on, and many of them hastened to express their loyalty to Hitler in the most abject terms. The power of Himmler and the SS was enhanced. Himmler was responsible for the arrests and for the investigation of those suspected of participation in the conspiracy, prior to their summary condemnation by a special court which made no pretence of impartiality. He also achieved equality for the SS with the regular army, and himself assumed command, first of the Home Army and then of an army in the field. In 1934 the army had won from Hitler the promise that they should be the only 'bearers of arms' in the Reich (see p. 340 above). Ten years later the weakness of their position was only too apparent. Defeated in war, their advice unheeded, they were now little more than the technical military arm of an SS state.

The failure of the German Resistance does not detract from its heroism; nor was the 20 July plot its only manifestation. While it is almost impossible to assess how far there was any popular resistance among the people at large, or what acts of sabotage and passive resistance have gone unrecorded, there were occasional desperate but impressive public gestures of moral protest, as when in February 1943 the Munich students Hans Scholl and his sister Sophie distributed thousands of leaflets prepared by an underground student organisation, and declared that 'The German name is dishonoured for all time if German youth does not rise now to take its revenge.'[16] Given the difficulties of opposition in a totalitarian state (see p. 344 above), such actions as those for which the Scholls and their associates were executed or for which Stauffenberg and many others paid with their lives have at least given the Germans something on which they can look back with pride in the twelve dark years of Nazi terror.

Hitler's escape from assassination in July 1944 only helped to convince him of his providential role, but in the last months of his rule, as from January 1945 the enemy armies were closing in from east and west, he was increasingly out of touch with reality. Immured in his underground shelter in Berlin, surrounded by a few faithful followers, kept going by the injections and pills which his dubious doctor prescribed, Hitler seemed to some of his visitors a mental and physical wreck. By 22 April 1945 the Russians had surrounded Berlin. On 25 April the American and Russian armies met at Torgau on the river Elbe, north-west of Dresden.

Hitler's original plan had been to organise guerrilla resistance to the invaders of Germany and to set up a 'national redoubt' in the Bavarian mountains. Events moved too fast for this: and in any case the will of the German people to resist had now evaporated. Hitler himself, however, decided on 22 April to remain in Berlin to the last. Even some of his closest collaborators were now trying to save something from the wreckage. Goering had left for southern Germany and sent word to the Führer that he was prepared to take over the leadership of the Reich, since Hitler had decided 'to remain at [his] post in the fortress of Berlin'.[17] Himmler, to Hitler's bitter chagrin, made an unsuccessful last-minute attempt to open negotiations with the western Allies through the Swedish Red Cross representative 'in order to save as great a part of Germany as possible from a Russian invasion'.[18] Speer, who claims that at one point he was considering murdering Hitler by introducing poison gas into the ventilation system of the bunker, refused to obey the Führer's orders to destroy industrial plant, and tried to save some of Germany's productive capacity for the future.

Hitler himself, though by now with very little idea of what was going on outside, but with Russian shells falling on his bunker from 26 April, at last realised there was no hope. On 29 April he married his faithful mistress Eva Braun whom he had known since 1932, but who had remained discreetly in the background of his life. He dictated his political testament. This offered a defence of his policies in phrases very similar to those of *Mein Kampf*, expelled Goering and Himmler from the party, and appointed Admiral Doenitz, the Commander in Chief of the navy, as his successor. The testament ended revealingly and characteristically with the words, 'Above all I charge the leaders of the nation and those under them to scrupulous observance of the laws of race and to merciless opposition to the universal poisoner of all peoples, international Jewry.'[19]

On that same day Hitler received the news of Mussolini's death. As the German armies in Italy retreated, the area controlled by Mussolini's shadowy Fascist republic dwindled, while, all over northern Italy, the partisans were taking over. On 28 April 1945 members of the Resistance caught up with Mussolini near Lake Como, as he was fleeing northwards with a convoy of German troops to which he had attached himself. A summary execution order was produced by the Committee of National Liberation in Milan, and, in what they claimed to be an act of revolutionary justice, the partisans shot Mussolini and his mistress Claretta Petacci. Their bodies, riddled with bullets and drenched with rain, were taken to Milan, where they were displayed publicly to a hysterical and violent Milanese crowd. 'The shooting of Mussolini and his accomplices,' the Committee of National Liberation stated, 'is the necessary conclusion of a historical era which leaves our country still covered by material and moral scars, and the conclusion of an insurrectional struggle which signifies for the Fatherland the prerequisite of its rebirth and reconstruction.'[20]

Hitler at least escaped the humiliation of Mussolini's end. On 30 April 1945, after taking leave of his staff, he retired to his own rooms with his wife. There he shot himself and Eva took poison. Goebbels and his family, who had insisted on remaining with him in the bunker, also took their own lives, and their bodies were burnt along with Hitler's in the Chancellery garden. Of the other leading Nazis, Himmler committed suicide after being captured by the British; Martin Bormann, Hitler's deputy, and a very influential figure behind the scenes, disappeared. There is some evidence that he was killed in Berlin; but there have been doubts as to his fate, and repeated rumours that he escaped to South America, as many lesser Nazis succeeded in doing. The other principal leaders were eventually brought to trial in 1946 before a special international tribunal set up at Nuremberg by the victorious Allies. They were charged with crimes new to international law such as planning aggressive war and genocide, as were some of the military commanders and two of the early collaborators of the regime, Franz von Papen and Hjalmar Schacht. The two latter were acquitted, and the remainder were found guilty. Ten of them, including Ribbentrop, were executed: Goering managed to commit suicide shortly before execution. The others were sentenced to long terms of imprisonment.

The armies in Italy had surrendered on 29 April, with effect from 2 May; and on 7 May 1945 General Jodl signed an instrument of unconditional surrender by all German forces to the British, Americans and Russians. Within a week of Hitler's death the war in Europe was at an end.

15

EUROPE DIVIDED

In the spring of 1945 all Europe lay at the mercy of the three powers ·which had successfully and decisively defeated Germany. The Continent was disorganised and impoverished; millions of refugees, or 'displaced persons', as they were known in the language of the Allied bureaucrats, had to be given some sort of shelter and nourishment. It took months for the foreign workers in Germany to find their way home; and some of those whose countries were now occupied by the Russians were reluctant to return. There were millions of prisoners of war in Allied hands: many of those in the Soviet Union did not return home for years. During the war the German government had moved Germans from other parts of Europe back into the Reich, and they had expelled Slavs from the areas, such as western Poland and the Sudetenland, which they had incorporated into Germany. Now the movement started in the reverse direction: many Germans in the east fled from the oncoming Russian armies, while the German inhabitants of Czechoslovakia and of the provinces now allocated to Poland were expelled *en masse*, and western Germany had to cope with some ten to twelve million refugees. After the First World War the attempts made to secure the rights of national minorities had broken down: after the Second World War a more brutal solution was adopted, which ensured that in many of the disputed areas there were no more national minorities.

In the course of the war decisions had been taken by the Americans, British and Russians which to a large extent determined the territorial and political structure of post-war Europe. Moreover, as the war went on, the balance between the Allied powers shifted, with Britain becoming the weakest of the three, lacking both the immense economic resources of the Americans and the massive military power of the Russians. Britain's economic dependence on the United States had already been foreshadowed in the First World War. In 1916 Maynard Keynes, at that time serving in the British Treasury, noted 'It is hardly an exaggeration to say that, in a few months time, the American executive and the American public will be in a position to dictate to this country in matters that affect us more nearly than them.'[1] If this had in fact been an exaggeration in and after the First World War, it was certainly true by the end of the Second World War, and the 'special relationship' which successive British governments claimed to have with the United States was one of economic dependence as well as of political cooperation. By the end of the war, Britain's resources of manpower and her productive capacity had been mobilised to the limit, so that inevitably the Americans had to take over a larger share in financing and supplying the joint war effort. The result was an increase of American influence within the alliance, although this was not always immediately apparent, because of the contribution which Britain had already made, and because of the immense prestige and dominant personality of Winston Churchill. In spite of disagreements about strategy, however, and in spite of the increasing weight of American economic power, relations between the British and Americans were comparatively smooth. There was a real integration of strategic planning through the combined Chiefs of Staff in Washington, and General Eisenhower's headquarters, which ran the invasion of Europe, was a genuinely Anglo-American organisation.

With the Russians, however, no comparable closeness of collaboration was ever achieved. The British government in June 1941 immediately greeted the Russians as allies: 'Any man or state who fights on against Nazidom will have our aid,' Churchill said on the radio on 22 June 1941,[2] although in private he was more cynical: 'If Hitler invaded Hell I would make at least a favourable reference to the Devil in the House of Commons.'[3] Even before the United States entered the war, Roosevelt had begun to send supplies to Russia, and until the end of the war the Soviet Union received a substantial amount of aid under the lend-lease programme, the abrupt cancellation of which in May 1945, was one of the earliest signs of the deterioration of Soviet-American relations. (According to American sources, the USSR received a total of 9.1 billions of dollars' worth of aid in all, while the United Kingdom received 13.5 billion.)[4] Stalin, however, soon made it clear that economic aid was not enough, and during 1942 and 1943 relations between the Western Allies and the Soviet Union were largely concerned with Russian demands for the opening of a Second Front. The Russians were suspicious that the delay was due to a desire to see the Soviet Union weakened by the German assault, and the charge has been repeated by some American critics of United States foreign policy in the 1960s, but there were, as we have seen, good military reasons for postponing the invasion until success was reasonably certain. However, even when the Second Front had been created and the western and Russian armies were advancing on Germany, there was no real military coordination of plans. The Russians refused, for example, to allow the United States Air Force to use airfields in Hungary when bombing targets in central Europe. Such decisions as had to be taken were nearly always the result of direct communications at summit meetings between the heads of

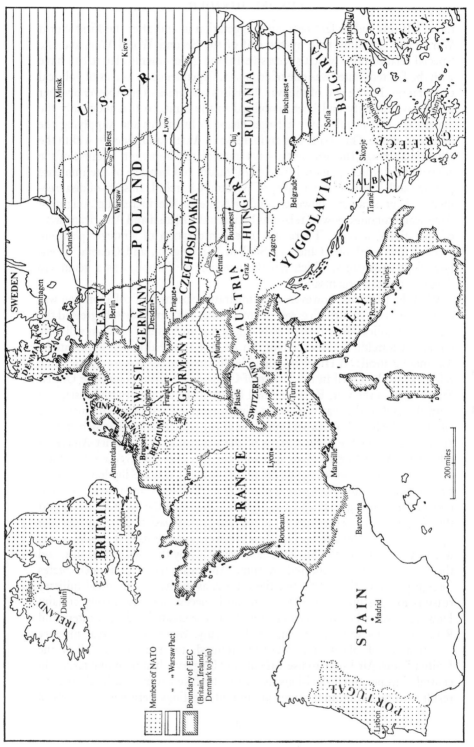

Europe in 1972

governments or their foreign ministers. And, as the war went on, these meetings revealed a growing discrepancy between Stalin's aims and those of the Anglo-Americans, in spite of the establishment of a certain ease and freedom of communication between Roosevelt, Churchill and 'Uncle Joe', a nickname symbolic perhaps of the wish of the British and American public to reduce to an acceptable stature the figure of the ruthless Russian dictator.

In August 1941, before America had entered the war, Churchill and Roosevelt met at sea off the coast of Newfoundland and drew up a document known as the Atlantic Charter, a general statement of liberal principles on which a post-war international settlement might be based. It was a declaration intended for the public in both countries, and it carefully avoided any specific commitments of the kind which had caused so much subsequent embarrassment in President Wilson's Fourteen Points. The two governments said that their countries sought 'no aggrandisement, territorial or other'; that they respected 'the right of all peoples to choose the form of government under which they will live'. And they expressed the hope that 'sovereign rights and self-government may be restored to those from whom it has been forcibly removed'. They looked forward to economic cooperation and to the free access for all countries to the raw materials of the world. They also spoke, deliberately somewhat vaguely – for the President knew that anything which seemed to recall the League of Nations would receive little support from the American public – of the establishment of a 'wider and permanent system of general security'.[5] On 1 January 1942, with America now at war, these principles were embodied in a Declaration of the United Nations which all the governments at war with Germany signed.

The application of the Atlantic Charter was to prove difficult, since the Soviet Union, although it subscribed to it on paper, interpreted its vague phrasing in quite a different way from the Americans and British. The Soviet Union not only played the biggest part in the fighting against Germany on land; it was also by the end of the war in occupation of most of Eastern Europe, and in a position to impose its own ideas about the post-war settlement. As Molotov said in January 1945, 'It was not necessary for the Soviet Union to conclude an armistice with Hungary since the Red Army was practically master of that country. It could do what it wished.'[6] While the war was actually going on, the differences between the three powers could be overlooked in the interest of defeating Germany, or, as in the meetings between Churchill, Roosevelt and Stalin at Teheran at the end of November 1943 and at Yalta in the Crimea in February 1945, postponed or muffled in an atmosphere of cordiality, and in agreements to which each side attached a different meaning, such as that at Yalta to hold free elections in the liberated countries.

As the war went on, and as the military advance posed immediate political problems about the systems of government and the future control of the territories from which the Germans had been driven out, the differences between the Soviet Union and its Western allies became more acute. The Russians were understandably extremely suspicious at anything which looked like an attempt at separate negotiations with any of their enemies. They resented their exclusion from the armistice negotiations with Italy in September 1943, though they were kept generally informed about them; and they were quick to use the precedent of Italy for excluding the Western Allies from any say in the administration of Roumania, Bulgaria and Hungary in 1945. Again, they were furious when in March 1945 they thought they might be left out of the first contacts in Switzerland between the Western Allies and representatives of the German High Command in Italy, which eventually led to the surrender of the German armies on the Italian front. They accused the Americans and British of making an agreement 'on the basis of which', in Stalin's words to Roosevelt, 'the German Commander on the Western Front ... has agreed to open the Front and permit the Anglo-American troops to advance to the east, and the Anglo-Americans have promised in return to ease for the Germans the peace terms'.[7] There was no basis for this latter assumption, since Britain and America were fully committed to the principle of unconditional surrender, though there were among the Allied leaders some, including Churchill, who were anxious for the Anglo-American armies to reach central Europe before the Russians, but it is typical of the growing mutual suspicions and of the increasing concern with the balance of power in Europe at the end of the war which both the Anglo-Americans and the Russians were showing by the spring of 1945.

The test case in relations between Russia and the West came over Poland. While Roosevelt and Churchill had accepted the fact that Russia was not going to give up the Baltic states, that she was going to insist on the annexation of some Finnish territory and that she was hoping to absorb part of the German province of East Prussia, they were increasingly worried about Russian intentions in Poland. The British had after all gone to war in 1939 ostensibly to defend Poland, while Roosevelt, with a presidential election, at which he was running for his third term, due in November 1944, was very conscious of the Polish-American voters. On the other hand they both realised that the intransigent insistence of the Polish government-in-exile on retaining the Polish eastern frontier as established after the Russo-Polish War in 1920 (see p. 247 above) was unrealistic, and might jeopardise not only immediate relations with the Soviet Union but also Soviet support for the establishment of the proposed United Nations Organisation.

The Russians had occupied eastern Poland in September 1939 and they were determined to keep it, in spite of the British government's declaration on 30 August 1941 that they 'do not recognise any territorial changes which have been effected in Poland since August 1939'.[8] No agreement had been reached between the Russian government and the Polish government-in-exile by the spring of 1943, when the situation between the two governments became even more difficult. In April 1943 the Soviet government refused to recognise the Polish government in London any longer and announced the establishment in the Soviet Union of a 'Union of Polish Patriots'. The immediate cause of the breach was an episode which illustrates the terrible situation in which the Poles found themselves as the result of the double occupation of their unfortunate country by the Germans and the Russians. The Germans had announced that they had found in the Katyn forest, in the part of Poland occupied by the Soviet Union until the German invasion, mass graves containing the bodies of thousands of Polish officers, murdered by the Russians. The Polish government, which had been unable to discover the fate of many former officers, accepted this report – and most subsequent Western historians have agreed with them – and asked the International Red Cross to investigate, a request which arrived simultaneously with a German demand for a Red Cross enquiry. The Russians immediately denied the charges as a fabrication by German propagandists, and accused the Polish government of collaborating with the Germans. Thus to the dispute between the Soviet government and the Polish government in London about the future Russo-Polish frontier was added a dispute about the credentials of the Polish government itself.

At the Teheran conference in November 1943 Churchill and Roosevelt accepted in effect, though without going into details, that the Russians should retain the eastern part of Poland and that the Polish state should, so to speak, be moved westwards and compensated with German territory up to the river Oder. Russian help would be necessary if the Poles were to take over and retain this area, and Polish dependence on the Soviet Union all the greater. By July 1944 the Red army had occupied a large part of eastern Poland and the question of Poland's future became even more acute. The Polish Committee in the Soviet Union moved to the Polish city of Lublin and was entrusted with the administration of the areas conquered by the Red army, while the Russians consistently decried the activities of the London controlled Polish Resistance. At the same time the British and American governments were urging the London Poles to reach agreement with the Russians and with the Russian-inspired Polish committee. Late in July 1944 the Polish Prime Minister Stanislaw Mikolajczyk went to Moscow to make the attempt. While he was there the Polish Resistance started on 1 August 1944 a major insurrection against the German occupiers in Warsaw. They hoped to speed the liberation of the city, in the expectation that the Red army, by now only a few miles away, would soon enter the capital; and at the same time they believed that, if the Home Army, loyal as it was to the Polish government in London, were in control of Warsaw when the Red army arrived, they would be in a much stronger position to negotiate with the Russians and their Polish protégés.

In fact the rising ended in defeat and tragedy after more than two months of bitter fighting. The Russian advance on Warsaw was halted. Whether this was for valid military reasons or in the hope of seeing the Home Army crushed and discredited is still argued among historians. It is certain however that the Russians expressed nothing but contempt for the non-Communist Resistance and that they refused repeated requests from the Western Allies for permission for their planes, attempting without much success to fly from their distant bases in Italy to drop supplies to Warsaw, to land on Soviet airfields.

This tragic episode, which cost thousands of Polish lives and led to the deportation of some 350,000 Poles to Germany, as well as leaving the city of Warsaw in ruins by the time the Red army finally reached it, demonstrated clearly the limits of British and American power in Eastern Europe. It also increased the pressure which the British and United States governments were applying on Mikolajczyk to be realistic and to accept Russian demands about the frontier in the hope of retaining for his government some say in the eventual determination of the new Polish regime. Churchill visited Moscow in October 1944 and suggested that Mikolajczyk should also come, and in the discussions there showed himself almost more categorical than Stalin in his insistence that the Poles should accept the Russian demands, telling the Polish Prime Minister that the Poles were trying to start another European war which would cost twenty-five million lives. The question took up a great deal of time at the summit conference at Yalta in February 1945 and was carried over to later meetings at San Francisco in April and Potsdam in July. The cession of Poland's eastern territories and the acquisition of the German provinces in the west was approved in principle, though the British and Americans insisted that the final delimitation of the frontier should await a peace conference: and it was agreed that a 'Provisional Government of National Unity' should be formed. In the event, when such a government was created in June 1945, with Mikolajczyk, who had resigned from the London Polish government, as Deputy Prime Minister, the key posts were already in the hands of the Communists, although Mikolajczyk may well have hoped that the strength of his supporters in the Peasant Party would be sufficient to redress the balance when elections came to be held. However, less than two years later elections organised under Communist direction gave the Communists an overwhelming majority, and Mikolajczyk's Peasant Party was heavily defeated. Mikolajczyk resigned and went into exile once more. By 1948 Poland was a Communist state.

The Polish story was particularly humiliating for the Western Allies because of their original commitment to Poland and because of the substantial help which the Polish armies and air force had given, especially in the Italian campaign. But the Soviet leaders had made it equally clear elsewhere in Eastern Europe by the end of the war that they were not going to tolerate any Western interference in areas which they regarded as their legitimate sphere of influence. Churchill indeed at times seems to have been prepared to accept this. For him the important thing was that such spheres of influence should be clearly defined. When he was in Moscow in October 1944, he said to Stalin, as he reports in his memoirs,[9]

> Let us settle about our affairs in the Balkans. Your armies are in Roumania and Bulgaria. We have interests, missions, and agents there. Don't let us get at cross-purposes in small ways. So far as Britain and Russia are concerned, how would it do for you to have ninety per cent predominance in Roumania, for us to have ninety per cent of the say in Greece, and go fifty-fifty about Yugoslavia?

He added, jotting down his proposals on a half sheet of notepaper, a fifty-fifty share in Hungary and a 75 per cent Russian share in Bulgaria. Churchill says that this was intended to deal with 'immediate wartime arrangements' and would be subject to revision in a final peace settlement, but such an agreement was bound to affect the longer-term post-war situation. Certainly the understanding soon had practical results, though Churchill had been optimistic if he really expected the Russians to give the West a half share in Hungary and a quarter share in Bulgaria. The British and Americans found themselves squeezed out of their share in the Allied Control Commissions which were supposed to take over the responsibility for these countries after surrender, and Russian influence remained wholly dominant there. On the other hand, the Russians stuck to the agreement as far as Greece was concerned, and did not protest or interfere directly when the British gave active support to the Greek royalist government in their civil war against the Communists between 1947 and 1949.

These war-time decisions started the division of Europe which has lasted ever since. They were decisions based on a realistic assessment of the limits of Western power and of the strength of the Russian position. The disillusionment to which they gave rise came about because there were many people in Britain and America, including perhaps President Roosevelt himself, who thought that Soviet and Western ideas about democratic constitutional development could be compatible and that cooperation between the great powers could be carried over from war to peace-time. In the last months of the war, however, there were areas of Europe where the situation was still fluid. For this reason, as the war drew to an end, Churchill was constantly pressing for a rapid advance to capture the key cities of central Europe – Vienna, Prague, Berlin – before the Russians could get there, though in fact he was deflected by military arguments, especially by General Eisenhower, from putting these plans into operation. By April 1945 the Russians were in occupation of Vienna, where they had installed a government under the aged Social Democrat Karl Renner (who had filled the same post on the establishment of the Austrian Republic in 1918), with a Communist Minister of the

Interior. In Prague, partly as a result of Beneš's belief that the future of Czechoslovakia depended more on Russia than on the West, the Communists held eight posts in a coalition government. The future of these two countries was still not settled, although it was agreed that Russia, the United States, Britain and France should all share in the occupation of Austria. But the main problem which the three allies now had to face and the real test of their policies towards each other was Germany.

At the beginning of the war the British government had declared that it was not fighting against the German people, but only against the Nazis. With the spread of German power and the experience of German air attack, bitterness against the Germans grew, and British intentions towards post-war Germany became more severe. Accordingly, after the invasion of Russia it was comparatively easy to reach agreement with Stalin on the general way in which Germany should be treated after the war. Germany must be disarmed and demilitarised, and the Nazis must be removed. Stalin was obsessed with the fear of a German revival, and was even more determined than the French had been at the end of the First World War to ensure that the Germans should not be capable of military recovery. Thus, when the British Foreign Secretary Anthony Eden visited Moscow in December 1941, he raised no objection to the Russian proposal to detach the Rhineland, Bavaria and East Prussia from the rest of Germany, and positively supported the restoration of Austrian independence. From then on the dismemberment of Germany in one form or another became one of the Allied war aims, at least until they were actually in a position to carry it out.

President Roosevelt was also enthusiastic about the idea of breaking up Germany, though not all his advisers were. Both he and Churchill believed, as Edward Grey had in 1914, that 'Prussian militarism' was one of the main causes of the war, and that there might now be a chance of removing Prussia from the map of Europe, overlooking, perhaps, the fact that Hitler and indeed many of his ideas were Austrian in origin and that the Nazi movement had first developed in Bavaria while it was members of the old Prussian military caste who led the nearly successful attempt to overthrow Hitler on 20 July 1944. As early as September 1941 Stalin had also raised the question of reparations. This was not a matter in which the Americans had any very direct interest, and the British, remembering the endless difficulties caused by the exaction of reparations after 1919, were able to agree with the Russians that this time reparations from Germany should be paid in kind rather than in cash. There was also agreement that after the unconditional surrender of Germany an Allied Control Commission, composed of representatives of the three powers, should take over the administration of the country.

By the end of 1943 therefore, when the summit conference met at Teheran, it was easy to reach agreement on these general lines, but there was still no final decision as to what form the dismemberment of Germany should take or just how the Allied occupation should be organised. In September 1944 at an Anglo-American meeting in Quebec the Americans proposed, and Churchill accepted, an extremely drastic plan for Germany, originally devised by the Secretary of the Treasury, Henry Morgenthau Jr. This plan, in addition to detaching German territory and giving it to Poland, the Soviet Union, France and Denmark and then dividing the rump of Germany into two states, one in the north, one in the south, proposed what Churchill called the 'pastoralisation' of Germany – the destruction of all its heavy industry and its conversion into a primarily agricultural country. This extreme proposal was soon abandoned when the members of the two governments and their advisers considered its practical implications, and the danger of having a discontented rural slum in the middle of Europe which would affect the whole European economy. The Morgenthau Plan marks the extreme point in the Anglo-American belief in a punitive peace which would lead to the permanent crippling of Germany, and none of the subsequent suggestions, to say nothing of the actual treatment of Germany under the occupation, went nearly as far.

The decision about zones of occupation was finally approved at the Yalta Conference. The main discussion had been between the British and Americans as to who should have the north-west and who the south-west zones. It was accepted – and there was no alternative – that the Russians should occupy eastern Germany, and it was finally agreed that the British should be assigned the north-west zone and the Americans the south-west. Berlin was to be occupied by all three powers, although the details of access to it for the British and Americans across the Russian zone were left rather vague, with serious consequences later when relations between Russia and the Western powers deteriorated. These occupation zones were envisaged as temporary military dispositions, pending a decision about the way in which Germany should be dismembered, but they ended up by determining the pattern for that dismemberment.

These discussions about the future of Germany had as one consequence a discussion about the future place of France in Europe, both because of de Gaulle's insistence on having a say, and because the French army as reconstituted after the liberation could provide a force which might help in the control and demilitarisation of Germany, especially since Roosevelt realised that the United States government would be under great pressure to withdraw American troops from Europe as soon as the war there was over. In spite of American reluctance to recognise de Gaulle's authority in France, the events of the liberation had forced them to accept him. De Gaulle had landed in France in June 1944 in a mood of rage against the Allies. He had been furious at being subjected to the ban on all communications between Britain and the outside world which was imposed for the sake of security in the days preceding the invasion, and which delayed messages between the Free French in London and in Algiers. He had been deeply offended because the bank notes printed by the Allies for use in France did not bear the name of France or refer to the *République Française*. However the activity in these weeks of the French Resistance, now called the French Forces of the Interior and conducting a vigorous campaign of sabotage of German installations and communications, as well as the contribution made in the campaign by the regular divisions of the French army and by the French civilians to the administration of liberated territory, all showed the backing which de Gaulle undoubtedly had. His triumphal entry into Paris on 25 August 1944, with German and collaborationist snipers still firing from the roof-tops and from the gallery of the cathedral of Notre Dame, where he went for a solemn thanksgiving on the next day, demonstrated that he was the undoubted leader of France. The first year after the liberation was what one historian of France has called 'a dictatorship by consent'.[10] As a result of the obvious strength of its position and the support which it commanded, in October 1944 the French Committee of National Liberation was recognised by Britain, the United States and the USSR as the provisional government of the French Republic.

De Gaulle was very anxious to obtain for France equality of status with the other Allies. He was not invited to Yalta or to the summit conference at Potsdam in July 1945, and, although in one of those gestures of diplomatic independence he was always fond of making, he went to Moscow in December 1944 and signed a Franco-Soviet treaty of alliance, he failed to win Stalin's backing for his demands to annex German territory west of the Rhine, while Stalin failed to persuade him to recognise the Polish Lublin government. At Yalta, in the absence of the French, Churchill had proposed the allocation of an occupation zone in Germany to France, and a seat on the Control Commission. Stalin agreed to this provided that the French zone was taken from the areas allotted to Britain and the United States. Thus, on the German surrender, the French army moved into an area of west Germany, and French representatives took their place on the Control Commission, remaining firm advocates of the idea of dismembering Germany, even after this had been abandoned by the other Allies.

The Allied leaders had to produce some plan for Germany when they met in July 1945 at Potsdam, the former royal and military headquarters of the vanished state of Prussia, since they were now in total control of the country and had not encountered the fanatical popular resistance which they had expected. The United States was now represented by Harry S. Truman, who had succeeded as President in April 1945 on the death of Roosevelt; and during the conference itself a general election in Britain overthrew Churchill, so that his place was taken by the leader of the Labour Party Clement Attlee. The Americans came to Potsdam with the knowledge that at any moment they would learn of the explosion of the first experimental atomic bomb in the desert of New Mexico. The news was in fact brought to Truman on the day before the formal opening of the conference, and he received a full report five days later, as well as an assurance that the bomb could be used against Japan within the next few weeks. There had been some delay in arranging the Potsdam meeting and some writers believe that Truman had deliberately postponed it because he was waiting for the result of the atom bomb test, in order to strengthen his hand in negotiating with Stalin, at a time when United States relations with the USSR were clearly going to be more and more difficult, and when the USA might have to face the problems which would arise if the Russians intervened in the war against Japan, as they clearly had every intention of doing.[11] Truman himself maintained that he needed the time to become familiar with problems which as Vice-President he had not had occasion to study, as well as to prepare the budget; and he was also perhaps awaiting the result of a direct approach to Stalin by a special envoy, Harry Hopkins, whom he had sent to Moscow in May. It is certain that, although Stalin did not appear to react strongly to the news of the atom bomb explosion when he was finally, after some hesitation, informed about it, the possession of this new weapon, the effects of which were seen at Hiroshima and Nagasaki on 6 and 9 August 1945, was thenceforth never far from the minds of the American, and doubtless of the Russian, leaders.

The agenda of the Potsdam Conference was a wide one, dealing with Poland, the settlement with the former German satellites and the question of Russia's entry into the war against Japan, but it was the German question which demanded the most immediate and far-reaching decisions. With the assumption of responsibility for the day-to-day running of Germany and for its future, all the Allies had had second thoughts about breaking up the German state. Churchill was worried by the potential growth of Russian influence: 'I hardly like to consider dismembering Germany until my doubts about Russian intentions have been cleared away,' he said in March 1945.[12] And in May he wrote – coining a phrase which has since become a commonplace – that 'an iron curtain is drawn down upon their front. We do not know what is going on behind.'[13]

Stalin too had changed his mind, and declared on 8 May 1945 that 'the Soviet Union does not wish to dismember and destroy Germany'.[14] He was determined to exact reparations from Germany, and especially from the industrial area of the Ruhr, now in the British zone, and he may also well have hoped that he might succeed in establishing a permanent influence over a united Germany. In spite of the hatred and fear which the invading Red army had inspired among the Germans, the Russians were busily looking for German support. Leading members of the pre-1933 German Communist Party, including Wilhelm Pieck and Walther Ulbricht, had been flown back from their exile in Moscow as soon as the occupation started, and in June

1945 the Russians had authorised 'the formation and activity of all anti-fascist parties having as their aim the final extirpation of all remnants of fascism and the consolidation of the foundation of democracy and civil liberties in Germany'.[15] The Communists were active in reminding the Social Democrats of the damage caused to the German working class by the division between the two parties at the time of the rise of the Nazis, and in April 1946 a new Socialist Unity Party was founded in the Soviet zone. In the western zones, on the other hand, the British and Americans were committed to rebuilding local government from the bottom and did not at first permit the formation of political parties except on a limited and local base. The first free elections to be held in Germany since 1932 were local elections in the American zone in January 1946. In September and October the Russians organised and managed local elections in their zone in which the Socialist Unity Party won and in November 1946 all local administration in the eastern zone was handed over to Germans. The political and ideological division between the two halves of Germany was becoming firmly established within eighteen months of the Potsdam agreement that there should be 'uniformity of treatment of the German population throughout Germany'.[16]

The Americans had rapidly withdrawn from the extreme punitive attitude towards Germany embodied in the Morgenthau Plan. By the time of the Potsdam meeting, the question of the immediate future of Germany could no longer be postponed, as Roosevelt had hoped in the last days of his life. While laying down, in the words of the directive to the United States Commander in Chief in Germany in April 1945, that 'It shall be brought home to the Germans that Germany's ruthless warfare and the fanatical Nazi resistance have destroyed the German economy and made chaos and suffering inevitable, and that the Germans cannot escape responsibility for what they have brought upon themselves,'[17] and forbidding, as the British also did, 'fraternisation' between their soldiers and the Germans, American policy tended to follow a different direction. This can be summed up in the advice which Henry L. Stimson, the Secretary for War, gave the President in May 1945: 'Punish . . . war criminals in full measure. Deprive [Germany] permanently of weapons, her General Staff and perhaps her entire army. Guard her governmental action until the Nazi educational generation has passed from the stage . . . but do not deprive her of the means of building up ultimately a contented Germany interested in following non-militaristic methods of civilisation.'[18] As things turned out, even this was to prove too radical a policy.

At Potsdam, therefore, it was agreed that the unity of Germany – or rather of the rest of Germany, after the Russians had incorporated part of East Prussia into the Soviet Union, and Poland had taken the area up to the line of the Oder and western Neisse rivers, including the port of Stettin west of the mouth of the Oder, and the industrial area of Silesia – should be preserved. This was a formidable loss to Germany of much undisputably German territory, and included 17 per cent of her previous industrial capacity. It was only with the greatest reluctance that the Western leaders, and especially Churchill, accepted a frontier well to the west of the one which had been accepted in principle at Yalta, but as in all questions affecting Poland there was nothing they could do.

As far as the rest of Germany was concerned, however, there was apparent agreement on the need for demilitarisation and denazification, for the restoration of local self-government and, although for the time being no central German government was to be established, for the setting up of central administrative departments. Above all the country was to be treated as a single economic unit. This still left the question of reparations, again agreed in general principle at Yalta, but not worked out in detail. In the final agreement the Russians were allowed to take 15 per cent of the industrial capital equipment in the western zones, while the Western powers renounced any reparations from east Germany. In fact the exaction of reparations from Germany, although it added in the short term to the difficulties of the German economy, turned out to be a brief if painful operation, for in 1946 the Americans ceased to allow any further dismantling for reparations purposes in their zone, leaving the Russians to draw what they could from east Germany.

The discussions of the question demonstrated the differences of approach between the Russians and the West. The Russians felt that, in quibbling about their demands, the British and Americans showed themselves more interested in German than in Russian recovery and were insensitive to the appalling damage which the Germans had done to the peoples of the Soviet Union. To the British and Americans, on the other hand, the Russians now seemed more interested in the consolidation of their own position than in any general European settlement. For all the apparent agreement on the maintenance of German unity and on 'the eventual reconstruction of their [the German people's] life in a democratic and peaceful Germany', Allied aims in Germany were farther apart than ever before. From 1945 on the German question became a central issue in the 'Cold War' – a phrase first used in 1947 in a speech by the American statesman Bernard M.Baruch. Within three years of the Potsdam agreement the economic division of Germany was complete; and by October 1949 two separate states had been formally set up. It was not only Hitler's Third Reich which came to an end in 1945; it was also the Germany established by Bismarck in 1871.

The experience of occupation, collaboration and resistance had led many Europeans to think about social and political problems in a new way, and to hope for a new order in Europe which would be a reality and not the sham which Hitler's new order had been even for those people who had placed their hopes in it. In a few of the occupied countries – Norway, Denmark, the Netherlands – the old political and social structure was restored with little change once the collaborators had been punished. But elsewhere there were revolutionary changes, even if these sometimes did not go far enough to satisfy the more idealistic members of the resistance. In Spain and Portugal alone little seemed to have changed as a result of the war. Spain had succeeded in obtaining supplies first from Germany and then from the United States as the price for neutrality. The end of the war was followed by a period of great economic hardship. Nevertheless Franco's authoritarian regime seemed as firmly established as ever, to the disappointment of those liberals and socialists in Western Europe who continued for some years to express their disapproval, and to the still more bitter chagrin of the many Spanish Republican exiles who had hoped that the end of the fascist dictatorships in Germany and Italy would somehow inevitably entail the fall of Franco.

It was in Eastern Europe that the post-war revolution was most complete and the effects most profound. This was, except in the case of Yugoslavia, less because the local communist parties themselves made revolutions than because the Russians were at the end of the war in a position to impose changes in the political, social and economic systems and to ensure the external and internal security of the Soviet Union by controlling the foreign and domestic policies of their neighbours. By the end of 1948 Poland, Hungary, Roumania, Bulgaria, Czechoslovakia and eastern Germany were all more or less securely under communist control. In September 1947 an international communist 'information bureau', the Cominform, was founded, as a rather less imposing successor to the Comintern, which Stalin had dissolved in 1943 as a gesture to his Western allies.

However, there were limits to the expansion of Russian influence. The Communists were defeated in a bitter civil war in Greece, largely because Stalin, in accordance with his 1944 agreement with Churchill (see p. 429 above) refrained from intervening. Above all Stalin had failed to maintain control over the Communist Party of Yugoslavia, where Tito had fought a successful guerrilla war against the Germans and had, with material assistance from the British and Americans, virtually liberated his country before the arrival of the Red army. In the years immediately after the war the Russians criticised Tito's economic policies, his insistence on developing an indigenous Yugoslav industry and his refusal completely to abolish the private property of the peasants and to enforce total collectivisation on the Russian model. The Russians disliked, too, Tito's initiative in foreign policy, his attempts to establish independent relations with his neighbours, and his proposal to form a Balkan league. These differences however were perhaps a pretext for Russian pressure on Tito rather than its cause, since Stalin jealously and suspiciously resented Tito's independence and his previous contacts with the British, as well as his refusal to accept total Russian control of all aspects of

436

Yugoslav life. Although Tito tried to preserve good relations in spite of this, Yugoslavia was expelled from the Cominform in June 1948. In spite of the disillusionment caused by the hardship of life in Yugoslavia after the war and rigorous control by the secret police, Tito's support inside the Yugoslav Communist Party was still unassailable, and his determination that Yugoslavia should solve her problems without interference from outside was widely admired by non-communists as well as by nearly all members of the party. The Russians, having failed to find anyone more pliable to replace him, had to face the fact that, unless they were prepared to invade Yugoslavia and install a government of their choice by force of arms (as they were to do in Hungary in 1956 and in Czechoslovakia in 1968), there was nothing they could do. Since such intervention might well have provoked intervention by the British and Americans, Stalin still hoped to force Yugoslavia to change her course by political intrigues and economic pressure. He was unsuccessful; and there was now a state which was undoubtedly communist but which did not accept Russian control.

Two countries which had seemed in danger of coming under Russian control at the end of the war succeeded in remaining outside the Soviet system: Finland and Austria. In Finland, which was not occupied by the Red army and where the Communists in the coalition government failed in 1948 to take over power, the Russians had to be content with some additions to the territory annexed in 1940, and the lease of a naval base which was evacuated in 1955 as a result of the reassessment of Soviet foreign policy which took place after Stalin's death in 1953. In the absence of a strong Communist Party, and faced with a Social Democratic Party determined to maintain its independence both from the Finnish Communists and from the Soviet Union, as well as with a national will for independence, the strength of which the Russians had experienced in the 'Winter War' of 1939-40, the Soviet government was prepared to settle for an independent but neutral Finland.

All the Allies had agreed during the war to the reestablishment of an independent Austria: and the Russians had hastened, without previous consultation with the British and Americans, to establish and recognise an Austrian government (see p. 429 above). However, the country was occupied by the Americans, British and French as well as by the Russians, and when elections were held in November 1945 the Communists only won five per cent of the votes. A government was formed in which the Communists held one post, and which was in effect a coalition between the People's Party (successors to the Christian Social Party of the period before 1938) and the Social Democrats. The two parties, which had been bitter rivals between the wars, now realised that, in a situation where their electoral support was almost equal, they had more to gain by cooperating than by quarrelling about the past and about basic political doctrines.

There had been long delays in reaching agreement on a final treaty establishing the new state, partly because the Russians were reluctant to relinquish the economic control which military occupation gave them and also because occupation of Austria carried with it the right to garrison troops in Hungary to ensure communications with the Russian zone of Austria. The Russians claimed as reparations those industrial installations which they were able to classify as 'German assets' and continued to take their products, including oil, for their own use. It was only in 1955, again in the changed international atmosphere after Stalin's death, that a treaty with Austria was finally signed and Russian troops withdrawn. It was by then finally clear that there was no chance of the Austrian Communist Party taking over the government; and the link between the occupation of Austria and that of Hungary had now been replaced by direct ties between the Soviet Union and the Communist government in Budapest, which allowed Russian troops to remain in Hungary as allies. Accordingly, as in Finland, the Soviet government was prepared to accept a genuinely independent Austria provided – and this was explicitly written into the treaty – it remained permanently neutral.

The change in Austria's position since 1938 had been a substantial one. Government from Berlin between 1938 and 1945 had created for the first time since 1918 a genuine sense of Austrian nationality. The union with Germany – particularly with the divided and impoverished Germany of the immediate post-war years – had lost its attractions. Moreover, the discovery of oil in eastern Austria and German development of heavy industry as part of their programme of removing factories out of range of Allied bombers, had transformed the Austrian economy and, with a rapidly recovering tourist industry, laid the basis for the economic stability which had been denied to the First Republic.

Austria, Finland, Yugoslavia and Greece were the only countries of Eastern Europe to escape Soviet domination. Elsewhere it was firmly established by the end of 1948. Many people had felt the need for a social and economic revolution and for an end to the power of the old ruling class, and especially of the landowners, but few of them were communists or wanted a communist revolution. For them a revolution meant land reform and the establishment of an independent peasantry, with higher wages and better conditions for the industrial workers. Indeed, in the first stages after the arrival of the Red army, the Soviet government made a point, as they had in their policy towards Italy, of encouraging the formation of popular fronts and coalition governments, and they had appeared to give way to Western pressure in favour of holding free elections. In Hungary this policy proved embarrassing to them. A provisional government, set up in December 1944 and composed of former supporters of Horthy with some members of the Smallholder's (peasant) Party and two Communists, enacted under the direction of the Communist Minister of Agriculture a far-reaching agrarian reform, and then in November 1945 held elections which turned out to be a victory for the Smallholders' Party, associated in the minds of the electors with the idea of land reform. Although the Smallholders, who had won sixty per cent of the seats, were given half the posts in the new government, the Russian head of the Control Commission which, under the agreement between the Allies, had the right to supervise Hungarian affairs, insisted that a Communist, Mátyas Rákosi, a veteran of the 1919 Hungarian Soviet republic, should be a deputy prime minister, together with a leading socialist committed to collaboration with the Communists. A Communist was also given the post of Minister of the Interior. During the next two years the Smallholders' Party was under increasing Communist attack and in 1947 members of the party were accused by the Security Police – an organ of the Communist Minister of the Interior – of conspiracy and espionage. The Prime Minister went to Switzerland for a cure and did not return, and Rákosi became, in fact if not in name, the undisputed holder of power, even if the pretence of a coalition was maintained a few months longer. Among the tragic victims of these events was Michael Károlyi, the leader of the liberal revolution in 1918 (see pp. 247-8 above), who had returned to Hungary from twenty-six years of exile and had been appointed Ambassador in Paris, only to be obliged to resign in 1949 in protest against the purges, so that he ended his days in exile once more, a sad symbol of the fate of genuine liberals in Eastern Europe.

In Bulgaria elections were also held in November 1945 and the British and American representatives in the country protested without effect against communist intimidation in the election campaign, and reported that the votes had been fraudulently counted. Within a year a referendum was held abolishing the monarchy and establishing Bulgaria as a 'People's Republic', the name now given to the communist regimes of Eastern Europe. There was in Bulgaria an old revolutionary tradition, and there had been an active Communist party as well as a radical peasant movement in the 1920s; and the Communist regime, under a veteran of the old Comintern, Georgi Dimitrov, who in 1933 had been charged by the Nazis with responsibility for the Reichstag fire (see p. 338 above), seemed to be as strongly based there as anywhere in Europe. In Roumania, the pattern was similar, though the process of establishing a communist state took rather longer. King Michael was forced to abdicate after an uneasy two years of coalition government, and Roumania was proclaimed a People's Republic, in spite of the fact that the Communist Party had been in a minority and that here, as in Hungary, the impetus behind the land reform carried out in 1945 came from the radical agrarian 'Ploughman's Front'.

These were all countries which, however reluctantly, Britain and the United States recognised as lying within the Soviet sphere of influence. Hungary, Roumania and Bulgaria had all fought on Germany's side, so that by 1945 Churchill, though not all his colleagues, 'had never felt that', as he wrote later, 'our relations with Roumania and Bulgaria in the past called for any special sacrifices from us'.[19] Poland and Czechoslovakia were another matter. We have already seen (see p. 426-8 above) how the Polish question became in the eyes of the British and Americans a test case in their relations with the Soviet Union, since Poland was an ally to whom Britain had been committed since 1939. The British also felt under a special obligation to Czechoslovakia, since the Czechs had been the victims of British and French policy in 1938, and Beneš and the Czechoslovak government and army in exile had fought loyally on the Allied side, so that the British felt emotions of both guilt and gratitude towards them.

In Poland the Western Allies had been forced to accept an arrangement by which the Russians agreed to a few Polish politicians from among the exiles, and a few from inside Poland not already in the government, becoming ministers in a predominantly Communist government. When the elections were finally held in January 1947 under the auspices of a Communist Minister of Public Security and a Communist Minister of 'Regained Territories', who had made sure that the settlers in the newly acquired lands from which the Germans had been expelled were loyal Communist voters, and that the new provinces received a disproportionately large number of seats, the Communists and their socialist allies won a large majority. Many members of the old ruling class had been liquidated by the Germans and Russians between 1939 and 1944; many officers of the Home Army had been arrested by the Soviet authorities – some of their leaders after accepting an invitation to discussions at the Russian army headquarters; many remained in exile. Of the old forces in Polish life, only the Roman Catholic Church remained in being as an organised body, and continued to provide, under the skilful leadership of Cardinal Wyszynski, a centre of opposition and a rival focus of loyalty.

It was, however, the case of Czechoslovakia which caused the most alarm in the West. At first it seemed that the country might remain on good terms with the Soviet Union, while at the same time keeping a liberal democratic constitutional system. The Russian troops were withdrawn after a few months. President Beneš returned from exile in Britain. Indubitably free elections were held in May 1946, in which the Communist Party, which had been among the largest in Europe before 1938, won thirty-eight per cent of the votes. As a result a coalition was formed under a Communist Prime Minister and a Communist Minister of the Interior, but with a majority of non-communist members. The country's economy had suffered less from the war than that of most occupied countries, in spite of the problems caused by the expulsion of the Germans from the Sudetenland, an important industrial area. The government, even before the elections and the Communist success, had embarked on a programme of land reform and had started to nationalise industry. The Slovak question was still a difficult one, especially as many Slovaks had supported the autonomous Slovak state set up by the Germans and resented the decision to hang its former president as a traitor. Still there seemed to be real prospects for economic development and political stability, with Beneš as President and Jan Masaryk, the son of the republic's founder, as Foreign Minister, and it seemed possible that, as in France and Italy in the immediate post-war period, the Communists might show themselves prepared to work within the limits of a democratic, liberal multi-party system.

These hopes were destroyed in 1948. First the Russians made it clear that, if Czechoslovakia were to join in the plan for European economic recovery with American help, proposed by the United States Secretary of State General Marshall in June 1947 (see p. 452 below), this might be interpreted as a blow to the friendly relations between her and the Soviet Union, so that the government felt obliged to withdraw its acceptance of Marshall's invitation. Then it became clear that within the coalition government the Communists were strengthening their hold on the administration, and in particular were purging the police force to fill it with their own nominees. In protest against this, in February 1948 the members of the government, other than the Communists and their Socialist allies, resigned. The Communists and Socialists still had a majority in parliament, however, and, in an atmosphere of mounting tension, with massive demonstrations showing that the Communists did in fact command strong support in much of the country, President Beneš decided to accept a Communist-dominated government, and Jan Masaryk agreed to stay on as Foreign Minister. Within a few weeks however Masaryk was dead, having fallen from a window in his ministry in circumstances which are still obscure and which still leave it uncertain whether he killed himself or was murdered, or even, as has been maintained in Czechoslovakia, lost his balance accidentally. Beneš himself resigned a few months later, already very ill, and died soon afterwards. In Czechoslovakia, as in the rest of Eastern Europe, the Communists were in undisputed power, and, as events twenty years later were to show only too clearly, the Russians in undisputed control over them.

These revolutionary changes in Eastern Europe were profound and lasting, and it is as yet hard to strike a balance in assessing them. Land reform and industrialisation have transformed the economy of the area, but the strict bureaucratic control of the economic system and the demands and needs of the Soviet Union have inhibited economic growth. There have been repeated complaints about shortages, especially of consumer goods. On the other hand, many people would argue that the standard of living for the majority of the population is higher in most of these countries than it was before the war; and in any case a return to an economic system based on private capitalism and private ownership of land is not only very unlikely, but does not seem to be demanded even by those critical of the present regime. Even those who took part in movements of protest or revolt, in Poland and Hungary in 1956, in Czechoslovakia in 1968, attacked the methods used to run the planned socialist economy rather than the socialist economic system as such, and hoped to humanise communism rather than abolish it altogether.

As the economic structure of the communist one-party state was changed by industrialisation, so there have been pressures on the political structure to change too. As yet these have not had much effect, except in Yugoslavia, where there has been a genuine attempt at decentralisation and at granting administrative power in the factories to workers' councils as well as allowing the development of nearly autonomous state industrial corporations. These innovations have been possible there because, as we have seen, Tito succeeded in freeing the country from Soviet control so that it could find its own way to communism. The other communist countries have not shown the same degree of flexibility, or else, when they have tried to do so, this has been part of a general movement of reform, such as provoked Soviet intervention in Hungary in 1956 and Czechoslovakia in 1968. The Soviet rulers have been anxious to preserve political, economic and intellectual uniformity to reinforce the stability of communist party control in Russia itself and have been worried by any example anywhere in the communist world which might encourage criticism within the USSR itself.

In Eastern Europe the post-war revolution followed a pattern imposed by the Soviet Union in the conviction that both the internal security of the Soviet system and its external defence against a possible military revival of Germany and against American attempts to extend American influence and to fight communism, demanded the creation of a group of communist satellite states on Russia's western frontiers. But both in Eastern and Western Europe revolutionary change was also the result of the need for reconstruction after the appalling material damage caused by the war and of the need for political reform caused by the disruption in many countries of the old political system and the discrediting of the old political elites.

In Britain, where the political and administrative machinery had shown itself capable of considerable flexibility in mobilising the resources of the country, so that by 1945 there was a stronger and more centralised control of economic and social life than had ever been seen before, the experiences of bombing, of universal military and civil defence service as well as the sense of dangers survived in common, all contributed to a desire for social reform and for a new society which might embody some of the ideals of equality and social justice which had been much discussed during the war. Even before the end of the war plans had been laid by the government – a coalition between the Conservatives, Labour and the now tiny Liberal Party – for substantial changes after the war. They had accepted in 1943 most of the recommendations of a report prepared by a committee headed by Sir William Beveridge, in his earlier days a close friend of Sidney and Beatrice Webb, proposing a new system of universal social security, while in the following year they had passed a new Education Act, for which the Conservative R.A.Butler was mainly responsible, raising the school leaving age and substantially extending the range of free secondary education. These hopes of social change and social justice led to the victory of the Labour Party in the elections of July 1945 and to the defeat of Churchill, who, for all his immense prestige and personal popularity, belonged to the generation of pre-First World War politicians and was rightly thought by many of the electors to be out of sympathy with programmes of radical reform.

In practice the reforms introduced by the Labour Party between 1945 and 1951, when they were defeated by the Conservatives who then remained in power until 1964, were largely an extension on a much wider scale of the ideals of the welfare state first introduced forty years before by the Liberal government, of which Churchill had been a member. The aim was to provide a comprehensive system of social security 'from the cradle to the grave', which would protect everyone against the worst disasters caused by unemployment, illness or old age. Perhaps its most striking feature was the introduction of a national health service, which provided all medical and hospital services free. Other more specifically socialist measures included nationalisation of about a fifth of British industry, notably the coal mines, gas and electricity undertakings, and the railways (in the latter case bringing Britain into line with many European countries, such as Germany, where the railways had been owned by the state almost since they were first constructed).

What seemed at the time, and to some extent in fact was, a social revolution was nevertheless rapidly accepted by the Conservative Party and at least until 1970 successive Conservative governments in general adopted the principles of the welfare state and the use of heavy taxation to pay for social security, and for the most part did not return nationalised industries to private ownership. In practice both the Labour and the Conservative parties were faced with the same economic problems which limited their freedom of political manoeuvre, and both followed the advice of the same permanent officials in trying to deal with them, so that much of their political controversies had a certain air of unreality about them. Britain was confronted with a shortage of foreign currency and a chronic contrary balance of payments, and had great difficulty in exporting enough to earn foreign currency with which to pay for her imports. Nearly all British holdings of gold and dollars had had to be spent during the war, and much of the accumulated capital of what had in the nineteenth and early twentieth century been the world's greatest trading and banking centre had been used up. At the same time industrial growth after the war was never as fast as was hoped, partly perhaps because British industrial plant was by now often old-fashioned compared with that which for example was replacing the ruined equipment of Germany, partly because of the instincts of conservatives among both management and labour, who were slow to realise that Britain's industrial supremacy could no longer be taken for granted.

One of the most important results of this change in Britain's international economic position was increased dependence on the United States. With the end of the war the lend-lease programme, which had to a large extent solved Britain's supply problems and counteracted the exhaustion of her currency reserves and foreign assets, came to an end; and the British government had to negotiate a large dollar loan to launch the post-war economy. It was clear – and this was to remain a basic condition of the international monetary situation for more than twenty years – that the dollar was the currency in relation to which other currencies would be valued. For the British this was acknowledged by the devaluation of the pound sterling in 1949 and by the British refusal to allow the free conversion of sterling balances held in Britain into other currencies. Internationally the new organisations set up at the end of the war – the International Monetary Fund and the World Bank – also operated on the basis that the dollar, backed by the large stocks of gold in the vaults of Fort Knox, was now the basic world currency. The American loan helped to save the British economy and, as we shall see, from 1948 onwards American aid became the basis of the recovery of the rest of Western Europe.

The leaders of the British Labour Party had been members of the war-time coalition government, and their programme in 1945 was in part an implementation of plans made during the war, as well as making permanent the war-time machinery of central government planning and control. The economic difficulties of the late 1940s and early 1950s perhaps made the continuation of war-time controls – rationing of food and fuel, restrictions on imported goods – inevitable, but for the Labour Party this had the unfortunate effect of linking, in the minds of many electors, socialism with shortages and austerity.

Most of the other countries of Western Europe however did not have a comparable administrative structure on which to build, and had to face as well the total disruption and dislocation of their economic systems. This disruption gave hope to those who thought that it would now be possible to build a revolutionary new order, and that the dreams of a new world which had heartened many members of the Resistance might now be realised.

The effect of these hopes was to strengthen the Communist Parties in France and Italy. But they also helped to encourage the Catholics to develop new social ideas and new forms of political activity, notably by forming new parties, the Christian Democratic Union in Germany, the Christian Democrat Party in Italy and the *Mouvement Républicain Populaire* (MRP) in

France. Between 1945 and 1948, as the economic situation in Europe grew worse, the Communist Parties in France and Italy, with their resistance record to add to their revolutionary appeal, won an increasing number of supporters, and so had to face the old question of the role of a mass communist party within a democratic system. In France, where a Constituent Assembly to draft a new constitution was elected in November 1945, the Communists won a quarter of the votes and became the largest single party, and a year later, in the elections to the new National Assembly after the constitution of the Fourth Republic had finally been approved, raised their share of votes to twenty-eight per cent. For the first three years after the end of the war a Communist victory in France seemed a practical possibility.

In Italy too the Communists had won great influence in the struggle against the Germans after the Italian surrender in September 1943. By the end of the war they controlled the Committees of National Liberation in many important cities. As in France they had members in the first post-war governments and were working hard to create a united front with the socialists. Moreover, in Italy the socialists were at first mostly less suspicious of such cooperation than they were in France. In the municipal elections in the spring of 1946 – the first free elections in Italy since 1921 – they joined forces in many areas; and soon after, a general election in June 1946, held at the same time as a plebiscite which finally decided by a small majority that Italy should be a republic rather than a monarchy, gave the Socialists and Communists between them just under forty per cent of the votes, while the Christian Democrats won about thirty-five per cent. The result however was to start a series of splits in the Socialist Party, which had shown itself to be slightly stronger than the Communists. Some socialists believed that they could only hope to maintain their position by adhering to the doctrine of 'no enemies on the Left' and collaborating closely with the Communists, while others believed they were strong enough to dissociate themselves from the Communists. Over the next years fresh splits and regroupings among the socialists had the effect of leaving the Communists as the strongest mass working-class party, and its relations with the government and its attitude to the constitutional system still remain the central issue in Italian politics.

The rise of new Catholic parties in France and Italy meant that, for a few years in the case of France, and throughout the quarter of a century after the end of the war in the case of Italy, the main conflict seemed to be between these new mass Catholic movements and the Communists and such socialists as were prepared to vote with them. In Italy the fragmentation of the socialists and the fact that the Communists, though strong, were not indispensable to the formation of a parliamentary majority, meant that since 1947, when the government was reconstituted without the Communists, the Christian Democrats have been in effect the ruling party and have dominated the coalition governments in which they have been the strongest element.

The result has been that the real political struggles in Italy have been those within the Christian Democratic Party, in which the differences between the right and left wings, in addition to embodying personal feuds and rivalries, have been the differences between a deep, old-fashioned Catholic conservatism and a genuine movement towards social and governmental reform. In both France and Italy in the period immediately after the war the new Catholic parties provided a political home for some conservatives who would have preferred to join groups further to the Right, but who realised that for the time being the Right had been largely discredited through its links with Fascism or with the Vichy regime. It took several years in Italy before there was a party openly claiming descent from the Fascists, and over twenty years before this became a force to be taken seriously. In the meantime the Christian Democrats have often found genuine efforts at reform hampered by the necessity of keeping a coalition together, and by their own internal rivalries, as well as by an administrative, judicial and educational system, much of which dates from before the Fascist era and which has not been able to cope successfully with the changes in Italian society resulting from the very successful industrial development, the migration of workers from the south to the north and the slow awakening, economic and political, of the southern provinces and of Sicily and Sardinia.

In France the emergence of the MRP as a major political force in the elections in 1945 and 1946 surprised everybody, including the MRP's own supporters: and, as the Socialists and Communists, although for a time prepared to collaborate on certain issues, grew more critical of each other, there were three political forces active while the constitution of the Fourth Republic was being drafted. There was also General de Gaulle, indisputably in 1944 and 1945 the leader of the French people, but suspected by some (including many Americans) of authoritarian and even fascist views. While he undoubtedly always preserved a sense for the Rights of Man and for the rule of law, his pride, his political style and his undisguised impatience with ordinary politicians made it hard for him to collaborate with parliamentary leaders accustomed to other methods, and the General found himself more at home with those who had been his associates since the early days in London rather than with the members of the political parties. As one of the Socialist leaders, who admired him and was anxious to work with him, put it, 'We want him to stay in office, but we also want him to acquire the habits of democracy.'[20] This was something which de Gaulle proved never wholly able to do. The immediate result was that in January 1946 he resigned when he was faced with the three powerful political parties unable to agree on a new draft constitution and unwilling to let the General take decisions without them. Although this led to more than twelve years of political retirement, de Gaulle's name and ideas remained a force in French politics. In two speeches during the months immediately after his resignation, he called for the creation of a strong executive independent of parliament – not wholly unlike the President of the United States – and for the retention and reorganisation of the French Empire. The MRP, which till then had appeared to be the party whose ideas were closest to those of de Gaulle, found itself outflanked by a new movement, the *Rassemblement du Peuple Français* (RPF), started by de Gaulle's personal supporters with his approval, although he withdrew from political activity in 1953. The RPF in practice developed into a strong conservative party, with the paradoxical result that it was in a Gaullist party that many former supporters of Pétain found their eventual political place.

The French Communist Party had taken the line in 1944 that it was not going to attempt to seize power by insurrection, but that it would cooperate, as the Italian Communists were doing, in the establishment of a coalition government and of a new democratic constitution. Consequently, in the discussions in the Constituent Assembly the Communists aimed at producing a system which would give power to parliament to make and break ministries and to control every detail of governmental action, since such an all-powerful national assembly – besides being in the revolutionary tradition of Rousseau and the Convention of 1792 – would give the Communists and the Socialists, who they still hoped would be their allies, control over all aspects of government. The MRP, on the other hand, were anxious to avoid what seemed to them to be the danger of a collective dictatorship. They wanted a strong and independent executive and also the devolution of government on a regional basis, while some of them had hopes of putting into practice Catholic ideas of a corporate state, ideas which in the final constitution found expression only in the creation of an 'economic council' which governments were supposed to consult, but which never played any significant role.

In the event the only thing on which the French political parties – with the exception of the now much weakened Radicals, who were discredited in many people's minds because they were associated with the failures of the Third Republic, but who nevertheless would have been quite happy to return to it – could agree was that there should be a new constitution. The draft which emerged from the Constituent Assembly, however, was rejected by a plebiscite. A second freshly elected Constituent Assembly in which the Socialists were slightly weaker and the Communists slightly stronger, and in which the MRP was now the largest party, produced a revised version which was finally approved by a very small majority and without much enthusiasm in a referendum in October 1946. The Fourth Republic was in being. It turned out to be surprisingly like the Third. Although the parties were larger and better disciplined, and there were procedural measures to stop a government being overthrown by a snap vote, it was still in practice hard to dissolve the Assembly, and in any case governments now had to be formed by coalitions between those of the parties who believed in the constitutional system –

447

Socialists, MRP and Radicals, with a few smaller groups. The trouble was that, as in the Weimar Republic in Germany, there was a large body of opinion, represented by the Communists and the Gaullist RPF, which had no desire to make the Fourth Republic work and wanted to abolish it and replace it by something else.

The Communists had finally been dropped from the government in May 1947, when they found themselves in disagreement with the other parties over wages policy and over colonial policy. Soon after leaving the government they called a general strike, which was firmly dealt with by a Socialist Minister of the Interior and which led to a split in the Communist-led CGT, with the old syndicalist leader Léon Jouhaux forming a new, though smaller, group of unions, the *Force Ouvrière*. The limits of Communist strength had been demonstrated.

The Fourth Republic achieved a great deal, in spite of its ignominious collapse in 1958. The French economy was transformed and modernised (a process already started under de Gaulle's provisional government in 1944–5), partly as a result of an ambitious plan for nationalisation and technological development devised by Jean Monnet, who then went on to try and do something similar on the international scale and became president of the European Coal and Steel Community and a leading advocate of European unification. A system of social security was introduced on a scale never seen in France before. The standard of living rose, and although there remained many backward pockets in French economic life, for example among some of the peasants and small provincial shopkeepers, France was overcoming the economic and technological gap which had been one of the sources of her weakness in the 1930s. The goal of Franco-German reconciliation which had eluded the politicians of the inter-war period was finally achieved, and important steps, to be discussed later, were taken towards the economic unity of Western Europe.

The intractable problem which finally caused the overthrow of the Fourth Republic was the Algerian question, and this was bound up with the question of the relation of the army to the republic. From 1947 to 1954 the French army was engaged in a war in Indo-China, in an effort to re-establish French control in the face of an effective nationalist movement. It was a war in which many officers felt that the prestige of the army was involved, but it was also a war which aroused little popular enthusiasm in France outside military and right-wing circles. A major military defeat at Dien Bien Phu in May 1954 showed the futility of the attempt to retain Indo-China by force. Early in June 1954 the ablest of the younger politicians in the old Radical Party, Pierre Mendès-France, formed a government on the basis of a promise to end the war within four weeks or else to resign. 'To govern', he believed, 'is to choose';[21] and this was something which most governments of the Fourth Republic proved unable to do. A conference of the Americans, Russians,

British, French and Chinese was already holding sessions at Geneva to discuss Far Eastern problems, and, after the Americans had given up the idea that they might intervene directly in Indo-China or supply the French with nuclear weapons so as to encourage them to continue the war, Eden and Molotov, the British and Russian representatives, were able to obtain agreement on an armistice in Vietnam, Cambodia and Laos and on the creation of two zones in Vietnam, north and south, pending elections for the whole country which was now to become an independent state – a provisional arrangement which lasted far longer than the two years originally intended and which turned out to have disastrous consequences. For the French, however, the Geneva agreement brought an end to an expensive and costly war, although many French military leaders regarded it as a bitter humiliation which must not be allowed to recur elsewhere in the French Empire.

As it was, Mendès-France was able during his ministry to reach agreement on autonomy for Tunisia, which soon became completely independent, as did Morocco in 1956. The test for French policy in North Africa was, however, Algeria, which was far more closely linked to France than either Tunisia or Morocco had been. It was constitutionally part of metropolitan France; its deputies, one half representing the French inhabitants and the other half the Arabs, sat in the National Assembly, even though it was underrepresented in proportion to its population. There were a million European settlers, ranging from large landowners to small employees. There was also an increasingly radical nationalist movement among the Arabs, the revolutionary wing of which launched a revolt in November 1954. By 1956 this had become a full-scale war. It was a war which the leaders of the army and of the French settlers were determined to win. The army, defeated in Indo-China, forced to see the abandonment of colonial territory in North Africa, Madagascar and elsewhere and believing that their brief expedition against the Egyptians at the time of the Suez crisis in the autumn of 1956 had been stopped from a victorious advance on Cairo by the cowardice of the politicians in Paris and the treachery of their British allies, were determined to hold Algeria at all costs. Many army leaders were ready to make a *coup d'état* against the republic rather than risk the surrender by the politicians to the demands of the Algerian nationalists.

On their side, the Algerian revolutionaries in the National Liberation Front (the FLN) used terrorist methods both against the French and against those Algerian Moslems who did not support them and, as the war went on, their attacks spread to metropolitan France. The army and the settlers demanded firm action by the government, and embarked on a programme of counter-terror. Successive governments, unable to make any compromise agreement with the FLN, and forced to tolerate methods of repression, including the torture of prisoners, which were repugnant to much of French opinion, and at the same time threatened with a military revolt, seemed increasingly helpless. By May 1958 it was questionable whether the police, for example, would any longer obey the Minister of the Interior. In Algiers itself on 15 May 1958 a group of officers and civilians led by the Commander in Chief constituted themselves as a Committee of Public Safety.

This was the moment for which de Gaulle had been waiting. His criticism of the constitution of the Fourth Republic appeared to be justified. Above all he had at that particular moment the ability to convince almost everyone that he wanted what they wanted. To the French settlers in Algiers, who had demanded his return to power, shouting their slogan of '*Algérie Française*', de Gaulle started his speech with the words '*Je vous ai compris*'; and they did not go on to listen to the carefully ambiguous phrases which followed this opening. To those who wished to see the war ended, de Gaulle seemed the only man with the prestige to overrule the army. To the soldiers he seemed to be one of themselves. On 15 May 1958 de Gaulle made a press statement summing up his position and his view of his own historic role:[22]

The degradation of the state inevitably leads to the estrangement of the associated peoples, to uneasiness in the fighting forces, to national dislocation and to the loss of independence. For twelve years, France, at grips with problems too difficult for the regime of the parties, has been entangled in this disastrous process.

In the past, the country, from its very depths, trusted me to lead it in unity to its salvation.

Today, in the face of the ordeals which mount anew before it, let the country know that I hold myself ready to assume the powers of the Republic.

For ten years, until his retirement after failing to get his way over a minor constitutional change, in 1968, two years before his death, de Gaulle wielded those powers. After being invested as Prime Minister under the Fourth Republic constitution and entrusted with full powers for six months, he won parliamentary approval for drafting a new constitution. The proposals, based on a strong presidency and a weak parliament, were approved by a large majority in a referendum in October 1958. Sixty-eight per cent of the voters of metropolitan France, Algeria and the overseas territory voted in favour, and the main opposition came from the Communists, though their hostility soon became muted as de Gaulle moved towards ending the Algerian War, and, more important, showed that he was going to conduct an independent and often anti-American foreign policy.

It took a long period of careful manoeuvring by de Gaulle to reach an Algerian settlement. The extremists on the Right had to be isolated, and some of them (the 'Organisation of the Secret Army', OAS) embarked on a series of terrorist bomb attacks in Paris and elsewhere in metropolitan France. The military leaders associated with their views had to be replaced. The FLN had to be perusaded to negotiate. De Gaulle himself originally hoped for some solution which would keep Algeria in close association with

France, but when it was clear that the Algerian nationalists would no longer consider this, he was realistic enough to see that nothing short of complete independence would lead to peace, and he had sufficient prestige and influence to get away with what amounted to a reversal of his own previous position. In June 1961 a referendum approved self-determination for Algeria: the war finally came to an end in March 1962. It was perhaps de Gaulle's greatest achievement, since it is hard to see how France could otherwise have avoided a military dictatorship and perhaps even civil war, or at least a reopening of all the bitter political feuds of the previous twenty-five years.

At the end of the war Germany was the area in which the Russians and the Western Allies were committed to common action by the fortunes of war and by the Potsdam agreement; yet it was in Germany that their rivalry became most apparent and most dangerous, so that Germany was the central problem in the development, both economic and political, of Europe after the Second World War. The political structure of post-war Germany was determined by the occupying powers, and the total responsibility for German life and society which they had assumed at the end of the war soon forced them into practical decisions which had profound consequences. Above all the economic collapse of Germany obliged the Americans and British to take action which deepened the divisions between west and east Germany and led to the development of two separate German states.

At the beginning of 1947 the British and American occupation zones were combined into a single economic unit, after it had become clear that the intention expressed at Potsdam of treating Germany as a single whole was not, at least in the immediate future, going to be fulfilled. The British and American governments felt that no economic recovery was possible without some degree of centralisation, and they were very conscious that they were supplying the basic imports necessary to maintain a minimum standard of living in western Germany without any return, while the Russians continued to remove industrial equipment as part of their reparations. The fusion of the British and American zones (the French joined a few months later) was at once sharply criticised by the Russians, who were told that it was always open to them to allow their zone to join too. From the early months of 1947 each side was accusing the other of responsibility for the breakdown of the Potsdam agreement, and at the same time with the first elections in Germany the two political systems were growing further apart. In 1947 and 1948 all these differences came to a head, and the iron curtain fell across Germany.

In the spring of 1947 the whole European economy was in a critical state. Productivity was still much lower than before the war. Currencies were unstable, and in the absence of confidence in the economy, capital investment was low. While the situation of Germany was worse than that elsewhere, the

451

factors which had disrupted the Germany economy were to be found almost everywhere else in Western Europe – physical destruction of industrial plant, a transport system damaged or worn out by the war, inflation and an unstable currency, political uncertainty and a flourishing black market. There seemed to be some basis for the Communists' belief that the West of Europe might be about to collapse economically and politically, and for American and British fears that conditions might become so bad that the Communist Parties would be able to take over, especially in France and Italy where they were strong and influential mass movements.

In June 1947 the American Secretary of State General George Marshall announced a plan of aid to restore the European economy:[23]

> The remedy [he said] seems to lie in breaking the vicious circle and restoring the confidence of the people of Europe in the economy of their own country, and of Europe as a whole . . . It is logical that the United States should do whatever it is able to do to assist in the return of normal economic health in the world, without which there can be no political stability and no assured peace. Our policy is directed not against any country or doctrine, but against hunger, poverty, desperation and chaos. The purpose shall be the revival of a working economy in the world so as to permit the emergence of political and social conditions in which free institutions can exist.

This proposal served American political and economic interests. It came three months after President Truman had offered United States support to 'free people who are resisting attempted subjugation by armed minorities or by outside pressures'.[24] The specific reference in Truman's speech was to the situation in Greece, where the civil war was still going on, but where the British were no longer able to support the cost of intervention against the Communists, and to Turkey, which was being pressed in vain by the USSR to grant a naval base on the Dardanelles and to surrender territory adjacent to the Russian border in the Caucasus. The general implication of what became known as the 'Truman Doctrine' seemed to be that the Americans were now committed to resisting Russian expansion and communist influence everywhere. The offer of economic aid made by Marshall was ostensibly open to all countries of Europe, including those of Eastern Europe, but to the Russians it seemed an attempt by the Americans to secure economic control of the Continent; and they showed their attitude clearly when they virtually forbade the Czechoslovak government to attend the conference organised to discuss the European response to Marshall's offer (see p. 441 above).

The Marshall Plan served the American policy of containing communism. It also served the interests of the American economy: a prosperous Europe would provide a market for American exports and a field for American investment; and the Marshall Plan was followed by a successful attempt to reduce European trade barriers against United States imports. But, whatever the motives behind these developments in American policy, the Marshall Plan undoubtedly made the recovery of Western Europe possible, and began the process of spectacular growth which was characteristic of the West European economy over the next twenty years. The initiative in organising the European response to the American offer was taken by the British, and especially by Ernest Bevin, Foreign Secretary in the Labour government, and it resulted in the formation of the Organisation for European Economic Cooperation (OEEC), and in an impetus to further economic unification. While the greatest measure of economic unity and the strongest political organisations for that end were the result of later negotiations between the six nations of continental Western Europe – France, Italy, West Germany, Belgium, Luxemburg, the Netherlands – it was the creation of the OEEC which started the movement and it continued to provide an institutional framework for the cooperation of the other European countries – Britain, Austria, Switzerland and the Scandinavian countries – with the six states who set up the European Economic Communities between 1951 and 1957 (see pp. 461-3 below).

Marshall aid, and the American commitment to Europe which it implied, emphasised the division of the Continent. The effects were rapidly felt, above all in Germany. A meeting of the Foreign Ministers of the United States, the USSR, Britain and France in December 1947 broke down without reaching any agreement, and this was soon followed by the end of the four-power Control Commission in Germany, after the Russian representative walked out on 20 March 1948. By this time it was accepted by the Americans and British that West Germany must be included in the general plan for European economic recovery, but the first step in the rescue of the German economy was the creation of a currency which commanded some public confidence. In the post-war collapse money in Germany had virtually lost all value: people were not prepared to work to earn it and preferred payment in kind; the everyday economy was to a large extent based on a barter system, in which the cigarette was a more realistic unit of currency than the mark. There was general agreement that there must be a currency reform, and it was originally intended that this should be introduced by the four-power Control Commission for all the occupation zones simultaneously. However, negotiations broke down, officially on the question whether the new notes should be printed outside Germany, as the Americans wanted, or in the eastern zone, as the Russians proposed. Some critics of American policy have suggested that the Americans were too rigorously insistent on an unimportant point, while, on the other hand, the Russians have been accused of delaying the currency reform because they feared that a rise in the standard of living in Germany would drive the country irrevocably into the Western camp. In any case the Western powers took the initiative alone, and in June 1948 a new currency was substituted for the old in the western zones.

453

The economic effect was remarkable: goods which had been carefully hoarded appeared in the shops; people started to work for wages which at last had some purchasing power; farmers sent produce to be sold rather than keeping it for bartering on the black market. West Germany began a period of rapid economic recovery, which Germans understandably referred to as 'the German miracle'. The political results, however, were serious. Not only did the Russians immediately carry out a currency reform in their own zone, and thus complete the economic division of the country, but they immediately denounced the Western powers: 'With the aid of a separate currency a separate west German state is being created according to a plan, integrated into the western bloc and made into an economic and military deployment area of the Anglo-American western bloc.'[25] More seriously they attacked the weakest point in the Western position in Germany – Berlin.

The Americans, British, French and Russians were each occupying and administering a sector of the city, on the assumption that it would one day once more become the capital of a united Germany, but the exact terms of the Western powers and rights of access to Berlin had never been precisely defined (see p. 431 above). Thus the Soviet government, when its representatives left the Control Council, began to interfere with Western military traffic to the city. Then at the time of the currency reform they insisted on the use of the east German currency for the whole of Berlin. When the Western Allies refused, they cut off gas and electricity supplies to the western sector and then stopped all rail, road and canal traffic from the west. It was the first open trial of strength in the 'Cold War' and it was the first moment, coming as it did three months after the Communist take-over in Czechoslovakia (see p. 441 above), when the European public began to fear that a war between America and Russia might be imminent. The Americans, British and French were determined to stay in Berlin, and, while the American commander in Germany talked of sending an armed convoy up the *Autobahn*, the solution adopted was the organisation of a massive air lift, which, to the surprise of many observers, including perhaps the Russians, succeeded in keeping the Western sectors of the city supplied with food, fuel (including fuel for the power stations) and raw materials for a whole year. The success of the airlift, which enabled the links with West Berlin to be maintained without the use of force, and which put the Russians in the position where all they could have done to interfere was to shoot down Western aircraft, with the probability that this would lead to war, finally resulted, after long secret diplomatic negotiations, in the lifting of the blockade. The Western sectors of Berlin continued to be occupied by the Americans, British and French, and now had their own municipal government. Although later there were renewed Russian challenges to Berlin's position these were never as serious as that of 1948, and West Berlin has remained a Western enclave behind the Iron Curtain.

The West appeared to have won the first open and dramatic confrontation with the Soviet Union and the American government was encouraged in its tough policy of containing Russian expansion by going to the brink of war if necessary. Moreover, the blockade of Berlin completed the division of Germany. By the autumn of 1949 there were two separate German states and two separate municipal administrations in Berlin. Within the city, contacts between East and West remained comparatively easy until 1961, when the East Germans erected a heavily guarded wall between the two halves of the city to stop the flow of refugees from their zone.

The formal establishment of two separate German states, the German Democratic Republic (*Deutsche Demokratische Republik* – DDR) in the east and the German Federal Republic (*Bundesrepublik Deutschlands*) in the west, was completed by the end of 1949. The Communist government in the east depended on Russian support for its existence, and the industrial resources of the country were of great economic importance for the whole of the Soviet bloc, so that the Russians were never likely of their own accord to renounce their control. Thus the pretence that there was more than one party was soon abandoned, and the government remained firmly in the hands of loyal Communists, the most prominent of whom, Wilhelm Pieck and Walther Ulbricht, had been leaders of the party in Germany before 1933 and had survived Stalin's purges while exiles in Moscow. Ulbricht's government managed to overcome serious difficulties. By June 1953 there was widespread discontent with the economic situation and with the slow rate of recovery, especially compared with West Germany, while the party itself had publicly admitted mistakes in the transition to a socialist system. At the same time Stalin's death in March 1953 had everywhere started rumours about liberalisation and about changes in Soviet foreign policy, which might, it was thought, lead to a change in the relations between the two halves of Germany and to a general *détente* in Europe. In this atmosphere of expectancy the East German government made the mistake of announcing to the German workers, already tired and exasperated by the unremitting hard work which had been expected of them without a break since the end of the war – and indeed before – that they would have to work even longer hours and that their norms of production would be raised. The result was a general strike and impressive demonstrations against the regime in Berlin and a number of other cities of the eastern zone. For the first time the experience – to be repeated in Hungary in 1956 and in Czechoslovakia in 1968 – of Soviet tanks attacking the workers once more showed unmistakably the strength of the Russian hold over Eastern Europe and the ruthlessness with which Stalin's successors were prepared to deal with any attempt at insurrection or even reform in the area they controlled.

In West Germany the Social Democrats had resisted the overtures of the Communists to form a joint party, largely at the insistence of their leader

Kurt Schumacher, an intransigent and impressive figure who had survived ten years in concentration camps. Until his death in 1952 he remained equally suspicious of Western and of communist intentions towards Germany, and was determined to keep his party free from the taint of association with either capitalists or communists. He himself came from eastern Germany, and he also realised that in a divided Germany the Socialists would be deprived of some of their traditional centres of support in Berlin, Saxony and Thuringia, so that he was always opposed to any step which suggested that the reunification of Germany might be postponed indefinitely. His successors proved more flexible, and the German Social Democratic Party rapidly lost its tactical and ideological rigidity. In 1958 it broke with its Marxist past in a new programme approved at a party congress at Godesberg, which, in the words of the party's leading economist, allowed for 'Competition as far as possible – planning as far as necessary'[26] and turned the party into a reformist one, working within the liberal capitalist system, and, like the British Labour Party whose example was important especially for those of the German socialist leaders who had spent their years of exile in Britain, drawing its strength from a wealthy and pragmatic trade union movement.

During the formation and establishment of the West German state the Social Democrats were out-manoeuvred by the Christian Democratic Union (CDU), whose leader Konrad Adenauer proved to be one of the shrewdest and toughest statesmen of post-war Europe. He was a devout Catholic from the Rhineland who had already been responsible for the distribution of food supplies in the area at the beginning of the First World War. In the Weimar Republic he was Mayor of Cologne and a Centre Party politician who had been spoken of as a possible Chancellor in the late 1920s. He had again become Mayor of Cologne in 1945, but had soon been dismissed by the British military administration, allegedly for incompetence – an experience which had left him with a certain, perhaps justified, scepticism about British intentions and policies. In the negotiations to create a new Christian Democratic party, no longer, as the old Centre Party had been, exclusively Roman Catholic, but with a Protestant wing, he emerged as undisputed leader, and after the first parliamentary elections the CDU was the largest single party in the newly created Federal parliament, the *Bundestag*. Adenauer, leading a coalition of his own party and the small Free Democratic Party – the successor of the liberal parties of the Weimar Republic – remained continuously in office from 1949 until his somewhat reluctant retirement at the age of eighty-seven in 1963, four years before his death.

Under Adenauer's government the Federal Republic made a rapid economic recovery which seemed to demonstrate the vitality of a system of capitalist free enterprise. Some doubts were expressed whether the personal ascendancy of the Chancellor, and the uninterrupted rule of his party and their associates, gave West Germany a true experience of democratic parliamentary government, since many of the real issues had to be fought out within the government rather than between government and opposition, while the age and temperament of Adenauer himself encouraged the image of a benevolent paternalism. There were, too, a number of political scandals and obvious personal manoeuvres for office which by the 1950s were leading some people to express doubts about the future of the parliamentary system in Germany – doubts which were partly dispelled after 1969, when the Social Democrats, after a period of shared power in a coalition with the Christian Democrats, formed a government under the leadership of the Mayor of West Berlin, Willy Brandt – though again with the support of some members of the flexible Free Democratic Party.

The fourteen years of Adenauer's administration gave West Germany a period of political stability and economic growth during which most citizens of the Federal Republic showed themselves more interested in an improved standard of living than in wider political and ideological issues. The local politics of the *Länder*, the component states which made up the Federal Republic, were often as important as the activities in Bonn, the small town on the Rhine which was chosen as a temporary capital in the hope, repeatedly deferred, that at some time Berlin would once more become the capital of a reunited Germany. The most striking feature of German domestic politics has been the absence of the extremism which wrecked the Weimar Republic. The Communists, largely because of their association in the mind of the public with the Red army and the brutalities of the initial Russian occupation, had comparatively little success in the elections of 1949 and none in those of 1953. In 1956 the Federal Constitutional Court, the highest judicial authority, on the plea of the government declared the Communist party to be illegal, since under the constitution, in an obvious effort to prevent a recurrence of what happened to the Weimar Republic, associations committed to the overthrow of the constitutional system could be banned. Although a small communist party was formed again later with a revised programme, there has been remarkably little active opposition on the extreme Left, except in the late 1960s in the comparatively isolated world of the universities and the student movements.

On the Right too, although parties have appeared which played on the frustration and bitterness of the refugees from the east, and which tried to revive some of the old nationalist, *völkisch* attitudes as well as taking up points in the Nazi programme, they have so far only had limited success. The most significant of them, the National Democratic Party, formed from a fusion of several groups in 1964, although it only won 2 per cent of the votes in the 1965 elections (approximately the same as the Nazis in 1928) and 4.3 per cent in 1969, appeared to be growing in subsequent local elections but has not yet won a significant volume of mass support. This comparative failure of right-wing radicalism is perhaps due in part to the fact that there are enough Germans in the West aware of the dangers these parties represent and partly too because the Germans who have grown up in the west since the war do not respond to *völkisch* appeals and have either been realistic enough tacitly to accept the division of Germany and the loss of the eastern territories or else, when they have adopted romantic radical views, have turned to a kind of revolutionary anarchism which has as its immediate target the values and institutions of a successful, materialistic capitalist society.

It has been argued that one of the guarantees against a revival of right-wing radical nationalism in West Germany has been provided by the foreign policy initiated by Adenauer. While no German politician could openly declare that hope of German reunification must be abandoned, and while the Adenauer government officially refused to accept the existence of the East German regime, and even broke off diplomatic relations with states which recognised the German Democratic Republic, in practice, since Adenauer's retirement, German policy has moved towards the acceptance of the situation in the east. Adenauer's great achievement in foreign policy was to find a new role for Germany in relation to Western Europe. This policy was based on retaining American support and on the achievement of a genuine reconciliation with France, in spite of the intransigence of the French government in the early months of the occupation and of French hopes – finally abandoned in 1957 – of acquiring control over the industrial area of the Saar basin, which had been one of their aims in 1919. Some of Adenauer's critics suggested that his own roots in Catholic West Germany made him less enthusiastic than other politicians about reunion with a largely Protestant or socialist East Germany, in which his own position and that of his party would be less secure; and indeed he seems to have felt a genuine feeling of sympathy with the leaders of Christian Democratic parties in France and Italy and with the ideals of a closer association of the Catholic countries of Western Europe. But in fact it was events outside Europe which gave West Germany the opportunity to become a major European power again and forced a radical change in American policy towards Germany, so that within five years of American insistence on total and permanent disarmament of Germany the American government was looking for ways of persuading the Germans to build up an army and of making this acceptable to the French and the other Western European countries which had vivid recent memories of German military occupation. Events outside Europe were giving a new impetus towards a union of West European states.

In June 1950 troops from North Korea invaded South Korea, and the Americans and some of their allies came to the assistance of the South against the communist North. The lessons for Europe appeared to the American government to be obvious. In the Far East, the division of Korea into communist and non-communist zones had led to the invasion by the Communists of the non-communist, American-sponsored half of the country, and perhaps a similar attack might be expected in Germany where a comparable division existed. For the American government therefore the provision of a strengthened local defence for West Germany appeared to be an urgent need: and it seemed both practical and economical that the West Germans should themselves play a part in that defence.

A military threat from the Soviet Union had already been recognised in April 1949, when the North Atlantic Treaty Organisation (NATO) was set up, but the Korean War seemed to create a new and more pressing need for the consolidation of the defence of Western Europe, especially since the Americans, British and French only had four divisions in Germany at a moment when it was estimated that the Russians could produce 175 divisions for an attack from East Germany. The Soviet Union now had nuclear weapons, so that the deterrent on which the American government had relied was now less potent than five years before. By the autumn of 1950 therefore the American government had decided that the rearmament of Germany was necessary in order to prevent a local attack without the use of atomic weapons. In December 1950 the American, British and French foreign ministers agreed in principle to the creation of a German army. In fact it took nearly five years of diplomatic negotiations to overcome opposition to the proposal and to settle the way in which it should be carried out, so what was believed in 1950 and 1951 to be an immediate threat was in fact met by an increase in the number of Allied troops in Germany, by the strengthening of the machinery of NATO and by the appointment of General Eisenhower as supreme commander in Europe.

Opposition to the idea of German rearmament was natural enough. Both the experiences of the countries which had been occupied by Germany and the years of propaganda against German militarism made the suggestion a shocking and unwelcome one to many people, while, for the Russians and for the communist parties of Europe, the proposal seemed to confirm all their suspicions of American intentions. It was opposed in West Germany not only by the Social Democrats, but by a whole generation which reacted against the old Germany and genuinely hoped to be able to opt out of a nationalist and militarist society. The solution proposed to this dilemma was to permit German rearmament within the framework of the movement towards the unification of Western Europe, though it has been argued by some writers that the introduction of this difficult and emotional question into the discussions about European unity delayed rather than hastened the advance of the European movement.[27]

The immediate practical impetus towards the unification of Western Europe had been economic, and it was in the organisation to make use of the Marshall aid programme that the first steps were taken towards common action, just as it was the East European rejection of Marshall's offer that marked the extent to which the division of Europe had become a basic fact of international relations (see p. 453 above). Economic reconstruction of Western Europe was necessary not only on practical and humanitarian grounds; it also seemed to be a way of limiting the appeal of the communist parties and of forestalling the danger of social revolution.

At the same time, however, the experience of occupation and liberation as well as Hitler's destruction of the old European state system made many people impatient of national barriers and anxious to create a genuine new order in Europe in place of Hitler's spurious one. Some people stressed the practical advantages of European union, political, economic and technological; some of them had a sense of the common historical experience – and especially the Roman Catholic experience – of Western Europe, which gave a special tinge to their beliefs in a united Europe, and at first alienated many socialists and others who did not share their Catholic faith. The leading politicians who took the decisive steps towards the creation of a united Western Europe, Robert Schuman, the Foreign Minister and Prime Minister in a number of French governments between 1948 and 1952, and Alcide de Gasperi, Italian Prime Minister from 1945 to 1953, were old enough to have known earlier loyalties and to have a sense of the artificiality of national boundaries: Schuman was an Alsatian who had served in the German army in the First World War, while de Gasperi had grown up as a citizen of the Austro-Hungarian monarchy. They were devout Catholics, as was Konrad Adenauer, who was very willing to join them in thinking in terms of a new Western European system, predominantly Catholic, which would give West Germany a new status and a new role, even if the unification of West and East Germany had to be delayed indefinitely.

While Churchill when in opposition had spoken enthusiastically of Franco-German reconciliation and had in a famous speech at Zurich in September 1946 spoken hopefully of a future United States of Europe, and while the Labour Foreign Secretary Ernest Bevin had been most active in organising the European response to Marshall's offer, Great Britain remained aloof from this movement towards a united Western Europe, and still hoped to reassert its world-wide role on the basis of the Commonwealth and of a close association with the United States. In fact in his Zurich speech Churchill did not speak of British membership of a European community but said, 'Great Britain, the British Commonwealth of Nations, mighty America, and, I trust Soviet Russia – for then indeed all would be well – must be the friends and sponsors of the new Europe and must champion its right to live and shine.'[28] It took nearly twenty years before the British government finally decided that this role as a great power friendly to, but outside, Europe was no longer possible.

In 1949 these ideas about the future of Western Europe found expression in the formation of a Council of Europe, which included Britain and the

Scandinavian countries, but its role was strictly limited to the discussion rather than the execution of policy, largely because the British were not prepared to join on any other terms. Its very existence, however, showed that ideas which between the wars had been regarded as the property of enthusiastic utopian publicists, such as the half-Austrian, half-Japanese Count Coudenhove-Kalergi, or which had been dismissed as cynical tactical manoeuvres when Aristide Briand produced a plan for European Union in 1930, were now at least treated seriously by governments.

However the most important practical steps were economic, and began in May 1950 (just before the outbreak of the Korean War) with a proposal by Robert Schuman for the establishment of a European Coal and Steel Community which came into being in July 1952. It had long been felt that the mines and factories of northern and eastern France, Belgium, Luxemburg and West Germany formed a single economic unit. Between 1870 and 1914, when Lorraine was under German rule, many of its steel mills were still financed by French capital. In spite of national differences and French resentment there were still ties between the industrialists who controlled the resources of the area; and one of the leading families of industrialists was called de Wendel on one side of the frontier and von Wendel on the other. In the First World War German industrialists had dreamed of bringing the industrial wealth of the rest of Lorraine and of Belgium under their control, and the French had hoped in 1919 and in 1945 to include the Saar in the French industrial sphere. The Coal and Steel Community was a truly supranational organisation for the regulation of the industry and was, in effect, a vast international cartel. It could close down inefficient plant and it planned the pattern of industrial development in the member countries. Freedom of trade in coal and steel over a large area suggested that there might be advantages in similar freedom for other commodities. The idea of a West European tariff union and of a West European 'common market' was now a practical possibility.

The Coal and Steel Community served a political as well as an economic purpose. Robert Schuman had hoped that it would be 'the first stage of European Federation'[29]; and, although these wider hopes were for the time disappointed, it at least enabled West German industrial power to be integrated into that of Western Europe; and this would it was hoped, prevent German industry from being used, as in both World Wars, as a basis for military expansion and conquest. It seemed to some European statesmen in 1950 that a similar pattern might be followed in respect of German rearmament and a new German army. If a European defence force could be created which would be genuinely international, then a German army might be integrated into it without danger to Germany's neighbours. In fact the proposal for a European Defence Community was not accepted because, when it came to the point, the French National Assembly refused to ratify it.

Opposition to German rearmament prevented the formation of a European army, but did not prevent the formation of a German army. Moreover, the proposal to rearm Germany hastened the recognition of the full sovereignty of the German Federal Republic. The Treaty of Bonn, signed in May 1952 and ratified by the German Parliament in spite of opposition from the Social Democrats, who believed that the formal establishment of a West German state and the creation of a German army would make reunification by agreement with the Soviet Union harder, ended the occupation of Germany and marked the acceptance of the Federal Republic into the new West European system. It had been intended that the Bonn Treaty would be ratified simultaneously with the treaty establishing a European Defence Community, but when this was rejected by the French National Assembly, some other solution to the problem of German rearmament had to be found. A compromise was reached in 1954 with the establishment of an association of sovereign states, of which a rearmed Germany was one, in a Western European Union, and with German entry into NATO.

However, the German government voluntarily undertook not to manufacture nuclear, bacteriological or chemical weapons, and it was very careful to make the new German army look quite different from the old: uniforms were not worn except on duty; parade-ground drill, with its associations of the Prussian goose-step and the 'corpse-like obedience' (*Kadavergehorsamkeit*) of the Prussian military tradition, was largely abolished, and stress was laid on the soldier's role as a citizen-in-arms. As one of the officers responsible for implementing these reforms wrote, 'The German soldier must be given the feeling that he is a member of a free nation standing on the side of freedom.'[30] There were indeed problems in creating an army of technicians in which conditions of service were made as much like civilian employment as possible so that it faced the competition of industry in attracting volunteers. Conscription was introduced in 1956; and in the later 1960s the military authorities were sometimes embarrassed to find that young conscripts in a citizen army were just as liable to revolt against the society in which they found themselves as their contemporaries in the universities.

The long discussions about German rearmament and the failure to create a European Defence Community revealed that the political union of Western Europe for which the enthusiasts in the European movement were working was still unattainable; and it was again in the field of economics that progress in the direction of unification was made. In June 1955 a conference of the foreign ministers of the six countries – France, Germany, Italy, Belgium, the Netherlands and Luxemburg – associated in the Coal and Steel Community met at Messina in Sicily, and prepared the way for the establishment of a European Atomic Energy Community, and, of much more importance, a European Common Market. The governments passed a resolution[31]

That it is necessary to work for the establishment of a united Europe, for the development of common institutions, the progressive fusion of national economies, the creation of a common market and the progressive harmonisation of their social policies. Such a policy seems to them indispensable if Europe is to maintain her position in the world, regain her influence and prestige and achieve a continuing increase in the standards of living of her population.

In March 1957 the signature by the six countries of the Treaty of Rome achieved two at least of these aims: it established a Common Market and it carried a stage further the development of common institutions. It was in the development of these institutions and of the self-confident bureaucracy serving them that progress towards a limited degree of unity among the six states was made. A Commission, appointed by the governments, but whose members are appointed for four years and cannot normally be removed, is responsible for the formulation of policy, which has to be approved by a Council of ministers from the member countries. Although the governments of the individual states have the last word and cannot be overruled against their will, since the French refused to consider substituting a majority vote for the unanimity required of the Council in its first year of existence, the Commission has been in many cases able to make regulations which imposed common economic and social policies on the members of the community. Any move towards greater political unity however was firmly and successfully opposed by General de Gaulle after his return to power in 1958. The French government from 1958 onwards, although prepared to accept the advantages of economic unification, provided that special provisions were made for the protection of French agriculture, was insistent that Europe should remain what de Gaulle called '*l'Europe des patries*', an association of sovereign national states whose identity would not be lost in any supra-national organisation. The question also arose of the extension of the European community to include new members. The British, who had refused to join at the beginning, began by 1961 to have second thoughts, and, rightly or wrongly, to see in the Common Market a possible solution to their endemic economic difficulties: but here again de Gaulle made it clear that British membership was unacceptable. The British application was rejected in January 1963, and again when it was renewed by the Labour government in 1967, largely because of de Gaulle's personal suspicion, at a time when he was determined to demonstrate France's independence of the United States, of the British 'special relationship' with America, and of British attempts at cooperation with America in the field of nuclear weapons. It was only after de Gaulle's retirement that Britain, under the Conservative government of Edward Heath, who had been the principal negotiator in the first attempt, was in 1971 successful in obtaining agreement to the admission of Britain into the European community.

The creation of NATO and the moves towards Western European unification had the effect of emphasising the division of Europe as a whole still further.

The communist states in Eastern Europe created a kind of mirror-image of the West, with a Council for Mutual Economic Assistance (COMECON), first set up in 1949 and later given institutional machinery, and a military alliance, the Warsaw Pact, signed in 1955 as an answer to NATO. From the point of view of the East European countries, these moves served to strengthen Soviet influence. The Warsaw Pact ensured that the Red army could maintain its military control with the consent of the other governments concerned: COMECON attempted to organise the East European economy so as to meet Russian needs rather than those of the individual members of the organisation. For the Soviet leadership there was, from 1948 on, when the Cold War in one form or another became the main fact of international life, a two-fold problem, that of their relations with the West and that of maintaining the solidarity of their own communist bloc. Apart from the Berlin question the main points of confrontation with the West occurred outside Europe – most dramatically in the Cuban crisis of 1962.

In Western Europe Russian policy concentrated on making the most of the spontaneous and understandable movements against nuclear armament, while asserting that it was American aggression and West German militarism which were responsible for the division of Europe and the maintenance of international tension. From time to time there were proposals for 'disengagement' in Europe, while negotiations between America and the Soviet Union about nuclear disarmament and a ban on nuclear testing were never totally abandoned. In 1955, while there was still a hope that Stalin's death might be followed by a genuine solution of the problem of European security, the British Prime Minister Anthony Eden, who had just succeeded the aged and ailing Churchill, proposed the establishment of a zone on both sides of the Iron Curtain which should be open for inspection and control; in 1957 the Polish Foreign Minister Adam Rapacki suggested that there should be an area in central Europe in which no nuclear weapons should be stationed. Not much came of these proposals, although a limited treaty banning certain kinds of nuclear tests was signed in 1963, since neither side trusted the other sufficiently to believe that they would implement them seriously and honestly. During the years from 1953 to 1959 in which John Foster Dulles was the American Secretary of State, the United States government was committed to the refusal of any serious concessions to the Russians and to a belief in the universal aggressiveness of Communist intentions.

Moreover, any settlement of the problem of European security presupposed a settlement of the German question. The Western powers insisted that the way to German unification was to hold free elections for both parts of the country, and, although in 1955, as part of the negotiations for a lessening of tension in Europe and in an attempt to postpone West German rearmament, the Soviet government agreed to 'reunification of Germany by means of free elections . . . in conformity with the national interests of the German people and the interests of European security',[32] it was in fact quite clear that, since the Communists would never win a majority, free elections were not in the interests of the Russians, while for the Western powers any German unification would have to be subject to guarantees that the country would not fall under communist control as Czechoslovakia had in 1948, and these the Russians would not be prepared to give. As a result negotiations for elections for the whole of Germany came to nothing.

Russian relations with the communist states of Eastern Europe were not only conditioned by the economic and strategic needs of the Soviet Union; they also reflected the internal situation in Russia itself. After Tito had shown that it was possible for a communist state to free itself from Russian control, Stalin was determined to stop other countries from following Yugoslavia's example. In Poland, Hungary, Czechoslovakia, Roumania and Bulgaria, old communists who might have taken an independent line were put on trial, following the pattern of the Soviet purges of the 1930s. They were accused of espionage, of conspiracy against the state, of Trotskyism and of the latest heresy, Titoism; in many cases these attacks had a marked anti-Semitic side. Stalin clearly intended that any independent centre or group of communists who might question Moscow's orders or think in a different way from that in which he wanted them to think must be broken up or destroyed. At the same time, in the Soviet Union itself, the atmosphere of terror was intensified. The assertion of party control in the newly annexed regions in the west, the regimentation of the economy to end the local independence and initiative which the peasants had shown in some areas, and to maintain the pace of industrial production, the disciplining of the intellectuals, especially those who, in the days of Russia's alliance with the West, had shown enthusiasm for Western styles and models, all showed that Stalin and his associates were determined to suppress any possible criticism or opposition and to maintain the hold of the party on all aspects of life.

There was plenty of ground for criticism; although the production of heavy industrial products recovered reasonably quickly from the damage caused by the war, consumer goods were extremely scarce and housing conditions very bad. On the land the reimposition of collective discipline on the peasants failed to raise production or to improve the standard of living. At the same time the exercise of authority with the aid of the secret police was as severe as ever.

Stalin himself, always suspicious and tyrannical, had become even more so. He personally participated in the regimentation of the intellectuals and artists which had been initiated by A.A. Zhdanov, the head of the Agitation and Propaganda (Agitprop) directorate, who died in 1948 – in circumstances which, like the death of most prominent Soviet personalities in this period, seemed to be mysterious. Stalin personally endorsed the erroneous genetic theories of the botanist T.D. Lysenko, which maintained that environment rather than heredity alone determined the mutation of species. He published a pamphlet attacking the prevailing Soviet theory of linguistics, because it paid insufficient attention to the unique historical characteristics of the Russian language, at a moment when he was appealing to Russian nationalism. He publicly contradicted the views of the most eminent Soviet economist, Eugene Varga, because Varga (like the old revisionist Social Democrats) thought that the revolution might not be necessary and that social reforms and colonial liberation might be achieved by cooperation between Communists and non-communists, whereas Stalin at this point was proclaiming the total hostility between Russia and the West, and his belief that the final crisis of capitalism was approaching and an era of revolution and war about to dawn.

By the beginning of 1953 it looked as though a renewed purge on the lines of that of the late 1930s might be under way. A 'doctors' plot' was unearthed, and nine eminent physicians were accused of poisoning Zhdanov and of planning to murder a number of military leaders. Then, however, on 5 March 1953 Stalin died suddenly of a stroke, aged seventy-three, and the usual suspicions were expressed that the death was not a natural one. Stalin had dominated the Soviet government and the Communist Party of the Soviet Union as well as the international communist movement for so long that his sudden death led to a period both of confusion and of hope – confusion because the rivalries in the higher party leadership now came into the open, and hope because it seemed that a possibility now existed of more liberal policies both inside Russia and in the Soviet Union's relations with the world outside.

The immediate result of Stalin's death was an attempt to assert the principle of collective leadership, with G.M.Malenkov as Chairman of the Council of Ministers. However within four years Malenkov was dismissed and Nikita Khruschev had established his ascendancy, first in partnership with N.A.Bulganin, and then on his own, until he too fell victim of party rivalries and to his failure to solve Russia's economic problems, and was forced to retire in 1964. It was Khruschev who, although he himself had made his successful career as a result of Stalin's favour and had as the party boss in the Ukraine in the 1930s been a main agent in carrying out the purges there, launched the attack on the 'cult of personality' and, by his disclosures at the Twentieth Party Congress in 1956, revealed the truth about some of the atrocities of Stalin's regime, and made some attempt at rehabilitating a few of Stalin's victims. At the same time, the signing of the Austrian State Treaty in 1955, the end of the occupation of military bases in Finland and a restoration of comparatively good relations with Tito all suggested that there might be a genuine change in Soviet foreign as well as internal policies.

These hopes were largely disappointed. There was a certain relaxation inside the Soviet Union; legal procedures were more carefully observed; the powers of the secret police were somewhat curbed, and its chief, Beria, put on trial; and it was significant that most of the other leading members of the government and party who fell from power – Malenkov, Molotov and in his turn Khruschev – were at least allowed to retire without being tried, imprisoned or executed. Intellectuals and artists seemed to have more freedom, but it soon became clear that any criticisms, even friendly ones, of the workings of the Soviet system and any over-eager adoption of Western models would lead to trouble. Equally, the reconciliation with Tito did not mean that other communist states would be allowed to take their own roads to communism as Yugoslavia had done. The Russian government was prepared to intervene with troops to prevent this – in Hungary in 1956 and in Czechoslovakia in 1968 – but it did not usually need to go as far: even where, as in Poland after 1956, there seemed to be a greater measure of freedom, this was closely controlled and could always be revoked, as the vicissitudes of Polish life in the past fifteen years have shown. Russian political and economic pressure was generally enough to ensure conformity. Only Roumania in the later 1960s seemed to have succeeded in winning a certain freedom in its foreign relations, and it may be that the apparent Russian tolerance of this was due to the fact that, unlike Hungary or Czechoslovakia, the Roumanians adopted a more flexible foreign policy without at the same time becoming more liberal in their internal arrangements.

Although the Soviet Union was not prepared to relax its control over Eastern Europe or to go very far in breaking down the authoritarian rigour of its rule, Western Europe was by 1970 perhaps becoming less important to the Russian rulers. They were in direct competition with the United States in the construction of nuclear weapons and in defence against them, as well as in their programme for launching men and machines in space. And from 1964 on they were also in direct competition for the leadership not only of the communist world but also of the under-developed states of Africa, Asia and Latin America, with the other imponderable factor in the world balance of power – China. As the presuppositions of the Cold War broke down and a new pattern in international relations began to emerge, so the role of the lesser states – Egypt and Israel or India and Pakistan – became more important, while the possibility began to be discussed of a new independent role for Western Europe in the 1970s.

16

EPILOGUE

The meeting of the American and Russian armies on the river Elbe in April 1945 symbolised the extent to which the future of Europe was now dependent on the policies of these two powers and on the relations between them. There is a sense in which the end of the Second World War marked what has been called 'the end of European history' (the title of the English translation in 1947 of the book by the German historian and social scientist Alfred Weber (brother of Max Weber) called in German, *Abschied von der bisherigen Geschichte* (Farewell to Previous History, 1946)). Although European problems, and especially that of Germany, have been at the centre of American–Russian relations in the last quarter of a century, events outside Europe – in Korea, in Cuba, in Vietnam, in the Middle East – have become increasingly important in the development of international relations. The most striking example of the changed position of Europe in the world, however, has been the end of European imperialism and of European colonial rule overseas. At the end of the nineteenth century, the public in the great states of Europe took for granted the right and indeed the duty of Europeans to rule the less developed territories of the rest of the world. By the end of the Second World War this confidence had largely vanished and the political will to dominate had gone. With a surprising rapidity the great colonial empires of Britain, France, the Netherlands and Belgium disappeared, and Portugal alone of the old imperial powers of Europe has succeeded in maintaining control, for the time at least, of vast areas of Africa, perhaps just because the government has so far been able to insulate its subjects at home and abroad from the prevailing ideas about progress and political independence.

In this process the rise of Japan as a world power has been of obvious importance and Japanese success in 1941 and 1942, in spite of later defeat and the terrible experience of nuclear bombardment in 1945, left its mark permanently on the rest of Asia. The rapid Japanese victories over the British in Malaya and Singapore, the ease with which, after the defeat by Germany of the Netherlands and France, the Japanese were able to occupy and control Indonesia and Indo-China, confirmed the lesson of the Russo-

Japanese War earlier in the century. The myth of the Europeans' natural right to rule was broken once and for all, and the former imperial powers, in their attempts to influence the politics and economics of Asia and Africa, have had to find new forms of expression and new formulae with which to justify themselves. In this connection the attitude of the United States has often seemed paradoxical. During the war American disapproval of European imperialism was frequently and clearly expressed – at Teheran for example, when Churchill impatiently brushed aside a proposal by Roosevelt that Britain should not regain her colony of Hong Kong (still in 1972 one of the few remaining British Crown Colonies) after the end of the war. The Dutch attempt to reestablish their hold on Indonesia was unsuccessful less because of their lack of material resources to retain an effective physical presence than because of the pressure of world opinion, led by the United States. Just as British liberals had hoped in the nineteenth century and until the 1920s that the establishment of a number of small independent national states in central and eastern Europe in place of the Ottoman and Habsburg Empires would contribute to internal stability, only to find that instead they added a new element of instability to international life, so the dream that new independent nations would help to preserve a balance of power has proved as unreal in Asia or Africa as it did in the Balkans before the First World War or in central and eastern Europe after 1919, and the Americans have been obliged to use methods in pursuit of their world policy very similar to those which they had earlier criticised when employed by the British or the French.

When the Labour Party came to power in Britain in the summer of 1945, it was already committed to granting independence to India. This had not only long been an avowed aim of Labour Party policy; it had also been the ostensible goal of the Conservatives, who in the 1930s had introduced a measure of self-government, though never enough to satisfy Gandhi and the other Indian leaders; and the argument had been about the speed and manner of the transfer of power rather than about the necessity of carrying it out at some time. In August 1947, from a mixture of genuine political idealism and a practical sense of the impossibility of finding the resources, or the popular support in Britain, to maintain control over an increasingly restless sub-continent, the British government handed over in India, not, as had been hoped, to a single central administration under the leadership of Gandhi's Congress Party, but to two governments and two states, India and Pakistan, since the differences between Hindus and Muslims had proved insuperable. Independence was followed by bloody communal massacres and a hostility between the two states which has not diminished since the British left. The British withdrawal from India was perhaps the grandest and for the historian the most significant of all the gestures of retreat from empire, both because of the size and long historical traditions of the area involved, and because of the importance of the link with India over the past two centuries for so many aspects of British life.

In fact, the granting of independence to India and indeed the giving up of political control over most of the rest of the British Empire which followed over the next few years, while of some emotional and political importance, had comparatively little practical effect in Britain. Much of the capital invested in Indian industry had already passed into Indian hands, but the Indian and Pakistan governments still needed foreign investment for industrial and military development. During the war, India had accumulated a large sterling balance in London, owed for goods imported by Britain, and this meant that the financial links with India and Pakistan remained as long as sterling was still a world currency and as long as successive British governments made it difficult to convert it into any other money. India and Pakistan remained members of the British Commonwealth, which at least provided a means for consultation about international questions, even if over the next decades it became increasingly shadowy and increasingly devoid of all but a vague emotional content except when it coincided with the tangible economic ties of the sterling area.

Within twenty years, at an even faster pace, most of the rest of the British Empire became independent. The Conservatives, returned to power in the election of 1951, although emotionally they would have liked to retard the change, were realistic enough to accept it. As their Colonial Secretary said in 1956, in a revealing remark, 'if only nationalism were a patient, gentle, amenable creature – a kind of cocker spaniel',[1] things might be different. As it was, the new Conservative attitude was summed up by Prime Minister Harold Macmillan in 1960, when, on a visit to the Union of South Africa, he said, 'The most striking of all the impressions I have formed since I left London a month ago is of the strength of this African national consciousness. In different places it may take different forms. But it is happening everywhere. The wind of change is blowing through the continent.'[2] (These were not sentiments likely to arouse any sympathy among his hosts, and in 1961 indeed South Africa left the British Commonwealth because of the objections to its racial policies expressed by other members.)

It was this wind which blew away the intermediate stages on the road to total independence which British governments, both Labour and Conservative, would have liked to see erected, and the pattern established in British dealings with Ireland between 1919 and 1922 soon became familiar, by which a nationalist leader was first imprisoned and then released by the British to become president or prime minister of a new state. Twenty years after the end of the Second World War all that remained of the British Empire were those territories which were too small or too isolated to be capable of political or economic independence or which were on such bad terms with their neighbours that British colonial rule seemed preferable to absorption by them. The example of decolonisation by the largest empire in the world had its effect elsewhere. Thus in 1960 the Belgian government precipitately granted independence to the Congo, even though its policy up to then had been based on maintaining direct imperial rule for an indefinite period, so that they had taken good care that scarcely any Congolese had been educated above the primary level.

The areas where the process of decolonisation continued to cause political difficulty to Britain were those which were either thought to be of strategic importance (as for example Aden) so that the British government believed that it needed bases there, or those where the succession was disputed, as it was in Palestine by Arabs and Jews, or in Cyprus by Greeks and Turks. When it proved impossible to reach any compromise solution, the British, increasingly conscious of the economic cost of maintaining a military presence all over the world, gave up the ungrateful task, hoping that their withdrawal might precipitate a solution or that the United Nations Organisation might be successful where they had failed. It was in the unstable situation in the Middle East resulting from the British withdrawal from Palestine, the establishment of the state of Israel and the Israeli-Arab War of 1948 that the last old-style gesture of British imperialism was attempted. In 1956, after the last bases which the British had retained in Egypt had been handed over, the Egyptian government under Gamal Abdul Nasser national-ised the Suez Canal. The British government owned forty-four per cent of the shares, and they were very conscious of the importance for their economy of free passage of ships through the canal, especially for tankers carrying oil from the Persian Gulf. Moreover Eden, the Prime Minister, who had succeeded as leader of the Conservative Party on Churchill's retirement, was haunted by historical precedents, and saw in Nasser the equivalent of Hitler. If Britain was not to repeat the errors of the policy of appeasement in the 1930s, Nasser must, he believed, be resisted before it was too late. Inspired in part by this dubious historical parallel, the British government decided, in association with the French and the Israelis, to launch a military attack on Egypt, which, though it brought some gains to the Israelis (and might have brought more had it not been called off as a result of American pressure), achieved nothing for the British and French, and only led to the final expulsion of the British and most of the other Europeans from Egypt and to an end to British prestige and influence throughout much of the Arab world.

The end of the British Empire, whatever psychological effect it may have had on the British people, did not for the most part arouse passionate political debates. This was largely because there were very few parts of the colonial empire where the British had settled permanently and it is significant that the one country the status of which is still unresolved and which has remained at the centre of international controversy – Rhodesia – is the one in which there is a firmly entrenched minority of permanently resident white settlers. In this respect the British were more fortunate than the French, since it was the large French population in North Africa which made the Algerian question so intractable, and caused a prolonged crisis in France with important political consequences. In Indo-China, too, the French were on the defensive from the moment of their resumption of control after the Japanese surrender and their attempt to keep the country within the French Union under a government friendly to France ended in 1954 with the military defeat by the Vietcong at Dien Bien Phu. In their black African empire, on the other hand, they were successful in solving for the time at least, some of the problems left behind by the process of decolonisation. They maintained cultural and educational links with the new independent states (the first President of Senegal, Leopold Sedar Senghor, for example, has a considerable reputation as a poet writing in French and once taught French in a Paris *lycée*). They contributed a larger share of their economic resources than any other European country in aid for the development of their former colonies.

The difficulties of the new relationship between the imperial powers and the new states which had just won independence were considerable. The European countries were anxious to keep their economic advantages, especially in countries such as the Belgian Congo where there were important mineral resources, and therefore to retain enough political influence for this to be possible, while the African intelligentsia, and especially those members of it who grew up in the later stages of the movement for independence, were deeply resentful of the technological superiority of the whites and of their own dependence on them – a resentment given eloquent expression in the writings of the black French West Indian writer Frantz Fanon, in *Les Damnés de la Terre* (The Wretched of the Earth, 1961). On the other hand the new states needed foreign capital for the industrial development which, accepting without question European models and European standards of progress, their governments regarded as essential. For the European states investment in aid to the new states might well increase the market for the export of steel or industrial and agricultural equipment; but much of this expenditure was not likely to produce immediate financial returns, and stemmed rather from motives of political prestige, and, more important, from a general belief that economic growth at home depended on economic growth in the rest of the world. Yet the imbalance between the new states and Europe, marked by the instability of the prices of the primary materials which are the main assets of the developing countries, and on which their economy depends, and by the fact that even generous foreign aid can do little to raise the basic standard of living in many Asian and African countries, remains an obvious and disturbing fact. Here too the United States now plays a more important role than Europe, while the new states, ever on the look-out for what they regard as 'neo-colonialism', in an attempt to avoid the political implications of accepting aid from America or from the former imperial powers of Europe, turn to the Soviet Union and to China for help.

Although the French and Belgians were successful in making special arrangements with the European Economic Community for many of the African states which formerly belonged to their empires, the relations between Europe and the former colonies are still unsettled and uncertain. It is perhaps too soon to strike a balance of the effects in Europe of decolonisation, or even to estimate the direct economic results in any clear or incontrovertible terms. The colonial situation allowed of a variety of different relationships, some of which survived political independence, at least for a time. Moreover those countries which were forced most rapidly to abandon their colonies were those which were most active in spreading in their possessions a knowledge of European ideas and techniques, and who, whether they wanted to or not, provided their subjects with the tools with which to challenge their rule. The century between 1870 and 1970 saw the extension of European power and of European ideas to all parts of the world. The power waned; the ideas stayed. The concepts of equality and of national self-determination which inspired nationalist movements everywhere are European in origin, as are the Marxist doctrines of the class struggle and of the nationalisation of the means of production which form part of the official ideology in many of the new states. Most of them subscribe to European economic theories about growth based on industrialisation. Moreover those imperialist countries which spread these ideas and techniques, notably France and Britain, were those where an enlightened liberal opinion at home was the most critical of the increasingly severe and brutal methods needed to maintain colonial rule, and accordingly made it very hard for their governments to pursue these policies. The very nature and history of the decline of European rule overseas is the greatest tribute to the strength and vitality of European ideas.

The changes in Europe's relations with the rest of the world and Europe's division as a result of the Cold War have led to much discussion both about the nature of European civilisation and about Europe's political role in a world which seemed to be dominated strategically and culturally by the United States and the USSR.

As the survival of a separate cultural identity for Europe became more and more doubtful, West Europeans reacted in different ways. Some – in Scotland, Wales or Brittany for example – tried to revive a local national culture and to ensure the survival of languages spoken by a minority, both in the hope of achieving political autonomy and of meeting the threat of a growing standardisation by the assertion of a local cultural identity. The success of such movements was limited, both because complete independence was impractical either politically or economically, and because, even where political

473

independence had been achieved, as in Eire, the attractions of an international, transatlantic culture still proved strong; decades of inculcating Irish as an official language failed to make it a living one. Sometimes these movements expressed themselves in acts of terrorist violence; and in the case of the Basques in north-east Spain such violence was a natural response to the severe repression of the Basque provinces since the end of the Spanish Civil War. In Belgium the increasing insistence of the Flemish-speaking members of the population on the use of their own language threatened the stability of the state, as well as imposing on the small country the expensive necessity of duplicating many of its institutions, such as the radio and television services, in order to provide for both the Flemish- and French-speaking Belgians, who began to feel less in common with each other even if no alternative political arrangement seemed possible.

The movement for European unity seemed to some a way of asserting Europe's identity and of restoring Europe's place in the world when European rule in Africa and Asia was coming to an end and when the individual states of Europe were no longer powerful enough to equal America or Russia. There was much talk in the early 1950s of turning Europe into a 'Third Force' in world politics which would hold the balance between the United States and the Soviet Union. This has not come about, largely because both the political allegiance of the liberal capitalist democracies (as well as of the oppressive capitalist autocracies such as Greece or Spain) inevitably lies with America rather than with the Soviet Union. Nuclear weapons, and the immense cost of constructing and maintaining them, have obviously introduced a new and overwhelming element of strategic imbalance. Europe without nuclear weapons – and those constructed by France and Britain have been as much objects of national prestige as of effective strategic use – must rely on one or other of the super-powers, so that the countries of Europe have been obliged by the strategic necessities of the Cold War to choose sides. At the same time the increasing economic control of European industry by American capital, resulting from the complexity and expense of contemporary technological organisation, make it hard for dreams of European independence to be realised. Even de Gaulle, who went further than any West European leader since the war in trying to act independently of the United States, did not succeed, in spite of the French nuclear weapons and the attempt to unsettle the dollar by the accumulation of gold, in freeing French industry from American influence; and France remains a country in which a high proportion of investment in the most important and the most modern industries is in American hands.

The search for a middle way between Soviet communism and American capitalism has continued to be the main preoccupation of the Left in Western Europe – and indeed in Eastern Europe too, whenever there has seemed a chance to take 'different roads to socialism', as in Poland in 1956 or

Czechoslovakia in the spring of 1968. The old Social Democratic parties are now pragmatic and reformist, and have, notably in West Germany, deliberately eschewed ideology and concentrated on practical political programmes. In West Germany, where there is no Communist competition, this has won votes for the Social Democrats, but in France and Italy it has posed problems about their relations with the Communist Parties: the French Socialists have declined in strength, and by 1970 seemed more conservative in many respects than the left wing of the Radical Party. The opportunity of forming a mass working-class party has also posed problems for the Communists as it did in the 1920s. Since the death of Stalin the Communists both in France and Italy have had to face serious internal crises, both as a reaction against Soviet repression of attempts at an independent form of communism in Hungary or Czechoslovakia, and even more as a result of the emergence of Peking as a rival to Moscow as capital of the communist world.

Although the Communist leaders in France and Italy have retained their hold over their parties, this has been, especially in Italy, at the cost of permitting a wide measure of free discussion within the party. The loosening of Soviet control has also forced these parties to decide what their role is to be in the day-to-day politics of their own countries. Both in France and Italy the result has been that, for the time at least, the Communist Parties appear by no means revolutionary. In France, when in May 1968 the students' revolt had detonated an explosion of social unrest throughout the country, the Communists came out firmly against those industrial workers who were conducting sit-in strikes on syndicalist lines, and appeared paradoxically in the role of the upholders of order and of constitutional methods. In Italy the Communist Party in the late 1960s has also been anxious to show its devotion to the parliamentary system and to establish the possibility that it might play a part in a coalition government. Although in France there have been extensive ideological discussions of Marxist philosophy, and attempts to define the relationship between Marxism and such later doctrines as Existentialism and Structuralism, just as in the 1920s there were endless attempts to relate Freud and Marx, and although in Italy there has been a revival of interest in the works of Antonio Gramsci, who died in a Fascist prison in 1937 and who suggested the possibility of a more humanistic communist doctrine, the dilemma of the Western communist in a prosperous capitalist society has not found an ideological answer, but has led rather to concentration on short-term political action and organisation.

In Eastern Europe the changes and developments within the communist parties are harder to detect than in the West, where democratic processes and the need to appeal competitively to a mass electorate produce a certain publicity of discussion even within the communist parties. The one-party state minimises the electoral process which is central to the political institutions of the West European countries, apart from Spain and Portugal, but elections perhaps seem less important where, as in some of the Balkan countries, they were between the wars conducted in an atmosphere of cynical political pressure and fraud in which they would hardly be described as free. The atrophy of the electoral process has focused attention upon the communist party itself. Changes of policy in communist countries have been the result of changes of balance within a narrow ruling group, changes which are often hard to detect and difficult to analyse. However the nuances of policy, the shifts towards and away from greater freedom of intellectual activity or artistic expression, have all taken place within a rigid framework which has so far, over more than twenty-five years, stood the strain imposed on it by hostile local traditions or external examples as well as by objective social and economic problems. For the last quarter of a century the development of Eastern Europe has been wholly different from that of Western Europe, institutionally, socially, economically and intellectually, in spite of a growing amount of trade and in spite of attempts at intellectual and academic contacts. How long this can remain the case is one of the great, as yet unanswered questions of contemporary history.

As the official communist parties in Western Europe have become more bureaucratic, so there have been attempts to start revolutionary movements independent of them. Young radicals, especially among students, have tried to form a New Left which will embody the ideals which the communist parties have lost.

This movement was inspired in part by enthusiasm – often based on ignorance and misunderstanding – for the revolutions in China and Cuba, but it also had serious intellectual origins in the teachings of social critics such as the philosopher Herbert Marcuse and the sociologist Theodore W. Adorno, who had been young radicals in the Weimar Republic, and who had been forced to emigrate, so that their influence was felt in the United States (where Marcuse continued to teach after the Second World War) as well as in Germany. The radical student movement has been an international one which has affected Europe, America and Japan. In Europe it had its most dramatic expression in the students' revolt in Paris in the spring of 1968, and in Germany in the late 1960s its violence brought the work of several universities to a stop for a long period. Behind the hysteria and intolerant dogmatism which was often a typical feature of these movements, especially in Germany, there was a genuine criticism of society. The socialist ideal of a society organised on the basis of the rule 'to each according to his need' could not be achieved, Marcuse suggested, until men's needs had been changed. In the world of today men's desires have become so hopelessly corrupted by the existing social and economic system, so debased by the influence of the mass media, that any reorganisation of society is pointless unless it is preceded by a revolution in human nature. The destruction of the existing system – the exercise of what Marcuse once called 'the liberating function of negation' – must be accompanied by a personal revolution in the values of the individual. Thus the attack on society – and for each individual the immediate target is that section of society immediately confronting him, so that the student's first objective is the destruction or transformation of the university – is accompanied by an insistence on a new style of life, expressing itself in a style of dress or more seriously in the organising of a new communal pattern of group living. Those observers who remember the enthusiasm with which German students in the early 1930s adopted the mindless violence of the Nazis, and enthusiastically burnt the books by writers of whom they disapproved, were understandably shocked by the intolerant anti-intellectualism of some of the student radicalism. But this movement, apart from being based on a genuine criticism of contemporary society, has as yet had no links outside the universities and has so far failed, except briefly in France in 1968, to perform the function of a detonator which would set off a revolution among the mass of workers.

The division of Europe politically and economically has been accompanied by a cultural division. In Eastern Europe the domination of a dreary, conventional and mechanical Marxism, an official dogma to which everyone had formally to subscribe, meant that intellectuals and artists were limited in their activities and hampered to a greater or lesser degree, which changed from time to time and from country to country, in their contacts with the West. A few, especially in Germany, moved from the German Democratic Republic to the Federal Republic, and these included some interesting and important radical thinkers and social critics, such as the philosopher Ernst Bloch. A few had sufficiently high international reputations to be allowed a certain freedom of expression and movement, at least for reasons of prestige and propaganda. It was not a climate in which original philosophy or the creative arts could easily flourish; and those artists who lived in the communist countries, even when, like Bertolt Brecht in East Berlin, they had chosen to work there, were under considerable strain. Some Russian writers, as well as the composer Dmitri Shostakovich, managed to win an international reputation: but the award of the Nobel Prize for Literature to the poet Boris Pasternak in 1958, after the publication in the West of his novel *Doctor Zhivago*, a detached, poetic and melancholy account of life during the revolution, and in 1970 to Alexander Solzhenitsyn, the author of brilliant and painful novels about the plight of the dissident members of Soviet society, only served to bring them into deeper disgrace.

In the other East European countries artists had a little more freedom, and the doctrine of Social Realism, which had killed the visual arts in the Soviet Union, was not as rigidly enforced, so that in Poland for example painters were able to work in the styles current among advanced artists in the West, and the Poles were able to produce some of the most original films in the history of the cinema, while in Hungary composers were able to work in advanced idioms. The most important means of control over artistic and intellectual life was the direct dependence of scholars, writers and artists on the state. This ensured that those who had received the necessary professional training and those whose work was acceptable to the authorities were treated as privileged members of society: their livelihood was secured, and they enjoyed the benefits of belonging to an officially recognised elite. The disadvantage however was that, if the authorities disapproved of the activities of a university teacher or an artist, the victim of this disapproval had no alternative open to him except to seek, if he was lucky, such menial employment as was permitted to him, once he was deprived of his membership of the state-run bodies responsible for the organisation of intellectual and artistic activities. For the original thinker and the independent artist life was in the most literal terms a struggle for survival, and his works could, especially in the Soviet Union itself, often only become known through underground channels, and circulate in typescript copies passed from hand to hand.

If intellectual and cultural life in Eastern Europe reflected, with local and temporary modifications, the rigid and authoritarian structure of the Soviet system, the culture of Western Europe after the Second World War was deeply influenced by the United States. Many European scholars and artists had taken refuge there before and during the war and had introduced ideas and movements which had then contributed to original developments in America itself. The Americans had absorbed for example the teachings of European psychologists or sociologists, or the style and views of the Surrealists, while the leading architects of the *Bauhaus* (see pp. 308–9 above), notably Gropius and Mies van der Rohe, became influential teachers in American architectural schools. This in turn fitted in with attempts in Europe, especially in Germany, to pick up the threads of cultural development where they had been broken off in the early 1930s, and with the revival of some of the ideas and styles of the 1920s – Surrealism for example and the rediscovery, in such enterprises as the 'Theatre of the Absurd' and in some aspects of 'Pop' art, of the iconoclasm and mockery of Dada. By the 1950s the Americans were themselves pioneers of new methods in social analysis and new ways in social thought which soon dominated many aspects of European political science. In the visual arts a school of New York developed which was to supersede the school of Paris as the focal point of new art in Europe as well as America. As new styles in art succeeded each other in ever more rapid succession, it became almost impossible to decide what had originated in Europe and what in America. The old European masters of the twentieth century – Matisse who died in 1954, Braque who died in 1963 and Picasso who celebrated his ninetieth birthday in 1971 – had long been great international figures, and the younger artists now belonged as much to America as to Europe. Styles and markets were both international and, as American methods of marketing and advertising became more and more prevalent in Europe, so too the applied arts provided a common substratum of popular taste for North America and Western Europe, to which many especially of the young people in Eastern Europe looked with envy.

If artists and intellectuals in most of Eastern Europe were imprisoned within a rigid ideological framework, in the West there were scarcely any points of reference at all. There was no universally accepted style in the arts: a number of styles existed side by side or followed each other with extreme rapidity. The old conservative cultural values, derived from the classical and the Christian traditions, which had provided the core of European education for centuries were no longer taken for granted, and even sometimes almost totally forgotten. Even in the most disciplined intellectual system of the Western world, the Roman Catholic Church, demands for reform – for the permission of contraception, for the end of the celibacy of the clergy, for priests who would be found side by side with the workers in the factories – began to be heard, especially from Catholics in the Netherlands, in Britain and in France, where the challenge of the Protestant and secular traditions were strongest.

This eclecticism and confusion of ethical and aesthetic standards, in which observers remarked 'the end of ideology' and the emergence of 'the permissive society', was spread and encouraged by the growth of television, which was daily bringing a flow of heterogeneous images into the homes of the inhabitants even of remote areas of the advanced countries of Western Europe. Between the wars radio had become a powerful political and cultural instrument, as Goebbels' skilful exploitation of it had shown only too clearly. The first television services in Germany and Britain had started on a very limited scale in 1935 and 1936; but it was not until twenty years later that television became the most potent and widely influential of all the mass media, providing a supply of vicarious experiences to millions of viewers. The television networks of Western Europe were sometimes owned by the State and sometimes by private companies, dependent on advertising for their revenue, but this made little difference to the programmes they offered, except in France where de Gaulle kept a sharp eye on the output of the Radio and Television Organisation.

In contrast to the growing flow of mass communications, the bombardment of a continuous stream of images and concepts, some writers and artists have reacted – as in the remarkable plays of the Irish writer Samuel Beckett, such as *Waiting for Godot* (1955) – by stressing the essential incommunicability of human experience and the failure of individual men to make any real contact with each other. The Existentialist message about man's search for his own identity has been reinforced by the sense of alienation which many people have felt in the face of the complexity of technological society and the ceaseless assault by the mass media. As some of the radical critics of Western

479

society in the 1960s pointed out, liberalism has reached a point of permissiveness in which the limitations on personal behaviour are almost non-existent, but in which the economic and political structure of an older society remains untouched. In such a situation it is very easy for individualism simply to turn into a vague revolt against everything, a 'dropping out' of a materialist society and a rejection of all organised movements or groups, even revolutionary ones. Whereas at the end of the nineteenth century some anarchists made heroes out of bandits who, by robbing from the rich and giving to the poor, performed an act of social justice, many young people have taken as their model the tramp, the down-and-out vagrant (such as the protagonists of some of Samuel Beckett's plays and novels) who has eschewed all contact with society and finally opted out of an irredeemably acquisitive world.

In contrast to the belief in the total isolation of the individual and the incommunicability of any common experience, some thinkers have tried to discover the common element in the way individuals think and express themselves and in the way different societies are organised. The French anthropologist Claude Lévi-Strauss has tried to show from his studies of 'primitive' societies, in books such as *La Pensée Sauvage* (The Savage Mind, 1962) and *Le Cru et le Cuit* (The Raw and the Cooked, 1964) – the first volume of a trilogy called *Mythologies* – that there are certain conceptual structures which are common to men of highly different environments, while the development of the study of linguistics has also suggested ways of looking for common features in the structure of different languages. 'Structuralism', in its emphasis on the search for models which are applicable to all human experience and on what is common to all mankind, stands in contrast to Existentialism, which it succeeded as the dominant intellectual doctrine in France and other parts of Western Europe. At the same time European philosophical systems and methods from Marxism to Structuralism have provided American thought with the framework of ideas which the pragmatic American tradition has lacked; and it is increasingly hard to say what are the cultural debts which America owes to Europe and what are owed by Europe to the United States.

It is too soon to see, in the flux of styles, fashions and philosophies which have succeeded each other in Western Europe since the end of the Second World War, which will be the lasting movements and which will seem to later historians to have affected the quality of European society, just as it is impossible to predict how far the rejection of traditional artistic activities and of old-established codes of behaviour may yet go. Will there be a *rappel à l'ordre*, a new puritanism in morals and aesthetics for which conservatives have been calling? Will the often inchoate movements of revolt or self-expression turn into an organised revolutionary wave? Are we witnessing the beginnings of a new revolt against materialism, hypocrisy and authoritarianism? Will the gap between advanced artistic expression and popular culture, which has worried artists throughout the twentieth century, be narrowed? Is it true that the economic achievements of Western Europe, a rising standard of living and the development of uniform patterns of consumption and social behaviour for much of Western Europe are producing a society in which the search for personal material satisfaction has led to 'an end of ideology'? Or are young people in the 1970s in fact looking for an ideology which will provide a basis for revolt against the material acquisitiveness of our society? And in Eastern Europe also it is too soon to predict the future of communist society and of communist ideology, or to foresee what modifications may occur or how far Russian control may be loosened and a variety of types of socialism develop, now that there is an alternative repository of communist orthodoxy in Peking, and now that the Chinese are challenging not only Russia's role in world politics, but also her ideological leadership of the communist movement.

The uncertainty of the political future of Eastern Europe affects any prediction one might make about Western Europe. If for example the status of East Germany were to change, and the reunification of Germany seemed a practical possibility, it would be hard to maintain the present form of the West European community, since the natural economic, demographical and geographical strength of Germany would be such as to threaten the European balance, and make the only form in which Europe might be able to unite that of a Europe under German hegemony. The history of Europe in the hundred years since 1870 has been dominated politically by the German question, by the need, and the failure, to absorb the economic resources and the productive capacity of Germany into an acceptable European political framework. An attempt to solve this problem has been the great achievement of the European Movement and the great historical contribution of Konrad Adenauer. The new pattern will be strengthened by the adherence to the European Common Market of three new members, Britain, Ireland and Denmark; but could it contain a reunited Germany without confronting the old German question all over again?

To some people the Europe of the Treaty of Rome seems rather a provincial affair. It remains to be seen whether it will stay as an inward-looking small grouping, linked for certain specific and limited purposes, or whether it is capable of expansion and growth. It is true that functional institutions create vested interests; and there is much talk of the development of a European spirit among the bureaucrats in the administrative and political centres of the European organisations in Brussels, Luxemburg and Strasbourg. But vested interests can restrict growth and inhibit change, so that here too the effects of enlarging the membership of the European institutions are unpredictable. Nor does a look at previous historical instances of the development of federations tell us much: both Switzerland and the United

States had to fight civil wars over constitutional issues before emerging in their present form, while political scientists are still arguing over the extent to which the German Customs Union, the *Zollverein*, contributed to the movement for German unification between the 1830s and 1860s. In history each set of events is unique; and if we are to see a united Europe, then this will be something new, for which past examples are of little relevance.

In 1918 the German writer Oswald Spengler published the first version of his enormous best-seller *Der Untergang des Abendlandes* (*The Decline of the West*). It is a book which caught the pessimistic imagination of the Europeans, and especially the Germans, of the 1920s, just as a not dissimilar (though even more rambling and disordered) work of a generation earlier, *Rembrandt as Educator* (see pp. 152-3 above), had done. In this diffuse, repetitive, pretentious but imaginative work Spengler proclaimed that European civilisation was nearing its end: its creativity in science, in the arts, in philosophy and law and politics was exhausted. Its culture was being killed by its own achievements: 'Democracy has by its newspapers completely expelled the book from the mental life of the people.'[3] Its cities, essential for the development of a civilisation, were causing its destruction: 'The giant city sucks the country dry, insatiably and incessantly demanding fresh streams of men, till it wearies and dies in the midst of an almost uninhabited waste of country.'[4] Spengler's message about the corruption of culture and the pollution of the environment is one which is familiar enough fifty years later. His own work soon became discredited outside Germany because of the apparent similarity of many of his ideas to those of the Nazis – although by the time of his death in 1936 Spengler had fallen out of favour because in his last works he expressed certain misgivings about National Socialist policies and behaviour.

Between 1934 and 1954 the English historian Arnold Toynbee published his *Study of History*, a vast work in which the details are always more convincing than the general message. Toynbee was engaged in a search for the patterns according to which civilisations rise and decay and believed, perhaps wrongly, that he was proceeding according to empirical methods. By all the criteria he had established (though these have not satisfied the majority of professional historians), European civilisation at the end of the Second World War might well be expected to succumb in the near future. While for Spengler, with his organic, quasi-biological vision of the life and death of cultures, the only salvation seemed to be a stoical assertion of firmness in treading a predestined path, trusting in the inherent virtues of race for salvation, for Toynbee, whose assumptions were gentler and more humane, the only hope lay in some form of religious conversion and in a vague and eclectic Christianity. If Toynbee's influence was a salutary one in that it directed attention to the importance of studying the history of other cultures as well as that of Europe, its general message, like that of Spengler, was that European civilisation had reached its appointed end.

It was the spectacle of Europe during and between the two world wars which had inspired the construction of these gloomy metaphysical systems; and anyone who looked at Europe at the end of 1945 might have felt that the most pessimistic prophecies were justified, and that the symptoms of decay as described by Spengler and Toynbee were visible on every side. Many of the physical and moral achievements of Europe had been destroyed in the experiences of the war. The economic resources of Europe seemed to be at an end, and it was only help from outside that made recovery possible and gave new hope to much of the Continent. The hopes of a new society which had inspired many members of the Resistance were soon disappointed.

Yet twenty-five years later it is possible to take a less apocalyptic view. The economic recovery of Europe has been startling, its inhabitants, including those of Eastern Europe, have achieved a higher standard of living than anywhere else in the world outside North America, Australia and New Zealand, and more recently Japan. Indeed this high standard of living poses a question of conscience with regard to Europe's relations with and duties towards the under-developed world and has also raised ugly problems of race relations, as workers from poorer lands have been attracted to the cities of Western Europe. Moreover among the countries of Western Europe economic interests have encouraged the move towards unification and the establishment of common institutions – though even on the economic level these have not always achieved as much as had been hoped: by 1971 they had still failed to produce a common monetary policy for example. In the view of many people a new Europe has been born.

The cost of achieving major technological ambitions, such as a space programme, has so far, perhaps fortunately, exceeded what the countries of Europe can afford, but the technological skills and the artistic vitality of Europe still remain worthy of the great European tradition. The pressures on Eastern Europe leave its inhabitants with less scope to develop these talents or to solve their own social, political and intellectual problems, but even this situation may change. In Western Europe the possibility of utilising in its own way its great economic and intellectual resources still exists. By the end of the 1960s the people of the United States were acutely aware of their own problems, domestic and international, and no longer as certain as before that they had solutions for the rest of the world. The result may be to make the relationship between the United States and Europe both more ambiguous and more reciprocal. The original encouragement of the movement towards the unification of Western Europe may give way to suspicion if the European Common Market erects barriers to American trade and does not need more American investment; and in the eyes of many Europeans the attraction of a united Europe lies in the prospect which this offers of greater political and economic independence from the United States. Yet as the practical and cultural links between the two continents become closer, the speed of travel greater and its cost smaller, so it becomes increasingly hard to differentiate two separate civilisations. For all Europe's apparent political weakness compared with the United States and Russia, it has continued to retain its intellectual and artistic importance. And perhaps each crisis of confidence in the United States increases the confidence of Europeans in their ability to organise their own future, as well as making much of Western Europe seem to many Americans an attractive place in which to live.

It has sometimes been suggested that the Europeans, who have made history for so long, might at last opt out of history into a comfortable and passive neutrality. However Europe's geographical position, her wealth and her inventiveness, especially if these can be organised and mobilised on a supra-national basis, make this policy of resignation a hard one. The role of Europe in world history is still different from that of any other continent. The danger is that any shift in the world balance of power might deprive Europe of the breathing-space needed to find its new role by plunging it into a third world war which would end in obliteration. There were signs in the early 1970s that international tension in Europe itself might be reduced and Europe's breathing-space prolonged.

Yet any hopes about the future course of European history can only be guarded or limited ones. The optimistic belief in progress, humanity and toleration which was characteristic of most European thought in 1870 was largely killed by the experiences of two world wars and of the methods and policies of the European dictatorships. But hope dies hard: some people in Europe still believe that all problems have solutions, that there is nothing which science and technology rationally applied cannot cure and that continuing economic growth is both inevitable and desirable. However as the Europeans look beyond their own countries and beyond their own continent, and even at the growing congestion, noise and squalor of their own great cities and the increasing pollution of their rivers, lakes and seas, the basis for optimism is not easy to find. Beyond the immediate fear of destruction by nuclear war lies a longer-term danger caused by world population growth and the exhaustion of the world's supplies of raw materials. The price of Europe's industrial success and technological achievements may still have to be paid. The immediate prophecies of the decline of the West of fifty years ago have not perhaps been justified and the standard of living in Europe is probably higher than ever before, but when we try to look beyond say the year 2000, our confidence in the future quickly fades away. If the forebodings of the most pessimistic demographers, geographers and ecologists are correct, the historian will have to face not just the end of European history but the end of world history as we have known it. The last hundred years of European history have been a period of splendours as well as of miseries: let us hope there will still be historians left a hundred years from now to assess whether the past century was just the end of an epoch or the beginning of a new one.

NOTES

Chapter 1

1 MICHAEL HOWARD, *The Franco-Prussian War* (paperback edn, London 1967), p. 10.
2 Quoted in JOHANNES ZIEKURSCH, *Politische Geschichte des neuen deutschen Kaiserreiches* (Frankfurt-am-Main 1927), II: *Das Zeitalter Bismarcks (1871–1890)*, p. 317.
3 Quoted in FEDERICO CHABOD, *Storia della Politica Estera Italiana del 1870 al 1896* (Bari 1951), I: *Le Premesse*, p. 189.
4 ALBERT SOREL, *La Question d'Orient au 18e Siècle* (Paris 1878), p. 309.
5 Laboulaye in Assemblée Nationale, 28 January 1875, quoted in J.E.C. Bodley, *France* (London 1898), I, p. 54.
6 SIR E.GREY in House of Commons, 3 August 1914. *Hansard*, Fifth Series, LXV, p. 1822.
7 Quoted in ASA BRIGGS, *The Age of Improvement* (London 1959), p. 453.
8 Quoted in ALEXANDER GERSCHENKRON, 'Agrarian Policies and Industrialisation: Russia 1861–1917', in *Cambridge Economic History of Europe* (Cambridge 1965), VI, p. 710.
9 Quoted in GERSCHENKRON, in *Cambridge Economic History of Europe*, VI, p. 765.
10 SIR E.GREY, letter to President Theodore Roosevelt, December 1906, in G.M.Trevelyan, *Grey of Fallodon* (London 1937), pp. 114–15.

Chapter 2

1 Quoted in A.SARTORIUS VON WALTERSHAUSEN, *Deutsche Wirtschaftsgeschichte 1814–1914* (Jena 1923), p. 134.
2 ADNA FERRIN WEBER, *The Growth of Cities* (New York 1899; reprinted Ithaca 1963), p. 446.
3 WEBER, *Growth of Cities*, p. 347.
4 *Neue Freie Presse*, 23 December 1909, quoted in James Joll, *Intellectuals in Politics* (London 1960), p. 73.
5 J.L.GARVIN, *The Life of Joseph Chamberlain* (London 1932), I, p. 549.
6 Quoted in A.M.MCBRIAR, *Fabian Socialism and English Politics* (Cambridge 1962), p. 241.

7 Quoted in CHARLES SEIGNOBOS, *L'Evolution de la 3e République, Histoire de France contemporaine*, ed. Ernest Lavisse (Paris 1921), VIII, p. 149.
8 POPE LEO XIII, *Encyclical Letter on the Condition of Labour : Rerum Novarum* (Official tr., London 1891), p. 3.
9 MAX BONNAFOUS (ed.), *Oeuvres de Jean Jaurès : Etudes Socialistes I 1888–1897* (Paris 1931), p. 236.

Chapter 3

1 Quoted in CHARLES THOMANN, *Le Mouvement Anarchiste dans les montagnes neuchâteloises et le Jura bernois* (La Chaux de Fonds 1947), p. 52.
2 KARL MARX, *Address of the General Council of the International Working Mens Association on the Civil War in France, 1871* (reprinted Peking 1966), p. 99.
3 GUSTAV MAYER, *Friedrich Engels : eine Biographie* (The Hague 1934), p. 352.
4 FRIEDRICH ENGELS, *Socialism : Utopian and Scientific* (1892), in *Essential Works of Marxism*, ed. Arthur P. Mendel (New York 1961), p. 82.
5 Proceedings of the International Socialist Congress at Amsterdam, Friday 19 August 1904. Quoted in James Joll, *The Second International, 1889–1914* (London 1955), p. 103.
6 *Protokoll über die Verhandlungen des Parteitages der Sozialdemokratischen Partei Deutschlands 1891*. See also Carl Schorske, *German Social Democracy* (Harvard 1955), ch. 1.
7 Quoted in ADAM B.ULAM, *Lenin and the Bolsheviks* (paperback edn, London 1969), p. 283.
8 A translation of the Stuttgart Resolution is printed in Joll, *Second International*, pp. 196–8.

Chapter 4

1 LEONARD WOOLF, *Imperialism and Civilisation* (London 1928), pp. 34–5.
2 L.BRUNSCHWIG, *Mythes et réalités de l'impérialisme colonial français* (Paris 1960), p. 9.
3 BRUNSCHWIG, *Mythes et réalités*, p. 23.
4 BRUNSCHWIG, *Mythes et réalités*, p. 24.
5 SALISBURY to Sir E. Baring, 5 February 1892. GWENDOLEN CECIL, *Robert, Marquis of Salisbury*, (London 1931), III, p. 218.
6 *The Letters of Queen Victoria 1896–1901*, Third Series (London 1932), III, p. 181. See also Max Beloff, *Imperial Sunset*, (London 1969), I pp. 20 ff.
7 BEATRICE WEBB, Diary entry, 25 June 1897, *Our Partnership*, ed. Barbara Drake and Margaret I. Cole (London 1948), p. 140.
8 SIR E.GREY to President Theodore Roosevelt, December 1906, in G.M. Trevelyan, *Grey of Fallodon* (London 1937), pp. 114–15.
9 Quoted in GUY CHAPMAN, *The Third Republic of France : The First Phase 1871–1894* (London 1962), p. 247.
10 Quoted in CHRISTOPHER SETON-WATSON, *Italy from Liberalism to Fascism* (London 1967), p. 138. See also William L. Langer, *The Diplomacy of Imperialism* (2nd edn, New York 1951), p. 272.

11 SETON-WATSON, *Italy from Liberalism to Fascism*, p. 179.

12 Quoted in A.J.P.TAYLOR, *Bismarck*, paperback edition (London 1961), p. 221.

13 GARVIN, *Life of Joseph Chamberlain* (London 1933), III, p. 508.

14 LORD ROSEBERY, Rectorial Address, Glasgow University, 16 November 1900. See also Wolfgang J. Mommsen, 'Nationale und ökonomische Faktoren im britischen Imperialismus vor 1914', *Historische Zeitschrift*, 206/3 (June 1968).

15 A.M.GOLLIN, *Proconsul in Politics* (London 1964), p. 131.

16 *Jeunesses royalistes de France*, December 1898, quoted in Eugen Weber, *Action Française* (Stanford 1962), p. 25.

17 ANDRÉ BLUMEL, *Léon Blum, Juif et Zioniste* (Paris 1951), p. 5. Quoted in James Joll, *Intellectuals in Politics* (London 1960), pp. 5-6.

18 PETER G.J.PULZER, *The Rise of Political Anti-Semitism in Germany and Austria* (London 1964), p. 204.

19 WALTHER RATHENAU, 'Staat und Judentum' in *Gesammelte Schriften* (Berlin 1918), I, pp. 188-9. See also Joll, *Intellectuals in Politics*, p. 65.

20 NORMAN COHN, *Warrant for Genocide* (London 1967), p. 18.

21 THEODOR HERZL, 13 August 1900, M. Lowenthal (ed.), *The Diaries of Theodor Herzl* (New York 1956) p. 330. See also Walter Laqueur, *A History of Zionism* (London 1972) p. 112.

Chapter 5

1 The phrase is taken from the title of the important book by H. Stuart Hughes, *Consciousness and Society: The Reorientation of European Social Thought 1890-1930* (New York 1958; Eng. paperback edn, London 1967).

2 JOHN MORLEY, *Life of Gladstone* (London 1903), III, p. 512.

3 VON HOETZENDORFF, *Aus meiner Dienstzeit* (Vienna 1923), IV, p. 153.

4 SETON-WATSON, *Italy from Liberalism to Fascism* (London 1967), p. 197.

5 SETON-WATSON, pp. 266-7.

6 *I Manifesti del Futurismo* (Milan 1920), I, p. 36.

7 *La Stampa*, 15 May 1924, quoted in Enrico Falqui, *Il Futurismo: Il Novecentismo* (Turin 1955), p. 16.

8 GAETANO MOSCA, *Elementi di Scienza Politica* (Turin 1923), p. 145.

9 DENIS MACK SMITH, *Italy: a Modern History* (Ann Arbor 1959), p. 139.

10 VILFREDO PARETO, *Manuel d'Economie Politique* (1909), printed in *Vilfredo Pareto: Sociological Writings*, ed. S.E.Finer (London 1966), p. 154.

11 V.PARETO, *Les Systèmes Socialistes* (1902) in Finer, *Vilfredo Pareto*, p. 134.

12 V.PARETO, *The Mind and Society*, ed. A.Livingston (4 vols, London 1935), IV, para. 2255.

13 V.PARETO, *Les Systèmes Socialistes* in Finer, *Vilfredo Pareto*, p. 139.

14 V.PARETO, *The Mind and Society*, IV, para. 2274.

15 HERBERT SPENCER, *Social Statics* (London 1892), p. 31. See also Philip Rieff, *The Triumph of the Therapeutic* (London 1966), p. 7.

16 WOLFGANG MOMMSEN, *Max Weber und die deutsche Politik* (Tübingen 1959), p. 70.

17 EMILE DURKHEIM, quoted in *Varieties of Classic Social Theory*, ed. Hendrik M.Ruitembeck (New York 1963), p. 332.

18 STUART HUGHES, *Consciousness and Society*, p. 280.

19 HERBERT SPENCER, *The Study of Sociology* (2nd edn, London 1874), p. 328, quoted in J.W.Burrow, *Evolution and Society : A Study in Victorian Social Theory* (Cambridge 1966), p. 198.

20 HENRI BERGSON, *Matière et Mémoire* (Paris 1900), p. 218.

21 H.BERGSON, *Introduction to Metaphysics* (Eng. tr., London 1913), p. 8.

22 A.B.WALKLEY, *The Times Literary Supplement*, 4 December 1913, quoted in George D.Painter, *Marcel Proust : A Biography* (London 1965), II, p. 251.

Chapter 6

1 DAVID S.LANDES, *The Unbound Prometheus* (Cambridge 1969), p. 323.

2 THORSTEIN VEBLEN, *Imperial Germany and the Industrial Revolution* (New York 1915), p. 124.

3 WALTHER RATHENAU: *Zur Kritik der Zeit, Gesammelte Schriften* (Berlin 1918), XI, pp. 75–6.

4 W.RATHENAU, *Briefe* (Dresden 1926), II, p. 280.

5 LEO TOLSTOY, *What then must we do?* (Eng. tr. Worlds Classics edn, London 1950), p. 311.

6 FRITZ STERN, *The Politics of Cultural Despair* (Berkeley and Los Angeles 1961), p. xvii.

7 STERN, *Politics of Cultural Despair*, p. 116.

8 [JULIUS LANGBEHN], *Rembrandt als Erzieher, von einem Deutschen* (Leipzig 1890), quoted in Stern, *Politics of Cultural Despair*, p. 135.

9 LANGBEHN, *Rembrandt als Erzieher*, p. 199.

10 LANGBEHN, *Rembrandt als Erzieher*, p. 272.

11 LANGBEHN, *Rembrandt als Erzieher*, pp. 315–16.

12 W.KINDT (ed.), *Grundschriften der deutschen Jugendbewegung* (Düsseldorf 1963), p. 63. See also R.H.Samuel and R.Hinton Thomas, *Education and Society in Modern Germany* (London 1949), p. 28.

13 See WALTER Z.LAQUEUR, *Young Germany* (London 1962).

14 LAQUEUR, *Young Germany*, p. 80.

15 EUGEN WEBER, 'Pierre de Coubertin and the introduction of organised sport in France', *Journal of Contemporary History*, Vol. 5, No. 2 (1970).

16 *Die Grosse Politik der Europäischen Kabinette* (Berlin 1924), XVI, p. 267.

17 LT GEN. R.S.S.BADEN-POWELL, *Scouting for Boys* (rev. edn, London 1909), p. 267.

18 BADEN-POWELL, *Scouting for Boys*, pp. 270–1.

19 *Architectural Review* (July 1905), quoted in Reyner Banham, *Theory and Design in the First Machine Age* (London 1960), p. 47.

20 NIKOLAUS PEVSNER, *Pioneers of Modern Design* (rev. edn. London 1960), p. 181.

21 PEVSNER, *Pioneers of Modern Design*, p. 30.

22 BANHAM, *Theory and Design*, p. 72.

23 BANHAM, *Theory and Design*, p. 80.

24 See JOLL, *Intellectuals in Politics*, pp. 179–84.

25 HOETZENDORFF, *Aus meiner Dienstzeit*, IV, pp. 128–9.

26 J.J.RUEDORFFER (pseudonym for K.Riezler), *Grundzüge der Weltpolitik in den Gegenwart* (Stuttgart and Berlin 1914), p. 23.

27 Gollin, *Proconsul in Politics*, pp. 128–9.
28 Quoted in HALVDAN KOHT, *The Life of Ibsen* (London 1931), II, p. 173.
See also Michael Meyer, *Henrik Ibsen* (London 1971), II: *The Farewell to Poetry 1864–1882*, p. 299.
29 Preface to *Heartbreak House* (1919). See also Samuel Hynes, *The Edwardian Turn of Mind*, p. 339.
30 *Il Pensiero Romagnolo* (November–December 1908), quoted in G.Pini and D.Susmel, *Mussolini – L'Uomo e l'Opera* (Florence 1950), I, p. 117.
31 VLADIMIR DEDIJER, *The Road to Sarajevo* (London 1967), p. 288.
32 From the notes put together by Nietzsche's sister after his death under the title *Die Wille zur Macht* (The Will to Power). *Vorrede* (Prologue) in *Friedrich Nietzsche, Werke in zwei Bänden*, ed. A. Messer (Stuttgart 1930), p. 315.

Chapter 7

1 *Treaty of Versailles*, Article 231.
2 HOETZENDORFF, *Aus meiner Dienstzeit*, I, p. 379, quoted in Gerhard Ritter, *Staatskunst und Kriegshandwerk* (Munich 1963), II, p. 302.
3 *Die grosse Politik der europäischen Kabinette*, XXVI/ii, no. 9493, p. 724.
4 Quoted in C.A.MACARTNEY, *The Habsburg Empire 1790–1918* (London 1968), p. 789.
5 Quoted in RITTER, *Staatskunst und Kriegshandwerk*, II, p. 311.
6 SIR SIDNEY LEE, *King Edward VII* (London 1927), II, p. 615.
7 WINSTON CHURCHILL in House of Commons 26 March 1913. *Hansard*, Fifth Series, I, pp. 1749–91. See E.L.Woodward, *Great Britain and the German Navy* (Oxford 1935), p. 408.
8 *Manchester Guardian*, 31 July 1914, quoted in Lawrence W.Martin, *Peace without Victory* (New Haven 1958), p. 47.
9 G.P.GOOCH and HAROLD TEMPERLEY (eds), *British Documents on the Origins of the War* (BDOW) (London 1927–36), III, No. 299.
10 BARON SCHILLING, *How the War began in 1914* (London 1925), quoted in Luigi Albertini, *The Origins of the War of 1914* (Eng. tr., London 1957), III, p. 290.
11 O.HOETZSCH (ed.), *Die Internationalen Beziehungen im Zeitalter des Imperialismus*, First Series (Berlin 1931–4), V, p. 37, quoted in Albertini, *Origins of the War of 1914*, II, p. 350.
12 BDOW, XI, No. 293.
13 DAVID LLOYD GEORGE, *War Memoirs* (new edn, London 1934), I, p. 41.
14 EMILE VANDERVELDE, 'La Guerre Italo-turque et l'Internationale', *Revue Socialiste* LIV (1911), p. 492, quoted in Georges Haupt, *Der Kongress fand nicht statt* (Vienna 1968), p. 59.
15 BDOW, XI, No. 367.
16 *Protokoll über die Verhandlungen des Parteitages der Sozialdemokratischen Partei Deutschlands* (Berlin 1891), p. 285.
17 EMILE VANDERVELDE, *Souvenirs d'un Militant Socialiste* (Paris 1939), p. 171.
18 J.A.SPENDER and CYRIL ASQUITH, *Life of Lord Oxford and Asquith*, p. 83.

19 NORMAN STONE, 'Army and Society in the Habsburg Monarchy, 1900–1914', *Past and Present*, No. 33 (April 1966), p. 100.

20 *Die Grosse Politik*, XXXIX, p. 364.

21 VISCOUNT GREY of Fallodon, *Twenty-Five Years 1892–1916* (London 1925), II, p. 20.

22 WALTHER RATHENAU, *Staat und Vaterland* (October 1918), p. 43.

23 Quoted in FRITZ STERN, 'Bethmann-Hollweg and the War', *The Responsibility of Power*, eds L.Krieger and F.Stern (New York 1967), p. 267.

24 FRIEDRICH MEINECKE, *Strassburg–Freiburg–Berlin 1901–1919* (Stuttgart 1949), p. 137.

25 *Why we are at War : Great Britain's Case* by Members of the Oxford Faculty of Modern History (Oxford 1914), p. 120.

26 *Le Temps*, 11 August 1914, quoted in Romain Rolland, *Journal des Années de Guerre* (Paris 1942), p. 37.

27 M. CORDAY, *Anatole France* (Paris 1927) p. 217, quoted in Annie Kriegel, *Aux origines du parti communiste français 1914-20* (Paris 1964) I, p. 83.

28 Bergson to the Académie des Sciences Morales, quoted in Rolland, *Journal*, p. 39.

29 RUPERT BROOKE, 'The Dead', *1914 and Other Poems* (London 1915).

30 JEAN JAURÈS, *Oeuvres*, ed. M.Bonnafous, *Pour la Paix II* (Paris 1931), p. 247.

Chapter 8

1 V.I.LENIN, 'Letters from Afar' I: *Collected Works* (New York 1932), XX, p. 28.

2 *Correspondenzblatt* 1 January 1916, quoted in Gerald D.Feldman, *Army, Industry and Labor in Germany 1914–1918* (Princeton 1966), p. 109.

3 D.W.BROGAN, *The Development of Modern France* (London 1914), p. 479, n. 1.

4 Quoted in MARC FERRO, *La Grande Guerre 1914–1918* (Paris 1969), p. 292.

5 BERNARD GEORGES and DENISE TINTANT, *Léon Jouhaux : Cinquante ans de syndicalisme* (Paris 1962), I, p. 320.

6 Quoted in ARTHUR MARWICK, *The Deluge : British Society and the First World War* (paperback edn, London 1967), p. 68.

7 BENITO MUSSOLINI, *La Mia Vita* (Rome 1947), p. 200.

8 FRITZ FISCHER, *Griff nach der Weltmacht* (1st edn, Düsseldorf 1961; Eng. tr., *Germany's Aims in the First World War*, London 1967).

9 A.J.P.TAYLOR, *The Struggle for Mastery in Europe 1848–1918* (Oxford 1954), p. 556.

10 Quoted in JOHN W.WHEELER-BENNETT, *Wooden Titan : Hindenburg in Twenty Years of German History 1914–1934* (New York 1936), p. 88.

11 Quoted in WHEELER-BENNETT, *Wooden Titan*, p. 90.

12 WOODROW WILSON, Address to Joint Session of the two Houses of Congress, 2 April 1917. Printed in *Official Statements on War Aims and Peace Proposals*, ed. James Brown Scott (Washington 1921), p. 92.

13 SIEGFRIED SASSOON, 'Memorial Tablet Great War' (1918), in *Selected Poems* (London 1925).

14 *Briefe im Kriege*, 4 May 1915, quoted in John Willett, *Expressionism* (London 1970), p. 105.

15 GIUSEPPE UNGARETTI, 'Veglia'. An English version is given in *The Penguin Book of Italian Verse* (London 1958), p. 366.

16 See GUY PEDRONCINI, *Les Mutineries de 1917* (Paris 1967).

17 Quoted in J.HAMPDEN JACKSON, *Clemenceau and the Third Republic* (London 1946), p. 170.

18 HAMPDEN JACKSON, *Clemenceau*, p. 190.

19 Report of the *Büro für Sozialpolitik*, 31 March 1917, quoted in Feldman, *Army, Industry and Labor*, p. 334.

20 Reichstag resolution, 19 July 1917, printed in *Dokumente der deutschen Politik und Geschichte von 1848 bis zur Gegenwart*, ed. J.Hohlfeld (Berlin n.d. 1952 ?), II: *Das Zeitalter Wilhelms II*, p. 354.

21 MICHAEL T.FLORINSKY, *The End of the Russian Empire* (New Haven 1931), p. 90.

22 FLORINSKY, *End of the Russian Empire*, p. 205.

23 GEORGE F.KENNAN, *Russia Leaves the War* (Princeton 1956), pp. 14–15.

24 E.H.CARR, *The Bolshevik Revolution 1917–1923* (New York 1951), I, p. 83.

25 Quoted in EDOUARD DOLLÉANS, *Histoire du Mouvement Ouvrier* (Paris 1946), II: 1871–1936, p. 235.

26 PIERRE LAVAL, in Chamber of Deputies Secret Session 1 June 1917, quoted in Geoffrey Warner, *Pierre Laval and the Eclipse of France* (London 1968), p. 12.

27 FLORINSKY, *End of the Russian Empire*, p. 246.

28 CARR, *Bolshevik Revolution*, I, p. 90.

29 CARR, *Bolshevik Revolution*, I, p. 78.

30 V.I.LENIN, 'State and Revolution', *Collected Works* (New York 1932), XXI, Bk II, p. 168.

31 LENIN, 'State and Revolution', p. 220.

32 LENIN, 'State and Revolution', p. 247.

33 JAMES BUNYAN and H.H.FISHER, *The Bolshevik Revolution 1917–1918 : Documents and Materials* (Stanford 1934), p. 378.

34 BUNYAN and FISHER, *Bolshevik Revolution*, p. 125.

35 DAVID LLOYD GEORGE, *War Memoirs* (London 1936), V, p. 2520.

36 WOODROW WILSON, Address to the Two Houses of Congress, 8 January 1918, printed in *Official Statements on War Aims and Peace Proposals*, pp. 237–8.

37 BUNYAN and FISHER, *Bolshevik Revolution*, p. 527

38 KÜHLMANN, 24 June 1918, printed in *Official Statements on War Aims and Peace Proposals*, p. 347.

39 Quoted in SIEGFRIED A.KAEHLER, 'Vier Quellenkritische Untersuchungen zum Kriegsende 1918', *Studien zur deutschen Geschichte des 19. und 20. Jahrhunderts*, ed. Walter Bussmann (Göttingen 1961), p. 261.

40 Imperial proclamation of 30 September 1918, printed in *The Memoirs of Prince Max of Baden* (Eng. tr., London 1928), I, p. 366.

Chapter 9

1 *The Memoirs of Prince Max of Baden* (Eng. tr., London 1928), II, p. 11.
2 *Foreign Relations of the United States, 1918* (Washington 1933), Supplement I, I, p. 383.
3 WILHELM GROENER, *Lebenserinnerungen* (Gottingen 1957), quoted in F.L.Carsten, *The Reichswehr and Politics 1918–1933*, p. 6. See also John W. Wheeler-Bennett, *The Nemesis of Power* (London 1953), pp. 22 ff.
4 W.GROENER, *op. cit.*, p. 458.
5 WALTHER RATHENAU, *Der Neue Staat* (Berlin 1919), p. 49.
6 Quoted in CARSTEN, *Reichswehr and Politics*, p. 11.
7 FRIEDRICH EBERT, *Schriften, Aufzeichnungen, Reden* (Dresden 1926), II, pp. 127–30. See also Wheeler-Bennett, *Nemesis of Power*, p. 31.
8 C.SEYMOUR (ed.), *The Intimate Papers of Colonel House* (London 1926–8), IV, p. 405. See also Carr, *Bolshevik Revolution* (New York 1953), III, p. 128.
9 RUDOLF L. TÖNÉS, *Béla Kun and the Hungarian Soviet Republic* (New York 1967), p. 143.
10 TÖNÉS, *Béla Kun*, p. 203.
11 JANE DEGRAS (ed.), *The Communist International 1919–1943 : Documents* (Oxford 1956), I, pp. 168–72.
12 ANNIE KRIEGEL, *Aux Origines du Communisme Français 1914–1920* (Paris 1964), I, p. 434.
13 KRIEGEL, *Communisme Français*, p. 774.
14 KRIEGEL, *Communisme Français*, pp. 275–6.
15 *L'Humanité*, 15 November 1918, quoted in Joel Colton, *Léon Blum* (New York 1966), p. 42.
16 EKKI, Letter to the Italian Socialist Party, 27 August 1920, printed in Degras, *Communist International*, I, pp. 188–91.
17 Quoted in JOHN M.CAMMETT, *Antonio Gramsci and the Origins of Italian Communism* (Stanford 1967), pp. 97–8.
18 CAMMETT, *Antonio Gramsci*, p. 106.
19 F.BELLINI and G.GALLI, *Storia del Partito Communista Italiano* (Milan 1953), pp. 84–5.
20 E. H. CARR, *Bolshevik Revolution*, III, p. 385.
21 CARR, *Bolshevik Revolution*, III, p. 289.
22 SETON-WATSON, *Italy from Liberalism to Fascism*, p. 587.
23 LEONARD SCHAPIRO, 'The Concept of Totalitarianism', *Survey*, No. 73 (1969), pp. 93–4.
24 SETON-WATSON, *Italy from Liberalism to Fascism*, p. 661.

Chapter 10

1 LLOYD GEORGE in House of Commons, 16 April 1919, *Hansard*, Fifth Series, CXIV, p. 2936.
2 WOODROW WILSON to Joint Session of Congress, 11 February 1918. Printed in *Official Statement on War Aims and Peace Proposals*, p. 269.

3 Meeting of Council of Four, 6 June 1919, *Foreign Relations of the United States : Paris Peace Conference 1919* (Washington 1946), VI, p. 212.

4 WINSTON S.CHURCHILL, *The Second World War* (London 1948), I: *The Gathering Storm*, p. 7.

5 Meeting of Council of Four, 5 April 1919, *Foreign Relations of the United States : Paris Peace Conference*, V, p. 27.

6 *An Ambassador of Peace : Lord D'Abernon's Diary* (London 1929), II: *The Years of Crisis June 1922–December 1923*, p. 167.

7 Quoted in E.H.CARR, *The Interregnum 1923–1924* (New York 1954), p. 180.

8 GUSTAV STRESEMANN, *Vermächtnis*, 3 vols (Berlin 1933), III, p. 266.

9 STRESEMANN, *Vermächtnis*, II, p. 172.

10 LT GEN. F.VON RABENAU, *Seeckt: Aus seinem Leben* (Leipzig 1940), II, p. 341. See also Wheeler-Bennett, *Nemesis of Power*, p. 108, and F.A.Carsten, *The Reichwehr and Politics*, ch. 4.

11 *An Ambassador of Peace : Lord D'Abernon's Diary*, II, p. 290.

12 STRESEMANN, *Vermächtnis*, I, p. 416.

13 AUSTEN CHAMBERLAIN in House of Commons, 18 November 1925, *Hansard*, Fifth Series, CLXXXVIII, pp. 431–2.

14 FRANZ BORKENAU, *The Communist International* (London 1938), p. 279.

15 ANDRÉ TARDIEU, *La Paix* (Paris 1921), p. 437.

16 Theses of the Sixth Comintern Congress August 1928, printed in *Communist International 1919–1943*, ed. Degras (Oxford 1960), II: *1923–1928*, p. 456.

17 LLOYD GEORGE in House of Commons, 16 April 1919, *Hansard*, Fifth Series, CXIV, pp. 2936–45.

Chapter 11

1 HENRI BARBUSSE, *Le Couteau entre les Dents* (Paris 1921), p. 54, quoted in David Caute, *Communism and the French Intellectuals 1914–1960* (London 1964), p. 77.

2 *The Autobiography of Bertrand Russell, 1914–1944* (London 1968), p. 124.

3 ISAAC DEUTSCHER, *The Prophet Unarmed : Trotsky 1921–1929* (London 1959), p. 190.

4 See SHEILA FITZPATRICK, *The Commissariat of Enlightenment : Soviet Organisation of Education and the Arts under Lunacharsky* (Cambridge 1970).

5 K.MALEVICH, 1919, quoted in Camilla Gray, *The Great Experiment : Russian Art 1863–1922* (London 1962), p. 283.

6 ALEXEI GAN, 'Constructivism', 1920, quoted in Gray, *The Great Experiment*, pp. 285–6.

7 See *Catalogue* of Vladimir Tatlin exhibition, Moderna Museet, Stockholm, 1968.

8 Quoted in V.MAYAKOVSKY, *The Bedbug and Selected Poems*, ed. Patrick Blake and tr. by Max Hayward and George Reevey (London 1961), p. 14.

9 V.MAYAKOVSKY, 'Too early to rejoice' (December 1918), quoted in Fitzpatrick, *The Commissariat of Enlightenment*, p. 125.

10 V.MAYAKOVSKY, 'Back Home!', in Blake, *Bedbug*, pp. 182–19. See also Introduction, p. 12.

11 P.BLAKE, *Bedbug*, p. 48.

12 *Program des staatlichen Bauhauses in Weimar*, 1919, quoted in Barbara Miller Lane, *Architecture and Politics in Germany 1918–1945* (Harvard 1968), p. 50.

13 Quoted in LANE, *Architecture and Politics in Germany*, p. 67.

14 LANE, *Architecture and Politics in Germany*, p. 49.

15 ADOLF HITLER, *Mein Kampf*, with an introduction by D.C.Watt, tr. by Ralph Manheim (London 1969), p. 240.

16 K.VON OSSIETZKY, *Das Tage-Buch*, 20 September 1924, quoted in Istvan Déak, *Weimar Germany's Left Wing Intellectuals* (Berkeley and Los Angeles 1968), p. 59.

17 R.DE JOUVENEL, *La République des Camarades* (Paris 1934).

18 L'Echo de Paris 12 June 1915, quoted in Rolland, *Journal*, p. 211.

19 FRANCIS STEEGMULLER, *Apollinaire, Poet among the Painters* (New York and London 1963), Appendix I. See also John Golding, 'Guillaume Apollinaire and the Art of the Twentieth Century', *Baltimore Museum of Art News*, XXVI, No. 4, XXVII, No. 1 (1963).

20 Printed in STEEGMULLER, *Apollinaire*, Appendix I.

21 Quoted in ROBERT S.SHORT, 'The Politics of Surrealism 1920–36', *Journal of Contemporary History*, I, No. 2 (1966).

22 ANDRÉ BRETON, *Manifestes du Surrealisme* (Paris 1969), p. 37.

23 ERNEST JONES, *The Life and Work of Sigmund Freud* (abridged edn, ed. by Lionel Trilling and Steven Marcus, London 1964), p. 649.

24 KARL JASPERS, 'Reason and Existenz', printed in *Existentialism from Dostoevsky to Sartre*, ed. Walter Kaufmann (Cleveland and New York 1956), p. 162.

25 LEIBNIZ, *Principes de la Nature et de la Grace*, quoted in Martin Heidegger, 'What is Metaphysics?', Kaufmann, *Existentialism*, p. 220.

26 J.P.SARTRE, *Existentialism and Humanism* (1948) in *The Age of Analysis*, ed. Morton White (New York 1955), pp. 125–6.

27 KARL-DIETRICH BRACHER, *Die Deutsche Diktatur* (Cologne 1969), p. 293.

28 SARTRE, in White, *Age of Analysis*, p. 128.

29 J.M.KEYNES, *Two Memoirs* (London 1949), p. 83.

30 ANDRÉ GIDE, *Journal 1889–1939* (Pléiade edition, Paris 1939), p. 1160.

31 EKKI, XIII Plenum, *Theses and Resolutions* (London 1934), p. 5.

Chapter 12

1 J.M.KEYNES, *The General Theory of Employment, Interest and Money* (New York 1936), p. 372.

2 KEYNES, *General Theory*, p. 381.

3 KEYNES, *General Theory*, p. 383.

4 DEGRAS (ed.), *Communist International*, II, p. 481.

5 DEGRAS (ed.), *Communist International*, II, pp. 484–5.

6 See FRANZ NEUMANN, 'Anxiety and Politics', in *The Democratic and the Authoritarian State* (New York 1957).

7 A.J.P.TAYLOR, *The Origins of the Second World War* (London 1961), p. 69.

8 *Mein Kampf*, p. 629.

9 *Mein Kampf*, p. 164.

10 HERMANN RAUSCHNING, *Hitler Speaks* (Eng. tr., London 1939), p. 209.

11 *Mein Kampf*, pp. 600–1.

12 *Mein Kampf*, p. 596.

13 HERMANN RAUSCHNING, *Die Revolution des Nihilismus* (rev. edn, Zurich 1938), pp. 83–4.

14 *Mein Kampf*, p. 238.

15 ADOLPH WAGNER, Speech at Brunswick 9 July 1930, quoted in Wheeler-Bennett, *Nemesis of Power*, p. 225.

16 Quoted in ALAN BULLOCK, *Hitler, A Study in Tyranny* (rev. edn, London 1962), p. 205.

17 ANDRÉ FRANÇOIS-PONCET, *Souvenirs d'une Ambassade à Berlin, Septembre 1931–Octobre 1938* (Paris 1946), pp. 52–3. See also Wheeler-Bennett, *Nemesis of Power*, p. 246.

18 WHEELER-BENNETT, *Wooden Titan*, p. 395.

19 WHEELER-BENNETT, *Nemesis of Power*, p. 339.

20 HITLER, Speech at Munich 19 March 1934, in *The Speeches of Adolf Hitler April 1922–August 1939*, ed. N.H.Baynes (London 1942), I, p. 211.

21 Quoted in CARL J.FRIEDRICH and ZBIGNIEW K.BRZENSKI, *Totalitarian Dictatorship and Autocracy* (2nd edn, Cambridge, Mass. 1965), pp. 95–6.

22 HANNAH ARENDT, *The Origins of Totalitarianism* (2nd edn, London 1958), p. 323.

23 Quoted in FRIEDRICH and BRZENSKI, *Totalitarian Dictatorship*, p. 301.

24 A.ROSENBERG, *The Myth of the Twentieth Century*, quoted in Robert Cecil, *The Myth of the Master Race : Alfred Rosenberg and Nazi Ideology* (London 1972), p. 113.

25 Quoted in RAYMOND CARR, *Spain 1808–1939* (Oxford 1966), p. 564.

26 *Le Populaire*, 1 June 1936.

27 S.HEALD (ed.) in conjunction with J.W.Wheeler-Bennett, *Documents on International Affairs 1936* (London 1937), pp. 299–300. See also Bullock, *Hitler*, p. 355.

28 See GEORGE BULL, 'The Vatican, the Nazis and the Pursuit of Justice', *International Affairs*, 47, No. 2 (April 1971), p. 355.

29 ROBERT CONQUEST, *The Great Terror* (paperback edn, London 1971), Appendix A.

Chapter 13

1 *Mein Kampf*, pp. 595–6.

2 *Documents on German Foreign Policy* (DGFP), Series D (Washington 1949), I, p. 34.

3 See GERHARD L.WEINBERG, *The Foreign Policy of Hitler's Germany* (Chicago and London 1970), pp. 102–6.

4 Quoted in BULLOCK, *Hitler*, pp. 431–2.

5 DGFP, Series D, II, p. 358.
6 *Documents on British Foreign Policy* (DBFP) Third Series (London 1949), II, p. 276.
7 *Documents on International Affairs 1938*, ed. Monica Curtis (London 1943), II, p. 270.
8 DGFP, Series D, VII, p. 247.
9 DBFP, Third Series, VII, p. 171.
10 DGFP, Series D, VII, p. 205.
11 J.R.M.BUTLER (ed.), *History of the Second World War*, United Kingdom Military Series, II: *Grand Strategy*, by J.R.M.Butler (London 1957), p. 97.
12 PAUL REYNAUD, *La France a sauvé l'Europe*, 2 vols (Paris 1947), II, pp. 330–1. See also William L.Langer and S.Everett Gleason, *The Challenge to Isolation* (paperback edn, New York 1964), II, p. 534.
13 PHILIPPE PÉTAIN to National Assembly 10 July 1940, quoted in William L.Langer, *Our Vichy Gamble* (New York 1947), p. 73.
14 CHARLES DE GAULLE, Broadcast Appeal 18 June 1940. *War Memoirs* (Eng. tr., London 1955), I: *The Call to Honour 1940–1942 Documents*, p. 12.
15 CHURCHILL in House of Commons, 4 June 1940, *Hansard*, Fifth Series, CCCLXI, pp. 745–6.
16 FRANZ HALDER, *Hitler as Warlord* (London 1950), quoted in Bullock, *Hitler*, p. 598.
17 WINSTON CHURCHILL, *The Second World War* (London 1949), II: *Their Finest Hour*, p. 518.
18 BULLOCK, *Hitler*, p. 625.
19 BULLOCK, *Hitler*, p. 663.

Chapter 14

1 ALAN S.MILWARD, *The New Order and the French Economy* (Oxford 1970), pp. 71–2.
2 J.W.D.TRYTHALL, *Franco* (London 1970), p. 179.
3 JEAN-PAUL SARTRE, *Situations III* (Paris 1949), pp. 11–14. See also Peter Novick, *The Resistance versus Vichy* (New York, 1968), p. 21.
4 HANS-ADOLF JACOBSEN, 'The *Kommissarbefehl* and mass execution of Soviet Russian prisoners-of-war', in H.Krausnick, H.Buchheim, M. Broszat, H.A.Jacobsen, *Anatomy of the SS State* (Eng. tr., London 1968), p. 510.
5 *Mein Kampf*, p. 620. See also Helmut Krausnick, 'The Persecution of the Jews', *Anatomy of the SS State*, p. 21.
6 KRAUSNICK, 'Persecution of the Jews', p. 43.
7 BRACHER, *Die Deutsche Diktatur*, p. 459.
8 HERMANN RAUSCHNING, *Die Revolution des Nihilismus* (1938) (Eng. tr., *Germany's Revolution of Destruction*, London 1939).
9 HENRI MICHEL, *La Guerre de l'Ombre* (Paris 1970), p. 84.
10 F.W.DEAKIN, *The Brutal Friendship: Mussolini, Hitler and the Fall of Italian Fascism* (rev. ed., New York 1956), p. 129.
11 DEAKIN, *The Brutal Friendship*, p. 36.

12 SIR CHARLES WEBSTER and NOBLE FRANKLAND, *The Strategic Air Offensive against Germany, 1939–1945* (London 1961), I, p. 366.

13 WEBSTER and FRANKLAND, *Strategic Air Offensive*, p. 236.

14 FELIX GILBERT (ed.), *Hitler directs his War* (New York 1951), pp. 105–6. See also Bullock, *Hitler*, p. 755.

15 BRACHER, *Die Deutsche Diktatur*, p. 497.

16 Quoted in WHEELER-BENNETT, *Nemesis of Power*, p. 541.

17 H.R.TREVOR-ROPER, *The Last Days of Hitler* (London 1947), p. 145.

18 COUNT FOLKE BERNADOTTE, *The Curtain Falls* (New York 1945), quoted in Bullock, *Hitler*, p. 791.

19 BULLOCK, *Hitler*, p. 795.

20 CHARLES F.DELZELL, *Mussolini's Enemies* (Princeton 1961), p. 543.

Chapter 15

1 ROSS GREGORY, *Walter Hines Page* (Lexington 1970), p. 175.

2 WINSTON CHURCHILL, *The Second World War* (London 1950), III: *The Grand Alliance*, p. 332.

3 CHURCHILL, *Second World War*, III, p. 331.

4 HERBERT FEIS, *Churchill, Roosevelt, Stalin* (Princeton 1957), p. 648, n. 21.

5 CHURCHILL, *Second World War*, III, pp. 393–4.

6 Quoted in FEIS, *Churchill, Roosevelt, Stalin*, p. 548.

7 CHURCHILL, *The Second World War* (London 1954), VI: *Triumph and Tragedy*, p. 392.

8 SIR LLEWELLYN WOODWARD, *British Foreign Policy in the Second World War* (London 1971), II, p. 613.

9 CHURCHILL, *Second World War*, VI, p. 198.

10 GORDON WRIGHT, *The Reshaping of French Democracy* (paperback edn, Boston 1970), p. 51.

11 See, for example, GAR ALPEROVITZ, *Atomic Diplomacy: Hiroshima and Potsdam* (New York 1965). For a valuable survey of the literature, see Charles S.Maier, 'Revisionism and the Interpretation of Cold War Origins', *Perspectives in American History*, IV (1970), pp. 313–47.

12 Quoted in FEIS, *Churchill, Roosevelt, Stalin*, p. 619.

13 CHURCHILL, *Second World War*, VI, p. 498.

14 Quoted in FEIS, *Churchill, Roosevelt, Stalin*, p. 620.

15 B.RUHM VON OPPEN (ed.), *Documents on Germany under Occupation 1945–1954* (London 1955), p. 38.

16 *Foreign Relations of the United States 1945* (*Conference of Berlin* (*Potsdam*)) (Washington 1960), II, p. 1502.

17 Directive of the US Chiefs of Staff (JS 1067) in *Documents on Germany under Occupation 1945–1954*, p. 15.

18 HENRY L.STIMSON and MCGEORGE BUNDY, *On Active Service in Peace and War* (London n.d.), p. 337.

19 CHURCHILL, *Second World War*, VI, p. 181. See also Diane Shaver Clemens, *Yalta* (New York 1970), p. 98.

20 Quoted in GORDON WRIGHT, *Reshaping of French Democracy*, p. 128.

21 PIERRE MENDÈS-FRANCE, *Gouverner c'est Choisir*, 3 vols (Paris 1954–8).

22 *Le Monde* 17 May 1958 printed in Charles S.Maier and Dan S.White, *The Thirteenth of May : The Advent of De Gaulle's Republic* (New York 1968), p. 284.

23 GEORGE MARSHALL, Speech at Harvard, 5 June 1947, printed in *Documents on International Affairs 1947–1948*, ed. Margaret Carlyle (London 1952), p. 25.

24 Message to Congress, 12 March 1947, printed in Carlyle (ed.), *Documents*, p. 6.

25 *Documents on Germany under Occupation 1945–1954*, p. 295.

26 Quoted in MICHAEL BALFOUR, *West Germany* (London 1968), p. 227.

27 E.g. WILFRID KNAPP, *A History of War and Peace 1939–1965* (London 1967), p. 291.

28 WINSTON CHURCHILL, Speech at Zurich, 19 September 1946, in *The European Common Market and Community*, ed. Uwe Kitzinger (London 1967), p. 37.

29 Quoted in JACQUES FREYMOND, *Western Europe since the War* (New York 1964), p. 80.

30 WOLF GRAF VON BAUDISSIN, 'The New German Army', *Foreign Affairs* (October 1955). See also Richard Hiscocks, *Germany Revived* (London 1966), p. 187.

31 Resolution adopted by the Ministers of Foreign Affairs of the Member States of the European Coal and Steel Community at their Meeting at Messina on 1 and 2 June 1955, printed in Uwe Kitzinger, *European Common Market*, p. 69.

32 *Documents on International Affairs 1955*, ed. Noble Frankland (London 1958), p. 48.

Chapter 16

1 J.LENNOX BOYD, quoted in W.N.Medlicott, *Contemporary England 1914–1964* (London 1967), p. 570.

2 P.N.S.MANSERGH (ed.), *Documents and Speeches on Commonwealth Affairs 1952–1962* (London 1963), p. 345. See also Wilfrid Knapp, *History of War and Peace*, pp. 511 ff.

3 OSWALD SPENGLER, *The Decline of the West* (one-volume edn, New York 1932), II, p. 461.

4 SPENGLER, *Decline of the West*, II, p. 102.

SOME SUGGESTIONS FOR FURTHER READING

The literature on the most recent period of European history is vast and is growing all the time as new source material becomes available and new research is carried out. (For example the British government archives for the period of the Second World War were opened in 1972.) No attempt has therefore been made to provide an exhaustive bibliography. The following list is merely intended to suggest a few books in English in which readers can pursue some of the subjects touched on in this volume and which may serve as a basis for further and more detailed reading, as well as providing further bibliographies.

The notes on pages 485–498 give the references for the actual quotations cited in the text; and the books from which these are taken should of course be consulted in addition to the works listed below.

1 General
a. More detailed general accounts are available in the following volumes of the series *The Rise of Modern Europe*, edited by W.L.LANGER:
CARLTON J.HAYES, *A Generation of Materialism 1871–1914* (1941)
ORON J.HALE, *The Great Illusion 1900–1914* (1971)
RAYMOND SONTAG, *The Revolt against the Old Order 1919–1939*
GEORGE LICHTHEIM, *Europe in the Twentieth Century* (1972) is particularly valuable for its account of philosophy and science.
GORDON WRIGHT, *The Ordeal of Total War 1939–1945* (1968)

There are also useful chapters in *The New Cambridge Modern History*:
Vol. XI *Material Progress and World Wide Problems 1870–1898* (1967)
Vol. XII (2nd edn) *The Shifting Balance of World Forces 1898–1945* (1968)

b. The history of international relations is covered in:
A.J.P.TAYLOR, *The Struggle for Mastery in Europe 1848–1918* (1954; paperback edn, 1971)
R.A.C.PARKER, *Europe 1919–1945* (Eng. edn, 1969)
WILFRID KNAPP, *A History of War and Peace 1939–1965* (1967)

c. A useful general cultural and intellectual history is:
GEORGE L.MOSSE, *The Culture of Western Europe : The Nineteenth and Twentieth Centuries* (1961)

d. An original and exciting introduction to the economic history of the period is:
DAVID S.LANDES, *The Unbound Prometheus: Technological Change and Industrial Development in Western Europe from 1750 to the Present* (1969)
WILLIAM ASHWORTH, *A Short History of the International Economy since 1850* (1952; 2nd edn, 1962) is a useful general survey.

11 The following general histories of individual countries or areas are recommended:

Austria–Hungary and the Successor States
C.A.MACARTNEY, *The Habsburg Monarchy 1790–1918* (1969)
ALAN PALMER *The Lands between: A History of East-Central Europe since the Congress of Vienna* (1970)
HUGH SETON-WATSON *Eastern Europe between the Wars* (new edn, 1962); *The East European Revolution* (rev. edn, 1956)

England
R.C.K.ENSOR *England 1870–1914* (1936)
A.J.P.TAYLOR *English History 1914–1945* (1965)
(The last two volumes in *The Oxford History of England*, ed. by Sir G. Clark)
W.N.MEDLICOTT *Contemporary England 1914–1964* (1967)

France
D.W.BROGAN *The Development of Modern France* (1870–1939) (1940)
Still a valuable, erudite and entertaining account: strongest on the period before 1918.
GORDON WRIGHT *France in Modern Times* (1960)

Germany
MARSHALL DILL JR *Germany: A Modern History* (1961)
AGATHA RAMM *Germany 1789–1919* (1967)
A.J.NICHOLLS *Weimar and the Rise of Hitler* (1968)
K.D.BRACHER *The German Dictatorship* (1969; Eng. tr., 1970)
MICHAEL BALFOUR *West Germany* (1968)

Italy
DENIS MACK SMITH *Italy: A Modern History* (1959)
CHRISTOPHER SETON-WATSON *Italy from Liberalism to Fascism* (1967)

Poland
ANTHONY POLONSKY *The Politics of Independent Poland* (1972)

Russia
HUGH SETON-WATSON *The Russian Empire 1801–1917* (1967)
IAN GREY *The First Fifty Years: Soviet Russia 1917–1967* (1967)
LEONARD SCHAPIRO *The Communist Party of the Soviet Union* (1960)

Spain
GERALD BRENAN *The Spanish Labyrinth* (1943; paperback edn, 1960)
RAYMOND CARR *Spain 1808–1939* (1966)

Yugoslavia
PHYLLIS AUTY   *Yugoslavia* (1965)

III The following are some of the books dealing in detail with some topics raised in the individual chapters of this volume

1 *The New Balance of Power*
JOHN CLAPHAM   *Economic Development of France and Germany 1815–1914* (4th edn, 1936; reprinted 1945)
ALEXANDER GERSCHENKRON   *Bread and Democracy in Germany* (1943)
A.J.P.TAYLOR   *Bismarck : The Man and the Statesman* (1955; paperback edn, 1961)
WILLIAM L.LANGER   *European Alliances and Alignments* (1931)

2 *Social Change and Social Reform*
W.O.HENDERSON   *The Industrial Revolution on the Continent, Germany, France, Russia 1800–1914* (1961)
E.J.HOBSBAWM   *Industry and Empire : An economic history of Britain since 1750* (1968)
ADNA FERRIN WEBER   *The Growth of Cities in the Nineteenth Century* (1899; reprinted 1963)
PETER HALL   *The World Cities* (1966)
IVO N.LAMBI   *Free Trade and Protection in Germany* (1963)

3 *The Socialist Challenge*
G.D.H.COLE   *A History of Socialist Thought*: Vol II *Marxism and Anarchism 1850–1890* (1954); Vol. III *The Second International 1889–1914* (1956)
GEORGE LICHTHEIM   *Marxism* (1961; rev. edn, 1964)
JAMES JOLL   *The Second International 1889–1914* (1955); *The Anarchists* (1964)
CARL SCHORSKE   *German Social Democracy 1905–1917* (1955).
PETER GAY   *The Dilemma of Democratic Socialism : Eduard Bernstein's Challenge to Marx* (1952)
J.P.NETTL   *Rosa Luxemburg* (2 vols 1966; abridged paperback edn, 1969)
STEWART EDWARDS   *The Paris Commune 1871* (1971)
AARON NOLAND   *The Founding of the French Socialist Party* (1956)
HARVEY GOLDBERG   *The Life of Jean Jaurès* (1962)
J.L.H.KEEP   *The Rise of Social Democracy in Russia* (1963; reprinted 1966)

4 *Imperialism*
WILLIAM L.LANGER   *The Diplomacy of Imperialism* (2nd edn, 1951)
MAX BELOFF   *Imperial Sunset* Vol. I: *Britain's Liberal Empire 1897–1921* (1969)
HENRI BRUNSCHVIG   *French Colonialism 1871–1914 : Myths and Realities* (1960; Eng. tr., 1966)
W.L.MONGER   *The End of Isolation: British Foreign Policy 1900–1907* (1963)
PETER G.J.PULZER   *The Rise of Political Anti-Semitism in Germany and Austria* (1964)

R*

NORMAN COHN   *Warrant for Genocide : The Myth of the Jewish World-Conspiracy and the Protocols of the Elders of Zion* (1967)
ROBERT F.BYRNES   *Anti-Semitism in Modern France* (1955)
MICHAEL R.MARRUS   *The Politics of Assimilation : A Study of the French Jewish Community at the time of the Dreyfus Affair* (1971)
GUY CHAPMAN   *The Dreyfus Case* (1955)
DOUGLAS JOHNSON   *France and the Dreyfus Affair* (1966)
EUGENE WEBER   *Action Française : Royalism and Reaction in Twentieth Century France* (1963)
MICHAEL CURTIS   *Three against the Republic : Sorel, Barrès and Maurras* (1959)

5 and 6 *Liberalism and its Enemies. The Industrial Society and its Critics*
H.STUART HUGHES   *Consciousness and Society : The Reorientation of European Social Thought 1890–1930* (1958; paperback edn, 1967)
JAMES H.MEISEL (ed.)   *Pareto and Mosca* (1965)
RICHARD WOLLHEIM   *Freud* (1971)
FRITZ STERN   *The Politics of Cultural Despair* (1961)
GEORGE L.MOSSE   *The Crisis of German Ideology* (1964)
WALTER S.LAQUEUR   *Young Germany : A History of the German Youth Movement* (1962)
SAMUEL HYNES   *The Edwardian Frame of Mind* (1968)
NIKOLAUS PEVSNER   *The Sources of Modern Architectural Design* (1968)

7 *The Coming of the First World War*
LAURENCE LAFORE   *The Long Fuse* (1965)
L.C.F.TURNER   *Origins of the First World War* (1970)
LUIGI ALBERTINI   *The Origins of the War of 1914* (3 vols, Eng. tr. 1952–7)
FRITZ FISCHER   *Germany's Aims in the First World War* (1961; Eng. tr. 1967)
LUDWIG DEHIO   *Germany and World Politics in the Twentieth Century* (1955; Eng. tr. 1959)
VLADIMIR DEDIJER   *The Road to Sarajevo* (1967)
GERHARD RITTER   *The Schlieffen Plan* (1956)

8 *The European Crisis, 1914–1918*
B.H.LIDDELL HART   *History of the First World War* (2nd edn, 1970)
SIR LLEWELLYN WOODWARD   *Great Britain and the War of 1914–1918* (1967)
ARTHUR MARWICK   *The Deluge : British Society and the First World War* (1965; paperback edn, 1967)
ARTHUR ROSENBERG   *The Birth of the German Republic* (1931)
JERE C.KING   *Generals and Politicians* (1951); *Foch versus Clemenceau* (1960)
ARTHUR J.MAY   *The Passing of the Habsburg Monarchy 1914–1918* (2 vols, 1966)
Z.A.B.ZEMAN   *The Break-up of the Habsburg Empire 1914–1918* (1961)
GEORGE KATKOV   *Russia 1917 : The February Revolution* (1967)
ADAM B.ULAM   *Lenin and the Bolsheviks* (1965)

SOME SUGGESTIONS FOR FURTHER READING

E.H.CARR   *The Bolshevik Revolution 1917–1923*, Vol. I (1950)
ISAAC DEUTSCHER   *The Prophet Armed: Trotsky 1879–1921* (1963)
ARNO J.MAYER   *The Political Origins of the New Diplomacy* (1959)

9 *Revolution and Counter-Revolution*
ARNO J.MAYER   *The Policy and Diplomacy of Peacemaking* (1968)
F.L.CARSTEN   *Revolution in Central Europe 1918–1919* (1972)
E.H.CARR   *The Bolshevik Revolution*, III (1953)
GERHARD SCHULZ   *Revolution and Peace Treaties 1917–1920*
(German ed. 1969: English ed. 1972)

10 *The Search for Stability*
A.J.P.TAYLOR   *The Origins of the Second World War* (1961)
F.P.WALTERS   *A History of the League of Nations* (1952; reprinted in 1 vol., 1960)
F.L.CARSTEN   *The Reichswehr and Politics 1918–1933* (1966)
E.H.CARR   *The Interregnum 1923–24* (1954); *Socialism in One Country 1924–1926* (4 vols, 1958–71)
ISAAC DEUTSCHER   *The Prophet Disarmed: Trotsky 1921–1929* (1959)

11 *The New Spirit*
DAVID CAUTE   *Communism and the French Intellectuals 1914–1960* (1964)
JOHN WILLETT   *Expressionism* (1971)
HENRY RUSSELL HITCHCOCK   *Architecture, Nineteenth and Twentieth Centuries* (1958)
PETER GAY   *Weimar Culture* (1968)

12 *Fascism, Communism and Democracy, 1929–1937*
EUGENE WEBER   *Varieties of Fascism* (1964)
F.L.CARSTEN   *The Rise of Fascism* (1967)
STEWART WOOLF (ed.)   *European Fascism* (1968)
ALEXANDER HAMILTON   *The Appeal of Fascism* (1971)
ALAN BULLOCK   *Hitler – A Study in Tyranny* (1952; rev. edn, 1962)
JOHN W.WHEELER-BENNETT   *The Nemesis of Power: The German Army in Politics 1918–1945* (1953)
J.S.CONWAY   *The Nazi Persecution of the Churches 1933–1945* (1968)
DAVID SCHOENBAUM   *Hitler's Social Revolution* (1966)
JOEL COLTON   *Léon Blum* (1966)
HUGH THOMAS   *The Spanish Civil War* (1961; rev. edn, 1965)
STANLEY G.PAYNE   *The Spanish Revolution* (1970)
ROBERT CONQUEST   *The Great Terror: Stalin's Purge of the Thirties* (1968)
ISAAC DEUTSCHER   *The Prophet Outcast: Trotsky 1929–1940* (1963)

13 *Hitler's War*
GERHARD L.WEINBERG   *The Foreign Policy of Hitler's Germany* (1970)
E.M.ROBERTSON   *Hitler's Pre-War Policy and Military Plans* (1963)
WILLIAM L.LANGER and S.EVERETT GLEASON   *The Challenge to Isolation 1937–40* (1952); *The Undeclared War* (1953)
ELIZABETH WISKEMANN,   *The Rome–Berlin Axis* (1949)

B.H.LIDDELL HART   *A History of the Second World War* (1970)
ALAN S.MILWARD   *The German Economy at War* (1965)
PETER CALVOCORESSI AND GUY WINT   *Total War: Causes and Course of the Second World War* (1972)

14 *Collaboration, Resistance and Liberation*
ROBERT ARON   *The Vichy Regime* (1955; Eng. tr. 1958)
RAOUL HILBERG   *The Destruction of the European Jews* (1961)
M.R.D.FOOT   *SOE in France* (1966)
ALAN S.MILWARD   *The New Order and the French Economy* (1970)
WERNER WARMBRUNN   *The Dutch under German Occupation 1940–1945* (1963)
ALEXANDER DALLIN   *German rule in Russia* (1957)
HERBERT FEIS   *Churchill, Roosevelt, Stalin* (1957)
CHARLES F.DELZELL   *The Italian Anti-Fascist Resistance* (1961)
F.W.DEAKIN   *The Brutal Friendship: Mussolini, Hitler and the Fall of Italian Fascism* (1962; rev. edn, in 2 vols: I. *The Brutal Friendship*; II. *The Six Hundred Days of Mussolini*, 1966)
H.R.TREVOR-ROPER   *The Last Days of Hitler* (1947; 2nd edn, 1950)
MARGARET GOWING   *Britain and Atomic Energy 1939–1945* (1964)

15 *Europe Divided*
WALTER LAQUEUR   *Europe since Hitler* (1970)
M.M.POSTAN   *An Economic History of Western Europe 1945–1964* (1967)
MICHAEL KASER   *Comecon* (1965)
ANDREW SHONFIELD   *Modern Capitalism* (1965)
RICHARD MAYNE   *The Recovery of Europe* (1970)
PHILIP WILLIAMS   *Crisis and Compromise: Politics in the Fourth Republic* (1955; 3rd edn, 1964)
PHILIP M.WILLIAMS and MARTIN HARRISON   *De Gaulle's Republic* (1960)
H.STUART HUGHES   *The Obstructed Path: French Social Thought in the Years of Desperation 1930–1960* (1966)
RICHARD HISCOCKS   *Democracy in Western Germany* (1957); *Germany Revived: An Appraisal of the Adenauer Era* (1966)
HENRY C.WALLICH   *Mainsprings of the German Revival* (1955)
ELIZABETH WISKEMANN   *Italy since 1945* (1971)
GHITA IONESCO   *The Politics of the European Communist States* (1967)
JOHN WHEELER-BENNETT AND ANTHONY NICHOLLS   *The Semblance of Peace: the Political Settlements after the Second World War* (1972)

INDEX

505